# THE
# DISCOVERY
# OF THE
# AMAZON

*Edited by*

José Toribio Medina

*Translation from the
Spanish by Bertram T. Lee,
Edited by H. C. Heaton*

DOVER PUBLICATIONS, INC., *New York*

Published in Canada by General Publishing Company, Ltd., 30 Lesmill Road, Don Mills, Toronto, Ontario.

Published in the United Kingdom by Constable and Company, Ltd., 10 Orange Street, London WC2H 7EG.

This Dover edition, first published in 1988, is an unabridged and slightly altered republication of the second printing (February 1935) of the work originally published in 1934 by the American Geographical Society, New York, with a title page reading: *American Geographical Society / Special Publication No. 17 / Edited by W. L. G. Joerg // The Discovery of / the Amazon / According to the Account of / Friar Gaspar de Carvajal / and other Documents // As Published with an Introduction / By José Toribio Medina // Translated from the Spanish / By Bertram T. Lee / Edited / By H. C. Heaton / Professor of Romance Languages, New York University.* The errors listed in the Errata of the original edition have been corrected directly in the text in the present edition.

Manufactured in the United States of America

Dover Publications, Inc., 31 East 2nd Street, Mineola, N.Y. 11501

### Library of Congress Cataloging-in-Publication Data

Descubrimiento del río de las Amazonas. English.

   The discovery of the Amazon / José Toribio Medina ; translated from the Spanish by Bertram T. Lee ; edited by H. C. Heaton.
   p.      cm.

   ISBN 0-486-25589-1 (pbk.)

   Reprint. Originally published: The discovery of the Amazon : according to the account of Friar Gaspar de Carvajal, and other documents / as published with an introduction by José Toribio Medina. New York : American Geographical Society, 1934. Originally published in series: Special publication / American Geographical Society ; no. 17.

   Translation of: Descubrimiento del río de las Amazonas.
   Includes index.

   1. America—Discovery and exploration—Spanish. 2. Amazon River—Discovery and exploration.   3. Orellana, Francisco de, d. ca. 1546.   4. Carvajal, Gaspar de, 1504–1584.   I. Medina, José Toribio, 1852–1930.   II. Carvajal, Gaspar de, 1504–1584.   III. Heaton, H. C. (Harry Clifton), b. 1885.   IV. Title.
   E125.06D4713    1988
   981'.101—dc19                                              87-30322
                                                                     CIP

# CONTENTS

## MEDINA'S "DISCOVERY OF THE AMAZON RIVER"

(translated by B. T. L. and H. C. H.)

### Part I: Introduction by Medina

## Part II: Carvajal's Account

## Part III: Documents

(a) *Relating to Orellana's Descent of the Amazon, 1541–1542*

(b) *Relating to Orellana's Expedition to New Andalusia*
*(lower Amazon Valley), 1545–1546*

## APPENDIX

### SELECTIONS FROM OVIEDO'S "HISTORIA DE LAS INDIAS" BEARING ON ORELLANA'S TWO EXPEDITIONS

(translated by H. C. H.)

## LIST OF ILLUSTRATIONS

# EDITOR'S PREFACE

It must have been during the last few months of the year 1894 that the late José Toribio Medina prepared for publication his book on Francisco de Orellana's voyage down the Amazon River and the ill-fated expedition which this leader subsequently organized to go back up that river and establish colonies on its shores in the name of Spain. Notwithstanding the mark of courteous and professional deference contained in a footnote at the end of the third chapter of the author's Introduction, the writing of the book seems to have been occasioned very largely by the publication, in the now defunct Spanish fortnightly, *Ilustración Española y Americana*, of an article, in several instalments, by Marcos Jiménez de la Espada under the title "La traición de un tuerto" ("The Treason of a One-eyed Man"), the first four chapters of this documented study having appeared in the number for August 22, 1892, and the remaining twelve in three numbers in the latter part of the summer two years later, or only a few months before the publication of Medina's book. The longest chapter, entitled "Orellana's 'Treason,'" in Medina's lengthy Introduction, and the one in the writing of which the author plainly put forth his best effort, is devoted in part to combating Jiménez de la Espada's thesis, to which historians for more than three centuries had been clinging almost unanimously, that Orellana was a despicable traitor.

Rehabilitation of the memory of Orellana, therefore, seems to have been the main purpose of Medina in hastening to lay the matter once more before the public with a different interpretation, this time not in a series of magazine articles, but in a book of five hundred pages. He proceeded to reproduce from the originals several of the very documents which Jiménez de la Espada, in his development of the treason theory, had studied and in part published; but Medina was able to add to them some very important ones which Jiménez de la Espada either did not know or had not had access to. Among these latter, the one to which Medina gave precedence in the body of his work, drawing from it the title of his book and publishing it in its entirety, the one which undoubtedly offered the greatest interest to the reading public, was a manuscript version, little known up to that time, of the account of that first voyage down the Amazon, written by a Dominican friar, Gaspar de Carvajal, who had been a member of the group of some fifty or more men comprising the expedition—a version largely quite distinct in text, though differing relatively little in content, from the one which had been made readily accessible for the first time by the publication of the fourth volume of Gonzalo Fernández de Oviedo y Valdés' *Historia general y natural de las Indias* in 1855.

Relying upon the tone of veracity which pervades each of the two versions of the Dominican friar's account, and particularly upon bits of evidence scattered throughout the first nine of the nineteen documents which, in whole or in part, he was publishing for the first time in most instances, Medina made out what appears to be a plausible case for Orellana, pleading in favor of discarding thenceforth the term "treason" in connection with the manner in which his hero got started upon his independent voyage of "discovery"; and at the same time he rectified not a few errors commonly found in print relative to the discoverer's entire career. But although it is now already forty years since Medina's book came from the press, authors of works on the fall of the Inca Empire, contributors to encyclopedias, etc., have continued to subscribe, sometimes half apologetically it must be admitted, to the judgment of Orellana's conduct pronounced by the early chroniclers and reiterated by writers who have relied for their information upon these latter; and they have gone on repeating the errors of fact. It thus appears that Medina's work has not produced the result which the author seems to have looked forward to. This may be due, to some extent, to the fact that only two hundred copies of the book were printed, with the result that the work does not appear to be very widely known and is rarely cited in bibliographies.

These considerations, in addition to the inherent importance in the history of exploration of the expedition with which these original records deal, amply justify the decision of the American Geographical Society to place the book anew in the hands of interested readers, this time in an English version thanks to the generous gesture of Señor Medina, shortly before his death on December 11, 1930, in accepting Mr. Lee's offer to prepare a translation amplified by such comments and supplementary information as the translator might choose to include.

The task of the editor in seeing this translation through the press has been twofold: first, to collaborate with the translator in the effort to reproduce in English both the story as Medina tells it in his very thorough Introduction and the testimony of the sixteenth-century documents which he published, whereby the English reader may have ready access to the material on which the author based the greater part of his assertions and opinions; and, secondly, to check Medina's references and cross-references. In this latter connection a few explanatory remarks are necessary.

The prolific Chilean scholar must have worked with great haste during the writing of what is essentially his own contribution to the volume, namely the Introduction, composing it, apparently, as stated above, during the autumn months of the year 1894; for he made considerable use of the instalments of Jiménez de la Espada's article published in the *Ilustración Española y Americana* under date of August 22 and August 30 of that year (but not of the concluding part in the September 8 number of that magazine), and the book was off the press by February 9 of the following year, as stated in the colophon (not reproduced in the present translation). The almost inevitable result was errors, inaccuracies, etc., in no small number. These consist of wrong dates for published works, references to non-existent editions, inaccuracy or incompleteness in the citing of titles of printed books, wrong page and chapter references, even references to works in which a given quotation is not to be found at all, etc. Then, too, in several scores of cases in which phrases and paragraphs are quoted Medina furnishes no references or cross-references whatsoever. Finally, Medina frequently indulges in the annoying habit of altering, to a greater or less degree, the text of a passage which he quotes, in order to make it fit in with his own phraseology or development of thought.

To remedy all this, and also, it is hoped, to add to the value of Medina's book as represented by the present English version, various methods have been adopted. In the first place, all matter of any considerable length or importance added by the translator or editor has been bracketed, with the annotation "TRANSLATOR" or "EDITOR" in each instance. In the case of minor errors or omissions on the part of Medina, corrections and additions have been made without recourse to any editorial device to indicate this fact:

this procedure has been followed principally in the correcting of dates of printed books, references to editions, page and chapter references, etc., and generally in the completing of bibliographical data. For all direct quotations inserted by Medina in his own text, references or cross-references not furnished by the author himself have been supplied, between brackets immediately after the quotations or in editorial footnotes, accompanied by remarks whenever they seemed called for, in every case in which the source either in the various documents which Medina publishes or in some other printed work to which he refers elsewhere has been found, the absence of such a reference indicating either that the source of a quotation is an unpublished document (probably in the Archives of the Indies, in Seville, in most cases) or that its existence in print is unknown to the editor. This latter procedure is, of course, a purely arbitrary one, but one which will be found, by such readers as may be interested in this question, to be a sufficient guide for running down Medina's sources for practically all important points brought out in his development of the story, so frequent are his direct quotations. With regard to the quotations themselves, in all cases in which Medina has taken liberties with the text which he quotes, they have been restored, before being translated, to the form in which they occur in the original texts, slight changes being introduced, whenever necessary, in Medina's own phraseology, most frequently with a remark explaining the change.

A word about the translation itself. In the Introduction, that is in that part of the book which comes largely from Medina's own pen, liberties have had to be taken at times with the author's sentence structure and with his mode of expression; and his "we," whenever it appears to be used editorially, is regularly rendered by the first person singular. Throughout all the rest of the book, as well as in Medina's numerous quotations from early sources, the reader who turns the pages of the present volume will be struck by the very frequent use, not to say abuse, of brackets. The presence of these brackets in such large numbers is due to the effort which has been made to hold as closely as possible to the text of the frequently poorly written documents and chroniclers' accounts of the sixteenth century which constitute the major part of the source material of the book, and at the same time to remedy what appear to be defects of composition by supplying modifiers, explanations (introduced by "i.e."), and even connecting phrases wherever, so it is believed, such editing clarifies the meaning or produces smoother reading. The reader will perceive that in general it is possible, if he wishes, to omit the words or phrases between brackets, whereby he will get an impression of the style of the originals, faulty as it frequently is. In other words, he may take his choice between two ways of reading this part of the work.

There remains but one more point to cover regarding the translation, namely a question of terminology. Orellana's exploit in going down the Amazon River, like the exploits of many other conquistadors, is called in Spanish a "descubrimiento"; and this is the term used on the title-page of Medina's book and, together with the corresponding verb "descubrir," throughout the entire volume. Literally translated, "descubrimiento" means "discovery." Now, inasmuch as the location of the Amazon (or Marañón) River, so far as its mouth is concerned, had been known for nearly half a century at the time that Orellana went down it, it may be argued that this Spanish captain did not *discover* that river in the ordinary sense of the word. This is true. Nevertheless, Orellana did discover, or did establish for the first time, the fact that the waters of certain headwater streams of unknown destination, on the slope of the Andes east of Quito, flowed from one river into another until they emptied into a great river of (until then) unknown source coming out in the Atlantic on the other side of the continent, namely what is now called the Amazon. It is not inappropriate, therefore, to use, with reference to Orellana's accomplishment, the term "discovery" (with its cognates "discover" and "discoverer") in the present translation; and, since it is thus a semi-technical term, it has been adopted in the present volume in other connections also as the equivalent of the corresponding Spanish word, although the use of an appropriate synonym has frequently been resorted to. Similar explanations could be offered to justify the use of several other semi-technical terms, such as "conquest," "pacification," etc., and their cognates.

The work of correcting the proofs for the present volume was well advanced when it was decided, as stated in the footnote on page 8, that it would be advisable to take advantage of the publication of the volume to make accessible to English readers interested in the career of Orellana the important material contained in the work of the first official chronicler of the Indies, Gonzalo Fernández de Oviedo y Valdés, abundantly drawn on by Medina in his Introduction. An English version of all that Oviedo has to say bearing directly or indirectly upon Orellana and his two expeditions, as well as of the version of Friar Carvajal's account of the first of these inserted by the official chronicler in his *Historia*, has therefore been added in the present volume as an Appendix.

The editor is pleased to acknowledge his indebtedness for kind assistance to the following: Dr. Homero Serís, of the Centro de Estudios Históricos, Madrid; Dr. Theodore F. Jones, Director of the New York University Library at University Heights, New York City; and Dr. Ralph G. Lounsbury, of the Department of History in New York University. To Mr. Carlos Korlowski-Figarola, teacher of Spanish in the New York City high schools, he desires to express his warmest thanks for valuable assistance lent during the final reading of the proof. He takes particular pleasure in recording his appreciation of the generous collaboration of Mr. W. L. G. Joerg, Editor of the Research Series of the American Geographical Society and geographical editor of the present volume, who not only suggested the inclusion of a translation of the version of Carvajal's account published in Oviedo's *Historia* but also furnished material for many a supplementary footnote.

H. C. HEATON

NEW YORK UNIVERSITY

# DESCUBRIMIENTO

### DEL

# RÍO DE LAS AMAZONAS

### SEGÚN LA RELACIÓN

#### HASTA AHORA INÉDITA

## DE FR. GASPAR DE CARVAJAL

#### CON OTROS DOCUMENTOS REFERENTES

## Á FRANCISCO DE ORELLANA Y SUS COMPAÑEROS

#### PUBLICADOS Á EXPENSAS

## DEL EXCMO. SR. DUQUE DE T'SERCLAES DE TILLY

con una Introducción histórica
y algunas ilustraciones

## POR JOSÉ TORIBIO MEDINA

*de la Academia Chilena, Correspondiente de las Reales Academias de la Lengua
y de la Historia, de la de Buenas Letras de Sevilla y del Instituto
Geográfico Argentino.*

SEVILLA
Imprenta de E. RASCO, Bustos Tavera, núm. 1
MDCCCXCIV

# DISCOVERY

## OF THE

# AMAZON RIVER

### ACCORDING TO THE ACCOUNT
#### HITHERTO UNPUBLISHED

## OF FRIAR GASPAR DE CARVAJAL

#### WITH OTHER DOCUMENTS RELATING

## TO FRANCISCO DE ORELLANA AND HIS COMPANIONS

#### PUT INTO PRINT AT THE EXPENSE

## OF HIS EXCELLENCY THE DUKE OF T'SERCLAES DE TILLY

with an historical introduction
and illustrations

## BY JOSÉ TORIBIO MEDINA

*of the Chilean Academy, Corresponding Member of the Royal Academies of Letters
and of History, of the Academy of Letters of Seville, and of the
Argentine Geographical Institute*

SEVILLE

Press of E. RASCO, Bustos Tavera, 1

MDCCCXCIV

## THE DUKE OF T'SERCLAES DE TILLY

*It is my pleasant duty to make known here that to you exclusively belongs the credit for the idea of publishing Friar Carvajal's* Account *with which this collection of documents relative to the River Amazon begins. It was you who persisted in putting upon my unworthy shoulders the task of preparing these documents for the press, and, although my inclinations were prompting me to give my attention to other occupations, I found it both impossible and inadvisable to excuse myself from undertaking so honorable a commission even though it was altogether uncertain that I could carry it out in a fitting manner.*

*These documents, more or less important, are, with the possible exception of one or two of them, absolutely unknown. The history and geography of America are therefore indebted to you from now on for their appearance in print and for the contribution which they constitute to the store of first-hand material for the study of an historical period whose sources have begun to become known only recently.*

*I now present these documents to you, together with the results of my researches in the Archives and a summary of the new information which I have found concerning the discoverer of the Amazon, the chronicler of his expedition, and the men who took part in it.*

*Kindly accept this work, then, as an homage which preëminently is your due and as a testimonial of the high esteem of your most affectionate friend*

José Toribio Medina

Seville, December 6, 1894

# PART I
# INTRODUCTION BY MEDINA

# INTRODUCTION

## I

## DOCUMENTARY SOURCES ON ORELLANA'S VOYAGE*

THE documents that are included in the present volume are divided into two well-defined series: the first comprises matter relative to the voyage of Francisco de Orellana down the Marañón River, and the second has to do with his later expedition for the exploration and conquest of the regions bathed by that river and officially named New Andalusia. The second series, from No. X on,† begins with the preliminaries of the pact which the Estremenian captain made with the King and concludes with the last accounts that we have of the outcome of that unfortunate expedition. The documents of this second series abound in details touching on the antecedents of the expedition, but they are found to be quite insufficient when one attempts to follow that enterprise incident by incident, owing to the fact that the only one bearing upon the expedition after it had gotten under way is the deposition of Francisco de Guzmán,‡ one of the expeditioners, poorly written, without coördination of dates, the original even appearing without signature. Yet this document, such as it is, is the only one dealing with that event that seems to have come down to us from Herrera's time.§

For this paucity of documentation covering the expedition of Orellana to New Andalusia, however, a ready explanation is at hand. During it there perished its principal protagonist, leaving no heirs who might some day make use of it as one of the bases for

*[In the original of Medina's Introduction each chapter is preceded by a brief topical summary of the subject-matter of the chapter. These summaries are repeated in Medina's table of contents. In the present translation they have been omitted from both places inasmuch as the index especially prepared for this translation, in its comprehensive analysis, includes all the topics enumerated in the summaries.—EDITOR.]

†[The numbered documents constitute the third part of the present volume. Document No. X is on pp. 320–328.—EDITOR.]

‡[Document No. XVII, on pp. 361–374.—EDITOR.]

§[Before the volume was actually printed, and even before Medina had written the last pages of Chapter 10 of the present Introduction, two additional documents relating to the expedition proper were communicated to the author and by him incorporated in the work. See, *infra*, p. 361, second footnote.—EDITOR.]

honors to which they might eventually seek to lay claim; and in fact the expedition was so unfortunate, so unfruitful in its results, and all in all such a complete failure, that to none of those who figured in it did it occur later to have a judicial inquiry put through covering their services (a procedure of the sort so common in those times in the Spanish colonies of America), by which they could have made known the part they had taken in it.

I might have completed this series with the loan conditions laid down for Orellana by the Genoese merchants of Seville, as they are preserved in the Archives of the Indies, and with two other pieces relative to the inspection of the fleet the day before its departure from Sanlúcar; but, as the former did not go into effect and as the latter have been published in the last volume of Torres de Mendoza's *Colección*,* I have preferred to omit them so as not to make this volume too bulky.

The documents of the first series call for a more careful study. It is clear that the chief document among them is Friar Gaspar de Carvajal's *Account*, of which two versions are known: the one which the chronicler Gonzalo Fernández de Oviedo inserted in his *Historia general de las Indias*,[1] making some changes, and the one which is now given to the public for the first time. Until the publication of that chronicler's complete work in 1851–1855, the account had remained unpublished, in either of its forms, so that it was not known save to a few persons; and it is indeed extremely strange that it did not come to the notice of the diligent Prescott, who in his *Conquest of Peru*, in referring to the voyage of Orellana, was obliged to avail himself of the scant information given by Zárate

---

*[*Colección de documentos inéditos relativos al descubrimiento, conquista y organización de las antiguas posesiones españolas de América y Oceanía, sacados de los archivos del Reino, y muy especialmente del de Indias*, 42 vols., Madrid 1864–84; see Vol. 42, pp. 268–290.—EDITOR.]

[1] The *Relación* of Friar Carvajal takes up pages 541–573 of Volume 4 [as Ch. 24 of Book L] of the work of the first chronicler of the Indies. [I.e. *Historia general y natural de las Indias, islas y tierra-firme del Mar Océano*, edited by José Amador de los Ríos, 4 vols., Real Academia de la Historia, Madrid, 1851–55. This version of Carvajal's account will hereafter be referred to in the present volume as the *Relación*, in contradistinction to the version which Medina published and which is here presented in English translation under the title of *Account*. On the relation of the *Relación* to the *Account* see the foreword to the Appendix, *infra*, pp. 387–389.

Gonzalo Pizarro's expedition to the Land of Cinnamon, Orellana's descent of the Amazon, and Orellana's subsequent expedition to New Andalusia, which form the subject-matter of Chapters 6–8 and 10 of Medina's Introduction, are independently described by Oviedo in the same work, namely in Book XLIX, Chs. 1–6 (Vol. 4, pp. 381–394). Because of its importance and because, so far as known, it has not yet been published in English, a translation of the *Relación* by the editor has been added to Medina's work in the present volume as an Appendix (pp. 405–448, *infra*). This is preceded by a translation of Oviedo's brief accounts of the three expeditions. In the quotations from Oviedo that occur throughout the following pages of the Introduction no cross-references are given to the Appendix as the reader may locate the passages by means of the page numbers in the 1851–55 edition of Oviedo there inserted in their proper places.—EDITOR.]

and the not always trustworthy accounts printed by the Inca Garcilaso de la Vega, his favorite author.

Antonio de Herrera, however, had it before him and followed it very closely, almost word for word, in accordance with his system of epitomizing the documents placed at his disposal.[2]

Of that form of the account which remained in manuscript there exists an incomplete copy in the collection of documents gathered together by Muñoz and preserved in the Royal Academy of History; its state of incompleteness may possibly go back to the original[3] from which this indefatigable historian made his transcript but is more probably due to carelessness on the part of the binder. In any case, the fact is that no complete copy had been known until now, and we might have remained ignorant of this one for who knows how long, had it not been for the excellent idea of my illustrious friend, his Excellency the Duke of T'Serclaes de Tilly, who with his love for letters and his proverbial generosity has desired that the copy which he possesses be given to the public in print.[4]

Having, then, had both copies before me, I have proceeded to publish this latter, noting the variants of any importance which examination and collation have brought to my attention. This comparative study brings me to the conclusion that both are the product of the same hand, a fact which in no manner whatsoever can be doubted, and that the variants are to be explained, in part, in one of two ways: either the copies were made from dictation by amanuenses who were not very expert, or the author suppressed in one or added in the other words and even phrases which he thought more expressive or nearer to the truth.

[2] As a proof of this fact, here are three quotations from Decade VI, Book IX, Chapters 4, 5, and 6 of his work:

"Friar Carvajal affirms that these Indians put up such a stubborn defence," etc.;

"Friar Carvajal affirms that a bird followed them," etc.;

"and as Friar Carvajal relates, they sailed down it," etc.

[Antonio de Herrera, *Historia general de los hechos de los castellanos en las islas y tierra firme del Mar Océano*, first published in Madrid, in four volumes, 1601–1615. The beginning of Pizarro's expedition to the Land of Cinnamon and all of Orellana's voyage are described in Decade VI: Book VIII, Chapters 7–8, and Book IX, Chapters 2–6, respectively. A free translation of Book IX, Chapters 2–6, was published by Sir Clements Markham in 1859 in the publications of the Hakluyt Society, London (First Series, No. 24, pp. 23–40). In the present footnote Medina gives the Decade and Book numbers erroneously as V and VIII respectively, repeating this error in footnotes 12 and 34.—EDITOR.]

[3] It is not easy to verify this assumption because in the transcript to which I refer there is no indication whatsoever as to the source from which it was taken.

[4] The *Account* owned by the Duke is not, in my opinion, in the handwriting of Friar Carvajal, even though the characteristics of the writing correspond in all respects to the epoch in which it must have been written. The two or three lacunae that appear in it are due to the fact that, after it had been bound up with other papers, the knife of the binder cut off a few words at the edge of the page.

With the exception of the first few paragraphs which Friar Carvajal devotes to relating the arrival of Orellana at Gonzalo Pizarro's camp, all of the *Account* was written by its author as an eyewitness.[5] It was not known how long that voyage down the course of a hitherto unexplored river which wound through those immense unknown regions could take; the expeditioners did not even know the names of the tribes through whose territories they would have to pass, much less the languages which the inhabitants spoke; they were absolutely ignorant of the climate, the trees that grew along the banks of the river, the animals so strange to them which they saw at every turn, the fishes that they saw jump from the water alongside the brigantine on which they had embarked; but they did know very well that they were on a voyage of discovery, and that, in order to leave behind them a record of the event, and with foresight for the future, it were well to note down day by day the incidents of that hazardous enterprise; and it was precisely this task that Friar Carvajal took upon himself.

His *Account* takes in, then, from the end of December, 1541, when Orellana and his companions separated from the expeditionary corps of Gonzalo Pizarro, to September 11 of the following year, when the brigantine in which the Dominican friar had embarked arrived at Nueva Cádiz on the island of Cubagua. The *Account* being restricted to the chronicle of the events of the voyage, there is no reason whatsoever why it should not receive full credence on our part, albeit at times the author attributes certain facts to supernatural causes and at other times shows himself to be an overenthusiastic admirer of his chief and fellow-Estremenian. "I . . . have chosen," he himself says at the end of his *Account*, "to take upon myself this little task and [recount] the progress and outcome of our journey and navigation, not only in order to tell about it and make known the truth in the whole matter, but also in order to remove the temptation from many persons who may wish to relate this peregrination of ours or [publish] just the opposite of what we have experienced and seen; and [what] I have written and related is the truth throughout . . . " [*infra*, p. 234f.]

Fernández de Oviedo, who better than anyone else was in a position to estimate at its proper value what Father Carvajal

[5] " . . . and although all that I have told up to now I neither saw nor took part in, still I gathered up information from all those who came with the said Captain, because I was with the said Gonzalo Pizarro and I saw him [i.e. Captain Orellana] and his companions come in in the manner that I have said; but what I shall tell from here on will be as an eyewitness. . . . " (*Account*, pp. 168–169).

asserted, accepts everything in his account, saying, not without some show of scoffing at certain fastidious critics: "And I say that I should have been happy to see him and know him well; for to me it seems that such a one as he is worthy to write of things of the Indies, and that he should be believed by virtue of those two arrow shots, one of which tore out or destroyed one of his eyes; and with that single one [which he still has left], not to mention his personal prestige and qualities, which are very fine according to the affirmations of those who have had dealings with him, I would believe [him] more than [I would] those who, with two eyes and without knowing what they are talking about or understanding what the Indies are and without having visited them, staying at home in Europe, are continually babbling and have written down many tales . . . "[6]

[6] *Historia general y natural de las Indias*, Vol. 4, p. 574.

# II

## FATHER GASPAR DE CARVAJAL, CHRONICLER OF ORELLANA'S EXPEDITION

THE author of this document bore the name of Friar Gaspar de Carvajal. Born in Trujillo, Estremadura,[7] about the year 1504,[8] he had already taken orders in one of the Dominican monasteries of Castile, probably in that of San Pablo of Valladolid, when by a royal decree of September 30, 1535, the Monarch charged the general of the order to take the necessary measures toward having ten of its members go over to Peru in company with Friar Vicente de Valverde, who is so well known in history for the part he played in the imprisonment of Atahualpa and who was soon to return to Peru as bishop of that country.

The general hastened to carry out the recommendation of the Sovereign, assembled eight of the ten friars asked of him, and placed them under the immediate command of Friar Gaspar de Carvajal; and they took up the work so actively that already towards the end of that year the royal officials in Seville were charged to give and pay to the clergymen who were to go with Valverde all that was just and reasonable[9] as befitted persons of their standing, although through circumstances for which the expeditioners were in no wise responsible, and particularly through delay in the arrival of the bulls for Friar Valverde, who was finally obliged to depart without having received them, they had to remain in Seville until the beginning of the second year following,

[7] I have been unable to find the name of Friar Carvajal either in the *Catálogo razonado y crítico de los libros . . . que tratan de las provincias de Extremadura*, Madrid, 1865, or in the *Aparato bibliográfico para la historia de Extremadura*, 3 vols., Madrid, 1873–77, by the learned Vicente Barrantes. That he was an Estremenian is affirmed by the chronicler of the order in Peru, Meléndez, in his *Tesoros verdaderos de las Indias*, Rome, 1681, Vol. 1, p. 369; and of the fact that he was born in Trujillo we are assured by Oviedo, *Historia general y natural de los Indias*, Vol. 4, p. 385. There is, besides, one piece of evidence furnished by Father Carvajal himself, in which he, too, very clearly makes this fact known, namely when, in giving testimony in connection with a judicial inquiry, on the subject of services rendered, put through at the request of Francisco de Valverde in Lima in 1579, he states that "he had known his [i.e. Valverde's] parents and grandparents and all his family from [the time when he, Carvajal, was still in] Trujillo."

[8] I deduce this date from the testimony just mentioned [footnote 7], in which, in speaking of his age, he said that he was then seventy-five years old.

[9] Royal decree of December 8, 1535.

when they were at last able to set sail headed for Nombre de Dios and Panama.[10]

[10] By royal decree of July 7, 1536, the officials of the House of Trade [the famous Casa de la Contratación in Seville] were ordered to pay for the passage of the clergymen, and the same order was again issued to them on November 3; nevertheless, there is proof that on December 9 they had not yet started. For this reason I am inclined to believe that the departure probably took place in January, 1537.

The fixing of this date is not as easy as it would seem. The chronicler Meléndez states that Carvajal crossed over to Peru with the ten monks taken along by Friar Juan de Olías in 1533. [The words of Menéndez (Tesoros, etc., Vol. I, p. 369) are: "towards the end of the year 1533."—EDITOR.] This has hitherto been the only statement that we possessed regarding this point, and the one which modern historians had been compelled to repeat, as was the case with my friend González Suárez in his Historia del Ecuador (7 vols. and atlas, Quito, 1890–1903), Vol. 2, p. 296.

In a letter from the officials of the House of Trade, dated Seville, January 13, 1533 [Is this an error for "1534" or a later date?—EDITOR], the following paragraph may be read: "We are sending herewith to Your Majesty the account which exists in this House relating to the friars who have gone over to the Indies since the Emperor, our master, departed for Italy." In this document I had hoped to find either the confirmation of the assertion of the Dominican chronicler or proof to the contrary; but unfortunately this list of the friars is not to be found in the Archives of the Indies.

With the same idea in mind, I have gone through the records of bookings of passengers who had gone to the Indies, the files of investigations of personal qualifications in connection with these bookings, and the collections of decrees, both of the "Indiferente General" and the "Audiencia" of Lima, but also without success. In view of this, and for lack of other data, I was about to accept perforce the date fixed by Meléndez, when I came upon a letter from Friar Carvajal, written to the King on April 9, 1561, in the care of the Viceroy, the Marquis de Cañete, in which he says that his report will be given without passion, "as I have done," he states, "for twenty-five years in all matters relative to this realm, whither I was sent by the very Christian emperor, father of Your Majesty, with the first clerics that came over to settle in this province." On the basis of these figures I find that, this letter having been written in 1561, as I have said, the sending of Carvajal to Peru had taken place twenty-five years before, that is in 1536, a date which corresponds perfectly with that which I have cited in the text. [The text says, by inference, 1537.—EDITOR.]

The information given above is supplemented by another piece of evidence which is also furnished by Carvajal himself, namely his declaration in connection with the judicial inquiry, covering Valverde's services, put through in Lima, to which I have already referred and in which he says literally "that he came over from Spain in company with Bishop Valverde when he [i.e. Valverde] journeyed to Castile, and [that] soon after that this witness [i.e. he] came over, with friars of his order, as their vicar-general to establish the Order of Saint Dominic in this realm."

I have recently found a document that disposes of the doubt in a definitive manner: it is the entry at the bottom of the decree which charged the royal officials of the House of Trade to pay the passage of the Dominican friars, and in it are mentioned their names and even that of the ship on which they set sail. I feel that I must quote this decree, together with the prompt measures to which it gave rise.

"The Queen.—To our officials who reside in the city of Seville in the House of Trade of the Indies:—The reverend father Friar Vicente de Valverde, bishop-elect of the province of Peru, has written to me to remind me how I had commanded you to provide with passage and ship-stores certain friars of his order whom he is taking over with him to the said province of Peru for the instruction of the natives there in the things of our Holy Catholic faith, and that you are providing them poorly with what they need, because while each one of them needs twenty ducats, you are giving them only six, with which it is even said they have not wherewith to buy bread and wine, beseeching me to order that they be provided as may seem best to him; and because the friars whom the aforesaid bishop-elect is thus taking along with him are persons of good life and good example, and [men] by whom we are confident God Our Lord will be well served in the said instruction, wherefor I have a desire to show them favor in whatever there may be any occasion for and wish them to be well treated and aided, I order you, in conformity with the opinion of the said bishop-elect, to provide the aforesaid friars with whatever they may need for their passage and ship-stores, and [to see to it] that both in this matter and in everything else that relates to them in your city you assist and favor them, so that they may be provided with all that is necessary in an orderly manner, for in this you will serve me. From Valladolid, on the third day of the month of November, One Thousand Five Hundred Thirty-six. I the Queen. By command of Her Majesty, Joan de Samano." And on the reverse side of the said decree there are three signature initials.

We have no record of the exact date of Friar Carvajal's arrival in Peru; but on the other hand we know that he succeeded perfectly in justifying the confidence placed in him by the general of his order in his mission to go out and establish the first Dominican monastery in that country. In fact, in November, 1538, we find him as vicar-provincial in Lima, defending the right of asylum of the monastery which he had founded against the pretentions of a lieutenant who wished to remove a prisoner from there—an incident in which he proceeded with as much circumspection as firmness.[11]

He was in Lima, therefore, when Gonzalo Pizarro passed through there on his way to Quito to take over the governorship formerly conferred upon Sebastián de Benalcázar, having already formulated in his mind the plan of going out to explore the rich territories where cinnamon grew on the eastern slopes of the Andes.

Carvajal was a man from Gonzalo Pizarro's own home province, that is, he was an Estremenian like him; until then the new governor had had no chaplain to say mass to his soldiers and to hear their confessions in the moments of danger, which were undoubtedly not infrequent; Carvajal was young, strong, courageous, and

"By virtue of the aforesaid decree of Her Majesty, transcribed above on the ninth day of the month of December of this present year One Thousand Five Hundred Thirty-six, we handed over as an item of account to Francisco Tello, treasurer of this House of Trade of the Indies, eighty-two gold ducats, which is the equivalent of thirty thousand seven hundred and fifty maravedis, which he is to give and pay to Friar Toribio de Oropesa, and Friar Alonso Daza, and Friar Gaspar de Carvajal, and Friar Alonso de Sotomayor, and Friar Antonio de Castro, and Friar Pedro de Ulloa, and Friar Gerónimo Ponce, and Friar Francisco de Plazencia, who are eight monks of the Order of Saint Dominic appointed by Friar Vicente de Valverde, bishop-elect of the province of Peru, in the number of those whom he holds a commission from Her Majesty to take over to the said province, for their ship-stores from here to the port of Nombre de Dios, at the rate of ten ducats to each one, in accordance with our agreement with the said bishop, who was present at the fixing of the aforesaid allowance for victualing; and the two ducats are for two chests in which to carry the said stores; which eighty-two ducats aforesaid the said treasurer Francisco Tello is to give and pay by virtue of the above decree of Her Majesty; which [decree], together with a receipt of payment from the said monks, and provided that the said bishop-elect certify, signing with his name on it, that these stores have been furnished in conformity with his wishes, and [with] the certificate of appointment by the aforesaid bishop of the said eight monks, he [Francisco Tello] is to take into his possession as his voucher. These eight monks sailed on the ship named *Santiago*, the master of which is Ginés de Carrión, with whom we entered into an agreement to the effect that the officials of Tierra Firme should pay him twenty-three thousand maravedis, seven thousand five hundred for a cabin and sixteen thousand for their persons, at two thousand maravedis for each one."

(Archives of the Indies, Trade, Accounts of the Treasurer Don Francisco Tello, 1530 to 1537, 2–3-2 /3.)

[11] *Lawsuit of Hernando González and others as bondsmen of Francisco Boscán*, etc., writs which are on file in the Archives of the Indies.

In view of this incident, in which Carvajal is called provincial and in which the witnesses designate him by this title, as well as because of the words of Carvajal which I quoted in the preceding note, there can be no doubt that he was in fact the founder of the Order of Saint Dominic in Peru, and the first vicar-provincial to hold the office there, a fact until now completely unknown, even to Friar Meléndez, and one which brings great honor to our author.

endowed with personal prestige, so that it was a foregone conclusion that Pizarro would invite him to accompany him on an enterprise in which God and the King could be served so well, in the exploration of a region which was supposed to be as thickly populated as it was rich. In company with Pizarro, therefore, he set out from Quito, and when along towards the end of that year, 1541, Pizarro resolved to send Captain Orellana down the waters of the Coca with the sick in search of food, in the brigantine which they had built but a short time before, Carvajal and the other cleric who was with them, perhaps out of consideration for their priestly calling, were also given places on board.

It has been thought by many, or, to be more accurate, by practically all of those who have related the voyage of Orellana, as we shall see more in detail further on, that when this captain decided to abandon Gonzalo Pizarro and continue his journey down the river, Friar Carvajal was the only one, with the exception of Hernán Sánchez de Vargas, to oppose such a plan, and that by way of punishing them the irritated captain abandoned them in those solitary regions.

The absurdity of such an assertion will be readily understood now. Carvajal followed Orellana in his fate, discharging with integrity and exactness the functions of his sacred ministry, and was destined to take part in all the combats which so frequently jeopardized the lives of that handful of fearless adventurers; and in one of these fights he met with such bad luck, that, as he himself tells it, "they hit no one but me, for they planted an arrow shot right in one of my eyes, in such a way that the arrow went through to the other side, from which wound I have lost the eye[12] and [even now] I am not without suffering and not free from pain, although Our Lord, without my deserving it, has been kind enough to grant me life so that I may mend my ways and serve Him better than I had done hitherto . . . "[13]

At last, about the middle of September, 1542, he arrived at the island of Cubagua.*

There he learned that Bishop Valverde, his friend and prelate, had been slain by the Indians of the island of Puná in the Gulf of

---

[12] ". . . a thing which caused them all much grief," says Herrera, "because this father, besides being a good priest, with his courage and prudence helped out greatly in the midst of these hardships" (*Historia general de los hechos*, etc., Decade VI, Book IX, Ch. 5).

[13] *Account, infra*, p. 216.

*[Off the coast of what is now Venezuela, in longitude 64° W., after the two vessels carrying Orellana and his men had skirted the mainland westward from the mouth of the Amazon (see map, Fig. 1a, on p. 48).—EDITOR.]

Guayaquil and that Francisco Pizarro had been murdered by members of the Chilean (i.e. Almagro) faction[14]—circumstances which perhaps explain why he did not accompany Orellana back to Spain and the capital.[15] The fact is that, without even going to Santo Domingo,[16] he took the first ship for Nombre de Dios, went on to Panama, and arrived at last in Lima, in good health, although with one eye less.[17]

Whether it be on account of the high office that he had been holding, or on account of his personal qualities, the fact is that he must have passed for a man of importance, when we observe the part that it fell to his lot to play in the events which took place in Lima in connection with the disagreements between the Judges of the Audiencia and the Viceroy Blasco Núñez Vela. He possessed, apparently, the confidence of both sides, to such a degree that he received from the Judges the commission to go and call upon the Viceroy to present himself on the steps of the Cathedral, where they were waiting for him in the midst of the people who surrounded them; and although Friar Carvajal undoubtedly knew already that the intention of the Judges was to take the Viceroy prisoner, he performed his task, and as soon as Blasco Núñez Vela was made a prisoner, he admonished him to prepare his soul and set his conscience aright, and in the next instant received from the afflicted magnate another mission to perform, which a contemporary author recounts in the following terms:

"And the Viceroy, fearing that the Judges might further transgress the bounds of justice with him, sent Friar Gaspar de Carvajal

[14] This we know from what Friar Carvajal relates in the testimony which he gave in connection with the legal proceedings of which I have already spoken, this testimony containing, however, no statement as to whether at the time of his arrival at the island news of these deeds had yet been received, although it is most probable that such was the case in view of the fact that the death of Pizarro had taken place on June 26, 1541, about one year before. [Valverde had been killed in November or early December, 1541 (Prescott, *Conquest of Peru*, Book IV, Ch. 6), while fleeing from the wrath of the Almagro party, which he had incurred by aiding his brother-in-law, Juan Blásquez, to escape from Lima. The latter also was killed at the same time as Valverde.—TRANSLATOR.]

[15] It seems strange indeed that Orellana did not take Friar Carvajal with him, for his testimony would have lent great weight to his account of the voyage. In my opinion, if the Dominican did not go to Spain, it could not be for any other reason than that he understood very well that his presence in Lima was indispensable under those circumstances, in order to protect the interests of his order in the midst of the profound political upheavals that were developing in Peru and at a time when Bishop Valverde, who might have protected those interests, had just been killed.

[16] This may be deduced from what Fernández de Oviedo, who was residing there at that time, states: "I should have been happy to see him and know him well . . ." [*Historia . . . de las Indias*, Vol. 4, p. 574]; the conclusion to be drawn is that Carvajal had not even stopped in that city.

[17] The itinerary of the return voyage is deduced from data furnished by question 12 of the interrogatory for the judicial inquiry on the subject of Ginés Hernández's services (see *infra*, p. 285), for it is natural to suppose that the Marañón expeditioners who returned to Peru journeyed together.

(of the Order of the Dominicans) with a ring of his, which was well known, to the end that without regard for any consideration whatsoever the fleet be delivered over to the Judges. When Friar Gaspar got there, he talked a long time with Diego Álvarez, insistently urging him to do this for the sake of the liberty and life of the Viceroy; but Diego Álvarez would not consent to do so."[18]

These events took place in the last months of the year 1544. Friar Carvajal was then sub-prior of the monastery of Lima, and it is probable that he filled this office for a period of four years; at all events, it is known that on October 26, 1547, he was present at the battle of Pucará[19] and that during the following year[20] he was a prior in Cuzco, where he was on fairly intimate terms with the Licentiate Pedro de La Gasca, as he himself has taken pains to relate.[21]*

From this time on one may say that Friar Carvajal had terminated his intervention in the political affairs of Peru, and that his old life of adventure was succeeded by one for which he was

---

[18] Diego Fernández [known as "el Palentino"], *Primera y segunda parte de la Historia del Perú*, Seville, 1571, Part I, fol. 20v. The arrest of the Viceroy took place on September 18, 1544: *ibid.*, I, fol. 19v. On board the ships of the fleet anchored in the harbor of Callao, Núñez Vela was holding as hostages the children of Francisco Pizarro. [The immediate caretaker of the two children whom Núñez Vela was holding was their aunt, Doña Inez Muñoz, widow of Francisco Martín de Alcántara, half-brother of Pizarro, killed with him on June 26, 1541. Doña Inez married, in 1543, Antonio de Ribera, who had acted as campmaster for Gonzalo Pizarro in the expedition with which the present work deals. The Diego Álvarez referred to was Diego Álvarez de Cueto, brother-in-law of the Viceroy.—TRANSLATOR.]

[19] In the declaration cited above Friar Carvajal does not state whether in this clash of arms he was on the side of Gonzalo Pizarro or of Diego Centeno, but it may be reasonably supposed that he was associated with the latter, against his old friend and fellow-Estremenian, as were all the others who had taken part in the Amazon expedition and whose subsequent careers are partly known to us through the extant records of judicial inquiries covering their services. If such had not been the case, it seems to me that he could not have enjoyed the friendship of La Gasca.

[We may also feel assured that on the part of Gonzalo Pizarro there was a great deal of ill feeling, for without doubt he believed that Orellana and his companions had basely deserted him. There exist among the La Gasca papers in the Henry E. Huntington Library, San Marino, California, several letters from Friar Carvajal to Gonzalo Pizarro. One, not dated, but belonging to the year 1547, is an offer of services to Gonzalo, and another, dated at Cuzco, January 8, 1547, is similar to it; but I am inclined to believe they were written to pull the wool over the eyes of Gonzalo and permit Carvajal to move about as a secret emissary of La Gasca, engaged in bringing home to the followers of Pizarro the advisability of returning to allegiance to the Crown.—TRANSLATOR.]

[20] In the declaration which I have already cited he states that he was present when La Gasca granted certain Indians to Pero López de Cazalla, the title to them having been given in Cuzco, August 19, 1548

[21] ". . . that there he visited him many times while he was prior of the monastery of Saint Dominic in the said city" (declaration cited above).

*[It is more than likely that Carvajal was active in the royal cause during all the troubles of the revolution of Gonzalo Pizarro and that he aided by carrying letters and information from the agents of La Gasca to those who were lukewarm in the cause of Pizarro, in an endeavor to alienate them from that chieftain—troubles that culminated in the triumph of the royalist cause at the battle of Xaquixaguana on April 9, 1548. He very likely served in the entourage of La Gasca in the endeavor of that wily prelate to placate the many claims of the captains and soldiers who had fought against Pizarro or had deserted him at the last moment and who all claimed compensation for their help.—TRANSLATOR.]

suited as a member of a religious order that had such a vast field before it at that time in America for putting its teachings into practice.

Indeed, it is stated by Father Meléndez that Carvajal was sent by La Gasca to Tucumán with the title of protector of the Indians, and that this appointment was confirmed by a royal decree of July 16, 1550;[22]† and that in the provincial chapter for 1553 he was made vicar-general of that monastery and of the buildings already erected or to be erected in those districts, and preacher-general of the monastery of Huamanga.[23]

[22] In none of the collections of royal decrees that are in the Archives of the Indies, however, was I able to find the slightest reference to such a document; nevertheless this is no proof that it does not exist. [Carvajal's appointment is referred to in a letter from La Gasca to the Council of the Indies dated at Lima, September 21, 1549, stating: "On the 13th of the said [month of] August there was sent off, with the official rank of protector, and in order that the pacifying and colonizing of Juaima might be carried out with the aid of his advice and opinion, Friar Gaspar de Carvajal, a friar-preacher of the Order of Saint Dominic and a man of letters and conscientiousness, and one who has had experience in matters pertaining to the Indians, and there was given to him the set of instructions which I am sending herewith; it seemed wise to do this in order that the said pacifying and colonizing might be carried out with a greater guarantee of conscientiousness" (Letter from the Licentiate La Gasca to the Council of the Indies, etc., in Roberto Levillier, editor, Gobernantes del Perú: Cartas y papeles, Siglo XVI, Vol. 1, Madrid, 1921, pp. 221–229; see p. 223).—TRANSLATOR.]

† [This, in fact, is true. Before La Gasca left Peru he opened escape valves to lessen the pressure from the loud-mouthed claimants and resorted to the device of Vaca de Castro: he gave out corregidorships, notarial positions, public offices, and, in supreme instances, in order to free the cities from the soldiers who had soon descended to a state of vagabondage when they found themselves without employment, he gave them lands to conquer and settle. On June 19, 1549 (Roberto Levillier, Nueva crónica de la conquista del Tucumán, Vol. 1, Lima, 1926, especially pp. 171 and 175; also pp. 179, 200, and 203), La Gasca signed a decree in Lima, stating that "beyond the Villa de la Plata, in the province of the Charcas in our realms of Peru, there is a province which in the Indian tongue is called Tucumán" and ordering Juan Núñez de Prado to go to that region and there found a city. He started out towards the end of 1549 from Potosí, Carvajal without doubt being a member of his party, and it is related that, owing to his evangelistic ideas, the expedition got on well with the Indian inhabitants; but a party of soldiers under Francisco de Villagra, entering the village of Tepiro on November 10, 1550, destroyed and robbed the village in spite of the fact that the crosses erected by Carvajal were in plain view, giving as a pretext that the country belonged to the jurisdiction of the governor of Chile, who at that time was Pedro de Valdivia, whose lieutenant Villagra was. It is not my purpose to inquire into the matter beyond the point of stating that in all the conversations and interviews between Villagra and Núñez de Prado as to the rights of one and the other, Friar Carvajal took an active part as ambassador from the camp of Núñez de Prado on various occasions. On October 8, 1551, Valdivia appointed Captain Francisco de Aguirre to replace Villagra, and the new man in command, immediately upon his arrival, expelled Núñez de Prado, Gaspar de Carvajal, and others from Tucumán, and sent them to Chile, all this happening in the middle of the year 1553. From here Friar Carvajal undoubtedly returned to Peru, for the provincial chapter meeting of the order held that year in Lima appointed him vicar-general in charge of the monastery in Tucumán and of the buildings already erected or to be erected there, and preacher-general in the monastery of Huamanga. It is quite likely that it was on his return from Chile that he was sent to Huamanga, to watch from that central point the intrigues leading up to the uprising of Francisco Hernández Girón, which broke out in 1554, and to send in information to his superiors for transmission to the Royal Audiencia in Lima. There exists a document dated at Lima, September 9, 1557, in which Carvajal as provincial of the order gives instructions to Friar Melchior de Villagómez to represent the order in a certain lawsuit (The Harkness Collection in the Library of Congress, Washington, 1932, p. 215).—TRANSLATOR.]

[23] We must confess, however, that the two positions seem hardly to be compatible with each other, in view of the enormous distance separating Huamanga from Tucumán, unless it be that the rank of preacher-general is to be considered as merely honorary.

I do not know whether or not, in compliance with this appointment, Friar Carvajal betook himself to those remote regions; but I do know that towards the end of July, 1557, in a chapter held in Lima, he was elected provincial of his order, and that, in fulfillment of the duties of his office, he visited many of the monasteries of the province.

It will be worth while to hear what one of the friars has to say of Carvajal and his administration. This friar was at that time only a simple student, but in the course of events he became bishop of Concepción in Chile:

"This wise and learned man (Friar Domingo de Santo Tomás) was succeeded by the great Friar Gaspar de Carvajal, a priest of great valor and of no less virtue—a plain and unaffected virtue —who left all the monasteries to which he went on his tours of inspection improved both spiritually and temporally, God favoring him; in his time, or during a part of it, the prior of this house was the very religious master Friar Tomás de Argomedo, a man of learning and of good example, who in the year [15]60 gave me the frock; and, no matter who we were, he used to take away our names and give us others, saying that for the new life new names were required; my name was Baltasar, but he commanded me to go by the name of Reginaldo, and with that name I have remained unto this day. This very religious man was the first in our monastery to begin to bring order into the choir; until then there had been none because there were no friars to keep it up; within a few months we took in, and gave the frock to, more than thirty, with whom, together with the rest of the priests in the monastery, there began both by day and by night, as in the strictest monastery in Spain, the maintaining of the observance of the faith; and the same was undertaken in all the rest of them in this city, because prior to this year [15]60 the number of priests in the monasteries was very small: so that you may see in how short a time the hand of the Lord had come most favorably upon all of them.— My profession of faith was received by the Provincial Friar Gaspar de Carvajal, when I had finished my year as a novitiate, and I wish that I had persevered in the simplicity that was then mine."[24]

[24] In Chapter 38 of this same work, which treats of the Monastery of the Incarnation, the name of Friar Carvajal is also mentioned in connection with an incident which cannot fail to be interesting: "They observe the profession and rules of the nuns of San Pedro de las Dueñas in Salamanca, subjects of the Ordinary; they tried with all their might to become our nuns, but they never could succeed in getting Friar Gaspar de Carvajal, of whom we have written briefly above as provincial, to receive them, although the prior of the monastery, Friar Master Tomás de Argomedo, favored them in all that was possible, and for many days they did not lose hope and they observed our

One of the towns which we know were visited by the Provincial Carvajal was Huánuco in the north of Peru. Nevertheless, Friar Carvajal's absence from Lima cannot have been an extended one, since on September 2, 1559, there was held in the capital, Lima, an extraordinary chapter meeting in which several measures were adopted for the interior administration of the province.*

In the chapter meeting immediately following, which must have been held in July or August, 1561, Carvajal, having ended his term as provincial, was elected one of the four members of the governing committee of the province; and in that of 1565 he was chosen to go as proctor to Spain and Rome, though the chronicler of the order doubts, and rightly so, that he made such a journey, since in the chapter meeting of 1569 he was promoted to the rank of candidate for the degree of master of divinity.[25]

For the next few years nothing more is heard of Carvajal, but in 1575 we find him subscribing to a document greatly to his credit, in which, addressing the King "as a Christian and a priest," he asks him to look to the protection of the Indians. I cannot refrain from transcribing this document, which reads as follows:

"To His Royal Majesty: As soon as Don Francisco de Toledo arrived here as viceroy of these realms, he called together prelates and counselors, and it seems that they decided and gave as their opinion that it was lawful to compel the Indians to hire themselves out for work in the mines, and so it has been done and is being done; and for four years now they have been compelling them, and carrying them off by force, to work in these mines, from which they receive notable injury and harm, particularly in the work in the quicksilver mines. It is taken for granted that Your Majesty is not informed of this matter, since you do not order it to be remedied, it being, as it is, so contrary to divine and natural right

order of prayer and followed the rules of our nuns, until finally, having lost hope, they adopted those which they now have and profess; they celebrate in this monastery the Transit of Our Lady" (*Libro que compuso Fr. Baltasar de Ovando*, Ch. 28 [Is it Ch. 28 or Ch. 38 (see beginning of this footnote)?—EDITOR], etc. National Library, Madrid, Dept. of Manuscripts, J-41).

*[I have also seen documents in the National Archives of Peru in which he asks aid for schools, and it may be stated almost as a fact that he gave instruction in the University which had been founded by his predecessor and which functioned for many years in the Dominican monastery of Lima until its definite establishment by the Viceroy Toledo on April 25, 1577, in its own building.—TRANSLATOR.]

[25] The reason at hand for Friar Carvajal's not undertaking the journey was never found out by Meléndez. It is my conviction that it could have been none other than the news which the Peruvian fathers must have received to the effect that the Chilean fathers were sending for the same purpose Friar Cristóbal Núñez, who on passing through Lima was given the power of attorney in this matter by the Peruvian fathers. This power of attorney, signed in Lima on July 1, 1569, among others by Friar Carvajal, is still preserved (Archives of the Indies).

that free men should be forced and compelled to perform tasks so trying, so injurious to their health, so endangering to their lives and so obstructive to the gospel preaching and to the faith which we are endeavoring to urge upon them, not to mention many other great difficulties that result from such compulsion; in view of which considerations and out of due respect to others, the Emperor our master, of glorious memory, with great judgment had commanded, by means of his special orders and decrees, that such systems of compulsion and such wrongs should cease. We have discussed this matter with the Archbishop of this city and with other prelates, and all state that none of them has ever been of the opinion that it is lawful to compel the said Indians to labor in the mines. We have felt that, as Christians and priests of the Order of our father Saint Dominic, who have always had special care to look after the interests of these natives, in view of the service which thereby accrues to God and Your Majesty, we were under obligation to advise Your Majesty of this matter in order that you may give orders that a proper remedy be put into effect, for the acquitting of your royal conscience, and in order that these natives, vassals of Your Majesty, may be freed from this compulsion and violence which they are being subjected to, and may be better instructed in the things of the faith. May Our Lord protect the Royal person of Your Majesty for many years, granting him an increase of states and dominions in His holy service, as we your vassals desire.—Los Reyes (Lima), March 17, 1575— To H.R.M. Humble chaplains and servants of Your Majesty who kiss his royal feet. *Friar Gaspar de Carvajal, Friar Alonso de la Cerda, Friar Miguel Adrian.*"

What resulted from this charitable gesture on the part of the Dominicans of Peru, who in this respect were following the path of the most famous man the order ever had in America, Friar Bartolomé de las Casas, is not a matter which falls within the province of the biographical study which we have in hand. It probably did set its signers at odds with the "encomenderos," those eternal exploiters of the native race; but there can be no doubt that it increased, in the public mind, the high esteem in which Friar Carvajal was held. His years no longer permitted him to go on the long journeys which constitute the dominating feature of his long career, and there in the monastery of Lima, which he had founded and which for so long a time had been the quiet refuge of his old age, he died in 1584, his funeral being honored with the presence of all who were notable in the civil and religious life of the city and country.

His *Account* of the voyage of Orellana, even if it is written without art, is the faithful reflection of his own impressions and of what he saw and is the only document that has been brought to light up to now relating in full that memorable event.[26]

[26] The principal biographer of Friar Carvajal has been until now Friar Juan Meléndez, who in Vol. 1 of his *Tesoros verdaderos de las Indias*, which he caused to be printed in Rome in 1681, devotes many pages [369–388; i.e. Book IV, Chs. 6 and 7] to relating the life of the chronicler of Orellana; but, as the reader has probably observed, he falls at every step into grave errors. Let it suffice to state that he supposes that Friar Carvajal was abandoned by Orellana when the latter resolved to begin the voyage down the Marañón, and that, consequently, Friar Carvajal did not take part in it.

Basing himself on the testimony of this author, Don Federico González Suárez has sketched in a few lines the life of Friar Carvajal in his *Historia del Ecuador*, Vol. 2, pp. 296–297.

Even before Meléndez another Dominican, Friar Reginaldo de Lizárraga, had briefly touched upon Friar Carvajal, without including anything which may be considered of importance.

Friar Alonso Fernández, general chronicler of the Spanish Dominicans, does not even mention Friar Carvajal in his *Historia eclesiástica de nuestros tiempos*, Toledo, 1611, folio, so interesting from many points of view; and the biographers of the Order of Saint Dominic, among them Quétif and Echard, had not even heard of the *Account* by our author.

# III

# AUTHORS WHO HAVE WRITTEN ABOUT ORELLANA'S VOYAGE

FRIAR CARVAJAL'S *Account* is followed in the present volume by: Gonzalo Pizarro's letter in which he denounces to the King the flight of his subordinate; the legal papers drawn up by Orellana at the time when he separated from his chief, for the purpose of being able later to justify his conduct, these papers, as well as the letter just mentioned, being documents whose existence was made known to me by Jiménez de la Espada through the columns of the *Ilustración Española y Americana;* Orellana's petition presented to the corporation of Quito, which was also utilized by the eminent writer on American history whom I have just named and which is of capital importance for the proper understanding of the facts in the public life of our hero in Peru; the judicial inquiries covering the individual service records of several of the expeditioners, the first in importance, from the point of view of chronological order and extent of content, being that of Cristóbal de Segovia, put through immediately upon the conclusion of the voyage of discovery and containing Orellana's own statements regarding some of the important details of his career; and, finally, a fragment from Toribio de Ortiguera's unpublished book, of interest because it recounts the various incidents of the expedition as they were told to him by some of the expeditioners who figured in it.

This is all the first-hand material of which I have any knowledge in connection with that memorable voyage of discovery; but, unfortunately, this is far from constituting all the documentation to which the event gave rise.

Orellana's desertion stirred up in Pizarro and his comrades the deepest indignation, which, as one will well understand, was bound to manifest itself in writing and in the form of attestations consonant with the judicial procedure in use at that time. Pizarro, it is known, did not limit himself to addressing to the King the declaration which I have mentioned; he had affidavits drawn up covering Orellana's action and sent them to the capital as the beginning of court proceedings against the captain who had revolted against him. ". . . it has been brought to my attention," says Orellana shortly after his arrival in Spain, "that letter-affidavits[27] coming from Gonzalo Pizarro have been presented, stating that I separated from the expeditionary force where he was [in command], and that I ran off with a brigantine and canoes filled with men and property belonging to him, and that as a consequence of my having revolted a certain number of men died of hunger"; and yet, immediately after, he shows himself to be less certain that what he suspects is accurate, requesting that in any case he be heard, "because . . . it would not be just for the said Gonzalo Pizarro to report [on this matter] in the manner in which he is reporting, [namely] with [the testimony of] witnesses chosen by him when he was governor, for they, in conformity with the nature of the matter involved, were bound to say, in order to exonerate themselves, all that they would be asked to say . . . "[28]

I for my part feel convinced that these affidavits did exist and that without any doubt Pizarro would have had others drawn up on his return to Quito, if on arriving there he had not been met with the grave news of the death of his brother, the Governor, a circumstance which of course called for his undivided attention and which, awakening ambitious designs in his heart, gradually drew him on to the point where he dreamed of setting up a kingdom independent of the mother country, comprising the vast regions discovered and conquered, as he said, by his family.

Still, the fact is that no such affidavits are to be found; and, if documents furnishing evidence in accusation of Orellana are thus lacking, on the other hand others which could have been brought forth in his defense appear also to have been lost. First among these latter to be mentioned is the account of his voyage which Orellana himself submitted; its existence at one time is attested by the following fragments of official texts.

In an autograph letter from the secretary Juan de Sámano to the "Comendador Mayor" of León, Francisco de los Cobos, dated May 31, 1543, there is a paragraph as follows: "As regards matters of the Indies there is nothing to be said until the arrival of Martín Alonso, whose coming is the most important one that is to be desired now. There has arrived from Peru one who came out by going down

[27] This is literally what Orellana says. Did he mean to say "letters and affidavits," or does he refer only to documents of the latter sort? I am inclined to think it more natural that both sorts were meant, judging from the normal usage in such cases and from what we know the practice was.

[28] P. 252 of the present volume.

a river, for he navigated a distance of one thousand eight hundred leagues and came out at the Cape of Saint Augustine, and, because the particulars which he has brought with him covering his voyage are such as Your Lordship will not listen to without fatigue, I shall not relate them, since he will shortly come himself"; and in the margin, apparently in the handwriting of Cobos himself, may be read: "would like account sent for His Majesty; let it be sent . . . "[29] And by way of reply to this annotation Sámano wrote shortly after: "The memorandum and account of the voyage that was made by the man who came from Peru is not going along with this, because it is being copied and is very long; it will be taken along by the first [messenger to go to you], and it is not of so much importance in my opinion as not to be more prejudicial [to our interests] than advantageous, as I shall write to Your Lordship when the account goes forward."[30]

Let us pass over for the time being this last reflection of Sámano's, founded on the fear that the new discovery might create complications with the government of Portugal. However, I have brought forth explicit evidence showing that Orellana presented before the Council of the Indies a long account of his voyage—an account which is not to be found today in the Archives. Was this account based on Friar Carvajal's notes? It is quite probable that it was, though I cannot but believe that it differed from either of the two versions of the Dominican friar's story which we now have, for to the friar's general outline Orellana probably added his own observations and personal impressions. It would be absurd to suppose that it was the chronicler's account which he presented, when we know the eulogistic terms in which Friar Carvajal expresses himself at every step in regard to his "Captain."

Moreover, it can be safely affirmed that López de Gómara and Herrera knew this account of Orellana's. The first of these two authors, in fact, mentions it, qualifying it as "full of lies," although, as has already been noted by Pinelo-Barcia,[31] he does not state on what he bases his assertion. But this is not difficult to discover. Carvajal in his notes and Orellana in his statements in the capital had spoken of the Amazons; and, as the existence of these women

<hr/>

[29] Archives of Simancas, State, Docket 61, fol. 208. This letter bears no indication as to year, but as it is among papers of 1543 it cannot belong to any other year.

[30] Letter of June 7, 1543.—Docket quoted, fol. 213.

[31] *Biblioteca oriental y occidental* [i.e. Antonio de León Pinelo. *Epitome de la bibliotheca oriental y occidental, nautica y geográfica* (second edition extensively added to and published by Andrés González de Barcia Carballido y Zúñiga, 3 volumes in one, with consecutive numbering of columns) Madrid, 1737-38], col. 683.

could be nothing but a fiction, a serious charge was raised against both Orellana and his chronicler for having sponsored a fable destitute of all verisimilitude.

"Among the extravagant statements which he made," says López de Gómara, to quote his own words, "was his claim that there were Amazons along this river with whom he and his companions had fought. That the women there should take up arms and fight is no novelty, for in Paria, which is not very far off, and in many other parts of the Indies, they used to do that; I do not believe either that any woman burns and cuts off her right breast in order to be able to shoot with the bow, because with it [i.e. the right breast] they shoot very well; or that they kill or exile their own sons; or that they live without husbands, being as they are very voluptuous. Others besides Orellana have proclaimed this same yarn about the Amazons ever since the Indies have been discovered, and never has such a thing been seen, and never will it be seen either, along this river. Because of this imposture, already many write and say the 'River of the Amazons,' and there have gathered together so many parties to go there."[32]

And in the same manner as López de Gómara, several of the old writers poke fun at the credulity manifested by Orellana and Carvajal in this matter.

Nevertheless, I believe that these inculpations launched against Orellana and the chronicler of his expedition start from a false premise. It is an undeniable fact that among the Indians with whom they had to fight along the river they had seen a certain number of women marching in front of their fighting squadrons; but between this and vouching for the existence of the Amazons there is a long way to go. Friar Carvajal limits himself to setting down the answers which the Indian questioned by Orellana gave relative to the manner of life of those women, but nothing more,[33] without saying whether or not he for his part believed such a tale. For this reason, I believe that the one who hits upon the truth in this matter is Antonio de Herrera when he says that "in regard to the Amazons, many have expressed the opinion that Captain Orellana ought not to have given this name to those women who fought nor have affirmed on such a slim foundation that they were Amazons, because in the Indies it was not a new thing that the women

---

[32] Rivadeneyra edition, p. 210. [See footnote 46, *infra*.]

[33] So it was understood also by Oviedo when he says: "From an Indian whom this Captain Orellana took along with him . . . they learned that in the country where these women are ruling persons," etc. (*Historia general y natural de las Indias*, Vol. 4, p. 389). This cunning Indian who so completely fooled the expeditioners died later in Cubagua.

should fight and draw their bows, as has been seen in some of the Windward Islands and in Cartagena and its neighborhood, where they showed themselves to be as valorous as the men."[34]

In addition to the very important document of which I have been speaking [namely, Orellana's own account of the voyage], I must mention also the absence of the "memoriales"[35] resulting from the expedition—documents which Herrera succeeded in seeing but which he did not utilize—as well as of the depositions or letters of the two friars who were members of the expedition, the existence at one time of these documents being known from the same source.[36]

From the island of Cubagua, Orellana went to Santo Domingo, where Gonzalo Fernández de Oviedo talked with him and learned from his own mouth the first story of the voyage of discovery. That voyage, following the current of the greatest river in the world over a distance of eighteen hundred leagues, was an event so important for the history of geography (being, as that chronicler at that time said,* "one of the greatest things that have happened to men") that it was deemed worth while to make it known in Europe at once. Consequently, the chronicler of the Indies took his pen in hand and in a long letter to Italy announced the event to Cardinal Bembo, who at that time enjoyed the favors of the celebrated Lucrezia Borgia—a letter which the compiler Giovanni Battista Ramusio inserted, in an abridged form, in the third volume[37] of his collection of voyages, *Delle navigationi e viaggi*, first published in 1555; this abridgment, in turn, was translated into Spanish by Gabriel de Cárdenas, and the manuscript of it was conserved for some time in Barcia's bookstore, according to the compiler of the *Biblioteca oriental y occidental*.[38]

[34] *Historia general de los hechos de los castellanos*, Decade VI, Book IX, Ch. 4. It would serve no purpose for us to try to substantiate what Herrera says relative to the Indian women who used to go into battle with their husbands, because this is a well-known fact in the case of many American tribes. See my *Aboríjenes de Chile* [Santiago de Chile, 1882], in which I have brought together much documentary evidence on this point.

[35] Herrera, in fact, says: "This business about the Amazons I reproduce as it is found in the 'memoriales' of this expedition" [*ibid.*, Decade VI, Book IX, Ch. 4].

[36] "The two priestly fathers who took part in this voyage affirmed . . ." [*ibid.*, Decade VI Book IX, Ch. 6].

* [Oviedo, *Historia general y natural de las Indias*, Vol. 4, p. 384.—EDITOR.]

[37] Page 345, edition of 1605. [In the edition of 1556 (Venice; also 1565, in the same place), fols. 415-416.—EDITOR.]

[38] Picatoste y Rodríguez, under number 257 of his *Apuntes para una biblioteca científica española del siglo XVI* [Madrid, 1891], mentions this letter of Oviedo, although he supposes mistakenly, following Pinelo-Barcia, that it formed part of his *Historia . . . de las Indias*. Oviedo's letter bears the date January 20, 1543, and was written, therefore, before two months had passed after the arrival of Orellana at Santo Domingo. In Pinelo-Barcia it is stated that the letter filled twenty-four folios, while Ramusio's extract occupies only two. [Orellana arrived at Santo Domingo probably on November 20, 1542 (see footnote 174, p. 125, *infra*).—TRANSLATOR.]

Oviedo himself further states that some of the incidents of Orellana's expedition became known to him "through letters which came after this Captain Orellana had arrived at this city of Santo Domingo, written in the city of Popayán" on August 13, 1542,[39] all of these being documents of which we have no knowledge at present.

In view of what has been said up to this point, it is easy to see that the first author to write[40] about Orellana's voyage was the chronicler Fernández de Oviedo, whom I have been quoting. The fact that he happened to be in Santo Domingo when the hero of the voyage landed there with some of his comrades enabled him to learn from a good source[41] many of its details, among them some which Friar Carvajal had not included in his notes and which, moreover, Oviedo inserted integrally, as has been shown, at the end of his work; but this work remained unknown until our own time. Let us hear what Oviedo himself has to say in this connection:

" . . . and, because this voyage and discovery of the Marañón will be described *ad plenum* where I have said, I shall not stop here to discuss the matter, except for certain particulars which, in addition to that which as an eyewitness a devout friar of the Order of Saint Dominic wrote down, I have since learned in this city of Santo Domingo from Captain Francisco de Orellana himself and from other cavaliers and hidalgos who came in with him. These particulars the said friar did not write down in his account because he did not remember to do so, or [because] it did not seem to him that he ought to concern himself with them; I shall tell it all as I heard it from this captain and his companions."[42]

[39] *Historia . . . de las Indias*, Vol. 4, p. 385.

[40] I hardly need to call attention here to the fact that in this summary review of the authors who have treated the subject of Orellana's voyage, I do not mention the articles in dictionaries, nor the histories of Brazil and the books in Portuguese in which the matter is touched upon incidentally, nor the accounts of travels, etc. Among these latter, however, mention must be made of the *Relation abrégée d'un voyage fait dans l'intérieur de l'Amérique Méridionale* by La Condamine, who appears to have made use of Orellana's *Account*, according to a statement of his on page 10 of the Paris edition of 1745. Among the works in Portuguese we must also make an exception, because of the special character of the matter which it treats and because of its rarity, in the case of the *Relaçao Svmaria das covsas do Maranhao, Escrita pello Capitao Symao Estacio da Sylueira*, em Lisboa, com todas as licenças necessarias, por Geraldo da Vinha, anno de 1624. Orellana's expedition, mentioned in a few brief lines, is found on page 3. [This account has been reprinted by Candido Mendes de Almeida in his *Memorias para a historia do extincto estado do Maranhão*, Vol. 2, Rio de Janeiro, 1874, pp. 1-31; cf. the short Chapter 7 entitled "Jornada de Gonçalo Pizarro e Francisco Orelhana" on pp. 9-10.—EDITOR.]

[41] "I learned from this Captain Orellana and his companions," etc. "As to the great size of the Marañón River, I was assured by Captain Orellana and his companions, who came here," etc. (*op. cit.*, Vol. 4, p. 387).

[42] Vol. 4, p. 384.

Thus we find that the two works, that of the Dominican friar and that of the chronicler of the Indies, supplement each other.

Pedro de Cieza de León is another of the historians of Orellana's voyage. The case of this author is exactly the same as that of Fernández de Oviedo. His work, entitled *Guerra de Chupas*, which contains valuable data concerning the itinerary followed by Orellana from the time he departed from Guayaquil until he joined Gonzalo Pizarro (data which would be sought for in vain elsewhere), remained unpublished and unknown until it was printed in the *Colección de documentos inéditos para la historia de España*.[43]

In the same situation as Cieza de León and Oviedo is Toribio de Ortiguera, author of a special work entitled *Jornada del Río Marañón, con todo lo acaecido en ella y otras cosas notables dignas de ser sabidas acaecidas en las Indias Occidentales del Pirú*, from which I publish here the fragment which deals with Orellana's voyage.[44]

Having been a witness of many of the important events which had occurred in Peru in his time and being anxious to offer to his prince (later Philip III) a more or less orderly and detailed account of the events whose scene of action had been the banks of the Amazon, Ortiguera wrote his book using, in so far as it dealt with Orellana's expedition, the testimony of some of those who had taken part in it.[45]

[43] It occupies, under the title of *Guerras civiles del Perú: Guerra de Chupas*, pp. 1–371 of Vol. 76 of this collection; the volume was published in Madrid in 1881. [For Pizarro's expedition, see Chs. 18–22 on pp. 61–82; for Orellana's voyage, see the first paragraph of Ch. 21, on p. 73. The work has been rendered into English by Sir Clements R. Markham, this translation being published as No. 42 of the Second Series of works issued by the Hakluyt Society, London, 1918: see pp. 54–77.—TRANSLATOR.] [The *Guerra de Chupas* forms Book II of Part IV of Cieza de León's *Crónica del Perú*.—EDITOR.]

[44] Pp. 310–320 of the present volume. [This entire account can now be read in the second volume of M. Serrano y Sanz's *Historiadores de Indias* (2 vols., Madrid, 1909, forming Vols. 13 and 15 of the *Nueva biblioteca de autores españoles*), Vol. 2, pp. 305–422. From statements contained in Ch. 14 it appears that the account proper was written in 1581, while Ortiguera was still in Quito; but the introductory paragraph containing the dedication of the work to Prince Philip could not have been written before 1585.—EDITOR.]

Ortiguera went to the Indies in 1561 as a captain of troops in the city of Nombre de Dios, and in the following year to Panama to serve against the rebels Rodrigo Méndez and Francisco de Santisteban, and after the rout and death of these latter, to Peru, "coming forward promptly," as he himself tells us, "in full earnestness and with all my strength on all occasions which arose in connection with the service of His Majesty, with my arms and [my] horse, at my own expense, not only in the positions of state which I held, but also outside of them . . . " [*infra*, p. 311]. It is on record that, having returned to Spain in 1585, he was living in Seville in 1595, where "he had built and fitted out a frigate from the keel up," which he wished to send out to the Indies—a project which was not carried out. (From a document preserved in the Archives of the Indies.)

[45] " . . . according to information which I obtained from some of those who took part in the affair, who were persons of reputation and good faith, such as were the Governor Andrés Contero, and Juan de Vargas, treasurer of the royal exchequer of Guayaquil, and Andrés Durán Bravo, head justice of the peace in this city, and Captain Juan de Llanes (Illanes), a citizen who holds

More fortunate than those whom I have mentioned so far were López de Gómara and Zárate,[46] for their works were published during their lifetimes and were drawn on, as sources for the account of these deeds, by the Inca Garcilaso de la Vega, who also had an opportunity to utilize the testimony of "many of those who accompanied Gonzalo Pizarro on this voyage of discovery," wherefore "I shall relate," he says, "what happened, borrowing now from the one and now from the other."[47]

Garcilaso de la Vega has been the favorite author drawn upon, for data concerning Orellana, by Friar Juan Meléndez in his *Tesoros verdaderos de las Indias;** by the Jesuit Manuel Rodríguez in his *Marañón y Amazonas*, published in Madrid in 1684, in which, as he himself says, he copied Garcilaso "almost in his own words";[48] and finally by Prescott, who for this reason, in so far as this part

an *encomienda* within the jurisdiction of the city of Quito, and Pero Domínguez Miradero" (p. 316 of the present volume).

This affirmation on the part of Ortiguera is entirely accurate in so far as it concerns Illanes, Domínguez Miradero, and Andrés Durán, who actually accompanied Orellana on his voyage. The Juan de Vargas to whom he refers I believe to have been the son of another man of the same name who went with them; and as for Captain Andrés Contero, it is known, in fact, that he made an expedition into the provinces of Quijos, Zumaco, and La Canela about the year 1561. Without doubt it was from him that Ortiguera gained his notions of the topography of the region, but this does not imply that Contero accompanied Orellana. The fact is that the judicial inquiries covering Contero's service record, now in the Archives of the Indies, do not mention any such participation in the expedition.

[46] Francisco López de Gómara, *Historia general de las Indias* (originally published at Saragossa in 1552), p. 243 ff. [also p. 210] of the Rivadeneyra edition [i.e. Vol. 22 (*Historiadores primitivos de Indias*, Vol. 1), Madrid, 1852, of *Biblioteca de autores españoles desde la formación del lenguaje hasta nuestros días*, 70 vols., M. Rivadeneyra y Cia., Madrid, 1846–78.]

Agustín de Zárate, *Historia del descubrimiento y conquista de la provincia del Perú*, Book IV, Chs. 2, 3, 4, and 5 [see Rivadeneyra edition: *Biblioteca de autores españoles*, Vol. 26 (*Historiadores primitivos de Indias*, Vol. 2), Madrid, 1853, pp. 493–495].

[47] Garcilaso de la Vega, *Comentarios reales de los Incas*, Second Part, Book III, Ch. 2. The *Primera Parte* of this work was first printed in Lisbon in 1609, while the Second Part, or the *Historia general del Perú*, came out in Cordova, Spain, in 1617. The work was reprinted [by Andrés González de Barcia Carballido y Zúñiga] at Madrid, 1723, and a later edition came out in Spain in 1829. A French translation [by Jean Baudoin] was published in 1633 and went through several editions. [The work was translated into English by Sir Paul Rycaut (London, 1688), and more recently (First Part only) by Sir Clements R. Markham for the Hakluyt Society of London (2 vols., Nos. 41 and 45 in the First Series of works issued by this society, London, 1869 and 1871). Moreover, Book III of the Second Part, dealing with Gonzalo Pizarro's expedition to the Land of Cinnamon and, briefly, with Orellana's voyage, has also been sketchily translated by Markham, in the same series, No. 24, London, 1859, pp. 3–20.—TRANSLATOR.]

*Vol. 1, Rome, 1681, pp. 373–375.

[48] This author, as is well known, incorporated into his book (pp. 103–141 and 425–428) Friar Cristóbal de Acuña's *Nuevo descubrimiento del gran río de las Amazonas* [Madrid, 1641], a work of which I have no occasion to speak, inasmuch as it does not treat of the personage who is the subject of my investigation. [Apparently, Medina did not consult this work itself, for the fact is that on the recto and verso of fol. 1 of the edition of 1641 there is a short chapter devoted chiefly to Orellana. Acuña's work was translated by Sir Clements Markham in the publications of the Hakluyt Society, First Series, No. 24, pp. 41–142, London, 1859. The chapter devoted to Orellana is on pp. 47–48.—EDITOR.]

of his work is concerned, has impaired the value of his masterly and artistic *History of the Conquest of Peru*.

Better informed than Garcilaso is Antonio de Herrera, who devotes to the expedition of Orellana Chapters 2, 3, 4, 5, and 6 of Decade VI, Book IX, of his *Historia general de los hechos de los castellanos en las Islas y Tierra Firme del Mar Océano*. He has presented to us a fairly complete picture of the event, although he did not utilize to as full an advantage as he might have done the documents which he had at his disposal, some of which have since disappeared.[49]

In Spanish America we have, as historians who only incidentally touch upon Francisco de Orellana, the Jesuit Juan de Velasco, Pedro Fermín Cevallos, and Pablo Herrera, all Ecuadorians; Lorente and Mendiburu in Peru; and finally, the canon of Quito, Federico González Suárez, who in his history of Ecuador has devoted several pages of interest to Orellana, even though they are not entirely irreproachable.[50]

Finally, Marcos Jiménez de la Espada, a man thoroughly familiar with the regions which were the scene of Orellana's exploits and the most profound and most conscientious of the Spanish scholars

---

[49] Herrera's work was printed in Madrid in the years 1601–1615 in four folio volumes; it was reprinted in Amsterdam in 1728, and a second time in Madrid sometime between 1726 and 1730. There is a French translation by N. de la Coste, 3 vols., Paris, 1660–71, large quarto.

Orellana's voyage has been poorly dealt with by foreign authors. Robert Kerr, in his *General History and Collection of Voyages and Travels*, Edinburgh, 1812, Vol. 4, pp. 447–449, does no more than translate Zárate's version; Captain John Stevens translates Herrera's version in his *General History of the Vast Continent and Islands of America*, Vol. 5, London, 1726, pp. 251–265; and Markham includes both the Inca Garcilaso's and Herrera's versions in his selection of documents entitled *Expeditions into the Valley of the Amazons*, London, 1859 (works issued by the Hakluyt Society, First Series, No. 24), pp. 1–40.

Neither in Thévenot's collection of voyages, nor in Van der Aa's, nor in Churchill's, nor in any other, so far as I know, with the exception of that of Ramusio of which I have already spoken, will one find the slightest mention of Orellana's voyage. [The collections to which Medina here refers are presumably the following: Melchisedech Thévenot, *Relations de divers voyages curieux, qui n'ont point été publiées*, etc., Paris, 1663 ("Seconde partie," Paris, 1664), and later editions; Pieter van der Aa (bookseller), *De aanmerkenswaardigste en alomberoemde Zee- en Landreizen der Portugeezen, Spanjaarden, Engelsen en allerhande Natiën*, etc., 8 vols., Leyden, 1706–27; Awnsham and John Churchill, *A Collection of Voyages and Travels, Some Now First Printed from Original Manuscripts, Others Now First Published in English*, 6 vols., London, 1732.—EDITOR.]

[50] Federico González Suárez, *Historia general de la República del Ecuador*, 7 vols., Quito, 1890–1903 (plus a volume with subtitle *Atlás arqueológico*): see Vol. 2, pp. 283–296.

Juan de Velasco, *Historia del reino de Quito en la América Meridional*, 3 vols., Quito, 1844, 1841, 1842: see Vol. 2, pp. 155–159.

Pedro Fermín Cevallos, *Resumen de la historia del Ecuador desde su origen hasta 1845*, 2nd edit., 5 vols., Guayaquil, 1886: see Vol. 1, pp. 387–396.

Pablo Herrera, *Apuntes para la historia de Quito*, Quito, 1874: see pp. 68–72.

Sebastián Lorente, *Historia de la conquista del Perú*, Lima, 1861: see pp. 417–422.

Manuel de Mendiburu, *Diccionario histórico-bibliográfico del Perú*, 8 vols., Lima, 1874–90 see Vol. 6 (1885), pp. 164–171.

interested in America (let this be said in detriment to none) has given us several valuable articles which have thrown considerable light upon many of the incidents in connection with the discovery of the Amazon.[51]

I shall close here this dry though necessary review of the historians of Orellana. By way of rounding it out, I shall now see how a reputable dramatist in olden times took hold of the figure of Orellana and how in a fit of irritation he represented it amidst the applause of the spectators in the theaters.

[51] I may state here that if I had known that my distinguished friend was thinking of publishing these articles, I should not have undertaken the present task, for I can easily believe that the results which I have obtained are incommensurate with the effort which it has required of me.

Jiménez de la Espada's first article appeared in the *Ilustración Española y Americana*, August 22, 1892, and the others came out exactly two years later. It is doubly to be regretted that the series of articles has remained unfinished and that they have not been brought together in book form. [On this point see, above, Editor's Preface, pp. vii and ix.—EDITOR.]

As a mere curiosity, but for no other reason, I shall also mention here Gómez de Arteche's article *Orellana y el río de su nombre*, with which his *Revista del Centenario* was started in 1892.

# IV

## ORELLANA IN THE DRAMA

THE portentous feats performed by the Spanish adventurers, the vast setting in which these deeds had been accomplished, the interest which they were destined to arouse—all this contributed toward making it evident that here were ready-made scenes and characters for such authors as might desire to seize upon them and present them on the stage. And so we have, as one after the other they tread upon the boards, Hernán Cortés, García Hurtado de Mendoza, the illustrious Alonso de Ercilla, the Pizarros, and later Núñez de Balboa, Almagro, and even Columbus himself.

Material for an interesting monograph could undoubtedly be obtained from a study of these dramatic pieces, in which history and the characters of the personages were ordinarily falsified in the most absurd manner and the most stupendous anachronisms were perpetrated, while the plays themselves (and this is an even worse feature about them) were at times inspired by sentiments quite distinct from those which are popularly supposed to adorn poets.[52]

Francisco de Orellana is one of the personages handled in this manner, although his rôle in the dramatic trilogy composed by the master Tirso de Molina under the title of *Hazañas de los Pizarros* is in the nature of a mere recounted incident.

It would be foreign to my purpose, as well as displeasing to the reader, for me to go into an analysis of a work so preposterous; I must limit myself, therefore, to reproducing for my readers the passages which relate more particularly to our hero.

In the second part of that trilogy of "famous comedies," the one entitled *Las Amazonas en las Indias*, there are presented to us as interlocutors Vaca de Castro and Francisco de Carvajal, the latter being Gonzalo Pizarro's bloodthirsty campmaster, and they carry on a dialogue which begins as follows:*

Vaca de Castro:—And because I should like to hear about the wonderful, though unsuccessful expedition to La Canela [Land of Cinnamon], and because

[52] An analysis of those dramatic pieces which concern Chile, and in particular Ercilla, may be found in my *Historia de la literatura colonial de Chile*, Santiago, 1878, Vol. I, pp. 111–116.

*[The original is in verse.—EDITOR.]

I see that you are as much interested in peace as you are valiant in arms, I beg you to tell us about it, for it is only just that we extol the triumphs of this man Pizarro.

Carvajal:—If deeds of valor be proper stuff for ecclesiastical harangues and it be my turn to preach, I will obey, so on with the sermon. Desirous of extending the imperial power of Spain, the Marquis Pizarro, then residing in Lima, relinquished in favor of Don Gonzalo the governorship of Quito, whose provinces at that time formed the outermost limit of the Christian conquests. He gave him five hundred soldiers composing the most splendid body of men that ever valor and cupidity enlisted for these parts. Supported by these men, then, and by his own magnificent courage, he leads eastward four thousand Indians [well] armed and joyful over the report that when once the mountains had been crossed [we should arrive] at the borders and shores of the monarch of the waters, of that undulating dropsy which swallows up so many Niles and glides on over a distance of a thousand leagues, its gold, liquid in [the form of] syrup, [thus constituting] seas of immense expanse: to it they give the name of Marañón (may Your Lordship pardon me if I go to extremes in my exaggeration, for nowadays discourses in plain language and without an abundance of hyperboles are eschewed, and only words with long locks on them are approved by the crowd). So, I say, lured by the greed inspired by the generally accepted fame of the cinnamon trees which grow on those rocky slopes, we marched on to the sound of beating drums as far as the territory which the Inca Gainacano brought under his control and which is called, I believe, Quinja.

And the author continues in his own manner, making use exclusively of Garcilaso's book, to relate the march of Gonzalo Pizarro up to the time when the brigantine was constructed, and then says:

To Francisco de Orellana, because he was a person of high esteem and a man of his own blood and from his own native region, he entrusts the command of the vessel, and orders him, with fifty Spaniards, to carry on the discoveries down the Marañón with all haste and to wait eighty leagues farther on, for he is informed that there two rivers end by becoming part of the Marañón. The treacherous relative started off, and as soon as he is out of sight he seizes the vessel for himself, incites all the men to mutiny and puts ashore Father Carvajal, of the Holy Family [i.e. Order] of the best Guzmán of Spain, because he [i.e. Father Carvajal] had reproached him for his undue abuse of power, and it was through a great piece of luck that he did not perish of hunger, for he had nothing to eat for four days. Eight days later, by traveling overland, we reach the above-mentioned region, and, when we find the friar, he tells us the story of the flight [of Orellana], unbecoming to such a man and to one of such noble birth, whereby in fact he robs us of more than a hundred thousand gold pesos which the conquests had brought us.

From these fragments of the play it is easy to form an opinion as to the historical truthfulness to which it pretends to adhere and to see how the figure of Orellana is brought forth merely for the purpose of enhancing that of Gonzalo Pizarro. The latter, finally, reaches the domains of the Amazons, where one of these, who is given the name of Menalipe, courts Gonzalo, and in an effort to persuade him to remain in her company, says to him:

> The treacherous relative has carried off your vessel, your treasure, and your clothing; without him, how are you going to win, even though in these wilds you accomplish formidable and seemingly impossible deeds, either on land or on the waters of this, as it were, vast sea?

These remarks do not succeed in convincing the Spanish captain, and he replies to them in these terms:

> Captain Orellana ran off with my brigantine and left us naked—an act of stupid and base disloyalty: my men, if I yield to your flattering advances, will not look with favor upon my not going back to Quito.[53]

But it is now time for me to leave the field of poetic fictions and, with the historical materials that I have been able to gather together, turn my attention to the discoverer of the Amazon himself.

---

[53] The first part of the trilogy by Father Téllez [the real name of this member of the Order of Mercedarians, Tirso de Molina being his pen name] is entitled *Todo es dar en una cosa y hazañas de los Pizarros;* the third, *La lealtad contra la envidia y hazañas de los Pizarros.* The second, to which belong the passages which I have quoted, was printed for the first time in the *Parte cuarta de las comedias del Maestro Tirso de Molina,* Madrid, 1635. It was reprinted in Madrid in the eighteenth century, separately, no year, in a quarto edition which I do not find mentioned in the *Catálogo bibliográfico del teatro antiguo español* by the erudite scholar Barrera y Leirado. [The play is now readily accessible in the two-volume collection of *Comedias de Tirso de Molina,* Madrid, 1906–07 (Vols. 4 and 9 of *Nueva biblioteca de autores españoles*), published by Emilio Cotarelo y Mori: see Vol. I, pp. 551–578.—EDITOR.]

# V

# BIOGRAPHICAL DATA RELATING TO
# FRANCISCO DE ORELLANA

FRANCISCO DE ORELLANA was born in Trujillo,[54] Estremadura, about the year 1511,[55] of a family related to that of Francisco Pizarro, and was always considered a "persona principal" (i.e. a prominent man of good family), to use the phrase applied by a chronicler who may be supposed to have been well informed on this subject.[56] He must have been very young, almost a child,[57] when he crossed over to the Indies, because, as he himself tells us, as early as 1542 he was in a position to testify to the deeds

[54] This is vouched for by Fernández de Oviedo, *Historia general y natural de las Indias*, Vol. 4, p. 384, and by Cieza de León, *Guerra de Chupas* [for bibliographical details of latter work, see footnote 43, *supra*.]

[55] This date is deduced from the sworn declaration of Orellana himself, made when he was on the island of Margarita in October, 1542, in connection with the judicial inquiry on the subject of Cristóbal de Segovia's services, wherein he declares that he was at that time thirty years old, more or less [see, *infra*, p. 270]. This will be sufficient evidence to contradict those who have maintained that Orellana was already an old man when he went on his voyage down the Amazon. That he must be thought of, independently of the item of evidence which I have just recorded, as having been quite young at this time we shall see later on when we come to the reasons which he had for marrying after he returned to Spain.

Desiring to verify the date of Orellana's birth, I have had a friend examine the baptismal records of Trujillo; but it so happens that these do not go back further than 1548.

[56] Fernando Pizarro y Orellana, *Varones ilustres del Nuevo Mundo*, Madrid, 1639, p. 351. Orellana, in his petition to the city corporation of Guayaquil, boasts (p. 264 of the present volume) also of being "a gentleman of noble blood and a person of honor," and the city magistrates, in their turn, certify that he is "an hidalgo of known ancestral estate" [*infra*, p. 265].

[According to the Spanish historian Clodoaldo Naranjo y Alonso, in his work *Trujillo y su tierra*, Madrid, 1925, there were three branches of the Pizarro family which had descended from Gonzalo Sánchez Pizarro (supposed to have been born in the last third of the thirteenth century), the second, or the Pizarro Orellanas, being the progenitors of the famous group that gave so many of its sons for the New World discoveries and conquests. A genealogical tree prepared by this historian shows that among the children born to Hernando Alfonso Pizarro and Isabel Rodríguez, one, namely Gonzalo Pizarro, was the father of Francisco the conquistador, and Estefanía Pizarro, his sister, was married to Francisco de Orellana. It is more than likely that our hero was the fruit of this marriage, or possibly a grandson of the couple; this would make him either a first cousin or a nephew of Francisco Pizarro and his brothers Hernando, Juan, and Gonzalo, the last-mentioned being his chief at the time when his famous expedition started off. He probably hailed from the village of La Zarza, which is situated four leagues from Trujillo, the ancient seat of the Pizarros; and as a boy he had undoubtedly played with the younger members of that clan.—TRANSLATOR ]

[57] Notwithstanding the fact that there is apparently no room for doubt on this point, inasmuch as it is vouched for by the person in question in his own deposition, which has every appearance of being authentic, it behooves us to bear in mind that the signers of such depositions regularly fall into striking self-contradictions in the matter of dates and ages. I happen to know of the case of one who stated that he was forty years of age, yet is known to have taken part in actions thirty-five years prior to the date of his declaration. However, I am obliged to accept data secured from documents apparently authentic, and therefore there remains for me no recourse but to accept what I state in the text.

accomplished by some of the conquistadors in those lands during the preceding fifteen years.

But to what part of the Indies did he go first? If, to abide by his own figures, his departure took place in 1527, his destination could not have been Peru, which at that time was not yet discovered. It is true that his relative Francisco Pizarro had at this period already gained a certain reputation and that he figured among the principal captains who were in Panama perfecting their plans for explorations in the lands which extended toward the south and which, according to the tales of the indigenes, were literally strewn with gold and inhabited by men much more civilized than any others known up to that time to be dwelling along the shores of the sea discovered by Núñez de Balboa. The general trend of explorations was towards the north, towards the lands which lay between the isthmus and the great empire of the Aztecs, destined to be the scene of the exploits of Hernán Cortés; in a word, towards Nicaragua. There exists, in fact, a strong likelihood that Orellana first landed somewhere in these regions and that it was here that he performed his first feats of arms as a conquistador.[58]

Be that as it may, there can be absolutely no doubt that at least he participated "in the conquests of Lima and Trujillo and Cuzco and in the pursuit of the Inca and in the conquest of Puerto Viejo

[58] I shall endeavor to point out here the reasons for my assumptions. In the judicial inquiry covering Cristóbal de Segovia's service record, to which I have already referred, the second question runs as follows: "*Item*, whether they know, believe, have observed, or have heard say that for something like twenty-three years, slightly more or less, I have resided in the provinces of Nicaragua and New Spain and Peru and other adjacent provinces," etc. [*infra*, p. 267]; and in reply to this question Orellana declares that he has known Segovia for the past fifteen years, "not only by sight but also by accounts that he had heard about him; and [he said that] he knew this man had been engaged in the wars which had been fought, both in New Spain and in Peru . . . ; and [that] during all this he knew that he had done everything," etc. [*infra*, p. 270].

It is unfortunate that, contrary to the usual thing in such cases, the witness was not asked how he knew all this, although when a question was answered by an avowal on the part of the witness that he did not *know*, the statement was always added that so it had been reported by hearsay. We may believe, then, that Orellana *knew* about these activities through having participated in them, and this appears to be confirmed by his deposition in reply to the next question, when he states that "what was mentioned in this question he had not [actually] witnessed, but that he had heard it related publicly," etc. [*infra*, p. 270].

Desirous of clearing up a point so interesting, I have carefully examined all the judicial inquiries in connection with services rendered which were put through in those days by the conquistadors of Panama, Nicaragua, and Mexico, although without finding anything; this does not prove, however, that Orellana was not associated in some way with these men, for it is possible that he either was not asked to testify or had already gone off to Peru. Besides, he must have been averse to figuring in proceedings of this sort, if we may judge from the testimony which he gave in the case of Segovia, wherein he plainly shows his reluctance to making sworn declarations, notwithstanding the fact that this particular service inquiry was one in which he was so directly interested, since it had to do with his voyage down the Amazon.

and its outlying territory,"[59] this last-mentioned city having been founded on March 12, 1535; and that in the course of these operations, if he did win for himself much honor, in exchange for it he lost an eye.[60] Having settled down in this town, he built his home there, which was always an asylum and a refuge for the Spaniards who came there from the north attracted by the fabulous riches of the Empire of the Incas.[61] There he was staying when

[59] Petition presented to the city corporation of Guayaquil, p. 262 of the present volume. [The conquest of Lima, as Orellana calls it, was not, properly speaking, a conquest.

A careful examination of the order in which Orellana makes his statement may help to establish the route which he probably followed in coming to Peru. When Francisco Pizarro, after leaving the island of Puná, landed on the South American mainland at Túmbez, the three ships which accompanied him were sent back, in part, to Panama for supplies, as had been previously done from Coaque, where many of the original members of the expedition had died in the early months of 1531. The report was not long in spreading regarding the great wealth whose existence had been suspected by the conquistadors at Coaque. At Puná, Pizarro had been joined by Hernando de Soto, who had come from Nicaragua: later, Captain Gabriel de Rojas started out from the same land, only to be cornered by the *Adelantado* Pedro de Alvarado and forced to join the expeditionary outfit which that captain sold at Quito to Diego de Almagro, sent hurriedly by Pizarro to repel the invasion of his territory. While Pizarro was at Cajamarca, a large force under Diego de Almagro arrived in April, 1533, composed of men recruited in Panama. I am inclined to think that it was either as a member of De Soto's expedition or of the last-mentioned one of Almagro's that Orellana arrived in Peru. The fact that he does not appear as having a share in the ransom of the Inca Atahualpa may be explained in both cases. If he was with De Soto, it may well be that he was a "companion" of some other conquistador and that it is the other's name which appears, the booty to be divided later by virtue of a form of brotherhood very common among the early conquistadors in America. If he came with Almagro, it is only necessary to recall that this group was given a lump sum. When he further says: "and in the pursuit of the Inca," it is more than likely that he is referring to one of the several expeditions sent out by Pizarro late in 1533 and early in 1534 in pursuit of the forces under Quiz-quiz, the Quito general of Atahualpa who resisted for some time.

From documents in the Library of Congress in Washington it is known that De Soto commanded one of these expeditions from Cuzco in 1534. In September, 1534, when Pizarro returned to Jauja and proceeded from there to Pachacamac to await the results of Almagro's expedition against Pedro de Alvarado, it may well be that Orellana accompanied him. In January, 1535, shortly after Alvarado had come to Pachacamac to receive the 100,000 castellanos which were to be paid him for the transfer of his fleet and for desisting from the conquest of the South Sea, Pizarro went to found Lima on the site where it now stands. However, no document shows that Orellana was present or that he was made a citizen of that city or given a piece of land whereon to erect his house. In February, 1535, Pizarro embarked for Trujillo to finish the work of founding that city, which had been laid out by Almagro and named Trujillo in honor of the birthplace of Pizarro, he having come from Quito to Pachacamac in December, 1534; but the name of Orellana does not appear in any of the lists of citizens who were then given building lots, as was the custom. It may be that when Pizarro, deciding that the Point of Santa Elena, one of the first capes to be sighted by a ship cutting across from Panama to the mainland near Túmbez, would be a good site for a port of call, sent an expedition to found such a town, Orellana was a member of the expedition. Only in this way can his own statements be reconciled with the facts as they are known.

An uncle of Francisco Pizarro, who was presumably also an uncle of Orellana, was in Guatemala. It may well be that our hero accompanied him as a page.—TRANSLATOR.]

[60] López de Gómara [*Historia general de las Indias*, Saragossa, 1552; Rivadeneyra edition, Madrid, 1852 (cited in full in footnote 46, *supra*), p. 210], therefore, is in error when he states that Orellana lost his eye during the Amazon voyage; he is evidently confusing him with his chronicler, Friar Gaspar de Carvajal.

[61] ". . . because it was during the time when the said Captain was residing in the said town that there flocked to these parts the horde of persons who came all worn out and in great distress from their journeyings, and they found refreshments in the house of the said Captain Francisco de Orellana, and he gave them food, and he sustained them in their moments of sickness and distress, and it was believed that if it had not been for him many would have perished. . . ." From the statement of the corporation of Guayaquil, pp. 264–265 of the present volume.

news came to him that the cities of Lima and Cuzco, commanded respectively by Francisco and Hernando Pizarro, were being besieged by the Indians, who had risen up en masse to destroy with one single blow that handful of intrepid adventurers. Matters were in such a bad way that no time was to be lost. Scarcely had the call for help reached Orellana when without any delay he purchased ten or twelve horses (which in those days and in those regions were worth a goodly sum of pesos),[62] distributed them among his comrades, borrowed money, gathered together more than eighty men, infantry and horsemen together, whose debts he paid, and began hurriedly his march by land toward Lima to succor the besieged.

Orellana with his men actually did reach Lima; but did he get as far as Cuzco? This seems to me very doubtful. From the history of those events we know that of the captains* dispatched by Francisco Pizarro to aid his brother in Cuzco none completed the journey except Alonso de Alvarado, who, having set out from Lima in April, 1537,† had gone as far as the valley of Amancay,‡ in the vicinity of the city for which he had started out, when it was found that Manco Inca had raised the siege.§  It is quite true that Orellana, in the memorandum of his services, goes no further than to say that he returned to the north, "having left the said cities freed from siege" [infra, p. 263], whereby, of course, he may have been referring to an event which had already taken place without his having had any part whatsoever in it.

But a matter which Orellana intentionally neglects to mention in his memorandum is the rôle that it fell to his lot to play in the quarrels of the two governors, Pizarro and Almagro‖—quarrels which had such a fatal ending for Almagro at the battle of Las Salinas, fought on April 26, 1538, in which Orellana took part after

---

[62] From 500 to 1000 gold pesos each.  [Equivalent to from $6,000 to $12,000. Cf.: " . . . [the price of] the one which cost the least in those days exceeded 500 gold pesos of 22 and one half carats, and others double that much  . . . " (Toribio de Ortiguera, infra, p. 313).—TRANSLATOR.]

*[There were several expeditions sent by Pizarro from Lima to raise the siege of Cuzco.  One, commanded by an officer who is presumed to have been his cousin, Diego Pizarro, was annihilated by the Indians at Parcos; a second, commanded by Juan Mogrovejo de Quiñones, met with a similar fate in the valley of Jauja; a third, under Captain Gaete, was exterminated in a pass of the Andes; while a fourth, under Francisco de Godoy, returned precipitately to Lima after having met Indians in great force in Huarochiri.—TRANSLATOR.]

†[He had been called back to Lima from his expedition beyond the "río grande" (i.e. the Marañón) into the territory of the Chachapuyas.—TRANSLATOR.]

‡[The spot which he had then reached was in the valley of the Apurimac River, near the site of the present Abancay.—TRANSLATOR.]

§[The city of Cuzco was now in the hands of Diego de Almagro, with Hernando and Gonzalo Pizarro as his prisoners —TRANSLATOR.]

‖[These quarrels were caused by Almagro's claim that Cuzco fell within the limits of his jurisdiction as governor of New Toledo.—TRANSLATOR.]

having been ensign-general of the seven hundred foot and horse soldiers sent by Francisco Pizarro from Lima to protect his brother Hernando.[63]    Eight days after the battle (i.e. on May 4, 1538), Orellana was on his way to Lima as the bearer of a letter from Doctor Sepúlveda* for the Governor Pizarro, in which the writer advised him as to what he thought "ought to be done in order that this land might not be totally ruined."†

Testimony to these activities is furnished by Cieza de León and Fernández de Oviedo, both well-informed historians and, on this point, impartial ones.‡   What is the explanation of this silence on the part of Orellana?   As has been observed by Jiménez de la Espada, the reason can be none other than the displeasures with which that action was viewed back in the capital and the legal proceedings which as a consequence of it were launched against Hernando Pizarro as soon as he arrived in Spain; for news of these legal proceedings had undoubtedly reached Peru by February, 1541, the date of Orellana's petition to the municipal corporation of Guayaquil.   At this time Orellana undoubtedly was thinking of asking for compensation for his services, and naturally it was to his advantage to make no mention of the rôle which he had played at Las Salinas.

With the destruction of the Almagro party, or of "the Chile faction," as it was called, many captains who had served under the

---

[63] See Cieza de León, *Guerra de las Salinas*, Ch. 58. [The *Guerra de las Salinas*, published in Madrid in 1877, forms Book I of Part IV of this author's *Crónica del Perú* (see footnote 43, *supra*). It has been translated into English by Sir Clements R. Markham in the publications of the Hakluyt Society, as No. 54 of its Second Series, London, 1923.   The only thing said regarding Orellana in Chapter 58 is that he was commissioned ensign-general, though it is not stated that this was done in connection with the setting out of Hernando Pizarro "with his laden Indians and 700 men, horse and foot" (Markham translation, p. 183); and in the account of the battle of Las Salinas a few chapters further on (Ch. 68) many names are mentioned, but not Orellana's.   In Fernández de Oviedo's account of these events there is no mention of Orellana until after the battle, and the brief statements made here (*Historia general*, etc., Vol. 4, pp. 336–337) have to do with the decision to send Orellana on an expedition to La Culata and with the manner in which he was dispatched *from Cuzco* with a letter, etc., as Medina states below.   Yet the fact that Orellana was in Cuzco available for this special mission eight days after the battle makes it seem highly probable that he had taken part in the fight, as indeed the passage published by Medina (note on the founding of Guayaquil, *infra*, p. 236 ff.) from a judicial inquiry on the subject of the services of one Rodrigo de Vargas seems to prove, though even here it is not specifically stated that Orellana had taken part in the fighting.—EDITOR.]

*[Hernando de Sepúlveda, "protomédico" of the island of Santo Domingo, promoted to be the first to hold that office in Peru, and an intimate friend of Pizarro and one of his most faithful counselors.   He died in Lima in 1539.—TRANSLATOR.]

†[Oviedo, *op. cit.*, Vol. 4, p. 337.—EDITOR.]

‡[And all the more deserving of consideration is Fernández de Oviedo when it is borne in mind that he held the power of attorney from Almagro and was appointed one of the executors of his will dated at Cuzco, July 8, 1538, the day of his execution.   It is quite conceivable that Oviedo harbored no hard feelings against Orellana for whatever part he may have taken in the quarrels and that he blamed all on the Pizarros.—TRANSLATOR.]

banners of Pizarro found themselves without occupation. To leave them inactive was extremely dangerous when the leaven of civil disturbances was latent and might ferment at the least threat; and, besides, it was necessary to reward them in some manner for their services in the cause of Pizarro. Fortunately, in Peru there were still immense expanses of territories not yet discovered or explored, some of which rumor painted as very rich; and nothing could better flatter the ambition for glory and the covetousness of those tireless adventurers than to obtain a title permitting them to carry out those new discoveries. It was, then, a very clever measure, both practically and politically, on the part of Pizarro to distribute as premiums to his helpers and his friends grants whereby, when these men were dispersed in all directions, the country would remain tranquil and the aspirations of all would be satisfied. In this distribution there fell to Orellana the province of La Culata, which was picked out for him with the special commission that he should found a city there.[64]

In accordance with this decision Orellana, taking with him such persons as he could pick up round about him, among whom were to be counted several "persons of distinction" [infra, p. 236], set out "at his own expense and on his own initiative" [infra, p. 265] from Lima headed for the north, shortly after the middle of the year 1538.[65] The conquest of the country which had fallen to him in the distribution was not of the easiest sort. Traversed by several rivers carrying much water, strewn with great swamps in which both men and horses sank, this region presented a further difficulty, namely that the Indians who inhabited it had become emboldened as a result of the defeats which they had inflicted upon other captains; but Orellana triumphed over all these obstacles, and in accordance with his instructions, after having reduced the

[64] He "ordered me and gave official instructions to me to set out to conquer [territory] in the name of His Majesty and in his own, and to conquer, with the rank of Captain-General, the province of La Culata, in which I was to found a city . . . " (p. 263 of the present volume).

[65] The battle of Las Salinas was fought on April 26, 1538, and Orellana started out from Cuzco headed for Lima on May 4: it must be assumed that a number of days went by after that before he could receive his commission and, above all, before he could get his men together. This is why I believe that his departure for the north could not have taken place before July of that year. If we possessed the document containing Orellana's appointment by Pizarro, the date could be arrived at with a little more precision; but unfortunately this document is not to be found in the archives.

[The date of Orellana's departure can be approximately arrived at from the deed of charter of the *San Pedro*, of which Benito de la Feria was master (*The Harkness Collection in the Library of Congress*, Washington, 1932, p. 80). The ship was to carry Orellana and his Spaniards to the Point of Santa Elena, and the document is dated at Lima, June 8, 1538. It is to be supposed that Orellana did not long delay his departure after signing this document.—TRANSLATOR.]

Indians to submission to the Spanish arms, he proceeded to found the city of Santiago de Guayaquil on a more advantageous site than that on which it had been attempted on previous occasions.[66]

Pizarro received with a considerable amount of satisfaction the news that at last there had been successfully founded a city which was destined to open up to Quito a door of communication with the sea, and at the same time he showed himself to be quite pleased with the manner in which Orellana had carried out his commission. Consequently, he sent him procurations and appointments, making him captain-general and lieutenant-governor in the new city and in Puerto Viejo.[67] As to how well Orellana filled these posts there exist no detailed accounts; but in one incident which occurred at that time in the district under his rule, and which constituted a serious outrage against public morals, he knew how to conduct himself with the energy which the nature of the case required.[68]

He was getting along quietly with the administration of these posts and was perhaps beginning to be bored by the inaction which had already lasted more than two years, when he learned that his friend, relative, and fellow-Estremenian, Gonzalo Pizarro, had presented his title of governor of the provinces of Quito, including Guayaquil and Puerto Viejo, to the municipal corporation of that capital on December 1, 1540.

Gonzalo Pizarro had come to replace Sebastián de Benalcázar, having been appointed by his brother the Marquis, with the idea in mind of organizing there a great expedition to the lands of El Dorado and La Canela (Cinnamon). As soon as Orellana learned that Gonzalo Pizarro had entered upon the exercise of his office of governor, thus becoming his new chief, he went to Quito to

---

[66] ". . . continuing my services," says Orellana in this connection, "I established and founded in the name of His Majesty a city to which I gave the name of City of Santiago . . . " (p. 263 of the present volume).

From what has been said it will be seen that Cieza de León and Antonio de Herrera were mistaken when they affirmed that the founding took place in 1537. See Note 1 to Friar Gaspar de Carvajal's *Account*, *infra*, pp. 236–238.

[67] This appointment must have been made, at the very latest, in October, 1539, because on November 10 Orellana signed in Guayaquil the title to an *encomienda* of Indians of the town of Quilca, in favor of Juan de Mogollón, doing so as "lieutenant-governor and captain-general in these provinces of the City of Santiago and Puerto Viejo and their outlying districts" (Archives of the Indies, 1-6-4/9).

[68] "Being in the capital, Valladolid, on February 6, 1544, he declared over his signature, at the request of the Licentiate Villalobos, attorney-general of the Council of the Indies, with reference to his having proceeded against certain persons for the nefarious crime of sodomy, at the time when he was lieutenant-governor of Puerto Viejo, that he had burned two of them and confiscated their goods; and that he had employed the same method of procedure, for the same crime, against another resident of that place, named Bartolomé Pérez, who fled and was now in Valladolid" (Jiménez de la Espada's article, already mentioned).

"see him and put him in possession of the said territory," which he had hitherto held from the Marquis, and at the same time to offer to accompany him on the proposed expedition, saying "how he wished to go with him in the service of His Majesty and take his friends along and spend his personal wealth in order better to serve . . . "[69]  Pizarro accepted the offer, as was to be expected, and thereupon Orellana returned to Guayaquil to arrange the affairs of the towns which he had had in his charge, to recruit the men who were to accompany him, and to get everything ready that he needed for the expedition.[70]

Among these preparations we must count the drawing up of his memorandum of past services, which he had dispensed with till then but which could be very useful to him in petitioning the King to give him the governorship of some province as a reward for his services, for nothing less than this was the goal of his aspirations; and in fact he had hardly arrived back home when, on February 4, he appeared before the magistrates of the city which he had founded, with a "memorial" wherein he had set down those services which he thought it politic to enumerate, in order that these gentlemen might without any delay express the opinion which they had of him on the basis of these services—an opinion which, it is superfluous to say, was bound to be entirely favorable to him. " . . . and in view of other things which they had seen and did know," to quote their opinion in the words in which it has been preserved for us, "regarding the said Captain and his person and his virtues, they declared that the said Captain was a person capable of, and qualified for, whatever commissions and offices His Majesty might be pleased to intrust to him, be it a governorship or any others whatsoever. . . . " [infra, p. 265].

These words coming from the city fathers of Guayaquil could not but be highly pleasing to Orellana. His mind had already been seized with the idea, which harassed him at all hours, of ruling over some independent district. He did not wish henceforth to depend on anyone, even though it were a relative and friend; and in order to attain his object he needed to go in person to present

[69] I take these statements from the *Account* [*infra*, p. 167f.] of Friar Carvajal, who must have known perfectly well what he was saying and whose testimony I am following, naturally, as against the opinion of all the historians who affirm that Orellana joined Pizarro in the course of the expedition without there being any previous understanding between the two men.

[70] Orellana's trip to Quito, including going and coming, must have taken place between the middle of December, 1540, and the end of January of the following year.

himself before the King and make known to him how deserving he was of that which he was soliciting.[71]

Let us leave Orellana giving the final touches to his preparations for his journey, and let us see what Gonzalo Pizarro in the meanwhile was doing in Quito.

[71] In Orellana's "memorial" to the corporation of Guayaquil there is a phrase which does not leave room for the slightest doubt as to his intention of going to Spain with the object in mind which I have mentioned: "and because I wish to go or send [someone] to beseech His Majesty, as a King and master who will be grateful for my services and for those that I hope to perform for him henceforth, to grant me in return for them [certain] favors, which I do not wish to state here, [preferring to wait] until I can beg and beseech His Majesty [to grant] them," etc. [*infra*, p. 264].

It is evident, then, that what he wanted first of all to do was to go in person to the capital, and it was only in case he could not go that he was willing to send some one to represent him. The reason which he had for not stating the favors that he thought of asking for can also be plainly deduced: he was anxious not to displease Pizarro, who could not have looked with kindly eyes upon the idea that one of his subordinates should cease being subject to his command.

# VI

# FRANCISCO DE ORELLANA AS A MEMBER OF GONZALO PIZARRO'S EXPEDITION

THERE can be no doubt that the principal motive which had actuated Gonzalo Pizarro when he requested his brother to make him governor of Quito, La Culata, and Puerto Viejo is to be found in the reports which were circulating at that time regarding the riches said to exist in the countries extending towards the east and called El Dorado and La Canela (Land of Cinnamon), where, according to the assertions of "prominent and very aged chiefs" [*infra*, p. 245], whose statements were confirmed by certain Spaniards, there were also many settlements. Immediately after his arrival at Quito the first occupation of the new governor was to investigate more closely the truth of these pleasing reports; and as the official accounts which came to him then coincided exactly with what he had been told while he was still far away from there, he embraced with fervor the project of undertaking a great expedition into the interior.

Having taken charge of his office of governor on December 1, 1540, as I have said, he made such haste with his preparations and had advanced so far in them by the end of a month and a half,* that on February 18 he was ready to delegate his authority to Pedro de Puelles to act as governor in his absence; and preparations were entirely completed three days later, February 21, when we find the corporation of Quito directing the attorney for the city to summon Pizarro to cause to be struck off from the Indians the chains and shackles in which he had been keeping them as a means of holding them ready to take along with him on his expedition.[72]

By that time he had succeeded in gathering together close on to four thousand of these unhappy people, as well as 220[73] Spaniards,

---

*[Evidently, Medina meant to say two and a half months.—EDITOR.]

[72] Pablo Herrera, *Ensayo sobre la historia de la literatura ecuatoriana*, [Quito], 1860, pp. 105–106.

[73] There is considerable discrepancy among the historians as to the number of Spaniards who accompanied Pizarro. Cieza de León says that there were 220 [*Guerra de Chupas*, ed. Madrid, 1881, p. 62], Oviedo 230 [*Historia general y natural de las Indias*, Vol. 4, p. 383] and Ortiguera 280 [*infra*, p. 313]. Among these figures I have preferred the first, because Pizarro in his letter to the King limits himself to stating that they were more than 200 strong.

It is scarcely necessary for me to remark that I do not propose to relate here the story of Pizarro's expedition in all its details, but merely in outline and by way of explaining the antecedents of Orellana's voyage of discovery.

this latter being a very respectable number for those times, "for, when one considers the small number of Spanish persons that there were in the land then, it was a great achievement to have been able to get them together" [*infra*, p. 313]; these were nobles of the highest ranks and leading citizens of the realm who, because of the personal prestige of the leader and the great notoriety given to the proposed new expedition of discovery, hastened to enlist under his banners.  He assembled also almost an equal number of horses, which alone were then worth a fortune; arquebuses, cross-bows, munitions of all kinds in abundance; llamas as beasts of burden, destined to serve also as food; more than two thousand[74] live hogs, and almost as many dogs, efficient aids for hunting, as well as, whenever the occasion should present itself, for turning loose on hostile Indians (for "dogging" them, as they put it).* As guides, he took along natives possessing an expert knowledge of those regions, and with them Gonzalo Díaz de Pineda and some of his comrades who some three years previously had marched over some of this country; as campmaster, Don Antonio de Ribera; Juan de Acosta as ensign-general; and, besides all these, he hoped soon after to be able to take advantage of the coöperation of Francisco de Orellana and of the soldiers whom this latter had offered to bring with him.

The soul of the expedition was naturally Gonzalo Pizarro.  Brave, handsome in person, an excellent horseman, he was looked upon, on the other hand, as a man who knew little and as being "close and not generous," according to the portrait which a contemporary has left us of him.†

With souls full of hope and minds filled with dreams of wealth, the first soldiers of that imposing expedition started out from Quito, towards the end of the month of February, 1541,[75] "each

---

[74] Cieza de León puts the number of hogs at five thousand. [See below, p. 55. Herrera, *Historia general de los hechos de los castellanos*, Decade VI, Book IX, Ch. 7, repeats this figure.]

*[The term "aperrear" (from "perro," meaning "dog") is used by Cieza de León, *op. cit.*, p. 66. Markham, in his translation of this work (Hakluyt Society publications, Second Series, No. 42, London, 1918), p. 60, contents himself with "devour" as an English equivalent.—EDITOR.]

†[The contemporary to whom Medina refers is obviously Pedro Pizarro, author of a *Relación del descubrimiento y conquista de los reinos del Perú*, etc., written, or at least finished, in 1571 and published in 1844 in *Colección de documentos inéditos para la historia de España*, Vol. 5 (pp. 201-388: see p. 311), who furnishes all the elements of Medina's characterization of Gonzalo Pizarro, including "close and not generous" ("apretado y no largo").  Mr. Philip A. Means, in his translation of Pedro Pizarro's *Relación* for the Cortes Society (2 vols., New York, 1921), Vol. 2, p. 341, renders these Spanish qualifiers as follows: "a compact man, not large."—EDITOR.]

[75] The day of Pizarro's departure is not known with certainty either; while some say March, Ortiguera [*infra*, p. 313], who had opportunities to investigate the matter carefully, gives it as February, a date which I also accept, at least for the departure of the advance guard.  The injunction of the procurator of the corporation of Quito also inclines one to the belief that this is correct.

one carrying nothing but a sword and a shield, and a small sack which he carried underneath, in which their food was carried by them."[76]

The advance guard commanded by Antonio de Ribera, who had orders to·head straight for the province of Quijos, advanced, in fact, as far as the town of Atunquijo. Pizarro, who had intrusted the rear guard to Cristóbal de Funes, was in the middle with the bulk of the soldiers, who a short time after they had left Quito and when they had scarcely advanced seven leagues,* had to cross a snow-covered mountain range where there perished from the cold more than one hundred Indians; and from there they began to march over a very rough region, traversed by several rivers and almost all covered with forests, through which they had to open a road with axes and machetes; and in this manner they marched on until they came to the valley of Zumaco, at a distance of thirty leagues from Quito,[77] this being the most thickly populated spot and the one best supplied with provisions that they had come upon. ". . . there I halted the expeditionary force," says Pizarro himself, "in order to allow it to get rested, both the Spaniards and the horses, for all were quite worn out in consequence of the great hardships which they had gone through in climbing up and going down the great mountains, and because of the many bridges which had been built for the crossing of the rivers" [infra, p. 245].

It was at this point, or not much farther on, that Orellana and the men that he was bringing with him joined the expeditionary

[76] Cieza de León, *Guerra de Chupas*, ed. Madrid, 1881, p. 63. [Cf. p. 57, Markham translation cited above, p. 29. It is not clear what Cieza de León means by "underneath" ("debajo").—EDITOR.]

* [The Spanish league was reckoned at four Roman miles of 1000 paces each. If the Roman mile is assumed to have been equivalent to 1617 English yards, a league was therefore 19,404 feet, or about 3⅔ statute miles, long. Although the value of the Spanish league has fluctuated, the figure of 3⅔ statute miles (used in the scale of the map, Fig. 1a, p. 48, *infra*) is, it is believed, a close approximation of the length of the league in use during the first half of the sixteenth century and may be employed in converting the distances mentioned in Father Carvajal's *Account* and elsewhere in the present volume.

The fluctuation in value was due in part to the difference between the theoretical concepts of the cosmographers and the values determined from practical experience by the mariners and in part to the growing realization of the fact that the earth was larger than at first thought, which resulted in increasing the value of the terrestrial degree, between the fifteenth and the eighteenth century, from 17½ to 20 Spanish leagues. For a critical discussion of the problem see Hermann Wagner, *Zur Geschichte der Seemeile* (*Ann. der Hydrogr. und Marit. Meteorol.*, Vol. 41, 1913, pp. 393–413 and 441–450), pp. 393, 397, and 443–445. Wagner, p. 444, cites a letter written in 1543 by Juan Ginés Sepúlveda to Prince Philip (later King Philip II) stating that the league is equal to four miles and not to three, "as commonly believed even by learned men."—EDITOR.]

[77] Pizarro says in his letter to the King [infra, p. 245] that the distance covered up to this point was a good sixty leagues—an exaggeration which in this case and in similar instances throughout the rest of his account must be attributed, as Jiménez de la Espada observes, to the fact that, with the hardships they endured, the distances seemed much greater to him than they really were.

The settlement of Zumaco, according to Ortiguera [infra, p 314], was located on the site where in his own time the city of Avila had been founded.

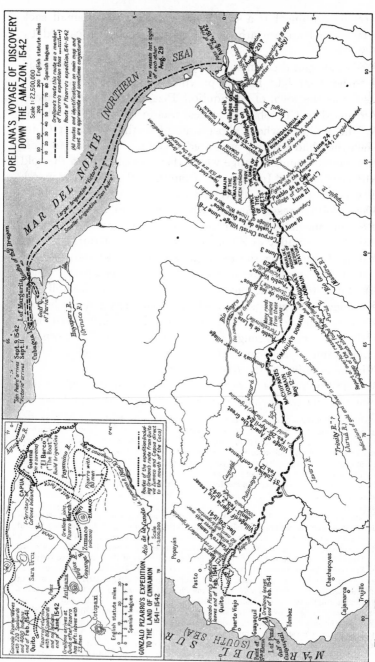

Fig. 1a—Map showing the route of, and features connected with, Orellana's voyage of discovery down the Amazon in 1542 (scale, 1:22,500,000) and, in the inset (1:3,000,000), the route of Gonzalo Pizarro's expedition to the Land of Cinnamon, 1541-1542. Based on the Oviedo and Medina versions of Carvajal's account and on other contemporary documents. All routes and identifications are approximate, and some of them are conjectural.

force. Let us now see the causes of his delay and the vicissitudes which attended his journey up to this point.

At the beginning of February he was busy, as has been said, in Guayaquil putting in order the documents on the basis of which he had hopes of obtaining a governorship from the home government; but in spite of all the haste which he applied to the completing of his preparations (for he knew that Pizarro would lose no time in getting started from Quito), whether it was as a result of the natural delays bound to occur in the fitting out of the soldiers who were to accompany him or as a consequence of the difficulty of securing the equipment which he needed for the journey, at a cost amounting, it is said, to the very considerable sum of forty thousand pesos,[78] the fact is that when he arrived at Quito he was surprised to find that Gonzalo Pizarro and his army had already departed. The citizens of the city and persons familiar with the route which Pizarro had taken then pointed out to him how dangerous it would be to risk continuing the march with so few men accompanying him, saying that in the event of their escaping the ambuscades of the Indians (and there had been many examples of this sort of thing), they were almost certain to perish from hunger.

But Orellana was not the type of man to be held back by these gloomy prognostications. His mind was made up to accompany Pizarro; he had given him his promise, and it was to his interest to keep that promise, so that there was no room for vacillation in his mind. What would his chief say of him on seeing him fail almost at the very outset to live up to the pledges which he had solemnly made?[79]

So, following in Gonzalo's footsteps, he set out from Quito with twenty-three[80] companions; but after going a short distance he must have become convinced that the warnings which had been given to him were not without foundation. The Indians came forth to attack him on several occasions and placed him in some very difficult situations. The few provisions with which he had started

[78] There is reason to believe that the sum was even greater, because Fernández de Oviedo states that in horses (14) and equipment alone Orellana lost the forty thousand pesos on the journey from Quito to Zumaco [*op. cit.*, Vol. 4, p. 542; this passage is in Carvajal's *Relación*.—EDITOR.]

[79] " . . . although the Spaniards dwelling in the country tried to dissuade him from doing so because he would have to pass through a hostile and rough country and because they feared that they [i.e. the natives] would kill him as they had done others who had gone [in there] with a very large force of men; yet notwithstanding this, for the sake of serving His Majesty, he determined in spite of all this risk to go on and catch up with the said Governor; . . . " (Friar Carvajal's *Account, infra,* p. 168).

[80] Oviedo cuts this number down to twenty; but Friar Carvajal, who saw them come into the camp at Zumaco, says that there were twenty-three of them.

out began to dwindle; in all those regions there was absolutely no way of securing anything because everything had been razed along the line of march of Gonzalo Pizarro's expeditionary army, and to such extremities did he fear that he would be reduced that from some point along his line of march he dispatched emissaries to Pizarro to inform him of the distressful situation in which he found himself, exposed to the danger of perishing from hunger if aid in the form of food were not sent back to him.

Without delay, Gonzalo transmitted to his campmaster, Antonio de Ribera, the alarming news which had come to him from Orellana, ordering him to dispatch someone to his relief, "and Don Antonio," the chronicler of these events tells us, "sent Captain Sancho de Caravajal to go and carry food relief which would enable Orellana to push on as far as that place; and Sancho de Caravajal departed at once to look for him, and as soon as they met they [i.e. Orellana and his men] rejoiced to see him and particularly [to see] the food which had been brought, of which he was sorely in need."[81]

Along the way he and his soldiers had lost all that they had started out with in the form of supplies, so that when they arrived at Gonzalo Pizarro's camp "he still had left only a sword and a shield, and his companions likewise . . . " [infra, p. 168].

Pizarro received Orellana with manifestations of great satisfaction, and, by way of giving evidence of the high esteem which Orellana had won from him and possibly in fulfillment of what the two men had agreed upon in the interview at Quito, he promptly made him his lieutenant-general.[82]

After this appointment had been made, the leaders and principal captains were called to council in the camp for the purpose of determining what should be done under the existing circumstances. Orellana and his companions had arrived all worn out; on the other hand, for many days already the expeditionary force had been halted there; heavier and heavier rains were beginning to fall, and so the necessity of continuing the march imposed itself beyond contention. It was then decided that Pizarro should go on ahead

[81] Cieza de León, *Guerra de Chupas*. pp. 64–65 [cf. Markham translation, p. 58]. I am following this author for the account of these events, since he is the only one who has taken the trouble to record them.

[82] On what date did the meeting of Orellana with Gonzalo Pizarro take place? To determine this it would be necessary to know how long it took Pizarro to reach Zumaco and how long the expeditionary force had been camped there before the arrival of Orellana. Many days had elapsed since they had reached this settlement, according to Cieza de León. The same author says that Orellana and his companions arrived at Zumaco after leaving Quito "at the end of a few days"— a statement which leaves us in the same uncertainty as before. It is probable that the meeting took place before the end of March.

with eighty men on foot, it being impossible for the horses to get through the woods, and that, taking with him some Indian guides, he should march directly to the east to see what there was farther ahead.

This plan was actually put into execution, and at the end of seventy days of marching, "during which," to quote Pizarro's own words, "we endured great hardships and spells of hunger on account of the roughness of the country and the dissension among the guides, in consequence of which hardships a few Spaniards died,"* Pizarro's advance guard found the cinnamon trees[83] which they were looking for. But this find amounted to a disillusionment. The plant which they prized so much was seen to be scattered over great stretches of land and was in reality scarce, and at one glance the disenchanted expeditioners perceived that trading in it could bring in no profit whatsoever. Among these mountains they also found some Indians who were thorough savages and who lived in miserable dwellings; these Pizarro questioned on the subject of whether farther ahead there were valleys and plains, because his fixed idea was to find a road suitable for the horses; and, irritated when these Indians could not give him the kind of answer that he wanted, he delivered some of them over to be torn to pieces by the dogs, while others he caused to be burned alive.

Gonzalo Pizarro's companions began to feel discouraged over this first disillusionment. Nevertheless, guided by their chief, they pushed on until they came to a river whose banks were in the form of a sandy beach, and here they determined to pass the night. Here they were sleeping when a sudden freshet caused the water to rise and they were compelled to take refuge in all haste on the slopes behind, not without the loss of a part of their equipment.

Being now thoroughly disillusioned, they started to go back over their tracks to see if it was possible to find a more open trail through some other part of the country. When they were within four leagues of where Zumaco was, Pizarro ordered his men to halt and then head straight for the settlement of Capua, thus avoiding contact with the main body of the expedition, in order, perhaps, not to infect the others with the dejection which had also begun to dominate him as well, although he had strength enough to conceal it. Having started off on this new line of march, they

*[Document I, *infra*, p. 246.]
[83] Known in natural history under the name of *Nectandra cinamomoides*.

came upon a very large river which they could not ford; but they saw that its waters were dotted with canoes manned by Indians, and on the other side of the river they caught sight of a certain number of Indians who were watching them. The Spaniards then began to call out to them, telling them to have no fear and to come over, as indeed some fifteen or twenty of them did, bringing at their head their chief whom Pizarro then presented with some trinkets highly pleasing to the savages, in order to get him to tell him whether he knew of any good country beyond, even though it might be far off. Being duly put on his guard by what he knew had happened to other Indians, Delicola, as the chief was called, then told him, fully conscious that he was lying, that farther on there were great settlements and regions very rich, ruled over by powerful overlords; and, by way of rewarding the chief for what he had related, Pizarro ordered him to be held a prisoner for such services as he might later furnish as a guide.

In view of this information, which the Spaniards held to be accurate, eager as they were to believe such reports, confidence in ultimate success was revived in all of them, and joyfully they started to proceed up along the bank of the river to a place where it formed some narrows and where the Indians tried to check their passage, with the loss of several of their men who perished from the shots of Pizarro's arquebusiers. The far bank of the river being now free of enemies, the Spaniards threw a bridge across these narrows, and proceeding along the other side they found a few insignificant settlements[84] and a very small quantity of provisions and at last came to some savanas two leagues long, surrounded on all sides by forests apparently as impenetrable as those they had just passed through.

Having pitched his camp there, Gonzalo determined to send for the companions who still remained in Zumaco; and, as soon as they were all together again, he dispatched the campmaster with fifty soldiers to go and explore the country that could be seen on ahead, "and he was fifteen days going and coming," says Pizarro, "and he brought back a story [to the effect] that he had found a great river, that there were houses right on the edge of the water, and that on the river he had seen many Indians wearing clothes, going about in canoes, and that it seemed to him that that province was a thoroughly settled one, because the Indians whom he had

---

[84] The most important of these, and the one in which camp was pitched, was called Quema or Guema, and, according to Friar Carvajal's obviously erroneous statement [*infra*, p. 169], was situated one hundred and thirty leagues from Quite.

seen wore clothes and [were] quite civilized. And, as soon as he came with this story, I set out and came to this province that is called Omagua, passing through great marshes and crossing over many creeks."[85] Hence, they must have followed the shores of the river for a distance of twenty leagues, stopping at last in some settlements which were "not very large" [*infra*, p. 169].

Once he had arrived there, Pizarro's first care was to win the natives over on peaceful terms, for their friendship in these circumstances was so important to him for the procuring of food. The Indians, who kept going up and down the river in their canoes, were agreeable to this at first and began bartering with the Spaniards; but presently they got angry and the greater part of them disappeared, not including, however, the chief nor the important persons, whom Gonzalo had caused to be closely watched. Hostilities having broken out, the expeditioners succeeded in taking possession of a few canoes, with which they went about, from one place to another, in search of provisions; yet they did not dare to venture afar along the river, because there were frequently as many as one hundred or even one hundred and fifty canoes on the water, all manned by Indian warriors, whom it was not possible to equal in dexterity and agility in the handling of that kind of craft.

Finding themselves on the banks of that river, and "reflecting that of all the servants they had brought from Quito," says one of the chroniclers, "not one remained, nor could any be found where they were, the land being so bad, [they] came to the conclusion that the best plan would be to build a craft, on board of which their supplies might go down the river, the horses following by land, in the hope of reaching some region of plenty . . . "[86] On board this boat they could also load all the sick, the munitions, the axes and adzes, and other necessary articles, because already the greater part of the Indians brought along as servants had perished* and there remained no one to carry all this equipment. Then, too, in that maritime warfare, if we may call it such, the proposed brigantine would of course be a powerful weapon which the frail canoes of the Indians could not oppose, and, if all the effort which its construction was to entail should turn out in the

---

[85] Letter of Gonzalo Pizarro, p. 246 of the present volume.

[86] Cieza de León, *Guerra de Chupas*, p. 70 [Markham's translation, *op. cit.*, p. 64].

*[Undoubtedly this was a result of their having taken highland Indians. The Spaniards soon found out that these residents of the high Andes, when brought down to lower regions, promptly fell sick and died of fevers, while the taking of lowland Indians to the higher regions resulted in pneumonia and death.—TRANSLATOR.]

end to be fruitless for the immediate objects they had in view, they might as a last resort put all the men on board the brigantine and, by following the current of the river, "come out in the Northern Sea" in it.[87]

Orellana, who, as his chronicler states, was opposed[88] to the construction of the brigantine, when once this had been decided upon showed himself more active than anyone else in getting together the material that was needed for it; he went in person through the whole camp searching for iron for nails, allotted among the soldiers the various tasks that fell to them in the work, sent the Indians to cut the necessary timber in the forests, etc.; so that in a short time, with the help of all, the brigantine was finished, "water-tight and strong, although not very large."[89]   In memory of this feat, they named this village El Barco.[90]

The command of the craft was intrusted to Juan de Alcántara. "They shipped as much stuff as she could stow, and the Spaniards with the horses followed down stream, along the bank.   They met with some small settlements where they got maize and *yuca*, and they found a quantity of guavas which afforded no small help to them in their need.   Continuing their journey down the river bank, they sometimes wished to diverge in one direction or another to see what the country was like, but the morasses and other obstacles were so great that they could not, and so they were obliged to keep along the river bank, though with much difficulty, for the creeks in the swamps were so deep that swimming the horses through them was an arduous task.   Some Spaniards and horses were drowned.   The Indian men and women carrying loads could not cross these swamps on foot, so they looked for some of the canoes which the natives had hidden.   When the bad places were narrow they made bridges of trees, and crossed in that manner.

[87] Pizarro so states in definite terms: "all of which I did with the end in view, if we did not find any good country wherein to found colonies, of not stopping until I should come out in the Northern Sea" [*infra*, p. 247].

[88] According to Friar Carvajal's *Account* Orellana opposed the construction of the brigantine "for several good reasons," being of the opinion that the thing to do was to return to the savanas where the camp had been pitched and search for the roads which could bring them to Pasto and Popayán [see *infra*, p. 169].

I do not know whether, in expressing himself in this manner, the Dominican friar wished to remove even the suspicion that Orellana had meditated ever abandoning his chief; for, in regard to "the good reasons," there does not seem to be any possibility of taking them seriously.

[89] Ortiguera, pp. 314-315, below.   We do not know, therefore, either the capacity of the brigantine or the exact time spent in its construction.   [It could hold 20 men (Oviedo, p. 545).—EDITOR.]

[90] "This village . . .   is situated on the shores of this river, on the left, on a high bank, safe from the freshets that are usual with the winter rains, and is estimated to be about 70 leagues from the city of Quito . . .   " (Ortiguera, p. 315 of the present volume)

In this way they advanced down the river for forty-three marches,[91] and there was not a day when they did not come upon one or two of these creeks, so deep that they were put to the labor we have described, each time. They found little food and no inhabitants, and they began to feel the pangs of hunger, for the herd of swine they brought from Quito, numbering more than 5000, all were eaten."*

But it is now time to hear from the mouth of Pizarro himself what happened upon their arrival in this uninhabited region, which was said to be only a foretaste of a still greater one ahead. At the same time we shall see the rôle played by Orellana in this affair.

"And pushing on down the river by the route which the guides told us [to follow], being now seventy leagues inside this province, I was informed by the guides whom I had with me that there lay [ahead of us] a great uninhabited region in which there was no food whatsoever to be had; and, learning this, I gave orders for the expedition to halt and for us to lay in all the food that could be obtained; and, the men being thus engaged in searching for food-stuffs, there came to me Captain Francisco de Orellana, and he told me how [he had questioned] the guides that I had placed in his charge for better protection and in order that he might talk to them and from them get information regarding the country beyond, as he had nothing to do, for it was I who looked after matters pertaining to fighting; and he told me that the guides said that the uninhabited region was a vast one and that there was no food whatsoever to be had this side of a spot where another great river joined up with the one down which we were proceeding, and that from this junction one day's journey up the [other] river there was an abundant supply of food; from the said guides I in turn sought information, and they told me the same as they had told Captain Orellana; and Captain Orellana told me that in order to serve Your Majesty and for love of me he was willing to take upon himself the task of going in search of food where the Indians said [that it was to be had], for he was sure that there would be some there; and that, if I would give him the brigantine and the canoes manned by sixty

91 " . . . and we went down the river another fifty leagues, at the end of which we found no more inhabited regions, and we were now suffering very great privation and lacked food . . . " (Carvajal's *Account, infra,* pp. 169–170).

"This arrangement and this method were kept up for a distance of 50 leagues, in the course of which they found along the shores of it [i.e. of the river] several settlements from which they kept supplying themselves with the food that they needed, and when once these had been passed they came upon an uninhabited region . . . " (Ortiguera, *infra,* p. 315).

*[Cieza de León, *op. cit.,* p. 71. The above is Markham's translation, *op. cit.,* pp. 64–65.— EDITOR.]

men, he would go in search of food and would bring it for the relief of the expeditionary force, and that, as I was to continue on down and he was to come back with the food, the relief would be quick [in coming], and that within ten or twelve days he would get back to the expeditionary force.

"And being confident that Captain Orellana would do as he said, because he was my lieutenant, I told him that I was pleased at the idea of his going for the food, and that he should see to it that he returned within the twelve days and in no case went beyond the junction of the rivers but brought the food and gave his attention to nothing else, inasmuch as he had the men to do it with; and he answered me saying that by no means would he exceed what I had told him and that he would come with the food within the time that he had stated. And with this confidence that I had in him, I gave him the brigantine and the canoes and sixty men, because it was reported that there were many Indians going about the river in canoes; telling him also, inasmuch as the guides had said that at the beginning of the uninhabited region there were two very large rivers that could not be bridged over, to leave there four or five canoes to ferry the expeditionary force over; and he promised me that he would do so, and so departed.

"And paying no heed to what he owed to the service of Your Majesty and to what it was his duty to do as he had been told by me, his captain, and to the well-being of the expeditionary force and of the enterprise [itself], instead of bringing the food he went down the river without leaving any arrangements [for the aid of those who were to follow on], leaving only the signs and choppings showing how they had been on land and had stopped at the junction of the rivers and in other parts, without there having come in any news of him at all up to the present time, he [thus] displaying toward the whole expeditionary force the greatest cruelty that ever faithless men have shown, aware that it was left so unprovided with food and caught in such a vast uninhabited region and among such great rivers, carrying off all the arquebuses and crossbows[92] and munitions and iron materials of the whole expeditionary force, and after great hardship the expeditionary force arrived at the junction where he was to await

[92] Pizarro fell into a grave exaggeration when he made this assertion, for Orellana had on board only three arquebuses and four or five crossbows, as may be inferred from the following passage of Friar Carvajal's *Relación* published in Oviedo: "The next day, in the morning, the Captain commanded that all be on the alert and arm themselves and have ready the *three arquebuses and four or five crossbows* that there were among the companions" (*Historia de las Indias*, Vol. 4, p. 544).

me.  And when the members of the expeditionary force, having gone that far, saw the junction and [realized] that there was no relief [there] for them in the way of food, because he had gone on and there was no way of finding any food whatsoever, they became greatly discouraged, because for many days the whole expeditionary force had eaten nothing but palm shoots and some fruit stones which they found on the ground [and] which had fallen from the trees, together with all the various kinds of noxious wild beasts which they had been able to find, because they had eaten in this wild country more than one thousand dogs and more than one hundred horses, without any other kind of food whatsoever, from which cause many members of the expeditionary force had become sick, and some were weak, while others died of hunger and from not being in a condition to go on any farther."[93]

[93] Pizarro's letter, pp. 247–249 of the present volume.

Comparing this passage, which we might call the act of accusation of Orellana, with Friar Carvajal's *Account*, one can easily see that they are in perfect agreement.

# VII

## ORELLANA'S "TREASON"

WE have now reached the culminating point in the life of Francisco de Orellana, the moment of that decisive act which was to be the origin of his glory and the cause of the terrible accusations that have been made to weigh upon his name. In order, then, to arrive, after employing all the scrupulousness which so grave a matter demands, at a true evaluation of the circumstances, places, and age in which there was acted out that drama whose stage was the virgin forests of the New World and the actors in which were that handful of fearless adventurers, I shall endeavor to make clear here, availing myself of the evidence at my disposal, when, how, and where the initial act of the voyage of discovery which I have undertaken to study took place.

The expeditioners had departed from Quito, as will be remembered, in the last days of February, 1541, and, after wandering in uncertainty and almost without any fixed direction in mind about the regions to the east which lie a little to the south of the equinoctial line, had finally halted, nearly ten full months later,[94]

[94] "We set out from the camp on the second day of the Feast-tide of the Nativity of Our Redeemer Jesus Christ, Monday, the year and the day being the second of One Thousand Five Hundred and Forty and Two," or December 26, 1541, because the final "and Two" is, to all appearances, a printer's error (Carvajal's *Relación*, printed in Oviedo, *Historia general y natural de las Indias*, Vol. 4, p. 542). [It should be borne in mind that the Spaniards of this time held their elections, etc., at Christmas time, and that not infrequently they referred, from that time on, to the year as being that of the one during which the new officials were to exercise the offices to which they had been elected.—TRANSLATOR.]

[December 26, 1541, was, indeed, a Monday. The correlation between days of the week and dates in such historical documents as Carvajal's *Account* affords a valuable means of arriving at precision in the interpretation of the chronology of the events related. A useful guide, among many others, in establishing this correlation with regard to the years here under consideration is H. Grotefend, *Taschenbuch der Zeitrechnung des Deutschen Mittelalters und der Neuzeit*, 4th edition, Hanover, 1915. According to calculations based on this source (pp. 128–129), some of the significant dates referred to in the present volume occurred on the days of the week cited in the following list (it should be borne in mind that 1540 and 1544 were leap years):

| | | | |
|---|---|---|---|
| January 1, 1540 | Thursday | February 26 | Quadragesima Sunday |
| December 1 | Wednesday | March 5 | Sunday |
| February 21, 1541 | Monday | March 19 | Sunday (St. Joseph's day) |
| December 26 | Monday | March 25 | Saturday (Annunciation) |
| January 2, 1542 | Monday | April 2 | Palm Sunday |
| January 8 | Sunday | April 5 | Tenebrae Wednesday |
| February 2 | Thursday (Candlemas) | April 6 | Maundy Thursday |
| February 12 | Sunday (St. Eulalia's day) | April 7 | Good Friday |
| February 22 | Ash Wednesday (beginning of Lent) | April 9 | Easter Sunday |
| | | April 16 | Quasimodo Sunday |

at a wide, deep-flowing river that ran through the valley of the Coca—a name which it has preserved down to the present time.[95]

With this fact established (and it is indisputable), it is averred by some that, since the Napo of the geographers of today, or the Canela of the conquistadors, is the first large river with which the Coca unites its waters, the junction to which Gonzalo Pizarro refers can be none other than that of these two rivers.

But to what degree is this accurate?

From Friar Carvajal's *Account* we know that a short time after leaving the camp Orellana found the waters of the Coca swelled by "many other rivers which emptied into it on the right from a southerly direction."[96]

Friar Carvajal knew what he was talking about when he said "rivers"; and, what is more important still, the names of these rivers are known to us from Friar Carvajal's *Relación* as published by Oviedo. "With this river," says the Dominican friar, speaking of the Coca, "other mighty rivers unite, such as the one they call the Cosanga (*by which we also passed*), as well as another which is called the Payamino, *and the Canela*."[97] Since these names

| | | | |
|---|---|---|---|
| April 25, 1542 | Tuesday (St. Mark's day) | August 6 | Sunday (Transfiguration) |
| May 6 | Saturday (Day of St. John Ante portam latinam) | August 25 | Friday (St. Louis' day) |
| May 18 | Thursday (Ascension) | August 29 | Tuesday (Beheading of St. John) |
| May 28 | Whitsunday (Pentecost) | September 11 | Monday |
| June 4 | Trinity Sunday | January 1, 1543 | Monday |
| June 8 | Thursday (Corpus Christi) | January 1, 1544 | Tuesday |
| June 22 | Thursday | January 1, 1545 | Thursday |
| June 24 | Saturday (St. John the Baptist's day) | May 11, 1545 | Monday |

With the aid of this list the reader may himself check the correctness or otherwise of weekday-date correlations by Medina, Carvajal and others. For this reason attention will not necessarily be called to discrepancies where they may occur in the remainder of this volume.—EDITOR.]

[95] The early chroniclers who speak of this river call it, without exception, by this name. Friar Carvajal in his *Account* calls it the "great river that comes down from Quijos." [Medina has erred here, for in neither of the two printed versions of Carvajal's account is this expression to be found; nor is it probable that he took it from the Muñoz copy, for precisely where Carvajal might be expected to speak of this river there is a long lacuna in the Muñoz copy (see Medina's foot-notes, *infra*, pp. 168 and 176). On the other hand, the expression is used (with the verb "viene" for Medina's "baja") by the scrivener of Orellana's expedition proper at the beginning of the document which records the appointment of this scrivener by Orellana and which was published by Medina himself (see *infra*, p. 253). There can be little doubt that it was from here that Medina took this designation of the river down which Orellana set out.—EDITOR.] On Pedro Maldonado's remarkable map published in 1750 [*Carta de la Provincia de Quito y de sus adjacentes*], immediately after the name of Coca, is found the following annotation: "River which Gonzalo Pizarro navigated, and from which Orellana discovered the Marañón." In spite of these testimonies, Prescott believed it was the Napo; but Jiménez de la Espada, who has visited these places, is of the same opinion as the chroniclers.

[96] P. 171 of the present volume.

[97] Oviedo, Vol. 4, p. 542. [The italics are Medina's.—EDITOR.]

are still preserved on the modern maps,[98] with the exception of the last mentioned, which has been changed to Napo,[99] the fixing of the starting point of Orellana is exceedingly easy.

If we accept, therefore, as we cannot help accepting, the data furnished by the Dominican chronicler, we shall find that the expeditioners very soon passed the Cosanga, and then the junction of the Coca with the Napo, and that the spot where they stopped, therefore, was much below this last point.

The spot where they stopped, in my opinion, is the confluence of the Napo with the Aguarico; that is, a place farther on downstream by a distance which in a straight line would be approximately equal to double that which separates the mouth of the Cosanga emptying into the Coca from the mouth of this latter emptying into the Napo.

Moreover, in connection with this *Relación* of Friar Carvajal's, there are to be noted two circumstances which I consider of importance and which in my humble but sincere opinion virtually substantiate my assertion.

If at the time when the expeditioners came to a stop they had not yet passed the junction of the Aguarico with the Napo, it seems to me quite certain that the Dominican friar, in telling us, as he always did in such cases, about the rivers which emptied one after the other into the one whose course they followed, would, when the time came, have had abundant reason for mentioning that copious river by some appellation or other. Yet he did not do so—a circumstance which I can explain only by assuming that the junction just beyond which they found the Indian village and the desired food supplies was that of the Aguarico and the Napo.

[98] The most recent among these maps is Doctor Teodoro Wolf's [*Carta geográfica del Ecuador*], published in Leipzig in 1892. This is the one which I have before me. [Wolf's map does not extend far enough east to show these headwater tributaries of the Coca. The most recent representation of this whole region is to be found on the maps (Fig. 1 and Pl. 3) accompanying the article by J. H. Sinclair entitled *In the Land of Cinnamon: A Journey in Eastern Ecuador* and published in the *Geographical Review*, Vol. 19, 1929, pp. 201–217. In its northeastern quarter Sinclair's map is superseded by the map of the headwaters of the Coca by General L. T. Paz y Miño accompanying his article *La Exploración al Reventador* in *Boletín de la Academia Nacional de Historia*, Vol. 12, pp. 175–184, Quito, 1931. The inset map in Fig. 1 on p. 48 of the present volume is based on the maps by Sinclair and Paz y Miño.—EDITOR.]

[99] "The Napo, another river which was not called by its present name in olden times but was known as the River of the Canela, as far as its confluence with the Santa Ana, a locality which now goes by the name of Juntas del Coca" (Jiménez de la Espada, article already mentioned [*Ilustración Española y Americana*, August 22, 1894, p. 110]).

And let it not be said that this statement in Carvajal's *Relación* contains an absurdity as regards the Payamino, a river which, even though it runs almost parallel to the Coca, actually empties its waters into the Napo. [Medina apparently interprets Carvajal's statement to mean that the Payamino and the Canela (Napo) form a single stream before uniting with the Coca.—EDITOR.]

To this piece of evidence, which is negative, so to speak, I shall now add another which is very precise and definite, taken from the Dominican's *Account* as printed herein. It can be seen from this document, in fact, that right after they had set out and when they had not yet gone more than "something like twenty leagues, . . . there joined with our river another one from the right, not very wide, on which river an important overlord named Irrimorrany" (or Irimara) "had his abode . . . And because of its [i.e. this other river's] strong current and [because] it emptied in with such a great onrush and force, ours [i.e. our force, our strength] was not sufficient for going up through it in the boat and the canoes . . . ; rather, we barely escaped drowning in getting past the junction of the rivers in [the midst of] a great jam of logs which the current had brought down."[100]

When we read a description like this and then take a look at the map, we readily perceive that this river can be none other than the Curaray, not only because no other river of such importance flows into the Napo from the right anywhere down to the latter's junction with the Amazon, but also because, as has been well said by Jiménez de la Espada, "all the elements of this description, and in particular the copiousness of its outflow, exactly fit the great Curaray, the most abundant of all the southern tributaries of the Napo, or, as it was formerly called, the Santa Ana."*

If we read on a little further in Friar Carvajal's journal, we shall also see that on Saint Eulalia's day,† "there having already gone by eleven days of February since we had departed from the place where the nails were made, *two* rivers united with the river we were navigating, and they were wide, in particular the one which came in on the right side as we came downstream, which did away with and completely mastered the other river, and it seemed as if it swallowed it up within itself, because it came on with such fury and with so great an onrush that it was a thing of much awe and amazement to see such a jam of trees and dead timber as it brought along with it, such that it was enough to fill one with the greatest fear [just] to look at it, let alone to go through it."[101]

---

[100] P. 179 of the present volume. [But beginning with: "And because of its . . . " Medina is quoting, not from the *Account* as published by him, but from the version inserted by Oviedo in his *Historia*, etc. (Vol. 4, p. 546).—EDITOR.]

*[*Ilustración Española y Americana*, August 30, 1894, pp. 126-127.]

†[February 12.—EDITOR.]

[101] Carvajal's *Relación* in Oviedo [Vol. 4, pp. 547-548. The italics are Medina's.—EDITOR].

Jiménez de la Espada, when he comes to this passage, makes it refer to the Curaray. But in so doing he neglects to take into consideration two important facts: first, that Friar Carvajal notes most explicitly that there were *two* rivers which here emptied together into the one navigated by the expeditioners up to this point, or which absorbed this latter; and, second, that Friar Carvajal goes on to say that the current "was so wide from bank to bank from here on that it seemed as though we were navigating launched out upon a vast sea."* Now if we examine the map of these regions, we shall see, in fact, that at the precise point of the confluence of the Napo with the Marañón the course of this latter is divided in two by a large island which, when seen from this point, has the effect of making it seem as if there were two rivers, and not just one, coming in from the west. And what else could this wide river be which from there on made the expeditioners believe that they were navigating launched out upon a vast sea?

On February 12 the crew of the brigantine were thus furrowing the waters of the Marañón, and it was now many days since they had left the Curaray behind them.

It is evident from the foregoing that I am now able to point with absolute precision to Orellana's stopping place, which must have been, according to my deductions, twenty leagues above the confluence of the Curaray with the Napo, and a short distance below the junction of this latter with the Aguarico, as I said at the beginning.

Another matter which it is well to take into consideration in this connection, and one which Jiménez de la Espada has made use of in attempting to prove his case, is the question of the ethnographic center in which were located the Irimaraes, the inhabitants of the village of Aparia, where Orellana made port. Let us hear what my learned friend has to say on this subject:

"The *Irimarais*, *Irimais*, or *Irimarases* (in all these three ways do I find this name written) belonged, beyond doubt, to the Omagua nation. The area of dispersion of this tribe, descendants of the prolific Carib race, extended at that time along the shores of the Napo or Santa Ana as far north as the regions above the drainage basin of the Coca; and even as late as the year 1700, approximately, the great missionary among these peoples, the Jesuit friar, Father Samuel Fritz, got to know, and had dealings with, a certain Irimara, chief of the *Ticunas*, the clever manu-

*[Oviedo, Vol. 4, p. 548.]

facturers of the 'curare' poison. This chief resided a little below the junction of the Napo with the Marañón. 'Irimara,' Friar Carvajal tells us in his manuscript itinerary, was also the name of another chief or overlord who lived in the middle region of the first of the above-mentioned rivers. The Irimarais settlement, where Orellana's little fleet put into harbor and made its head-quarters, is designated in the itinerary of the same friar (copied by Fernández de Oviedo) as *Ymara;* but in a more reliable document, namely the first one that Orellana signed on the day of his landing and exactly nine days after he had separated from his superior, it is called the *village of Aparia*, or in other words, the village ruled over by Chief Aparia. This name, in my judgment, is composed of 'abbá,' father, patriarch, lord, in the Omagua tongue, and 'Aria,' 'Arian,' 'Ariana.' For it must be borne in mind that the Omaguas living on the banks of the Napo between the Coca and the Aguarico, according to Father Fritz, were at the end of the seventeenth century still called 'Arianas'; and another missionary of the Company, the author of the *Noticias auténticas del famoso río Marañón* [Authentic Information Regarding the Famous Marañón River], supplements Father Fritz's statements, asserting that at the beginning of the seventeenth century there were some Ariana Indians living around the headwaters of the *Tiputini*, a river which flows in on the south side, between the Coca and the Aguarico at an equal distance from one and the other, and runs almost parallel to, and close to the right bank of, the Napo. Now then, Friar Carvajal, in his itinerary already mentioned, distinguishes between two chiefs or overlords by the name of Aparia, i.e. Aparia the *Lesser* and Aparia the *Great*, whose residences and dominions were situated respectively upstream and downstream from the mouth of the *great Curaray*, a tributary of the Napo, the distance separating the two dominions from each other being nineteen day-stages[102] by boat, more or less; and it must be further observed that the dominion of Aparia the Great took in territories on both banks of the Curaray. From all this one may conclude, after counting nineteen day-stages back upstream from the Curaray River, that the capital of the dominion of Aparia the Lesser, that is to say, the village of Aparia where Orellana put into port, must have been situated very close to the junction of the

[102] Jiménez de la Espada is in error here, for the nineteen day-stages were counted by Friar Carvajal from the time of his arrival at Aparia the Great to his departure from Pizarro's encampment. I shall have occasion to return later to these figures. Let it suffice for my purpose, for the time being, to note the area of dispersion of the Irimaraes.

Coca [with the Napo].* About this there can be no doubt, or else Friar Carvajal has deceived us, and that I do not believe, however much he may attempt to do so in connection with other episodes mentioned in his account . . . "†

For my part, far from believing, in the presence of all this, that the village of Aparia lay near the junction of the Coca [with the Napo], I draw the conclusion that the ethnographic center of origin of these people was precisely upstream and downstream from the mouth of the Curaray, or northward as far as the confluence of the Napo with the Aguarico and southward as far as a point a little below the junction of the Napo with the Marañón.

The center must have been the Curaray, a name from which "curare" is perhaps derived, as the poison with which these Indians poisoned their arrows was called.

Supposing my hypothesis to be correct, I find that Orellana must have started out from a point above the junction of the Cosanga with the Coca,[103] and that he had gone on to a spot a little below the junction of the Napo with the Aguarico before stopping.

If the data, both geographic and ethnological, regarding places and rivers which have been utilized by the latest historian of Orellana in making his calculations, just as they have been used by me also, were well authenticated and not founded upon conjectures which are only more or less accurate, there could be no doubt whatsoever in regard to the distance traveled by Orellana on this first journey of nine days' duration: in one case it would be a distance of sixty leagues and, in the other, close on to three times that distance. But as we possess other sources of information and enlightenment, it is necessary to examine these also.

Pizarro writes that when he reached the spot where he was supposed to join Orellana again, he found himself in the province of the Omaguas. This is a very vague piece of information and one which turns out to be even more uncertain if we consult the modern maps, where this name is put down at the confluence of the Napo with the Marañón, a spot which is undoubtedly altogether too far away from the one Pizarro meant; and this only confirms what I

---

*[The bracketed phrase has been added by the present editor to indicate the confluence he believes Medina meant.—EDITOR.]

†[*Ilustración Española y Americana*, August 22, 1894, p. 110.]

[103] This is the opinion of González Suárez, a distinguished Ecuadorian prelate who has traveled extensively in his country. In his book [see *supra*, p. 31, footnote 50], speaking of the rivers encountered by the expeditioners, he mentions not only the Cosanga, but also the Quijos, which is still farther to the east.

have already said regarding how risky it is to rely on such sources.[104]

Agustín de Zárate,* followed in this matter by the Inca Garcilaso, states that the river junction to which Orellana was ordered to go was eighty leagues beyond the spot where Pizarro was encamped, although the latter of these two authors also claims that the distance was covered [by Orellana] in only three days.[105]  Antonio de

[104] According to Cieza de León [Pizarro, rather; p. 246f., *infra*], it was in the province of Omagua that Pizarro seized the fifteen canoes from the Indians and had the brigantine built. This, indeed, substantiates what I state in the text; and, if all that I say above is not sufficient proof, one will only have to look into the question of the time it took Pizarro and his followers to get to the junction of the Coca with the Napo, the farthermost point reached by him. Pizarro in his letter to the King [p. 249, *infra*] limits himself to saying that he went as far as that spot, as I have said; and Oviedo says [Vol. 4, p. 385] that his arrival there occurred within a few days after Orellana's departure. This being the case, how could the stopping-place of the expeditioners who were on board the brigantine possibly have been the junction of the Coca with the Napo, when Pizarro and his followers arrived there, and after great hardships at that, as he tells us, within a few days?

But actually the time it took Pizarro and his followers to arrive at the mouth of the Coca must have been much longer than what the chronicler of the Indies tells us. In order to convince one's self that this is so, it will suffice, in fact, to remember how and by what route the small expeditionary army advanced and to recall that a short time prior to this, according to the testimony of Cieza de León, in advancing fifty leagues (and this is a great deal, it is thought) he had spent forty-three days; and it is for this reason, no doubt, that the Inca Garcilaso sets this time down as two months.

Diego Gómez and Álvaro de Sepúlveda, both of whom were soldiers of Pizarro's, testifying under the eleventh question in the judicial inquiry covering Ginés Hernández's service record [p. 289 f., *infra*], state that they waited for Orellana's return forty-odd days; but they do not speak of the time that it took the expeditionary force to arrive at the junction, nor do they state whether these forty days should be counted from the time of Orellana's departure up to the day when Pizarro started off on his return journey to Quito, disillusioned by Orellana's failure to come back. I believe this latter supposition to be a safe one, because it is the most plausible one.

I am still discussing this matter from a point of view based on the assumption that the distance was a short one, much less than the sixty leagues estimated by Jiménez de la Espada, inasmuch as it took Pizarro only a few days, or else two months, to get down to the junction. If the statement that he was two months on the way be accepted, it becomes necessary to assume that Orellana had gone on much farther down the river before stopping; but, then, how is one going to reconcile this with Friar Carvajal's assertion that Orellana started out, not from the neighborhood of this junction, but from a point above the Cosanga? If, however, all this could be shown to be true, we should find, for one thing, that the calculations of the expeditioners themselves were closer to the truth and that consequently they were right in estimating the distance at about two hundred leagues.

*[Medina gives Francisco de Jerez as the first of the two authorities whom he cites in this sentence, apparently not having noticed that this conquistador's account, in so far as it deals with events in the Indies, does not go beyond the year 1533. Evidently, Medina was a little careless in using Vol. 2 of Enrique de Vedia's *Historiadores primitivos de Indias* (*Biblioteca de autores españoles*, Vol. 26, first printed in 1853), in which are reproduced both Francisco de Jerez's *Verdadera relación de la conquista del Perú y provincia del Cuzco* (pp. 319–346) and Agustín de Zárate's *Historia del descubrimiento y conquista de la provincia del Perú* (pp. 459–574). He made the same error, quoting Zárate's exact words, in his footnote 109 and again in his text on p. cxvi (p. 80 of the present translation). In the present case, then, he most certainly took this mention of the distance of eighty leagues from Book IV, Ch. 4, of Agustín de Zárate's *Historia*, etc. (p. 494 of the above-mentioned volume); but it should be noticed that Zárate states that Pizarro merely "had been informed" beforehand that this was the distance.—EDITOR.]

[105] It would seem almost unnecessary to state here that Pizarro did not go beyond the junction of the Coca with the Napo, where the only signs that he found of Orellana's having been there were blazes on the tree trunks made with machetes. Oviedo, therefore, is exaggerating when he says that Pizarro found "huts and other signs" [Oviedo, Vol. 4, p. 393] showing that Orellana had stopped at the place agreed upon. [Nevertheless, when one has seen how the Indians, of whom Orellana must have had a certain number with him, can in a few minutes erect a good shelter out of poles and palm thatch, one must admit that the statement of Oviedo is not to be treated too lightly.—TRANSLATOR.]

Herrera, without voicing any personal opinion, merely remarks that Orellana and his companions, when they were in the village of Aparia, believed themselves to be three hundred leagues from their starting point; but this is obviously an exaggeration and does not agree at all with what they themselves tell us.

Appealing now to the testimony of the men themselves who made the trip, we find that, according to the calculations of the seamen who were among them, during the nine days[106] that it took them to advance to a spot below the junction, if we take the junction itself as the stopping point, they traveled two hundred leagues.[107]

Let us leave to one side for a moment the question of the estimate which they made of the distance, and let us take up the matter of the number of days of navigation, for, as Jiménez de la Espada has rightly observed, "the only sure fact that we possess in all this is that it took Orellana and his detachment nine days to reach by water a spot a little beyond the place at which he was to have put an end to his honorable and dishonored mission."* In this way it ought to be possible to check up on the computation of the distance covered by taking as a basis the average daily run during these nine days.

In making this calculation we must take into account one important circumstance, namely that as a result of the torrential rains of that season of the year in those regions the river which Orellana and his companions were navigating was swollen and swift, and that to the current such as it was at the beginning of

---

[106] That the number of days was nine may be gathered from Friar Carvajal's *Account*, and it is expressly recorded as such in one of the documents signed by the companions of Orellana: "and harassed by this shortage [of food] we journeyed on for nine days" (p. 258 of the present volume).

[107] This estimate was not made by Carvajal but, as he himself says, by "the seamen who happened to join our party," who, he says, "kept charting the river and taking notes, and they calculated our daily runs and affirmed that each day, rowing downstream, we navigated twenty-five leagues or more" (*Relación*, Oviedo [Vol. 4, p. 543]). A like assertion is made by the signers of the petition which is printed on pp. 258 ff. of the present volume: "and [we refused to follow], it being evident to us that the return up the river was impossible because of the great length of the journey, for we were informed by men who were best qualified to know about this that it was around two hundred leagues from the said village to where the said Governor was remaining behind, . . . ."

In Friar Carvajal's *Account* as published in the present volume [*infra*, p. 178] there is a different reading from that of the Muñoz copy of the same: in this latter it reads two hundred leagues; in the one published here, one hundred and fifty.

[From personal experience on Amazon rivers, the present translator is able to affirm that a canoe will make 60–70 miles (16–19 leagues) per day downstream, according as the quantity of water in the stream is greater or less. Also, it should be taken into account that while on the map a distance between two points may appear, for example, to be fifty miles, in order to get from one of these points to the other, following the innumerable curves and bends of the stream, one must navigate possibly three times that distance. The rivers of the Amazon lowland are very sinuous and meander a great deal, and this is characteristic of streams in such a country.—TRANSLATOR.]

*[*Ilustración Española y Americana*, August 22, 1894, p. 110.]

their journey there were added, within a very short time after they had set out, the waters of many other rivers.

With this in mind, we next have to establish, in order to solve our problem, how much time they spent every day in navigating. From Friar Carvajal's *Account* no conclusion whatsoever can be drawn on this point, at least as regards these first nine days of the voyage. But when one recalls that they were driven on, in the beginning, by the desire to arrive quickly at the end of the voyage, the success of which meant the immediate and eagerly awaited relief of their companions remaining behind, and that within a short time they were seized with the fear that they themselves were going to perish from hunger, one can readily believe that, except for the few moments when they stopped, first to repair the damage done to the boat (an incident which I shall speak of later) and afterwards to look for roots or wild fruits with which to placate their hunger, they must have hurried on rapidly. And as a matter of fact, it is recorded that they rowed from sunrise to sunset, and so vigorously that, as members of the crew said afterward, the great amount of rowing, together with their small rations of food, brought them to the point of death.[108]

In view, then, of the fact that they were carried along by the current and that they rowed with all their might the whole day long, it seems to me that there is no exaggeration in the figures which the seamen manning the brigantine gave, when they told Friar Carvajal that in nine days they had gone down the river two hundred leagues. When it comes to choosing between this estimate and the idea that the distance covered in this time and under these conditions was only sixty leagues, I, frankly, do not hesitate for a moment.

Besides, this question of the number of leagues they covered is merely incidental in judging the conduct of the Estremenian captain; and, even if the correct figure were sixty, it would be of no importance in connection with passing judgment upon his act, if he and his companions really *believed* that they were two hundred leagues away from Pizarro's camp.

In order to form, with all the facts before us, an opinion regarding the circumstances bearing upon the arraignment in connection

---

[108] " . . . those of us who were spared became quite ill from the said suffering, because, as Your Worship knows, it was very great, not only as a consequence of not eating but also because of the constant rowing from sun to sun [i.e. from sunrise to sunset], for this alone was sufficient to kill us . . . " (p. 258 of the present volume).

Daylight in those latitudes and in that month was a little more than twelve hours long.

with which the term "Orellana's treason" has come to be used, but which I, for my part, should more aptly designate as the rehabilitation of his name, it behooves us now to look into the conditions under which he accomplished this nine-day voyage.

The brigantine was loaded up with the heavy objects, as we already know, and on board it were placed also a part of the clothing and bedding of the expeditioners[109] and a very small quantity of food supplies.[110] Orellana left behind him, in Pizarro's

---

[109] Orellana has been accused of having appropriated, not only this clothing and bedding, but also the money and emeralds belonging to Pizarro's companions. Agustín de Zárate (Book IV, Ch. 4) [of work cited in footnote 46, *supra*, reprinted in *Biblioteca de autores españoles*, Vol. 26; reference on p. 495] tells us, in regard to this, that Orellana carried off "much gold and silver and [many] emeralds, whereby he had money to spend during all the time that he went about soliciting for and equipping himself for this [expedition of] conquest" (i.e. the conquest of New Andalusia [undertaken by the new expedition organized later in Spain]). López de Gómara states that "he went off down the river with the clothing and bedding, the gold and the emeralds which they had intrusted to him"; and further on he says that "he spent the emeralds and the gold that he had with him" [work cited above in footnote 46, reprinted in *Biblioteca de autores españoles*, Vol. 22; reference on p. 210]. Oviedo, referring to letters he had received, adds: "and it has even been stated in writing that the men in the boat also carried off a great wealth of gold and [precious] stones" [Oviedo, Vol. 4, p. 386].

We shall see later what Orellana did with the clothing and bedding which were loaded upon the brigantine. As for the gold, silver, and emeralds, these statements can be nothing but pure calumny and are contradicted by the most ordinary common sense. In the course of their march the expeditioners had not found any one of these commodities, and it is difficult to imagine them carrying such things along with them, unless it be supposed that they had merely brought them along from Quito for safekeeping; and that would be equally absurd, for, if they attached so much importance to them, they would hardly have intrusted them to persons who were separating themselves from the camp and about whose return nothing could be known in advance. Nor does it seem likely that these precious possessions would be so heavy for their owners that carrying them would eventually become unendurable, much less so because we know that as a matter of practice the soldiers were accustomed to carrying their emeralds in a small sack hung from their necks underneath their clothing, several cases being known of the finding of such a sack when a soldier's body was being prepared for burial. [A notable case of this kind is recorded in connection with the death of Pizarro's famous pilot, Bartolomé Ruiz. When he was dying on the outskirts of Cajamarca in April, 1533, an emerald was found on him in just such a sack and was confiscated by the Crown *veedor* García de Salcedo, who alleged that the royal levy of one fifth had not been paid on it. As to the presence of precious stones in Orellana's party, it is doubtless true that all of Pizarro's expeditioners had their little fortunes tied around their necks, and it is quite probable that Orellana in his campaigns on the coast of what is now Ecuador had secured some large emeralds, as that was where the largest stones in the world came from at the time of Pizarro's first trip; and it is quite likely also that the sale of these emeralds covered his expenses later.—TRANSLATOR.]

Oviedo, who likewise could not help seeing the absurdity of the sort of allegation which I have quoted, limits himself to saying that "there were placed on board the brigantine a few loads of clothing and bedding," and he adds later: "Here (in Santo Domingo), this captain and his followers publicly stated that they had come here poor . . . ": and this was the truth. [Medina is again slightly mixed up in his references. The first of the two statements which he claims to have taken from Oviedo is not to be found anywhere in this historian's account of these events; but it appears to be Medina's variation of what Friar Carvajal, in the *Relación* as reproduced by Oviedo (Vol. 4, p. 542), has to say regarding this matter: "going off in search of inhabited country and of food, in a boat and several canoes, in which there were likewise taken along *a few loads of clothing and bedding* belonging to the expeditionary force. . . . " The second statement, minus the phrase between parentheses, is to be found in Oviedo, Vol. 4, p. 386.—EDITOR.]

Let us, then, leave out of the arraignment of Orellana the ugly charge that he was a thief, with which an attempt has been made to stain his memory.

[110] " . . . for, as we had expected to return quickly," says Friar Carvajal (*infra*, p. 171). "we had not laid in a supply of food. . . . "

camp, the small amount of personal belongings not lost in his disastrous march from Quito to Zumaco; in a word, all he owned.[111] Ten of the fifteen[112] canoes belonging to the expedition were either manned or tied to the sides of the boat. Then Orellana, the Dominican friar Gaspar de Carvajal, Friar Gonzalo de Vera of the Order of Mercy, the sick, and the soldiers who had been selected to go on this special expedition, to the number of 60 persons[113] all told, went on board.

[111] Orellana "told him [i.e. Gonzalo Pizarro] how he was determined to leave behind him the little that he had with him and go on down the river . . . " (Carvajal's *Account*, p. 170, *infra*).

[112] Friar Carvajal does not state how many canoes were turned over to Orellana. Pizarro says, that he asked him at the time of his departure "to leave there four or five canoes to ferry the expeditionary force over; and he promised me that he would do so, and so departed" [*infra*, p. 248]; but he does not say categorically whether Orellana fulfilled his promise or not. But a little further along in his letter he states that after the departure of Orellana he sent men out to search for food, "in five canoes which by a miracle I personally captured from the Indians" [*infra*, p. 249], without saying, however, in a clear manner, whether he captured them after Orellana had departed, or whether they were part of the squadron which he had taken possession of earlier.

It would seem as if Oviedo, on this point, must have read Pizarro's letter, for as a matter of fact his words are almost the same as those employed by Gonzalo: "and, because Gonzalo Pizarro had to cross over two great rivers, he told him to leave for him four or five canoes out of those which they were taking with them, so that those who were proceeding with him [i.e. Pizarro] might be able to cross over; and Orellana told him that he would do all that, and he departed." [Oviedo, Vol. 4, p. 393].

It is my conviction that Orellana could not have neglected, even if he had desired to do so, to carry out the orders of his chief in this matter; and that, aside from this, it would have been a rare coincidence (it being supposed now that Orellana had taken along all the canoes) that Gonzalo Pizarro should immediately after capture the same five canoes which he had asked Orellana to leave for him. Nor does it seem natural that Orellana should wish to be encumbered with a greater number of craft of this sort than he might really need. No doubt a few were indispensable to facilitate his operations along the river, but fifteen would seem to be too many. For this reason I believe that Domínguez Miradero, one of the companions of Orellana, is exaggerating when he states that there were twenty-two of them (see p. 292 of the present volume).

But let us look at the question from another angle. Inasmuch as Orellana's plan of flight, if we accept for a moment the thesis of his accusers, was not formulated in his mind until later, I can see no way of attributing his disobedience to evil-mindedness; but, even if there was some such evil-mindedness on Orellana's part, we must not overlook the fact that Pizarro, with all his resentment, did not prefer charges against him on grounds on which there were none to be preferred; and we must not forget that Orellana was going in search of food and that, in the event of his finding some, he would think it best to have at his disposal all the means of transportation that the expeditionary force disposed of.

[113] Regarding the number of persons who went along with Orellana, see the chapter after next of this Introduction. The presence of the friars on an expedition having nothing to do with their ministry is explained in the following way, according to Oviedo: in addition to the above-mentioned, "there were others [four in number] who went aboard this same boat to go and wait for the rest of the army in a certain place where the said Captain Gonzalo Pizarro was to go shortly" [Oviedo, Vol. 4, p. 384]. [The "four in number," added parenthetically by Medina, seems to be based exclusively on the difference between the two figures 50 and 54 used by Oviedo!!—EDITOR].

Did Orellana take with him some of the guides who were in his care and custody in camp?

These Indians were the ones who, according to Gonzalo Pizarro, had reported, first to Orellana, and later on to himself when he in his turn questioned them, that they would find food at the junction of the rivers. Jiménez de la Espada deduces from this fact that Pizarro formulated a charge against his subordinate on this score also, because through the guides "he could be instructed with greater exactness and detail than his superiors and comrades as to what there was ahead of them" [*Ilustración*, etc., August 22, 1894, p. 107]. If Orellana had not communicated to his chief the information that he got from the Indians, there is no doubt that for such conduct he could have been qualified as disloyal and would have deserved to be denounced to the King by Pizarro; but not only did Orellana transmit to Gonzalo the reports of the Indians, but Pizarro (and this proves

When Orellana took leave of his chief he told him that "if luck favored him to the extent that he should find an inhabited region and foodstuffs whereby all might be succored, he would let him know about it; and that, if he [i.e. Pizarro] should see that he [i.e. Orellana] tarried, he should not be concerned about him, and that, meanwhile, he should turn back to where food was to be had, and that there he should wait for him three or four days, or as long as he should see fit, and that, in case he [i.e. Orellana] did not come, he should not be concerned about him" [*infra*, p. 170]. In reply, Pizarro merely told him, according to Friar Carvajal who must have been present at the leave-taking, to do what he thought best; but Pizarro states, as we have seen above, that he told him to return within the twelve days that were considered sufficient for the trip, and by no means to go beyond the junction of the rivers; and he adds that Orellana promised him that he would do so.

On the second day of their advance the expeditioners began to see in a practical way the difficulties presented by the journey down the river; the boat struck the trunk of a tree that seemed to be stuck up in the middle of the current, a plank was smashed, and water began to come in to such an extent that, if they had not happened to be close to land, the expedition would have ended there; but they quickly hauled the boat out on shore, repaired the damage, and promptly continued the voyage in great haste.

Three days later they had not yet come upon any settlement of any sort, the food supplies had been used up, the distance already covered was considerable, and, since in the last analysis they did not know where they would finally stop nor whether or not they were going to find what they were looking for, Orellana

his lack of confidence in what his subordinate announced to him) decided to question them for himself, thereby getting definite proof of the truthfulness of Orellana in what he had said. This being the case, Pizarro would have been quite wrong in accusing his lieutenant on this score, and in fact he did not do so; and one may be sure that he would not have failed to do so if it had been possible, irritated as he was against him at the time that he wrote his letter to the King.

With this detail established, and clearly so, in my opinion, let us return to our question: Did Orellana take along with him some of the guides? That he was in a position to do so, and that he even had a good reason for doing so, there can be no doubt. Since it was they who affirmed that there was food farther ahead at a spot the location of which they specifically indicated, it was a mere matter of foresight that they should be taken along by the expeditioners on the brigantine so that they might point out the place that they had indicated. In this connection they were not needed back in the camp, but on board the brigantine, particularly as it was expected that they would all return soon.

In spite of these considerations, it is my conviction that Orellana did not take along a single one of these guides, and I should even be inclined to say that in not doing so he committed a veritable act of imprudence. They could have been consulted, in fact, in moments of vacillation, as when Orellana thought he heard sounds coming from distant settlements; and he would have reprehended them for not having found, when he arrived there, what he was looking for at the junction of the rivers. But the fact is that Friar Carvajal never speaks of any such guides, as he does later when farther on down the river Orellana procured a few.

and his companions got together to discuss the question of whether, in view of the way things were going, it were not well to turn back from there; but, in the belief that the place designated by the guides could not now be far away, they decided amongst themselves to continue the journey. But day after day passed, and along the shores they found nothing with which to placate their hunger, nor did they catch sight of one single Indian hut among the trees. Friar Carvajal says that it was then that he celebrated mass and begged God to take pity on them, "beseeching Him . . . to deliver us from such manifest hardship and [eventual] destruction" [*infra*, p. 171]. They were now gradually beginning to understand that the return, which they had considered easy, was becoming increasingly difficult on account of the river current, and that to attempt to go back by land was perhaps impossible. The situation was discussed by all on board, in an attempt to arrive at some conclusion as to what they should do under such circumstances; and they finally agreed to go forward "and follow the river, [and thus] either die or see what there was along it . . . " [*infra*, p. 171].

Hunger was harassing them now to such a degree that they were reduced to eating hides, straps, and the soles of their shoes cooked with certain herbs; and many were so weak that they could not even stand up. In order to procure food, when the boat tied up, some on hands and knees and others leaning on staffs went into the forest in search of roots with which to appease their hunger; but, as they did not know the edible ones, not a few were poisoned and were at the point of death, "because they were like mad men and did not possess sense"[114] [*infra*, p. 172].

On January 1, 1542, as if the new year wished to regale them with a moment of joy, the men who were proceeding in one of the canoes thought they heard afar off the sound of drums—a sure sign that they would soon arrive in an inhabited district. A sad illusion! In vain did they row with renewed energy, bringing strength out of weakness, because neither on that day nor on the following day was the sound repeated. Their short-lived enthusiasm was followed by the most profound discouragement, for they believed that nothing remained for them to do but to die. But finally, on the night of this second day (January 2)[115] when,

---

[114] These were treated "by means of a little oil that was found among certain medicines that happened to be on board, and which belonged to the surgeon of the expedition" (Carvajal's *Relación*, in Oviedo [Vol. 4, p. 543]).

[115] In Friar Carvajal's *Account*, p. 172 we read: ". . . it being Monday evening, which by count was the eighth [day] of the month of January,"—obviously an error in the original which we must get around by saying that this Monday was the second day of the month and that they had now been navigating for eight days.

filled with sadness, they were supping on a little wheat and flour which Friar Carvajal had kept for use as a host and which was the last resort for them in their distress, the sound of the drums reached the boat with undeniable clearness and kept getting louder as they advanced along the river. Fearful lest the Indians should attack them by night and take them by surprise, Orellana arranged for the first time to have the little company guarded by watches as in time of war, and saw to it that on the following morning they should all have ready their missile weapons, which were not more than three arquebuses and four or five crossbows. Having taken these precautions, they started out in search of the village, and they had scarcely advanced two leagues when they saw coming up the river four canoes filled with Indians, who, on catching sight of the Spaniards, turned back in great haste to give the alarm in the near-by settlements. Orellana, eager to arrive at these settlements before the Indians could have time to gather, ordered the oarsmen to make haste. The Indians, however, were already waiting for these hitherto unseen people who presented themselves so unexpectedly before their eyes; but, on seeing the Spaniards leap out on land and come forward resolutely towards them, they lost courage and, fleeing in terror, were soon out of sight among the bends of the river.

The weakened expeditioners were in dire need of repairing their strength, worn down as they were by the days of fasting and by the moral suffering that they had just gone through; but Orellana issued orders to the effect that before eating they should first inspect the village so as to be certain that no enemies were hiding in it. Set at ease on this score, they at once began to eat the food and drink the beverages which the Indians had prepared for themselves, their shields slung over their backs and their swords under their arms. At two o'clock on the afternoon of that day, January 3, the Indians began to show themselves on the river, doubtless with a view to investigating what was going on in their homes; and, when Orellana saw them, he climbed up on the river bank and, availing himself of the native words that he knew,[116]

[116] Orellana was a remarkable linguist, for "with great perseverance, after he came to these Indies, he always made it a point to get to understand the tongues of the natives and made his own elementary primers for his guidance; and God endowed him with such a good memory and excellent natural aptitude, and he was so expert in interpreting, that, notwithstanding the numerous and varying tongues that there are in those parts, although he did not understand all the Indians entirely and perfectly, as he wanted to, still, as a result of the perseverance which he applied to this matter, devoting himself to this practice, he was always understood in the end, and he himself understood quite accurately so far as the matter in hand concerned us" (Carvajal's *Relación*, in Oviedo [Vol. 4, p. 548]).

began to call out to them, telling them to come near without fear, as he wished to speak with them. On this invitation two of the most daring of these Indians came up close to Orellana, who wheedled them as best he could and, giving them a few articles of trifling value, asked them to go get their overlord. The latter came at once, "very much decked out" [*infra*, p. 175]; the Spaniards embraced him, to the great satisfaction of the Indian; Orellana presented him with a costume and other things, all of which seemed to please him greatly, for he offered in exchange to give them all they needed; and when they told him that they wanted only food, he sent his men off to get some; and in a short time they appeared bringing meat, partridges, wild turkeys, and fish of many kinds. The Indian told them that the village where they had landed was called Aparia, and that the territories along the river at this point were ruled over by thirteen chiefs belonging to the race of the Irimaraes.

Such was the journey made by Orellana and his companions as far as the village of Aparia.

The events that had occurred up to now had been characterized by such unforeseen turns; what might happen farther along appeared so uncertain; the measures that Orellana was planning to take were of such importance, that, in accordance with a practice invariably followed by the conquistadors in those days, he thought it indispensable to legalize, in so far as circumstances would permit him to do so, if not what had already happened, at least what might happen in the future. With this end in view, on the day following his arrival, in his capacity of lieutenant-governor of Gonzalo Pizarro and in the name of the latter and of the King, he appointed Francisco de Isásaga to the position of scrivener, in order that he might furnish an affidavit in due legal form covering everything that "may occur and come to pass" [*infra*, p. 253] in his presence; and the document containing this appointment was drawn up in the presence of seven of the leading men who were in the party.[117]

The first act of the new functionary, in conformity also with what the conquistadors were in the habit of doing in such cases, was to record how Orellana, still calling himself Pizarro's lieu-

[117] I include in this volume a facsimile reproduction of this document [Fig. 2 on p. 255], reduced, as in the case of the one which will be found a little farther on, to approximately one half of the size of the original. In this document the reader may decipher the signatures of Orellana and Friar Carvajal, [the latter apparently as "Carauajal," the form implied by Medina in his transcription of the signature of Document II, 4, p. 254, *infra*.—EDITOR].

tenant, when three or four of the chiefs had barely come into his presence took possession of them and of their villages, Aparia and Irimara, in the name of the King.

That same day Orellana called a meeting of all the expeditioners in order to harangue them on the subject of what the best procedure under those circumstances would be, "what steps it was proper to take in the interests of their expedition and their salvation and [even the saving of] their lives, giving them a long talk, bolstering up their courage with very strong words" [*infra*, p. 176]. He added that, so far as he was concerned, his mind was made up in favor of going back up the river.

In reply Orellana heard from the mouths of his comrades some very kind words in praise of the energy that he was displaying under these conditions; but immediately after, through the intermediary of the scrivener, they presented to him a petition in which they informed him that, as a consequence of his determination to go back up the river, they could not refrain from pointing out to him that that was something impossible, in view of the distance they had come, the dangers they had encountered, and the lack of food in those uninhabited regions, all this having brought them to the point of perishing; and "how much more danger of death there would be for us," they said, "if we were to go with Your Worship back up the river!" [*infra*, p. 254]. They concluded with the request that he should not put them in the compromising situation in which they would be obliged to disobey him and in which they would be made to appear as traitors, saying that on the other hand they were ready to follow him by any other route by which at least their lives might be saved.[118]

Orellana put the petition away for future reference, and on the following day, calling the scrivener before him, he declared that, since the petition was just and it was impossible to return up the river, he could not follow any other course, although it was against his will, than to look for another route that would lead

[118] The second petition or summons addressed to Orellana by his men two months later, on March 1, furnishes further evidence to the truth of what Father Carvajal is telling us here [Medina's recital is apparently based on the text of the first petition (*infra*, p. 254ff.), rather than on Carvajal's *Relación* in Oviedo, where the episode is dealt with (Vol. 4, p. 545) in more general terms.—EDITOR]: ". . . there was great need, for the sake of our welfare, of resting a certain period of time, and this was not granted or conceded to us by Your Worship, rather Your Worship attempted right then to put into operation the plan of turning back, as Your Worship actually did start to do, and [Your Worship wished] to go in search of the Governor dead or alive; and [we refused to follow], it being evident to us that the return up the river was impossible . . . ; we decided to assemble, and we did assemble, and [we resolved] to summon [Your Worship], as it will appear from our summons, not to turn back up the river . . . " (pp. 258–259 of the present volume).

them to a region where there were Christians, whence all together, with him at their head, they could go and present themselves before his chief and inform him of all that had happened; but this was to be on one condition, namely, that they should wait for the latter there where they were for two or three months, or as long as they could find sustenance; and that while their stay lasted they should utilize the time in the construction of a brigantine "in order that the said Governor may continue on down the river, or that we ourselves [may do so] in his name in case he does not come," concluded Orellana, "inasmuch as in no other way except down the said river can our lives be saved" [*infra*, pp. 256–257].

And so on the same day he ordered that a proclamation be made to the effect that all those who had in their possession clothing or any other objects belonging to the companions who had remained behind in Pizarro's camp should bring them to him, under penalty of being looked upon as thieves, "because it is well," says this document, "that in all matters there be good order and good behavior and that no one derive personal profit from what belongs to some one else" [*infra*, p. 257]. This was the procedure followed by that man who has been accused of being a thief!

"And in order not to lose time nor waste the food in vain," Friar Carvajal goes on to say, "the Captain decided that a start should at once be made on what was to be done, and so he gave orders to prepare the necessary materials, and the companions said that they wanted to begin their task at once; and there were among us two men to whom not a little [credit] is due for having done something which they had never learned [to do], and they came before the Captain and told him that they with the help of Our Lord would make the nails that were needed, and [asked him] to order others to make charcoal. The names of these two companions were, the one, Juan de Alcántara, an hidalgo hailing from the town of Alcántara, and the other, Sebastián Rodríguez, a native of Galicia; and the Captain thanked them, promising them reward and payment for such an important piece of work; and he at once ordered some bellows to be made out of buskins, and in a like manner all the other tools, and the other companions he commanded in groups of three to prepare good kilnfuls of charcoal, all of which was promptly put into execution, and each one took his own tool and they went off to the woods to cut wood and bring it on their shoulders from the woods to the village, [a distance] which must have been about half a league, and they made their pits, and this with very great toil. As they were weak and not expert in that line of work, they could not bear up under the burden, and the other companions who had not the strength to cut wood worked the bellows and others carted water, while the Captain worked at everything, so that we all had something to which to give our attention. Our company gave such a good account of itself in this village in the organization of this task that in twenty days, with the help of God, two thousand very good nails and other things were made, and the Captain put off the construction of the brigantine for some other place where he might find a greater need for it and better facilities" [*infra*, p. 177f.].

While the work in connection with the building of the brigantine was going on, Orellana took advantage of the presence in the village of eleven chiefs from the surrounding districts, who of their own free will came in bringing food for their guests, to take possession of them in the name of the King and of Gonzalo Pizarro.

Up to the time when the preliminary work towards the construction of the proposed brigantine was completed, at the end of January[119] at the latest, Orellana and his companions had received no news whatsoever from Gonzalo Pizarro, and the situation for them was beginning to become unbearable. From the hardships which they had endured seven men had died; the Indians were no longer serving with the same good will as before; and, what was worse still, the food supplies they had laid in were diminishing in an alarming manner. Under these circumstances Orellana decided to make one last attempt to get in communication with Pizarro: he offered to give one thousand gold castellanos, as well as two negroes and some Indians to help at the oars, to any six soldiers who would volunteer to go in search of Pizarro. But only three accepted[120] the offer, and the proposal could not be carried out.

[119] Orellana having given the order to construct the brigantine on January 5, and the work having been begun at once, I think that I am safe in concluding that the two thousand nails and other instruments were finished by the end of that month. It is well to bear this circumstance in mind.

[120] The names of these three valiant men are not recorded in the documents; but this is probably the origin of the tale which Garcilaso recounts, of how, when Orellana expressed his desire to continue on down the river, some opposed him, among them Friar Carvajal and a young gentleman from Badajoz, whom he calls Hernán Sánchez de Vargas and whom Orellana, as punishment for his insolence, abandoned there at the junction of the rivers. This tale, in so far as it has to do with Hernán Sánchez de Vargas, has been copied by all the authorities who have written on this subject, including Prescott and González Suárez. I do not know where Garcilaso could have got this piece of pure invention; but the fact is that neither did Orellana start out from such a junction, as we have seen, nor did Pizarro find anyone there, nor does any such name figure in any document whatsoever. Let us strike out, then, another of the mean acts attributed to the discoverer of the Amazon.

Finally, to enter now definitely into the matter of passing judgment upon the acts on the basis of which charges are brought against Orellana, the only thing still left for us to examine is his action in resigning from the command which he held in the name of Gonzalo Pizarro, together with the manner in which he was again chosen by his soldiers to be their leader. All this, although it took place when almost a month had passed after he had left Aparia, must be examined here because it constitutes complementary evidence in connection with the charges formulated against him.

On March 1st, to be precise, Orellana relinquished[121] into the hands of the whole company the lieutenancy with which Pizarro had invested him; and, immediately after, his former subordinates proceeded to beg him and summon him to continue to be their chief in the name of His Majesty, threatening to make him responsible for all the losses, disturbances, deaths among the men, and "other outrages of the sort that are accustomed to take place in such a case as a result of the situation created when they [i.e. soldiers] have no captain" [*infra*, p. 259] if he did not accept, while promising him, on the other hand, that they would take the oath and obey him in that capacity.

Orellana having accepted the commission, thereby taking a step "essential to [the proper functioning of] the service of God . . . and of His Majesty, and in order to serve him" [*infra*, p. 262], the signers, to the number of forty-seven, or practically the whole body of men encamped there, with the two friars serving as witnesses of the act and the scrivener as administrant of the oath, "placed their hands on a mass-book and formally swore by God . . . , by the sign of the Cross, [and] by the four sacred Gospels, to have as their captain the said Francisco de Orellana, and to obey [him] as such in all that they should be commanded in the name of His Majesty [to do]" [*infra*, p. 262]; and Orellana in his turn, placing his hand on the missal, took the oath to be just with them and do for them all that befitted the service of God.

---

121 López de Gómara is the only author who has spoken of this relinquishment: ". . . he resigned the lieutenancy which he held from Pizarro," etc. [*Biblioteca de autores españoles*, Vol. 22, p. 210]; and Jiménez de la Espada, quoting the foregoing passage, adds: "There was no such resignation, although, when once the man had started to sham, there would have been nothing strange about this new piece of trickery" [*Ilustración*, etc., August 30, 1894, p. 127]. Call the incident what you will, it is impossible to deny the fact. The mere circumstance that the text of the relinquishment does not exist is no proof that the thing did not happen; for it was precisely because Orellana had relinquished his command that his subordinates signed that petition in which they re-elected him their chief, and the facts can be read very plainly in that document: ". . . and just recently we have seen Your Worship *resign* the said commission which Your Worship held from the Governor . . . , and . . . being *without a captain* in these forest regions and lands of infidels, . . . we *appoint you now to be our captain again*," etc. [*infra*, p. 259; the italics are Medina's]. In my opinion, nothing more conclusive could be asked for.

Such are the indisputable facts, as they are recorded in legal documents. Well, then, was Orellana proceeding in all this matter in good faith, or had he, from the time of his arrival at the village of Aparia, been staging a miserable farce? I for my part declare, without any circumlocution or beating around the bush, without any impassioned feeling or preconceived notion, that Orellana, in order to justify his conduct in the midst of those truly dramatic circumstances which fate alone had wished on him, did not need any such documents; that his part in the drawing up of these documents, moreover, stands out very clearly; but that for all this we must nevertheless not brand him a deceiver and a hypocrite, much less a traitor. What Orellana in all his actions was looking out for was not an alteration of the truth; on the contrary, for the very reason that what had happened to him was so extraordinary, and because his conduct might seem anomalous, he saw the necessity of providing himself right there with documentary proofs for the time which would come when he would have to give account of his acts before someone—before the Council of the Indies in Spain or before the Pizarros in Peru. We must furthermore keep in mind the routine formalities of those days in America, when everything was reduced to a file of papers, when the most insignificant vessel did not go to sea without having a scrivener on board, when the smallest event of everyday life was recorded in a notary's office. To whom would it occur today to have a judicial inquiry covering his past services put through the court? And yet, what was more common than this among the Spaniards in America in the sixteenth and even a part of the seventeenth century? The huge mass of papers which, in consequence of this method of procedure, has come down to us from those times is precisely what enables us now to see what their life was like, even in its most insignificant details; and it is these papers that constitute today the wealth of the Spanish archives.

Such are the facts regarding the documents. Let us now examine the more serious aspects of the matter, namely, the validity of the claims made by Orellana and particularly the charge, which has been repeated with such unusual persistency, that he was a traitor.

Naturally, the first of his accusers was likely to be, as in fact he was, Gonzalo Pizarro. An impassionable man, violent, and at that time profoundly irritated over not having found his former lieutenant at the spot where he expected to, he denounced him to the King in terms with which we are already familiar; "and he said," adds Oviedo, "that Francisco de Orellana had shown the greatest cruelty that any faithless man could indulge in, in abandoning Gonzalo Pizarro [i.e. him] and the others in those wildernesses among so many rivers and without food."[122]  He did not utter, therefore, a single word of excuse in his favor, nor did he show that he entertained the slightest suspicion that, if he had been abandoned, it might have been either because Orellana and his men had encountered insurmountable obstacles or had been shipwrecked or, in short, had perished; for any of these things could easily have happened to them, and yet Pizarro was unwilling to consider them at all.[123]  His own expedition, moreover, had been a disaster[124] of a sort such that none other like it in America could be recalled: it was necessary to put the blame upon someone for what had happened, and that someone was Orellana.  This explains why Orellana, who could do nothing else but reject energetically such an accusation coming from his former chief, said to the Council of the Indies: " . . . above all, attention should be called to the little need that there is for his bringing these charges against me by way of attempting to clear himself . . .  "[125]

And in the same tone as that employed by Pizarro the historians who have written on the subject, using unmistakable terms, accuse the discoverer of the Amazon of disloyalty, venturing at best some timid plea in his favor but without even daring to voice it as their own.  Thus López de Gómara says: "Orellana went along with Gonzalo Pizarro on the conquest, called the conquest of La Canela . . . ; he went in search of food supplies to an island of this same river with a brigantine and a few canoes, taking along fifty Spaniards, and when he saw that he was far away from his captain he went off down the river, with the clothing and bedding, the gold and the emeralds which they had intrusted to him; although he [afterwards] stated here that, being held back by

---

[122] Vol. 4, p. 393.

[123] It would seem logical for him to attribute Orellana's failure to come back to any one of these possible calamities; and that is why one of Pizarro's soldiers informs us that when they did not see Orellana and his companions return "they had taken it for granted that they had died . . . " (declaration of Diego Gómez in connection with the judicial inquiry on the subject of Ginés Hernández's past services [see *infra*, p. 289]).  Simply to accuse Orellana when he had no news about him is an indication of only one thing, namely, a great prejudice against him on the part of Pizarro; and there was nothing which could justify this attitude in an unimpassioned mind.

[124] The truth of the matter is well stated by Cieza de León: "This exploration and conquest by Gonzalo Pizarro . . . was the most laborious expedition that has been undertaken in these Indies, in which the Spaniards endured great hardships, famine, and miseries . . . " (*Guerra de Chupas*, ed. Madrid, 1881, p. 63).  [The translation given is Markham's in the Hakluyt Society publications, Second Series, No. 42, London, 1918, p. 56.—EDITOR.]

[125] Orellana's presentation of the case before the Council of the Indies, June 7, 1543; see p. 252 of the present volume.

the great current and descent of the water, he had not been able to turn back upstream."*

Agustín de Zárate, after telling us about the supposed abandonment of Friar Carvajal, omitting, however, the significant episode of Sánchez de Vargas, continues: "And so he went off . . . , practically a mutineer and a rebel; because many of those who had gone along with him implored him not to transgress the orders of his general."† And, a little further on, this same author, copying López de Gómara almost word for word, states‡ that Orellana "carried away in the brigantine much gold and silver and [many] emeralds, whereby he had money to spend during all the time that he went about soliciting for and equipping himself for this [expedition of] conquest" (i.e. the conquest of New Andalusia, undertaken by the new expedition organized later in Spain).§

The Inca Garcilaso, without being so explicit and final, nevertheless does condemn Orellana; but, as if to condone Orellana's conduct to a certain extent, he goes into greater detail in relating the circumstances under which the desertion took place, giving them just as the accused man himself had recounted them. He states, therefore, that Pizarro's companions stored away in the brigantine more than one hundred thousand pesos and many emeralds; that Orellana left Sánchez de Vargas helpless and abandoned and maltreated Friar Carvajal; that he did not find the food supplies that he was looking for; that he believed the distance which separated him from the encampment to be more than one hundred leagues; " . . . and being of the opinion that, if he tried to return with the news to Gonzalo Pizarro, he would not navigate

---

*[*Biblioteca de autores españoles*, Vol. 22, Madrid, 1852, p. 210.]

†[*Biblioteca de autores españoles*, Vol. 26, Madrid, 1853, p. 494. It is not, as Medina says, *after* Zárate tells us about the supposed abandonment of Friar Carvajal that the historian in question speaks of Orellana as a mutineer and rebel, but *before* these latter remarks, for immediately after the quotation above Zárate continues: "in particular Friar Gaspar de Carvajal, . . . whom, because he insisted more than the others that he [i.e. Orellana] should wait, he treated very badly both by deed and by word of mouth."—EDITOR.]

‡[*Ibid.*, p. 495.]

§[Two paragraphs in Medina have here been fused into one and some changes have been made in order to retain the actual wording of the sources drawn upon. The second of the two quotations, and also the last part of the first one, beginning: "in particular," etc. (but in a modified form existing, apparently, only in Medina's own notes), are attributed by Medina to Francisco de Jerez, by the same error to which attention has been called above (p. 65, asterisk footnote). Let it suffice to state here that Francisco de Jerez could hardly have copied López de Gómara, as Medina would have us believe, for the reason that the former's *Verdadera relación*, etc., was first published, in all probability, in 1534 (second edition in 1547), while the latter's *Historia general de las Indias* was not printed until 1552. Agustín de Zárate, on the other hand, whose *Historia del descubrimiento . . . del Perú* was first published in 1554 (according to *Biblioteca de autores españoles*, Vol. 22, p. 8, or in 1555, according to Palau y Dulcet, *Manuel del librero hispano-americano*, 7 vols., Barcelona, 1923–27), may well have copied López de Gómara —EDITOR.]

in one year, owing to the violent current of the river, the distance they had navigated in three days; and that if he were to await him there, there was nothing to be gained for the ones nor the others. And not knowing how long it would be before Gonzalo Pizarro would arrive there, he decided to change his plan, without talking the matter over with anyone, and he hoisted sail and went on his way forward. . . . "

And right after that he condemns Orellana in these terms: " . . . he relinquished the authority which he held from Gonzalo Pizarro in order not to do anything as his subordinate, and he caused himself to be chosen a captain responsible directly to His Majesty, without dependence upon anyone else—a deed (which might better be styled an act of treason) of the sort that others, great titled gentlemen, have perpetrated in the campaigns of conquest in the New World . . . "*

Pizarro y Orellana condemns him in even stronger terms: " . . . and in consequence of his not having found the food supplies that he had expected to find . . . he made up his mind to commit one of the greatest iniquities of this kind that ever happened in that land, failing to keep faith with his relative, captain, and friend."[126]

Friar Manuel Rodríguez, the historian of the Amazon, even though he follows Garcilaso, goes still further and says on his own account:

"Having found the junction of the rivers, and [having discovered] that at that spot there were no food supplies and no inhabitants whatsoever, and being of the opinion that if he returned to Gonzalo Pizarro with the news he would not navigate in one year, because of the strong current of the river, the distance he had navigated in three days; and that to wait for him there was a course which would not profit the ones or the others, he decided, without talking it over with anybody, to unfurl his sails and continue on his journey, renouncing [his allegiance to] Gonzalo Pizarro, and coming on to Spain to petition for the governorship of that province for himself. He concealed this latter part of his plan, but proclaimed the first part, [namely] to continue on navigating. Almost all the men opposed him in this, and many suspected his evil intention and told him not to transgress the orders of his captain-general nor

*[*Comentarios reales de los Incas* (see *supra*, p. 30, footnote 47), Second Part, Book III, Ch. 4. Cf. also Markham's translation, Hakluyt Society publications, First Series, No. 24, London, 1859, pp. 12 and 13.—EDITOR.]

[126] *Varones ilustres del Nuevo Mundo*, Madrid, 1639, p. 352.

abandon him in such a time of need, by taking away from him
the support represented by that brigantine.  The one who pressed
him most was a monk named Friar Gaspar de Caravajal [*sic*], together with a young cavalier, Hernán Sánchez de Vargas, a native
of Badajoz, who along with others who joined in would have come
to an open fight with Orellana, if the others had not calmed them
down for the time being with kindly words; and, after he had won
them over with bribes and with great promises, he maltreated both
by word of mouth and by deed the good friar and Hernán Sánchez
de Vargas; and, with the idea of punishing this latter with the
cruelest form of death, he did not stab him to death but left him
alone in that wilderness, cut off on the one side by two very wide
rivers, without there being any possibility of his crossing over
them, and on the other side by those wild forest regions, and left
him there without anything to eat.

"Having committed this act of cruelty, Francisco de Orellana
continued on his way, and the next day, revealing his intention,
he relinquished the authority that he held from Gonzalo Pizarro,
together with his commission, so as not to do anything as his
subordinate, and he caused himself to be elected by his soldiers
a Captain directly responsible to His Majesty, a deed or an act of
revolt [of the sort] that others perpetrated in those campaigns
of conquest, as told by the historians who have written about
these.  In this way he continued on in his navigating. . . . "*

It would be a waste of time for me to stop to point out how
many exaggerations and how many stupid falsehoods are contained
in some of the condemnations which I have just been transcribing,
because it is quite probable that the reader has already perceived
them, if luck has favored me to the extent of allowing him to put
the proper interpretation upon the documents and grasp the facts
which I have set before him in the foregoing pages; for up to this
point my aim has been simply to acquaint him, as far as my knowledge goes, with all that has been said against Orellana, omitting
the opinions of a few modern historians who, in treating this subject,
have limited themselves to copying the older ones, without adding
anything of their own to the controversy.  Nevertheless, among
both groups there have not been wanting here and there writers
who accept Orellana's excuses, albeit their words either have not
yet found an echo or have been severely criticized.

*[*El Marañón y Amazonas*, Madrid, 1684, p. 9; on this work see Medina's comment in footnote
48, *supra*.—EDITOR.]

In the olden times, as a matter of fact, we have Antonio de Herrera already lopping off from the charge the supposed theft of money and adding that Orellana and his men "wanted to go back to where they had started from, but they considered that to be something impossible, on account of its being a distance of three hundred leagues: and, justifying this [i.e. the step which he was about to take] with a few explanations, Orellana made up his mind to go forward, and he came upon that great River Marañón, or Fresh Water Sea as some call it . . . "*

And among the moderns, the English historian William Robertson says that Orellana's crime "is, in some measure, balanced by the glory of having ventured down the river under the conditions in which he did";[127] a very poor argument indeed, being, as it is, beside the question and one which the accused man, I am sure, would have rejected as contrary to moral law.

The truth of the matter is, after all, as the reader has probably observed from all that I have set down so far, that not one of these authors frankly voices an opinion of his own or pronounces a judgment having any foundation in fact. It is incumbent upon me, therefore, to examine now the opinions of those who occupy the middle ground and who are naturally the most to be feared when the memory of Orellana is involved. Let the first be Gonzalo Fernández de Oviedo, whose words must be admitted to have great weight when we realize that he talked personally with Orellana and his companions right after the events had taken place. Now this is what he says: " . . . and this man could not come back, because a certain river down which he had gone was so cold (*sic*) that within two days they found themselves so far separated from Gonzalo Pizarro's army that it seemed best to this Captain and his companions to proceed onward with the current in order to go in search of the Northern Sea with the idea in mind of [at least] getting out of there with their lives  That is what he gave me to understand, but *others say that he could have turned back, had*

---

*[*Historia general*, etc. (see footnote 2, *supra*), Decade VI, Book VIII, Ch. 7. Medina takes liberties here with Herrera's text to the extent of changing the verbs "wanted" and "considered" from plural to singular in order to make them apply to Orellana alone, instead of to the whole party as Herrera does. For this reason the words: "and his men" have been added in the present translation of Medina's statement introducing the quotation from Herrera.—EDITOR.]

[127] *The History of America*, London, 1777, Vol. 2, p. 214. [In the words: "down the river," etc., Medina has condensed the following: "upon a navigation of near two thousand leagues, through unknown nations, in a vessel hastily constructed, with green timber, and by very unskilful hands without provisions, without a compass, or a pilot." Medina could have found more to censure as "contrary to moral law" in Robertson's next sentence, which is as follows: "But his courage and alacrity supplied every defect."—EDITOR.]

*he so wished, to where Gonzalo Pizarro had stopped, and this I be-lieve. . . . "*

Such was the basis for the opinion of Oviedo: that certain persons said that Orellana, if he had so wished, could have turned back upstream; but that is all, and there is no backing up of this opinion with facts, calculations, or other detail.†

An historian to whose account great importance is attached is Toribio de Ortiguera, who wrote some forty odd years after these events, but who got his information from some of the men who had accompanied Orellana; among them he mentions Juan de Illanes and Pedro Domínguez Miradero. "And as they talked the matter over," says this author, "all or the greater part of them objected very strongly to [any suggestion of their] being able to go back up the river; others remarked that, considering the large number of persons who had remained behind with Gonzalo Pizarro and the small amount of food that they still had on hand, there could be no possibility of their [still] being where they had left them, because they could not find nourishment for themselves there, or [read: and (?)] they were probably all dead from lack of food supplies. But all [these remarks] were [merely] arguments which they were putting forth in [support of] their case, for they could with ease have gone back up the river with the brigantine, according to information which I obtained from some of those who took part in the affair, who were persons of reputation and good faith . . . And at the conclusion of all these agreements among themselves, they decided to go off down the river to look for the sea, for that was what best fitted in with the desires of the greater part of them."[128]

By a rare piece of luck, we are able to draw directly on the affirmations made in court by the only persons cited by Ortiguera that are known to have really taken part in the expedition;[129] and their statements, strange to say, happen to contradict absolutely and in the most conclusive manner all that we have just heard Ortiguera say.

One of the persons whose testimony was invoked by Ortiguera was Pedro Domínguez Miradero. Now the fact of the matter is that in one of the statements which Domínguez Miradero makes in connection with the judicial inquiry covering his past services

---

*[Oviedo, Vol. 4, p. 384. The italics are Medina's.—EDITOR.]

†[However, the passage just quoted from Oviedo ends with the words "for reasons that will be set forth farther on." See the Appendix, p. 392, *infra*, and the later pages.—EDITOR.]

[128] *Jornada del Río Marañón*, etc. [see *supra*, p. 29]: see p. 316 of the present volume.

[129] See footnote 45 to this Introduction.

put through the court at his request in the city of Quito in September of 1564, that is to say at the very same time that, according to our historian,* he affirmed that Orellana could have returned upstream, he categorically declares just the opposite: " . . . and on the said expedition of exploration, on the way down the Marañón River . . . he [Gonzalo Pizarro] sent me in company with Captain Francisco de Orellana . . . to explore the country down the river, *and, we not being able to go back by the same river* owing to the force of the currents and the [heavy] rains and the [bad] weather conditions and the skirmishes with the Indians, I traveled on," etc.

Such is his statement in the memorandum which precedes the list of questions; and in the sixth question itself he repeats this statement: "on the way down the Marañón River . . . , *not being able to go back upstream* on account of the force of the currents and the heavy rains and the [bad] weather conditions and the skirmishes with the Indians, we traveled on," etc.[130]

And all this was not merely Domínguez Miradero's own view, well grounded as it apparently was; but it was also the opinion of Alonso de Cabrera, another of those who had accompanied Orellana, for in replying to the aforesaid question he said that everything contained therein was true; and it was likewise the view of other soldiers, namely some who had remained behind with Pizarro and had talked with the companions of Orellana after they had got back to Quito.

But will an entirely different sort of statement be found, perchance, in the record of the judicial inquiry covering the past services of Juan de Illanes, whose testimony is likewise invoked by Ortiguera? Illanes had this official inquiry put through the court four years after Domínguez Miradero, also in Quito, the place from which the entire expedition had started out and to which many of the soldiers who had accompanied both Pizarro and Orellana had returned after it was over, and where, consequently, it was not possible to risk any hoax whatsoever. For this judicial inquiry Juan de Illanes availed himself of the testimony, among

---

*[But Medina is voicing a gratuitous supposition when he states that Ortiguera interviewed Pedro Domínguez Miradero at about the same time that the latter was having the judicial inquiry on the subject of his past services put through the court. Ortiguera wrote his account in Quito in 1581 (see editor's addition to footnote 44, *supra*, p. 29), at which time Domínguez Miradero was still living in that city, now a man past seventy (see *infra*, p. 113), and Ortiguera's interview with him could very well have been of recent date. And between 1564 and 1581 circumstances may have arisen to cause Domínguez Miradero to give a different slant to his testimony at this later date.—EDITOR.]

[130] For these two statements see pp. 292 and 295 of the present volume. [The italics are Medina's.]

others, of his former comrades Alonso de Cabrera and Domínguez Miradero, who without any discrepancy affirmed under oath that they *had not been able to return* upstream.[131]

Need anything more be said? Ortiguera could have quoted also, among the persons from whom he obtained information in Quito regarding matters connected with Orellana's voyage, Alonso de Cabrera, who was living there at that time; and, although Ortiguera does not mention him by name in this connection, I cannot refrain from emphasizing the fact that, as we have just seen, his opinion coincided in every particular with that of his comrades.[132]

Among documents of this sort I can also present the declarations of other reliable witnesses who had either stayed behind with Gonzalo Pizarro or followed Orellana on his daring voyage of discovery. Here we have the judicial inquiry covering Ginés Fernández's* service record, wherein we find: " . . . as a means of protecting themselves against the fury of the river, which was so great that they could not turn back upstream, rather they continued on down the said river . . . "[133] And lastly, there is

---

[131] See the judicial inquiry covering Illanes' record of services, p. 298 ff. of the present volume.

[132] Cabrera also had a judicial inquiry on the subject of his past services put through, and extracts from this I am likewise publishing in the present volume. In it one does not find this same question put in a categorical way, for Cabrera has occasion to say only that "continuing the said journey he went with Captain Francisco de Orellana down the Marañón . . . " [*infra*, p. 305], although in his sworn declaration in connection with the judicial inquiry covering Domínguez Miradero's service record we find him assenting to everything that the latter affirms. [Cf. p. 297.]

In this very vagueness one senses—and this is quite natural—the attitude of mind of the witnesses presented by Cabrera: Bonifaz de Herrera, for example, even seems to wish to give the impression that some of Orellana's soldiers did return with relief to Pizarro's camp, where this Bonifaz de Herrera was at the time, or that it was because they could not *all* return that they did not come back with food supplies for Orellana and his men, for either of these two interpretations is possible if I have not misunderstood what he means by the following: " . . . the said Alonso de Cabrera had gone off in a brigantine with Captain Francisco de Orellana, who had set out with fifty men to look for food to succor the expeditionary force, following [the return of] which this witness [i.e. he] had in the course of time learned from the others who had gone with the said Captain Orellana that they had all been unable to come back with the said relief on account of the many uninhabited regions and the fighting Indians that they had come upon . . . " [*infra*, p. 310]. But what is more probable is that in this paragraph there are one or more errors in redaction attributable to the scrivener who wrote it down. [The present editor does not believe that it is possible to accept for the passage quoted here the first of the alternative interpretations proposed by Medina. To get this meaning Medina apparently takes the words: "the others who," etc., to refer to those who had gone on with Orellana (as against those few who, if this is true, did come back), whereas they seem to mean merely those other members of *Pizarro's expedition* who went off with Orellana. Medina does not seem to take into consideration either, the fact that "no pudieron todos volver" (literally, "they could not all come back") may be interpreted as: "they all failed to come back." The crux of the difficulty with the passage seems to lie in the rather loose way in which "donde" is used, which in the sixteenth century could mean "whence" as well as "where."—EDITOR.]

*[Or Ginés Hernández. the alternative form of the name used in Document V, pp. 282–291 *infra*, and elsewhere.—EDITOR.]

[133] This judicial inquiry of Fernández's was put through the court in Zamora de los Alcaides on February 14, 1564, and extracts from it will be found on pp. 282 ff. of the present volume. [For the passage quoted above, see p. 285.]

the judicial inquiry on the subject of Cristóbal de Segovia's past services, put through the court on the Island of Margarita shortly after the conclusion of the voyage; and, in testifying in connection with it, all the witnesses who made such declarations as were called for unanimously assert that "as the currents were strong we went on down at an enormous risk and [at the cost of much] hardship for a distance of more than two hundred leagues, enduring great hunger . . . " and that "desirous though we were of returning to the [encamped] expeditionary force there where the said Governor had remained behind, it [nevertheless] being, as it was, impossible to go back because of the fact that the currents were so strong, . . . the said Captain Francisco de Orellana ordered a brigantine to be built," etc. [*infra*, p. 269]. And in replying to the questions formulated by Segovia not only does Orellana himself, who was cross-examined on this point, affirm that this was true, but so also do Cristóbal de Aguilar, Juan de Elena, Hernán González, Benito de Aguilar, the Ginés Fernández already mentioned, the Comendador Cristóbal Enríquez, and Blas de Medina, all men from among the most distinguished that had taken part in the expedition and all now declaring under oath that what was stated in the questions was exactly what had taken place.

When we consider such pieces of testimony as these, what is left of the opinions of Oviedo and Ortiguera? Can we, without entering into a spirit of partiality, prefer their judgment to the explicit and categorical declarations of the very participants in the events?

Perhaps someone will say that it was to the personal interest of these men to hide the truth; but from whom, and with what object in view? Besides, how does it come about that all as one man affirmed the same thing? At the time when they made their declarations, Pizarro and Orellana were already dead; in Peru there was no longer left, in a position of power, one single partisan of Pizarro to cause them to misrepresent the facts; and, as for the home government back in Spain, it could hardly have furnished the expeditioners any occasion for offering apologies for a line of conduct which no one back there had condemned.

There remains for us to examine, in conclusion, the judgment which Orellana's procedure has brought down upon him at the hands of his most recent biographer—one whose opinions should have all the more weight for the reason that, along with his vast knowledge of history, he possesses the advantage of having also traveled about a part of the country which was the scene of action of Pizarro's expedition and of having followed the course of the rivers down which Orellana proceeded on his voyage of discovery. What this judgment is can be guessed at once from a mere knowledge of the fact that the title which he has given to his study is: "The Treason of a One-eyed Man."[134]

But let us listen to the summing up of the conclusions at which Jiménez de la Espada arrives in his scholarly study.

"Is it not a strange and incomprehensible thing, and one that arouses suspicion in our hearts," he says, "that those cavaliers, hidalgos, and churchmen, just as they were about to fulfill the mission intrusted to them, and at the best and most favorable moment for bringing it to a conclusion, should conceive the idea of protesting that they could not carry it out? And was it not a manifest piece of impudence and unequaled shamelessness for them to dare to add that to take the opposite stand was a thing not befitting the service of God and the King, saying that by means of their protest they were clearing themselves of the charge of being traitors, of being disobedient to their superiors in the King's service in not following their leader on the return voyage up the river? And is it not a scandalous thing that these protesting men, with the idea of making the return to Pizarro's camp appear to be humanly impossible, should have raised to more than two hundred leagues their estimate of the distance from the camp to the village where they had put into port after nine days of navigation and had found the relief in the form of food supplies which Pizarro and his helpless companions were waiting for? The entire course of the Coca, with its multiple curves and deflections, does not equal eighty leagues. I grant that Orellana and his men may have separated from Pizarro at a spot close to the halfway point on this river. If we counted the two hundred leagues on this basis, the village of Aparia would unequivocally have to fall far beyond the confluence of the Napo (or Santa Ana) and the Amazon. That would be absurd. From Pizarro's camp to the port of Aparia the distance must have been approximately sixty leagues; and this distance, moreover, fits in well with the length and number

[134] Just as in the case of Juan Pizarro, who was a natural enemy of Orellana's and who applies the same epithet to him but goes no further in qualifying him. [Medina undoubtedly means Pedro (not Juan) Pizarro, who, in his *Relación del descubrimiento . . . del Perú* (see dagger footnote on Pedro Pizarro, p. 46 above), in the few lines (*ed. cit.*, pp. 350–351) which he devotes to Gonzalo Pizarro's expedition, introduces the leader of the party which went down the Amazon as "Orellana the One-eyed." The point which Medina is making is that in spite of the fact that Pedro Pizarro was an enemy of Orellana's and manifested a certain attitude toward him by using the epithet "one-eyed," it did not occur to this writer to call him a traitor.—EDITOR.]

of the daily runs in the itinerary as described by the Dominican vicar and chronicler, who, apparently, forgot what he had signed a year before.* The fears of certain death were also a willful exaggeration, and in truth not very becoming to soldiers of conquest. I do not say that it would have been an easy thing or a matter of a short period of time to pilot a brigantine loaded with victuals sixty leagues back up the river; but to send a few canoes as advice-boats, a part of them to go light, a part laden with a small quantity of victuals, to meet Pizarro, or to go as far as his camp in case he had not moved on, in order to bring him some quick relief thereby, would have been mere play, a pleasant boat ride for Indians of the Omagua race, makers and owners of the sleek big canoes which furrowed those rivers and so expert in handling them that they were called the pirates of the Amazon. Orellana and his comrades must have known all that, just as he must have known that, so far as plowing through a current is concerned, its great swiftness is not an insurmountable obstacle in the wide rivers carrying much water, such as we now know that the Coca was from well above the spot at which he separated from Pizarro. It is all a question of time and a matter of skill and experience on the part of the Indian *bogas* or paddlers who, sticking close to the banks and taking advantage of the backwaters and eddies, now paddling, now poling (they have a special term for this, namely, *launar*), do three leagues daily. Consequently, the trip would have taken, at the most, twenty days; and that, under those circumstances, had nothing long or dangerous about it . . . ."†

Then he applies the phrase "gross fabric of falsehoods and barefaced protests (which a loyal and punctilious leader could so easily have torn down)" [*loc. cit.*, p. 126] to the summons which Orellana's subordinates handed to him; he characterizes as "a second scene of the ignoble and ridiculous farce staged by Orellana"

---

*[It seems as if Jiménez de la Espada must be confused here. Friar Carvajal states, in the version of his story inserted by Oviedo in his *Historia* (Vol. 4, p. 543)—the other version accessible to Jiménez de la Espada (the Muñoz copy) has a lacuna here—that Orellana's party moved on at the rate of "twenty-five leagues or more" per day; and he also states (p. 544) that, when they arrived at the village where they made their long stop, they had been on their way for nine days. (In reality, they had traveled eight days and a fraction, and, according to the version printed by Medina—see *infra*, p. 173—, the distance still to be covered on the morning of the ninth day was only two leagues.) The distance roughly calculated on this basis would be, not sixty leagues, as Jiménez de la Espada says, but two hundred leagues, as Friar Carvajal himself says (Oviedo version, p. 545). It is evident, therefore, that "the Dominican vicar and chronicler" did *not* forget "what he had signed a year before," if by these words Jiménez de la Espada is referring to the petition addressed to Orellana by his men in Aparia on January 4, 1542 (Document II [4], p. 254, *infra*)—a petition which Friar Carvajal joined in signing and in which the men claimed that they were then two hundred leagues from Gonzalo Pizarro's camp.—EDITOR.]

†[*Ilustración Española y Americana*, August 30, 1894, p. 126.]

[*loc. cit.*, p. 126] his action in not waiting for Gonzalo Pizarro the two months that he had declared necessary in his reply to the summons; and, after denying that Orellana relinquished the post of lieutenant under orders from Gonzalo Pizarro, he qualifies his new acceptance of the post, and the events which led up to it, as "perfidious machinations" [*loc. cit.*, p. 127], stating further that in this way "he brought his farce to a conclusion and gave it a suitable dénouement by parodying the action of Hernán Cortés in San Juan de Ulúa." "In conclusion, and by way of summing up," he tells us, "Francisco de Orellana could have returned from Aparia (perhaps with the brigantine) to join his chief, or at least could have sent him some message. The priest, Friar Gaspar de Carvajal, says that he attempted this alternative and even smoothed out many of the difficulties in connection with the service to be thus rendered by offering two negroes as oarsmen and one thousand gold castellanos or pesos to each one of the messengers, but that nobody consented to go. But as this circumstance is not recorded in the affidavits prepared by Orellana in his exculpation, I am inclined to doubt it. However that may be, what I do not doubt, but on the contrary believe in all sincerity, is what Toribio de Ortiguera has to say about the matter (except as to the date) . . . " [*loc. cit.*, p. 126], and with this I have already acquainted my readers.

The reader who has followed me in this historical investigation, carried out to the best of my ability, will now be in a position, I imagine, in view of all that I have set forth, to form an opinion of his own regarding the accuracy of the remarks which I have just finished copying. But I do not wish a final decision to be pronounced until certain other considerations bearing on the case shall have been presented also, together with a full résumé of my own judgment of the matter.

Let us place ourselves for one moment in the situation of the accused man. Orellana sets out from Pizarro's camp, leaving behind him all that he possesses in the world; in a spirit of courtesy toward his comrades he offers to go in person to reconnoiter the place where the Indian guides had guaranteed that food would be found; before the end of the third day of his advance and already fearing that he may not be able to go back, he calls together all his companions in order to put before them the question of whether it would not be advisable to turn back from this point, lest they find themselves in the position of being unable to do so farther on; all of one accord decide to advance a little farther in the hope of not failing to achieve the object of the journey; and, finally, immediately upon their arrival at the village, the leader's first care is to see about getting together the required food supplies to send to the relief of Gonzalo Pizarro. All these are facts which do not admit of doubt and which show that Orellana acted in a manner befitting a man of foresight, diligence, vigor, and loyalty.

When the time comes for actually starting back, he finds that the distance traveled over, in the estimation of the seamen whom he has taken along with him, is much greater than they had imagined when they started; and, in the meantime, how limited have become the means at his disposal for undertaking the risk!

As for attempting to go up the river with the brigantine, that was not to be thought of. There remained the canoes. But even supposing that he could have loaded them with food (it must not be forgotten that very soon their own supply gave out), whom could he send with them? To abandon the boat at that place seemed to be madness when it had cost so much effort to build it; and, in view of the fact that it was the only means on which they could count for getting about in those regions, it was necessary to preserve it at all cost; and for this reason they were obliged to man it with a sufficient force to defend it from the Indians, who, if they had seen that it was possible to take possession of it, would not have failed to do so at once, so earnestly did they covet it.

Supposing the small force were thus divided and supposing a certain number, or as many as one half, of Orellana's companions had embarked in the canoes, with Indians as paddlers, would a sufficient number of these paddlers have been found? And if these paddlers were found, was it not evident that Orellana's men thus distributed among the canoes were exposed to the danger of being massacred in the first moment of inattentiveness? Could not their paddlers, when the party was half way up the river on its journey, in the heart of this uninhabited country, slip away into the forest and leave them again to the mercy of the currents? Was it, after all, an easy task to go upstream, with the canoes loaded, on a river whose waters were swollen owing to the season of freshets?

The physical and moral state to which, besides, Orellana's companions found themselves reduced could not be more lamentable. Weakened by the hardships of a painful campaign of ten months, they found themselves with their strength exhausted, with their spirits profoundly depressed, and some of them so sick that there in Aparia within the space of a few days seven died, that is, more than twelve per cent of their total number.

There remained another difficulty still, an even greater one, if that is possible. Inasmuch as Pizarro and his entire force had come to be without provisions, and inasmuch as farther downstream from this camp, as Orellana and his men had ascertained, there were none to be had, was it not extremely probable that Pizarro and his men had turned back in search of something which he did not actually find downstream, but which was to be had farther back? And in this case, where would Orellana's emissaries find them? Would not the food transported at the cost of so much effort turn out, in the end, to be of utterly no use?

Besides, what reason was there, to quote Orellana's own remarks, "why I should revolt, inasmuch as I was the principal man in the expeditionary force [next to Pizarro himself], and was not taking a chance on [securing] some personal gain by going, surrounded by so many dangers, down a river, starving, through a country which I knew nothing about . . . " [infra, p. 252]? If he had been sure of the way which lay before him; if at the end of his expedition he could have counted on arriving in safety at some settlement where there were Spaniards; if his equipment for launching out on the adventure had been proportionate to its magnitude, we might say that he was deserting his chief. But the facts were just the opposite.

To view the case from another angle, he was leaving behind him, and was destined to lose beyond recall, the favor of the Pizarro family, at that time all-powerful in Peru; the Indians that he held and which constituted his wealth; the administrative charge in which he held sway; in a word, his position and his worldly goods. This is exactly what Friar Carvajal had already in his time called attention to when he wrote that Orellana, in following the river's current to wherever it might lead, was abandoning his government position at Guayaquil "where he owned many Indians, and good ones, by right of grant, and other property and livestock and everything necessary for becoming a man of high rank and power."*

The only personal interest that Orellana could have in deserting, if we come right down to it, was a possible desire to get back to Spain quickly, eager as he may have been to turn his services to account at the earliest possible moment in order to obtain the governorship to which he aspired. But to take advantage, with

---

*[Carvajal's *Relación*, in Oviedo, Vol. 4, p. 542.]

this ultimate aim in view, of that combination of circumstances which chance laid before him was madness, and at the same time an act of stupidity of which I cannot believe him capable. The route which he was going to follow might lead him to his death, and not to the Spanish capital; and in any case by that route he would arrive there poor—a most unfavorable situation to be in for soliciting anything, and an absolutely impossible one for assembling means and equipment for any sort of expedition.

It would have been much better for him to go back to Pizarro, to bend his efforts toward deriving some profit from the influence of the latter's family, at that time one of great importance in the entourage of the Emperor, and to present himself in the capital pompous and money-laden, as it befitted an hidalgo aspiring to a governorship. Moreover, to push his claims all he needed was a proxy, "well instructed and well supplied with expense money," to borrow a forensic phrase commonly used in such cases.

Let us also glance at the man's moral make-up. He was gentle, affable, impressionable, inclined to believe whatever was told him and to act accordingly;[135] and it is this which makes me believe that—in spite of all that he, so far as he personally was concerned, proclaimed himself, right up to the last moment, ready to do in obedience to his chief—what won out with him in the end, and possibly as the result of pressure, was the attitude of his subordinates, who were for the most part professed opponents of the idea of returning, preferring, beyond doubt, the risk involved in the journey downstream, with all its dangers, to turning back toward Pizarro's camp, where only a new series of hardships awaited them with no prospect of any personal gain. For this reason, one should admire all the more in Orellana the firmness of his conduct during the voyage, because he perhaps understood that without this firmness all were doomed to perish; and quite different would have been his second expedition, of which I shall speak later, if it had been conducted in the same manner.

But how did it come about that, after proposing to wait two or three months in Aparia for his chief, in accordance with what he

[135] This picture of the character of Orellana is one which I am borrowing from what Friar Pablo de Torres, the King's trusted confidant who accompanied Orellana on the expedition to New Andalusia, wrote from Seville under date of November 20, 1544: "The Adelantado" (Orellana) "is so kind-hearted that every time that a person tells him something he believes it and acts on it, and [he fails to see that] so much gentleness at times is of little profit to one" [*infra*, p. 352]. [In this footnote Medina gives the date of this letter as November 30. In the present translation it is changed to conform to what one finds at the end of the letter as published by Medina himself, namely "the twentieth of November."—EDITOR.]

announced in replying to the summons which his subordinates handed to him immediately after their arrival there, he sailed away twenty-six days later? I have already stated my convictions on this point, and I reiterate them now: the document in which this proposal is found was not drawn up in connection with a farce inspired by him, but was on the contrary the instrument which he manipulated in staving off the demands of his subordinates, who threatened him with rising up in rebellion and considering him a bad servant of the King, if he did not come around to their point of view. Orellana was sincere in his proposal and no doubt hoped to be able to carry it out in view of the good will with which the Indians, with the scanty resources which he had found in the village, had begun to serve him. Yet this was only an illusion of the moment, enabling him to get out of the difficulty for the time being. But within a short time he had to admit that his plan was not feasible: when he saw that seven of his soldiers had perished within a few days; when the food supplies, which in the beginning he had thought were plentiful, began to run low in the village; when the Indians, who in the first moments had come joyfully to help them, for two weeks now had not put in an appearance; when the tasks at which he had meanwhile kept his men busy were finished (and this had been a measure of lofty foresight in its purpose, and one productive of excellent results in maintaining discipline among his soldiers); when, in short, he saw what the situation had come to be, he decided to make one last attempt at least to send word to his chief about the position in which he found himself; and when, finally, this attempt failed, then only, and without renouncing his position as the representative of another man, but still proposing to send him a report from the first Spanish settlement to which fate should guide him, then only, I say, did he cause the brigantine and the canoes to sheer off, only then did he plunge into the unknown down the river. The time had come when to wait there any longer was useless in so far as it affected the companions whom he was going to abandon back up the river, and of no avail, nay, even dangerous, for themselves. There was nothing for the leader to do but surrender and accept the only compromise that the force of circumstances imposed upon every one of them, and strike out at the mercy of the currents. What awaited them beyond was the dangers of the unknown, the whirlpools, the difficult narrows, hostile settlements, hunger, maybe death; but there was no way of avoiding all that.

"Treason!" they say. Treason, when a few days after the departure from Aparia Orellana resigns the lieutenancy which he has been holding from Pizarro, and his subordinates of their own free will, in a general assembly and in the name of the King, re-elect him to the position? A measure of great importance, say I, aimed at guaranteeing the successful completion of the dangerous voyage. Let us stop to reflect on where that handful of men was lost among the forests, far, very far, from any effective and constituted authority that could, if the case arose, punish the acts of misbehavior that were to be expected from men of that class, in whom the ties of obedience must have been observed to be thoroughly loosened, as evidenced by certain phrases in the Aparia summons which made it all the more necessary for the commander who was leading them to feel this obedience tightened in order to be able to make them obey him blindly in the midst of the perils in which they were staking their lives every day in the face of the obstacles of nature and the combats with the savages; and, if this was so, what more effective or wiser step could be taken by him who bore the responsibility for them all than to get these men themselves, by an act of their own free will, to bind themselves and swear to preserve that obedience?[136]

It is hard for me to condemn Orellana in view of all this. Was he condemned, perchance, by the Council of the Indies when he went back to Spain? It just happened that Hernando Pizarro was there at that time, facing charges himself, it is true, but nevertheless quite free to appear in court and file an accusation, as in truth he did file accusations against not a few who back in Peru had been enemies of his or of his family; but, during the period of more than two years that Orellana's stay in the Peninsula lasted, Hernando did not say a word about any treason committed against his brother, a treason of which, if he had considered it as such, he would not have failed to take advantage in order to make the Estremenian captain responsible for the failure of his brother's expedition to La Canela. Nor was anything said either by the Council, which better than anyone else must have known what had happened (for two years was ample time in which to find it out), its attorney-general at that time being the Licentiate Villalobos, an active man, zealous in matters pertaining to the royal prerogatives and showing himself to be tireless in prosecuting all the

---

[136] I could cite several cases in which the Spanish chiefs in America in those years, who came far from ever being in Orellana's difficult situation, proceeded in exactly the same manner, without anyone's branding them as traitors for that.

traitors of Peru and even persons who were not traitors. Far from this being the case, the Monarch recalls the successful outcome of the voyage, recognizes the services of Orellana, makes a contract with him whereby he may return to undertake the exploration and conquest of those regions, and grants him finally the title of Adelantado, "in order to add prestige to his person."[137] Is it believable that all this could have been done for a man who was a traitor?

[137] Royal decree of February 13, 1544. [Again in this footnote Medina seems to have erred in the matter of the exact date, giving it as February 17. The change is made here on the assumption that the few words quoted above are Medina's own variation of a phrase which occurs in the *Articles of agreement*, etc., dated Valladolid, February 13, 1544, and published (or rather, re-published) by Medina in the present volume (see *infra*, p. 328 ff.), wherein the expression reads as follows: "by way of adding prestige to your person" (*infra*, p. 331)—EDITOR.]

# VIII

# THE VOYAGE OF DISCOVERY

IF the conduct of Orellana in his relations with Pizarro has brought upon him the grave accusations that I have described, from the time he departed from the village of Aparia his steady endurance of hardships, his qualities as a prudent and watchful chief, his firmness and energy, the courage with which he met trials in that perilous and daring voyage of discovery, entitle him to an indisputable glory, disputed, in fact, by no one up to the present time.

I should have to copy here point by point the *Account* of Friar Carvajal if I were to enter into the details of that famous expedition; but, as that would be too long, I must limit myself to relating here its principal incidents, clarifying, in so far as my ability permits me to do so, all questions relative to the dates and places of occurrence of those incidents.

I have already said that Orellana and his companions left the Indian village on February 2, 1542,[138] and that soon after, some twenty leagues farther on, they reached the mouth of the Curaray River, the abode at that time of an important chief of the Irimaraes, whom Orellana was desirous of visiting, "because he was an Indian and overlord of much intelligence" [*infra*, p. 179] and had come to see him, bringing him a few presents; but he had to abandon his idea because of the violence of the waters at the confluence of the two rivers, for it was so great that the eddies which they formed and the tree trunks which they brought down placed the frail boats in grave danger of foundering.

Not very far from there two of the canoes carrying eleven of the expeditioners went on ahead among some islands and were not able to get back to the main body of the expedition until two days later, after they had already been given up for lost and were all in the state of distress which can readily be imagined.[139] After a day of rest they started out again and on the following morning

---

[138] In the text of the *Relación* in Oviedo [*Historia general y natural de las Indias*, Vol. 4, p. 545] it is stated, however, that their departure took place on the first of this month.

[139] In consequence of this incident Orellana at once ordered, under severe penalties, that those who manned the canoes should not separate from the brigantine a distance greater than a crossbow shot.

came upon some Indian settlements which were glad to receive the Spaniards, giving them turtles and parrots and other provisions of which they were sorely in need. They passed the night in another village near-by, which they found abandoned, and from there early in the morning the expedition on account of the mosquitoes moved on toward a larger village visible just below, where they stayed three days, fêted by its inhabitants.

Finally, on the following day, Sunday, February 11, 1542, the little squadron entered upon the waters of the Marañón,[140] or Amazon.

[140] Friar Carvajal, in the version of his *Account* which I am publishing here, says [*infra*, p. 181] that their entrance upon this great river, which at this point divides into two arms and at first sight seems to be two distinct rivers, took place on Sunday, while in the *Relación* which Oviedo inserts in his *Historia de las Indias* one reads: "On Saint Eulalia's day, there having already gone by eleven days of February" [Oviedo, Vol. 4, p. 547]. The two manners of indicating the day are in agreement because, in fact, the eleventh of February, 1542, was a Sunday. [It was February 12 and not February 11 that was Sunday. Saint Eulalia's day falls on February 12, which corresponds exactly with Friar Carvajal's statement that eleven days of February had already gone by. The two different designations of the day are hence indeed in agreement, but one day later than stated by Medina. In the very next paragraph Medina characterizes February 26 as a Sunday, which is correct and which agrees with February 12 as a Sunday date. See also editorial addition to footnote 94, *supra*.—EDITOR.]

It also appears from both versions of the account that, the expeditioners having left Aparia on the second of that month, in order to arrive at the point which I have indicated it took them only seven days of actual traveling, inasmuch as they rested four; and, moreover, on the day on which they found their companions who had gone forward and got separated from them they had stopped early. I can make allowances for the time that they lost in trying to go up the river on which resided the friendly chief whom I have mentioned, and even grant that the departure from Aparia may have taken place on the first of February and not on the second; the result of my calculation would still be that the number of days in question was not more than eight.

Now then, if we suppose that the starting point was, as Jiménez de la Espada will have it, just a short distance below the junction of the Coca, we shall find ourselves face to face with the absurdity that in seven days or in eight at the most they had gone a distance three times greater than that established for the first journey of nine days. (I do not speak in terms of leagues, because in view of the windings of the river any calculation of this sort would be quite unreliable). I find here, therefore, a new argument in support of my belief that the village of Aparia was situated at the junction of the Aguarico, or in other words almost at the halfway point in the course over which Orellana passed from the time he left Gonzalo Pizarro's camp until he entered the Marañón. This is practically proven by the number of actual traveling days spent in both journeys—nine in the first and seven or eight in the second.

Did Orellana, or those who were with him, suspect perchance that the river which they had just entered upon was the Marañón? In the records of the judicial inquiries covering past services put through the courts at the request of several of the expeditioners at various dates after the voyage was over it is stated simply that "they came upon the Marañón River"; but, as there were some among them who were seamen, and as the mouth of a great river already called by the name of Marañón or Fresh Water Sea was known to exist approximately in that latitude, they must have comprehended from the first moment that this river which appeared from its imposing width to be a sea could be none other than the one which on the maps of the time was labeled the Marañón [Medina here leads one to infer that the expression which he encloses between quotation marks, with "came upon" as its verbal element, occurs frequently in the documents of this sort which he publishes. As a matter of fact, it is found (in the first person plural instead of the third) only once, namely in the first part of the first of these documents (see *infra*, p. 269). Elsewhere throughout these particular documents the expression used in this connection, most frequently some form of the verb "to go" followed by "down the said river" or "down the Marañón River," is too general in meaning to serve as a basis on which to formulate an opinion in reply to Medina's query. Moreover, Carvajal says (Oviedo, Vol. 4, p. 557), long after the expeditioners had entered upon the waters of the Marañón: "although we did not know what river it was."—EDITOR. ]

For two weeks they continued on downstream in sight of various villages which could be seen situated along the shores; on Sunday, February 26, in the morning, a few canoes occupied by Indians came out to meet them, bringing as presents some turtles, birds, and fish sent by Aparia the Great, whose abode was near-by; and here Orellana, guided by the Indians, made port. After a conversation in which the Spanish captain made known to the Indians there gathered together his plan of continuing on down the river, claiming that he and his companions were children of the Sun, the god whom those river people worshipped, they begged him to remain there and said that they would provide him with the things that he might need, beginning by taking all the inhabitants out of the village so that he might go into quarters there.

Considering this to be a favorable opportunity, Orellana called together his companions in order to present to them the advisability of constructing the brigantine there, to which proposal all assented joyfully; for they understood how important it would be for them to be able to navigate from this point on in boats which would enable them to resist the future attacks of hostile Indians and later to defy the pounding of the waves of the sea. He apportioned the work, consequently, among all the men under the immediate supervision of the Sevillian Diego Mexía. At the end of a week the required timber was already cut; they then made the charcoal needed in order that they might resume the manufacture of the nails and other iron pieces, using for this purpose a forge "which an ingenious companion," says Carvajal, "had made, for all that he was no blacksmith";* cotton was used for oakum; resin from the forest trees, which the Indians found for them, served as tar; and so, thanks to the enthusiasm of all, in forty-one days[141] they built the

*[Oviedo, Vol. 4, p. 550.]

[141] In Carvajal's *Account* as published in this volume the Dominican friar says [*infra*, p. 185] that it took thirty-five days, but in this there is an error; and the checking up of the figure as given in the Oviedo version will enable us to establish the fact that they started the work the day following their arrival and also to establish a few dates which are at least worthy of notice in this connection.

Since Orellana had put in at Aparia's capital on Sunday, February 26, and had departed from there on April 24, his stay there had lasted 57 days. "The time it took to build this brigantine," according to the *Relación* published in Oviedo, "and to repair the boat which we already had was forty-one working days, leaving out the Sundays and feast days and Maundy Thursday and Good Friday and Easter, when the companions did not work; . . . " [Oviedo, Vol. 4, p. 551]. These non-working days were, therefore, Sunday, the day of their arrival, February 26; the 5th, 12th, 19th, and 26th of March, and the 2nd, 9th, 16th, and 23rd of April, which were also Sundays; Maundy Thursday and Good Friday, the 13th and 14th of April; the first three days of the week after Easter, the 17th, 18th, and 19th of the same month; and the two feast days of March, Saint Joseph's (the 19th) and the Annunciation (the 25th): the total of non-working days thus being 16, which, when subtracted from the 57 that they remained there, leaves 41 working days. In the year 1542 Ash brigantine, which turned out to be considerably better and much larger than the one which they already had and which also had to be repaired, because it was already rotting.*

During the days spent there Orellana took possession, in the name of the King, of a few other chiefs; had Friar Carvajal preach on the more solemn feast days; and chose as ensign an hidalgo named Alonso de Robles, who by the manner in which he subsequently carried out the duties of his commission was a credit to the good tact of his commander. All confessed their sins to the two friars of the expedition; and, finally, with the preparations all completed and their consciences cleared, Orellana gave orders for departure for the 24th of April.

Again on the following day Aparia in person came to bring provisions to him in a village of his farther below, and good treatment at his hands lasted throughout all the time that they were traversing regions subject to him. "From here on," says Friar Carvajal, "we endured more hardships and more hunger and [passed through] more uninhabited regions than before, because the river led from one wooded section to another wooded section and we found no place to sleep and much less could any fish be caught, so that it was necessary for us to keep to our customary fare, which consisted of herbs and every now and then a bit of roasted corn" [*infra*, p. 189].

Amidst all these hardships they were proceeding, when on May 12 they caught sight of the villages of Machiparo, of which they had already been informed in Aparia. Here the Indians came out to attack them at an inopportune moment, for, their powder being

Wednesday fell on March 1st, Easter on the 16th of April, and Quasimodo Sunday on the 23rd. And on the day following this last mentioned, i.e. on the 24th, Orellana was again on his way!

[Although Medina's reckoning fits in well with an assumed stay of 57 days in Aparia's village, it should be pointed out that according to Gauss's rule for finding the date of Easter and according to other sources (e.g. A. Cappelli, *Cronologia e calendario perpetuo*, 2nd edit., Milan, 1930) Easter in 1542 came on April 9 and not on April 16 and hence Ash Wednesday on February 22 and not on March 1, as indicated in the list of dates in footnote 94 *supra*. In itself this would only involve a shift of dates by one week, but a difficulty arises from the fact that Carvajal's *Account* indicates that the village was reached on a Sunday (p. 180), that the whole of Lent was spent there (p. 186), and that the date of departure was April 24 (p. 188). This would seem to call for arrival on the Sunday before the beginning of Lent, i.e. February 19. From this date to April 24 is 64 days —a period difficult to reconcile with Carvajal's narrative. On the other hand Medina, farther on (p. 102), by dating the day before Trinity Sunday (on which Carvajal states—p. 204 *infra*—the mouth of the Río Negro was passed) as June 3, implies acceptance of April 9 as Easter, inasmuch as Trinity Sunday is the Sunday following Pentecost, or, in other words, falls eight weeks after Easter.—EDITOR.]

*[To this day the Amazon Indians will cut the timber they need for their building purposes only in the last quarter of the moon. They know from experience that timber cut in any other quarter will soon rot and be eaten by insects. Possibly this fact, coupled with the use of inappropriate woods, caused the brigantine to need repairs so soon after its construction.—TRANSLATOR.]

damp, the Spaniards could not use their arquebuses but only their crossbows, which, however, were sufficient to drive off the enemy and to permit them to make port in a village in which the Indians still put up a defense for some time but which, on the other hand, happened to be well stocked with provisions.

But the task of gathering together the turtles kept there in pools, as well as other provisions, was not an easy one. Against Cristóbal de Segovia and some others to whom Orellana had assigned this task the Indians launched a furious assault; they attacked at the same time those Spaniards who had remained in the village and those who were still on board the brigantines, and the day's fighting cost the Spaniards eighteen wounded, some of whom were placed on board wrapped in cloaks like bales of goods so that the enemy might not become emboldened, one man being so seriously wounded that he died a week later; they lost also one arquebusier who was left incapacitated as a result of the wounds that he received. At last when they were all on board the brigantines they went out onto the river, followed by numerous canoes filled with Indians who continued to harass them all that night. When the sun rose they perceived a great number of very large villages, from which fresh Indians came out to take the places of their companions who were getting fatigued; and, as by mid-day the situation was becoming untenable for the Spaniards, tired out as they were after the hazards of the day before, many of them being wounded and all worn out from so much rowing, Orellana decided, in order to let his men get some rest and in order to make it possible for them to eat, to pull up with the brigantines alongside a deserted island in the middle of the river; but they had scarcely begun to prepare their meal when it was seen that the Indians were attempting to attack them both from land and water, whereupon they had to change their plans and again strike out downstream, thinking that they could thus defend themselves better. Pursued all the while by the Indians, they came to a narrows made by the river. Here many of the Indians had posted themselves and thus had the brigantines at their mercy, and these would probably have been definitely held up there with their crews had it not been for the good aim of Hernán Gutiérrez de Celis, who with a shot from his arquebuse knocked over the Indian in command of the canoes; for the Indian's companions, in rushing to him to see how badly he was hurt, allowed time for the brigantines of the Spaniards to get out of that dangerous pass. Nevertheless, the Indians still continued to harass them for two days and two nights, without giving them a moment of repose, at the end of which time Orellana and his men reached the farthest limit of the dominions of the warlike Machiparo.

Farther on down they came upon another village belonging to a different tribe, and this the expeditioners had to take by force of arms in order to procure for themselves a much-needed rest; and after resting in it for three days and after providing themselves with biscuit and various kinds of fruit, they resumed their journey on May 16,[142] always avoiding, whenever they could, any encounter with the inhabitants of the numerous villages which they saw on both shores of the river, all of which lay within the territory ruled over by Omagua, until they came to the country belonging to Chief Paguana, whose people received them in the most hospitable manner. On the 29th of that month they landed in a small village which they occupied without resistance, and on June 3 they came in sight of the mouth of the Río Negro. They rested the following day, which was Sunday, and on Monday the 5th they made port in a medium-sized village, and afterwards in others, where they continued to lay in food supplies, without there occurring any other incidents of importance until the 7th, when they sustained a night attack from the Indians, with the result that several Spaniards were wounded and a certain number of Indians were taken prisoners and hanged at once.

The 8th, which was Corpus Christi day, and the following day were given up to resting. Early in the morning of the 10th they came to the mouth of a river of great volume emptying into the one down which they were proceeding; they gave it the name of Grande, but it is known today as the Madeira. On the 13th they saw a fairly large village, strongly fortified and situated on a high spot; by the form of construction of its buildings it "showed by its style that it was the frontier of other provinces,"* and on the 14th they caught sight of another village, which they captured in order to procure food and in which they set fire to a large hut, causing several women and children to be burned to death. On the 24th they were again engaged in combat by the Indians, captained this time by the so-called Amazons, the result of the fighting being that several Spaniards were wounded, among them Friar Carvajal, who was hit "in the side with an arrow, which," as he

---

142 Through an error the month is given as March in Oviedo [Vol. 4, p. 556].
*[Oviedo, Vol. 4, p. 560.]

tells it, "went in as far as the hollow part, and had it not been for the folds in my clothes, through which the arrow first passed, they would have killed me."* This day the good father had preached in honor of St. John the Baptist; but it was God's will that he should be unlucky, for in another combat that was fought later they put out one of his eyes.[143]

Hard pressed in this way, Orellana was obliged to redouble his precautions and continue the journey without landing in any settlement, even though the provisions were becoming very scarce, for fear that the Indians might kill some of his soldiers; but all these precautions did not suffice to prevent one of his men, Antonio Carranza, from being wounded by a poisoned arrow shot, shortly after the beginning of the new month.[144] To put a stop, so far as possible, to this unpunished wounding of his soldiers by the Indians, Orellana had the brigantine moored to the trees of an island in the mouth of a great river which emptied in on the right (apparently the Tapajóz) and had a sort of railing built around the top of the sides of the boats to defend his men against the poisoned arrows of the savages; but even this was not sufficient, for shortly after, as they were passing opposite the mouth of one of the arms of the Paranaiba,† the Indians with their arrows shot another soldier named García de Soria, who died from the poison within twenty-four hours.

In the midst of these misfortunes, however, the expeditioners were beginning to feel more cheerful on noticing that they had now reached waters in which the rise and fall of the tide could be felt, indicating that they could not be far from the Atlantic. They then crossed over to the opposite side of the river, still avoiding the inhabited places, and there, having gone on downstream for several leagues, keeping away from the shore, through a region in which the villages that they saw were some distance inland from the river and the country was beginning to appear cleared

---

*[Oviedo, Vol. 4, p. 563. The words in the *Account* are closely similar (*infra*, p. 213f.).—EDITOR.]

[143] "They hit no one but me," says Carvajal, "for Our Lord permitted them, because of my faults, to plant an arrow shot over one of my eyes, the arrow passing through my head and sticking out two fingers' length on the other side behind my ear and slightly above it; from which wound, besides losing the eye, I have endured much suffering and worry, and even now I am not free from pain . . . " [Oviedo, Vol. 4, p. 563; for the parallel passage in the *Account* see *infra*, p. 216—EDITOR.]

[144] The date of this misfortune is not recorded, but it must have occurred at the time that I am talking about. From June 25 on the chronology of the voyage becomes difficult to establish because the chronicler ordinarily limits himself to saying: "a few days later" [Oviedo, Vol. 4, pp. 566 and 568], "not many days after" [*ibid.*, p. 570], etc.

†[It is not clear which river Medina had in mind. No river of this name is readily identifiable on good recent maps.—EDITOR.]

of the woods which usually covered the banks, they rested two days. From this point on, the aspect of the scenery changed radically; the savanas and the high banks were replaced by lowlands, and the river was seen to be cut up by numerous islands occupied by very few inhabitants; and they began to row among these islands, procuring food wherever they could do so without danger, "and, owing to the fact that the islands were numerous and very large," says Friar Carvajal, "never again did we manage to reach the mainland either on the one side or on the other all the way down to the sea . . . " [*infra*, p. 228].

"Continuing on our journey in our customary way," continues the chronicler a little further on, "as we were getting to be very weak and in great need of sustenance we set out to capture a village which was situated on an estuary; at the hour of high tide the Captain gave orders to steer the large brigantine toward that place; he succeeded in making port in good form and the companions leaped out on land; [those on board] the smaller one did not see a log that was covered by water, and it struck such a blow that a plank was smashed to pieces, so badly that the boat was swamped. Here we saw ourselves in a very trying situation, one more trying than any into which we had fallen along the whole [course of the] river, and we thought we should all perish, for from all sides [evil] fortune was heaping blows upon us; because just as our companions leaped out on land they encountered the Indians, and they made them take to flight and, thinking that they were safe, started in to collect food. The Indians, as they were in great numbers, came back at our companions and went at them in such a manner that they made them fall back to where the brigantines were, with the Indians in pursuit of them; yet on the brigantines little security did they have, because the larger one was high and dry, for the tide had ebbed, and the smaller one [was] sunk, as I have stated . . . " [*infra*, pp. 228–229].

To escape from this difficult situation Orellana arranged to have half of his men present a front to the Indians, while the others beached the damaged brigantine and repaired it. In charge of the large one, which was pushed out from the shore, there were left on board only the commander, one other soldier, and the two friars. By a piece of good luck, at the end of three hours the Indians retired just as the damage to the small brigantine had been repaired.

The following day they took refuge in some thick woods and

started to work on preparing the small boat so that it might be in condition for navigating at sea, beginning by making the extra nails that were needed. These tasks took eighteen days, during which time hunger brought them to such a pass that they distributed the grains of maize by count; but they were saved from dire distress by the opportune catch of a tapir recently killed and brought down the river by the current.

The large brigantine still remained to be repaired, and to do this they went on downstream in search of a beach where they could haul it out; and, when they had found one, in fourteen days both brigantines "were entirely repaired and rigging for them was made out of vines, as well as the cordage for the sea [voyage], and sails out of the blankets in which we had been sleeping, and their masts were set up"; and these were "days of continuous and regular penance," the Dominican friar recalls, "due to the great hunger [that we were enduring] and to the little food that was to be had, for we did not eat anything but what could be picked up on the strand at the water's edge, which was a few small snails and a few crabs of a reddish color of the size of frogs; and these one half of the companions went to catch, while the other half remained working . . . " [*infra*, p. 231].

At last, on August 8,* they moved away from that place, using their sails in the hours of ebb tide and tacking from one side to the other; but as they lacked anchors they tied the boats to stones, with the result that it sometimes happened that the tide picked them up and carried them back in one hour the distance that they had covered in a whole day. They still found a few villages inhabited by tractable Indians who had hidden their stores, Orellana and his men being obliged for this reason to content themselves at times solely with certain roots, and "if we had not found these, we should all have perished from hunger," says Friar Carvajal [*infra*, p. 232].

Finally, on the 24th of August, they came to the mouth of the river. After all the obstacles that nature and men had placed in their way up to that time, they still had to endure the terrible rainstorms of those regions. They rested there one day and one night, if it can be called resting to busy one's self with the making

*[A difficulty arises as to dates in this period in view of what appears to be an internal contradiction in Carvajal's *Account* (p. 231, *infra*) and *Relación* (Oviedo, Vol. 4, p. 570). Carvajal states in both versions that they reached on Transfiguration Day (the date of which is August 6) the beach where the large brigantine was repaired, stayed there fourteen days, and left on August 8.—EDITOR.]

of cables and ropes for the rigging of the brigantines, "and, as they had been made out of piecings, there was always some piecing to be done on them . . . And, as the rest of the things with which we fitted ourselves out were imitations and made by the hands of men without experience and unaccustomed to such a profession, they lasted a very short time; and, as they were not to be found everywhere, it was necessary to keep on toiling and fitting [ourselves] out at random.  In this manner, in one place the sail was made, in another the rudder, in another the pump, and in another the rigging, and in the case of each one of these things, as long as we did not have it, it meant being in great danger."*

"I am leaving out," continues Carvajal, "many other things we lacked, such as pilots and sailors and a compass, which are necessary things, for without any one of them there is no man, however devoid of common sense he may be, that would dare to go to sea, except ourselves, to whom this rambling voyage came by accident and not by our will."†

At this place the expeditioners took on water, "each one a jarful, and some half an *almud* of roasted maize and others less, and others [supplied themselves] with roots, and in this manner we got ready to navigate by sea wherever fortune might guide us and cast us, . . . " [*infra*, p. 232].

With this equipment, on the 26th of August, a Saturday,‡ early in the morning before dawn, the two brigantines spread their sails and put out to sea between the large island of Marajó and another smaller one that lies towards the north.¹⁴⁵  During four days they navigated in convoy, sometimes in sight of land, at other times a bit distant from the coast; but on the night of the 29th "one brigantine got separated from the other,¹⁴⁶ so that never again did we succeed in sighting each other," says Carvajal, "wherefore we concluded that they [i.e. those on the other brigantine] had got

---

*[Oviedo, Vol. 4, p. 571].

†[Oviedo, Vol. 4, p. 571.]

‡[Carvajal says in the *Account* (p. 233, *infra*) that they sailed out on August 26, St. Louis' day.  St. Louis' day is on August 25.  In the *Relación* in Oviedo (Vol. 4, p. 572) the date is given as Saturday, August 26.  This correlation of weekday and date is correct.—EDITOR.]

¹⁴⁵ This is deduced from the following passage in the *Relación* published by Oviedo: "This mouth of the river, from cape to cape, is four leagues wide, and we saw other wider mouths than the one through which we went out to sea; and to the minds of experienced men, and in view of the pattern of the many islands and gulfs and bays which the river formed fifty leagues back before we got out of it, it was quite evident that there remained other mouths to the right as we came down, . . . and notwithstanding all the diligence that was applied to searching for the mainland bordering upon the river, never could it be reached: so that we were forced to go out between islands on the one side and the other through the aforesaid mouth" [Oviedo, Vol. 4, pp. 571–572].

¹⁴⁶ The smaller one they had christened *San Pedro*, and the other *Victoria*.

lost, and, at the end of nine days that we had been sailing along, our sins drove us into the Gulf of Paria, we believing that that was our route, and when we found ourselves within it we tried to go out to sea again; getting out was so difficult that it took us seven days to do so, during all of which [time] our companions never dropped the oars from their hands, and during all these seven days we ate nothing but some fruit resembling plums, which are called 'hogos'; thus it was that with great toil we got out of the Mouths of the Dragon (for so this may [well] be called for us), because we came very close to staying inside there [forever]. We got out of this prison; we proceeded onward for two days along the coast, at the end of which [time], without knowing where we were nor whither we were going nor what was to become of us, we made port on the island of Cubagua and in the city of Nueva Cádiz, where we found our company and the small brigantine, which had arrived two days before, because they arrived on the ninth of September and we arrived on the eleventh of the month with the large brigantine, on board which was our Captain: so great was the joy which we felt, the ones at the sight of the others, that I shall not be able to express it, because they considered us to be lost, and we [so considered] them" [*infra*, pp. 233–234].

In this way they brought to an end their "navigation and experience" which "had been entered upon unintentionally and turned out to be so extraordinary," says Oviedo,* "that it is one of the greatest things that ever happened to men."

*[Vol. 4, p. 384.]

# IX

## ORELLANA'S COMPANIONS

WHAT was the total number of Orellana's companions in his voyage down the Amazon? The historians, as ordinarily happens in such cases, are in disagreement on this point. López de Gómara, who is followed by Garcilaso de la Vega and by Father Rodríguez,* says that they were not more than 50 in number; Oviedo, who is the one that has gone most extensively into details in the matter, brings the number up to 53, naming the men one by one; Antonio de Herrera affirms that there were 60 of them; and finally, Friar Carvajal expressly states that there were 57 of them.† I shall try to determine, therefore, which one of these chroniclers in my opinion was right.

Those who attached their names to the two longer documents drawn up during the voyage,‡ if one counts *all* the signatures, total 61. Of these, 35 signed both pieces; in addition, 14 signed the first one and not the second, while on the other hand in this latter there appear for the first time the names of 12. To these 61 could be added the names of two others who are found mentioned only in Oviedo,[147] so that the total number of the discoverers of the Amazon, inclusive of Orellana, would turn out to be 64.

Now, how can one reconcile the figure given by Friar Carvajal, who states definitely that the number of companions taken along by Orellana was 57, with the one which I get from my count? Taking as a minimum basis for my calculation the actual signatures to the two documents mentioned above, I am bound to get at least 61, as I have already stated. Did Friar Carvajal, therefore, make a mistake in his count? Did some of the signers manage, perchance, to get their names affixed twice to the same document? In order to understand how it is permissible to entertain a suspicion as to this latter possibility, one has only to bear in mind two cir-

---

*[Manuel Rodríguez, *El Marañón y Amazonas*, Madrid, 1684; see footnote 48, *supra*.]

†[This is the figure given by Carvajal in the *Account* as published by Medina (see *infra*, p. 170); but in the version inserted in Oviedo's *Historia general y natural de las Indias*, etc., the round number of 50 is used three times (Vol. 4, pp. 541, 542, 543).—EDITOR.]

‡[Documents II [4] and II [7], *infra*, pp. 254-257, 258-262.]

[147] These are Juan Carrillo and Andrés Martín, the latter a native of Palos. "Perucho," a Biscayan, a native of Pasajes, and "Joanes," also a Biscayan, a native of Bilbao, who, says Oviedo (referring only to the latter), died during the voyage, are probably Pedro de Acaray and Pedro de Empudia, Oviedo having assumed that the latter's Christian name was Juan.

cumstances: first, that some of the expeditioners did not know how to sign, and that consequently someone else had to do it for them;[148] and, second, that in these two documents, which I reproduce in this volume, I actually find signatures repeated, namely (not counting the case of Juan de Alcántara)* those of Hernán González and Juan Bueno. Finally, there is the possibility that in some cases I have not solved correctly the question of the Christian name with respect to the surname to which it belongs. In connection with this last point let it suffice to recall that Oviedo himself errs in giving the Christian names of several of the men.

Taking this latter uncertainty into consideration and attributing to the circumstances just noted the excess number needed to bring the figure up to the total which I have given above, I choose to abide by the assertion of the chronicler of the expedition, who in the course of several months of intimate association with his companions was in a position to count them accurately and who, consequently, can not be suspected of having made an error in a matter of so much importance as this.[149]

[148] This assertion of mine can be checked up in two ways. In the first place, it can be seen at a glance that the last few signatures are manifestly in the same handwriting, more plainly so in the second document [Fig. 3, pp. 260–261, *infra*] than in the first [Fig. 2, p. 255]. This sort of thing, though it may appear anomalous, was current in those times in America: in support of this statement I could cite many proofs. And in the second place, among the signers is to be found Juan de Elena, who could only make his mark, if we may draw this conclusion from the fact that this is what he did before a notary public when it came to signing his deposition as a witness in connection with the judicial inquiry covering the past services of Cristóbal de Segovia (see p. 274 of the present volume).

*[The double occurrence of this name among the signatures of the second document is not the result of repetition but is due to the fact, as Oviedo explains and as Medina admits below, that there were two men by this name.—Editor.]

[149] In case some reader might feel inclined to reject my hypothesis, let it be noted that to the names of Juan Carrillo and Andrés Martín, which Oviedo puts down, there should be added the following to complete the count of 62 which I give above: Juan Bueno, Francisco Elena, Alonso García, Alonso Gómez, and Hernán González.

[In this cryptic note of Medina's, intended to show how simple it is to reconcile all figures, there are several errors. In the first place, in no part of the discussion has Medina used the figure 62 which he here claims to have given above. At the very end of the second paragraph of the present chapter he states that the total number of the discoverers of the Amazon may possibly have been 63—a figure which in the present translation is changed to 64 for the obvious reason that 61 + 2 + 1 = 64. The only way to obtain the figure 62 is to take Medina's count of 61 signers of the two documents in question, and add 1 for Orellana himself; but in this case the names of Juan Carrillo and Andrés Martín are not to be taken into consideration at all.

In the second place, the matter under discussion is the number *of the companions* of Orellana. The leader's name should therefore not be taken into consideration either, and the only figures to be reconciled are 57 and 61. In other words, a difference of only 4 needs to be accounted for. For this purpose, the names Francisco Elena and Alonso García can not be used: Francisco Elena (signer of the second document) is identified by Medina (see No. 20 in the biographical notes below) with Juan de Elena (signer of the first document), the two names being thus taken by Medina to constitute one of the 35 cases of signatures common to both documents (see the second paragraph of this chapter); and the same thing has been done with the name Alonso García (occurring *once* among the signatures of *each* of the two documents), in spite of what Medina says in connection with this name in the biographical notes below. But the above-mentioned difference

"And because," to borrow Oviedo's words,* "it is not right that after a feat so remarkable, after such a long and dangerous voyage, the names of those who took part in it all should be forgotten and passed over in silence, I shall put them down here, . . . "[150]

1. ACARAY (Pedro de).—This is possibly the Biscayan Perucho to whom Friar Carvajal refers in his *Account*.[151]

of 4 is sufficiently accounted for by the remaining three names listed in the present footnote by Medina, namely those of Juan Bueno (whose signature occurs twice in the second of the two documents in question), Hernán González (whose signature occurs twice in *each* of the two documents), and Alonso Gómez (who signed the first document only but who is identified by Medina below, under No. 30 in the biographical notes, with Alonso Gutiérrez, likewise a signer of the first document only, both signatures being so uncertain that Jiménez de la Espada, in publishing this document in the *Ilustración Española y Americana*, has apparently deciphered one of them as "Alonso Lagares").

After all, is Medina right in juggling with these signatures in the way that he does in order to keep the number of Orellana's companions down to Carvajal's figure of 57? Is it not possible, and even probable, that when Carvajal, using an exact figure and not a round number, says that Orellana "took fifty-seven men with him," he meant only the soldiers, thus not including himself and the other priest Friar Gonzalo de Vera? To bring the number of soldiers alone up to 57, one has only to count Alonso Gómez as a distinct person (i.e. *not* to be identified with Alonso Gutiérrez) and to take the names Juan de Elena and Francisco Elena as designating, not, as Medina thinks, a single person, but two distinct individuals.

Then again, is it necessary to stop at the figure given by Carvajal? Is it logical to believe, as Medina seems to do, that it just so happened that all of the men, including those who reached Aparia in such a weakened condition that they died before the expedition moved on from that village, managed to sign one or the other of the two documents, when not all of the signers signed both of them? And is it possible to reject the names of Juan Carrillo and Andrés Martín, recorded by Oviedo in his list of members of the expedition, when we know that this chronicler got his information from Orellana himself and from other direct sources right after the conclusion of the voyage? To return to Carvajal's figure, is it not possible that 57 was the number of men actually decided upon by the commander (possibly in a sort of council meeting at which Carvajal would be apt to be present) to make up the body of the expedition, but that a certain number of others, driven to disobedience by the irresistible desire to get to a place where food was said to exist, managed to join the party either right from the start or within a few hours after it had gotten under way?

In any case, it is certain that the careful reader who may wish to check up on Medina with the aid of Oviedo and of the lists of signatures on pp. 254, 256, 259 of this volume will expect to find all the names from all the sources in the alphabetically arranged biographical notes below. For this reason, in the present translation those names which were either omitted by Medina or elsewhere explained away by him are inserted in their proper places, together with a brief note or cross-reference. These added names are bracketed and left without numbers in order that Medina's enumeration of the men composing the party as he has worked it out may remain intact. —EDITOR.]

*[Oviedo, Vol. 4, p. 384. Oviedo's numbered list of names is on pp. 384-385.—EDITOR.]

[150] For one who has not had experience in handling the papers in the Archives of the Indies it is almost impossible to get an idea of the difficulties which present themselves at every step to the investigator who is assembling biographical data relating to the soldiers of the Conquest, on account of the strange identity of names which constantly confronts him. Only after a scrupulous examination of the documents in hand can one distinguish at times which data pertain to one and which to another of two persons having exactly the same name, having taken part in the same events, and being in some cases of the same age. A good proof of this assertion will be found in what I have to say below about Juan de Illanes. [In the present translation of Medina's work this point can not be checked up because of the translator's decision to leave out a large part of the material included by Medina under the name of Juan de Illanes (see, below, editorial footnote under that name).—EDITOR.] For this reason, and with a view to avoiding errors, I have preferred at times to omit information which may apply to some of Orellana's companions but which I can not vouch for as really relating to them.

[151] See p. 227 of the present volume and my note 27 to Friar Carvajal's *Account*.

2. AGUILAR (Benito de), an Asturian.—Oviedo is in error in giving his Christian name as Blas. Benito de Aguilar was born about the year 1508. He crossed over to Peru around 1535 and there took part in the conquest of Quito and its vicinity and in the conquests of Popayán and the provinces of Lile, serving at the side of Cristóbal de Segovia and under the immediate command of Sebastián de Benalcázar. He was in Quito at the time when Gonzalo Pizarro's expedition to La Canela was being organized, and he set out from there with the expedition.

3. AGUILAR (Cristóbal de).[152]

4. AGUILAR (Juan de), a native of Valladolid.—He died during the voyage. Oviedo gives him the Christian name of García, but this is an error.

5. ALCÁNTARA (Juan de).[153]

6. ALCÁNTARA (Juan de).[154]

7. ARÉVALO (Rodrigo de), a citizen of Trujillo.—Oviedo calls him Juan de Arévalo. He appears to have died during the voyage.

8. ARNALTE (Juan de).—I believe that he was one of those who died during the voyage.

9. BERMÚDEZ (Diego), a native of Palos.—His given name is erroneously recorded by Oviedo as Alonso.*

10. BUENO (Juan), a native of Moguer.—In the documents two signatures in this form may be read, but I am inclined to believe that they refer to one and the same person.

[BUENO (Juan).—Possibly not the same man as No. 10, after all.—EDITOR.]

11. CABRERA (Alonso de).—He was born in Cazalla about the year 1517 and obtained permission by royal decree of November 27, 1534, to cross over to Peru. At the conclusion of the voyage

---

[152] See my note 13 to Friar Carvajal's *Account*.

[153] See my note 5 to Friar Carvajal's *Account*.

[154] See the last-mentioned note. [It is not evident on what basis Medina, at the end of the footnote to which he refers (p. 239 in the present volume), states that both of the men named Juan de Alcántara died during the voyage. Friar Carvajal does not say so. Can it be that Medina misinterpreted Oviedo? The latter (*op. cit.*, Vol. 4, pp. 384–385) gives the first Juan de Alcántara as No. 8 in his list but says nothing about him. No. 18 is as follows: "García de Aguilar, a native of Valladolid: he died during the voyage." No. 19 reads: "Another Juan de Alcántara, from the *maestrazgo* of Santiago: he also died during the voyage." His word "also" plainly connects his statement about the second Juan de Alcántara with what he has just said about García (read: Juan) de Aguilar, not with the bare name of Juan de Alcántara eleven numbers back.—EDITOR.]

*[The place of birth of this member of the expedition would lead us to believe that he was perhaps one of the seamen who, Carvajal says, accompanied Orellana.—TRANSLATOR.]

down the Amazon he returned to Quito, where six days after his arrival he was taken prisoner by command of Pedro de Puelles,* in the seizure and assassination of whom he later took an active part. He served, consequently, against Gonzalo Pizarro and was present at the battle of Xaquixaguana. He returned a second time to Quito, and at the time of the insurrection under Francisco Hernández Girón the *corregidor* of that city, namely Antonio de Osnayo, sent him with an advance detachment to the province of Los Cañaris. Later on he took up his abode in Cuenca, where he became a royal treasurer, although in 1568 he was temporarily in Quito and was definitely settled there by 1579, filling the offices of revenue collector and inspector of the Royal Exchequer. He also became a *regidor* (magistrate) of the city. In the month of March of the last-mentioned year he was sent, as the lieutenant of Captain Rodrigo de Salazar, to Guayaquil because of the fear then current that that port might be entered by the ships of Sir Francis Drake's fleet. He was esteemed a man of distinction and an hidalgo, although at this time he was now very poor and old. He was still living as a bachelor in February of 1583. On December 23 of this year it was voted in the Council of the Indies to send out a royal decree by virtue of which a pension of 800 pesos was to be paid to him—a tardy favor from which nothing probably ever came.

[CÁCERES (Cristóbal de).—See under Cristóbal de Segovia.—EDITOR.]

12. CARRANZA (Antonio de).[155]

13. CARRILLO (Gonzalo).—Oviedo, by error, calls him Gómez Carrillo.

[CARRILLO (Juan).—A man by this name is listed by Oviedo (*Historia* . . . , Vol. 4, p. 384) among the members of the expedition.—EDITOR.]

14. CARVAJAL (Friar Gaspar de).

15. CEVALLOS (Rodrigo de).

16. CONTRERAS (Gabriel de).[156]

17. DÍAZ (Gonzalo).

*[Pedro de Puelles was Gonzalo Pizarro's lieutenant in Quito at the time of the latter's rebellion.—TRANSLATOR.] [There is no statement in the selections from the judicial inquiry covering Alonso de Cabrera's past services published by Medina (*infra*, pp. 304 ff.) as to when and how Alonso de Cabrera obtained his release after being taken prisoner by Pedro de Puelles.—EDITOR.]

[155] See my note 24 to Carvajal's *Account*.

[156] See my note 12 to Carvajal's *Account*.

18. Domínguez Miradero (Pedro).—He was born in Palos about the year 1515* and along about 1535 went to Santa Marta with the Adelantado Pedro Fernández de Lugo. Under Captain Luis Bernal he took part in the expedition of exploration to the provinces of Ancerma; from there he went on to Cali with Captain Miguel Muñoz, and later to Quito, and participated in the expeditions of conquest and pacification in Macas, and in the quelling of other Indian insurrections in that part of the country. After his return from the Amazon expedition he aided in chastising the Indians of the island of Puná, who had revolted and had killed Bishop Valverde, and right after that he went on similar business to Caguasqui. On learning of the discovery of the mines of Santa Barbola, he went there, becoming "instrumental in bringing it about" [infra, p. 292] that some very good veins were discovered. He sided with the hunchback Rodrigo de Salazar against Pedro de Puelles, Gonzalo Pizarro's lieutenant in Quito, and in company with him went off to Jauja to join La Gasca.

He was present at the battle of Xaquixaguana, and returning again to Quito he served under Antonio de Osnayo against the Indians of Lita and Quilca. Having finally settled down in Quito, he was still living there in April, 1581, at which time he had a second judicial inquiry covering his past services put through the court, and the record of this he caused to be sent to the King, together with a letter from the Audiencia dated October 7 of that year which says: "Cesarean Royal Majesty:—Pedro Domínguez Miradero is a very honorable man and a person more than seventy years of age: he was one of the first discoverers of these realms and one of the fifty-seven who went down the Marañón with Captain Orellana during the expedition of conquest to La Canela. He afterwards returned to this province and served in the conquest of Quijos, Zumaco, and La Canela and Coca, and ever since has been engaged in making gunpowder. He is poor, unmarried, and supports himself with the aforesaid work: it seems from the law of nature as if he will live but a few years [more]: in view of this and of the fact that he has served long and that he has never failed in his duty, Your Majesty might grant him the favor of an income of one thousand gold pesos for the days that remain to him to live, in gratification for his services, or as Your Majesty might see most fit. Done in Quito on October seventh, One Thousand Five Hundred and Eighty-one.—*The Licentiate Diego*

*[Or 1510? Cf. the evidence furnished by the document quoted in the next paragraph.—Editor.]

*Ortegon.—The Licentiate Francisco de Anucibay.—The Licentiate Pedro Vargas de Cañaveral.*"[157]

19.  DURÁN (Andrés), a native of Moguer.—There was a man by this given name and family name who was an *alcalde* of Puerto Viejo by appointment by His Majesty and a resident of that town in 1534,* at which time he said that he was fifty years of age; and his deposition figures in the lawsuit which Marshal Diego de Almagro carried on against the Adelantado Pedro de Alvarado in the town of San Miguel in the month of October of that year.[158] Later he was chief constable of the city of Quito.

[ELENA (Francisco).—This name figures among the signatures of the second petition addressed to Orellana (see *infra*, p. 259); but cf. Medina's remarks on Juan de Elena.—EDITOR.]

20.  ELENA (Juan de).—It is probable that the man so designated and Francisco Elena were one and the same person: in the latter form the Christian name was probably so written by another person by mistake, for it is known that Juan de Elena did not know how to sign his name.  Juan de Elena was born in 1509, crossed over to Peru about 1534, and took part in the discovery and settlement of Quito, whence he went with Benalcázar to take part in the conquest of Popayán; and, returning to Quito, he set out from that city as a member of Gonzalo Pizarro's expedition to La Canela.

21.  EMPUDIA (Pedro de).[159]

22.  ENRÍQUEZ (Cristóbal).[160]

23.  ESTÉBAN (Alonso), a native of Moguer.—It is possible that this is the same soldier who later served brilliantly in the Araucanian wars of Chile.

[FERNÁNDEZ (Antonio).—See HERNÁNDEZ.—EDITOR.]

24.  FERNÁNDEZ [or HERNÁNDEZ] (Ginés), a native of Moguer.—

---

[157] For further details regarding the life of Domínguez Miradero see the extracts from his petitions and the record of the judicial inquiry covering his past services printed on pp. 291 ff. of the present volume.

*[The year of this lawsuit is given as 1584 in Medina's book, but this must be a mere printer's error, and not a correction of the date 1534 in Torres de Mendoza's *Colección de documentos inéditos* etc. (see asterisk footnote, p. 8, *supra*, Vol. 10, Madrid, 1868, p. 152, because Medina can hardly have failed to know that in 1584 Marshal Diego de Almagro was long since dead —EDITOR.]

[158] See Torres de Mendoza's *Colección de documentos inéditos*, etc., Vol 10, pp. 152ff.

[159] See my note 15 to Friar Carvajal's *Account*.

[160] See note 17 to this same *Account*.

It must have been in 1535,[161] when he was only nineteen years old, that he went to Peru, serving later in the district of Piura, in the conquest and pacification of Copiz, Cerrán, and Guancabamba, and part of the province of the Paltas, a tribe dwelling in the neighborhood of Loja in the days when this city had not yet been founded. After that, he set out for Quito, then recently founded, for "that was at the time when Captain Lorenzo de Aldana went to the said city with a commission from the Marquis Don Francisco Pizarro, in which [city] he stopped and resided a long time, helping to keep it up and going off to the wars of conquest and pacification of the said provinces which had risen up and were in revolt, and [which] every day kept revolting . . . " [*infra*, p. 283]. Shortly after this he went with Gonzalo Díaz de Pineda to explore Pelayo and Chalcoma, regions famous because of reports then circulating regarding the emeralds that were to be found there; on this expedition they suffered great hardships, and no results of any consequence came of it. After that, he went with the same captain, in 1536, to aid in exploring the provinces of Quijos, Zumaco, and La Canela, finally coming out in the district of Quito, whence he went and joined up with Lorenzo de Aldana, who had come to found the city of Pasto on behalf of the governor of Popayán. Under Captain Alonso Hernández he next went to the province of Yumbo bent on checking a revolt which the Indians were planning to launch, and this preventative measure, in fact, was successful in its effect; and a little later he went with Aldana to Tomebamba to help subdue a certain Captain Pedro de Vergara, who had gone in there from Bracamoros and was causing a great deal of annoyance to the natives. His last service before joining Gonzalo Pizarro was to go with Captain Rodrigo Núñez de Bonilla to take part in the conquest and pacification of the provinces of Macas and Quisna, the natives of which had revolted and had massacred a few Spaniards.

From the island of Cubagua Fernández crossed over to Nombre de Dios and Panama, sailed to the coast of Peru, whence he went into the province of Popayán and continued straight on to Quito, again promptly leaving that city to go out with Captain Rodrigo

---

[161] From question 2 in the judicial inquiry covering his past services put through in 1564 [Document V, *infra*, p. 282f.] wherein he says that he had come to Peru twenty-six years before, one would draw the conclusion that he must have come over in 1538. However, in this there is an error, for, as he himself declares further on [*infra*, p. 283], he accompanied Gonzalo Díaz de Pineda in his foray into the lands of La Canela, an expedition which was carried out in 1536, when Fernández had already been in Peru for some time. The true date of his crossing over to the Indies should therefore be set back at least as far as 1534 or 1535.

de Ocampo to serve in pacifying the provinces of Lita and Quilca. After his return to Quito we find him again taking part in a campaign, under the orders of Pero Martín Montanero, against the Indians of Canaribamba, who had also revolted and had robbed and killed many Spaniards. He was back in Quito in time to aid Captain Rodrigo de Salazar, who had come out in favor of the Crown and who assassinated Pedro de Puelles, Gonzalo Pizarro's lieutenant; and in company with this same captain he went to join La Gasca, who was then in the valley of Jauja, and fought under his standard in the battle of Xaquixaguana. The rebellion of Gonzalo Pizarro ending there, Fernández returned to Quito with Salazar, who had been commissioned to conquer and settle the provinces of Quijos, Zumaco, and La Canela; and, as this proposed expedition was not carried out, he went off to the one in Macas, where Captain Hernando de Benavente was. From there he proceeded to Tomebamba with the intention of pushing the aforesaid expedition of discovery, crossing over afterwards to Loja in order to join Captain Alonso de Mercadillo in exploring and conquering the region where they, in conjunction with Benavente, founded the city of Zamora de los Alcaides. In this town he at last settled down, became an *alcalde*, and was appointed magistrate many times, as well as treasurer for His Majesty, and held "other government offices which are customarily bestowed upon persons of importance . . . " [*infra*, p. 288], "keeping up his household on a large scale and maintaining the rank of citizen with his arms and [his] horse, constantly supporting in his house honorable men who help to keep up the town, all at his own expense and on his own initiative . . . " [*infra*, p. 287]. Although he had been the owner of an *encomienda* comprising five hundred Indians, granted to him at the time of the founding of the city, confirmed by the Viceroy Don Antonio de Mendoza, and increased by the Marquis de Cañete to the extent of another two hundred in 1564, these Indians had become so reduced in number that he asserted that he could not support himself on them and had thus come to be a man "very poor and plunged into debt" [*infra*, p. 288].

Ginés Fernández was a brother of Diego Fernández de Serpa, well known in history because of his expedition to Cumaná in 1568.

25.  FUENTERRABÍA (Sebastián de).—He died of sickness in the village of Aparia.

26. García (Alonso).—There are two signatures in exactly this form, but it is probable that they stand for one and the same person.*

[Gómez (Alonso).—He was one of the signers, along with Alonso Gutiérrez and the rest, of the petition handed to Orellana in Aparia on January 4, 1542, according to Medina's deciphering of the signatures (see *infra*, pp. 254 and 256); but see Medina's theory about this name under Alonso Gutiérrez, below.—Editor.]

27. González (Alexos), a Galician.

28. González (Alvar), an Asturian, from Oviedo.—He died a natural death during the voyage.

29. González (Hernán), a Portuguese.—There are two signatures composed of this given name and this surname, but the handwriting is exactly the same. Hernán González was born in 1504, and having gone to the New World in 1533 he took part "in the conquests of Peru and of Alcázares and of Popayán, associated, [while aiding] in conquering the said lands, with the governors of them . . . " [*infra*, p. 274]. He started out from Quito with Gonzalo Pizarro.[162]

*[This sentence is the translator's adaptation of Medina's puzzling statement, which literally rendered into English reads as follows: "There are two of this same given name and family name, but it is probable that they are a same person." From Medina's reproduction in print of the two documents in which these signatures are found (pp. 254 and 256, and 258–259, respectively), it is difficult to see on what he bases his assertion that there were two persons so named. Unlike the case of Juan Bueno, whose signature appears repeated in one of the documents, and that of Hernán González, who signed each of the documents twice, the name of Alonso García is found once among the signatures of each of the two documents, as in the case of at least thirty-one other men. If Medina found differences in the handwriting of the two signatures of Alonso García as they occur first in one document and then in the other, we should expect him to mention this fact and then to draw the conclusion that here was another man who either could not sign for himself or had someone else do it for him in one of the two cases. There remains, of course, the possibility that Medina did find this signature twice in one of the documents and that his reproduction in print of the documents fails to show this, either as the result of an oversight on his part or through a printer's error; but if this is so, he ought at least to have had the case in mind and to have mentioned it when in the third paragraph of the present chapter he stated his belief regarding the double occurrence of the signatures of Juan Bueno and Hernán González respectively. (Medina's facsimile reproductions are too faint to help solve the question.)

If, on the other hand, there was some reason for making Medina suspect that there may actually have been in the expedition two men by the name of Alonso García, this suspicion does not seem to rest on any evidence to be found in Carvajal's *Account*, or in the other documents published by Medina, or in Oviedo, or in Jiménez de la Espada's article. Can it be that in some other source, such as the papers in the Archives of the Indies (see footnote 150 above), Medina found evidence showing that two men by the name of Alonso García took part in the expedition, and that he chose to slight this evidence in order not to upset his count of fifty-seven companions?—Editor.]

[162] In the "List of those who followed Gonzalo Pizarro" one reads, under the name of Hernán González: "It is said that he also [at first] followed Pizarro, but that he was converted [to the royal cause] and was allowed to keep his Indians: he is a bachelor and a farmer." His place of residence is given as Lima. [The list to which Medina refers here is presumably the one which he mentions in his note 27 to Friar Carvajal's *Account* (*infra*, p. 242). Medina does not tell us where this list may be consulted.—Editor ]

[González (Hernán).—Medina's opinion to the contrary, certain differences in the handwritings of the two signatures, notably in the initials of the first name, are discernible in the facsimile reproduction of the signatures of the second petition addressed to Orellana by his men (our Fig. 3, pp. 260–261). It is therefore quite possible that at least at the beginning of the voyage there were two men who bore this name, or rather that there was a Portuguese named Fernan Gonçales (as the facsimile seems to show) and a Spaniard named Hernán González (to modernize this latter name, as Medina does).—Editor.]

30. Gutiérrez (Alonso), a native of Badajoz.—I am inclined to believe, from the abbreviations of the signatures, that this is the same person as Alonso Gómez.

31. Gutiérrez de Celis (Hernán).[163]

32. Gutiérrez Vayón (Juan).

[Hernández (Ginés).—See Fernández.—Editor.]

33. Hernández or Fernández (Antonio), a Portuguese.—Apparently he returned to Spain with Orellana and went back with him to the Indies after obtaining a recommendation in the form of a court order for use as occasion might arise.

34. Illanes (Juan de).—There were three captains by exactly this same name who figured in the history of Peru at this time.* The one who accompanied Orellana on his voyage down the Amazon was born in the village of Illanes in Asturias. He went to Peru about 1534 and took part in the conquest and settling of Guayaquil. At the conclusion of his voyage with Orellana he returned to Quito and served under the Viceroy Blasco Núñez Vela, and under La Gasca against Gonzalo Pizarro until the battle of Xaquixaguana was fought. Later he participated in the wars of conquest and pacification against the natives of Lita and Quilca and against other Indian inhabitants of the territory falling within the jurisdiction of Quito, in which city he finally settled. " . . . and at the time when Francisco Hernández Girón rose up in revolt in this realm . . . ," he says in his own words, "I remained

---

[163] See my note 18 to Friar Carvajal's *Account*.

*[The translator has wisely chosen to omit a little more than two pages (including footnote 164) of biographical material gathered together by Medina on the two captains named Juan de Illanes who had no connection with Orellana's voyage—Editor.]

in the village of Chimbo* belonging to this city under orders from its *corregidor*, guarding that pass with men whom I had received for that purpose; and I have served . . . in other affairs which have come up . . . with my arms and [my] horses and [my] servants, all at my own expense and on my own initiative . . . " [*infra*, p. 299]. In 1564 he was a member of the municipal corporation of Quito. When he was an old man, being now poor and without children, hoping to get some reward for his services, for which up to that time he had received no compensation whatsoever, he had a judicial inquiry covering his past record put through the court in Quito in September, 1568, extracts from which will be found among the documents published in the present volume (see pp. 298ff).

35. ISÁSAGA (Francisco de), a Biscayan, a native of San Sebastián.—He returned to Peru, became treasurer of Potosí, at least from 1549 to 1555, and in connection with his accounts carried on, through an attorney, a lawsuit in the Council of the Indies, a decision being given in 1568 ordering him to present certain vouchers. He seems to be the same person whom Garcilaso de la Vega calls Isásiga and of whom this author relates that while he was treasurer of the above-mentioned city he was taken prisoner by Egas de Guzmán and his followers.[165]

["JOANES," a Biscayan, a native of Bilbao, being one of those who died of illness during the voyage, according to Oviedo, Vol. 4, p. 385. Medina identifies him with Pedro de Empudia: see footnote 147 above.—EDITOR.]

[LAGARES (Alonso).—In this form Jiménez de la Espada has deciphered one of the signatures in the first of the two petitions addressed to Orellana in Aparia, but with a question mark. See the second paragraph of the editor's addition to footnote 149 above.—EDITOR.]

36. MANGAS (Juan de), a native of Puerto de Santa María.

[MANRIQUE ("Comendador" Cristóbal).—See under Cristóbal Enríquez, and the note referred to in footnote 160.—EDITOR.]

*[Medina here has "Chumbo" (but in Document VII (p. 299, *infra*), "Chimbo." Chimbo is correct. To judge from Maldonado's map (see footnote 95, p. 59 *supra*) interpreted in the modern terms of Wolf's map (see footnote 98, p. 60 *supra*) the village of Chimbo lies about 25 miles west of Riobamba and guards a pass leading from that town, and hence from the Ecuadorean plateau in general, through the valley of the Chimbo River to the coastal lowland at Guayaquil.—EDITOR.]

[165] *Comentarios reales de los Incas*, Part II, Cordova, 1617, Book VI, Ch. 24; cf. also Diego Fernández, *Primera y segunda parte de la Historia del Perú*, Seville, 1571, Part II, fol. 40.

37. Márquez (Alonso).

[Martín (Andrés).—A man by this name, a native of Palos, was a member of the expedition, according to Oviedo, Vol. 4, p. 385.—Editor.]

38. Matamoros (Diego de), a citizen of Badajoz, whose given name Oviedo did not know.

39. Medina (Blas de).[166]

40. Mexía (Diego).[167]

41. Moreno (Diego), a native of Medellín.—He died in Aparia. Oviedo erroneously lists him as Pedro Moreno.

42. Muñoz (Lorenzo), a native of Trujillo.—Oviedo gives his Christian name as Antonio.

43. Noguel (Alonso Martín de).

44. Ortiz (Alonso), a native of the Maestrazgo.*—Oviedo gives his first name as Juan.

45. Osorio (Baltasar), from the Maestrazgo.—He died in Aparia. Oviedo erroneously calls him Juan Osorio.

46. Palacios (Cristóbal de), a citizen of Ayamonte.—Oviedo calls him Juan Palacios, by mistake.

["Perucho," a Biscayan, from Pasajes, according to Oviedo, Vol. 4, p. 385. See under Pedro de Acaray above.—Editor.]

47. Porres (Pedro de).

48. Rebolloso (Mateo de), a native of Valencia.—He died of sickness during the voyage. He is listed by Oviedo erroneously as Juan de Rebolloso.

---

[166] See my note 14 to Friar Carvajal's *Account*.

[167] See my note 8 to this same *Account*.

*[The common noun *maestrazgo* designates the territory under the jurisdiction of a grand-master of a military order. Used here as a proper noun, "the Maestrazgo," it is not certain to which region the term refers. It may refer to the *maestrazgo* of Santiago (possibly Santiago de Carbajo, 20 miles west of, or Santiago del Campo, 25 miles east of the town of Alcántara), which Oviedo cites as the home of his second Juan de Alcántara (see footnote 154, p. 111 *supra*). This assumption would seem to be strengthened by the fact that Oviedo first uses "the Maestrazgo" in the immediately following entry (No. 20, "Juan" Osorio; No. 45 in Medina's list) as if it were a shorter form of designation of the home of the expeditioner listed in the preceding entry. He also uses the shorter form farther down in his list in the cases of "Juan" Ortiz (Medina's No. 44) and "Blás" Contreras (Medina's No. 16), to the homes of both of whom this assumption would therefore also apply. On the other hand, "the Maestrazgo" may refer to the mountainous region back of the Mediterranean coast in the northern part of the province of Valencia. Plausibility is lent to this assumption by the fact that at least one expeditioner hailed from this province, namely Mateo de Rebolloso (Medina's No. 48; Oviedo's No. 24).—Editor.]

49. ROBLES (Alonso de).[168]

50. RODRÍGUEZ (García).

51. RODRÍGUEZ (Sebastián).[169]

52. SEGOVIA (Cristóbal de), a native of Torrejón de Velasco.—
He went to Nicaragua in 1519 and took part in the exploration
of the Desaguadero under Captain Martín Astete, serving with
his own arms and horse. From there he continued on to New
Spain, on learning that a province had revolted, and went with
Captain Valdivieso to help conquer and pacify it, without pay and
again with his own arms and horse. From there he seems to have
returned again to Nicaragua, where he obtained the grant of a
few Indians, whom he left in charge of certain relatives in order
to go off to Peru. He was with Benalcázar at the founding of
Quito in 1534 and became one of its first settlers. Later he was
associated with this same Benalcázar in the conquest of Popayán
"and the provinces of Lile, and was one of the first conquistadors
and colonizers of it [i.e. all that country] . . . " [infra, p. 267].
From there he went on frequent expeditions through the territories of several chiefs who had revolted, and, continuing his march
with Benalcázar towards New Granada, he succeeded in defeating
the Indians in the vicinity of the Sierra de los Alcázares and captured from them enough provisions to be able to continue the
expedition still further. He took part in the founding of the town
of Timaná; then he accompanied Benalcázar until he left him on
board ship headed for Spain; and, shortly after, he joined Captain
Juan de Cabrera, who was on his way to found the city of Neiba,
where Segovia became a magistrate and received a grant of Indians.
Later on he returned to Quito to demand the restitution of the
Indians who were supposedly being kept in trust for him but of
whom he had been despoiled during his absence. From Quito
he accompanied Gonzalo Pizarro on his expedition to La Canela.
In connection, probably, with his plan to return to Spain, he had
a judicial inquiry covering his past services put through the court
on the island of Margarita, in October of 1542. He accompanied
Orellana on his voyage back to Spain and the capital and became
his associate in the preparations for the expedition to New Andalusia; but, having quarreled with his old commander, he separated
from the group and, I believe, went to Portugal. This Cristóbal

[168] See my note 9 to Friar Carvajal's *Account*.
[169] See my note 6 to Friar Carvajal's *Account*.

de Segovia is probably the same man whom Friar Carvajal in his *Account*, and afterwards the royal officials, called Maldonado, this being perhaps the second part of his family name.*

53.  SORIA (García de).—He was killed during the voyage by an Indian's arrow.[170]

54.  TAPIA (Alonso de).

55.  TAPIA (Francisco de).

56.  VARGAS (Juan de), a native of Estremadura.

57.  VERA (Friar Gonzalo de), of the Order of Mercedarians.— Friar Marcos Salmerón, in his *Recuerdos históricos*, etc. (Valencia, 1646), does not list the name of this brother of the Order of Mercedarians.

I should indeed be unjust if I did not also mention among the companions of Orellana two negroes who in the course of the voyage lent efficient service as oarsmen and whose names do not appear in any document.

It will be seen from the foregoing that of the fifty-seven Spanish soldiers† who set out with Orellana from Pizarro's camp three were killed by the Indians in the course of the voyage and that at least eleven died from illness.[171]

---

*[This is likewise presumably the same man whom Oviedo, in mentioning by name four of Orellana's companions with whom he talked in Santo Domingo at the conclusion of the voyage, calls "Cristóbal de Cáceres, a native of the town of Torrejón de Velasco" (Oviedo, Vol. 4, p. 573). In Oviedo's list of names of members of the expedition, the corresponding entry reads, however, "Cristóbal de Segovia, a native of Torrejón de Velasco."—EDITOR.]

[170] See my note 25 to Friar Carvajal's *Account*.

†[So says Medina, thus definitely ranking the two friars as soldiers.—EDITOR.]

[171] It is to be regretted that Friar Carvajal has neglected to tell us the names of these latter. Oviedo [Vol. 4, p. 385] affirms that there were eleven deaths in all, but he is undoubtedly mistaken in his count. There is no question with respect to the three killed by the Indians: these were Pedro de Empudia, Antonio de Carranza, and García de Soria. Deducting these three, we should have a remainder of eight; but as Friar Carvajal assures us that, out of these, seven died in Aparia, and as it is known that during the rest of the voyage the same fate overtook the two Alcántaras, Alvar González, and Mateo Rebolloso, who were still alive on the first of March, inasmuch as on this date they signed the summons presented to Orellana, it is evident that to the seven who died in Aparia there should be added these last four, the result being, consequently, a total of eleven men who died natural deaths during the voyage.

[Regarding the two Alcántaras see the footnote on No. 6 in the biographical notes above.]

Those who signed the petition addressed to Orellana on January 4, 1542, the day after the arrival of the expeditioners in Aparia (Document II [4], p. 254ff., *infra*) but did not sign the summons presented to him on March 1, a month after their departure from that place (Document II [7], p. 258ff. *infra*) are (exclusive of those who are known to have lived on after the departure, namely Antonio de Carranza, Friar Carvajal, Friar Gonzalo de Vera, and Francisco de Isásaga, and exclusive of Alonso Gómez, identified by Medina with Alonso Gutiérrez): (1) Juan de Aguilar, (2) Rodrigo de Arévalo, (3) Juan de Arnalte, (4) Sebastián de Fuenterrabía, (5) Alonso Gutiérrez, (6) Diego de Moreno, (7) Baltasar Osorio, (8) Sebastián Rodríguez. It seems improbable that the last-mentioned of these eight men was among the seven who, according to Carvajal's *Account (infra,*

p. 178), died in the village of Aparia (the Lesser), not only because Oviedo, who lists this man (p. 385), does not say that he died, but also because he (Sebastián Rodríguez) was, during the first few days spent in that village, in a state of health such that, as Friar Carvajal says (*infra*, p. 177), he was able to take an active part in the work of making nails, etc., to be used ultimately in the building of a new brigantine. With this name omitted, then, we have a list which at first sight might seem to be correct for the seven men who died in Aparia. Oviedo, in fact, explicitly states that Nos. 1, 4, 6, and 7 "died during the voyage" or "died of illness," but without specifying that they died in Aparia, although it seems fairly safe to assume that this latter was the case. (Medina states, in his biographical notes, that Nos. 4, 6, and 7 died in Aparia but does not give his authority; and his guess that Nos. 2 and 3 died during the voyage seems to be based on the absence of their signatures from the summons of March 1, coupled with the fact that he finds no further mention of these men.) It is not safe, however, to infer that Nos. 2, 3, and 5 are the other three men who died in Aparia (or that they died sometime during the voyage), inasmuch as Oviedo in listing them does not say that they died. On the other hand, to account for the other three men who died in Aparia out of the names which have come down to us, it is not possible to take any of the other four men whom Oviedo records as having died during the voyage, with the possible exception of the person whom he calls "Joanes," because all of these, with the exception just mentioned, signed the summons presented to Orellana a month after the departure from Aparia; and the same is true of the eight names found in the documents but unknown to Oviedo, namely Nos. 15, 24, 37, 43, 47, 50, 54, and 55 in Medina's biographical notes. The conclusion to be drawn is that there must have died in Aparia two, three, or more men whose names have not come down to us—a further reason for not accepting Medina's (or Carvajal's) figure of fifty-seven for the total number of Orellana's companions. Incidentally, in the version of Carvajal's story inserted by Oviedo in his *Historia*, etc., there is no statement to the effect that seven men died in Aparia.— EDITOR.]

# X

# ORELLANA'S EXPEDITION TO NEW ANDALUSIA

IT was stated above that Orellana and his companions made port on September 9 and 11, 1542, on the island of Cubagua. There they remained enjoying a rest they so well deserved after the fatigues and dangers[172] that they had experienced in that hard campaign of close on to two years from the time that they had departed from Quito and Guayaquil. The greater part of them returned, however, at the first opportunity to Peru to continue to play a rôle in the civil wars that were soon to sprinkle with Spanish blood the empire of the Incas, fighting under the royal banners against Gonzalo Pizarro, their old leader, and in the expeditions and "entries," as they were then called, which at that time afforded them an opportunity to satisfy still further their desire for adventure and enabled them to continue their search for wealth.

Orellana followed an entirely different course. The discovery so unexpectedly brought about by him and his soldiers; the great amount of information which he had obtained during his voyage regarding the vast extent and the wealth of the country; the great number of people that inhabited it—all contributed toward making him think that he was the person naturally called upon to undertake the exploration and conquest of those regions. But for this purpose it was necessary for him to give an account of everything to the King, and to persuade the latter to grant him the title of governor, which for a long time back had constituted the sole aspiration of his life. He needed, besides, to get together a certain amount of equipment indispensable for an enterprise of this magnitude, and this was something which he could procure only in Spain. Having resolved, then, to go to the seat of the home government, he chartered or bought a small ship in Trinidad[173]

[172] Oviedo relates how, "amidst their perils and hardships, besides their own special devotions they always called on and remembered Our Lady of Guadalupe, and they even vowed and promised to go on a pilgrimage to her shrine when it should please the Mother of God to give them an opportunity to do so" [*Historia general y natural de las Indias*, Vol. 4, p. 573].

[173] It is Garcilaso de la Vega (*Comentarios reales de los Incas*, Part II, Cordova, 1617, Book III, Ch. 4) [Markham translation, Hakluyt Society publications, First Series, No. 24, London, 1859, p. 13: see footnote 47, p. 30, *supra*] who informs us of this purchase made by Orellana, but without stating whether Orellana himself went to this island or whether he made his purchase through an agent. I am inclined to believe that he merely chartered the ship.

and, accompanied by the Comendador Enríquez, Cristóbal de Segovia, Alonso Gutiérrez, and Hernán Gutiérrez de Celis, he arrived in transit at the city of Santo Domingo on November 22, 1542,[174] continuing on his way to Spain as soon as it was possible.

Probably as the result of damage to his ship during the crossing, he was forced to land in Portugal, where the King of that country, who had heard of the expedition which Orellana had just brought to an end, detained him for fifteen or twenty days, "acquainting himself in very great detail with the facts in connection with this voyage of discovery and making advantageous offers to him in an effort to get him to stay there, it being his intention to make use of him in this matter . . . "[175] But the Spanish captain, far from yielding to such tempting offers and, apparently, confident now that his sovereign could not refuse him what a foreigner had already promised him, entered into an understanding there with a wealthy Portuguese, who took upon himself to furnish him a goodly supply of provisions when he should arrive at Cape Verde on his way to the province the governorship of which he hoped to obtain, on condition that Orellana would take along one of his sons on the expedition; and as soon as he could he continued his journey toward the Spanish capital, which was then Valladolid, where he arrived, at the latest, in the middle of May, 1543.[176]

The first impression produced by the account which he gave orally of his discovery was not as flattering as he had hoped. When he told how by sailing down a great river he had come out in the Atlantic, on the coast of Brazil, it was feared that that river fell within the limits of the territories assigned by Pope Alexander VI to Portugal, as shown by the most recent mariners' charts; and this fear was increased when they came to believe, and rightly so, that the river discovered by Orellana could be none other than the Marañón, the mouth of which was marked as clearly belonging to Portugal.[177]

This is why the secretary of Charles V, Juan de Sámano, declared that in his opinion Orellana's discovery did not seem to be of so much importance and that in the last analysis it would turn out to be more prejudicial than advantageous.[178]

[174] Oviedo, *Historia*, Vol. 4, p. 573. [On p. 384 Oviedo says Dec. 20. As neither of these dates was, as Oviedo says in both cases, a Monday, was it not Monday, Nov. 20?—EDITOR.]

[175] *The petition which Orellana presented*, *etc.*, reference on p. 323 of the present volume.

[176] This is deduced from the letter of Juan de Sámano to the "Comendador Mayor" of Leon, Francisco de los Cobos, dated May 31, 1543 [see *supra*, pp. 24–25.]

[177] See the opinions of the Council of the Indies, p. 323 of the present volume.

[178] Letter of Francisco de los Cobos, June 7, 1543. [See *supra*, p. 25. Medina says here: "Letter of," etc., but does he not mean: "Letter to," etc.?—EDITOR.]

Meanwhile Orellana was urged to submit a written and detailed account of his voyage, in which he could clear up in a precise manner the doubts raised in the Council with respect to the various serious questions regarding the geographical situation of the river, so that it might be determined whether or not it was included within the jurisdiction of Portugal. Orellana complied with what he was ordered to do, although it was considered that he had "not finished explaining the matter" [*infra*, p. 323] with respect to the point of controversy; and he presented at the same time as his account of his voyage a petition in which he declared that he had taken part in the exploration of the provinces of Peru and had been active in other parts of the Indies,[179] performing many services for the King in the various honorable commissions with which he had been intrusted, not only as captain, but as lieutenant-governor; he spoke of the expenses, amounting to more than forty thousand pesos, which he had incurred in connection with his preparations for going on the expedition to the regions of La Canela, and in general terms mentioned his departure from Pizarro's camp and his voyage down the river; "and because of the considerable amount of information which I had obtained," he said in conclusion, "regarding the great size and wealth of the country, and for the sake of serving God and Your Majesty and of exploring those vast provinces and bringing the peoples inhabiting them around to a knowledge of our holy Catholic faith, and of placing them under the rule of Your Majesty and of the Royal Crown of these realms of Castile, disregarding the danger to myself, and without [having in view] any personal gain whatsoever for myself, I launched forth on the adventure of trying to find out what there was in the said provinces, in the course of which enterprise there was discovered and there was performed [all] that which Your Majesty has become acquainted with through the account that I have laid before him covering it and [which] is also attested by several affidavits which I have with me; and considering the fact that the matter has been and [still] is as great [as], and [even] greater than, any matter ever [heard of] from the point of view of [extent of] population and [vastness of] country, and that the natives inhabiting it [i.e. this country] will [in this way] be able to come into

---

[179] This confirms, therefore, in a way that leaves no room for doubt, what I stated on p. 37 to the effect that he really had served in Nicaragua and perhaps in Mexico. It is to be regretted that Orellana did not present on this occasion the reports which he claimed he had brought with him from the Indies and in which his services were detailed in the regular form. His failure to present them undoubtedly explains why they are not to be found in the archives today.

[possession of] a knowledge of our holy Catholic faith, because the greater part of them are intelligent people, I beseech Your Majesty to see fit to give it to me as territory to be held by me as governor in order that I may explore it and colonize it on behalf of Your Majesty, and in case Your Majesty grants me the favors which I shall state below, I offer myself for undertaking what follows, for the sake of serving God and Your Majesty . . . " [infra, p. 321].

It would be useless to repeat these conditions here, as well as the expressions of opinion which they brought forth from the Councilors of the Indies, for the reader can see all this in Part III of the present volume; but I cannot refrain from setting forth the motives by which these men were guided when they decided to accept these conditions in the main.

With all the documents before it, the Council declared to the King that "according to the [said] account and [judged from] the location in which this river with the lands that he says he has discovered is, it might be a rich country and one by [the occupation of] which Your Majesty might be rendered a service and the Royal Crown of these realms be enhanced . . . " [infra, p. 323]; that some three or four years earlier the King of Portugal, thanks to the diligence of the treasurer Hernán Dálvarez, had built a fleet (which, however, had been wrecked) to go up the Amazon from the coast; that in the House of Trade in Seville it was rumored that as a consequence of Orellana's voyage another fleet was being fitted out for the purpose of penetrating up the river; "and it also seems quite likely to us," they added, "that, so far as may be judged from the indications that have been given out on the part of the King of France of a desire to look into matters connected with the Indies, if this thing should come to his notice he might have covetous designs in connection with it . . . " [infra, p. 323]; "and for this reason," they said in stating their findings, "it is the opinion of the greater part of the Council that it is advantageous to the service of Your Majesty that the banks of this river be explored and settled and taken possession of by Your Majesty, and that this be done within the shortest time and with the greatest amount of diligence possible, because, in addition to the service which is rendered to God Our Lord by the bringing of the natives of that land to a knowledge of our holy Catholic faith and evangelical law, upon which until now they have been without any enlightenment whatsoever, it is desirable in this way as tending toward the enhancement of the Royal Crown . . . " [*infra*, p. 323], and "it is the opinion of the majority of us that this [expedition of] exploration and colonization be carried out, and that it be intrusted to this [man] Orellana on account of his having discovered it [i.e. this river] and on account of his being informed on the subject . . . "[180] [*infra*, pp. 323–324].

At last, nine months after his arrival in Spain, Orellana succeeded in getting Prince Philip to accept the opinion of the Council of the Indies and grant him, on February 13, 1544, the royal decree which constituted the articles of agreement authorizing him to undertake the exploration and settling of New Andalusia. In this document the Monarch, after recalling in a few words the services rendered to the Crown by Orellana, the circumstances which had prevented him from going back to Pizarro's camp, and the laudable intentions which guided him in his desire to return to the regions that he had discovered, put upon him the obligation to take along on his new expedition: two hundred infantrymen and one hundred horsemen; the materials required for the construction of the ships needed for the purpose of proceeding up the river with the men and horses; eight friars who were to be selected for him by the Council of the Indies, in order that they might undertake the conversion and instruction of the natives, although he was forbidden to take along any of these latter as he was proceeding up the river, except such as might be indispensable as interpreters. Furthermore, it was stipulated that Orellana should attempt to build two towns, one just inside the entrance to the river, as soon as he should come upon the first inhabited region, at the spot which should seem most appropriate to him, to the friars, and to the royal officials, and the other at some distance inland; and he bound himself not to do anything to interfere with any Spanish captain who might be engaged in explorations in those regions, "so that there may be avoided," said the Prince, "those disturbances which have hitherto arisen out of such situations, both in Peru and in other parts . . . " [*infra*, p. 330]; and much less was he to do anything in violation of the treaties and agreements concluded with Portugal with regard to the established line of demarcation between jurisdictions in the Indies and to the apportioning of those territories.

[180] From this last opinion the Councilor Bernal dissented, stating that, Orellana being a poor man, "as they tell him that he is, and one trained in the kinds of warfare that have been practiced in the Indies, and taking along with him from them [i.e. from the Indies] men accustomed to that sort of thing, going on the expedition with arms and under pressure of want, he [i.e Doctor Bernal] does not believe that he will live up to the serious instructions that will be given to him . . . " [*infra*, p. 326].

On the other hand Orellana was given permission and power to conquer and settle, in the name of the Crown of Castile and Leon, the regions that stretched towards the south from the river that he had discovered, for a distance of two hundred leagues as the crow flies, with the right to select these lands three years after having commenced his explorations, on condition that these lands should be inside the lines of demarcation of Spanish jurisdiction. He was to have the title of governor and captain-general and have authority over all that he might discover, with a salary of five thousand ducats from the day the fleet should sail from Sanlúcar, the said salary to be paid to him out of the profits derived from the country that should be conquered and settled, plus one twelfth of the royal revenue from the same, but with the proviso that this should not exceed a million maravedis per year, this income to devolve also upon his heirs; together with the persons whom he was to take along with him, he was to be exempt for a period of ten years from the payment of customs taxes; and finally, he was authorized to take eight negro slaves across with him.

There was also attached to the articles of agreement, as was the custom in such cases, a summary of the laws and ordinances relative to the kind treatment he was to extend to the Indians; and with this condition duly stated, the Prince added by way of conclusion: "I do declare and promise that these articles of agreement and everything embodied in them will be lived up to in your favor, as a whole and in all details, in the form in which it is [all] stated above: and in the event of your not executing and fulfilling it [i.e. your part] in this way, His Majesty shall not be bound to live up to or fulfill in your favor that which is stated above, or any part of it; rather he will issue orders to punish you and to proceed against you as against a person who does not live up to and fulfill [what he has agreed to] and [who] transgresses the commands of his king and natural master."[181]

And Orellana, on his part, five days later submitted before a notary his acceptance of all that had been stipulated, pledging his person and his worldly goods that he would carry out all the obligations imposed upon him, with the express renunciation of the right to resort to any laws that might favor him, "in order that by the application of the full rigor of the law, which [in its working] shall be the quickest and most expeditious [possible],

<hr>

[181] *Articles of agreement which were drawn up in favor of Francisco de Orellana*, etc., pp. 328–334 of the present volume: see p. 334.

he may be forced to execute it [i.e. his part of the agreement], just as if by the final decision of a duly qualified judge he were sentenced to do so and [as if] the said decision were handed down in a case tried [in court] and allowed by him . . . "[182]

In addition, Orellana was given the titles. each independently of the other, of Adelantado[183] and of Governor and Captain-General, together with the command of the two fortresses that he might build subject to approval by the royal officials.[184] Other appointments were made as follows: Juan García de Samaniego, inspector; Juan de la Cuadra, keeper of accounts; Francisco de Ulloa, treasurer; Cristóbal Maldonado, chief constable, this appointment being at the request of Orellana; Vicencio de Monte, revenue collector, to whom were issued full instructions to which he was to conform in the discharge of his office and who was also given the title of magistrate of the town that was to be founded; and, lastly, the Dominican friar Pablo de Torres, inspector-general, "so that he may observe," reads his appointment, "how our Governor adheres to and carries out the articles of agreement which we ordered to be drawn up in his favor . . . ," this friar being intrusted, moreover, with a secret packet which contained the appointment of the person who should succeed Orellana in case the latter died.[185]

Thus Orellana at last saw his aspirations to a position of command satisfied, although in reality he could not have felt very highly flattered when he found out that there had been placed at his side a spy in disguise who, under the title of inspector-general, was to observe his actions and to whom he was actually subordinated in the exercise of his functions as commander.

But this was not the worst of it. He was authorized, it is true, to undertake the conquest of the regions bathed by the Amazon; but the Monarch, on his part, did not contribute in any manner whatsoever toward lightening the burdens of the expedition, the weight of which was thus to fall entirely upon Orellana, whose purse was not very well lined. The Monarch's action in leaving Orellana in such a plight was no fit reply to the warning issued by the Council when it pointed out the advisability of organizing

[182] *Declaration in writing by which Francisco de Orellana bound himself*, etc., pp. 334–335 of the present volume: see p. 335.

[183] Royal decree of February 17, 1544.

[184] Royal decree of March 7, 1544. [These appointments were made in conformity with the requests of Orellana himself (see *infra*, p. 321) and with the recommendations of the Council of the Indies (see *infra*, p. 324), which considered Orellana's various requests.—EDITOR.]

[185] There is no record in the documents of the name of the person who had been chosen to replace Orellana in the command.

the expedition without delay if it was thought desirable not to let the French or the Portuguese (in the case of these latter there was not the slightest doubt) get ahead of them.  At first Orellana remained silent, perhaps so as not to lose all, although very soon he saw that he would have to make known to the King the difficult situation that had been created for him by the refusal to give him any assistance.  Having transferred his headquarters without a moment's loss of time to Seville so as to start right in on his preparations, relying now on his own strength alone, sometime prior to May of that year he had already written to the King reiterating the request that he had formerly made to the effect that he, the King, should give orders that he be provided with the guns needed to arm his ships; "and in reply to this I was told," he states, "that there was no source from which they could be supplied . . . " [*infra*, p. 336].  Nor was any better reception accorded to his petition that he be permitted to press the sailors that he found ready at hand into going along with him; and he met with even less success in getting some Portuguese pilot to accompany him,[186] for among the Spaniards none could be found who knew that part of the coast where lay the mouth of the river to which he was going.  But all of Orellana's negotiations with this end in view and his claims of advantages to be gained thereby turned out to be of no avail, in spite of the fact that he did not tire of telling how important it was to take along a person who knew that coast: a serious error on his part, founded on a diffidence carried to extremes, destined in the end to contribute to the complete failure of the expedition organized at such a great cost and with so much effort.

Without becoming discouraged at these refusals, Orellana with all the speed that he could muster carried on the preparations for his departure, and by May he was able to give notice that he had two galleons and two caravels ready in the Guadalquivir, that the smaller boats which he needed for going up the river were being built, and that, consequently, his departure was bound not to be delayed very long; but this announcement was nothing more than an illusion created by his enthusiastic imagination, which caused him to consider as already overcome the great mass of difficulties with which he still had to contend.

[186] On the other hand, the Prince ordered the Councilors of the Indies to speak to the pilot Francisco Rodríguez to get him to go with Orellana, offering him flattering financial returns (Letter of the Council, June 30, 1544).  Without doubt it is to him that Orellana referred when he said in his letter to the King under date of May 30 of that year that the man who had been recommended to him had been spoken to, in fact, but that "this man talks less intelligently about the coast than any other . . . " [*infra*, p. 337].

As a matter of fact, on the very day that he had set as the probable date of his departure he found it necessary to write to the King, being worried by the whisperings which he supposed people had caused to reach the Monarch's ears relative to the bad treatment which, so it was said, he was dealing out to those who were associated with him, it being rumored also that "other things are being done which do not seem right . . . " [*infra*, p. 338]; and, fearful lest he should be molested for these reasons, on top of his protestations that he was a loyal servant of the royal person he exclaimed: " . . . if anything more is desired in addition to what I have already stated, [let it be recalled that] I little needed to pledge my person to the extent of more than four thousand ducats, as up till now I have done, for the sake of putting in complete order the affairs of the expedition . . . " [*infra*, p. 338].

With obstacles of this sort he was now beginning to struggle when there arrived in Seville the inspector Friar Pablo de Torres. Some echo of the remarks made by Orellana's detractors must have reached the King's ears, showing that Orellana had not been mistaken in his fears, when under date of August 23 a royal decree with special instructions was dispatched to the Dominican directing him to report on "what equipment Orellana has on hand and what ship-stores and other supplies he has procured, and whether the enterprise is in a state [of preparation] such that he will be able to go ahead with it . . . ;" " . . . and if you see that he will not be able to bring this enterprise to a successful conclusion," the decree went on to say, "do not give an opportunity to the men to ruin themselves in that city by spending their fortunes while waiting to go off in that fleet, nor allow money to be taken away from them [as the price to be paid by them] in order that they may be taken along in it, as it is said that up to now they [i.e. the organizers of the expedition] have been doing."

In answer to this, Friar Torres said: " . . . let Your Majesty be informed that on account of his poverty the aforesaid, having spent on expenses in connection with the expedition all that he has and [ever] did have in the form of funds in order to feed them and buy ships and not charter them, has been receiving money from those who were planning to go along, . . . as is customarily done in [the organizing of] other expeditions . . . If Your Majesty is of the opinion that this must not be done, the expedition will not be able to be carried out, for it is in this way that they are all carried out, even though the fitter-out may be rich . . . "

[*infra*, p. 342]. He then went on to state that already the provisions had begun to be put on board and that it was hoped that in the coming month of September everything would be ready for the departure. " . . . and owing to the dissension and to the secret and sly factions that have come into existence here between Maldonado[187] and those who accepted his views on the one hand, and the rest who were for the Adelantado and [the real interests of] the enterprise on the other, it was brought about that not only did certain ones, who were persons that had been helping a great deal toward the success of this enterprise, go off with the first fleet that departed for the Indies, but also many have become exasperated who are here in Seville [and] who had made up their minds to go, [and] who are [now] hesitating until they see whether the vessels are finally to be fitted out, and [this applies] even to many who both in Granada and in the rest of Andalusia were determined to go . . . " [*infra*, p. 341].

This situation which his enemies had created for Orellana was what most preoccupied him in the midst of all his labors, without his being able to discern whence came those shots fired by such skilful and cunning hands, as we may see from his own words:

" . . . and since in other [letters] I have given a long account of how in my negotiations I have had powerful enemies, and [these] in various connections, bent on obstructing an enterprise such as this one is . . . , I shall not go into details any more than to remark that those who have attempted to achieve this [i.e. the obstructing of the enterprise], now that they perceive the excellent progress that is being made in connection with whatever is needed, are at present pursuing very much more eagerly their evil purpose and intention, all to the detriment of the service of Your Majesty and to the demoralization of the men whom I am taking along; [in all of] which, because it is being done in such a concealed and tricky manner, there cannot be designated any particular person, [nor can one go] beyond speaking from conjectures and emphasizing the harm which their works are doing, because, if certain things have not been fully worked out in short order, it has been on account of this worm which has been in our midst . . . " [*infra*, p. 339]. •

In these terms he complained to the King of the obstacles that kept presenting themselves to him at every step, and to offset

187 This is Cristóbal Maldonado, or Cristóbal de Segovia, Orellana's former companion on his voyage down the Amazon [see No. 52 in the list of names, p. 121, *supra.*]

all this he limited himself to begging the King to have confidence in him, "since at all times," he said, "it has been and is my intention and determination to serve Your Majesty with every solicitude and with perfect fidelity . . . " [*infra*, p. 340].

In consequence, then, of these "manifestations of passion and the prattlings" [*infra*, p. 343], as the Dominican said, the preparations for the enterprise did not proceed with anything like the speed which would have been desirable and which Orellana had had visions of at the beginning. The "unusual weather conditions" [*infra*, p. 343] that had prevailed since May; the departure of the fleet for New Spain, in which had embarked some of those who had originally signed on for Orellana's voyage; the failure of the men recruited in Granada, in the Almendralejo,* and in other places to come to Seville; the payment that remained to be made of part of the price of the ships; the delay in getting all the food supplies loaded on the ships—all these were circumstances that made it necessary for Friar Torres, having complied with the orders which had been sent to him, to sum up the situation, in his letter to the King, as follows: "As to my replying definitely whether there exists an absolute certainty that this voyage is to become a reality, I really don't know; but of the probability of it I am convinced, for there are the required ships for four hundred men with ample room, [there are] foodstuffs and provisions to the value of two thousand ducats and more . . . " [*infra*, p. 343].

In the meantime this situation was beginning to worry the King, who, not content with asking Friar Torres for reports, turned also for the same purpose to the Councilors of the Indies. These latter informed him that in order to determine what stage had been reached in the fitting out of the fleet and what equipment had already been procured for the undertaking, they had called in Friar Torres, Orellana, and the royal officials who were to go along with him, and that at this meeting these persons had presented a full statement of what they already had and what they still lacked. With this memorandum before them, they reported that Orellana still owed more than one thousand ducats on the price of a ship of upwards of two hundred and forty tons and a galleon of ninety-six and a caravel of seventy-two; that when the passengers who kept coming in to take ship learned about this and found that the provisions were not yet on board and, what was worse, that

*[The Almendralejo is a region in the Guadiana basin of southern Estremadura centering about the town of the same name that lies about 30 miles southeast of Badajoz.—EDITOR.]

Orellana had no sailors, they did not dare to pay in their passage money; that he was not finding merchants to help him out and could not even count any longer on a certain person who had agreed to supply him with funds up to the amount of two thousand ducats; that Maldonado, one of "those who had gone down the river" [*infra*, p. 351] with Orellana, still remained in disagreement with him; and, finally, that others who had come there with the intention of going aboard, seeing that the departure was being delayed, had returned to their homes.

What was most needed, after money, was pilots. Orellana had engaged one Francisco Sánchez of Cadiz, a good sailor, but one who had not been on the New World coast; and a certain Portuguese who was familiar with that coast but who, by reason of the fact that he was a foreigner, would normally not be permitted to go, was being retained by Orellana until permission to accompany him might be obtained. The good name of the enterprise being now marred, the Councilors were quite right in fearing that in the end the expedition could not set sail.[188]

Orellana was in these straits when his stepfather Cosme de Chaves came to his aid, placing on sale thirty thousand maravedis that he had in annuities and quit-rents, in order to raise the eleven hundred ducats that were needed right away; and, not having found purchasers in Seville, he went and found some in Trujillo, where his family was located. Some Genoese merchants and others also offered to advance funds for the enterprise under certain conditions, and the search for money was continued "by the giving of bills of exchange, or through loans, or by means of notes payable out of the profits of the enterprise . . . " [*infra*, p. 347]; and they even went so far as to take over great quantities of merchandise and sell it immediately at less than cost price, all with the object of getting together the funds that were still lacking to finish paying for the ships and supplying them with the provisions needed for the expedition. But all this constantly fell to the ground before the occult machinations traceable "to a [single] person or to [several] persons," as Friar Torres asserted, "who are striving either to take charge of this enterprise themselves or to have friends of theirs take charge of it, or to some person to whom it is irksome that the Emperor our master be rendered this service and enjoy the profit that is expected to be forthcoming from this source and who finds no better expedient for the time being than to wreck this expedition from the start . . . " [*infra*, p. 348].

[188] Letter of September 11, 1544.

At last, at the beginning of October, Chaves arrived with the funds that were to be used to finish paying for the ships, though this did not mean the cessation of negotiations with merchants and private individuals in an effort to procure the money that was still needed for other purposes. In this way the enterprise was now in a state of preparation such that they could take on board the persons whom it had not been thought desirable to admit up till now or who were disposed to enlist for the expedition, among whom, as a matter of fact, figured certain individuals with objectionable antecedents to whom the inspector-general requested that access to the fleet be denied, giving as a reason the fact that "on other occasions, no heed having been paid to a contingency of this sort, mutiny and revolt have broken out in some expeditions among those who had gone along on them . . . " [*infra*, p. 346].

Such were the circumstances when there was received from Portugal a piece of news which heightened, if that was possible, the critical state of the affairs of the expedition. It was reported, in fact, that great preparations were being made in that country for an expedition to the Amazon in the name of a wealthy Castilian who had arrived from Peru and that among the organizers of the expedition had figured Don Juan de Almeda, son of the Count of Brandes, who later had been replaced by Don Juan de Sandi, generally looked upon as a swaggerer and reputed to be living constantly surrounded in his own home by cutthroats and troublemakers. It was said that the number of ships fitted out was four and that they were equipped with plenty of bronze guns, powder, stores, and victuals in abundance, and that the organizers were looking about for men who had been in those parts; and it was even rumored that they had spoken to one of Orellana's former companions on the Amazon voyage, who, in consequence of his having killed a man in Seville, had fled and was then in Lisbon.

This furnished the inspector a good excuse for begging the King to advance in his turn the money that was still needed and to supply the ships with the guns that they lacked, in order that Orellana might resist the attack of the Portuguese fleet which he was bound to meet; for, as the inspector very fittingly and wisely remarked, at times an attempt to economize costs dear. The Councilors of the Indies, in their turn, advised the Monarch on October 7, 1544, that they had learned from Orellana that he had received news, through a letter from a gentleman in Lisbon written to another in Seville, that the King of Portugal was preparing a fleet of four ships "for the Great River and the province of the Amazons"; and they stated that they were reporting this in order that in a matter so important he might issue such orders as he might think best adapted to the interests of his service, "because it would be a great nuisance if the expedition which is being made ready here were to find the Portuguese expedition inside the river, inasmuch as that river and that province fall within the line of demarcation of [territories belonging to] His Majesty"; and they added that they were hastening as much as possible to get the ships under way, giving all the encouragement and assistance that they could, and working with certain merchants, both Spaniards and foreigners, to get them to help Orellana, as some had offered to do, asking that for every hundred ducats of capital so advanced they be granted the earnings of one peon.

In regard to other particulars in connection with the expedition the reports that kept coming in to the Council were not very complimentary. The treasurer, Francisco de Ulloa, in a letter dated November 14, 1544, stated that, having gone to Seville to see where they were at toward getting the expedition off, discovered that Orellana had closed the transaction with the Genoese, but had accepted conditions to which he, the treasurer, finding them to be too hard, had not been willing to subscribe; that Orellana had under construction two brigantines to guide the ships up the river; and that the Adelantado had assured him that within a short time he would be equipped with all the rest that was needed for the expedition. "Any further clearer account," he concluded, "I am unable to give at this point, because in truth I do not understand either Orellana or the affairs of this fleet, nor do I believe that he understands them himself."

"As regards the affairs of our own expedition," added Friar Torres in his turn at about this time, "may Your Majesty be informed that the Adelantado has married,[189] despite my attempts

[189] When did Orellana's marriage take place? In a letter addressed to the King by Friar Torres under date of September 11, 1544, the following words occur: " . . . people are approaching the Adelantado here with marriage proposals . . . " [*infra*, p. 345]; and in the letter dated November 20, from which I am quoting, the friar informs the King that the event had taken place, just as Orellana himself, in a communication dated one day later, announced to the King in the following terms: " . . . so as better to perpetuate myself and be able to serve God Our Lord and Your Majesty in that land, I married . . . " [*infra*, p. 339]. The ceremony must have been celebrated, therefore, a few days prior to November 21, 1544.

The historians do not say what the name of Orellana's wife was, nor to what rank she belonged, although Friar Torres asserts that she was "exceedingly poor" [see below, p. 145]. I, however, have succeeded in finding out that her name was Ana de Ayala. She must have been very young when she married Orellana, because twenty-seven years later she declared [p. 375, *infra*] that she was only thirty-five—an obvious exaggeration which may be attributed to coquettishness on

to persuade him [not to], which were many and well founded,
because they did not give him any dowry whatsoever, I mean not a
single ducat, and he wants to take his wife along over there, and
even one or two sisters-in-law [also]: he alleged as an argument
on his side that he could not go off without a woman, and [that it
was] in order to have a female consort [that] he wanted to marry;
to all this I replied at considerable length in the manner that one
was bound to reply as a Christian, and in a manner that harmonized
with the interests of this enterprise, to the end that we might
not burden the expedition with women and with expenses on their
account.   He has been considering appointing as his [lieutenant]-
general and as his deputy one of the persons who arranged his
marriage, not a suitable man for the office or even a suitable one
to go along on the voyage, over which project of appointment
there certainly would have been some hard feelings if it had not
been forestalled.   He fixed his choice for a campmaster upon a
Genoese, in defiance of the laws and of the will of all, who are vexed
at the setting of an Italian over these men; at first the plan as discussed was to have him go along [merely] as the representative of
the Genoese to collect their shares [of the profits] which they are
demanding, and for this purpose permission had to be asked
of Your Majesty on account of his being a foreigner, and on top
of this he [i.e. Orellana] made him campmaster, and they tell me
that he handed some funds over to him; he said nothing to me
about this, and I reprimanded him before all the officials for this
and for other things.   Of everything that needs to be done for
this expedition and for the directing of it I shall notify Your Majesty
just as soon as he shall give orders as to what is to be done with
regard to the articles of agreement proposed by the Genoese"
[*infra*, pp. 351–352].

And as a climax to all these causes for discontent it was discovered that proper care had not been exercised in the purchasing
of the ships, and that the largest of them had to be rejected "because
it was found to be unseaworthy, and at the time when there were
funds available to finish paying for it," says Friar Torres, "I
insisted on looking it over thoroughly and I found it to be damaged,
and already certain other individuals knew about that and had not

her part, or to carelessness on the part of the scrivener who took down her statement, but an
exaggeration which in any case proves what I claim.  After seeing her husband die on board the
brigantine on which she had gone a certain distance up the Amazon with him, she reached port
with the other survivors on the island of Margarita, whence she went to Nombre de Dios and
later to Panama, probably with the intention of reclaiming the property that her husband had
left behind him in Guayaquil.  She was still living in 1572.

told me about it; but they were not among those who were to take part in the enterprise, and I reprimanded those who had purchased it [demonstrating to them] that they had not purchased one fulfilling the conditions stipulated, and [yet] when I came here they told me that it was sound and in good condition and that there was no defect in it; the purchase was made without plan, without order, absolutely blindly, and with little understanding: at present the Adelantado and those who sold it to him are litigating, and this is not as I should advise, because we are much to blame and there is not being done what needs to be done for the enterprise and we are wasting time on lawsuits . . . " [*infra*, p. 350]. It therefore became necessary to purchase another ship to replace the useless one, and for this purpose they took a very much smaller one which was scarcely half the size of the other.

While Orellana was being harassed by these new worries there arrived in Seville that Don Juan de Sandi who called himself the captain of the Portuguese fleet which was to go to the Marañón and whose presence here was inspired, it was feared, by a desire to come to spy on what was being done in the way of preparations on the part of Orellana or perhaps to find a way of taking away one or another of the Spaniards who might be familiar with the river; but when the Portuguese "captain" had returned, very shortly after, to the port of Santa María,* where his galleon lay at anchor, Orellana offered to arrest him, using his own captains who were there, because this individual was going about "like a cautious man, with an escort of ten or twelve men . . . "[190] And, as a matter of fact, this suspicious person was arrested and brought to Seville, his galleon in the meantime being attached, and he was set free only when it was believed that no harm could now come from him.[191]

And so at last, after all these hardships, vexations, toils, and struggles, occasioned for the most part by the absolute lack of protection afforded him by the Monarch, by the scanty means at his disposal for carrying out an enterprise which flattered his ambition but which was beyond his strength, and in no small part also, it must be said in all justice, by the limited talent as an organizer that he displayed during the whole month of March, 1545, in view of the fact that he had now been engaged in prepara-

---

*[A harbor on the northern shore of the Bay of Cadiz, about 30 miles by sea southeast of Sanlúcar de Barrameda, which was to be the port of departure of Orellana's ships (see below).—EDITOR.]

[190] Letter of the Council, December 31, 1544.

[191] Letter of the Royal Officials, April 4, 1545.

tions for more than a year, Orellana succeeded in getting his ships as far as Sanlúcar,* ready to set sail. Before he could give the signal for departure there remained one last formality to which he had to submit, but an indispensable one in such cases: the inspection which the royal officials were to make in the name of the King. The instructions which these men received in this case read that, if as a result of the examination which they were to make it was found that Orellana had complied with the stipulations in the matter of what he was ordered to take along with him, they should allow him to depart; and that, if the contrary was the case, he should be detained until such time as the Monarch, after being informed of the circumstances, should make a decision. In order to carry out their instructions the officials got in touch with Friar Torres, who was at the time in Sanlúcar, and when he had come to Seville they proceeded, in conjunction with other functionaries, to make their inspection;† "and because we concluded," they said, "that the vessels lacked a certain amount of equipment and a certain number of guns, and likewise certain supplies, we gave the Adelantado a statement of what we thought that he still lacked, in order that he might have the matter attended to, because without it [i.e. what they still lacked] the ships were not in condition to sail as they ought to . . . " [infra, p. 353]. They also discovered that the three hundred men that he was to take along were not all on hand,[192] nor more than twenty-four out of the hun-

---

*[Port at the mouth of the Guadalquivir River, about 55 miles below Seville.—EDITOR.]

†[Obviously this inspection took place in Sanlúcar, whither Friar Torres, who had been ordered by the officials to come all the way back to Seville in order that they might be sure to meet him (see infra, p. 353), had returned with the officials.—EDITOR.]

[192] At this point it is not out of place to attempt to determine how many companions Orellana took along on his expedition. Oviedo says that he sailed from Sanlúcar with more than four hundred men (Historia de las Indias, Vol. 4, p. 390); López de Gómara says: "At last he gathered together five hundred men in Seville and started out . . . " (Historia general de las Indias, ed. Rivadeneyra, p. 210); and Garcilaso de la Vega (Comentarios reales de los Incas, Part II, Book III, Ch. 4 [Markham translation, p. 14]) states that they were more than five hundred in number. Muñoz Ternero, in the petition which forms the beginning of the judicial inquiry covering his past services, likewise asserts that there were five hundred men in the expedition. [This statement is not included in the extracts from this document published by Medina: see infra, pp. 361 ff.— EDITOR.] Francisco de Guzmán (see p. 358f. of the present volume), whom Herrera follows word for word throughout his account of Orellana's second expedition (Historia general de los hechos de los castellanos, Decade VII, Book III, Ch. 8), says that "he started out with four ships complete, on board which he carried away four hundred fighting men . . . " And lastly, Juan de Peñalosa (p. 374 of the present volume) declares that Orellana "started out from the realms of Spain to undertake the said conquest and exploration with four hundred and fifty men and four captains . . . "—an assertion corroborated by Ana de Ayala, wife of Orellana, and by Antonio Pérez de Vivero.

In my opinion, these figures are greatly exaggerated. In the report on the inspection made by Friar Torres this important detail is not given; but from the one which the royal officials made a short time previously it can be clearly seen, as I state in the text, that in April, 1545, that is to say when everything was ready for the departure, Orellana had not yet on board the three hundred

dred horses. To this Orellana replied that he had the men scattered throughout Seville and Sanlúcar and the surrounding country; that in the Canary and Cape Verde Islands he expected to take on the balance of the horses; that as regards the small boats that he was supposed to build, he had all the material necessary for them including the nails, and also competent shipmasters, while as for the lumber and rigging, these were to be obtained much more readily at the mouth of the river, where he proposed to build the boats; that in addition to this he was taking along with him the lumber all cut and the rigging for two brigantines; that as for caravels for going up the river, the ships on which the expeditioners were sailing could serve for this purpose perfectly well; and finally that, in regard to the eight friars, these men were still in Seville awaiting the hour of departure of the fleet, and he would not fail to take them along.

But these explanations did not convince the royal officials, particularly as they could plainly see that pilots and shipmasters were still lacking; that the majority of the sailors still available, after they (the officials) had caused to be discharged those who turned out to be Englishmen and Portuguese, were Flemings and Germans; that the master of the flagship was a Ragusan, with whom they did not dare to use the same procedure, aware as they were that if they did so there would not remain on the ships a single person capable of keeping them under control; and, finally, that there was still needed at least a thousand ducats for the purchase of things that the expeditioners still had to procure. In consequence of all this, the officials found themselves obliged to notify Orellana

men that he was supposed to take along according to the terms of his contract: "and . . . [as for] the total of three hundred men, he had that many there in Sanlúcar and in Seville and in the villages of the above-mentioned region . . . " [*infra*, p. 353], referring, apparently, to the Canary and Cape Verde Islands or, perhaps, to Sanlúcar. This is conclusive evidence that they were not on board the ships. In this connection one must take into consideration what we already know about the innumerable difficulties with which Orellana had to contend in rounding up his men, so that, even if it be granted that what he declared to the royal officials was true, it seems to me quite probable that he could not have taken along more than a bare fifty in addition to the three hundred which he had sworn to take.

This estimate of mine may also be checked up by means of a study of the statistics regarding those who died during the voyage, according to the above-mentioned account of Guzmán. He tells us that of the 400 men who sailed from Spain, Orellana lost 98 in Cape Verde, 77 on the Brazilian coast, 57 in the Amazon, and later, 17 more, or a total of 249. To this number it is necessary to add 50 men who remained in Cape Verde, and 28 in places over on the other side when he separated from them to go up the river; so that there would have remained with him to man the brigantine in which he made the trip 73 men, seemingly too many, because those who really did accompany him and who later reached the Island of Margarita, although their number is not known with accuracy, could not, perhaps, have been more than 30 all told, when one considers both the capacity of the boat and the number of those who reached the Island of Margarita—a number which was small, according to a letter from the Audiencia of Santo Domingo, which I shall mention later.

that, under penalty of being fined ten thousand ducats and of being deprived of the commissions and favors that had been bestowed upon him, he was not to leave the port until the King should so order. This decision was communicated to him in complete secrecy, "because, if the men had learned that we were ordering him to be held back," said the officials, "they would have all left him and the expedition would have been ruined" [infra, p. 354]. And they summed up the situation by venturing the opinion "that, if this expedition is not sent on its way within a short time, it will wear itself out of its own accord and will become disintegrated, because, since the men have been here for so long a time already, they are quite exhausted and broken down" [infra, p. 354].

The Monarch approved in full the decisions of his delegates, seeing to it, in consequence thereof, that just as soon as Orellana should have made up for what he still lacked, "they should let him go on his way . . . " [infra, p. 358], and ordering Orellana in particular to take away from Vicencio de Monte and his brother the commissions of lieutenant and chief constable respectively with which he had invested them, and not to give them to any foreigner; furthermore, permission to accompany the expedition or even go on board the ships was to be denied to such persons as Friar Torres should designate.

In order to ascertain whether Orellana had carried out all that he had been ordered to do, the royal officials, one month after their first investigation, on May 5, 1545, ordered Friar Torres, in company with the supervisor of all ships bound for the Indies, to make a second inspection of the fleet, "with the understanding," reads the text of the order, "that you shall not allow him to put on the aforesaid ships or take along with him any pilot or master or other person who is French, or English, or Portuguese; and as regards the natives [i.e. Spaniards] that he is to take, even though you do not find the number complete, you shall not stop him from starting out on his voyage; and if he be not provided with other equipment as we have prescribed and commanded, you shall not send him off, and you shall advise us at once regarding the matter, so that proper action may be taken."*

In fulfilment of these orders Friar Torres and the other functionaries designated for that purpose presented themselves on board the ships on May 9 and proceeded to make an inventory of the supplies, equipment, etc., interrogating under oath various

---

*[Pp. 269–270 of the published version of the document cited below in footnote 194.—EDITOR.]

witnesses;[193] and as soon as their task was completed, they went to Sanlúcar in search of Orellana, who had not been found on any of the ships, in order to instruct him not to depart until the judges should see the result of the inspection; but in Sanlúcar they found no news of him save that he had gone off to the ships. During the night of this same day, which was Saturday, the inspector Rodríguez went aboard the ships but still failed to find Orellana; and in view of this, Friar Torres, on the afternoon of the following day, issued orders to the pilots whose special duty was to take ships over the bar not to lend their services, under heavy penalty, in taking the ships out; but it was all to no avail in the end, because on Monday, May 11th, at 10 o'clock, the four ships sailed two leagues outside the port, and there they remained anchored until six in the evening, when they hoisted their sails and stood out to the open sea.[194]

In this manner Friar Torres was obliged to remain on land, and with this excuse he took upon himself to write to the King and give him certain details regarding Orellana's flight, the condition in which the fleet was, and the fears that he entertained as to the fate which he suspected awaited Orellana. These are interesting details which I must record here before following the fugitive in his disastrous enterprise, begun under auspices as sad as they were lamentable.

This new letter informed the King that the accounts presented by Vicencio de Monte were false and that he, Friar Torres, had told Orellana that he guaranteed that he could point out a shortage of more than twelve hundred ducats in the three thousand which Orellana had received from the Genoese if he, Orellana, would allow him to examine these accounts. Friar Torres added that it seemed quite apparent to him that there was collusion between Orellana and the Genoese; that neither party could account for the money intended to be used in chartering ships; that the fleet had slipped away without having taken sufficient supplies on

[193] Orellana's ships were the following:

The caravel *Guadalupe*, which had on board as pilot Gil Gómez, a Portuguese, and a crew of ten others, master and sailors all told.

The Galician ship named *San Pablo*, which carried four culverins, being the only one, apparently, that had guns.

The ship *Bretón*, with a crew of 18 men, sailors and cabin boys, only two among them being Spaniards.

The flagship, which had a crew of 16 men, counting sailors and cabin boys.

[194] *Inspection of Francisco de Orellana's fleet*, published on pp. 268–281 of Vol. 42 (Madrid, 1884) of Torres de Mendoza's *Colección de documentos inéditos relativos al descubrimiento . . . de América y Oceanía*, with numerous errors of the kind that are frequent in this collection.

board, notwithstanding the contrary assertions of Orellana who said that he was taking along more than enough money to fit himself out after getting out to sea; and that it was known already that in their course thus far the expeditioners had seized a caravel and sacked it, "and this," he averred, "is what they will do with all those that they can lay hands on, because they are not carrying any kind of supplies . . . "[195]

And in another letter of the day before he had put down statements to the same effect: that the fleet "had gone [down to Sanlúcar] as thoroughly stripped as if it had been plundered . . . " [*loc. cit.*, p. 285]; that, having been listed as one of the persons to go on board the ships, he had left Seville for that purpose, and on arriving at Sanlúcar had found that the sails of one of the ships had been sequestered up to that day, and that in order to get them out they had had to sell some of their supplies; that on his last visit of inspection he had found the fleet as thoroughly dismantled as if it had been plundered by the French or the Turks; that he had sent for Orellana, and that the latter and all his men had shut themselves up on board the ships; that during the night from Saturday to Sunday they had gone ashore to steal cows, calves, sheep, and chickens, leaving the shepherds, etc., wounded; that on Sunday afternoon Orellana had sent word to him to come on board, and that on Monday, as the constable was going to put a certain exiled individual on board, the persons manning the ships, on seeing the constable with the rod of justice in his hand in the small boat, had hoisted sail, without having any licensed pilots or masters among them, without taking off the Portuguese and other persons who had been forbidden to go, without having assigned sailors or passengers to their proper places, without arms or munitions, with rigging made for the most part out of esparto grass; in short, with such limited equipment that, to quote Friar Torres' own words, "no organizer of an expedition would let him go [even such a short distance as] from here to Naples. Prior to this I lodged a protest with him, which he signed, as did also two others besides him, and I have it, and his answer along with it, and, to make a long story short, I do not wish to relate the infinite errors and frauds that have been perpetrated in connection

---

[195] Letter dated May 20, 1545. [This letter, and the one dated May 19 which is summarized and in part quoted by Medina in his next two paragraphs, have been printed, in inverse chronological order, in the above-mentioned volume (42) of Torres de Mendoza's *Colección de documentos inéditos . . . América y Oceanía*, pp. 282–290, in a text which appears to contain many errors (cf. Medina's remark in footnote 194 above). For the passage here quoted see p. 282.—EDITOR.]

with this enterprise; and the one who has completely ruined it is Amonte (*sic*), who has made himself rich out of the money of the Genoese, through charterings, through deals, and the Adelantado has been putting up with all this, or else between themselves they are dividing up the money and the profits. How can the fleet be well fitted out if to his own wife, [who is] exceedingly poor, they have given jewels and silks and embroideries, and if the Genoese have not handed over the three thousand ducats *in numerata pecunia;* if Amonte and the Adelantado have cash in their pockets while [the rest of] the expedition is perishing from hunger and thirst and 'armejos' (*sic*);* if receipts for payment in full are made out without the transfer of money and victuals; if he does not heed advice nor harken to reason, not to mention many other things whereby there are made manifest little obedience to Your Highness and peril to so many souls?'' [*loc. cit.*, p. 289].

He adds that a certain friar and a companion of the same, seeing the disabled condition of the fleet, had remained behind and that the others too would have done the same if Orellana had not fooled them and detained them by force. "I assure Your Highness," he concluded, "that he is not carrying enough water to reach the Canaries, nor jars in which to catch some if it takes them fifteen days to reach there . . . May it please Our Lord in the first place to keep their souls and give their persons time for repentance, for they are in great danger from all sides; and already they were beginning to give to every three men one pound of biscuit, and no wine or meat; and the poop of the largest ship, on which the Adelantado is sailing, is filled with women, and already he was placing a guard in order that no passenger might go to the poop, and they were quarreling, for such was the state of affairs when they were anchored outside the bar, as we learned from the pilots who took them over the bar . . . ''[196]

*[No explanation of this term, which apparently puzzled Medina also, has been found by the translator or the editor.—EDITOR.]

[196] Letter from Friar Pablo de Torres to the King dated May 19, 1545 [*loc. cit.*, p. 290].

The biographical information that we have concerning Friar Torres is not as complete as might be desired, and that which has been published by a few historians is full of errors.

Friar Alonso Fernández, in his *Historia eclesiástica de nuestros tiempos* (Toledo, 1611), p. 185, merely says: "The third bishop of Panama was Friar Pablo de Torres, from the Province of Spain, year One Thousand Five Hundred and Forty."

Gil González Dávila, in his *Teatro eclesiástico de la primitiva iglesia de las Indias occidentales* (2 vols., Madrid, 1649-55), Vol. 2, fol. 58*v*, takes it for granted that Friar Torres belonged to the Order of St. Jerome and states that he was bishop of Panama in 1560.

Antonio de Alcedo ["Alsedo" on the title-page], in his *Diccionario geográfico-histórico de las Indias occidentales* (5 vols., Madrid, 1786-89), Vol. 4, p. 34, contents himself with copying González Dávila, although rectifying the latter's error regarding the order to which Friar Torres belonged.

After the departure of Orellana, Friar Torres returned to Seville, and, so I believe, set out

With this poor equipment and with forebodings of this sort, carrying on board the germs of disorganization, with the prospect of hunger and death before them, there sailed away from the coast of Spain that squadron whose mission it was to conquer and colonize New Andalusia. Granted the shortcomings[197] of its organizer, it is plain to see, on the other hand, that a little assistance in the form of money coming from the one who could have supplied it would have saved this expedition,[198] the outcome of which

immediately for Valladolid to report personally to the Monarch on the result of the commission that had been intrusted to him; and it is certain that as early as May of the following year he was back again in Seville, having been appointed bishop of Castilla del Oro, for which locality he was supposed to start in company with the Licentiate Pedro de la Gasca, whom, however, in the end he was unable to accompany (Letter to the King, Seville, May 30, 1546).

In this same year he took possession of his diocese in Panama, and such was his conduct as a prelate that already in 1547 the attorney for the city of Nombre de Dios drew up a report to send to the King, covering the outrageous acts attributed to Torres. This document, together with another one relative to a similar matter, is to be found in the Archives of the Indies (bundle 52–1-1/32).

The Archbishop of Lima sent one of the canons from his cathedral to investigate him, and as a consequence of this there was instigated a lawsuit which had as a result the departure of Friar Torres from the diocese.

After arriving in Spain, he presented to the Council a long statement in which he declared that he had been away from his diocese since 1554, without cause, as he said, having stayed in Havana and Puerto Rico on account of storms which had prevented the ships from sailing, and that he had been more than two years in the capital, awaiting the termination of the war before going to Rome (whither he had been ordered to go by the Archbishop of Lima), at the same time watching to see if anyone was bringing any complaint against him before the King and the Council of the Indies. He adds that he had submitted testimonials in justification of his conduct and that he had performed great services during the rebellions of Gonzalo Pizarro and of the Contreras brothers, and in Milan back in the days of Leiva, and he concludes by asking certain favors and requesting that he be given a position in his profession.

[197] Among these the gravest of all, beyond all doubt, was that of having taken it upon himself to carry out an enterprise far beyond his power; and, in the second place, that of having consented to the presence of women on the ships, his own wife to begin with. Yet this latter circumstance was not a rare thing in those times, and on occasions these women lent good services to the conquistadors. In this manner Pedro Meléndez de Avilés was accompanied on his expedition to Florida; and Pedro de Valdivia, when he left Peru to undertake the conquest of Chile, carried before his saddle an image of Our Lady of Perpetual Succor, which is still venerated in Santiago de Chile, and behind him, on the croup, his mistress, Inés de Suárez. The usual way, and the one which would have been at the same time the most correct, was first to establish a home on New World soil and then send for the family, as was done by the majority of the soldiers of that epoch.

[198] Orellana's wife, with remarkable common sense and as one who could observe things close at hand, voiced the idea (and she was quite right, in my opinion) that the enterprise of her husband failed because of his not having received from the Crown the help which he needed and which could have saved it; "and . . . inasmuch as His Majesty had not given the said Adelantado any aid or financial backing, the said Captain Peñalosa could not have failed to come to the aid of the said Adelantado, . . . " [infra, p. 375].

To be sure, Prince Philip (later King Philip II) did order the royal officials not to let Orellana depart in case he had not gathered together the equipment which up to the last hour he still lacked in order to comply with the terms laid down in the articles of agreement; but it is also true that the dilemma in which Orellana saw himself thus placed was a terrible one. His resources gone, without any hope of securing any more, and fearful lest the men whom he had recruited and whose money he had already received should disband, there remained to him only these alternatives: either abandon the enterprise, and be left in poverty and misery and with his prestige gone, or take the risk of being saved by chance, as had already happened to him on the Amazon. But luck, which had favored him on the former occasion, was against him this time. His departure under such conditions indicated a grave lack of foresight and constituted a violation of the King's orders, and only death could redeem him.

might have been of incalculable consequences for the nation; but in view of its state of unpreparedness when it set out, totally unequipped as it was, one did not need to be a prophet to predict the fate that awaited it: for the Monarch, that enterprise, which was costing him nothing, by reason of its very cheapness was going to cost him dearly, as Friar Torres had already remarked; for Orellana and his men, it was to cost an infinite amount of suffering, the loss of their fortunes, and, in the end, their lives.

In accordance with the itinerary laid out, Orellana steered his course for the Canaries, stopping three months in Teneriffe, in the hope, no doubt, of finding a good chance to procure the things which he still lacked; and at the end of this period of time he went on to the Cape Verde Islands, where he was obliged to wait two months more. This delay was fatal to him, for he fell far short of finding what he hoped to find, the greater part of the persons on the ships became ill, ninety-eight of them dying, and out of the four ships that he then had it was necessary to abandon one in order to refit the remaining ones with hawsers and anchors to make up for those that they had lost. When the fleet again set sail, fifty more fighting men remained ashore, among them the camp-master and three of the captains, who either were not in a condition to continue the voyage, or did not dare to face the new and greater dangers that they believed awaited them.

Orellana, however, did not wish to give up and abandon an enterprise which it appeared to be madness to continue. About the middle of November[199] he ordered his sails to be spread again, heading for the coast of Brazil. During the crossing he was assailed by unfavorable weather; thirst began to be felt on board, and all would have perished had it not been for the tropical rainstorms which they were fortunate enough to come upon just in time. As a climax to his misfortunes, one of the ships, the one which carried seventy-seven persons, eleven horses, and a brigantine that was to serve to go up the river, was lost from sight, and nothing was ever learned of its fate.[200] Letting themselves be

[199] The chronology of the events of the crossing is difficult to establish, since only the dates of his departure from Seville and of his arrival at the mouth of the Amazon are known with accuracy. To fix the date which I give in the text I have estimated that Orellana must have arrived at Teneriffe at the end of May, and that after he had spent five months in the Canaries and at the Cape Verde Islands his departure from this last point must be considered as having occurred during the first fortnight of November, 1545.

[200] The words used by Francisco de Guzmán, and copied by Herrera, in speaking of this ship are: " . . . and amidst this hardship and struggling one [ship] put in toward land, [the persons on board] saying that they had no water, . . . regarding which said ship up to the present time nothing more has ever been heard . . . " [*infra*, p. 359]. Frankly, I do not understand what

carried on by the north wind, the ships hit upon the right course, and after sailing for some hundred leagues within sight of the coast they came upon fresh water, a sure indication that here was the mouth of the river which they were looking for.   Immediately the prows were turned towards land, and on the following day, December 20, 1545,[201] after having been at the point of being wrecked on the shoals and after having been obliged to avail themselves of their cannon as substitutes for anchors, of which they had none, they anchored the ships between two islands, the inhabitants of which supplied the expeditioners with maize, fish, and native fruits.   Some of the expeditioners then attempted to persuade Orellana of the advisability of giving a short rest to the men and horses, for they were quite worn out after that laborious voyage, and of putting together, in the meantime, the other brigantine which they had brought over in pieces, in order to reconnoiter the arm of the river up which they were to sail; but replying that he knew that from here on the country was thickly inhabited "and that there would be plenty of facilities for doing what is stated above . . . " [infra, p. 359], he started up the river with the two ships, covering a distance of one hundred leagues past flooded lands and rough woodlands and uninhabited regions, until, having arrived at some Indian huts, he ordered his men to proceed with the construction of the brigantine.   In this task the months of January, February, and March, 1546, were used up, it having been necessary to tear apart one of the ships in order to use its nails and planking; and, as soon as the brigantine was finished and properly manned, Orellana sent it off in search of food supplies, the shortage of which had made itself so strongly felt that already fifty-seven men had perished from want, after having eaten the dogs and horses which had formed part of their equipment; but their efforts were fruitless, and, after many of the crew had died also of hunger or from wounds received in the encounters which they had with the Indians, the survivors returned to the camp. The brigantine and the ship then started out in convoy in search of the

Guzmán and the chronicler of the Indies mean here by "put in toward land"; but the fact is that the boat became lost, either having been smashed to pieces on the coast of Brazil, or having been sunk during a storm, or, finally, having gone adrift after its crew had perished from thirst. [In the above rendering into English of Guzmán's words regarding what happened to this ship, the difficulty which Medina apparently finds with the text has been made, rightly or wrongly, to disappear. It seems, in fact, as if Medina must have been familiar with the verb "arribar" only in the sense of "reach shore" or "come into port," whereas the meaning of "put in toward land in time of stress," adopted in the present translation, is vouched for by several dictionaries.— EDITOR.]

    [201] Day of Our Lady of the O, according to Guzmán [see *infra*, p. 359].

principal arm of the river, for they had failed so far to find it; and scarcely had they gone twenty leagues when, at a moment when the ship was at anchor, the flood tide caused the only hawser it had to break and drove the ship ashore, whereupon the ship-wrecked men were compelled to take refuge on an island a little more than a league from the scene of the catastrophe, where by good fortune they were able to come to a peaceful understanding with the Indians who inhabited it. Under these circumstances Orellana decided to set out again in the brigantine in search of the principal arm of the river, leaving on the island twenty-eight or thirty of his soldiers; and twenty-seven days later, tired of wandering about in vain, he returned to the camp, where he could not find the soldiers who had remained behind, in spite of all the efforts that he exerted in an attempt to locate them.[202]

While Orellana was trying in vain to find the principal arm of the river, his companions who had remained on the island, seeing that the days were passing with no news whatsoever of the where-abouts of their commander and that, being so few in number, they were doomed in the end to die at the hands of the Indians or, what was perhaps worse, of hunger, resolved to proceed to build a boat which would enable them to go in search of Orellana and, if neces-sary, to a land where there were Christians, for which purpose, one of them tells us in connection with the building of the boat, "they had gone for nails and other needed materials to the ship which

---

[202] All these incidents in the experiences of the expeditioners during the time that they wandered about these regions appear greatly confused in the documents which have so far come to my notice. In regard to this whole question of the return of Orellana to the island, after his first departure, it should be pointed out that two distinct versions of the story are given.

According to Guzmán's account, Orellana did find the men who had been left behind on the island occupied in building a boat, and, after he had passed another month there, seeing that the task was not being completed, he went off again, saying that he felt ill, and that "he wanted to go back again to look for the branch of the river and go up as far as the point of San Juan . . . , and that if we felt like following him after our boat should be built, we should find [him] some-where around there . . . " [infra, p. 360].

The version of the story given in my text above is based on deductions which are apparently to be drawn from various statements contained in the next-to-last document which I am pub-lishing in part at the end of this volume. According to this version Orellana, after all—and this is just the reverse of what I say in the text—did not come back to the camp after he had once set out from there. " . . . in view of the fact that he was staying away a long time and no news was being had of him," says Muñoz Ternero in the ninth question of his interrogatory, "we built a boat at the cost of much [hard] work, in which we went a very long way up the said river in search of the said Orellana, . . . and on account of our having obtained no news of him . . . " [infra, p. 363]. On these points all the witnesses agree. Among these latter, however, there is one who particularly deserves to be mentioned, namely Juan Griego [John the Greek], "a shipmaster and pilot" [infra, p. 369], who accompanied Orellana on this excursion and who expressly affirms that he "had gone with the said Governor as far as a hundred and fifty leagues on up, and [that] when they had come back they had not found the said Diego Muñoz nor the rest of the men where the said Adelantado had left them, 'and we went about in search of them' . . . " [infra, p. 370f.].

had been abandoned as a wreck a league or a league and a half away from there, and . . . they had kept going back and forth on errands of this sort many times, and [also] to the forest to cut lumber for the said task, and had been in the habit of carrying it on their backs . . . " [*infra*, p. 368]. By dint of incessant toil, which lasted close on to three months, they at last succeeded in launching the craft on the river; but it turned out to be of such faulty construction, as was natural, that it let in water in all parts; yet, without being discouraged over this, they began to move upstream in search of their commander, accompanied by some Indians who also provided them plentifully with food on the strength of their understanding with the Spaniards that they would make war on the Indians' enemies who lived farther up the river; and in fact they got as far as a point a little below where the river divides into three large arms; but, seeing that they were so few in number, that the provisions were about exhausted, and that Orellana was not to be found, they resolved to return downstream. Forty leagues above the place where the river flows into the sea they came upon a spot which they thought belonged to the mainland, rather thickly populated and well provided with food, a supply of which they purchased from the Indians, who on this occasion dealt with them on terms of peace, and six of the twenty-eight men composing the crew of the boat stayed there; and later, four leagues farther down, four others ran away from the rest of the party in the small boat which had been taken along, "because they considered the country to be a good one . . . " [*infra*, p. 361], and because they were afraid to face the dangers of the sea in so fragile a boat. After searching for them and calling them to no avail, those who still remained in the larger boat continued on their way downstream; and scarcely had they sailed out of the mouth of the river, when one evening at nightfall, after the boat had been pulled out on dry bottom, the flood tide cast it up on the flooded lands of a mangrove swamp, where the men, believing themselves doomed because of the strong undertow that ran there, began nevertheless to build rafts in order to look about and see how they could save their lives; but after they had been for two or three days in such a dangerous situation, cruelly tormented by the mosquitoes, they managed to get out to sea again, and, sailing close to the coast, baling out day and night the water that came into the boat, weakened by the lack of nourishment, they finally arrived, in the last days of November or the first days of December,

1546,[203] at the Island of Margarita, where they found twenty-five[204] of their companions, and also Orellana's wife, "who told us," says Francisco de Guzmán, "that her husband had not succeeded in getting into the main branch which he was looking for, and [that] consequently, [and particularly] on account of his being ill, he had made up his mind to come to a land of Christians: and [that] during this time, when he was out looking for food for the journey, the Indians shot seventeen of his men with arrows. From grief over this and from his illness Orellana died . . . "[205] [*infra*, p. 361].

[203] For the fixing of this date I am relying upon statements made in the fourth question in the judicial inquiry covering the service record of Juan de Peñalosa [*infra*, p. 374 f.] and the answers given by the witnesses to the effect that the expeditioners wandered about lost on the banks of the river for eleven months, which must be counted as beginning on December 20, 1545, when they started up the Amazon River.

[204] Of all the expeditioners only 44 persons escaped alive, according to the testimony of Juan de Peñalosa and Doña Ana de Ayala [pp. 375, 376] and as the crew of the boat in question numbered 18, there must have been 25 in the brigantine; that is, in all, 43 men plus Orellana's wife.

[205] There is no way of knowing the exact date of Orellana's death, though it is not difficult to deduce it with some approximation inasmuch as we know that it occurred somewhere up the river and while he was searching for provisions in order to go out to sea; in other words, during the last days during which the crew of the brigantine remained on the Amazon, hence, probably, in the beginning of November, 1546.

As a consequence of the sufferings that they had experienced on the voyage, as soon as they arrived at the island of Margarita almost all the expeditioners fell seriously ill.

The Licentiate Cerrato, a judge of the Audiencia of Santo Domingo, in a letter which he wrote from that place to the King under date of January 25, 1547, announced in the following terms the disastrous end of the expedition to New Andalusia: "Orellana and those who went with him to the Marañón lost their way, and he died, and some of them, although only a few, reached Margarita, their health wrecked, and under separate cover accompanying this, so they tell me, there is an account of the whole matter, and for this reason I am not writing one." This document is not attached to the letter, but I believe it cannot be any other than the account by Francisco de Guzmán with which we are already familiar.

A short time later this same Audiencia of Santo Domingo, which was engaged at that time, in obedience to orders of the King, in getting together men and supplies to aid the expedition which La Gasca was undertaking to Peru, announced to the King, in a letter dated March 19th of that year, that they had sent to Margarita a ship "with another captain in order to bring from that island and from the district of the mainland all the soldiers that there might be there and to pick up a certain number of soldiers who had put in there from Orellana's expedition, and bring back the ship [which was] loaded with horses and provisions."

Some of these soldiers did not remain in Santo Domingo, for a few settled down in Panama, such as Juan de Peñalosa, who apparently had Doña Ana de Ayala henceforth as a companion; others went off to Peru, among them, besides Diego Muñoz Ternero (who continued to fill, in Lima, the office of clerk of the court which had been granted to him to be his occupation in New Andalusia); the pilot of the expedition, Francisco López [whom Pedro de la Gasca called the best chart maker in the South Sea—TRANSLATOR]; and, to mention only one more, Francisco de Ulloa, who had gone over to be the treasurer of the new province and who settled in Concepción, one of the southernmost cities of Chile.

The failure of Orellana did not discourage others from at least attempting the same undertaking. Under date of December 24, 1549, Diego de Vargas, a citizen of the village of Valverde, made a contract with the King, offering to take over to New Andalusia three hundred men in four or five ships, as well as horses and other supplies, with a view to making conquests and founding settlements one hundred and fifty leagues inland from the mouth of the river and along a stretch of twenty leagues on either side, "I having been informed," said the King on accepting the offer, "that along the river which they call the Amazon, which is the one by which Captain

Buried at the foot of one of those aged trees of the always verdant forests bathed by the current of the majestic river which he had discovered, he at last found rest from his toils and sufferings in the midst of that luxuriant nature which was a sepulcher worthy of his imperishable name.

Orellana passed out from the provinces of Peru on his way to these realms, there are many peoples who are without the light of the Faith." [The articles of agreement drawn up in favor of Diego de Vargas have been printed in Vol. 23 of *Colección de documentos inéditos* . . . *América y Oceanía*, pp. 132–144. The quotation is from p. 132.—EDITOR.]

# XI

## CONCERNING THE NAMES OF THE RIVER DOWN WHICH ORELLANA WENT

WHEN was the Marañón River discovered? What is the origin of this name? Here are two historical questions which deserve to be studied in any discussion of Orellana's expedition.

The first is easy to answer on the authority of the documents at our disposal; not so the second, which down to the present day has remained enveloped in the mystery of the past, notwithstanding the positive opinions which have been expressed regarding it—opinions which, as we shall see, cannot be considered as well-founded or conclusive.

Let us look into the question of how and when the Marañón was discovered.

Vicente Yáñez Pinzón was navigating in the waters north of the equator in the month of February, 1500, and, having encountered fresh water in the sea forty leagues out from land and being desirous of learning the cause of a phenomenon until then never before seen by him, he steered his course towards the coast and discovered that "this water," as Herrera says, "came from that very renowned Marañón River . . . " He anchored his ships inside the mouth of the river but was promptly compelled to move away from there because the place appeared to him to be dangerous, though not until he had seized as prisoners thirty-six of the trusting islanders who dwelt on its shores.[206]

Diego de Lepe, who, one might say, did little more than follow in the tracks of Yáñez Pinzón, also arrived very shortly after this at the same river, started to ascend it, found the natives up in arms because of the piratical acts of his predecessor, and it was then that its shores were stained for the first time with Spanish and Indian blood.

To Vicente Yáñez Pinzón, therefore, belongs the title of first discoverer of the river, which at that time was called the Mar Dulce [i.e. Fresh Water Sea]; and this fact was expressly recognized by the Monarch when, in causing to be drawn up in his favor the

[206] Antonio de Herrera, *Historia general de los hechos de los castellanos*, Decade I, Book IV, Ch. 6.

articles of agreement under date of September 5, 1501, he put into this document the following words: " . . . you followed the coast that runs to the northwest of the Río Grande, to which you gave the name of Santa María de la Mar Dulce . . . ."[207]

The geographers contemporaneous with Yáñez Pinzón had, therefore, no choice but to accept the name by which it was then called. The pilot Juan de la Cosa, in fact, when he made his celebrated world map of 1501 right after the discovery of the river, placed its mouth approximately in the position where it is actually located and designated it the Mar Dulce; and by this name, so it appears, they went on calling it until the beginning of 1513.*

During the lawsuit instigated by Diego Columbus, the prosecuting attorney, in 1512, brought in a list of questions, in No. 6 of which he says, in reference to Yáñez Pinzón's discoveries, that the latter "entered the mouth of the Río Grande, where they found the fresh water that flows out to sea . . . " And the witnesses, in replying to this question, express themselves as follows: Andrés de Morales says that "he got into the fresh water in the sea of the Río Grande . . . "; and Cristóbal de Barros states that "he had heard it said that the said Vicente Añez and the others had found the Río Grande with its fresh water which goes out into the sea . . . "[208]

But as early as February of the following year (1513), while evidence was again being sought in connection with the same lawsuit in Seville, also by the prosecuting attorney, we have the declaration of the pilot, Juan Rodríguez, who, replying to the seventh question, said that he had gone with Diego de Lepe "at the time when he [i.e. Diego de Lepe] had gone on a voyage of exploration, by command of Their Highnesses, and had seen that the aforesaid Diego de Lepe and his followers had explored from the Cape of St. Augustine as far as Paria, skirting all along the

---

[207] Torres de Mendoza, *Colección de documentos inéditos relativos al descubrimiento . . . de América y Oceanía*, Vol. 30, Madrid, 1878, p. 536.—Pedro Martir de Anglería [Pietro Martire d'Anghiera], in speaking of Yáñez Pinzón's expedition, states: " . . . they say that they came upon a river called Marañón . . . " [For an English translation of Pietro Martire d'Anghiera's work see F. A. MacNutt, *De Orbe Novo: The Eight Decades of Peter Martyr D'Anghera*, 2 vols., New York, 1912: cf. Vol. 1, p. 163.] This author does not say, therefore, that it was Yáñez Pinzón and his companions who first called it the Marañón, nor does he state what the origin of the name was.

*[The Admiral's Map in the 1513 Strasburg edition of Ptolemy (reproduced in A. E. Nordenskiöld, *Facsimile-Atlas to the Early History of Cartography*, Stockholm, 1889, Pl. 36) carries the legend "Hoc mare est de dulci aqua" off the mouth of the "Río Grande."—TRANSLATOR.]

[208] *Colección de documentos inéditos relativos al descubrimiento . . . de las antiguas posesiones españolas de ultramar* [frequently referred to as the second series of *Colección* cited in footnote 207 above], Vol. 7 [*De los pleitos de Colón*, I], Madrid, 1892, pp. 194, 202, and 229 respectively.

coast, which means six hundred leagues of mainland, included in this being the Río Grande and the Marañón . . . "[209]

This is the oldest document that I am able to cite in which the name Marañón appears, though at that time the term could not have been in general use to any extent, in view of the fact that the other witnesses, all sailors like Rodríguez, in turn likewise refer to the river exclusively as the Río Grande.

However, from this date on, the name Marañón begins to come into much more general use. During the taking of evidence on behalf of Diego Columbus in Palos in February, 1515, Alonso Rodríguez de la Calba said that he had been with Diego de Lepe on an expedition to explore the River Marañón.[210]  In another document of this sort, drawn up in Seville in August of this year, Rodríguez de la Calba again states that from the bay to which they gave the name of San Julián "they sailed towards the west until they arrived at the River Marañón . . . "[211]  The Palos physician García Ferrando "said that he knew that the said Diego de Lepe had gone exploring on his own account and had gotten as far as the River Marañón . . . "[212]  Cristóbal García testified that "the said Diego de Lepe [and his companions] had gone on exploring, utilizing his [i.e. the leader's] skill and knowledge, following along off the coast, as far as Paria, and had been in [the mouth of] the Marañón . . . "[213]  Diego Fernández Colmenero "said that this witness [i.e. he] had seen the said Diego de Lepe start out on a voyage of exploration, and that he [i.e. Diego de Lepe] had made explorations of the mainland towards the south, down to what is called the Marañón . . . "[214]  Luis de Valle affirmed that Lepe and his companions "had gone on and explored more than seven hundred leagues, according to what the pilots said, and that they had finally reached the Río Grande, which is called the Marañón . . . "[215]

These declarations were brought forth as evidence in October, 1515, and it may be said that from this time on the name Marañón began to prevail almost exclusively, although at times there was

[209] *Ibid.*, p. 277.  "Marañó" is what the text as printed here says literally, probably because the "tilde" over the "o" has not been properly interpreted. [The voyage of Diego de Lepe was terminated in June, 1500.—Translator.]

[210] *Ibid.*, Vol. 8 [*De los pleitos de Colón*, II], Madrid, 1894, p. 43.

[211] *Ibid.*, p. 132.

[212] *Ibid.*, p. 190.

[213] *Ibid.*, p. 198.

[214] *Ibid.*, p. 207.

[215] *Ibid.*, p. 213.

confusion due to the fact that one of the two great arms which the river forms at its outlet was referred to as the Mar Dulce.

At all events, a little later another authority on the geography of this region no less famous than Juan de la Cosa, namely Martín Fernández de Enciso, in his description of the Marañón River in a work first published in 1519, places it seven and one half degrees north of the equator, stating that "it is more than xv leagues wide." "And eight leagues inland," he adds, "it has many islands." Inasmuch as the river had by that time been explored by Diego de Lepe for a distance of seventy leagues up into the interior, Enciso was able to include also a few details regarding its shores.

Then, a little further on, he says: "From this river Marañón to the one which they call the Mar Dulce there is a distance of twenty-five leagues. This river is seventy leagues wide at the mouth, and it brings down so much water that it goes out to sea for more than twenty leagues, for it does not mix with the salt water; this wide part extends inland for twenty-five leagues, and then it divides into two parts, the one going to the southeast and the other to the southwest."[216]

Thus we find that, from this date on, a certain river which was in seven and one half degrees north latitude began to be designated in print as the Marañón River and that this was considered to be distinct from the one which Yáñez Pinzón and Juan de la Cosa had named the Mar Dulce.

Not long after, this latter term also disappears almost entirely from the cartographic and official documents, and the name Marañón begins to be the one commonly used, the lamentable confusion established by Fernández de Enciso thus being eliminated. In fact, the Portuguese cosmographer Diego Ribeiro, in the service of Spain, on the map which he made in 1529 designates it exclusively as the Marañón; and in the articles of agreement which the King caused to be drawn up in favor of Diego de Ordaz on May 20, 1530, one may read: "Inasmuch as you have offered to explore and conquer the provinces that extend away from the Marañón River," etc.[217]

· And by this name it was now known not only in Spain but also in America. In a letter which the Archbishop of Santo Domingo

[216] [*Suma de geographia ꝗ̃ trata de todas las partidas e prouincias del mundo: en especial de las Indias* (first published in Seville in 1519)], ed. Seville, 1530, fol. 51 recto and verso. [The Spanish original of these quotations is to be found on the second of two folios numbered "lj" (i.e. signature g iij) in this irregularly foliated volume.—EDITOR.]

[217] Archives of the Indies, "Patronato," 1-1-1 /28, piece 46.

wrote to the King under date of August 11, 1531, he says: "By this Audiencia there has been given to Your Majesty an account of how Ordaz failed to establish a colony on the shores of the Marañón River . . . "

In a judicial inquiry on the subject of the past services of a nephew of Ordaz put through the court in November, 1533, in the fourth question, we read that "His Majesty granted him favors and made him governor of the Marañón."[218]

Among the lawsuits to which this expedition of Ordaz's gave rise there is one which deserves to be recalled here, namely the one which the district attorney of the Island of Pearls (in the Bay of Panama), Francisco Pereira, carried on there in 1531 to prove that Ordaz had usurped the jurisdiction which belonged to him (Pereira) by virtue of his contract with the King. In the course of this trial a very curious investigation regarding the distance which separates the mouth of the river from the province of Paria* was made. The preliminary instructions in connection with this investigation, together with the findings as contained in the deposition of the pilots, are as follows:

"On the twenty-third day of the said month of June of the said year the said chief justice of the peace, being in the building of the municipality of this city (Nueva Cadiz), in order better to get at the facts in connection with what had been requested by its [i.e. the city's] prisoner, for the purpose of being able better to arrive at a decision in this case, caused to appear before him the inspector Juan López de Anchuleta, and Gonzalo Martel, and Pero Sánchez, and Francisco Fernández Turifeño, and Cristóbal de Cea, pilots, at present stopping in the said city, as persons trained and expert in the art of navigation and having much experience, to whom he said that, as they knew, he had commanded them, each one by himself and all together, to scan their navigators' charts and their quadrants, and by means of them [i.e. the charts] and of the said quadrants and by the altitude and by all the other means which there are available to them and which they possess, to look into and confer on the distance and [the difference of] longitude that there is, and how many leagues [there are], from the said Marañón River down the coast as far as the province of Paria, where at present it is on record and [is a] well-known [fact] that the said Comendador Diego de Ordaz has settled,

---

[218] *Ibid.*, "Patronato," 1–6–1/24.
*[At the head of the Gulf of Paria, west of Trinidad.—Editor.]

together with the persons composing his expedition. And these men, being thus together in the said building of the municipality, conferred on the above-mentioned matter, and they brought along certain navigators' charts and a quadrant and a book of rules for sailing, and they figured it all out, together with the altitude; and having made their calculations, they came to an agreement, under [burden of an] oath which they took in legal form at the hands of the said chief justice of the peace, and in the presence of me the said scrivener, they testified as follows:

"These said, under burden of the aforesaid oath, that they had carefully looked at and examined the aforesaid ocean charts of theirs, and in particular [had studied the question] with the aid of a chart that has just recently been made and certified, which was brought in by the said Francisco Fernández Turifeño, who declared it to have been made by Don Ferdinand Columbus, and [they had relied upon it] because that one agrees with others; and having carefully conferred and deliberated with reference to the whole matter, being unanimous and in agreement, they said, under burden of the aforesaid oath, that from the said Marañón River down the coast in this direction as far as the Bay of Candón there are two hundred leagues . . . "

Furthermore, one of these pilots, Pero Sánchez, in giving his testimony as a witness said that he was certain of the correctness of these claims "because of having seen it on ocean charts recently *printed* and sent over from Castile and certified in the city of Seville by Don Ferdinand Columbus . . . "

There can therefore be no doubt that the name of the river was Marañón and that this name was the one by which it was now known on a printed geographical chart, which, unfortunately, has not come down to us.

Within a very short time after Ordaz's expedition the government of Portugal sent over another one to operate in those regions; of its disastrous outcome we are informed by the following letter from the Audiencia of Santo Domingo, written to the King of Spain on February 12, 1536, in which, as will be seen, the name Marañón continues to be applied to the river which in the beginning was called the Mar Dulce:

"In this month of November last it appears that there passed by the Canary Islands an expeditionary fleet from the Kingdom of Portugal composed of twelve ships, on board which there were one thousand five hundred men and one hundred and twenty horsemen, on their way, so they say, to found colonies along the Marañón River, which is within the territory marked off for Your Majesty; as they proceeded on their voyage, a small lighter with oars which the expedition was taking over to use in going up the river was lost from their sight [somewhere] out in the open sea, and so drifted about the ocean for more than two months without being able to get back toward the aforesaid Marañón River; and as a vessel carrying subjects of Your Majesty was coming through the same [part of the] open sea, it came upon it [i.e. the lighter] without food or water, and they [i.e. the persons in it] did not even know where they were, and it [i.e. Your Majesty's ship] brought it [i.e. the lighter] along to this port, where eight Portuguese sailors were made prisoners . . . The sailors of this lighter say that they had gotten as far as near the Marañón River, and that at the same time a ship of Don Pedro de Mendoza's expedition to the River Plate had arrived there, and that the Indians from the land had killed some of the Spaniards who had been on board that ship."[219]

Lastly, Pedro Cieza de León, writing in the year 1541 when as yet he had not heard of Orellana's voyage of discovery, also calls it the Marañón.[220]

In view of all this, I believe it to be quite evident that for a time after the river, or more properly its mouth, had been discovered by Yáñez Pinzón in 1500 it was called the Mar Dulce and that as early as 1515, in all the documents emanating from various sources, it takes on the name of Marañón. And at this point fits in the serious and obscure question to which I referred in the beginning of this chapter: what is the origin of this name?

Agustín de Zárate says in regard to this: " . . . and this river is called the Marañón because the first man who discovered it as a navigable stream was a certain captain named Marañón."[221]

Juan de Castellanos agrees with this opinion of the chronicler

[219] Letter from the Audiencia of Santo Domingo, February 12, 1536.

[220] *Crónica del Perú*, Part 1 (originally printed in Seville, 1553, and in Antwerp, 1554, Ch. 44. [A translation of Part I by Sir Clements Markham constitutes No. 33, published in 1864, of the First Series of the publications of the Hakluyt Society, London. The reference to the Marañón is on p. 165. This reference, which is of all the greater interest as it alludes to the upper part rather than to the mouth of the river, reads in Markham's translation " . . . to the east [of the Andean Inca province of Cañarís centering about the city of Tumebamba] is the great river Marañón, with its forests and some villages." This wording, especially the last phrase, may indicate that, contrary to Medina's belief, Cieza de León knew of Orellana's voyage when he wrote this and that it was hence written later than 1541. This contingency is possible in view of the fact that Cieza de León returned to Spain in 1550 and that his chronicle was not published until 1553. On Part IV of Cieza de León's work, see footnote 43, p. 29, *supra.*—EDITOR.]

[221] *Conquista de la provincia del Perú*, [see footnote 46, p. 30, *supra*], Book IV, Ch. 4.

Zárate, adding that the name came from certain captains who had accompanied Yáñez Pinzón:

> This name was giv'n to it by the Pinzóns
> From certain sailors named the Marañóns.[222]

A certain Portuguese writer also agrees with these authors in affirming that the name given to the river came from a captain named Marañón, who discovered its source in Peru.[223]

A French traveler quite well informed on matters pertaining to the Amazon, La Condamine, with whose account of a journey through those regions all are familiar, affirms that, when Orellana went down it, it had already become known as the Marañón, and as early as 1513, from the name of another Spanish captain, and that Orellana himself so calls it in his own account of his voyage.[224]

Such, then, is the version most current and most generally accepted, namely, that the river was called the Marañón in honor of a Spanish captain by this surname, and that this name began to be applied to it at least as early as 1513.

The opinion of the Portuguese writer Silveira, who supposes that the discovery by this captain Marañón was effected from the Peruvian side, is entirely untenable when one considers that the supposed discoverer would have had to guess that a river arising in Peru was the one which flowed out to sea there where

[222] Elegy XIV, Canto II, stanza 20. It will not be amiss to reproduce here the lines which Juan de Castellanos in his famous work *Elegías de varones ilustres de Indias* devotes to a description of the river and the different names that have been applied to it (*Biblioteca de autores españoles*, Vol. 4, p. 157):

"Its course is such a one and is so greatly spread out that no living man ever saw a greater one, and hence, because its great size is of such huge proportions, we generally call it the Fresh Water Sea; and it is said that it is sometimes erroneously thought that this onrushing stream is not the Marañón: this name was given to it by the Pinzóns from certain sailors named the Marañóns."

"They tried to land at a certain village which was seen on the shores, but were prevented from doing so by a warring people who rushed forth to meet them with ferocious energy, and by a male-like Indian woman who like a watchdog bravely defended her lands, and they called her an Amazon because she displayed great valor in her person.

"Out of these circumstances, Captain Francisco de Orellana later fabricated his stories in order to call it the Amazon River," etc.—Elegy XIV, Canto II, stanzas 20, 32, 33.

[223] Simão Estacio da Silveira, *Relação summaria das cousas do Maranhão*, fol. 1: "It took this name of "Maranhão" from the captain who discovered its source in Peru, . . . " [This work has been reprinted by Candido Mendes de Almeida in his *Memorias para a' historia do extincto estado do Maranhão* . . . , Vol. 2, Rio de Janeiro, 1874: cf. p. 5.—EDITOR.]

[224] *Relation abrégée d'un voyage fait dans l'intérieur de l'Amérique Méridionale*, Paris, 1745, pp. 9–10.

In La Condamine's *Extracto del diario de observaciones hechas en el viaje de la provincia de Quito al Pará por el río de Amazonas* [translated from French into Spanish by the author], Amsterdam, 1745, one may read (p. 3) a statement to this same effect: "The first name of the river of the *Amazons* was *Marañón*. So it is called by *Orellana* himself in his *Account*, when he says that he came upon the *Amazons* while sailing down the River *Marañón*, a name which had already been attached to it by a *Spanish* Captain having that surname . . . "

the Mar Dulce was situated, for the fact is that the determination of the course of the river did not take place until Orellana's time. Furthermore, it should be noted that if, in 1513, it was already called the Marañón, no Spanish captain could have so named it in Peru, for this country had not even been discovered at that time.

Was it really given the name of Marañón, as Juan de Castellanos thinks, in honor of the sailors named Marañón, who, he says, accompanied Yáñez Pinzón? To me this hypothesis does not seem to be admissible either, first because there is no record to the effect that any sailor by this name went with that navigator, and secondly because, on the contrary, documents show that it was precisely at this time that it came to be designated as the Mar Dulce.

How are we to explain the fact that none of the witnesses who testify in the lawsuit carried on by Diego Columbus, some of whom had taken part in the expeditions of Yáñez Pinzón and Diego de Lepe, do not mention this Captain Marañón even once, who, if he did exist, must have been a companion of them all?

There remains to be investigated the affirmation of La Condamine to the effect that the name was attached to the river in 1513 by a certain Captain Marañón who in that year, supposedly, went over its course. But what expedition was this? From an examination of the documents preserved in the Spanish archives it does not appear that at this time any expedition whatsoever to these regions was carried out. If there had been any such expedition, some trace of it at least would have remained.

If it were claimed that the name "Marañón" or "Maranhão" came from some Portuguese navigator, I for one would not be in a position to contradict such an assertion; but, as those who furnish this information affirm that the name is of Spanish origin, I find myself obliged to reject the whole theory.

There have not been lacking authors who, not taking these assertions and opinions into account, have ventured other hypotheses to explain the name Marañón. For example, Father Manuel Rodríguez says with considerable nonchalance that it was originated by the soldiers of Lope de Aguirre who deserted their flag and "endured such misfortunes, perplexities, and hardships, both when they went down in company with him and when they came up, turning back towards Peru, that in consideration of them [i.e. their hardships, etc.] and of the mix-ups and entanglements ['marañas'] that they went through in going up and down that river and its turns they called it the River of Entanglements

['Río de Marañas']; and by way of indicating that these [entangle-ments] were enormous ones, they went further and it came to be called the 'Marañón.' "[225]

Others try to tell us that the name Marañón comes from the cashew tree, *Anacardium occidentale*, or from its fruit, which in Puerto Rico is called *cajuil*, in Venezuela *merey*, in Cuba [and Peru] *marañón*, in Brazil *caju*, and in the Indian language *maran-i-hobo*, which in fact abounds in the forests along the banks of the Amazon.

The conclusion to all this is that, so far as I can see, it is not possible, on the basis of known documents, to explain in a satis-factory way the origin of this name Marañón.

In the years which followed Orellana's expedition the name Marañón, in its turn, was abandoned, and the river began to be more generally known as the River of the Amazons. At times, also, it was referred to under the name of its discoverer. An instance of this may be seen in the articles of agreement drawn up by order of the King, under date of August 11, 1552, empowering Gerónimo de Aguayo "to go to the provinces of the Aruacas and of the Amazons, who are located," as this document reads, "[in a region stretching away] from the mouth of the Orellana River, called by another name The Amazons."

And from this moment on we find more and more among the writers an extraordinary confusion in the names of the river, beginning with López de Gómara, who goes so far as to describe the Orellana and the Marañón as distinct rivers. Worse than this, it becomes a common practice to apply to it new names[226] completely forgotten today, and it even seems as if there were retrogression in geographical knowledge that had apparently been definitely acquired.[227]

It is strange that the anarchy which reigned right from the start in this matter of the names of the river subsists even today. From its source in Lake Lauricocha in the province of Huamalíes in Peru down to its mouth it has always been known under different names. Some call it the Marañón throughout its whole length;

---

[225] *El Marañón y Amazonas*, p. 18. [See p. 30, together with footnote 48 on the same page.—The noun "marañón" is an augmentative form of "maraña."—Editor.]

[226] In a certain appointment to a captaincy made by Fernando de Oruña y de la Hoz in 1604 this latter styles himself governor and captain-general for the King our master in these provinces of El Dorado, Guiana, and Gran Manoa, a land *which lies between the two rivers Pauto and Papamene*, which under other names are called *the Orinoco and the Marañón*.

[227] In an account made up by the House of Trade in Seville from reports by the Chief Pilot, the professor of cosmography, and other persons concerning the Marañón, it is worthy of notice that they all maintain that the Marañón is a river distinct from the Amazon, and that one of them even states that these two rivers are arms of the River Plate!

others, the Marañón or Amazon from where it receives the Hua-llaga down to where it flows into the sea, the part above this being known as the Tunguragua, etc.; and the confusion is still greater when one takes into consideration the various designations that it has received from the Portuguese and Brazilians, who distinguish in the course of the river at least three sections, reserving the name Solimões for that part which extends from Tabatinga to the city of Manáos, situated at the mouth of the Río Negro.

But the most current usage, and the one which the geographers now definitely accept, is to call the river the Marañón from its source down to where it joins the Ucayali and, from there on, the Amazon.[228]   The one thing that really can be affirmed with all certainty is, strange to say, that the name least commonly used today is that of its discoverer, Francisco de Orellana.

[228] A. Raimondi, *Apuntes sobre la provincia litoral de Loreto*, Lima, 1862, p. 14.

# PART II

# CARVAJAL'S ACCOUNT

# ACCOUNT

## WRITTEN BY FRIAR GASPAR DE CARVAJAL,

*a friar of the Order of Saint Dominic of Guzmán, of the recent voyage of discovery down the famous great river which Captain Francisco de Orellana, by a very great piece of good fortune, discovered, starting at its source and coming out at the sea, accompanied by fifty-seven men whom he took along with him, having launched forth at random upon the said river, which from the name of the captain who discovered it came to be called the Orellana River.*

## DISCOVERY OF THE ORELLANA RIVER

IN order that there may be a better understanding of the whole progress of events in connection with this voyage, it must first be explained that this Captain Francisco de Orellana was a captain and lieutenant-governor of the city of Santiago (1)*, which he in the name of His Majesty had founded and conquered at his own expense, and of Villa Nueva de Puerto Viejo (2), which is in the province of Peru; and because of the numerous reports which circulated regarding a country where cinnamon existed, out of a desire to serve His Majesty in exploring for the said cinnamon, having learned that Gonzalo Pizarro, in the name of the Marquis (3), was coming to be the governor of Quito and of the said territory over which the said Captain held jurisdiction, and in order to go along with the expedition in the exploration of the said country, he went to the town of Quito, where the said Gonzalo Pizarro was, to see him and put him in possession of the said territory. Having done this, the said Captain told the said Gonzalo Pizarro how he wished to go with him in the service of His Majesty and take his friends

---

*[The numbers refer to Medina's notes at the end of the *Account*, pp. 236–242, below (here moved to this position instead of being made to follow the Documents, as in Medina). Asterisk, dagger, etc., footnotes, when not enclosed in brackets, are also by Medina.—EDITOR.]

along and spend his personal wealth in order better to serve; and, this being agreed upon, the said Captain went back to the territory over which he held jurisdiction in order to resign from office and to leave in peace and quiet the said city and the said town, and in order to join the said expedition he spent over forty thousand gold pesos on things which he would require, and, being now ready, he departed for the town of Quito, where he had left the said Gonzalo Pizarro, and when he arrived there he found that he had already started out, for which reason the Captain was somewhat embarrassed* as to what he should do, and he determined to press forward and follow him . . . (torn), although the Spaniards dwelling in the country tried to dissuade him from doing so because he would have to pass through a hostile and rough country and because they feared that they [i.e. the natives] would kill him as they had done others who had gone [in there] with a very large force of men (4); yet notwithstanding this, for the sake of serving His Majesty, he determined in spite of all this risk to go on and catch up with the said Governor; and so [he did], suffering many hardships, both from hunger and from fights which the Indians forced upon him, for, he not having more than twenty-three men with him, many times they placed him in such straits that they considered themselves doomed to destruction and death at their hands; and in spite of these hardships he journeyed . . . (torn) leagues from Quito, before the end of which [journey] he had lost all that he had started out with, so that when he overtook the said Gonzalo Pizarro he still had left only a sword and a shield, and his companions likewise; and in this way he entered the province of Motín, where the said Gonzalo Pizarro was with his expeditionary force, and there he joined up with him and went along on the search for the said cinnamon; and although all that I have told up to now I neither saw nor took part in, still I gathered up information from all those who came with the said Captain, because I was with the said Gonzalo Pizarro and I saw him [i.e. Captain Orellana] and his companions come in in the manner that I have said; but what I shall tell from

* From this point on there is a passage missing in the Muñoz copy.

here on will be as an eyewitness and as a man to whom God chose to give a part in such a strange and hitherto never experienced voyage of discovery, such as is this one which I shall relate from here on.

After* the said Captain had joined the said Gonzalo Pizarro, who was the Governor, he [i.e. the latter] went in person to search for cinnamon, and he did not find any land or any resources wherewith he might render a service to His Majesty, and so he determined to go farther on, and the said Captain Orellana [followed on] after him with the rest of the force, and he caught up with the said Governor in a settlement that was called Quema, which stood in [the midst of] some savanas† one hundred and thirty leagues from Quito, and there they joined forces again; and the said Governor wishing to send someone down the river to explore, there were opinions to the effect that he should not do so, because there was no excuse for following a river and leaving the savanas which fell off behind the towns of Pasto and Popayán, where there were many roads; and yet the said Governor insisted on following the said river, along which we went twenty leagues, at the end of which we found some settlements not very large, and here the said Gonzalo Pizarro decided that a boat should be built to cross from one side of the river to the other for food, for that river was now half a league wide; and, although the said Captain was of the opinion that the said boat should not be built, for several good reasons, but rather that they should turn back to the savanas and that we should follow the roads that led to the said settled country, the said Gonzalo Pizarro would consent to nothing save that work on the said boat should be started, and so Captain Orellana, seeing this, went throughout all the camp securing iron for nails and apportioning to each one the timbers that he was to bring, and, in this manner and with the labor of all, the said boat was built, in which the said Governor Pizarro placed a certain amount of baggage and some sick Indians, and we went down the river another fifty leagues, at the

*[There is no paragraphing here in Medina's text.—EDITOR.]

†[This appears to be the only logical interpretation (confirmed by Ortiguera, p. 314, *infra*, line 14) of "cabanas" here and a few lines below. Possibly Carvajal actually wrote "çabanas."—EDITOR.]

end of which we found no more inhabited regions, and we were now suffering very great privation and lacked food, for which reason all of the companions were greatly dissatisfied and talked of returning and not going ahead any farther, because it was reported that there was a great uninhabited region [ahead]; and Captain Orellana, seeing what was happening and [perceiving] the great privation from which all were suffering and [considering] that he had lost all that he had had [at the start], thought it was not becoming to his honor to turn back after so great a loss, and so he went to the said Governor and told him how he was determined to leave behind him the little that he had with him and go on down the river and that, if luck favored him to the extent that he should find an inhabited region and foodstuffs whereby all might be succored, he would let him know about it; and that, if he [i.e. Pizarro] should see that he [i.e. Orellana] tarried, he should not be concerned about him, and that, meanwhile, he should turn back to where food was to be had, and that there he should wait for him three or four days, or as long as he should see fit, and that, in case he [i.e. Orellana] did not come, he should not be concerned about him; and thereupon the said Governor told him to do whatever he thought best; and so the said Captain Orellana picked out fifty-seven men, with whom he embarked in the aforesaid boat and in certain canoes which they had taken away from the Indians, and he began to proceed down his river with the idea of promptly turning back if food was found; all of which turned out just the reverse of what we all expected, because we did not find food for a distance of two hundred leagues, nor were we finding any [for ourselves], from which cause we suffered very great privation, as will be stated farther on; and so we kept going on, beseeching Our Lord to see fit to guide us on that journey in such a way that we might return to our companions. On the second day after we had set out and separated from our companions we were almost wrecked in the middle of the river because the boat struck a log and it [i.e. the log] stove in one of its planks, so that if we had not been close to land we should have ended our journey there; but matters were soon remedied [thanks to the energy of the men] in hauling the boat out of water and fastening a piece of plank on it, and we promptly started off on our way with very great haste; and, as the river flowed fast, we proceeded on at the rate of from twenty to twenty-five leagues [a day], for now the river was high and [its power] increased owing to the effect of many other rivers which emptied into it on the right from a southerly direction. We journeyed on for three days without [finding] any inhabited country at all. Seeing that we had come far away from where our companions had stopped and that we had used up what little food we had brought along, [too little] for so uncertain a journey as the one that we were pursuing, the Captain and the companions conferred about the difficulty [we were in], and the [question of] turning back, and the lack of food, for, as we had expected to return quickly, we had not laid in a supply of food; but, confident that we could not be far off [from some settlement], we decided to go ahead, and this [was done] at the cost of no little hardship for all, and, as neither on the next day nor on the following one was any food found nor any sign of a settlement, in accordance with the view of the Captain I said mass, as it is said at sea, commending to Our Lord our persons and our lives, beseeching Him, as an unworthy man [that I was], to deliver us from such manifest hardship and [eventual] destruction, for that's what it was coming to look like to us now, since, although we did wish to go back up the river, that was not possible on account of the heavy current, [and there was no alternative], for to attempt to go by land was out of the question so that we were in great danger of death because of the great hunger we endured; and so, after taking counsel as to what should be done, talking over our affliction and hardships, it was decided that we should choose of two evils the one which to the Captain and to all should appear to be the lesser, which was to go forward and follow the river, [and thus] either die or see what there was along it, trusting in Our Lord that He would see fit to preserve our lives until we should see our way out; and in the meantime, lacking other victuals, we reached a [state of] privation so great that we were eating nothing but leather, belts and soles of shoes, cooked with certain herbs, with the result that so great was our weakness that we could not remain standing, for some on all fours and others with staffs went into the woods to search for a few roots to eat and some there were who ate certain herbs with which they were not familiar, and they were at the point of death, because they were like mad men and did not possess sense; but, as Our Lord was pleased that we should continue on our journey, no one died. Because of this suffering as stated a number of the companions were quite disheartened, to whom the Captain spoke words of cheer, and he told them to exert themselves and have confidence in Our Lord, for since He had cast us upon that river He would see fit to bring us out to a haven of safety; in such a way did he cheer up the companions that they accepted that hardship.

On New Year's Day of [the year One Thousand Five Hundred and] Forty-two* it seemed to certain of our companions that they had heard Indian drums, and some said they did and others said no; but they became somewhat happier over this and pushed on with much [greater]† diligence than was customary with them; and, as neither on that day nor on the next was any inhabited country actually seen, it became evident [to all] that it was [a matter of pure] imagination, as in reality it was; and, in consequence of this, both the sick and the well were becoming so greatly downhearted that they thought that they could no longer escape with their lives; however, the Captain sustained them with the words which he spoke to them, and, as Our Lord is the father of mercy and of all consolation, who restores and helps him who calls on Him in the time of greatest need, [they took heart]; and so it was that, it being Monday evening, which by count was the eighth [day] of the month of January, while eating certain forest roots they heard drums very plainly very far from where we were, and the Captain was the one who heard them first and announced it to the other companions, and

*[For a list of significant dates during the expedition, correlated with days of the week and with religious feast days, see footnote 94, p. 58, *supra*.—EDITOR.]

†[Inserted by Medina.—EDITOR.]

they all listened, and they being convinced of the fact, such was the happiness which they all felt that they cast out of their memories all the past suffering because we were now in an inhabited country and no longer could die of hunger. The Captain straightway ordered us to keep watch by quarters with great care, because . . . (*torn*) it might be that the Indians had caught sight of us and would come at night and attack the party, as is their custom; and so that night a very heavy watch was kept, the Captain not sleeping, it being considered that that night transcended all the rest, because all were so eager for day to come, for they had had their fill of [living on] roots. No sooner had morning come than the Captain ordered the powder and arquebuses and crossbows to be made ready and all the men to be alert for arming themselves, because in truth not one of the companions here was without great worry as to how to do what they [read: he] had to. The Captain had his own [worry] and that of all [the others]; and so in the morning, everything being made quite ready and put in order, we started to go in search of the village. At the end of two leagues of advancing down the river we saw coming up the river to look over and reconnoiter the land four canoes filled with Indians, and, when they saw us, they turned about at great speed, giving the alarm, in such a manner that in less than a quarter of an hour we heard in the villages many drums that were calling the country to arms, because they are heard from very far off and are so well attuned that they have their [harmonizing] bass and tenor and treble; and at once the Captain ordered the companions who were at the oars to row with all speed, so that we might arrive at the first village before the natives had gathered together; and so it was that at very great haste we began to move on, and we arrived at the village where the Indians were all waiting to defend and guard their homes, and the Captain commanded that in very good order they [i.e. his men] should all leap out on land and that all should look after [each] one and [each] one after all, and that no one should exceed orders, and [that] as good [soldiers] they should look to what they had in hand to do, and that each one should do what he was supposed to do; so great was the courage which they all gained on seeing the village that they forgot all the past toils, and the Indians left the village and all the food that there was in it, which was no small relief and support for us. Before the companions should eat, although they had great need [of food], the Captain ordered them all to scout about the village in order that afterwards, while they were gathering food together and resting, the Indians might not turn back on us and do us some harm, and it was so done. Here the companions set about to make up for the past, because they did nothing but eat of that which the Indians had prepared for themselves and drink of their beverages, and this [they did] with so much eagerness that they thought that they would never satisfy themselves; and this was not done all unguardedly, because, although they ate like men all that they needed, they did not forget to take all precautions in everything that was incumbent upon them for the defense of their persons, for they all remained alert, their shields on their shoulders and their swords under their arms, watching to see if the Indians were turning back on us; and in this way we earned this rest, for such it may be called for us after all the hardship [which]* we had endured, until two hours past midday, when the Indians began to come on the water to see what was going on, and thus they kept moving about on the river like simpletons; and, this having been observed by the Captain, he got up on the bank of the river and in their language (for to a certain extent he could understand them) he began to speak with them and tell them to have no fear and to come near, for he wished to speak to them; and so two Indians came right up to where the Captain was, and he cajoled them and took away their fear and gave them something from his supplies and told them† to go get the overlord (for he wished to speak to him) and to have no fear that he would do him any harm whatsoever; and so the Indians took what was given them and went at once

---

*[Inserted by Medina.—Editor.]

†[Medina's text has: "y dijo que les fuesen á llamar," etc. This appears to be an error for either "les dijo que fuesen . . . " or "dijo que le fuesen . . . "—Editor.]

to inform their overlord, who came right away, very much
decked out, to where the Captain and the companions were
and was very well received by the Captain and by all, and
they embraced him, and the Chief himself manifested great
contentment at seeing the good reception that was given
him. At once the Captain ordered that he be given clothes
and other things, with which he was much pleased, and thereafter he became so happy that he told the Captain to decide
on what he needed, for he would give it to him, and the Captain told him to order nothing to be furnished him but food;
and straightway the Chief ordered his Indians to bring
food, and in a very short time they brought, in abundance,
all that was needed, including meats, partridges, turkeys,
and fish of many sorts; and after this, the Captain thanked
the Chief heartily and told him to depart with God's bless-
ing and to summon to him all the overlords of that land, of
whom there were thirteen, because he wished to speak to
them all together and announce the reason for his coming;
and although he [i.e. the Chief] said that the next day they
would all be with the Captain and that he was going to send
for them, and went away quite content, the Captain continued to put things in order as best befitted the welfare of
himself and his companions, arranging the watches in such
a way that, both by day and by night, every precaution
should be taken in order that the Indians might not fall
upon us and that there should be no oversight or laxity in
consequence of which they might be encouraged to attack
us either by night or by day. The next day, at the hour of
vespers, the afore-mentioned Chief came and brought with
him three or four other overlords, for the rest were unable
to come as they were far away, but would come the next
day; the Captain extended to them the same reception as
to the first and spoke to them at great length on behalf of
His Majesty and in the latter's name took possession of
the said land; and he did the same with all the others who
afterwards came [to him] in this province, for, as I have
said, there were thirteen of them, and in the case of all of
them he took possession in the name of His Majesty. When

the Captain perceived that he [now] had all the inhabitants and the overlords accepting peace and friendly toward him [and] that kind treatment was the proper procedure to be followed, [he took advantage of the fact that] they were all glad to come with peaceful intentions; and in this way he took possession of them and of the said land in the name of His Majesty; and, when this was done, he commanded all his companions to gather together so that he might talk to them on the subject of what steps it was proper to take in the interests of their expedition and their salvation and [even the saving of] their lives, giving them a long talk, bolstering up their courage with very strong words. After the Captain had given them this talk, the companions were very happy to see the good courage that the Captain had within him and to see with what patience he bore up under the hardships which were falling to his lot, and they spoke to him* also some very kind words, and with the words which the Captain spoke to them they went about so happy that they were not conscious of any of the hardships that they had endured.

After the companions had somewhat recovered from the effects of the hunger and suffering that they had undergone, being [now] in a mood to work, the Captain, seeing that it was necessary to make plans for what was ahead, gave orders to call all the companions together and repeated to them that they could see that with the boat which we were using and the canoes, if God saw fit to guide us to the sea, we could not go on out to a place of rescue and [that] for this reason it was necessary to apply our wits to building another brigantine of greater burden so that we might sail on the sea, and this [he advised] in spite of the fact that among us there was no skilled craftsman who knew that trade, for what we found most difficult [of all] was how to make the nails; and meanwhile the Indians did not stop offering aid and coming to the Captain and bringing to him foodstuffs in abundance, and all with as much orderliness as if all their lives they had been servants; and they came wearing their

*The lacuna in Muñoz's copy extends to this point.

jewels and gold medallions, and never did the Captain permit that anything be taken [away from them], or even merely looked at, in order that the Indians might not conceive the idea that we valued such things, and the more indifference we showed in this matter, the more gold did they put on.

It was here that they informed us of the existence of the Amazons and of the wealth farther down the river, and the one who gave us this information was an Indian overlord named Aparia,* an old man who said he had been in that country, and he also told us about another overlord who lived at some distance from the river, far inland, who, he said, possessed very great wealth in gold; this overlord's name is Ica; never did we get to see him, because, as I say, he kept away from the river where we were.

And in order not to lose time nor waste the food in vain, the Captain decided that a start should at once be made on what was to be done, and so he gave orders to prepare the necessary materials, and the companions said that they wanted to begin their task at once; and there were among us two men to whom not a little [credit] is due for having done something which they had never learned [to do], and they came before the Captain and told him that they with the help of Our Lord would make the nails that were needed, and [asked him] to order others to make charcoal. The names of these two companions were, the one, Juan de Alcántara (5), an hidalgo hailing from the town of Alcántara, and the other, Sebastián Rodríguez (6), a native of Galicia; and the Captain thanked them, promising them reward and payment for such an important piece of work; and he at once ordered some bellows to be made out of buskins, and in a like manner all the other tools, and the other companions he commanded in groups of three to prepare good kilnfuls of charcoal, all of which was promptly put into execution, and each one took his own tool and they went off to the woods to cut wood and bring it on their shoulders from the woods to the village, [a distance] which must have been about half a league,

---

*In other passages the reading is "Aparian" or simply "Parian." [This was Aparia the Lesser, to use Jiménez de la Espada's designation (p. 63, *supra*) not the same as Aparia the Great, met with later in the voyage.—EDITOR.]

and they made their pits, and this with very great toil.  As they were weak and not expert in that line of work, they could not bear up under the burden, and the other companions who had not the strength to cut wood worked the bellows and others carted water, while the Captain worked at everything, so that we all had something to which to give our attention.  Our company gave such a good account of itself in this village in the organization of this task that in twenty days, with the help of God, two thousand very good nails and other things were made, and the Captain put off the construction of the brigantine for some other place where he might find a greater need for it and better facilities.

We stayed in this village longer than we should have stayed, eating up all we had, with the result that this was the cause of our suffering great hardship from this point on, and this was [due to a desire] to see if in some way or manner we could get news from the expeditionary force; and, seeing that none could be had, the Captain decided to give one thousand castellanos to six companions if they would form a group and take the news to the Governor Gonzalo Pizarro, and in addition to this he would give them two negroes to help them row and a few Indians, in order that they might carry letters to him and give to the governor on his [i.e. Orellana's] behalf news of what was happening; and among them all only three were found, because all feared the death that was sure [to come] to them, in view of the long time that it was bound to take them to get back to where they had left the said Governor, and [they said] that he had probably turned back, because they had gone one hundred and fifty* leagues since they had left the Governor in the nine days that they had used up in going on [as far as here].

The task being finished, and in view of the fact that our food was becoming exhausted and that seven of our companions had died from the hunger endured, we departed on the day of Our Lady of Candlemas; we laid in what foodstuffs we could, because this was not the time to stay any longer in that village, on the one hand because, so it seemed,

*Two hundred, according to the Muñoz copy.

this was beginning to become irksome to the natives and they [i.e. Orellana's men] wished to leave them content, and on the other hand because of our desire not to lose time and use up our food without advantage, because we did not know whether we should need it; and so we began to move on through this said province, and we had not gone a distance of something like twenty leagues, when there joined with our river another one from the right, not very wide, on which river an important overlord named Irrimorrany* had his abode, and, because he was an Indian and overlord of much intelligence and because he had come to see the Captain and bring him food, he [i.e. the Captain] wanted to go to his country; but [in addition to other difficulties in the way of doing so] there was also the reason that the river came down very strong and with a great onrush; and here we were on the point of perishing, because, right there where this river flowed into the one on which we were navigating, the one stream battled with the other and [the waters thus stirred up] sent large pieces of driftwood from one side to the other, so that it was hard work to navigate up it, because it [i.e. the river] formed many whirlpools and carried us from one bank to the other; but by dint of hard work we got out of this danger, [though] without being able to reach the village, and we passed on toward where we had heard that there was another village which they told us was two hundred leagues farther on from there, all the country between being barren, and so we covered them [i.e. the two hundred leagues] at the cost of a great deal of suffering for our bodies, passing through many hardships and very extraordinary dangers. for example when there befell us a certain mishap and [one which caused us] no small worry for the time that we were held up by it, and this was that two canoes carrying eleven† Spaniards of ours became lost among some islands without knowing where we were and without our being able to find them; they were lost for two days without being able to locate us, and we, expecting never to see them again, for the time being experi-

*"Irimara," according to the above-mentioned copy.
†Twelve, according to the Muñoz copy.

enced very great grief; but at the end of the aforesaid time Our Lord was pleased that we should come together, so that there was no little rejoicing among [us] all, and in this way we were so overcome with happiness that it seemed to us that all the suffering endured had passed out of our memories. After resting a day at the spot where we found them, the Captain ordered us to continue on our journey.

The next day, at ten o'clock, we came to some settlements in which the Indians were in their houses, and in order not to disturb them the Captain would not permit us to go that far, and he ordered one of the companions to go with twenty others to where the Indians were and [instructed them] not to make a surprise attack on their houses nor to get out on land but rather with much kindness to tell them the serious plight which we were in and [to ask them] to give us food and come and speak with the Captain, who remained in the middle of the stream, for he wished to give them something taken from his supplies and state the reason for his coming. The Indians remained quiet and rejoiced on seeing our companions and gave them much food, consisting of turtles and parrots in abundance, and they told them to tell the Captain to go for lodgings to a village which was uninhabited, on the other side of the river, and [promised] that on the next day in the morning they would go to see him. The Captain was much cheered up by the food and more so by the good understanding of the Indians, and so we went off to occupy the lodgings, and we slept that night in the afore-mentioned village, where we did not fail to find great swarms of mosquitoes, which [circumstance] was the reason why, early the next day, the Captain went off to a larger village that appeared farther down the river; and, when we had arrived, the Indians did not put up any resistance, rather they remained quiet, and there we rested three days, whither the Indians came with peaceful intent to bring us large quantities of food. The next day, the three days being now passed, we left this village and went on down our river within sight of some fair villages; and as we were going along in this way, one Sunday morning, at a fork which the river made, for

it divided into two parts, there came upstream to see us some
Indians in four or five canoes which were laden with much
food, and they came close to where the Captain was and
asked for permission to approach because they wished to
speak with the said Captain, who ordered them to approach;
and so they did approach [and] they told him that they
were prominent persons and vassals of Aparia, and that
it was at his command that they were coming to bring us
food; and they began to take out of their canoes many partridges like those of our Spain, save that they are larger,
and many turtles, which are as large as leather shields, and
fish also of various kinds.  The Captain thanked them and
gave them something taken from his supplies, and, after
he had sold* it to them, the Indians remained very happy to
see the kind treatment that was being extended to them
and to see that the Captain understood their tongue, a fact
which was of no little consequence in connection with our
getting to a haven of clear understanding, for, had he not
understood it, we should have found our final escape [from all
our sufferings] to be a difficult one.  As the Indians were
desirous of taking leave [of us], they told the Captain to
go to the village where their chief overlord resided, whose
name, as I have said, was Aparia, and the Captain asked
them down which of the two arms he ought to proceed, and
they replied that they would guide us, [telling us] to follow
them; and so, within a short time, we saw the settlements
where the said overlord was, and, proceeding towards that
place, the Captain again asked the Indians to whom these
settlements belonged, [and] the Indians replied that there
dwelt the above-mentioned overlord of theirs, and then they
set off toward the village to give the message that we were
coming, and it was not long before we saw many Indians
come out of the aforesaid village and get into their canoes, in
the attitude of warriors, and it looked as if they were getting
ready to attack us.  The Captain ordered his companions,
who saw the manifestation [of hostility] that the Indians were
making, to be alert, with their weapons ready, so that in

*The copy in the Academia de la Historia says "given."

case they attacked us they might not be able to harm us; and in good order, rowing and with full power, we put into shore, and the Indians seemed to get out of the way. The Captain leaped out on land all armed, and after him all the others, and at this the Indians became quite frightened and came in closer to land. Inasmuch as the Captain understood them, for, as I have already said, his understanding of the language was, next to God, the deciding factor by virtue of which we did not perish [somewhere] along the river, [we got out of this difficult situation,] for, had he not understood it, neither would the Indians have come forward with peaceful intentions nor should we have met with success in these settlements; but, as Our Lord was pleased that such a great [venture into the] unknown and [feat of] discovery should be carried out and brought to the notice of His Cesarean Majesty, and [all] at the cost of so much hardship, the discovery *was* made, and [it is certain] that by no other method or [use of] force or [expenditure of] human energy could the discovery have been made, had not God put His hand to it [then] or until many centuries and years had elapsed.

After the Captain had called the Indians to him, he told them to have no fear, [but] to step out on land, and they proceeded to do so, for they came close in to land, showing on their faces that they rejoiced at our coming; and the overlord leaped out on land, and with him many important personages and overlords who accompanied him, and he asked permission of the Captain to sit down, and so he seated himself, and all his followers [remained] standing, and he ordered to be brought from his canoes a great quantity of foodstuffs, not only turtles, but also manatees (7) and other fish, and roasted partridges and cats and monkeys. The Captain, perceiving the polite manners of the overlord, addressed a few words to him, giving him to understand that we were Christians and worshipped a single God, who was the creator of all created things, and that we were not like them who walked in the paths of error worshipping stones and images made [by man]; and in this connection he told them many other things, and explained to them also how we were servants and vassals of the Emperor of the Christians, the great King of Spain, and [that] he was called Don Carlos our master, to whom belonged the territory of all the Indies and many other dominions and kingdoms existing throughout the world, and that it was by his command that we were coming to that land, and that we were going to make a report to him on what we had seen in it; and they were very attentive and with keen interest [went on] listening to what the Captain was saying to them, and they told him that if we were going to visit the Amurians, whom they call "Coniupuyara" in their tongue, which means "grand mistresses," to be careful about what we were doing, for we were few in number and they many, for they would kill us; [and they counseled us] not to stop in their country, for right here they would give us everything that we might need. The Captain told them that he could not avoid at least passing by at a distance, in order to give an account to him who was sending him, who was his king and master; and, after the Captain had spoken and it seemed as if the listeners were very content, that chief overlord asked who he was, and as, by way of seeing if the Captain showed any discrepancy in his words, he [also] asked to be better informed about what was being told to him, the latter told him in reply the same things that he had [just] explained to him, and he told him more, namely, that we were children of the Sun and that the object of our journey was to go down that river, as he had already told him. At this the Indians marveled greatly and manifested great joy, taking us to be saints or celestial beings, because they worship the Sun and hold him [i.e. the sun] to be their god, whom they themselves call "Chise." They then told the Captain that they were his [i.e. the Captain's servants] and that they wished to serve him, and [told him] to look into the matter of just what he and his companions had need of, for he [i.e. the overlord] would give it to him very willingly. The Captain thanked them well and then ordered many things to be given [to him] and to the other important personages, and in consequence thereof they were so pleased that henceforth not a single thing did the Captain ask for that they did not at once give to him; and they all stood up and told the Captain to take up lodgings in the village, for they would leave it free for them, and [then announced] that they wished to go to their homes and that each day they would come to bring us food. The Captain directed them to have all the overlords come to visit him, because he wished to give them something out of what he had [brought along with him]. The overlord said that the next day they would come, and so they did all come with a very great supply of food and were well received and treated by the Captain, and to all of them together he repeated what he had first told the principal overlord, and he took possession of them all in the name of His Majesty; and there were twenty-six overlords, and as a token of possession he ordered a very tall cross to be set up, in which the Indians took delight, and thenceforth the Indians came every day to bring us food and to speak with the Captain, for in this they took great delight.

When the Captain perceived the excellent conveniences and resources of the country and the favorable attitude of the Indians, he commanded all his comrades to come together and told them that, since there was a good supply of materials here as well as good will on the part of the Indians, it would be well to build a brigantine, and so the work got under way; and there was found among us a woodworker named Diego Mexía (8), who, though it was not his trade, gave instructions as to how the task was to be done; and thereupon the Captain ordered an apportionment [of the work] among all the companions whereby each man [in one group] was to bring one frame and two futtocks, and others [in another] to bring the keel, and others the stem pieces, and others to saw planks, so that all had enough to occupy themselves with, not without considerable physical toil, because, as it was winter and the timber was very far away, each had to take his ax and go to the woods and cut down the amount that he was supposed to and bring it in on his back, and, while some carried, others formed a rear guard for them, in order that the Indians might not do them any harm, and in this way within seven days all the timber for the said brigantine was cut; and when this task was finished another was immediately assigned, for he ordered [some of the men] to make charcoal in order to manufacture more nails and other things. It was a wonderful thing to see with what joy our companions worked and brought the charcoal, and in this same way everything else needed was supplied. There was not a man among all of us that was accustomed to such lines of work as these; but, notwithstanding all these difficulties, Our Lord endowed all of them with [the proper] skill for what had to be done, since it was in order to save their lives, for, had we gone on down from there using [only] the [original] boat and the canoes, coming, as we afterwards did, upon warlike people, we could neither have defended ourselves nor gotten out of the river in safety; and thus it became quite evident that it was because God had inspired the Captain that the brigantine was constructed in this village that I have mentioned, because farther on it was impossible, and this [village] was found to be very well suited to the purpose, because the Indians did not fail to continue to bring us food in abundance in proportion as the Captain asked them for these things. Such great haste was applied to the building of the brigantine that in thirty-five days it was constructed and launched, calked with cotton and tarred with pitch, all of which the Indians brought because the Captain asked them for these things. Great was the joy of our companions over having accomplished that thing which they so much desired to do. There were so many mosquitoes in this village that we were unable to aid one another either by day or by night, being thus at a loss as to what to do for one another,* [yet we managed to get along] because with the good lodgings and the desire we had of seeing the end of our expedition we did not [fully] realize our hardships. In the meantime, while we were engaged in this task, there came to see the Captain four

*[Medina calls attention, in a footnote, to the reading of the Muñoz copy for this passage, namely: "sin que . . . nos amosqueásemos" for "sin que . . . no sabíamos que hacernos" in the present text. The reading of the Muñoz copy, with its subjunctive, is more regular from the point of view of Spanish syntax, and its meaning is: "except by shooing the mosquitoes away from one another."—EDITOR.]

Indians, who approached us, and they were of such a stature that each one was taller by a span than the tallest Christian, and they were quite white and had very fine hair which reached down to their waists, [and they came] all decked out in gold and [splendid] attire; and they brought much food; and they approached with such humbleness that we were all amazed at their manners and good breeding; they took out a great quantity of food and placed it before the Captain and told him how they were vassals of a very great overlord, and that it was by his command that they came to see who we were or what we wanted or where we were going; and the Captain received them very nicely, and, before conversing with them, he commanded that they be given many trinkets, which they esteemed highly, and they were greatly pleased. The Captain told them all that he had told the overlord Aparia, whereat the Indians were not a little astonished; and the Indians said to the Captain that they wished to go and make a report to their overlord [and begged the Captain] to give them permission to depart. The Captain gave it to them, and [told them] to depart with his best wishes, and gave them many things for them to present to their principal overlord, and [asked them] to tell him that the Captain earnestly requested him to come to pay him a visit, because he would get a great deal of pleasure out of meeting him; and they said that they would do so, and they left, and nevermore did we learn anything as to where they were from or from what country they had come [on their way to this place].

We tarried at this same stopping-place all during Lent, when all the companions confessed their sins to us two friars who were there; and I preached every Sunday and every feast day [and] Maundy Thursday, Good Friday, and Easter, to the best that Our Redeemer chose by His grace to grant me understanding, and I endeavored to lend assistance and encouragement, to the best of my ability, in keeping up the good spirits of all those brothers and companions, reminding them that they were Christians and that they would render a great service to God and to the Emperor in carrying on the enterprise and in patiently bearing up under the present hardships and under those to come, until they should complete this novel voyage of discovery, particularly in view of the fact that this was a matter in which their lives and their honors were at stake; so that with this end in view I said what I thought best [to say] as fulfilling my mission and also because my [own] life depended upon the successful outcome of our peregrination. I also preached on Quasimodo Sunday and I can truthfully testify that not only the Captain but also all the other companions were possessed of so much forbearance and courage and saintliness of devotion toward Jesus Christ and His Holy Faith that Our Lord plainly showed it was His will to help us. The Captain requested of me that I preach and [see to it] that all attend to their devotions with great fervor, as persons who had very great need of asking God for His mercy. The small boat was also put in condition, because it had begun to rot, and so, everything being now well repaired and put in shape, the Captain ordered that all [the men] be ready and make up their ship-stores, because with the help of Our Lord he wished to depart the following Monday. In this village a thing happened to us which caused us no little amazement, and this was that on Tenebrae Wednesday and Maundy Thursday and Good Friday the Indians made us fast by force, because they did not bring us food until the Saturday before Easter, and the Captain asked them why they had not brought us anything to eat, and they answered that it was because they had not been able to get it; and as a result, on Saturday and on Easter Sunday and on Quasimodo Sunday so abundant was the food that they brought that we threw [some of] it away. And in order that everything might be as was fitting and entirely regular, he appointed to be his lieutenant an hidalgo quite competent for the post, named Alonso de Robles (9), whom, after we came to a hostile land, the Captain used to order to sally forth with a few companions to collect food for all, and the Captain used to stay behind to guard the brigantines, which were our only real asset on this journey and our protection, next to God, because the Indians desired nothing more than to take them away from us.

We departed from the stopping-place and the village of Aparia aboard the new brigantine (which was of nineteen *joas* (10), quite [large] enough for navigating at sea) on the eve of the Evangelist Saint Mark's day, the twenty-fourth of April of the year mentioned above, for [read: and] we come on down past the settlements belonging to that dominion of Aparia, which extended for more than eighty leagues, without our finding a single warlike Indian; on the contrary, the Chief himself came to talk to and bring food to the Captain and us, and in one of his villages we celebrated the above-mentioned Saint Mark's Day, whither the same overlord came to bring us abundant food, and the Captain gave him a good reception, and no ill treatment was meted out to him because it was the purpose and desire of the Captain, if it was possible, that that land and that barbaric people should continue in its friendly attitude as a consequence of our having come to know them, and without any dissatisfaction at all, for thereby God Our Lord and the King our master would be rendered a service, so that later on, when it should please His Majesty, our sacred republic and [our] Christian faith and the banner of Castile might with greater facility be glorified [in the eyes of the natives] and the country be found more tamed for pacification and for being reduced to obedience to his [i.e. our master's] royal service, in the way most fitting, because, at the same time that this was being done with tact and charity, the purpose was also to keep up as long as it should be necessary the kind treatment to be dealt out to the Indians in order [for us] to be able to go forward and in order that the expedient of arms might not be resorted to save when [recourse to] self-defense could not be avoided. Because of this, although we found the villages abandoned, seeing the kind treatment that was being given to them [i.e. the Indians], throughout the whole aforesaid province they provided us with sustenance. Within a few days the Indians ceased [to appear], and by this we recognized that we were [now] outside the dominion and tribal domains of that great overlord Aparia; and the Captain, fearing what might come to pass on account of the small food supply, ordered that the brigantines proceed with greater speed than had been the custom.

One day, in the morning, when we had just departed from a village, there sallied forth toward us two Indians in a canoe, and they came close up to the brigantine where the Captain was and came on board, and the older of them, as the Captain thought that he knew the country and that he could take us down the river, he ordered to stay on board, and the other he sent to his home, and we began to follow on down our river, which the Indian did not know nor had ever navigated, wherefore the Captain ordered him to be freed and given a canoe in which to return to his country. From here on, we endured more hardships and more hunger and [passed through] more uninhabited regions than before, because the river led from one wooded section to another wooded section and we found no place to sleep and much less could any fish be caught, so that it was necessary for us to keep to our customary fare, which consisted of herbs and every now and then a bit of roasted maize. Proceeding along, harassed by our usual suffering and great hunger, one day at noon we came to an elevated spot which looked as if it had been inhabited and possessed some natural advantages for supplying some kind of food, or [at least] fish, and that day was the day of Saint John Ante-portam-latinam, which was the sixth of May, and there an incident occurred which I should not have dared to write down if it had not been observed by so many witnesses who were present; and this was that a certain companion already mentioned, for it was the one who had directed the building of the brigantine (11), shot with a crossbow at a bird which was in a tree on the edge of the river, and the nut* sprang out of the stock and fell into the river, and, he having no idea of ever getting the nut back, another companion named Contreras (12) with a pole cast a hook out into the river and pulled up a fish five spans

*[Murray's Dictionary defines "nut" as "a projection from the lock of a crossbow, serving to detain the string until released by the trigger."—EDITOR.]

long, and, as it was big and the hook was small, it was necessary to extract it [i.e. the hook] with skill, and, [the fish] being opened up, in its belly the nut of the crossbow was found, and in that way it [i.e. the crossbow] was repaired, for which there was later no little need, because next to God it was the crossbows that saved our lives.

When twelve days of the month of May had gone by, we arrived in the provinces belonging to Machiparo, who is a very great overlord and one having many people under him, and is a neighbor of another overlord just as great, named Omaga, and they are friends who join together to make war on other overlords who are [located] inland, for they [i.e. the latter] come each day to drive them from their homes. This Machiparo has his headquarters quite near the river upon a small hill and holds sway over many settlements and very large ones which together contribute for fighting purposes fifty thousand men of the age of from thirty years up to seventy, because the young men do not go to war, and in all the fights that we had with them we did not see any, but it was the old men, and these [were] quite expert, and they have thin mustaches and not beards.

Before we had come within two leagues of this village, we saw the villages glimmering white, and we had not proceeded far when we saw coming up the river a great many canoes, all equipped for fighting, gaily colored, and [the men] with their shields on, which are made out of the shell-like skins of lizards and the hides of manatees and of tapirs, as tall as a man, because they cover them entirely. They were coming on with a great yell, playing on many drums and wooden trumpets, threatening us as if they were going to devour us. Immediately the Captain gave orders to the effect that the two brigantines should join together so that the one might aid the other and that all should take their weapons and look to what they had before them and take heed of the necessity on their part of defending their persons and fighting with the determination to come through to a haven of safety, and that all should commend themselves to God, for He would help us in that serious plight which we

were in; and in the meantime the Indians kept coming closer,
with their squadrons formed to catch us in the center, and
thus they were coming on in such orderly fashion and with
so much arrogance that it seemed as if they already had us
in their hands. Our companions were all [filled] with so
much courage that it seemed to them that four* Indians to
each one of them were not enough, and so the Indians drew
near to the point where they began to attack us. Immediately the Captain gave the command to make ready the
arquebuses and crossbows. Here there happened to us a
misfortune by no means slight when one considers the situation in which we were at the time, which was that the arquebusiers found their powder damp, in consequence whereof
they turned out to be of no use, and it was necessary for the
crossbows to make up for the deficiency of the arquebuses;
and so our crossbowmen began to inflict some damage on
the enemy, as they were close up and we [were] fear-inspiring;
and when it was seen [by]† the Indians that so much damage
was being done to them, they began to hold back, [yet] not
showing any sign of cowardice, rather it seemed as if their
courage were increasing, and there kept coming to them many
reinforcements, and every time that some came to them
they set about to attack us so boldly that it seemed as if they
wanted to seize hold of the brigantines with their hands.
In this manner we kept on fighting until we came to the
village, where there were a great number of men stationed on
the high banks to defend their homes. Here we engaged in
a perilous battle, because there were many Indians on the
water and on land and from all sides they gave us a hard
fight; and so, of necessity, although seemingly at the risk
of the lives of all of us, we attacked and captured the first
spot [we could], where the Indians did not cease to leap out
on land at [i.e. to attack] our companions, because they continued to defend it [i.e. the land] courageously; and had it not
been for the crossbows, which effected some remarkable shots
here (whence it became very evident that the incident in

*The copy to which I have several times referred says "a thousand."
†[Inserted by Medina.—EDITOR.]

connection with the nut of the crossbow was a stroke of divine providence), the landing would not have been won; and so, with this help already mentioned, the brigantines were beached and one half of our companions jumped into the water and fell upon the Indians in such a manner that they made them flee, and the other half stayed on the brigantines defending them from the other warriors who were out on the water, for they did not cease, even though the land was won, to fight on, and although damage was being done to them by the crossbows, they nevertheless did not give up [their attempt] to carry out their evil design. The beginning of the settlement being won, the Captain ordered the Lieutenant with twenty-five men to run through the settlement and drive the Indians out of it and look to see if there was any food [there], because he intended to rest in the said village five or six days in order to let us recover from the hardships which we had endured; and so the Lieutenant went and made a foray for a distance of half a league out through the village, and this [he did] not without difficulty, for, although the Indians were in retreat, they kept up a defensive fight like men whom it vexed to abandon their homes; and, as the Indians, when they do not meet with success in their intentions at the beginning, always run away until they feel the second impulse to return to a normal state of mind, they were, as I say, still fleeing; and, when the aforesaid Lieutenant had perceived the great extent of the settlement and of its population, he decided not to go on farther but to turn back and tell the Captain what the situation was; and thus he did turn back before the Indians could do him any damage, and, having got back to the beginning of the settlement, he found that the Captain was lodged in the houses and that the Indians were still attacking him from the river, and he [i.e. the Lieutenant] told him exactly how things were and [informed him] that there was a great quantity of food, such as turtles in pens and pools of water, and a great deal of meat and fish and biscuit, and all this in such great abundance that there was enough to feed an expeditionary force of one thousand men for one year; and the Captain, having observed what a good harbor it was, decided to gather food together in order to recuperate, as I have said, and for this purpose he sent for Cristóbal Maldonado* and told him to take a dozen companions and go and seize all the food that he could; and so he went, and when he arrived there he found that the Indians were going about the village carrying off the food that they had. The said Cristóbal Maldonado toiled hard to collect the food, and, when he had gathered together more than a thousand turtles, the Indians returned, and this second time there came a great number of men, and very determined† [they were] to kill them [i.e. Maldonado and his men] and push on to strike at the place where we were with the Captain; and when the said Cristóbal Maldonado saw the Indians coming back, he rallied his companions and attacked the enemy, and here they [i.e. Maldonado and his men] were held in check for a long time, because there were more than two thousand Indians and of the companions who were with Cristóbal Maldonado there were only ten, and they had much to do to defend themselves. In the end such superior skill was displayed that they [i.e. the Indians] were routed, and they [i.e. Maldonado's men] again started to collect the food, and two companions came out of this second fight wounded; and, as the country was very thickly settled and the Indians were constantly reforming and replenishing their ranks, they again came back at the said Cristóbal Maldonado, so resolutely that [it was evident that] they sought (and actually started) to seize them all with their hands, and in this assault they wounded six companions very badly, some being pierced through the arms and others through the legs, and they wounded the said Cristóbal Maldonado to the extent of piercing one of his arms and giving him a blow in the face with a stick. Here the companions found themselves in a very serious plight and need of help, for, as they were wounded and very tired . . . (torn), they could not go backward nor forward, and so they all considered themselves as good

*"De Segovia," according to the other manuscript.
†Here begins another lacuna in the manuscript to which I have frequently referred.

as dead and kept saying that they ought to return to where their Captain was, and the said Cristóbal Maldonado told them not to think of such a thing, because he for one had no intention of returning to where his Captain was, whereby the Indians would carry off the victory; and so he rallied around him those of the companions who were in a condition to fight, and put himself on the defensive, and fought so courageously that he was the means of preventing the Indians from killing all of our companions.

During this time the Indians had come around by the upper part [of the village] to strike at where our Captain was from two sides, and as we were all tired out from so much fighting and off our guard, thinking that we were protected from the rear because Cristóbal Maldonado was out there, it became evident that Our Lord had enlightened the Captain [by inspiring in him the idea] of sending out the aforementioned [Cristóbal Maldonado], for had he not sent him out, or had he [i.e. Cristóbal Maldonado] not happened to be just where he was, I hold it for certain that we should have run a great risk of [losing] our lives; and, as I am saying, our Captain and all of us were off our guard and with no armor on, so that the Indians had an opportunity to enter the village and fall upon us without being noticed [before we could get ready for them], and, when they were noticed, they were right in among us and had felled four of our companions, [leaving them] very badly wounded; and at this moment they were seen by one of our companions named Cristóbal de Aguilar (13), who took his stand facing them, fighting very courageously, giving the alarm, which our Captain heard, who went out to see what it was, with no armor on, with a sword in his hand, and he saw that the Indians had the houses where our companions were, surrounded; and, besides this, a squadron of more than five hundred Indians was in the square. The Captain began to call aloud, and so all our companions came out behind the Captain and attacked the squadron with so much intrepidity that they routed them, inflicting damage upon the Indians, but they [i.e. the Indians] did not cease from fighting and putting up a defense, so that they wounded nine companions with grievous wounds, and, at the end of two hours during which we had kept on fighting, the Indians were vanquished and routed and our own men [were] greatly fatigued. In this encounter many of our companions distinguished themselves who until now had not been aware of what they were good for, nor had we held them in any esteem, because all plainly showed [that they realized] the serious straits in which we were, because there was one man who with [nothing but] a dagger rushed in among the foes and fought so well that we were all astonished, and he came out with a thigh pierced through. This man's name is Blas de Medina (14).

When this was now all over, the Captain sent to learn what had become of Cristóbal Maldonado and how he was getting on, and they met him on the road coming to where the Captain was, he and all the rest being wounded; and one companion whose name was Pedro de Ampudia (15), who was with him, eight days later died of his wounds: he was a native of Ciudad Rodrigo.

The aforesaid Cristóbal Maldonado having arrived at the spot where the Captain was, the Captain now ordered that the wounded, of whom there were eighteen, be given medical treatment, and there was no other remedy but a certain charm (16), (and, with the help of Our Lord, within fifteen days all were cured except the one who died). At this juncture they came and told the Captain how the Indians were coming back and that they were close to us in a gully, waiting till they got reorganized; and, in order to drive them out of there, the Captain ordered a cavalier named Cristóbal Enríquez (17) to go there with fifteen men, and he went, and when he got there one of the arquebusiers that he had taken with him had one of his legs pierced; in that way we lost an arquebusier, because thereafter we could not make use of him. The said Cristóbal Enríquez promptly sent back someone to inform the Captain of what was taking place and to ask him to send more men, because the Indians were in great numbers and were being reinforced every hour; and the Captain at once sent orders to the said Cristóbal Enríquez*

*Here ends the above-mentioned lacuna in the other manuscript.

that, without showing that he was retreating, he should come along little by little to where they [i.e. the Captain and the rest] were, because now was not the time for them to risk the life of a single Spaniard, nor did they really have to do so, nor were he or his companions engaged in conquering the land either, nor was it his intention to do so, but inasmuch as God had brought them down this river, [his intention was] to explore the country in order that, in due time and when it should be the will of God Our Lord and of His Majesty, he [i.e. His Majesty] might send him to conquer it. And so, on that day, after the men had been called in, the Captain harangued them, recalling to them the hardships already endured and bolstering them up for those to come, instructing them to refrain from provoking the attacks of the Indians because of the dangers that might arise therefrom; and he determined still to continue on down the river, and he began to load food on board, and as soon as it was on board the Captain commanded that the wounded be placed on board, and those who were unable to go on their own feet he ordered to be wrapped in blankets and be carried aboard on the backs of other men, as if these latter were carrying loads of maize, so that they might not embark limping and so that the Indians on perceiving this might not regain so much courage that they would not let us embark; and after this had been done, the brigantines being ready and unmoored and the oars in hand, the Captain with the companions in good order went down [to the river], and they embarked, and he put off, and was not a stone's throw away when there came more than four hundred* Indians on the water and along the land, and, as those on the land could not get at us, they served no purpose but to call and shout; and those on the water attacked again and again, like men who had been wronged, with great fury; but our companions with their crossbows [and]† arquebuses defended the brigantines so well that they turned away those wicked people. This was around sundown, and in this manner, attack-

---

*Ten thousand, according to the other version.
†[Inserted by Medina.—EDITOR.]

ing us every little while, [they kept] following us all the night, for not one moment did they allow us a respite, because they had us headed off. In this way we kept on until it was day, when we saw ourselves in the midst of numerous and very large settlements, whence fresh Indians were constantly coming out, while those who were fatigued dropped out. About midday, when our companions were no longer able to row, we were all thoroughly exhausted from the cruel night and from the fighting which the Indians had forced upon us. The Captain, in order that the men might get a little rest and eat something, gave orders that we put in on an uninhabited island which was in the middle of the river, and, just as they began to cook something to eat, there came along a great number of canoes, and they attacked us three times, so that they put us in great distress. It having become evident to the Indians that from the water they could not put us to rout, they decided to attack us [both] by land and by water, because, as there were many Indians, there were enough of them for [undertaking] anything. The Captain, seeing what the Indians were making ready to do, decided not to wait for them on land, and hence embarked again and pulled out into the river, because there he thought he could better fight back, and thus we began to move on, with the Indians still not ceasing to follow us and force upon us many combats, because from these settlements there had gathered together many Indians* and on the land the men who appeared were beyond count. There went about among these men and the war canoes four or five sorcerers, all daubed with whitewash and with their mouths full of ashes, which they blew into the air, having in their hands a pair of aspergills, with which as they moved along they kept throwing water about the river as a form of enchantment, and, after they had made one complete turn about our brigantines in the manner which I have said, they called out to the warriors, and at once these began to blow their wooden bugles and trumpets and beat their

* The variant reading is: "more than a hundred and thirty canoes, in which there were more than eight thousand Indians."

drums and with a very loud yell they attacked us; but, as I have already said, the arquebuses and crossbows, next to God, were our salvation; and so they led us along in this manner until they got us into a narrows in an arm of the river. Here they had us in a very distressful situation, and so much so that [if luck had not favored us] I do not know whether any one of us would have survived, because they had laid an ambuscade for us on land, and from there they would have surrounded us. Those on the water resolved to wipe us out, and they being now quite determined to do so, being now very close [to us], there stood out before them their captain-general distinguishing himself in a very manly fashion, at whom a companion of ours, named Celis (18), took aim and fired with an arquebuse, and he hit [him] in the middle of the chest, so that he killed him; and at once his men became disheartened and they all gathered around to look at their overlord, and in the meantime we seized the opportunity to get out into the wide part of the river; but still they followed us for two days and two nights without letting us rest, for it took us that long to get out of the territory occupied by the subjects of this great overlord named Machiparo, which in the opinion of all extended for more than eighty leagues, for it was all of one tongue, these [eighty leagues] being all inhabited, for there was not from village to village [in most cases] a crossbow shot, and the one which was farthest [removed from the next] was not half a league away, and there was one settlement that stretched for five leagues without there intervening any space from house to house, which was a marvelous thing to behold: as we were only passing by and fleeing, we had no opportunity to learn what there was in the country [farther] inland; but, judged from its [apparent wealth of natural] resources and its [general] appearance, it must be the most populous that has been seen, and this was just what the Indians of the province of Aparia had told us that it was, [saying] that there was a very great overlord in the interior towards the south, whose name was Ica, and that this latter possessed very great wealth in gold and silver; and this piece of information we considered to be very reliable and exact.

In this manner and in spite of these hardships we made our way out of the province and great dominion of Machiparo and came to another no smaller [than that one], for here was the beginning of [the land ruled over by] Oníguayal*, and at the approach and entrance to this land stood a village on the model of a garrison, not very large, on an elevated spot overlooking the river, where there were many warriors; and the Captain, aware that neither he nor his companions could [any longer] endure the great hardship, which consisted not only of fighting but, in addition to this, of hunger (for the Indians, although we did have something to eat, did not leave us free to do so because of the excessive amount of fighting which they forced upon us), decided to capture the said village and so gave orders to steer the brigantines towards the harbor, and the Indians, seeing that an attempt was being made to capture the village, decided to put themselves fully on the defensive; and so it was that when we came up close to the harbor the Indians began to draw on munitions from their arsenal, to such an extent that they made us stop; and the Captain, seeing the defense put up by the Indians, gave orders that with very great haste the arquebuses and crossbows be brought into play and that the oarsmen row in such a way as to beach the boats; and thereupon they [i.e. the Indians] made way and rendered it possible for the brigantines to get our companions up on the beach and for them to leap out on land, and after that they fought on land in such a way that they made the Indians take to flight, and so the village was left in our hands along with the food that it possessed. This village was fortified, and, because it was so, the Captain said that he wished to rest there three or four days and get together some ship-stores for farther along, and so we relaxed in this way and with this idea in mind, although not without having to do some fighting, and [this] of such a dangerous sort that one day at ten o'clock there came a great number of canoes bent on seizing and unmooring the brigantines which were in the harbor, and, if the Captain had not had at his disposal

*Variant reading: "Omaguci."

crossbowmen to leap quickly on board, we believe that we should have been unable to defend them; and so, with the help of Our Lord and thanks to the great skill and luck of our crossbowmen, some damage was done among the Indians, who thought it best to go off and return to their homes; so we remained resting, regaling ourselves with good lodgings, eating all we wanted, and we stayed three days in this village. There were many roads here that entered into the interior of the land, very fine highways, for which reason the Captain was wary and commanded us to get ready, because he did not wish to stay there any longer, for it might come about that from our staying there some harm would result.

This idea having been voiced by the Captain, all began to get ready to depart when they should be ordered to do so. We had gone, from the time we left Aparia to this said village, three hundred and forty leagues, of which two hundred were [country] without any settlements. We found in this village a very great quantity of very good biscuit which the Indians make out of maize and yucca, and much fruit of all kinds.

To return to the story, I [next] state that on Sunday after the Ascension of Our Lord we set out from this said village and began to move on, and we had not gone more than two leagues when we saw emptying into the river another very powerful and wider river on the right; so wide was it that at the place where it emptied in it formed three islands, in view of which we gave it the name of Trinity River; and at this junction of the two [rivers] there were numerous and very large settlements and very pretty country and very fruitful land: all this, now, lay in the dominion and land of Omagua, and, because the villages were so numerous and so large and because there were so many inhabitants, the Captain did not wish to make port, and so all that day we passed through settled country with occasional fighting, because on the water they attacked us so pitilessly that they made us go down mid-river; and many times the Indians started to converse with us, and, as we did not understand them, we did not know what they were saying to us. At the hour of vespers we came to a village that was on a high bank, and as it appeared small to us the Captain ordered us to capture it, and also because it looked so nice that it seemed as if it might be a recreation spot of some overlord of the inland; and so we directed our course with a view to capturing it, and the Indians put up a defense for more than an hour, but in the end they were beaten and we were masters of the village, where we found very great quantities of food, of which we laid in a supply. In this village there was a villa in which there was a great deal of porcelain ware of various makes, both jars and pitchers, very large, with a capacity of more than twenty-five *arrobas*,* and other small pieces such as plates and bowls and candelabra of this porcelain of the best that has ever been seen in the world, for that of Málaga is not its equal, because it [i.e. this porcelain which we found] is all glazed and embellished with all colors, and so bright [are these colors] that they astonish, and, more than this, the drawings and paintings which they make on them are so accurately worked out that [one wonders how] with [only] natural skill they manufacture and decorate all these things [making them look just] like Roman [articles]; and here the Indians told us that as much as there was made out of clay in this house, so much there was back in the country in gold and silver, and [they said] that they would take us there, for it was near; and in this house there were two idols woven out of feathers† of divers sorts, which frightened one, and they were of the stature of giants, and on their arms, stuck‡ into the fleshy part, they had a pair of disks resembling candlestick sockets, and they also had the same thing on their calves close to the knees: their ears were bored through and very large, like those of the Indians of Cuzco (19), and [even] larger. This race of people resides in the interior of the country and is the one which possesses the riches already mentioned, and it is as reminders that they have them [i.e. the two idols] there: and in this village also there

---

*[One hundred gallons.—TRANSLATOR.]

†Out of palm leaves, according to the other manuscript.

‡[In Medina's text, the word here translated as "stuck," namely "metidos," which would qualify "brazos" ("arms"), appears to be an error for "metidas" to agree with "ruedas" ("disks").—EDITOR.]

were gold and silver; but, as our intention was merely to search for something to eat and see to it that we saved our lives and gave an account of such a great accomplishment, we did not concern ourselves with, nor were we interested in, any wealth.

From this village there went out many roads, and fine highways [they were], to the inland country: the Captain wished to find out where they led to, and for this purpose he took with him Cristóbal Maldonado* and the Lieutenant and some other companions, and started to follow them [i.e. the roads], and he had not gone half a league when the roads became more like royal highways and wider; and, when the Captain had perceived this, he decided to turn back, because he saw that it was not prudent to go on any farther; and so he did return to where the brigantines were, and when he got back the sun was now going down, and the Captain said to the companions that it would be well to depart at once from there, because it was not wise to sleep at night in a land so thickly populated, and [he gave orders] that all embark at once; and thus it was that, with the food and all [the men] on board the brigantines, we began to move on when it was now night, and all that night we continued to pass by numerous and very large villages, until the day came, when we had journeyed more than twenty leagues, for in order to get away from the inhabited country our companions did nothing but row, and the farther we went, the more thickly populated and the better did we find the land, and so we continued on always at a distance from the shore so as not to furnish the Indians any occasion for coming out to attack us.

We continued our progress through this country and dominion of Omagua for more than one hundred leagues, at the end of which we began to enter another country belonging to another overlord, named Paguana, who has many subjects and quite civilized [ones], for we arrived, at the beginning of the settled section of his country, at a village that must have been more than two leagues long [and] in which the

*"De Segovia," according to the other manuscript.

Indians let us go to them in their houses without doing [us] any harm or damage; on the contrary, they gave presents to us out of their belongings. From this village there were many roads leading into the interior, because the overlord does not reside [in a village] on the river, and the Indians told us to go there, for [they said] he would be quite pleased with us. In this country this overlord has many sheep of the sort found in Peru (20), and it is very rich in silver, according to what all the Indians told us, and the country is very pleasing and attractive and very plentifully supplied with all kinds of food and fruit, such as pineapples and pears, which in the language of New Spain are called "aguacates," and plums and custard apples and many other kinds of fruit and of very good quality.

We left this village and went on journeying past a very large inhabited region, for there was one day when we passed more than twenty villages, and this on the side where we were steering our course, because the other side we could not see for the reason that the river was so wide; and so we traveled on for two days along the right side, and afterward we crossed over and proceeded for two days more along the left side, for during the time we could sight one [side] we could not see the other.

On the Monday after Whitsunday, in the morning, we passed in sight of, and close to, a village very large and very flourishing, and it had many sections, and in each section [there was] a landing place down on the river, and on each landing place there was a very great horde of Indians, and this village extended for more than two and a half leagues, to the very end of which it was still of the type just stated; and, because the Indians of this village were so numerous, the Captain commanded us to pass by without doing them any harm and without attacking them; but they, having observed that we were passing by without doing them any harm, got into their canoes and attacked us, but to their detriment, because the crossbows and arquebuses made them go back to their houses, and they let us go on down our river. This same day we seized a small village where we found food, and here we reached the end of the province of the afore-mentioned overlord Paguana, and we entered into another province very much more warlike and one having a large population and one which forced upon us much fighting: in regard to this province, we did not learn what the name of its overlord was, but they are a people of medium stature, of very highly developed manners and customs, and their shields are made of wood and they defend their persons in a very manly fashion.

On Saturday, the eve of Holy Trinity, the Captain gave orders to make port at a village where the Indians put themselves on the defensive, but in spite of that we drove them from their homes, and here we procured supplies, and there were even a few fowl to be found. This same day, on leaving there, pursuing our voyage, we saw the mouth of another great river on the left, which emptied into the one which we were navigating [and] the water of which was as black as ink, and for this reason we gave it the name of Río Negro, which river flowed so abundantly and with such violence that for more than twenty leagues it formed a streak down through the other water, the one [water] not mixing with the other. This same day we saw other villages not very large. On the next day, which was Trinity, the Captain and all [the rest] celebrated the holiday in some fishermen's quarters in a village that was on a hillside, and here much fish was found, which was a help and a great relief for our Spaniards, because [many] days had passed since they had had such lodgings. This village was situated on a high spot back from the river as if on the frontier facing other tribes who made war on them, because it was fortified with a wall of heavy timbers, and, at the time that our companions climbed up to this village to seize food, the Indians decided to defend it and took up a strong position inside that inclosure, which had only one gate, and they set to defending themselves with very great courage; however, as we saw that we were in difficulty, we determined to attack them, and so in accordance with this resolution the attack was launched through the said gate, and, entering without any loss, they [i.e. our companions] fell upon the Indians and fought with them until they dispersed them, and then they collected food-stuffs, of which there was an abundance.

On Monday we continued on our way from there, all the time passing by very large settlements and provinces, procuring food as best we could whenever we lacked it. On this day we made port at a medium-sized village, where the inhabitants let us come right up to them. In this village there was a very large public square, and in the center of the square was a hewn tree trunk ten feet in girth, there being represented and carved in relief [thereon] a walled city with its inclosure and with a gate. At this gate were two towers, very tall and having windows, and each tower had a door, the two facing each other, and at each door were two columns, and this entire structure that I am telling about rested upon two very fierce lions, which turned their glances backwards as though suspicious of each other, holding between their forepaws and claws the entire structure, in the middle of which there was a round open space: in the center of this space there was a hole through which they offered and poured out *chicha* for the Sun, for this is the wine which they drink, and the Sun is the one whom they worship and consider as their god. In short, the construction was a thing well worth seeing, and the Captain and all of us, marveling at such a great thing, asked an Indian who was seized here [by us] what that was, or as a reminder of what they kept that thing in the square, and the Indian answered that they were subjects and tributaries of the Amazons and that the only service which they rendered them consisted in supplying them with plumes of parrots and macaws for the linings of the roofs of the buildings which constitute their places of worship, and that [all] the villages which they had were of that kind, and that they had that thing there as a reminder, and that they worshipped it as a thing which was the emblem of their mistress, who is the one who rules over all the land of the aforesaid women. There was also to be seen in this same square a house not very small, within which there were many vestments of feathers of various colors, which the Indians put on to celebrate their festivals and to dance when they wished to rejoice before this said hewn tree trunk, and it was there that they offered up their sacrifices with their wicked purpose.

We soon left this village and in little time came to another very large one which had a similar hewn tree trunk and symbolic device such as has been mentioned: this village put up a strong resistance, and for a period of more than an hour they did not let us get out on land; but in the end we did get out, and, as the Indians were numerous and were increasing in number* every hour, they would not surrender; but seeing the damage that was being inflicted upon them, they decided to flee,† and then we had an opportunity, although not for very long, to procure a certain amount of food, because already the Indians were turning back towards us; but our Captain did not permit us to wait [for their attack], inasmuch as we could gain nothing by trading, and so he ordered us to embark and go on, and that is what was done.

Having departed from here, we passed by many more villages where the Indians stood waiting for us ready to fight, like a warlike people, with their arms and shields in their hands,‡ crying out to us, asking why we were fleeing,§ for they were waiting for us there; but the Captain did not wish to attack where he saw that we could win no honor, particularly as we had a certain amount of food on hand, and, whenever there was some on hand, nowhere would he risk his life and those of the companions, and that is why in some places we fought, they from the land and we from the water; but whenever the Indians were in great numbers they formed a wall and our arquebuses and crossbows inflicted damage upon them, and so we passed on, leaving them with the information just mentioned [i.e. what we could do to them].

On Wednesday, the day before Corpus Christi, the seventh of June, the Captain gave orders to make port at a small settlement that was on the aforesaid river, and so it was

---

*"Were re-forming."
†"Nevertheless, at last, out of fear, they decided to flee."
‡"Who were anxious to defend their homes and shields . . . "
§"Why we did not go to where they were . . . "

seized without resistance, and there we found much food,
particularly fish, for of this there was found such a variety
and so plentifully that we could have loaded our brigantines up well, and this [fish] the Indians had drying, to be
transported into the interior to be sold; and all the companions, seeing that the village was a small one, begged the
Captain to celebrate there, since it was the eve of such a great
festival. The Captain, as a man who was familiar with
the ways of the Indians, said that they must not speak of
such a thing because he had no intention of doing it, for,
although the village seemed small to them, it had a large
outlying district whence they [i.e. the inhabitants] could
come to give aid and inflict injury upon us, but rather [was
he of the opinion] that we should go on as we were accustomed to doing and get to the wilderness to sleep; and our
companions again asked as a favor that he celebrate there.
The Captain, seeing that all were making the request, although
against his will consented to what they requested, and so
we stayed in this village resting until the hour when the sun
was going down, when the Indians came to see their houses,
because when we went ashore there were none but women,
inasmuch as the Indian men had gone off to attend to their
field occupations, and so, it being the proper time, they
were now coming back, and, as they found their homes
in the possession of someone whom they did not know, they
were greatly astonished and began to tell us to get out of
them; and at the same time that they said this they came to
an understanding among themselves and got ready to attack
us, and this they did; but at the moment when they started to
penetrate the camp, there stood facing the Indians four or five
companions, who fought so well that they succeeded in bringing it about that the Indians did not dare to enter where
our men were, and so they [i.e. our men] made them take to
flight, and when the Captain came out there was nothing
left to be done. Night had now fallen, and the Captain, sus-
pecting what might happen, gave orders that the guards be
doubled and that all sleep with their armor on, and that
was done; but at midnight, at the hour when the moon

came out, the Indians came back in great numbers upon us and fell upon our party from three sides; when they were discovered they had wounded the sentinels and were in among us, and, as the alarm was given, the Captain came out shouting, saying: "Shame, shame, gentlemen, they are nobody; at them!" and so our companions rose up and with very great fury they attacked those men, so that, although it was night, they were dispersed because they could not withstand our companions, and so they fled. The Captain, thinking that they were bound to come back, commanded that an ambuscade be laid along the way by which they would have to come and that the others should not sleep, and gave orders that the wounded should have their wounds dressed, and it was I who dressed them, because the Captain was busy going from one place to another, attending to everything necessary for the saving of our lives, for in this he was always zealous; and if he had not been so expert in things pertaining to fighting (for it seemed as if Our Lord was guiding him in what he was to do), many times they would have killed us: and in this manner we were occupied all the night, and, the day having come, the Captain commanded us to get into our boats and to go on, and [first] ordered certain persons whom we had captured there to be hanged, and so it was done; and this [was done] in order that the Indians from here on might acquire fear of us and not attack us. We got into our boats, and, when we were out on the river, there arrived at the village many Indians with the intention of falling upon us, and also by water there came many canoes; but, as we were proceeding well off from shore, they no longer had any opportunity to put into effect their wicked intention.

On this day we penetrated into a forest and rested on the following [day], and the next day we continued our voyage, and we had not gone four leagues when we saw emptying in on the right side a very great and powerful river, indeed greater than the one which we were following, and, because of its being so wide, we gave it the name of Río Grande; and we continued on, and on the left side we saw some very large settlements standing on a slope which reached down to the river, and in order to get a look at them the Captain gave orders that we steer toward there, and we went; and it being observed by the Indians that we were going towards that place, they decided, so it seemed, not to show themselves but to stay in hiding, thinking that we would leap out on land, and for this reason they kept the roads that came down to the river cleared. The Captain and a few companions understood the base action that they had planned, and he ordered us to continue on, keeping well away from shore; and the Indians, seeing that we were passing by well out from shore, rose up more than five thousand strong, armed, and they began to shout at us and challenge us and strike their weapons one against another, and with this they made such a great noise that it seemed as if the river were sinking [from under us]. We moved on, and, [having gone] something like half a league, we came upon another larger village, but here we steered our course well out in the river. This is a temperate land and one of very great productiveness: we did not get acquainted with their [i.e. its inhabitants'] manners and customs, because they did not furnish us any opportunity for that; and here this race of people came to an end, and we came upon another that gave us little trouble. We continued onward in our journey and always through settled country, and one morning at eight o'clock we saw on a high spot a fine looking settlement, which, from appearances, must have been the capital of some great overlord, and in order to examine it we should have liked, although at a risk, to pull in close there; but it was not possible because it had an island in front of it, and by the time we decided to try to go in there we had already left the entrance behind us upstream; and for this reason we passed by in sight of it, looking at it. In this village there were seven gibbets [which]* we saw were at certain distances apart from one another throughout the village, and on the gibbets [were] nailed many dead men's heads, because of which [circumstance] we gave to this province

*[Inserted by Medina.—EDITOR.]

the name of Province of the Gibbets [Picotas], which extended down the river seventy* leagues. There came down to the river from this village roads made by hand, and on the one side and on the other [were] planted fruit trees, wherefore it seemed probable [to us] that it was a great overlord who ruled over this land.

We proceeded onward and the next day we came upon another village of the same sort, and, as we were in need of food, we were forced to attack it, and the Indians hid in order to let us leap out on land, and so our companions did leap out, and, as soon as the Indians saw that they were on land, they came out from their ambuscade with very great fury. At their head came their captain or overlord spurring them on with a very loud yell. A crossbowman of ours took aim at this overlord and shot him and killed him; and [some of] the Indians, on seeing that, decided not to wait, but to flee, and others to fortify themselves in their houses, and there they put themselves on the defensive and fought like wounded dogs. The Captain, seeing that they did not want to surrender and that they had done us injury and wounded some of our companions, gave the order to set fire to the houses where the Indians were, and consequently they came out from them and fled and gave us a chance to collect some food, for in this village, praised be Our Lord, there was no lack of it, because there were many turtles of the kind already mentioned and many turkeys and parrots and a very great abundance [of all things], for bread and maize do not require any special mention; and we departed from here and straightway went off to an island to rest and enjoy what we had seized. There was captured in this village an Indian girl of much intelligence, and she said that nearby and back in the interior there were many Christians like ourselves and that they were under the rule of an overlord who had brought them down the river; and she told us how there were two white women among them [as wives of two of these Christians], and that others had Indian wives, and children by them; these are the people who got lost out of

*Twenty leagues, according to the Muñoz manuscript.

Diego de Ordaz's party, so it is thought from the indications which were at hand regarding them, for it was off to the north of the river (21).

We proceeded on down our river without seizing any village, because we had food on board, and at the end of a few days we moved out of this province, at the extreme limit of which stood a very large settlement through which the Indian girl told us we had to go to get to where the Christians were; but, as we were not concerned with this matter, we decided to press forward, for, as to rescuing them from where they were, the time for that will come.

From this village there came out two Indians in a single canoe, and they came close up to the brigantine aboard which our Captain was, without weapons, and they came near in order to observe closely and remained there looking on; and, no matter how insistently our Captain called on them to come aboard and in spite of the fact that many things were given to them, they would not do so, but on the contrary, pointing toward the interior of the country, they turned back.

We slept that night directly facing this village in our brigantines, and, when day had come and we had begun to proceed on our way, there came out from the village many men, and they got into their canoes and came out to attack us in the middle of the river. These Indians [like all the others from] now [on] have arrows, and they fight with them. We started off on our way without letting them come up to us; we kept on going, picking up food wherever we saw that they could not protect it, and at the end of four or five days we went and captured a village where the Indians offered no resistance. Here was found a great quantity of maize (and there was also found a great quantity of oats) from which the Indians make bread, and very good wine resembling beer, and this [sort of beer] is to be had in great plenty. There was found in this village a dispensing place for this wine, [a thing so unusual] that our companions were not a little delighted, and there was [likewise] found a very good quality of cotton goods. There was also found in this village a temple within which were hung many military adornments for use in war, and above all these in the highest place were two mitres, very well made [and yet] with [only] natural skill, resembling those which bishops wear: they were [made out of] woven [goods] and we do not know out of what [material], because the stuff was neither cotton nor wool, and they were of many colors.

We moved on from this village and went over to sleep on the other shore of the river, as was our custom, in the woods, and to this spot there came many Indians to give us battle from the water, but against their will they turned back. On Tuesday, the twenty-second of June, we saw a great deal of inhabited country on the left shore, because their houses were glimmering white, [but we could not see the inhabitants at that distance,] for we were going down the middle of the river; we wanted to go over there, but we could not because of the heavy current and the rougher waves, and there were more [of them] than at sea.

The following Wednesday we captured a village which stood in the bend of a small stream on a very large piece of flat ground more than four leagues long. This village was laid out all along one street and [had] a square half way down, with houses on the one side and on the other, and [there] we found a great deal of food; and this village, because it was of the sort already stated, we named Pueblo de la Calle [i.e. Village of the Street].

On the following Thursday we passed by other villages of medium size, and we made no attempt to stop there. All these villages are the dwellings of fishermen from the interior of the country. In this manner we were proceeding on our way searching for a peaceful spot to celebrate and to gladden the feast of the blessed Saint John the Baptist, herald of Christ, when God willed that, on rounding a bend which the river made, we should see on the shore ahead many villages, and very large ones, which shone white. Here we came suddenly upon the excellent land and dominion of the Amazons. These said villages had been forewarned and knew of our coming, in consequence whereof they [i.e. the inhabitants] came out on the water to meet us, in no friendly mood, and, when they had come close to the Captain, he would have liked to induce them to accept peace, and so he began to speak to them and call them, but they laughed, and mocked us and came up close to us and told us to keep on going and [added] that down below they were waiting for us, and that there they were to seize us all and take us to the Amazons. The Captain, angered at the arrogance of the Indians, gave orders to shoot at them with the crossbows and arquebuses, so that they might reflect and become aware that we had wherewith to assail them; and in this way damage was inflicted on them and they turned about towards the village to give the news of what they had seen; as for us, we did not fail to proceed and to draw close to the villages, and before we were within half a league of putting in, there were along the edge of the water, at intervals, many squadrons of Indians, and, in proportion as we kept on going ahead, they gradually came together and drew close to their living quarters. There was in the center of this village a very great horde of fighters, formed in a good squadron, and the Captain gave the order to have the brigantines beached right there where these men were, in order to go look for food, and so it came about that, as we began to come in close to land, the Indians started to defend their village and to shoot arrows at us, and as the fighters were in great numbers it seemed as if it rained arrows; but our arquebusiers and crossbowmen were not idle, because they did nothing but shoot, and although they killed many, they [i.e. the Indians] did not become aware of this, for in spite of the damage that was being done to them they kept it up, some fighting and others dancing: and here we all came very close to perishing, because as there were so many arrows our companions had all they could do to protect themselves from them, without being able to row, in consequence whereof they did [so much]* damage to us that before we could jump out on land they had wounded five of us, of whom I was one, for they hit me in one side with an arrow, which went in as far as the hollow region,

*[Inserted by Medina.—EDITOR.]

and, if it had not been for [the thickness of] my clothes, that would have been the end of me. In view of the danger that we were in, the Captain began to cheer up the men at the oars and urge them to make haste to beach the brigantines, and so, although with hard work, we succeeded in beaching the boats and our companions jumped into the water, which came up to their chests: here there was fought a very serious and hazardous battle, because the Indians were there mixed in among our Spaniards, who defended themselves so courageously that it was a marvelous thing to behold. More than an hour was taken up by this fight, for the Indians did not lose spirit, rather it seemed as if it was being doubled in them, although they saw many of their own number killed, and they passed over them [i.e. their bodies], and they merely kept retreating and coming back again. I want it to be known what the reason was why these Indians defended themselves in this manner. It must be explained that they are the subjects of, and tributaries to, the Amazons, and, our coming having been made known to them, they went to them to ask help, and there came as many as ten or twelve of them, for we ourselves saw these women, who were there fighting in front of all the Indian men as women captains (22), and these latter fought so courageously that the Indian men did not dare to turn their backs, and anyone who did turn his back they killed with clubs right there before us, and this is the reason why the Indians kept up their defense for so long. These women are very white and tall, and have hair very long and braided and wound about the head, and they are very robust and go about naked, [but] with their privy parts covered, with their bows and arrows in their hands, doing as much fighting as ten Indian men, and indeed there was one woman among these who shot an arrow a span deep into one of the brigantines, and others less deep, so that our brigantines looked like porcupines.

To come back to our own situation and to our fight: Our Lord was pleased to give strength and courage to our companions, who killed seven or eight (for these we actually saw) of the Amazons, whereupon the Indians lost heart, and they were defeated and routed with considerable damage to their persons; and because there were many warriors coming from the other villages to give aid and as they were bound to turn back [on us], since already they were again giving their calls, the Captain ordered the men to get into the boats with very great haste, for he did not wish to jeopardize the lives of all, and so they got into the boats, not without some trouble, because already the Indians were beginning to fight [again], and besides this there was approaching on the water a great fleet of canoes, and so we pushed out into the river and got away from the shore.

We had now traveled, from the spot from which we had started and at which we had left Gonzalo Pizarro, one thousand four hundred* leagues, rather more than less, and we did not know how much there still remained from here to the sea. In this village just mentioned there was captured an Indian trumpeter, who had been attached to the fighting force [and] who was about thirty years of age, who, when he had been captured, started in to tell the Captain many things about the country farther inland, and he [i.e. the Captain] took him along with him.

Once out in the river, as I have stated, we let ourselves go drifting along without rowing, because our companions were so tired that they did not have the strength to hold the oars; and while proceeding on down the river, when we had gone about a crossbow shot, we discovered a village not particularly small, in which no people were to be seen, because of which all the companions asked the Captain to go there, [saying] that we should procure some food [there], inasmuch as in the last village they had not let us obtain any. The Captain told them that he did not want to, that although to them it looked as if there were no people [in the village], it was there that we had to be more on our guard than where we could clearly see them; and so we again held council together, and I joined with all the companions in begging him to do this as a favor, and, although we had passed the village, the Captain, granting their wish, gave the order

*"One thousand four leagues."

to turn the brigantines toward the village, and as we went skirting along the shore, the Indians [were] in ambush hidden inside their tree-covered areas, divided up into squadrons and all ready to catch us in an ambuscade; and so, as we went close to shore, they had an opportunity to attack us, and hence they began to shoot arrows at us so ferociously that we could not see one another; but, as our Spaniards were equipped, from Machiparo on, with good shields, as we have already said, they did not do us as much injury as they would have done if we had not come equipped with the said protection; and, out of all [of us], in this village they hit no one but me, for they planted an arrow shot right in one of my eyes, in such a way that the arrow went through to the other side, from which wound I have lost the eye and [even now] I am not without suffering and not free from pain, although Our Lord, without my deserving it, has been kind enough to grant me life so that I may mend my ways and serve Him better than [I had done] hitherto; and in the meantime the Spaniards that were in the smaller boat had leaped out on land, and, as the Indians were so numerous, they had them surrounded, so that, had it not been for the Captain's coming to their aid with the large brigantine, they would have been done for and the Indians would have carried them off; and even so they [i.e. the Indians] would have done this before the Captain could have come up, if they [i.e. our companions] had not shown such fine skill in fighting with such bravery, but they were now worn out and placed in a very serious situation. The Captain called them back, and when he saw me wounded he ordered the men to embark; and so they did embark, because the Indians were numerous and were thoroughly stubborn, [so much so] that our companions could not withstand them, and the Captain feared losing some of them and did not wish to place them at such a risk, because he perceived very plainly (and this was quite evident) the certainty that there was that they would get help, in view of the extent to which the land was inhabited (and it was imperative to conserve the lives of all), for one village was not half a league away from another, and still less than that along that whole bank of the river on the right, which is the south bank; and I can add that inland from the river, at a distance of two leagues, more or less, there could be seen some very large cities that glistened in white, and besides this the land is as good, as fertile, and as normal in appearance as our Spain, for we entered upon it on Saint John's Day and already the Indians were beginning to burn over their fields. It is a temperate land, where much wheat may be harvested and all kinds of fruit trees may be grown; besides this, it is suitable for the breeding of all sorts of livestock, because on it there are many kinds of grass just as in our Spain, such as wild marjoram and thistles of a colored sort and scored, and many other very good herbs; the woods of this country are groves of evergreen oaks and plantations of cork-trees bearing acorns (for we ourselves saw them) and groves of hard oak; the land is high and makes rolling savanas, the grass not higher than up to the knees, and there is a great deal of game of all sorts.

To come back to [the story of] our journey: the Captain ordered us to go out into the middle of the river in order to steer clear of inhabited districts, which were so large that they stirred up fear [in us]. We named this province the province of San Juan [Saint John], because it was on his day that we had entered it, and I had preached in the morning coming down the river in praise of so glorious a herald of Christ, and I hold it to be certain that it was through his intercession that God granted me life.

When once we were in the middle of the river, the Indians set out by water in pursuit of us, wherefore the Captain gave the command to cross over toward an island which was uninhabited, and until night came on the Indians did not cease pursuing us; and in this way we arrived at the island after ten o'clock at night, where the Captain gave orders that we should not get out on land because it might happen that the Indians would come upon us; and consequently we passed the night on board our brigantines, and, the morning having come, the Captain gave the command for us to continue on our way in good order until we should

get out of this province of San Juan, which is more than
one hundred and fifty leagues long along the river front,
settled in the manner I have stated. And on the next day,
the twenty-fifth of June, we went in among some islands
which we [at first] thought uninhabited, but, after we got to
be in among them, so numerous were the settlements which
came into sight and which we distinguished on the said
islands that we were grieved; and, when they [i.e. their in-
habitants] saw us, there came out to meet us on the river over
two hundred pirogues, [so large] that each one carries twenty
or thirty Indians and some forty, and of these there were
many; they were quite colorfully decorated with various
emblems, and they [i.e. those manning them] had with them
many trumpets and drums, and pipes on which they play
with their mouths, and rebecs, which among these people
have three strings: and they came on with so much noise and
shouting and in such good order that we were astonished.
They surrounded our two brigantines and attacked us like
men who expected to carry us off; but it resulted in just
the reverse for them, for our arquebusiers and crossbowmen
made it so uncomfortable for them that, many as they were,
they were glad to stand off; and on land a marvelous thing
to see were the squadron formations that were in the villages, all [the persons who composed them] playing on instruments and dancing about, [each man] with a pair of palm
leaves in his hands, manifesting very great joy upon seeing
that we were passing beyond their villages. These islands
are high, although not particularly so, and have level land,
apparently very fertile, and so pleasing to the sight that
although we were worn out they did not fail to gladden us.
Along the shore of this island, which is the largest [of them
all], we kept skirting: it must be about six leagues long,*
it being in the middle of the river; what its width is we cannot say; and still the Indians kept following us until they
drove us out of this province of San Juan, whose length, as
I have said, is one hundred and fifty leagues, all of which we
covered while enduring much hardship from hunger, avoiding

*Fifty leagues, according to the other copy.

fighting, because, as it was thickly populated, there was no opportunity to go on land. All along this island the afore-said pirogues and canoes still continued in pursuit of us, attacking us whenever they [i.e. the men in them] felt like doing so; but, as they were constantly tasting the fruit of our shots, they accompanied us [only] for a distance. At the end of this island there was a district much more thickly settled, from which there came forth, as a reinforcement, many more pirogues to attack us: here the Captain, seeing himself in such a desperate plight and desiring peace with these people, endeavoring to see if we could take some time to rest, decided to speak to the Indians and appeal to them for peace, and, in order to bring them around to this [attitude of mind], he gave orders to place a certain quantity of barter goods in a gourd and to throw it into the water, and the Indians picked it up, but they valued it so little that they made fun of it; but, for all that, they did not cease following us until they drove us from their villages, which, as we have said, were very numerous.

That night we managed to get to a place to sleep, now outside of this whole settled region, in an oak grove which was on a large flat space near the river, where we were not without fearful apprehensions, because Indians came to spy on us, and toward the interior there were many well-populated districts and [there were] roads which led into it [i.e. the interior], for which reason the Captain and all the rest of us stayed on guard waiting for whatever might happen to us.

In this stopping-place the Captain took [aside] the Indian who had been captured farther back, because he now under-stood him by means of a list of words that he had made, and asked him of what place he was a native: the Indian answered that he was from that village where he had been seized; the Captain asked him what the name of the over-lord of this land was, and the Indian replied that his name was Couynco* and that he was a very great overlord and that his rule extended to where we were, and that, as I have already said, was [a stretch of] one hundred and fifty leagues.

*"Quenyuc" [in the other copy].

The Captain asked him what women those were [who]* had
come to help them and fight against us; the Indian said that
they were certain women who resided in the interior of the
country, a seven† day journey from the shore, and [that] it
was because this overlord Couynco was subject to them that
they had come to watch over the shore. The Captain asked
him if these women were married: the Indian said they were
not. The Captain asked him about how they lived: the Indian replied [first] that, as he had already said, they were off in
the interior of the land and that he had been there many times
and had seen their customs and mode of living, for as their
vassal he was in the habit of going there to carry the tribute
whenever the overlord sent him. The Captain asked if these
women were numerous: the Indian said that they were, and
that he knew by name seventy villages, and named them
before those of us who were there present, and [he added] that
he had been in several of them. The Captain asked him if
[the houses in] these villages were built of straw: the Indian
said they were not, but out of stone and with regular doors,
and that from one village to another went roads closed
off on one side and on the other and with guards stationed at
intervals along them so that no one might enter without paying duties.‡ The Captain asked if these women bore children:
the Indian answered that they did. The Captain asked him
how, not being married and there being no man residing
among them, they became pregnant: he said that these
Indian women consorted with Indian men at times, and,
when that desire came to them, they assembled a great
horde of warriors and went off to make war on a very great
overlord whose residence is not far from that [i.e. the land]
of these women, and by force they brought them to their
own country and kept them with them for the time that
suited their caprice, and after they found themselves pregnant they sent them back to their country without doing

*[Inserted by Medina.—EDITOR.]

†"Four or five."

‡In this passage there is a notable variation in the form of the two versions, although the general
sense is more or less the same. In general, from here on many discrepancies in the wording of
the two manuscripts are to be noted.

them any harm; and afterwards, when the time came for them to have children, if they gave birth to male children, they killed them and sent them to their fathers, and, if female children, they raised them with great solemnity and instructed them in the arts of war. He said furthermore that among all these women there was one ruling mistress who subjected and held under her hand and jurisdiction all the rest, which mistress went by the name of Coñori. He said that there was [in their possession] a very great wealth of gold and silver and that [in the case of] all the mistresses of rank and distinction their eating utensils were nothing but gold or silver, while the other women, belonging to the plebeian class, used a service of wooden vessels, except what was brought in contact with fire, which was of clay. He said that in the capital and principal city in which the ruling mistress resided there were five very large buildings which were places of worship and houses dedicated to the Sun, which they called "caranain," and [that] inside, from half a man's height above the ground up, these buildings were lined with heavy wooden ceilings covered with paint of various colors, and that in these buildings they had many gold and silver idols in the form of women, and many vessels of gold and of silver for the service of the Sun; and these women were dressed in clothing of very fine wool, because in this land there are many sheep of the same sort as those of Peru (23); their dress consisted of blankets girded about them [covering their bodies] from the breasts down, [in some cases merely] thrown over [the shoulders], and in others clasped together in front, like a cloak, by means of a pair of cords; they wore their hair reaching down to the ground at their feet,* and upon their heads [were] placed crowns of gold, as wide as two fingers, and their individual colors.† He said in addition that in this land, as we understood him, there were camels that carried them [i.e. the inhabitants] on their backs, and he said that there were other animals, which we did not succeed in understanding

---

*[Such appears to be the meaning of "tendido en su tierra." Or perhaps "tendido" is an error for "teñido," in which case the meaning might be: "dyed the same color as their soil."—Editor.]

†[These last three words represent imperfectly nothing more than a conjecture as to the meaning of "aquellos sus colores." The text appears to be defective.—Editor.]

about, which were as big as horses and which had hair as long as the spread of the thumb and forefinger, measured from tip to tip, and cloven hoofs, and that people kept them tied up; and that of these there were few. He said that there were in this land two salt-water lakes, from which the women obtained salt. He related that they had a rule to the effect that when the sun went down no male Indian was to remain [anywhere] in all of these cities, but that any such must depart and go to his country; he said in addition that many Indian provinces bordering on them were held in subjection by them and made to pay tribute and to serve them, while other [provinces] there were with which they carried on war, in particular with the one which we have mentioned, and that they brought the men [of this province] there to have relations with them: these were said to be of very great stature and white and numerous, and [he claimed that] all that he had told here he had seen many times as a man who went back and forth every day; and all that this Indian told us and more besides had been told to us six leagues from Quito, because concerning these women there were a great many reports, and in order to see them many Indian men came down the river one thousand four hundred leagues; and likewise the Indians farther up had told us that anyone who should take it into his head to go down to the country of these women was destined to go a boy and return an old man. The country, he [i.e. the captive Indian] said, was cold and there was very little firewood there, and [it was] very rich in all kinds of food: also he told many other things and [said] that every day he kept finding out more, because he was an Indian of much intelligence and very quick to comprehend; and so are all the rest [in that]* land, as we have stated.

The next day, in the morning, we departed from this stopping-place in the oak grove, not a little delighted, thinking that we were leaving all the settled country behind us and that we were going to have an opportunity to rest from our hardships, past and present; and so we started off again on our

*[Inserted by Medina.—EDITOR.]

customary way; but we had not gone far when on the left
we saw some very large provinces and settlements, and these
lay in the pleasantest and brightest land that we had seen
and discovered anywhere along the river, because it was high
land with hills and valleys thickly populated, from which
said provinces there came out toward us in midstream a very
great number of pirogues to attack us and lead us into a fight.
These people are as tall as, and [even] taller than, very tall
men, and they keep their hair clipped short; and they all
came forth stained black, for which reason we called this
the Province of the Black Men [Provincia de los Negros].
They came forth very gaily decked out and attacked us many
times; but they did no damage to us, while they themselves
did not get away without some. We captured none of the
said villages, the Captain not giving us an opportunity to
do so on account of the excessively large number of inhabitants that were there. The Captain asked the Indian already
mentioned to whom that land belonged and who held it
in subjection, and he said that that land and the settlements
which were in sight, together with many others that we
could not see, belonged to a very great overlord whose name
was Arripuna, who ruled over a great expanse of country;
that in a direction back up the river and across country
he possessed [territory so vast as to require] eighty days of
journeying [to cross it], as far as a lake which was off to the
north, [the country about] which was very populous, and that
this was ruled over by another overlord whose name was
Tinamostón; but he said that this one here [i.e. Arripuna]
was a very great warrior and that they [i.e. his subjects] ate
human flesh, which was not eaten in all the rest of the land
that we had gone through up to here. This aforesaid overlord [Arripuna] is not [the ruler] of [the territory surround-
ing] the lake, but he is [the overlord] of a distinct one [i.e.
territory]. It is he who holds under his control and in his
country the Christians whom we learned about farther back,
because this said Indian had seen them; and he said that he
[i.e. the said overlord] possessed and controlled a very great
wealth of silver and that they used it [i.e. silver] in all this

land, but [that] gold they were not familiar with; and in truth the very land warrants one in believing all that is reported, according to the [general] aspect and appearance that it has.

We went on pursuing our course down the river, and at the end of two days we came upon a small village where the Indians offered resistance to us, but we routed them and seized the food supplies and [then] continued on, and [we captured] another [village] that was close to it, a larger one: here the Indians put up a resistance and fought for the space of half an hour, so well and with such bravery, that before we had had a chance to leap out on land they killed on board the larger brigantine a companion whose name was Antonio de Carranza (24), a native of Burgos.   In this village the Indians were familiar with some kind of poisonous plant, for this became evident from the wound of the aforesaid man, because at the end of twenty-four hours he surrendered his soul to God.

To return to our story, I have to state that the village was captured and we collected all the maize that the brigantines could hold, because, when we saw [the effects of] the poison, we proposed not to put foot on land in a settled district unless it was from sheer necessity, and so we proceeded with more prudence than we had been exercising up to now.

We forged ahead at great haste, steering away from inhabited country, and one day in the afternoon we went off to get some sleep in an oak grove which was at the mouth of a river that emptied, on the right, into the one down which we were navigating and was a league wide.  The Captain gave orders to cross over in order to get our sleep where I have said, because it looked as if close to the shore of the said river there was no inhabited district and we could sleep without worry, although the country farther inland appeared to be thickly populated: of this we were not afraid, and we stopped in the said oak grove, and here the Captain gave orders for putting some railings on the brigantines in the manner of fortifications for protection against arrows, and of no little use did they turn out to be for us.  We had not been long in this said stopping-place when there came a great quantity of canoes and pirogues, to keep watch on us, without, on the other hand, doing us any harm, and in this manner they did nothing but keep going up and down. We stayed in this place a day and a half and thought of staying longer. Here was noticed a thing of no little amazement and augury to those of us who heard it, and that was that at the hour of vespers there alighted upon a tree under which we were quartered a bird whose cry was all that we ever got to know about it, and this it uttered rapidly, and it said distinctly: "huí,"* and this it said three times, in very rapid succession. I can also relate that this same bird, or another [like it], we heard in our midst from [the time we reached] the first village, where we made the nails, and it was accurate [in giving its warning] to the extent that, noticing that we were close to an inhabited spot, at the watch of dawn it used to tell us so in this manner: "huí," and this [happened] many times: this means† that this bird was so reliable with its cry that we now considered it [i.e. the fact that there was an inhabited district near by] as sure as if we had seen it; and so it was that when it was heard our companions were cheered, and particularly if there was a shortage of food, and they made ready to go all prepared for fighting. Here this bird left us, for nevermore did we hear it.

Soon after that the Captain gave the order for us to depart from this spot, because it seemed to him that there were many people about and that in the night, as he thought, they had put everything in order for falling upon us; it was a night which the Captain ordered us to pass tied to the oars, because no place was found to sleep in on land, and this was a heavenly grant, for, if they [i.e. our men] had found [a place] at which to go ashore, few of us would have remained, or [rather] not one, who could have given any news of the voyage, according to all appearances; and the fact is that, [the situation] being as I have said, the Indians came

*[In the version of Carvajal's *Relación* inserted in Oviedo's *Historia*, etc., Vol. 4, p. 566, it is explained that this word means "hut." It could also mean "Flee!"—EDITOR.]

†[In the original, "quiere decir" may possibly be an error for "quiero decir," i.e.: "I mean."—EDITOR.]

in pursuit of us by land and by water, and thus they went all around searching for us with a very great clamor, and so the Indians came close to us and there they were talking, for we heard them and saw them, and Our Lord did not permit them to attack us, because, if they had attacked us, there would not have remained alive a single one of us; and so we hold it to be certain that Our Lord blinded them in order that they might not see us; and in this situation we remained until day came, when the Captain ordered us to begin to move on. Here we recognized that we were not very far from the sea, because the flowing of the tide extended to where we were, whereat we rejoiced not a little in the realization that now we could not fail to reach the sea.

As we started to move on, as I have said, within a short time we discovered an arm of a river not very wide, out of which we saw coming forth two squadrons of pirogues with a very great clamor and outcry, and each one of these squadrons headed for the brigantines and began to attack us and to fight like ravenous dogs; and, if it had not been for the railings that had been built farther back, we should have come out of this skirmish decidedly decimated; but with this protection and with the damage that our crossbowmen and arquebusiers did to them, we managed, with the help of Our Lord, to defend ourselves; but after all we did not escape without damage, because they killed another companion of ours, named García de Soria, a native of Logroño (25); and in truth the arrow did not penetrate half a finger, but, as it had poison on it, he did not linger twenty-four hours and he gave up his soul to Our Lord. We went on fighting in this manner from the time the sun came up until it was somewhat past ten o'clock, for they did not let us rest one moment; on the contrary, there were more and more warriors every hour, indeed the river was all cluttered up with pirogues, and this [was] because we were in a land thickly inhabited and one belonging to an overlord whose name was Nurandaluguaburabara.* On the bank there was a very great horde of people, who were watching the "guazábara" (26),

* "Ichipayo" [in the other manuscript.]

so that [escape seemed all the more impossible for us, be-
cause] as they [i.e. the Indians in the pirogues] kept following
us they were gradually placing us in a very perilous situation,
to the point where they were now close to the brigantines.
Here there were fired two remarkable shots with the arquebuses, which had the effect of inducing that devilish mob to
abandon us; and one of them was fired by the Lieutenant, who
killed two Indians with one shot, and from fright at this
thunder-clap many fell into the water, of whom not one was
saved, because they were all slain from the brigantines;
the other [shot] was fired by a Biscayan named Perucho (27).
This was a thing worth seeing, in consequence of which the
Indians left us and turned back without helping those that
were in the water; not one of these, as I have stated, escaped
alive.

When this was over, the Captain ordered us to cross over
to the left side of the river to avoid the settled section of
country which was in sight, and this was done; we continued
to push on along the aforesaid side for several leagues past
some very fine country, except that down close to the shore
there were no settlements, for they all appeared to be in
the interior of the land; we did not find out what the reason
was. So we went skirting along the shore: we saw the inhabited section of country located where we could not derive
any profit therefrom, and it was seen to be rather a number
of fortresses scattered along on the tops of hills and for the
most part stripped bare, they being about two or three
leagues back from the river; we did not find out what overlord ruled this land, nothing beyond what the Indian told
us, namely that in those fortresses they fortified themselves
when war was waged against them, but we did not learn
who it was that made war on them.

When we had gone on a little farther, the Captain ordered
us to go on shore to get some recreation and see the resources
of that land which was so pleasing to our sight; and so we
stopped [a number of] days at this aforesaid place, whence
the Captain ordered [some men] to go and reconnoiter the
country toward the interior for a distance of one league in

order to see and determine what [sort of] country it was; and so they went, and they had not advanced a league when those who had started off [i.e. they] turned back; they told the Captain how the country kept getting better and better because it was all savanas and woodlands of the type which we have stated, and that there had been seen many traces of people who came there to hunt game, and that it was not wise to go on farther; and so the Captain was delighted at their having turned back.

Here we began to leave [behind us] the good country and the savanas and the high land and began to enter into low country with many islands, although not so thickly inhabited as those farther back. Here the Captain turned away from the mainland and went in among the islands, among which he gradually made his way, seizing food wherever we saw that that could be done without damage [to us]; and, owing to the fact that the islands were numerous and very large, never again did we manage to reach the mainland either on the one side or on the other all the way down to the sea, during which [part of our voyage] we covered, in and out among the islands, a distance of some two hundred leagues, over the full length of which, and a hundred more, the tide comes up with great fury, so that in all there are three hundred of tide-water and one thousand five hundred without tide; consequently the total number of leagues that we have covered on this river, from where we started out as far as the sea, is one thousand eight hundred leagues, rather more than less.

Continuing on our journey in our customary way, as we were getting to be very weak and in great need of sustenance we set out to capture a village which was situated on an estuary; at the hour of high tide the Captain gave orders to steer the large brigantine toward that place; he succeeded in making port in good form and the companions leaped out on land; [those on board] the smaller one did not see a log that was covered by water, and it struck such a blow that a plank was smashed to pieces, so badly that the boat was swamped. Here we saw ourselves in a very trying situation, one more trying than any into which we had fallen along the whole [course of the] river and we thought we should all perish, for from all sides [evil] fortune was heaping blows upon us; because just as our companions leaped out on land they encountered the Indians, and they made them take to flight and, thinking that they were safe, started in to collect food. The Indians, as they were in great numbers, came back at our companions and went at them in such a manner that they made them fall back to where the brigantines were, with the Indians in pursuit of them; yet on the brigantines little security did they have, because the larger one was high and dry, for the tide had ebbed, and the smaller one [was] swamped, as I have stated; and so there we were in this terrible plight without any way out other than [that which] God alone [might provide] and that [which might be effected by the work] of our own hands, which was the one that was destined to save us and lead us out of the difficulty which we were in; and at once the Captain gave orders for devising and putting immediately into operation a plan whereby we might not suffer any loss, and that consisted in the manner in which he ordered the men to be divided up, which was that half of all the companions should fight the Indians and the others should float the small brigantine and [see to it that] it got repaired; and then he ordered the large one to be pushed off so that it might float, and on it there remained the Captain with just us two friars who were there with him and another companion to watch over the said brigantine and be on the alert against the Indians on the side turned toward the river: that is how all of us were not without having much with which to occupy ourselves, in such a way that we had fighting on the side toward the land and luck on the side toward the water; it pleased Our Lord Jesus Christ to help us and favor us as He had always done on this voyage, and [to watch over us as one] who had brought us here like lost people, without our knowing where we were or whither we were going or what was to become of us. Here it was made clear in a very special and complete manner that our God made use of His pity, for without its being understood by anyone [among us] how [it was done], He showed His divine mercy, and through the working of His unbounded clemency and divine providence a way out was found and aid was lent, in such a way that the brigantine was mended and a plank was fastened on; and at this very same instant [that the repairing was completed] the warriors took to flight, and during the three hours that the said task had required they had not ceased fighting. O infinite and sovereign God, how many times did we find ourselves, in the throes of agony, so close to death that without Thy mercy it would have been impossible [for us] to obtain [sufficient] strength or [avail ourselves of] the counsels of the living in order to escape with our lives! From this village we secured a certain quantity of food, and the length of the day fitted in so exactly with the toils thereof, that the fall of night and the final act of our getting into our boats were one. This night we slept right out in the river on board the brigantines. The following day we made port in a wooded section. Here we set to work repairing the small brigantine in order that it might be fit for navigation, for [read: and] we were held up by the said task eighteen days, and once again, in this place, they made nails, where once more our companions toiled with no little amount of endeavor; but there was a very great shortage of food; we ate maize in rations counted out by grains. Once again, while we were in the midst of this suffering, Our Lord manifested the special care which He was exercising over us sinners, for He saw fit to provide [for us] in this [time of] shortage of food as in all other instances I have quoted; and it happened as follows: one day toward evening there was seen coming [i.e. floating] down the river a dead tapir, the size of a mule, and when the Captain saw it he ordered certain companions to go after it for him and to take a canoe to bring it in, and they did bring it, and it was divided up among all the companions in such a way that for each one there turned out to be enough to eat for five or six days, which was no small help, but on the contrary a great one, for all. This tapir had been dead for only a short time, because it was [still] warm, and it had no wound whatsoever on it.

The repairing of the [small] brigantine and [the making of] the nails being completed, in order to repair the large one we departed from this spot and kept pushing ahead and looking for [proper] facilities or a beach to haul it out of the water and repair it as it needed to be. On Holy Savior's Day, which is the Transfiguration of Our Redeemer Jesus Christ, we found the said beach that we were looking for, where both brigantines were entirely repaired and rigging for them was made out of vines, as well as the cordage for the sea [voyage], and sails out of the blankets in which we had been sleeping, and their masts were set up: the said work took fourteen days of continuous and regular penance due to the great hunger [that we were enduring] and to the little food that was to be had, for we did not eat anything but what could be picked up on the strand at the water's edge, which was a few small snails and a few crabs of a reddish color of the size of frogs; and these one half of the companions went to catch, while the other half remained working: in this manner and amidst hardships of this sort we finished the aforesaid task, which was no small [occasion for] joy for our companions, who had had so difficult a task put upon them.

We departed from this stopping-place on the eighth of the month of August, fitted out none too well [but] in proportion to the limited means at our disposal, because we lacked many things that we really needed; but, as we were in a spot where we could not secure them, we put up with our hardships as best we could. From here on we proceeded under sail, watching the tide, tacking from one side to the other, for there was a very considerable tide when one took into consideration the fact that it was at a place where the river was wide, although we were passing among islands; to be sure, we were in no small danger whenever we expected the tide; but as we had no irons,* we would fasten to stones. We kept steering our course through places where the water was shallow enough to allow us to make use of our

*[I.e. anchors.—TRANSLATOR.]

anchors,* and we held on so poorly that it happened to us very frequently to drag our [stone] anchors along the bottom and go back upstream in one hour a greater distance than we had covered during the whole day. Our Lord saw fit, not looking upon our sins, to bring us out of these dangers and to do us so many favors that He did not permit us to die of hunger or suffer shipwreck, which we were very close to many times, finding ourselves aground, we being now all out in the water, asking God for His mercy; and when one considers the [number of] times that bottom was struck and knocks were received, it may well be believed that God with His absolute power chose to save us so that we might mend our ways or for some other mysterious purpose that His Divine Majesty [held]† in store, which we mortals, consequently, did not grasp. We went on in our journey, continually passing by settled country, where we secured a certain amount of food, although only a small amount, because the Indians had carried it off, but we found a few roots which they call "inanes,"‡ [and so we remained alive], for, if we had not found these, we should all have perished from hunger: thus we came out of there very short of supplies. In all these villages the Indians met us without weapons, because they are a very docile people, and they gave us to understand by signs that they had seen Christians [before]. These Indians are at the mouth of the river through which we came out, where we took on water, each one a jarful, and some half an *almud* of roasted maize and others less, and others [supplied themselves] with roots, and in this manner we got ready to navigate by sea wherever fortune might guide us and cast us, because we had no pilot, nor compass, nor navigator's chart of any sort, and we did not even know in what direction or toward what point we ought to head. For all these things Our Master and Redeemer Jesus Christ made up, to whom we looked as to

*[This long phrase is admittedly a conjecture, based on the context and on the corresponding passage of the other version (see p. 444, *infra*), as to the meaning of Carvajal's "echábamonos por portalles," this last word not being in the dictionaries consulted.—EDITOR.]

†[Inserted by Medina.—EDITOR.]

‡[I.e. yams.—EDITOR.]

our true pilot and guide, trusting in His Most Holy Majesty that He would place us on the right way and bring us to a land of Christians.  All the tribes that there are along this river down which we have passed, as we have said, are people of great intelligence and [are] skillful men, according to what we saw and to what they appeared to be from all the tasks which they perform, not only in carving but also in drawing and in painting in all colors, very bright, such that it is a marvelous thing to see.

We passed out of the mouth of this river from between two islands, the distance from the one to the other being four leagues measured across the stream, and the whole [width], as we saw farther back, from point to point must be over fifty leagues: it sends out into the sea fresh water for more than twenty-five* leagues; it rises and falls six or seven fathoms.  We passed out, as I have said, on the twenty-sixth of the month of August, on Saint Louis' Day, and we [always] had such good weather that never in our course down the river or on the sea did we have squalls, and that was no small miracle which Our Lord God worked for us.  We began to proceed on our way with both brigantines at times in sight of land and then again [so far out] that we could see it, but not so [plainly] that we could determine where [we were], and on the very day of the Beheading of Saint John, at night, one brigantine got separated from the other, so that never again did we succeed in sighting each other, wherefore we concluded that they [i.e. those on the other brigantine] had got lost, and, at the end of nine days that we had been sailing along, our sins drove us into the Gulf of Paria,† we believing that that was our route, and when we found ourselves within it we tried to go out to sea again; getting out was so difficult that it took us seven days to do so, during all of which [time] our companions never dropped the oars from their hands, and during all these seven days we ate nothing but some fruit resembling plums, which are called "hogos"; thus it was that with great toil we got out

*"Twenty" [in the other copy].
†"Aparian" [in the other copy].

of the Mouths of the Dragon (for so this may [well] be called for us), because we came very close to staying inside there [forever]. We got out of this prison; we proceeded onward for two days along the coast, at the end of which [time], without knowing where we were nor whither we were going nor what was to become of us, we made port on the island of Cubagua and in the city of Nueva Cádiz, where we found our company and the small brigantine, which had arrived two days before, because they arrived on the ninth of September and we arrived on the eleventh of the month with the large brigantine, on board which was our Captain: so great was the joy which we felt, the ones at the sight of the others, that I shall not be able to express it, because they considered us to be lost and we [so considered] them.

Of one thing I am persuaded and assured: that both to them and to us God granted great favors, and very special ones, in having us under His care at this time of year, for at any other the fallen trees that float along this coast would not have permitted us to navigate, because it is the most dangerous coast that has ever been seen. We were as well received by the citizens of this city as if we had been their sons, because they sheltered us and gave us all that we were in need of.

From this island the Captain decided to go and give an account to His Majesty of this new and great discovery and of this river, which we hold to be the Marañón, because the distance from the mouth as far as the island of Cubagua is four hundred and fifty leagues by latitude, for so we figured it out after we arrived. Although there are, along the entire coast, many rivers, they are small ones.

I, Brother Gaspar de Carvajal, the least of the friars of the order of our brother and friar, Father Saint Dominic, have chosen to take upon myself this little task and [recount] the progress and outcome of our journey and navigation, not only in order to tell about it and make known the truth in the whole matter, but also in order to remove the temptation from many persons who may wish to relate this peregrination of ours or [publish] just the opposite of what we have experienced and seen; and [what]* I have written and related is the truth throughout; and because profuseness engenders distaste, so I have related sketchily and summarily all that has happened to Captain Francisco de Orellana and to the hidalgos of his company and to us companions of his who went off with him [after separating] from the expeditionary corps of Gonzalo Pizarro, brother of Don Francisco Pizarro, the Marquis, and Governor of Peru. God be praised. Amen.

*[Inserted by Medina.—EDITOR.]

(1) The city of Santiago de Guayaquil.—There is much confusion among the chroniclers in regard to the history of the various attempts at, and ultimate success in, founding this city; but one thing is certain, namely that neither in the archives of Spain nor in those of Ecuador is any authentic record of the facts to be found today.

Pedro Cieza de León says that the city was first founded in 1534 by Sebastián de Benalcázar, at the mouth of the River Babahoyo; but Alcedo maintains that it had been founded one year earlier, in the Bay of Charapoto. It is recorded that Benalcázar left a certain Diego Daza there as fortress governor and captain and that the Indians revolted, killing all the Spaniards with the exception of Daza and five or six others who managed to escape and get back to Quito. Wishing to give a lesson to the insurgents and found the town anew, Daza returned there in company with Captain Tapia and a few soldiers, but without being able to carry out his intention; and, as by this time Benalcázar had now gone off on new exploring expeditions to the north, Francisco Pizarro, as soon as he had heard what was going on, dispatched from Lima, for the same purpose, Captain Zaera, who had begun to busy himself with dividing up the natives of the surrounding districts of the town into *repartimientos*, when he was called back in all haste to the aid of the capital, which the Indians were holding in a state of siege, and consequently that place as a colony had to be abandoned once more.

This was the state of affairs when this same Pizarro dispatched Orellana, in 1538, with a larger number of soldiers and horses, as they used to say in those days, to build the town on a better and more suitable site, as in fact he did do, choosing the west bank of the river [the Guayas] from which the city was to get its name. Cieza de León (*La crónica del Perú*, [Part I], Ch. 55 [*Biblioteca de autores españoles*, Vol. 26, Madrid, 1853, p. 409; Markham translation, Hakluyt Society publications, First Series, No. 33, London, 1864, p. 202]), followed by Antonio de Herrera (*La descripción de las Indias occidentales*, p. 37 [in the edition of Madrid, 1730, a companion volume of the four-volume edition of his *Historia general de los hechos de los castellanos*, etc., Madrid, 1726–1730; or p. 49 in the original edition, Madrid, 1601, a companion volume of the two-volume edition of the first four Decades of the *Historia*, etc., same place and date]), says that this founding of the city took place in 1537, a date which is manifestly wrong, for, since it was after the battle of Salinas (April 25, 1538) that Pizarro authorized Orellana to undertake the conquest and settlement of the province, the founding of the city could not have taken place before this last-mentioned year.

I shall now bring forth a document which presents evidence as to the manner in which Orellana carried out his commission and one which confirms most amply the theory which I have just advanced.

This document is the record of a judicial inquiry, put through the court in San Francisco de Quito at the request of Martín Ramírez de Guzmán, covering the services rendered by his father, Rodrigo de Vargas. In this judicial inquiry the thirteenth question of the interrogatory reads as follows: "*Item*, whether they know that after the said founding of the said city mentioned in the question preceding this one, on the occasion of the [various] conquests and expeditions into the interior that had to be carried out, the said Rodrigo de Vargas served in them personally and at his own expense; and [that], when the battle of Salinas was over, the Marquis Don Francisco Pizarro being desirous of rewarding some of the persons who had been on his side against Don Diego de Almagro, the said Marquis sent off Captain Francisco de Orellana to conquer and settle the province of Guayaquil, inasmuch as it fell within the Yagual *repartimiento*, and [that] with him there came other persons of distinction for the said purpose, and [that] the said Rodrigo de Vargas was ordered to come with him, because he too had his *repartimiento* there; and [that] thus they came and [served together]

* These Notes have here been placed immediately after Carvajal's *Account* instead of after the Documents, as in Medina.—EDITOR.]

in the conquest and colonizing [of the territories] of the Chonos along the river and [suffered many hardships in subduing] the natives of the said province, owing to the fact that they were a warlike people and that the country was rough, being covered with swamps and mangrove forests, and [that] in this affair the said Rodrigo de Vargas served with distinction, enduring many hardships."

Here is what the witnesses declared in reply to this question:

Gaspar Ruiz, "that he had seen that Orellana, [the one] mentioned in the question, had come to be the lieutenant of the city of Puerto Viejo, by command of Don Francisco Pizarro, and [that], just as soon as he had arrived, he had gone with a certain force of men to conquer the province of Guayaquil, which belonged to the Guancavelicas . . . , which fact this witness [i.e. he] knew because he had [likewise] gone with the said Orellana and had [actually] seen that what he had stated had taken place."

Captain Diego de Sandoval, "that, coming from the city of Panama, he had arrived in the city of Puerto Viejo, where as captain [in command] of the city was Captain Orellana, who had come from where the question states, and [that] he had likewise seen that the said Rodrigo de Vargas was there with the said Orellana and [that] they had served [together] in the conquest of the said province. . . . "

Francisco de Illescas said that "this witness [i.e. he] had come with Captain Zaera to [take part in] the conquest of the province of Guayaquil and [that], when they had arrived there, as there had just come from the city of Puerto Viejo a captain with a certain number of men for the conquest of this said province, among whom was the said Rodrigo de Vargas, to whom belonged as an *encomienda* the Lemos settlement, the one force of Spaniards had joined up with the other, and [that] while the said Captain Zaera was there he [i.e. this latter] had decided, in agreement with his men and in obedience to orders from the said Don Francisco Pizarro, to turn back to the said City of the Kings [Lima] to aid it, because he had received news how all the natives of these realms were in revolt on the side of the Inca Manco, with whom [i.e. Captain Zaera] this witness [i.e. he] had gone off . . . . "

Francisco Pérez de Vivero stated "that he knew and had seen how the said Marquis Don Francisco Pizarro had sent Captain Francisco de Orellana with a force of men to come and conquer this province of Guayaquil, whither they [actually] had come and [whither] the said Rodrigo de Vargas and other citizens of the said city of Puerto Viejo, who had their *repartimientos* of Indians in this province of Guayaquil, had been ordered to come and take part in the conquest of it . . . . "

Juan de Vargas, who, apparently, was a son of the captain having the same Christian name and the same family name who accompanied Orellana on his voyage down the Marañón, said "that, after this witness [i.e. he] had arrived at the said city of Puerto Viejo, he had seen how, at the command of the said Marquis Don Francisco Pizarro, the said Captain Francisco de Orellana had come with a force of men for the conquest and pacification of this said city of Guayaquil, to which, owing to the fact that the Yagual *repartimiento* of the said Rodrigo de Vargas fell both within its territorial boundaries and within its jurisdiction, he [i.e. Rodrigo de Vargas] had been ordered to come and take part in the conquest and pacification of the said country . . . . "

Francisco Perdomo said "that he had come along with the said Captain Francisco de Orellana to [take part in] the said conquest of this province [and] that he [i.e. Orellana] had come to carry it out under orders and instructions from the said Marquis Don Francisco Pizarro . . . . "

[In the Library of Congress in Washington, among the documents composing the collection given by Mr. E. S. Harkness, there is one relating to the chartering of the ship which Orellana took to transport his company from Lima when he went to found the city of Guayaquil. This document (listed in *The Harkness Collection in the Library of Congress: Calendar of Spanish Manuscripts Concerning Peru, 1531–1651*, Washington, 1932, p. 80) states, under date of June 8, 1538, that "Francisco de Orellana, lieutenant-governor of the city of Santiago which is in La Culata," chartered the ship *San Pedro* from the ship-master Benito de la Feria for the sum of 1,000 pesos, payable in five months, "in consideration of the fact," to quote the words of the document, "that you have let to me by charter the ship *San Pedro* so that I may load [upon it] and put upon it all the Spaniards and clothing and horses and anything else that I may wish to carry in the said ship, God to bring it safely to port, as far as the Point of Santa Elena which is in the said province of La Culata." Another document in this collection (*op. cit.*, p. 80), under date of June 8, 1538, is a letter of payment to the merchant Alonzo Jiménez, for the amount of 86 pesos and one *tomín* for money advanced. In another (*op. cit.*, p. 96) the royal treasurer Alonso Riquelme, the crown inspector García de Salcedo, and the accountant Pedro de Avendaño give authority to the lieutenant-governor Francisco de Orellana to represent them in "the city of Santiago on the river Daule which he is now founding in the name of His Majesty." This is dated at Lima, April 10, 1539. Still another (*op. cit.*, p. 78) is a letter of payment for 100 gold pesos advanced by García de Salcedo, the crown inspector attached to Francisco Pizarro; it is dated at Lima, June 6, 1538, and is signed by Orellana.—TRANSLATOR.]

However, Guayaquil did not last long on the site selected by Orellana; it was later transferred to the place which they had named "Old City" and finally, in 1693, to the location where it stands today; "and because its citizenry has been considerably increased," says Antonio de Alcedo (*Diccionario geográfico-histórico de . . . América* [5 vols., Madrid, 1786–89], Vol. 2, p. 330), "they are making one [city] out of the two, which are, as it were, separate quarters . . ."

In the work by Dionisio de Alcedo ["Alsedo" on the title-page] y Herrera entitled *Compendio histórico de la provincia, partidos, ciudades, astilleros, rios y puerto de Guayaquil*, Madrid, 1741, in spite of the fact that one might expect much from its title and its author, there is not one word regarding the various enterprises resulting in the ultimate founding of the city.

(2) Villa Nueva de Puerto Viejo was founded, under the patronage of Saint Gregory, on March 12, 1535, by Gonzalo de Olmos in the name of Pizarro. Situated originally on the shore of the sea, it was moved in 1628 to a site four leagues away, in consequence of its having been sacked by the [Dutch] corsair L'Hermite. (Cf. Antonio de Alcedo, *Diccionario geográfico-histórico de . . . América*, Vol. 4, p. 317; Dionisio de Alcedo y Herrera, *Compendio histórico de . . . Guayaquil*, p. 55.)

(3) This is Don Francisco Pizarro. He has been called Marquis of Charcas, or more commonly Marquis of Los Atavillos. The truth of the matter is, however, that Charles V, when he created him a marquis, did not assign any lands to him along with the title or attach any qualifier to it whatsoever. In an imperial decree signed in Monzón on October 10, 1537, the Emperor says to him, in fact, after stating that he is charging Bishop Valverde to report to him (the Emperor) on the place where vassals could be assigned to him (Pizarro): "You shall see to it that this is done without delay, in order that, when it [i.e. the report] shall have come in, I may order that the title and the appointment be sent to you, and in the meantime you shall call yourself Marquis, in just the form that I am using in writing to you, for inasmuch as the name which the land that shall be given to you is to have is not known, the said title is not being sent now."

(4) " . . . they feared that they [i.e. the natives] would kill him as they had done others who had gone [in there] with a very large force of men. . . . " In my opinion, Friar Carvajal in these words can be referring only to Gonzalo Díaz de Pineda, who, as Herrera says, crossed over the great Cordillera in 1536, "entered into the country of Quijos and La Canela, and was the first [white] man that did so and that reconnoitered it. . . ." (*Historia general de los hechos de los castellanos*, etc., Decade V, Book X, Ch. 14.) And Oviedo adds: "This Pineda, with a party of Spaniards, penetrated as far as some very lofty mountains, but many Indians came from their lower slopes to prevent the Spaniards from advancing further. These Indians killed some of the Spaniards, and amongst them a cleric." [If this passage, in the Spanish as quoted

by Medina, is in Oviedo's *Historia . . . de las Indias* (cited in full in footnote 1 of the Introduction, p. 8, *supra*) it is not easy to find. In any case, the exact words given by Medina may be read in Chapter 18 of Cieza de León's *Guerra de Chupas* (in Vol. 76 of *Colección de documentos inéditos para la historia de España:* see p. 62). The above is taken from Markham's translation printed in 1918 in the Hakluyt Society publications (Second Series, No. 42, p. 55).—EDITOR.]

(5) Juan de Alcántara.—There were among Orellana's companions two men by this same given name and surname, as Fernández de Oviedo has already noted [*op. cit.*, Vol. 4, pp. 384–385]: the one who is mentioned here, and another from the *maestrazgo* of Santiago. It was to one of these that Gonzalo Pizarro intrusted the brigantine as soon as it had been built. Both of them died during the trip down the river. [Regarding this last statement of Medina's, see the editor's addition to the footnote on the second Juan de Alcántara on p. 111 of the Introduction.—EDITOR.]

(6) Sebastián Rodríguez.—His signature is to be found at the end of the document on pp. 254 and 256 of this volume, of which I also present a facsimile. [This last statement is an error, as Medina reproduces in facsimile the document numbered [2] on p. 253 (our Fig. 2 on p. 255) and the end of the document numbered [7] on pp. 258–267 (our Fig. 3, pp. 260–261) but not document [4] on pp. 254 and 256, which is the one to which is attached Rodríguez's signature.—EDITOR.] That he was a native of Galicia is the only fact regarding him that we can gather from the testimony of Friar Carvajal.

(7) There are two species of turtles that are found in the waters of the Amazon: the *Podocnemis expansa*, commonly called *charapa* in South America, and the *Podocnemis tracaxa*, very much smaller than the first species and for this reason known by the common name of *charapilla*. [*Charapilla* is a diminutive of *charapa*.—EDITOR.]

When Friar Carvajal says: "manatees and other fish," he falls into the error of supposing that these animals, because they live in the water, belong to the fish family. The Amazon manatees are mammals, and they are commonly known as "sea cows." There are two species of them, and the naturalists distinguish them by the two designations of *Manatus americanus* and *Manatus latirostris.*

Father José de Acosta could not accept without scruple the idea that the manatee was not an animal, particularly one Friday when some manatee flesh was served to him as fish. Here is what he has to say in this connection in Chapter 15 of the third book of his *Historia natural y moral de las Indias:* "In the islands which they call the Windward Isles, which are Cuba, Santo Domingo, Puerto Rico, and Jamaica, one finds the so-called 'manatee,' a strange kind of fish, if one may designate as a fish an animal which brings forth its young alive and has teats and milk with which it nourishes them, and feeds on grass in the fields; but the fact is that it ordinarily lives in the water, and this is why they eat it as fish, although I, when I ate some one Friday in Santo Domingo, almost had scruples, not so much for the reasons just stated, as because in color and in taste the chops from this fish did not seem to be anything but slices of veal and, in part, of ham: it is as large as a cow." [An English translation of this work of Father Acosta's, with the title literally translated as *The Natural and Moral History of the Indies*, was made by Edward Grimston and published in 1604; it has been reprinted, with notes and an introduction by Clements R. Markham, in the Hakluyt Society publications (First Series, Nos. 60 and 61, 1880). For Grimston's version of the passage just given, see No. 60, pp. 146–147.—EDITOR.]

Quite worth reading is the elegant description of the manatee which López de Gómara gives us, together with the romantic story which he relates about a tame one owned by an Amazon Indian (*Historia general de las Indias*, ed. Rivadeneyra [see Introduction, footnote 46, *supra*], pp. 174–175).

(8) Diego Mexía was a wood-cutter [or a stone-cutter?] according to Friar Carvajal, or a carpenter if we are to accept the authority of Oviedo [*op. cit.*, Vol. 4, p. 385]. The latter did not know his given name. Diego Mexía was a native of Seville.

(9) Alonso de Robles was a native of Don Benito [a town in Estremadura about 60 miles east of Badajoz.—EDITOR.] Being a man who had won the confidence of Orellana, he came to be chosen by the latter to be the lieutenant of the expedition.

(10) In Antonio de Herrera's *Historia*, probably as the result of a printer's error, the reading is goa. A *joa* or *jova* is "an addition which is joined on to the main timbers at the upper points which constitute the sides [of the ship]" (Thomé Cano, *Arte para fabricar, fortificar y aparejar naos de guerra y merchante*, Seville, 1611, fol. 54).

In Law 22, Title 28 of Book IX of the *Laws of the Indies*, which contains the rules for the building of ships, it is set down that a vessel of nine cubits breadth of beam, or of 80¾ tons, must measure "of *jova* half a cubit to bow, divided into as many equal parts as be the ribs that it would have from the second rib to bow: and the half [i.e. one half, but of what?] divided into the [number of (?)] ribs from the sixth [rib] to bow." [With the exception of what is here printed between brackets, this is a word-for-word translation.—EDITOR.]

I confess that, probably because I am not expert in nautical science, on the basis of this definition and these rules I am unable to guess what Friar Carvajal means when he speaks of nineteen *joas* to indicate the size of Orellana's brigantine. [It is probable that the *joas* were additions made to the ends of the ribs to carry the rail, and that consequently "nineteen *joas*" means "nineteen ribs."—TRANSLATOR.]

(11) The companion who took charge of the building of the brigantine was, it will be recalled, Diego Mexía, from Seville.

(12) The given name of this Contreras was Gabriel. Oviedo [*op. cit.*, Vol. 4, p. 385] erroneously gives it as Blas.

(13) Cristóbal de Aguilar was the son of the Licentiate Marcos de Aguilar and an Indian woman, "by whom he had him on this island of Hispaniola," affirms Oviedo [*op. cit.*, Vol. 4, p. 384], adding that he was "a young man handsome of person and an honest fellow." He was at this time about 27 or 28 years of age and had already had experience "in the military expeditions which had been carried out in the land of Peru . . . " [*infra*, p. 271]; and he had been with Benalcázar in the conquest of Popayán and the provinces of Lile.

(14) Blas de Medina was a native of Medina del Campo, where he had been born in 1519. He had been in Peru for the past seven or eight years, "exploring and colonizing new lands . . ." [*infra*, p. 280]; and he had seen service with Benalcázar in the provinces of Quito and had taken part in the conquest of Popayán and in the fighting occasioned by the later uprisings of the natives in the territory round about it, and in the founding of the town of Timaná.

(15) Ampudia or Empudia.—Friar Carvajal, it will be noticed, gives his Christian name as Pedro and asserts that he was a native of Ciudad Rodrigo. Fernández de Oviedo [*op. cit.*, Vol. 4, p. 385] calls him Juan de Empudia and makes him a native of Empudia. From his signature, which occurs at the end of each of the two documents which I transcribe on pp. 256 and 259, it is not possible to determine what his first name was, because he did not put it down.

Which of the two authorities is right? Inasmuch as Friar Carvajal was in daily contact with him over a period of several months, I feel that the preference should be given to his testimony over that of the chronicler of the Indies who never saw the man in question owing to the fact that he [Ampudia] died during the voyage, on May 20, 1542.

By a royal decree of January 31, 1539, an appointment to the position of magistrate in the city of Popayán was sent to a man named Juan de Empudia, with a proviso to the effect that he could have the position only on condition that he would present his credentials to the Municipal Council within the time limit of fifteen months; and by another decree of the same date the lieutenant-governor of the province of Quito was ordered to see to it that the Indians held by Empudia as a *repartimiento* should not be taken away from him without his being first beaten in court by due process of law (Archives of the Indies, 109–7–1).

It is possible that Oviedo confused this man with the Empudia (or Ampudia) who went with Orellana, in spite of the fact that he had been informed that the latter of the two had died somewhere along the Amazon at the hands of the Indians.

(16) ". . . and there was no other remedy but a certain charm. . . ." Independently of the question of the lack of medicines with which the expeditioners had to put up, it is certain that in those days and even much later this system of practicing cures was much used in America and that it contributed in a large measure toward the fomenting of superstition among Indians and negroes. Numerous were the accused persons who were tried on such charges before the tribunals of the Holy Inquisition in Lima, Mexico City, and Cartagena.

(17) Cristóbal Enríquez.—Oviedo [in his list of the men who accompanied Orellana] erroneously gives [*op. cit.*, Vol. 4, p. 384] this man's Christian name as Francisco, and at another time [*ibid.*, p. 573] speaks of him as Cristóbal Manrique. This member of Orellana's party was a native of Cáceres and was a *comendador* in some order which I have been unable to determine. Born in 1514, he had been in the Indies only three years when he started out from Quito with Gonzalo Pizarro.

(18) This man's full name was Hernán Gutiérrez de Celis, and he was a native of Celis, which is in the Montaña.

(19) "In addition to their being shorn, their ears were pierced [in that part] where women commonly pierce theirs for ear-rings; but they caused the hole to grow artificially . . . to an extraordinary size, incredible to one who has not seen it [i.e. this great size]. . . . And because these Indians had ears formed in the manner that we have stated, the Spaniards called them 'Orejones' "—Garcilaso de la Vega, *Comentarios reales*, etc., Part I, Book I, Ch. 22. [For title of and other bibliographical details concerning the *Comentarios*, see footnote 47 to the Introduction, p. 30, *supra*. "Orejones" means "Large Ears."—EDITOR.]

(20) This is the llama (*Auchenia lama*) which is very common on the plateaus of Bolivia and Peru and which even at the present day is used as a beast of burden. To own a large number of these native ewes or sheep, as the old chroniclers call them, was the special and exclusive right, in certain regions, of "the men of importance and power." See my book, *Los aboríjenes de Chile*, Santiago de Chile, 1882, pp. 181 ff. [The possession of large herds of llamas is still a sign of wealth in the Indian communities of the Andes.—TRANSLATOR.]

(21) At the beginning of the year 1531 Diego de Ordaz started out from Seville and, having gone as far as the "Río Marañón," it being his intention to begin his explorations from there, he was compelled to abandon the project on account of the calms, currents, and shoals among which he found himself. He therefore put on all sail in order to pull away from that region at once and sailed farther on for the purpose of starting his expedition proper from another and less dangerous spot; but his lieutenant-general, Juan Cornejo, although an experienced seaman, was not so successful in getting away, and he ran his ship on the rocks, with the loss of a certain number of men; "and although many have maintained," says the chronicler Antonio de Herrera (*Historia general de los hechos de los castellanos*, etc., Decade IV, Book X, Ch. 9), "that they managed to save their lives and get on land, they too were lost among the Indians."

Let us see how Juan de Castellanos, in his *Elegías de varones ilustres de Indias*, describes the shipwreck of Ordaz's comrades, observing the very sensible opinion which he expresses with respect to the complete absence of any foundation on which to base assertions of the sort made by Herrera. After stating that Ordaz had penetrated without difficulty into the mouth of the Marañón, he continues as follows [*Biblioteca de autores españoles*, Vol. 4, Madrid, 1847, p. 81; the original is in meter]:

"Ordaz through skillful managing escaped alive and reached the spot which had been his goal, but Juan Cornejo with others numbering more than three hundred failed to get away . . .

"Very close to land they were shipwrecked, but without suffering any loss from the dashing to pieces of their ships, and so 'tis said that they all escaped with their lives and penetrated into regions ne'er before looked upon by men, until they at last discovered and joined some great and powerful tribes, at a spot where they were later found and where they have prospered, constantly increasing in numbers and welfare.

"This report used to be peddled around as absolutely trustworthy by many whom I got to talk with and whom I have known well; but it is a plain and obvious fiction, and an idle tale in my opinion; for if these persons had not long since died, they would have turned up in a thousand places (?); hence it will not be speaking from blind judgment to say that they all soon perished."—Elegy IX, Canto I.

Even more difficult to believe is the idea that these Spaniards about whom Orellana heard were the ones who had taken part in Alonso de Herrera's expedition, as hinted by the chronicler whom I quoted above. This expedition, undertaken in 1535, had headed for the regions which extend northward from the Amazon.

(22) See what I have to say in the Introduction in my remarks on the Amazons [pp. 25–27].

(23) See Note 20.

(24) Antonio de Carranza, according to Oviedo [*op. cit.*, Vol. 4, p. 385], was a citizen of Frías, which is located, in fact, in the province of Burgos.

(25) García de Soria, according to Oviedo [*ibid.*], came from the town which bears his family name.

(26) "Guazábara: a battle, skirmish, combat. A general term, or one in quite general use throughout the American continent and even on the islands of Cuba and Haiti." (From a glossary of "American words used by Oviedo" at the end of the fourth and last volume [pp. 593–607; reference on p. 599] of the edition of the *Historia . . . de las Indias* published by the Royal Academy of History, Madrid [1855].)

(27) Oviedo also mentions [*op. cit.*, Vol. 4, p. 385] this Christian name Perucho without giving the surname of the man in question. Can this be Pedro de Acaray?

In a list of the followers of Gonzalo Pizarro (list attributed to the Provincial of Santo Domingo) [See editor's addition to footnote 162, *supra*.—EDITOR.] mention is made of a certain Garay, a Biscayan, unmarried, a resident of Guamanga, who finally consented to enter the service of the King and whose Indians were ordered left in his possession. It seems to me probable that this Biscayan "Garay" was the same person as "Perucho," or Pedro de Acaray. ["Perucho" is a familiar, or pejorative, form of "Pedro."—EDITOR.]

# PART III
# DOCUMENTS

# DOCUMENTS

## I

*Letter of Gonzalo Pizarro to the King, dated Tomebamba, September 3, 1542**

Sacred Cesarean Catholic Majesty:

From the city of Quito I wrote to Your Majesty telling how I had come over to that city to hold it as governor on behalf of Your Majesty, because the Marquis my brother, now deceased, by virtue of the power and authority which he received from Your Majesty, relinquished into my hands the governorship of Quito and La Culata and Puerto Viejo, as I have informed Your Majesty at greater length; and I did likewise inform Your Majesty how, because of the many reports which I had received in Quito and outside of that city from prominent and very aged chiefs as well as from Spaniards, whose accounts agreed with one another, to the effect that the province of La Canela and [the region around] Lake El Dorado were a very populous and very rich land, [I became interested,] for which reason I decided to go and conquer it and explore it, both in order to serve Your Majesty and in order to broaden and increase Your Majesty's realms and royal patrimony, and because I had been made to believe that from these provinces would be obtained great treasures whereby Your Majesty would be served and aided in meeting the great expenses with which Your Majesty is faced every day in his realms; and in my zeal and eagerness to do this I spent more than fifty thousand *castellanos* (for which amount, or for the greater part of which, I am now in debt), which I paid out in advances to the men whom I took along with me, both on foot and on horse.

And, in order of events, what happened on the expedition was that I started off with more than two hundred men on foot and on horse, together with many other elements of equipment and munitions of war required for such an expedition, leaving behind me, above all things, proper arrangements and the proper persons for the good administration of the cities and the capital and for [the proper functioning of] the service of Your Majesty; and, having gone a distance of about seven leagues from the city, we came to some very rugged wooded country and great ranges out of which we were obliged to open up roads anew, not only for the men but also for the horses, and we continued on our journey until we came to the province of Zumaco, which must be a good sixty leagues away [and] within which it was reported that there were a great number of people dwelling, though it was impossible to travel about there on horseback, and there I halted the expeditionary force in order to allow it to get rested, both the Spaniards and the horses, for all were quite worn out in consequence of the great hardships which they had gone through in climbing up and going down the great mountains, and because of the many bridges which had been built for the crossing of the rivers. And here I found the land to be abounding in food, although the dwelling places of the Indians

* Archives of the Indies, "Patronato," case 1, shelf 1, bundle 1/6, number 2, division 11. This letter was first published by Marcos Jiménez de la Espada in *Ilustración Española y Americana*, August 22, 1892, pp. 109–111.

245

were far apart from one another and located on the slopes of the mountain range, which [land] is uninhabitable [for Europeans] on account of the heavy rains and the marshes and the ranges of mountains that there are in it, and I had all the food supplies brought together that I could.

And as the rains were getting heavy I sought to find out in what direction lay the land of La Canela, from some Indians whom I had caused to be captured from among the natives, and these said that they knew where the land of La Canela was; and as it was a matter about which there circulated so many reports, and as it was reputed to be such a rich country, and in order that Your Majesty might be better and more accurately informed of the truth, I decided to go in person to see it with eighty foot-soldiers, without taking any horses along because the topography of the land and its ruggedness did not warrant my attempting to do so. And so I went about in search of the cinnamon trees and the province where it [i.e. this product] was to be found, for at least something over seventy days, during which we endured great hardships and spells of hunger on account of the roughness of the country and the dissension among the guides, in consequence of which hardships a few Spaniards died, owing [chiefly] to the heavy rains and the hunger spells that we had to endure; and at the end of this time we found the trees which bear cinnamon, which is in the form of flower buds, a sample of which [product] I am sending to Your Majesty; and the leaf has the same flavor, and neither the bark nor the rest [of the tree] has any flavor whatsoever; and these [trees] were on some mountainsides very rugged, unsettled and uninhabitable; and some of the trees were small and others somewhat larger in circumference, and they stood at long stretches one from another. It is a land and a commodity by which Your Majesty can not be rendered any service or be benefited in [any attempt to exploit] the business, because it [i.e. the cinnamon] is in small quantities and [would be a source] of even smaller profit.

From there I proceeded into another province which is called Capua, and from here I sent back for the expeditionary force and continued on my way toward where the guides said that the good country was, and all [this time I was advancing] through wooded regions and over ranges and making roads anew, and I came to another province which is called Guema, where I found a savana of something like two leagues in length and a quarter in width of flat land; and here I set about capturing some native Indians, and, when they had been captured, by means of them I brought the chief and overlord of this province around to an attitude of peace; and, on questioning him in regard to the country on ahead, I was informed by him that farther on down was the good country, and that it was very thickly settled with people, and that these wore clothes, for the people that I had come upon hitherto were naked.

And acting on the information which I got from this chief I sent Don Antonio de Ribera, the campmaster, with fifty men to investigate the matter and open up the road by which the expeditionary force could go ahead; and he was fifteen days going and coming and he brought back a story [to the effect] that he had found a great river, that there were houses right on the edge of the water, and that on the river he had seen many Indians wearing clothes, going about in canoes, and that it seemed to him that that province was a thoroughly settled one, because the Indians whom he had seen wore clothes and [were] quite civilized. And, as soon as he came with this story, I set out and came to this province that is called Omagua, passing through great marshes and crossing over many creeks.

After I had arrived here I set about to reduce to a peaceful attitude of mind the chiefs of the province, who were going about all excited and [were dashing here and there] on the water in their canoes; and I dealt with them from the water and they [finally] adopted an attitude of peace. And when I had thus gotten them into a peaceful attitude of mind, they became excited [just the same] in such a manner that the greater part of them fled, using the tricks and evil devices to which the Indians always resort; and [yet] they did not succeed in doing this with so much impunity but that there remained [in my hands] the chief and a few of the important persons, thanks to the skillful tactics which I employed in handling them. And here I looked for a way of capturing a few canoes from them, as [in fact] I did capture them, to the number of fifteen, and [these were not difficult to find] because the Indians of this province frequent one another and carry on their trade by water in their canoes, inasmuch as back inland [from the shore of the river] one can not get about, for it is all marshes and water in great quantities and they [i.e. the natives] all have their living quarters and homes right down on the water's edge. And so, in the canoes which I captured we were in the habit of going up and down the river to search for food, but nevertheless we were in no condition to dare to go too far out on the water, because there were frequently on the river [as many as] a hundred or a hundred and fifty canoes, [the occupants being] all warriors; and they are so skillful in propelling these canoes about and in steering them that for this reason no one stands any chance of doing them any injury or of being able to defeat them.

And owing to the vegetation of the country and the roughness of the woodlands, and since, on the basis of the reports which I had got regarding the country inland, we were obliged to go down the river (a journey which could not be made [by land] except by opening up a road anew), and in order to take the men along safe and better sheltered, and in order that the Indians might not harm the members of the expeditionary force [by attacking] from the water, I found it advisable to build a brigantine to protect and accompany the canoes which I had captured, and [also] because we were compelled to search for food for the expeditionary force and to cross over the river from one side to the other in order to look for it, and without this brigantine and the canoes the men of the expeditionary force could not have been kept in condition, both from the point of view of food and from the point of view of the problem of transporting their weapons and the munitions for their arquebuses and crossbows and the other things indispensable to the expeditionary force, and of taking along the sick, and the shoes for the horses, and iron bars and pickaxes and other necessary things, for already there had died from among our number the greater part of the servants [i.e. porters] that we had brought along, because this country is a very warm one; all of which I did with the end in view, if we did not find any good country wherein to found colonies, of not stopping until I should come out in the Northern Sea.

And pushing on down the river by the route which the guides told us [to follow], being now seventy leagues inside this province, I was informed by the guides whom I had with me that there lay [ahead of us] a great uninhabited region in which there was no food whatsoever to be had; and, learning this, I gave orders for the expedition to halt and for us to lay in all the food that could be obtained; and, the men being thus engaged in searching for foodstuffs, there came to me Captain Francisco de Orellana, and he told me how [he had questioned] the guides that I had placed in his charge for better protection and in order that he might talk to them and from them get information regarding the country beyond, as he had nothing to do, for it was I who looked after matters pertaining to fighting; and he told me that the guides said that the uninhabited region was a vast one and that there was no food whatsoever to be had this side of a spot where another great river joined up with the one down which we were proceeding, and that from this junction one day's journey up the [other] river there was an abundant supply of food; from the said guides I in turn sought information, and they told me the same as they had told Captain Orellana; and Captain Orellana told me that in order to serve Your Majesty and for love of me he was willing to take upon himself the task of going in search of food where the Indians said [that it was to be had], for he was sure that there would be some there; and that, if I would give him the brigantine and the canoes manned by sixty men, he would go in search of food and would bring it for the relief of the expeditionary force, and that, as I was to continue on down and he was to come back with the food, the relief would be quick [in coming], and that within ten or twelve days he would get back to the expeditionary force.

And being confident that Captain Orellana would do as he said, because he was my lieutenant, I told him that I was pleased at the idea of his going for the food, and that he should see to it that he returned within the twelve days and in no case went beyond the junction of the rivers but brought the food and gave his attention to nothing else, inasmuch as he had the men to do it with; and he answered me saying that by no means would he exceed what I had told him and that he would come with the food within the time that he had stated. And with this confidence that I had in him, I gave him the brigantine and the canoes and sixty men, because it was reported that there were many Indians going about the river in canoes; telling him also, inasmuch as the guides had said that at the beginning of the uninhabited region there were two very large rivers that could not be bridged over, to leave there four or five canoes to ferry the expeditionary force over; and he promised me that he would do so, and so departed.

And paying no heed to what he owed to the service of Your Majesty and to what it was his duty to do as he had been told by me, his captain, and to the well-being of the expeditionary force and of the enterprise [itself], instead of bringing the food he went down the river without leaving any arrangements [for the aid of those who were to follow on], leaving only the signs and choppings showing how they had been on land and had stopped at the junction of the rivers and in other parts, without there having come in any news of him at all up to the present time, he [thus] displaying toward the whole expeditionary force the greatest cruelty that ever faithless men have shown, aware that it was left so unprovided with food and caught in such a vast uninhabited region and among such great rivers, carrying off all the arquebuses and crossbows and munitions and iron materials of the whole expeditionary force, and after great hardship the expeditionary force arrived at the junction where he was to await me. And when the members of the expeditionary force, having gone that far, saw the junction and [realized] that there was no relief [there] for them in the way of food, because he had gone on and there was no way of finding any food whatsoever, they became greatly discouraged, because for many days the whole expeditionary force had eaten nothing but palm shoots and some fruit stones which they found on the ground [and] which had fallen from the trees, together with all the various kinds of noxious wild beasts which they had been able to find, because they had eaten in this wild country more than one thousand dogs and more than one hundred horses, without any other kind of food whatsoever, from which cause many members of the expeditionary force had become sick, and some were weak, while others died of hunger and from not being in a condition to go on any farther.

And when I saw how Orellana had gone off and had become a rebel, I set about searching for the [reported supply of] food and sent out some men not only by land but also by water, in five canoes which by a miracle I personally captured from the Indians, which canoes were the means of saving our lives by carrying us over the great rivers which we found; and those men whom I had thus sent out to search for food came in at the end of six days, without bringing any information whatsoever regarding food, on which account the expeditionary force was put to [even] greater suffering.

And when I saw the shortage of food and the great discouragement which the expeditionary force was experiencing, I took the canoes and seven or eight companions and launched forth down the river, with the determination not to stop until I should find food wherewith to succor the expeditionary force; and God saw fit to grant that on the day after I started out I should arrive at the junction of the rivers where Orellana was to stop and go no farther, and I went up the [other] river on which I had been told that food was to be had, which [in fact] I found in abundance; and with these news I returned to the expeditionary force, which I found now filled with the fixed idea that they were in no condition to go on any farther, not only on account of the lack of food but also because of the killing off of the many horses that had been eaten and because Orellana had carried off the weapons of the expeditionary force and the brigantine and the canoes, with which [equipment] we had been crossing the river from one side to the other to search for food, for without the brigantine and the canoes we were unable to do anything; and they had all determined to tell me that they would rather die than go on any farther.

Considering the unfavorable attitude of the men and the shortage of horses and the lack of weapons and of the other things which Orellana had carried off, I saw that I had no chance of being able to go on any farther, and [the change of plan was necessary] also on account of the great stretch of uninhabited territory which we should have had to traverse [if we had gone on] down the river, and so I determined to take the expeditionary force across the large river in the canoes, in which crossing much difficulty was encountered, accompanied by a loss of horses due to the great size of the river and the depth of the water, so that it took us eight days to get it [i.e. the expeditionary force] over on the other side. And as soon as the expeditionary force had been ferried over [we started off], going one day's journey up the river from the junction where the food which I had discovered had been found and where it was reported that Orellana must have found it, to a place where we members of the expeditionary force, together with the horses which had been spared, rested after a fashion, and we laid in a supply of food for another uninhabited stretch, which we likewise traversed at the cost of much hardship, in the course of which all the remaining horses, more than eighty in number, were finally eaten; and in this uninhabited stretch were found many rivers and creeks of considerable size, the greater part of which could not have been crossed without the canoes; and there were many days when there were built in the course of two leagues [of advancing] twelve, thirteen, fifteen, and [even] more bridges to take the expeditionary force across; and we kept advancing on foot, opening up the way anew, because the Indians and people dwelling in those provinces always go about and get in contact with one another by water in their canoes, for except right along the bank of the river one can not travel [in that land], because of the great amount of water and the marshes and the creeks that there are there; and there were many days when we waded through the water up to our knees, and for many stretches up to our waists and even higher.

And at the cost of great suffering and with the loss of everything that we had taken along with us we got back up to the land of Quito with only our swords and each with a staff in his hand, and [this we accomplished only] by constantly opening a road. And [from Quito] to where I turned back it must be more than two hundred and seventy leagues, and a much greater distance by the route by which we came back, during which return there likewise died a few Spaniards, from hunger alone: regarding all of which matter I am sending a report to Your Majesty. And with regard to all our hardships and losses neither did we feel any regrets nor do we feel any [now], except in the matter of not finding any wealth whereby the great expenses of Your Majesty might be met more easily.

In all this land which we traversed in this way there was not found any opportunity for establishing some [sort of] town, owing to the fact that the land was mountainous*, with great ranges, and characterized by ruggedness, and uninhabitable; nevertheless, some of those who traveled about there [and] who possessed a knowledge [of the country] said that there probably existed, and that there would be found, gold mines there.

And on arriving at Quito I found that during the time that I had gone off to serve Your Majesty after sacrificing in expenses so much of my personal wealth, and without there being any cause or authority [emanating] from Your Majesty that he could have for it, the Licentiate Vaca de Castro, in passing that way, had taken away from me that city of Quito together with La Culata and Puerto Viejo, which I had been holding under my administration as governor on behalf of Your Majesty, and had caused himself to be received as governor of all that territory, owing to which cause there have been in these towns many disturbances among the Spaniards as well as among the native Indians, and [all this] is the reason why the Indians of La Culata rose up in revolt and the town [which had been founded there] was abandoned and [the people on] the island of Puná rose up in revolt, and there were killed in the one affair and in the other more than one hundred Spaniards, among whom [is to be counted] the Bishop of Lima, [whom] they murdered, as Your Majesty has probably already heard. And in order not to cause any annoyance to Your Majesty or do anything contrary to his service, because my desire is none other than to serve Your Majesty always, as my ancestors and I have [always] done, I have not meddled with the affair with a view to taking possession again of the towns which, as already said, I [formerly] held under my administration as governor on behalf of Your Majesty, and I feel certain that on this account Your Majesty is bound to grant me a favor, as he has always done and is doing, and will not be pleased at what the Licentiate Vaca de Castro has been doing in the way stated, because no orders have been given to him by Your Majesty to the effect that from those who spend their lives and

*[Or, possibly, "forest covered."—EDITOR.]

their property in the service of Your Majesty there shall be taken away that which they held on behalf of Your Majesty, but rather that they shall be granted greater favors.

And I likewise learned how Don Diego de Almagro* and other persons had murdered the Marquis my brother and many other persons and had taken possession of the land and [had accompanied this act] with great robberies and outrages and acts of injustice (for he had a hand in all that), all to the detriment of the service of Your Majesty, and [he has] been the cause [which has brought it about] that the natives of these parts have risen up and rebelled, in injury to the service of Your Majesty. And seeing the great harm that is accruing from all this and that might accrue to the greater detriment of the service of Your Majesty, I decided on going, just as I was when I came out of the expedition to La Canela, with my sword and with my staff in my hand, with more than sixty companions to look for the Licentiate Vaca de Castro, Your Majesty's president, to do whatever I might be ordered to do by him in the name of Your Majesty, and to endeavor with all my strength to pacify the country and the natives who might be engaged in revolt and rebellion and again reduce them [to obedience] to the service of Your Majesty and attempt to bring it about that Your Majesty's president and judicial organization be maintained and obeyed as it is just that they should be; because I am informed that Don Diego and his associates do not obey the commands of Your Majesty nor those of his royal courts of justice, for as regards punishment for the murder of the Marquis my brother Your Majesty is so just that [in due time] he [i.e. Your Majesty] will order him [i.e. Don Diego] to be punished as the case requires and as shall best befit the service of Your Majesty.

This land of Quito is in a very bad way, for the disturbances in connection with Don Diego extend as far as here; and they say that all the land of Peru is in the same condition, which fact I have learned from persons who have come in from out there. I shall hasten as fast as I can to arrive where Your Majesty's president is, for inasmuch as these companions of mine are going on foot and I [am doing the same] to keep them company, we can not get there as quickly as I wish I could. And I trust that I shall be able to serve Your Majesty in this expedition, owing to the fact that I am familiar with the passes and corners of that country and am acquainted with all those who are out there and they with me, and owing to my having, as I do have, many friends in it [i.e. that country] who out of consideration for me and at my bidding will leave their homes and go to serve Your Majesty, exposing themselves to all the dangers that may arise.

Our Lord prosper the Sacred and Catholic person of Your Majesty with the addition to his crown of greater realms and dominions as it is desired by Your Majesty. From the town of Tomebamba, in the land of Quito, September 3rd of the year One Thousand Five Hundred and Forty-two.—The vassal who kisses the sacred feet and hands of Your Majesty.—*Gonzalo Pizarro*.

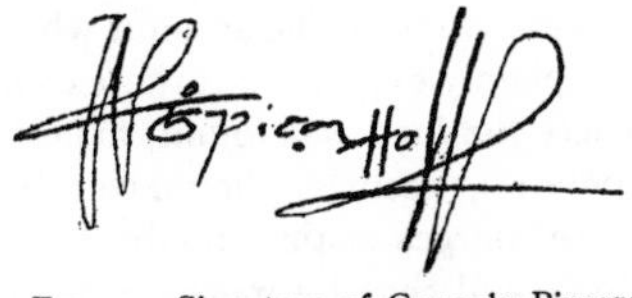

Fig. 1.—Signature of Gonzalo Pizarro from a document acquired by Bertram T. Lee, now in the Harkness collection in the Library of Congress.

*[The son of Diego de Almagro, known as "the Lad." He became leader of the anti-Pizarro faction after his father's execution in 1538. Instrumental in bringing about the death of Francisco Pizarro in 1541, he was in turn executed in late September, 1542.—Editor.]

# II

*Documents drawn up during Orellana's voyage and presented by him before the Council of the Indies on June 7, 1543* \*

[1]

Very powerful Sirs:

I, Captain Francisco de Orellana, declare: that it has been brought to my attention that letter-affidavits† coming from Gonzalo Pizarro have been presented, stating that I separated from the expeditionary force where he was [in command], and that I ran off with a brigantine and canoes filled with men and property belonging to him, and that as a consequence of my having revolted a certain number of men died of hunger; and because any report and petition that may have been made out and handed in to that effect is contrary to the truth, I beseech Your Highness‡ to order that there be examined a few affidavits which I bring from all the men who went along with me, wherein will be found definite information as to what actually took place in this affair; because, in view of the importance of my personal rank or [read: and (?)] of the matter [involved], it would not be just for the said Gonzalo Pizarro to report [on this matter] in the manner in which he is reporting, [namely] with [the testimony of] witnesses chosen by him when he was governor, for they, in conformity with the nature of the matter involved, were bound to say, in order to exonerate themselves, all that they would be asked to say, and I earnestly request that in this whole affair five things be considered: first, the testimony which I bring from all the men, who were so many in number, including both churchmen and laymen, and who were among the [most] honorable persons of the expedition, and [a testimony] which in all it says does not show any sign of a reference to personal advantages [to be gained], among which some-one may say that I could have been looking out for one [for myself]; second, that Gonzalo Pizarro himself gave me the men . . . (*torn*) . . . I had thought up such a piece of mischief, I should not have left behind me with the [encamped] expeditionary force my servants and my negroes and the few belongings that I had; third, that there was no reason why I should revolt, inasmuch as I was the principal man in the expeditionary force [next to Pizarro himself], and was not taking a chance on [securing] some personal gain by going, surrounded by so many dangers, down a river, starving, through a country which I knew nothing about, a fact which the experience [which I had] has demonstrated and which can be checked up from the account which I have handed in; fourth, the difficulty which it is plainly evident that there could have been in a return back up from the place where the food was found; fifth, that the currents themselves carried us on; and, above all, attention should be called to the little need that there is for his bringing these charges against me by way of attempting to clear himself, it having been God's will that by means of us who went over that route there should be discovered, unexpectedly, with so much risk and so much [relying on] luck, so many

---

\* Archives of the Indies, "Patronato," case 1, shelf 4, bundle 1/6, number 2, division 11. [Of these nine documents, Nos. 4 and 7 were first published by Jiménez de la Espada in *Ilustración Española y Americana*, in the numbers for August 22, 1894 (p. 111) and August 30, 1894 (p. 127) respectively.—EDITOR.]

† [See Introduction, p. 24, footnote 27.—EDITOR.]

‡ [I.e. the King, through the intermediary of the Council of the Indies.—EDITOR.]

peoples who will [now] be able to come to a knowledge of God, and [the fact being that] from this [adventure] there may come so much good to these realms; and so, I beseech Your Highness to command that my case be at once attended to as Your Highness may see fit, and I shall consider myself favored thereby.

*Action taken.*—[It is ordered] that this petition be attached to the affidavits and examined. Valladolid, June 7, 1543.

[2]*

In the village of Aparia, which is on this great river that comes down from Quijos, on the fourth day of the month of January in the year of the birth of Our Savior Jesus Christ One Thousand Five Hundred and Forty-two, Captain Francisco de Orellana, Governor's Lieutenant-General for the very honorable Gonzalo Pizarro, Governor for His Majesty, appointed Francisco de Isásaga† to be the scrivener of this expeditionary force which he [i.e. Orellana] is leading on behalf of the Governor, in order that everything that may occur and come to pass may take place before him [as a witness] and in order that he may bear witness to everything that may happen during the said expedition: the said Lieutenant gives authority to the said Francisco de Isásaga, in the name of His Majesty and of the said Governor, to exercise the said office of scrivener. Witnesses to all that is stated above, the Comendador Cristóbal Enríquez, and Father Friar Gaspar de Caravajal [*sic*], and Alonso de Robles, and Juan de Arnalte, and Hernán Gutiérrez de Celis, and Alonso de Cabrera, and Antonio de Carranza. The said Lieutenant signed it, and [so did] the witnesses.—*Francisco de Orellana.*— *Friar Gaspar Carvajal* [apparently *Carauajal*], Vicar-General.—*Xptoval Enriquez.* —*Alonso de Robles.*—*Juan de Arnalte.*—*Celis.*—*Carrança.*—*Alonso de Cabrera.*

And thereupon the said Lieutenant administered to, and received from, the said Francisco de Isásaga the formal oath, under the force of which he swore to exercise the said office well and faithfully and diligently; and the said Francisco de Isásaga said: "Yes, I swear" and "Amen": witnesses, [the same as] the aforesaid; and the said Francisco de Isásaga signed it with his name.—*Francisco de Orellana.*— *Francisco de Isasaga.*†

[3]

On this same day [of] the above-mentioned month and year the said Lieutenant requested me, the said scrivener Francisco de Isásaga, to bear witness for him and furnish him with true testimony to the fact that he in the name of His Majesty, and on behalf of the Governor Gonzalo Pizarro, does take possession, as the latter's Lieutenant-General, of the people of Aparia and of the people of Irimara and of all the other [peoples represented by the] chiefs who have come to a peaceful understanding [with him]; and to bear witness for him to the fact that they have come to where he is, and have served him and are serving him, and that he has taken the said possession without interference on the part of anyone. Witnesses who were present to see the said possession being taken: Father Gaspar de Carvajal, and the Comendador Cristóbal Enríquez, and Alonso de Robles, and Antonio Carranza, Alonso Cabrera, and Cristóbal de Segovia.

*[This document is reproduced in facsimile in Fig. 2, p. 255, *infra*.—EDITOR.]

† [Since written accents in signatures were not used in the sixteenth century they are omitted from these names in all cases where they occur as signatures in the present volume, although these accents, when added by Medina as editor in the documents which he publishes and in his own text, are retained. Medina himself was not consistent in the matter of using accent marks on the signatures.—EDITOR.]

I, Francisco de Isásaga, scrivener appointed by the said Lieutenant, do hereby bear witness and true testimony to the fact that on this said day [of] the above-mentioned month and year he [i.e. the said Lieutenant] took the rod of justice in his hand, and in the name of His Majesty, on behalf of the Governor Gonzalo Pizarro, took possession of this people of Aparia and [of that] of Irimara, which said possession he took without opposition of any sort: and, moreover, I do hereby bear witness to the fact that the said chiefs have accepted peaceful arrangements and have given obedience to His Majesty, and are rendering service and bringing food for the Christians. Witnesses, the aforesaid.—*Francisco de Isasaga.*

[4]

Honorable Francisco de Orellana:—We, the cavaliers and hidalgos and priests who are here with this expeditionary force with Your Worship, having become aware of Your Worship's determination to go up the river over the course down which we came with Your Worship, and having seen that it is an impossible thing [to do] to go back up to where Your Worship left Gonzalo Pizarro, our Governor, without risking the lives of us all, and that it is a thing which is not in keeping with the service of God or of the King our master, in the name of God and of the King we summon and beg Your Worship not to enter upon this so up-hill a journey, in which the lives of so many able-bodied men are placed in jeopardy, because we are assured by the seamen who are here in the boat and the canoes which have brought us here that we are two hundred leagues or more by land from the [encamped] expeditionary force of the Governor Gonzalo Pizarro, all [these two hundred leagues being] without road or settlement, but on the contrary very wild wooded regions, which we have come to know from [actual] experience and seen with our own eyes while coming down by water in the said boat and canoes, suffering great hardships and hunger; on which way and journey as we came downstream we have felt the fear of all losing our lives because of the privation and hunger that we suffered in the said uninhabited country; how much more danger of death there would be for us if we were to go with Your Worship back up the river! Therefore, we beseech Your Worship, and we beg him and summon him, not to take us with him back up the river, in view of what we have stated and pointed out to Your Worship; and let not Your Worship take the position of ordering us to do so, for that will be furnishing an occasion for our disobeying Your Worship, and for that disrespect which such [disobedient] persons ought not to have except [when faced] with the fear of death, [a death] which appears to us quite plainly [to be inevitable] if Your Worship tries to turn back up the river to where the Governor is: and if need be, again and again we summon Your Worship to do what is stated above, offering as an excuse to Your Worship [the necessity of saving] the lives of all; and we hereby exonerate ourselves from the charge of being traitors or even men disobedient to the service of the King in not following Your Worship on this journey: all of which we all request as of one voice and sign with our names, as will be seen from them below; and we request Francisco de Isásaga to bear witness to this, as the scrivener that he is of Your Worship; and we state that we are ready to follow Your Worship by any other route by which we may save our lives.—*Friar Gaspar de Caravajal* [*sic*], Vicar-General Ordinis Praedicatorum.—*Alonso de Robles.—Juan Gutierrez Bayon.—Mateo de Revolloso.—Cristobal Enrriquez.—Alonso de Cabrera.—Alonso Gutierrez.—Rodrigo de Arevalo.—Friar Gonçalo de Vera.—Carrança.—Alonso Garcia.—Francisco de Tapia.—Alonso*

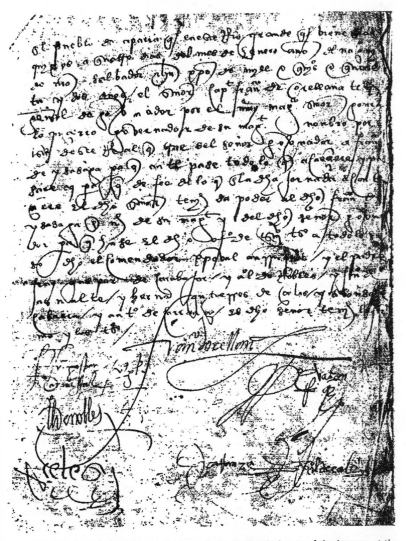

FIG. 2—Facsimile of the document drawn up during Orellana's descent of the Amazon, at the Indian village of Aparia on January 4, 1542, appointing Francisco de Isásaga scrivener of the expedition. The translation of the text is given on p. 253.

The Spanish text is transcribed (with partly modernized orthography) as follows by Medina:

En el pueblo de Aparia, ques en este río grande que viene de los | Quijos, á cuatro días del mes de Enero, año del nascimiento | de Nuestro Salvador Jesucristo de mill é quinientos é cuaren- | ta y dos años, el señor capitán Francisco de Orellana, Teniente | General de Gobernador por el muy magnífico señor Gonza- | lo Pizarro, Gobernador de Su Majestad, nombró por | escribano deste real que trae del señor Gobernador, á Francisco | de Isásaga, para que antél pase todo lo que acaeci- | ere y pa- | sare, y para que dé fee de lo que en la dicha jornada aconte- | ciere: el dicho señor Teniente da poder al dicho Francisco de | Isásaga, en nombre de Su Majestad y del dicho señor Goberna- | dor, para que use el dicho oficio de escribano: testigos á todo lo su- | sodicho, el comendador Cristóbal Enríquez, y el padre | fray Gaspar de Caravajal, y Alonso de Robles, y Juan de | Arnalte, y Hernán Gutiérrez de Celis, y Alonso de | Cabrera y Antonio de Carranza. El dicho señor Teniente lo fir- | mó, y los testigos.

*Gomez.—Alvar Gonçalez.—Pedro Dominguez.—Blas de Medina.—Cristoval de Segovia.—Alonso Marquez.—Gonzalo Diaz.—Garcia de Soria.—Graviel de Contreras.—Gonzalo Carrillo.—Hernan Gonçalez.—Alejos Gonçalez.—Alonso Ortiz.—Juan de Vargas.—Empudia.—Pedro de Porres.—Pedro de Aqaray.—Diego de Matamoros.—Juan de Arnalte.—Cristoval de Palacios.—Cristoval de Aguilar.—Celis.—Hernan Gonçalez.—Juan Bueno.—Juan de Yllanes.—Baltasar Ossorio.—Juan de Aguilar.—Sebastian de Fuenterravia.—Sebastian Rodriguez.—Diego Bermudez.—Francisco de Isasaga.—Andres Duran.—Diego Moreno.—Juan de Elena.—Juan de Alcantara.—Lorenço Muñoz.—Gines Fernandez.*

On the fourth day of the month of January, year of the birth of Our Lord Jesus Christ One Thousand Five Hundred and Forty-two, before me, Francisco de Isásaga, scrivener, there appeared all the cavaliers and hidalgos who came with Francisco de Orellana, Governor's Lieutenant, who was sent with them by the very honorable Gonzalo Pizarro, his Governor, to look for an inhabited district in order to succor the expeditionary force with food; and having appeared before me, they handed me this writing attached above in order that I, in the name of them all and in their presence, might read [it] and deliver [it] to Captain Francisco de Orellana, summoning him [to do] that which by its contents it summons him [to do], and they requested me to bear witness for them to all that is stated above; and I, the said scrivener, received the summons attached above on a [separate] sheet of paper with the signatures of the aforesaid persons, and in their presence and [in that] of the Lieutenant I delivered it personally [to him] and summoned him, as has been stated, in the name of all [to do] all that has been said above and is contained in the said writing, which is that he should not go back up the river by the route by which we came down in a boat and canoes through two hundred leagues and more of uninhabited forest country, without food [to nourish ourselves] or path [to follow]; and [I informed him] that by way of some other—an inhabited—part of the country they were ready and prepared to go with him to look for his Governor and his Captain: in evidence whereof, [this whole matter being] thus witnessed by me, [and] particularly [in the presence of] the said Lieutenant, I made my mark here, bearing, as I do bear, witness to the truth of it all, on the fifth day of the month of January, year of the birth of Our Lord Jesus Christ One Thousand Five Hundred and Forty-two.

The said Lieutenant and Captain Francisco de Orellana replied and said: that considering the summons and considering the fact that what they were requesting really was just, inasmuch as it was impossible to go back up the river again, he was ready, although against his desire, to look for another route to bring them out to a port of rescue and to a place where there were Christians, in order that from there they might go all together with the said Lieutenant to look for his Governor and render an account of what had happened; and he said that he gave this as his answer on condition that at this said stopping-place where we were at the present time we should wait for the Governor two or three months, [or] until we could no longer find sustenance for ourselves, because it might turn out that the said Governor would arrive there where we were, and, if it should happen that he did not find us, a serious risk would be incurred for his life, which was [of] great service to His Majesty; and [by way of improving our equipment] during the time that we are waiting here, the said Lieutenant orders that a brigantine be built in order that the said Governor may continue on down the river, or that we ourselves [may do so] in his name in case he does not come, inasmuch as in no other way except down the said river can our lives be saved; and this he said he was giving, and he did give, as his answer, and the said Lieutenant signed it with his name and requested me, the said scrivener, to bear witness to it for him. Witnesses: Father Carvajal, the Comendador Rebolloso (*sic*), Alonso de Robles, Antonio de Carranza, Francisco de Orellana. In evidence whereof I made my mark here. (*There is a mark to this effect in evidence of the truth of all this.*)

## [5]

The honorable Francisco de Orellana, Lieutenant-General of the very honorable Gonzalo Pizarro, Governor and Captain-General of the provinces of Quito and explorer of the provinces of La Canela and the Río Grande de Santa Ana, in the name of His Majesty [hereby] issues orders [as stated below] to all [individuals] and any persons whatsoever who may have taken or may have in their possession pieces of wearing apparel or any other articles whatsoever belonging to private persons who are remaining behind and are accompanying the Governor [on this expedition]: he orders them, in the name of the latter, to bring them [i.e. these articles] before him not later than tomorrow at any time during the entire day, under penalty [of punishment as follows, namely] that he who does not do so and conceals something shall be liable to and shall incur the punishment to which are accustomed to be liable those who keep another's property and who steal by force; and when the time limit which he orders for them is past, they [i.e. any persons having knowledge of such a case] shall come and denounce him [i.e. any person disobeying this order] or bring him before me, and he [i.e. the Lieutenant-General] will immediately proceed, as has been stated, [to take action] against the persons who shall have become rebels in this respect, because it is well that in all matters there be good order and good behavior and that no one derive personal profit from what belongs to some one else: in order that this may come to the notice of all and that no one may claim ignorance [in this matter], he orders it to be proclaimed publicly. Dated in this village of Aparia on the fifth day of the month of January, year of the birth of Our Saviour Jesus Christ One Thousand Five Hundred and Forty-two.—*Francisco Orellana.*—By order of the Lieutenant, *Francisco de Isasaga*, scrivener of His Majesty.

On the fifth day of the said month and year that which is contained [in the order] above was publicly proclaimed with the aid of a crier in the square of the village of Apariana,* in the presence of me, Francisco de Isásaga, scrivener of the Lieutenant, in a public place where that which is contained in the said proclamation could come to the notice of all. To the truth of which I bear witness and testimony, and I made my mark here in evidence of the truth. (*There is a mark.*)

## [6]

On the ninth day of the month of January [of the] year One Thousand Five Hundred and Forty-two the Lieutenant requested me, the said Francisco de Isásaga, scrivener, to bear witness and [furnish] true testimony for him to the fact that he is taking possession of eleven chiefs who have recently come to a peaceful understanding [with him], in addition to others whom I have [already noted down as having been] taken over, these eleven being: Hirimara, Paraita, Dimara, Aguare, Piriata, Ayniana, Hurumara, Aparia, Macuyana, Guaricota, Mapiare, and [to the fact that he has done this also] with all the other chiefs who have

---

* [*Sic* as printed by Medina.—EDITOR.]

accepted peaceful arrangements, and [he also requested me] to bear witness for him to the fact that they have come to where he is and have served him and that he has taken the said possession without interference from anyone. Witnesses who were present to see the said possession being taken: Father Friar Gaspar de Carvajal, and the Comendador Cristóbal Enríquez, and Alonso de Robles, and Antonio Carranza, [and] Alonso Cabrera, and Cristóbal de Segovia.

I, Francisco de Isásaga, scrivener of the Lieutenant, do [hereby] bear witness and [furnish] true testimony on the sixteenth day of the said month and above-mentioned year [to the fact that] the Lieutenant took possession, as Captain and Lieutenant-General [and] in the name of His Majesty and of the Governor Gonzalo Pizarro, of eleven chiefs who say that they are such, and these are: Hirimara, Parayta, Dimara, Aguare, Piriata, Ayniana, Hurumara, Aparia, Maluyana,* Guaricota, Mapiare, in this said village of Aparia; and this said possession he took without any opposition whatsoever; and besides this, I bear witness to the fact that the said chiefs have accepted peaceful arrangements and have served the Christians [by supplying them] with food. Witnesses, the aforesaid.— *Francisco de Isasaga*, scrivener of His Majesty.

[7]

Scrivener, who are here present, bear witness for us, the cavaliers and hidalgos, comrades, able-bodied men, whose signatures appear here, to the fact that we, on behalf of God Our Lord and of His Majesty, request and summon the honorable Francisco de Orellana to keep and protect us and maintain justice and tranquillity in the name of His Majesty, in view of the fact that he [i.e. Orellana] left the expeditionary force of the very honorable Gonzalo Pizarro, Governor and Captain-General of the provinces of Quito, and the expedition of exploration [which started out in quest] of cinnamon, [and that he] left [it] by his [i.e. Pizarro's] command to go in search of maize down the river at the river junction concerning which information was at hand, which junction everybody, and the Governor in particular, said might be at a distance of something like a four days' journey at the most; and we, coming in search of the said maize, [undertook this journey] without food or supplies, eating roots, herbs, [and] very dangerous unknown fruits, and harassed by this shortage [of food] we journeyed on for nine days, all [of them] through uninhabited territory, and at the end of them, God Our Lord having pity [on us], He saw fit to place in our path a village where, [upon investigation] in it, we found a certain supply of maize; and from the great hunger thus endured there died several Spaniards, and those of us who were spared became quite ill from the said suffering, because, as Your Worship knows, it was very great, not only as a consequence of not eating but also because of the constant rowing from sun to sun [i.e. from sunrise to sunset], for this alone was sufficient to kill us; there was great need, for the sake of our welfare, of resting a certain period of time, and this was not granted or conceded to us by Your Worship, rather Your Worship attempted right then to put into operation the plan of turning back, as Your Worship actually did start to do, and [Your Worship wished] to go in search of the Governor dead or alive; and [we refused to follow], it being evident to us that the return up the river was impossible because of the

*[*Sic* as printed by Medina, who gives "Macuyana" above.—EDITOR.]

great length of the journey, for we were informed by men who were best qualified to know about this that it was around two hundred leagues from the said village to where the said Governor was remaining behind, and in addition to this fact the currents and rapids are very strong; in consequence of all this we considered it to be better and more [in keeping with the] service of God and of the King to come on and [even] die down the river than to turn back up the river in the face of so much hardship; we decided to assemble, and we did assemble, and [we resolved] to summon [Your Worship], as it will appear from our summons, not to turn back up the river; and to all that is stated above Your Worship did consent as our Captain and Lieutenant-General, holding this commission, as Your Worship did, from the said Governor; and just recently we have seen Your Worship resign the said commission which Your Worship held from the Governor, with a view to getting relieved of the great amount of toil involved;* and we, perceiving and realizing the evil effects and great disorders that can prevail and come about [among men placed in the situation of] being without a captain in these forest regions and lands of infidels, again agree among ourselves and beseech [you] and once, and twice, and three times, and as many more times as are usual in petitioning in such cases, summon you, the honorable Francisco de Orellana, to keep and protect us in all peace and tranquillity, as you did keep us and command us before, and as in other parts you have kept and commanded Spaniards in greater numbers than [are] we who are here at the present time; because we appoint you now to be our captain again in the name of His Majesty, and so we wish to swear to it, and we shall swear to it, and for such a captain we wish to have you and obey you until such time as His Majesty shall decree otherwise: and by so doing you will render a service to God Our Lord and to His Majesty, and to us [you will do] favors; if you do not do this, we call attention by way of protest to all the harmful evils, tumults, homicides, [and] other outrages of the sort that are accustomed to take place in such a case as a result of the situation created when they [i.e. soldiers] have no captain. And thus we request you, the said scrivener who are here present, to bear witness for us to this effect and [furnish] testimony in such a way that it present incontestable evidence of what we are here requesting and soliciting.—*Alonso de Robles.—Xptobal Enrriquez.* —*Xptobal de Segovia.—Alonso de Cabrera.—Rodrigo de Zeballos.—Alonso Marques.* —*Gonzalo Diaz.—Matheo Revolloso.—Juan de Alcantara.—Juan Bueno.—Francisco de Tapia.—Garcia de Soria.—Juan de Alcantara.—Juan Bueno.—Francisco Elena.—Diego Matamoros.—Alonso Garcia.—Gabriel de Contreras.—Alonso de Tapia.—Gonçalo Carrillo.—Garcia Rodriguez.—Alejos Gonçalez.—Juan de Yllanes.—Blas de Medina.—Pedro Dominguez.—Empudia.—Pedro de Aqaray.— Juan Gutierrez Bayon.—Pedro de Porres.—Benyto de Aguilar.—Alonso Estevan.— Celis.—Mangas.—Cristoval de Aguilar.—Alonso Martin de Nogel.—Diego Mexia.—Lorenço Muñoz.—Antonio Fernandez.—Hernan Gonçalez.—Jines Hernandez.—Alonso Ortiz.—Hernan Gonçalez.—Alvar Gonçalez.—Juan de Vargas.—Diego Bermudez.—Cristoval de Palacios.—Andres Duran.*

On the first day of March [of the] year One Thousand Five Hundred and Forty-two, I, the said scrivener, gave notice of this summons to the said Francisco de

---

* [From this point on to the end of the first supplementary paragraph, ending, in the translation, with the words "This took place before me.—*Francisco de Isásaga*, scrivener of the expedition" (p. 262, *infra*), this document is reproduced in facsimile in Fig. 3, on pp. 260-261. —EDITOR.]

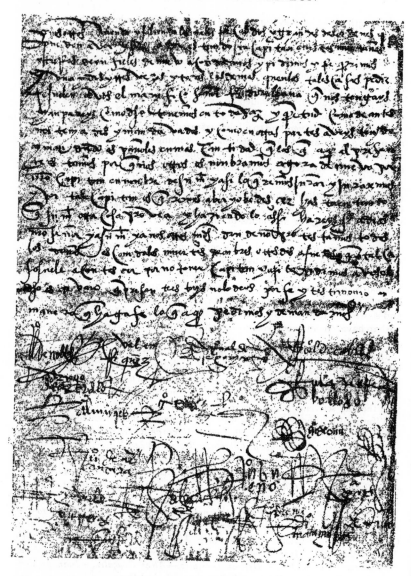

FIG. 3 (on this and the next page)—Facsimile of the end of the document dated March 1, 1542, in which the members of the expedition petition Orellana to resume the captaincy of the expedition. The translation of the section here reproduced is given on pp. 259 and 262.

The Spanish text is transcribed (with partly modernized orthography) as follows by Medina (pp. 104-105), beginning with the longer passage preceding the signatures:

y nosotros, viendo y sabiendo los malos recabdos y grandes desórdenes que | pueden haber y suceder estando sin capitán en estas montañas | y tierras de infieles, de nuevo acordamos y pidimos y requirimos, | una, y dos, y tres veces, y todas las demás quen los tales casos pedir | se suelen, de vos el magnífico señor Francisco de Orellana que nos tengáis | y amparéis como dicho tenemos en toda paz y quietud, como de antes | nos teníades y mandábades, y como en otras partes habéis tenido | y mandado españoles en más cantidad que los que aquí al presen- | te estamos; porque nosotros os nombramos agora de nuevo por | nuestro capitán en nombre de Su Majestad, y así lo queremos jurar, y juraremos, | y por tal capitán os queremos haber y obedecer hasta en tanto | que Su Majestad otra cosa provea; y haciéndolo así haréis servicio á Dios | Nuestro Señor, y á S.

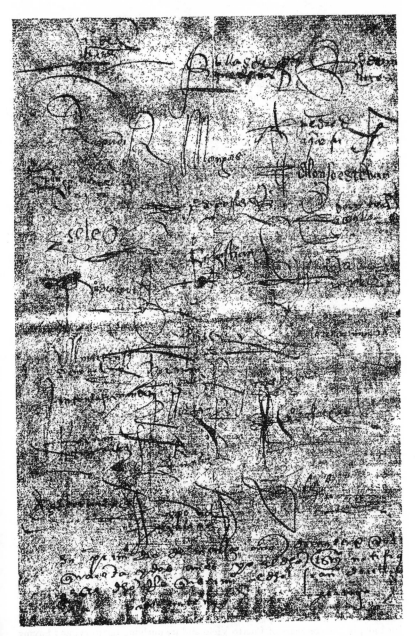

Majestad, y á nosotros mercedes; donde no, protestamos todos | los daños, escándalos, muertes de hombres, otros desafueros que en tal ca- | so suelen acontecer por no tener capitán. Y así lo pidimos á vos el | dicho escribano que presente estáis nos lo deis por fee y testimonio en | manera que haga fee lo que aquí pedimos y demandamos.

The short paragraph following the signatures reads:

En primero día de Marzo, año de mill é quinientos é | cuarenta y dos años, yo el dicho escribano notifiqué este | requerimiento al dicho Francisco de Orellana.— Pasó ante | mí.—
Francisco de Isásaga, escribano de la Armada.

Orellana.—This took place before me.—*Francisco de Isasaga*, scrivener of the expedition.

And then the said Captain Francisco de Orellana, having taken cognizance of the said summons, and [in the belief that] it [i.e. his acceptance] was essential to [the proper functioning of] the service of God Our Lord and of His Majesty, and in order to serve him, said that he accepted it [i.e. the summons, together with the position offered to him] and he did accept it in the name of His Majesty, and he signed it with his name.—*Francisco Dorellana.*—Before me, *Francisco de Isasaga*, scrivener of the expedition.

And then all those who have signed placed their hands on a mass-book and formally swore by God and by Holy Mary, by the sign of the Cross, [and] by the four sacred Gospels, to have as their captain the said Francisco de Orellana, and to obey [him] as such in all that they should be commanded in the name of His Majesty [to do]. Witnesses, Father Friar Gaspar de Carvajal and Father Friar Gonzalo de Vera. All of which took place in the presence of me, the said scrivener. —*Francisco de Isasaga*, scrivener of the expedition.

And then all together of one accord they requested the said captain to swear to keep them in [conformity with the laws of] justice: which said captain placed his hand on a mass-book and formally swore to do all that is befitting to the service of God Our Lord and of His Majesty, and to keep them in [conformity with the laws of] justice. Witnesses to all that which is [here] stated, the aforesaid priests, and in the presence of me, the said scrivener.—*Francisco de Isasaga*, scrivener of the expedition.

# III

*A statement, to be submitted to His Majesty, furnished by the Court and Council of the city of Santiago\* in this land of New Castile called Peru, covering the well-deserving services of Captain Francisco de Orellana, Governor's Lieutenant in the said city†*

In the city of Santiago in this [land of] New Castile called Peru, on the fourth day of the month of February [in the] year of the birth of Our Savior Jesus Christ One Thousand Five Hundred and Forty-one, there being together in council meeting, as is their usage and custom, the very distinguished gentlemen Rodrigo de Vargas, regular justice of the peace in the said city, and Gómez de Estacio, and Francisco de Chaves, and Pedro de Gibraleón, and Alonso Casco, and Juan de la Puente, and Cristóbal Lunar, magistrates of the said city, and in the presence of me, the scrivener whose name appears below, there appeared in person Captain Francisco de Orellana, Governor's Lieutenant-General in the said city, and he handed in a petition, the content of which is as follows:

Very distinguished gentlemen: I, Captain Francisco de Orellana, Governor's Lieutenant-General in this city, etc., and a citizen of it, present myself before Your Worships and state that [I desire to petition His Majesty for certain favors] as a reward for what I have done in the form of services to His Majesty in these parts of Peru during the time that I have been residing in it, having thus taken part in the conquests of Lima and Trujillo and Cuzco and in the pursuit of the Inca and in the conquest of Puerto Viejo and its outlying territory, and having

---

\* [I e. Santiago de Guayaquil.—EDITOR.]

† Archives of the Indies, "Patronato," case 2, shelf 2, bundle 1/6, piece 23.

lost an eye in them [i.e. these campaigns], and [believing that] likewise [there is bound] to be [well] known to Your Worships the service which I rendered to God Our Lord and to His Majesty in the said city of Puerto Viejo in the aiding of Spaniards who came freely to my house, and [that familiar also to Your Worships is] my having gone from the said Villa Nueva de Puerto Viejo, where I was a resident, with more than eighty men on foot and on horse, and my having taken along more than ten or twelve horses, which I purchased at my own expense and on my own initiative, and [my having] distributed them among some companions, because in the said town news had been received how the city of Cuzco, where Hernando Pizarro was, and that of Lima, where the Governor was, were being besieged by the Indians and [were] in great danger of being lost [by the Spaniards], [and] I recruited the said eighty men at my own expense and on my own initiative, paying their transportation and other expenses which they had incurred in the said town and putting myself in debt for a large amount and sum total of gold pesos, [and] I led them by land, at my own expense and on my own initiative, on which said expedition I accomplished much good and [rendered] a great service to the Royal Crown, as a person zealous [in looking after the interests] of it; and, having left the said cities freed from siege, and the said Governor and Hernando Pizarro being now out of their perilous situation, the Governor ordered me and gave official instructions to me to set out to conquer [territory] in the name of His Majesty and in his own, and to conquer, with the rank of Captain-General, the province of La Culata, in which I was to found a city, which task I accepted in order to serve His Majesty; and I set out on the said conquest, which I carried out with the aid of men whom I took along on it at my own expense and on my own initiative, and at the cost of many hardships on the part of myself and of those who went along with me, for the reason that the Indians of the said province were untamable and warlike and the land where they were [was one] of many rivers and [of rivers] having great volume of water, and [was a region] of great marshes, and because two or three captains had gone into it and they [i.e. the Indians] had routed them and killed many Spaniards, for which reason the Indians of the said province were very haughty; and, after I had conquered them and placed the said province under the yoke of, and under obedience to, His Majesty, continuing my services I established and founded in the name of His Majesty a city to which I gave the name of City of Santiago, in the establishing and founding of which I rendered and [have since rendered] a great service to His Majesty owing to the fact that I founded it in a spot so fertile and so rich and because of its being in a district [so conveniently situated] that through it provisions are furnished and carried to the towns of Quito and Pasto and Popayán, and it is expected [that through it also] they will supply the others that will be founded in the future, all of which could not have been done, if the said city had not been founded, without frequent slaughterings of Spaniards and great destruction and losses, because of the fact that the province was [formerly] outside of the [territory under] obedience to His Majesty, while at present the said provinces are traversed [freely] by one Spaniard or by two traveling alone and as they wish, without any risk for their lives and their property, and the said city [has the further advantage of] being in a spot where [the proximity of the sea is such that] ships come close up to it; and likewise the said Governor, seeing and understanding how [well] I had done all this, sent me powers and commissions by virtue of which I might hold the office of Captain-General and Governor's Lieutenant in this said city and in Villa Nueva de Puerto Viejo, which said office I accepted, and I have held and am holding the city and the town in [keeping with the laws of] righteousness and justice and I have exercised and am exercising the said functions well and faithfully and diligently, and of them I have given and am giving a good account; and because I wish to go or send [someone] to beseech His Majesty, as a King and master who will be grateful for my services and for those that I hope to perform for him henceforth, to grant me in return for them [certain] favors, which I do not wish to state here, [preferring to wait] until I can beg and beseech His Majesty [to grant] them, and because His Majesty does command through the medium of his royal [decrees of] authorization that whenever any person in these parts may wish to go or send [someone] to ask [him] to grant him favors in return for the services that he is rendering to his Royal Crown in them [i.e. these parts], he shall submit a statement of them* before the Court of the city, town, or place where the one who may wish to beg and beseech His Majesty [to grant] some such thing as this may be a resident, so that the said Court may say whether he is entitled to it and is a person to whom such a favor should be granted; and because I, the said Captain Francisco de Orellana, do not clearly state here what I wish to beg and beseech His Majesty [to grant me], and since I am a gentleman of noble blood and† a person of honor, and there are brought together in me the qualifications which are required [of me] in order that I may be able to hold and fill any office, such as that of governor or any other whatsoever that His Majesty might see fit to grant me, I beg Your Worships, in accordance with the said [decrees of] authorization, to reply and state my personal qualifications and my titles to a reward and my [past] services and [to say] whether I am a person such that any office or offices whatsoever might fittingly be held by me, and [I urge Your Worships] to state in reply, in all this matter, exactly what Your Worships think best, so that His Majesty may be truthfully informed in the [present] case; for which purpose, and to such an extent as may be necessary, I implore the very distinguished services of Your Worships, and I beg Your Worships to order that I be given one or two or more copies of this petition and of Your Worships' reply.—*Francisco de Orellana.*

And the said petition having been thus submitted in the form that is stated and having been read by me, the said scrivener, the said justice of the peace and magistrates declared that it was well known to them that the said Captain Francisco de Orellana took part in the conquests as stated in the said petition of his, and that he lost an eye in them, in which [conquests] he served His Majesty as a very good servant; and [that] likewise to several from among the said justice of the peace and magistrates, as persons who had been eye-witnesses of it, it was well known that the said Captain Francisco de Orellana rendered great service to God Our Lord and to His Majesty in Villa Nueva de Puerto Viejo, where he was [then] a resident, because it was during the time when the said Captain was residing in

---

* [In the text as printed by Medina this pronoun, namely the feminine "dellas," can apparently refer only to the favors ("mercedes") for which Orellana is going to petition. This interpretation, however, is illogical, since Orellana refuses to state here what favors he is going to petition for. It seems probable, therefore, that the feminine "dellas" is an error for the masculine "dellos," the antecedent of which would be "services," as the sense of the passage plainly requires.—EDITOR.]

† [The text here has "or," while in footnote 56 of Medina's Introduction (p. 36, *supra*), where this statement of Orellana's is quoted, the reading is "and." This latter conjunction appears to be the more logical one and is therefore retained in the translation here as well as in the Introduction.—EDITOR.]

the said town that there flocked to these parts the horde of persons who came all worn out and in great distress from their journeyings, and they found refreshments in the house of the said Captain Francisco de Orellana, and he gave them food, and he sustained them in their moments of sickness and distress, and it was believed that if it had not been for him many would have perished, for many were the sufferings which they endured; in which affair the said Captain spent a large amount of gold pesos, because the food supplies were at very unreasonable and high prices, and he purchased them at his own expense and on his own account; and [that] it was likewise certain and [was] known to them that the said Captain went to the relief of the cities of Lima and Cuzco with a considerable number of men, and that he spent a great deal in this undertaking, and that he also accomplished much good by his journey; and [that] it was likewise known to them that the said Governor sent the said Captain with a commission to conquer these provinces of La Culata, which he did conquer at his own expense and on his own initiative at the cost of a great deal of hardship to himself, at the conclusion of which said conquest he founded and established as a colony this said city, the great service which the said Captain has rendered to His Majesty by it [i.e. this city thus founded] being certain and well known, because it is in a district and [advantageous location] exactly as stated in the said petition of his; and [that] it was likewise known to them [that] the said Governor, having learned in what way the said Captain had served His Majesty and [what he had] accomplished in his service to the King, sent him letters of tenure so that he might hold, together with the said rank of Captain, the office of Governor's Lieutenant and Captain General in this said city and in Villa Nueva de Puerto Viejo, which letters of tenure are duly witnessed in the book of this Council; which said offices were occupied and exercised very well by the said Captain Francisco de Orellana, because he was a person of high honor, for some of the gentlemen of this Council knew him from his family connections, because he was a cavalier [and] an hidalgo of known ancestral estate, [and was a man] whom people saw and had seen exercise them [i.e. the said offices] well and faithfully and diligently and with prudence and wisdom; and in view of what is stated above, and in view of other things which they had seen and did know regarding the said Captain and his person and his virtues, they declared that the said Captain was a person capable of, and qualified for, whatever commissions and offices His Majesty might be pleased to intrust to him, be it a governorship or any others whatsoever, because he was a person who would give a good account of them or of any one of them and would discharge them as a servant of such a sort as that and [one who was] zealous [in performing the duties] of his service to the King: and they hereby beseech His Majesty, as a King and master who under all circumstances is grateful for the services which his subjects and his vassals render him, to see fit to grant the said Captain the favors which he may beg for and solicit, because he deserves all this by virtue of his personal qualities; [and they urge His Majesty to grant this petition] in order that the said Captain and others may be encouraged henceforth to render him other services of the same sort and [even] greater ones: all of which they signed with their names, and they ordered that there be given to the said Captain [all] the copies that he might wish to have of the said petition and of this their reply.—*Rodrigo de Vargas.—Gomez Estacio.—Fran.*co *de Chaves.—Pedro de Gibraleon.—Alonso Casco.—Juan de la Puente.—Cristobal Lunar.*

And I, Francisco Heres, scrivener of Their Majesties, and public [scrivener] and [scrivener] of the Council of the said city of Santiago, was present at what is stated, along with the said justice of the peace and magistrates, as it took place in my presence: and for this reason I made here my mark to that effect in evidence of the truth.—(*There is a mark.*)—*Fran.*$^{co}$ Heres, public scrivener and [scrivener] of the Council.

# IV

*Taking of testimony executed* ad perpetuam rei memoriam *before the Court of the Island of Margarita in the Indies of the Western Seas, on behalf of Cristóbal de Segovia, a conquistador, to be submitted to His Majesty, or wherever he may find that it suits him.*\*   October, 1542.

In the town of Espíritu Santo, port of the Island of Margarita in the Isles of the Indies of the Western Seas, on the twenty-fourth day of the month of October, One Thousand Five Hundred and Forty-two, before the distinguished gentlemen Francisco de Reina and Diego Xuarez, regular justices of the peace and [officers of the] Court on this said island for His Majesty, and before me, Rodrigo de Navarrete, scrivener of Their Majesties, there appeared in person Cristóbal de Segovia, as he said his name was, and he presented a writing [in the form] of a petition, and at the end an interrogatory with seventeen† questions, the contents of which [two writings] are respectively this which follows:

Very distinguished Sir, Francisco de Reina, regular justice of the peace on this Island of Margarita for His Majesty:—I, Cristóbal de Segovia, do come before Your Worship in the best way and form becoming to my rights, and declare, Sir, that I have good reason for wishing to have a certain taking of testimony *ad perpetuam rei memoriam* put through the court in order to inform His Majesty of the services that I have performed in these parts of the Indies, in order that as a reward for them he may bestow favors upon me; for which purpose I beg Your Worship to order that an oath be taken from the witnesses whom I shall present before Your Worship and that they be examined, and [I request] Your Worship to order that what they shall testify to and declare be given to me closed and sealed in [such] a way that it shall furnish true evidence, and that Your Worship bring to bear upon this matter his authority and his judicial sanction; and for whatever else [may be] necessary I implore the very distinguished services of Your Worship.

By means of the following questions shall be questioned the witnesses who shall be presented by me, Cristóbal de Segovia, in the judicial inquiry which I am having drawn up *ad perpetuam rei memoriam* before the Court of this town of Margarita in order to submit it to His Majesty.

1.   Let them first be asked whether they know me, the said Cristóbal de Segovia, and how long they have known me.

\* Archives of the Indies, case 53, shelf 1, bundle 10.

† [In reality there are eighteen questions, only the first four of them bearing numbers so far as may be judged from Medina's reproduction of this document.   The discrepancy between this number and the number of answers, always seventeen, of each of the eight witnesses is explained as follows: the fifteenth question does not seem to have been put to the first witness, namely Orellana, his 15th, 16th, and 17th answers corresponding to questions 16, 17, and 18 respectively, while in the case of each of the other seven witnesses the reply to question 18 is included in the 17th answer.—EDITOR.]

2. *Item*, whether they know, believe, have observed, or have heard say that for something like twenty-three years, slightly more or less, I have resided in the provinces of Nicaragua and New Spain and Peru and other adjacent provinces, being constantly occupied in the service of His Majesty, exploring and colonizing new lands, and during all this placing my person at every hazard and risk.

3. *Item*, whether they know that I took part, going with Captain Martín Astete, in explorations of the Desaguadero in Nicaragua, doing in the course of all this, with [my] arms and [my] horse, what any loyal man could and ought to do in the service of His Majesty.

4. *Item*, whether they know that, having learned that in New Spain there had risen up in revolt a province which is called Cocupotecas and [that the insurgents had] killed a certain number of miners, I went with Captain Valdivieso to subdue them and pacify them at my own expense and on my own initiative, with my arms and [my] horse, whereby I was instrumental in bringing it about that they settled down in peace and in [obedience to] the service of His Majesty.

[5]. *Item*, whether they know that in view of the services which I had performed for His Majesty, Pedrarias Dávila, governor of the said province of Nicaragua, granted me in *repartimiento* a certain number of Indians, whom I left in trust with certain relatives of mine in order to go off in the service of His Majesty.

[6]. *Item*, whether they know that after I left the said province of Nicaragua [to continue elsewhere] in the service of His Majesty, as I have already said, I was in the city and provinces of Quito and took part in the conquest and exploration of it [i.e. the city of Quito with its outlying districts] with my arms and [my] horse and [my] slaves and was one of the first colonizers of it, and [that] in view of my services Captain Sebastián de Benalcázar granted me in *repartimiento* some Indians, whom I left behind me in trust in order to go further on in the service of His Majesty, and [that] afterwards Francisco Pizarro took them away from me.

[7]. *Item*, whether they know that as I went forward on the said expedition of exploration with the said Captain Benalcázar I took part in the conquest of Popayán and the provinces of Lile, and was one of the first conquistadors and colonizers of it [i.e. all that country]; and [that] in consideration of all this the said Captain gave me in *repartimiento* a certain number of Indians, who, because I still continued to follow the said Captain instead of abandoning him, were taken away from me by a lieutenant who remained behind in the said city, there having been killed in the course of the said conquest two horses of mine, which had cost me four thousand gold pesos.

[8]. *Item*, whether they know that, when many Indians had risen up in revolt in the said provinces, I went forth many times as captain to subdue them, and I reduced to a state of peace many villages and provinces, compelling them to submit to [obedience to] the service of His Majesty.

[9]. *Item*, whether they know that, in order still to follow Captain [Benalcázar]*, I left behind me the Indians whom they had given me there also, and [that] in the course of the expedition, the men being in a state of great weakness from hunger in the provinces of Guachicuna, the said Captain pitched camp and from there sent out [for] supplies, and [that], because the inhabitants of the country were warlike, and he not daring to send out just a few men, he sent out a captain with thirty men, and [that] the Indians routed him and killed one man and

* [Added by Medina.—EDITOR.]

took their food away from them, in consequence of which the expeditionary force endured much suffering.

[10.] *Item*, whether they know that, after the Indians had routed the said captain and men, they came to be so warlike and haughty that no Christian dared to venture forth, for which reason the Captain-General sent me out with thirty men, with the aid of whom I routed the Indians and humbled their pride and brought in a large quantity of food, so that the expeditionary force was refreshed and stocked up after the great suffering from want that it had been experiencing, and [that] thanks to that relief we crossed over the snow-capped ranges as far as Alcázares, which is now called New Granada.

[11]. *Item*, whether they know, ever saw, [or] heard say that Captain Benalcázar, as he was going down the valley of Santa Marta, got reports about the country of Alcázares in the province which they call New Granada, and decided to go there; and whether they know that in order to make this said journey it was necessary to go through some very bad country, [it being] not only [one] of mountains and snow-capped ranges, but also [one] of very barren land [and one which is] lacking in foodstuffs.

[12]. *Item*, whether they know that I, the said Cristóbal de Segovia, went on this said journey with the said Captain Benalcázar, and whether they know that on the said expedition we endured many hardships, due not only to hunger but also to fights [with the Indians] and to other unbearable hardships, [all of] which I endured, although at the cost of great suffering, doing always what my captain ordered me [to do] as a servant of His Majesty; and whether they know that in all these expeditions I was always well mounted, serving as any hidalgo should serve his King and master.

[13]. *Item*, whether they know that after we had crossed over the snow-capped ranges the said Captain founded the town of Timana, and that I was one of the first who explored it [i.e. that region] and set up a colony there: let them tell what they know [about this].

[14]. *Item*, whether they know that after having founded this said town as a colony the said Captain decided to go and give an account [of what he had accomplished] to His Majesty, and that I went with him as far as to see him on board ship, and whether they know that after he had gone on board ship he sent Captain Juan Cabrera to found the town of Neiba, and that I, the said Cristóbal de Segovia, set out with the said Captain to found the said town, and we did found it, and [whether they know] how I was a magistrate in it and had some very fine Indians in *repartimiento* in it.

[15]. *Item*, whether they know that, later on, when I was on my way back from [the country of] the snow-capped ranges, passing along the route of the provinces which we had colonized and conquered [and stopping] in those places where I had left my Indians that had been given to me, as a conquistador, in *repartimiento*, when I appealed to the representatives of the law who had been left in those regions, they refused to give them to me, and I returned to the city of Quito, and from there I set out with the Governor Gonzalo Pizarro on an exploring expedition [in search] of cinnamon.

[16]. *Item*, whether they know that, as the said Governor Gonzalo Pizarro was proceeding with two hundred men on the said exploring expedition, having advanced as much as a hundred and thirty leagues, arriving at certain rivers and with supplies failing him and there being no possibility of getting any in that country

because it was barren, he sent the man who as his lieutenant served as captain-general, namely Francisco de Orellana, with fifty-odd men in pirogues and in a small boat which he had caused to be built, down the river in search of supplies, and [that] as the currents were strong we went on down at an enormous risk and [at the cost of much] hardship for a distance of more than two hundred leagues, enduring great hunger, in the course of which the Indians killed a certain number of Christians among us.

[17]. *Item*, whether they know that, desirous though we were of returning to the [encamped] expeditionary force there where the said Governor had remained behind, it [nevertheless] being, as it was, impossible to go back because of the fact that the currents were so strong, as I have already said, we being thus in a desperate situation, the said Captain Francisco de Orellana ordered a brigantine to be built, in spite of there being [among us] no master [shipbuilder] to build it, and [that] in it and in another small boat we continued on down the river until we came upon the Marañón River, and made our way down it out to the sea and came into port on this Island of Margarita, nearly dead from hunger and thirst, where God saw fit to bring us [and] where we found salvation for our lives and our consciences.

[18]. *Item*, whether they know that all that which is stated above is common knowledge and [facts] well known among persons who do know something and have heard about what is going on in general.

The said writing and interrogatory having been presented in the manner that is stated, the said justices of the peace declared that [whenever] the witnesses of whom it was proposed to make use in this taking of testimony [should be] present in person before them, they were ready to receive them and examine them in conformity with the said petition and interrogatory and would exercise justice in the matter as far as there should be any occasion [for so doing] in accordance with right.

And then the said Cristóbal de Segovia, on this said day [of the] above-mentioned month and year, before the said justices of the peace, and in the presence of me, the said scrivener, brought in as witnesses for the said purpose Captain Francisco de Orellana, and Cristóbal de Aguilar, and Juan de Elena, and Hernán González, to [all of] whom (and to each one of them) the oath was administered in due legal form, under the binding force of which procedure they promised to tell the truth about what they knew in regard to this matter for which they were being brought in as witnesses, and at the conclusion of the said oath they said: "Yes, I swear," and "Amen."

And [a few days] after what is stated above, on the twenty-eighth of the said month and of the said year, before the said justices of the peace, and in the presence of me, the said scrivener, there appeared in person the said Cristóbal de Segovia, and he brought in as additional witnesses for the said taking of testimony Benito de Aguilar, and Ginés Hernández, and the Comendador Cristóbal Enríquez, and Blas de Medina, to [all of] whom (and to each one of them) the said justices of the peace administered the oath in legal form, under burden of which they promised each one of them to tell the truth about what they knew in regard to this matter for which they were being brought in as witnesses, and at the close of the said oath they said: "Yes, I swear," and "Amen."

And what the said witnesses declared and testified to [in replying] to the questions of the said interrogatory, to all [of these questions] and to each one of them, is this which follows:

The said Captain Francisco de Orellana, a witness brought in for this taking of testimony, having sworn in accordance with legal form and being questioned as per the contents of the said interrogatory, said and testified as follows:

1.—[In reply] to the first question he said that he had known the said Cristóbal de Segovia mentioned in the question for the past fifteen years, slightly more or less, and had made his acquaintance in these parts of the Indies.

Being questioned by means of the general questions as required by law, he said that he was about thirty years old, slightly more or less, and that none of the general questions of the law affected him.

2.—Questioned as per the second question, he said that he, as he had already said, had known the said Cristóbal de Segovia for the past fifteen years, during which he had known him not only by sight but also by accounts that he had heard about him; and [he said that] he knew this man had been engaged in the wars which had been fought, both in New Spain and in Peru, devoting himself in the said wars to the service of His Majesty, exploring and colonizing new lands in the said provinces; and [that] during all this he knew that he had done everything that he owed to [his status of] a loyal vassal and servant of His Majesty.

3.—[In reply] to the third question he said that what was mentioned in this question he had not [actually] witnessed, but that he had heard it related publicly by many persons who knew the said Cristóbal de Segovia, and [that] this witness [i.e. he] considered it as exact.

4.—[In reply] to the fourth question he said that he did not know about [the matter referred to in] it.

5.—[In reply] to the fifth question he said that what was mentioned in this question he had heard related.

6.—[In reply] to the sixth question he said that what was mentioned in this question he had heard recounted by many persons and that it was regarded as common knowledge.

7.—[In reply] to the seventh question he said that what was mentioned in this question he had likewise heard recounted by many persons.

8.—[In reply] to the eighth question he said that he had heard about the matter mentioned in this question.

9.—[In reply] to the ninth question he said that he did not know about [the matter referred to in] it.

10.—[In reply] to the tenth question he said that he did not know about [the matter referred to in] it.

11.—[In reply] to the eleventh question he said that what was mentioned in this question he had heard recounted publicly by many persons.

12.—[In reply] to the twelfth question he said that he had heard about the matter mentioned in this question.

13.—[In reply] to the thirteenth question he said that what was mentioned in this question he had heard recounted by many persons.

14.—[In reply] to the fourteenth question he said that what was mentioned in this question he had heard recounted by many persons who had been associated with the said Cristóbal de Segovia.

15.—[In reply] to the fifteenth question he said that he was familiar with [the subject matter of] the question as it is stated therein: asked how he was familiar with it, he said that [it was] because it did happen exactly as the question stated, and because this witness [i.e. he] was the Captain Francisco de Orellana who had led the expedition into the interior down the river [as] stated in the question, and [that] it had taken place exactly as the question relates it.

16.—[In reply] to the sixteenth question he said that he was familiar with [the subject matter of] this question exactly as it is stated therein, because it did happen and was [so], exactly as the question states, and because he was the said captain who had led the said men and [these men] were at present on this island where they had come into port, and that it was so.

17.—[In reply] to the seventeenth question he said that what he had stated and declared in this his statement was what he knew and [was] the truth, under burden of the oath which he took; and he signed it with his name.—*Francisco Dorellana.*

Cristóbal de Aguilar, a witness brought in for this taking of testimony, having sworn in accordance with legal form, and being questioned according to the contents of the said interrogatory, stated the following:

1.—[In reply] to the first question he said that he had known the man mentioned in this question for the past seven years, slightly more or less, by sight and from relations and dealings which he had had with him during most of the said time.

Being questioned by means of the general questions, he said that he was from twenty-seven to twenty-eight years old, slightly more or less, and that none of the general questions affected him as a party [having a personal interest in the matter].

2.—[In reply] to the second question he said that this witness [i.e. he] had known the said Cristóbal de Segovia from the time mentioned in the question down to the present, and that he had known him as a man always active in the military expeditions which had been carried out in the land of Peru where he had seen him constantly enduring hardships as the question states and had seen him engaged in conquests in the said land of Peru and in establishing colonies in it.

3.—[In reply] to the third question he said that what was mentioned in this question he had heard related but that he had not been a witness to it.

4.—[In reply] to the fourth question he said that he had heard stated what was mentioned in the question but that he had not been a witness to it.

5.—[In reply] to the fifth question he said that he was not familiar with [the matter referred to in] it.

6.—[In reply] to the sixth question he said that what was mentioned in this question he had heard stated publicly by other conquistadors of the land and [that] this witness [i.e. he] believed it [to be true] because he had heard it stated publicly by many persons.

7.—[In reply] to the seventh question he said that he knew about the matter mentioned in this question, except that he had not seen more than one of his horses killed, notwithstanding the fact that he had heard stated that they did kill the other horse of his which the question mentions, and that at the time when they took the said *repartimiento* away from him this witness [i.e. he] had not seen it [i.e. how he was being treated then], and that the rest he knew and had seen as a man who had [himself] likewise been engaged in the said conquest where what was mentioned in the question took place.

8.—[In reply] to the eighth question he said that he knew that the said Cristóbal de Segovia had gone out many times to subdue the Indians whom the question mentions but that he did not know about the rest.

9.—[In reply] to the ninth question he said that what was mentioned in this question he had heard stated and that he considered it as certain.

10.—[In reply] to the tenth question he said that he had heard related what was mentioned in this question.

11.—[In reply] to the eleventh question he said that he was not familiar with [the matter referred to in] it.

12.—[In reply] to the twelfth question he said that he knew that the said Cristóbal de Segovia had always participated well mounted in the military operations and that he had seen him to be obedient to his captain, and [had observed that] he had always served as a loyal vassal and servant of His Majesty in participating in the said military operations.

13.—[In reply] to the thirteenth question he said that he had heard related what was mentioned in the question.

14.—[In reply] to the fourteenth question he said that he had heard related what was mentioned in this question.

15.—[In reply] to the fifteenth question he said that he knew that the said Cristóbal de Segovia had gone with Gonzalo Pizarro on the expedition of exploration [in search] of cinnamon, and [that] the rest he did not know about.

16.—[In reply] to the sixteenth question he said that he was familiar with the matter exactly as the question states it; asked how he knew about it, he said that he had been a participant in it and [that] this witness [i.e. he] was one of those who had set out in search of supplies down the river as the question states.

17.—[In reply] to the seventeenth question he said that he likewise knew about the matter mentioned in this question, and knew about it as a man who had taken part in it and was at the present time on the Island of Margarita where they had come into port, and that [all] this which he had said in this his statement was the truth and [was] what he knew, under burden of the oath which he had taken; and he signed it with his name.—*Cristobal de Aguilar*.

The said Juan de Elena, a witness brought in for this taking of testimony, having sworn in accordance with legal form, and being questioned according to the contents of the said interrogatory, made the following declarations:

1.—[In reply] to the first question he said that he knew the man mentioned in this question, who is Cristóbal de Segovia, whom he had known for the past eight years, slightly more or less.

Being questioned by means of the general questions, he said that he was thirty-two or thirty-three years old, slightly more or less, and that he was not a relative of the said Segovia and that none of the general questions affected him.

2.—[In reply] to the second question he said that this witness [i.e. he] had known the said Cristóbal de Segovia from the time mentioned in the first question, and that he had known him in the lands of Peru, and [that] at this time he had seen him engaged in war and in the service of His Majesty in conquering and colonizing the said lands.

3.—[In reply] to the third question he said that what was mentioned in this question he had heard many persons tell about.

4.—[In reply] to the fourth question he said that he had heard the matter recounted by many persons who knew the said Segovia.

5.—[In reply] to the fifth question he said that he had heard the matter related.

6.—[In reply] to the sixth question he said that what was mentioned in this question he knew about in just the form that it is stated therein: asked how he knew about it, he said that [it was] because this witness [i.e. he] had been there in person during a part of the time that the events mentioned in the question had occurred and [that] he had seen the Indians mentioned in the question taken away from him.

7.—[In reply] to the seventh question he said that he knew about the matter mentioned in this question: asked how he knew about it, he said that [it was] because he had been a witness to everything that the question mentions, except that he had not seen more than one horse of his killed, and that he had heard many persons say that they had killed another horse of his.

8.—[In reply] to the eighth question he said that he knew about the matter exactly as it is stated in the question: asked how he knew about it, he said that [it was] because he had been present at it all.

9.—[In reply] to the ninth question he said that he knew about [the subject matter of] this question as it is stated therein: asked how he knew about it, he said that [it was] because he had been right there and with his own eyes had seen it [take place].

10.—[In reply] to the tenth question he said that he likewise knew about the matter referred to in this question: asked how he knew about it, he said that [it was] because he had been right there and was one of the thirty men who had gone with the said Cristóbal de Segovia to penetrate into the interior to [fight] the Indians and [that] he knew about and had been a witness to what is mentioned in this question.

11.—[In reply] to the eleventh question he said that he knew about the matter in his capacity of a man who had participated in it.

12.—[In reply] to the twelfth question he said that he knew about most of the matters referred to in the question [as] stated because he had personally gone along on a part of the journey, and [that] this witness [i.e. he] had turned back from the journey, and [that] for this reason he knew about the matter which the question relates.

13.—[In reply] to the thirteenth question he said that he knew that they had made some explorations as per the statements made in the question and that the said Segovia was one of the first who had explored the said valley.

14.—[In reply] to the fourteenth question he said that he had heard the matter recounted.

15.—[In reply] to the fifteenth question he said that he knew about [the matter referred to in] it as it is stated therein: asked how he knew about it, he said that [it was] because he had participated personally in everything that is mentioned in the question.

16.—[In reply] to the sixteenth question he said that he knew about [the matter referred to in] it as it is stated therein: asked how he knew about it, he said that he had participated personally in it all and was one of the fifty men who had gone off in search of supplies with Captain Orellana.

17.—[In reply] to the seventeenth question he said that he knew about [the matter referred to in] it as it is stated therein: asked how he knew about it, he said that [it was] because it did happen that way, and [that] this witness [i.e. he] had been one of those who had gone off with him on the same journey and was at the present time on this Island of Margarita; and [he said] that what he had stated was what he knew, and [that it was] the truth, under burden of the oath which he had taken: and he affixed his mark.

The said Hernán González, a witness brought in for this taking of testimony, having sworn in accordance with legal form and being questioned according to the contents of the said interrogatory, made the following declarations:

1.—[In reply] to the first question he said that he had known the said Cristóbal de Segovia for the past eight or nine years, slightly more or less.

Being questioned by means of the general questions, he said that he was thirty-seven years old, rather more than less, and that none of the general questions of the law affected or offended him.

2.—[In reply] to the second question he said that during all the said time that this witness [i.e. he] had known the said Cristóbal de Segovia he had known him [while he himself had been taking part] in the conquests of Peru and of Alcázares and of Popayán, associated, [while aiding] in conquering the said lands, with the governors of them, and [that] he had seen the said Cristóbal de Segovia participating in the said war with [his own] arms and horse, serving as a good conquistador and exploring lands.

3.—[In reply] to the third question he said that he did not know about [the matter referred to in] the question, because he had not been in that land.

4.—[In reply] to the fourth question he said that he did not know about [the matter referred to in] the question, because [much] less had he ever been in the land of New Spain.

5.—[In reply] to the fifth question he said that he was not familiar with [the matter referred to in] it.

6.—[In reply] to the sixth question he said that he knew that the said Cristóbal de Segovia had taken part in the exploration of the province of Quito and other adjacent ones, and [that] he had heard it said that as a colonizer he had been granted his *repartimiento* of Indians, and [that] later on they had taken it [i.e. the *repartimiento*] away from him and given it to another and [had] taken them [i.e. the Indians] away from him.

7.—[In reply] to the seventh question he said that he knew that the said Cristóbal de Segovia had taken part in the exploration of the provinces mentioned in this question, and [that] he likewise knew that they had killed a horse of his while he was engaged in the said fighting in the said provinces, and that this [was what] he knew about [the matter mentioned in] this question.

8.—[In reply] to the eighth question he said that what he knew about [the subject-matter of] this question was that at the time when the said Segovia had been active in the said conquests with the said Governor Benalcázar he [i.e. the Governor] had sent him off, he [i.e. the witness] knew, several times as the leader of a certain number of men whom the said Benalcázar had sent out with their captains, and [that] he knew that the said Cristóbal de Segovia had always been a man who had served well in the said wars with [his own] arms and horse.

9.—[In reply] to the ninth question he said that he did not remember about the matter mentioned in this question.

10.—[In reply] to the tenth question he said that this witness [i.e. he] did not remember very well about the matter mentioned in this question; but [he said] that he did know that the said Cristóbal de Segovia, because he was a good man at fighting, had been many times intrusted with many tasks of this sort, such as going out to explore and bring in supplies, and [that] for this reason he believed that what is stated in this question probably did take place.

11.—[In reply] to the eleventh question he said that he knew about [the matter referred to in] this question just as it is stated therein: asked how he knew it, he said that [it was] because this witness [i.e. he] had taken part personally along with the said Benalcázar and the said Cristóbal de Segovia in the affair mentioned in this question.

12.—[In reply] to the twelfth question he said that he knew about [the matter referred to in] the question just as it is stated therein, because he had personally taken part in everything on the said journey; and [that] he knew that the said Cristóbal de Segovia had always been well mounted and had served as a loyal servant and vassal of His Majesty in the tasks which had been assigned to him by the said Benalcázar, by whom he had been highly esteemed, and [that] he [i.e. Benalcázar] had liked him very much.

13.—[In reply] to the thirteenth question he said that he knew that the said Cristóbal de Segovia had been one of the first explorers of [the region about] the town of Timana.

14.—[In reply] to the fourteenth question he said that he knew that the said Cristóbal de Segovia had gone with the said Benalcázar as far as to see him go on board ship when he [i.e. Benalcázar] was on his way to Spain, and [that] he knew that from there he [i.e. Segovia] had gone back with Captain Juan Cabrera [when the latter was sent] to form a colony at what is now the town of Neiba and [had thus helped] to found the said town as a colony, and [that] the rest he did not know about, because this witness [i.e. he] had come on down the river with Benalcázar.

15.—[In reply] to the fifteenth question he said that he knew that the said Cristóbal de Segovia had gone on the expedition of exploration [in search] of cinnamon with the Governor Gonzalo Pizarro, and [that] the rest he did not know about.

16.—[In reply] to the sixteenth question he said that he knew about [the matter referred to in] this question just as it is stated therein: asked how he knew about [the matter referred to in] it, he said that [it was] because this witness [i.e. he] was one of the fifty-odd men who had gone off with Captain Orellana in search of food.

17.—[In reply] to the seventeenth question he said that he knew about [the matter referred to in] this question just as it is stated therein: asked how he knew about [the matter referred to in] it, he said that [it was] because, as he had already stated, he was one of those who had been members of the party, and that they had come on with the said Captain Francisco de Orellana and had put into port in this land where the question states [that they had arrived]; and that what he had stated was the truth and [was] what he knew and [was] common knowledge and well known [facts], under burden of the oath which he had taken; and he did not sign because he said that he did not know how to write.

The said Benito de Aguilar, a witness admitted for this judicial inquiry, having sworn in accordance with legal form and being questioned according to the contents of the said interrogatory, declared as follows:

1.—[In reply] to the first question he said that he had known the said Cristóbal de Segovia for the past seven years, by sight, from relations, and from dealings which he had had with him during all the said time: being questioned by means of the general questions of the law, he said that he was thirty-three years old, slightly more or less, and that none of the questions of the law affected or offended him.

2.—[In reply] to the second question he said that this witness [i.e. he] had known the said Cristóbal de Segovia for the said past seven years, during which time he had known him [as a man] engaged in the wars in the provinces of Peru, where he had always seen him doing what he owed to the service of His Majesty, constantly active in the said wars, and that the rest of the matter mentioned in the question he had heard related.

3.—[In reply] to the third question he said that what is mentioned in this question he had heard related by many persons who are from Nicaragua, and particularly by his uncle Alonso de Segovia, and that this [was what] he declared regarding [the contents of] this question.

4.—[In reply] to the fourth question he said that he did not know about [the matter referred to in] it.

5.—[In reply] to the fifth question he said that he had heard many persons recount what is mentioned in this question.

6.—[In reply] to the sixth question he said that he knew about the matter mentioned in this question just as it is stated therein: asked how he knew about it, he said that [it was] because he had been present at everything mentioned in this question, inasmuch as this witness [i.e. he] had been one of the conquistadors of Quito and its outlying districts.

7.—[In reply] to the seventh question he said that he knew about [the matter referred to in] this question as it is stated therein; asked how he knew about it, he said that [it was] because he had seen it [take place] and had been present at it all.

8.—[In reply] to the eighth question he said that he knew about the matter mentioned in this question just as it is stated therein: asked how he knew about it, he said that [it was] because this witness [i.e. he] had taken part in it and because many times he had gone out to explore and to restore peace [in company] with the said Cristóbal de Segovia.

9.—[In reply] to the ninth question he said that he knew about the matter in his capacity of a man who had been present at it and had been a witness to it.

10.—[In reply] to the tenth question he said that he knew about [the matter referred to in] the question just as it is stated therein: asked how [he knew about it], he said that [it was] because he had seen it [take place] and had been right there and knew that during this expedition into the interior they had wounded the said Cristóbal de Segovia in one of his thighs.

11.—[In reply] to the eleventh question he said that he knew about [the matter referred to in] it just as it is stated therein: asked how [he knew about it], he said that [it was] because he had been present at it all.

12.—[In reply] to the twelfth question he said that he knew about [the matter referred to in] it because he had seen it [take place] in that way and had seen the said Cristóbal de Segovia do what it was his duty to do as a loyal servant of His Majesty, being always well mounted.

13.—[In reply] to the thirteenth question he said that he had seen [all] this [take place], being as he was a man who had been a witness to it.

14.—[In reply] to the fourteenth question he said that he was likewise familiar with [the matter referred to in] this question just as it is stated therein: asked how he knew about it, he said that [it was] because he had taken part in it and had seen the said Cristóbal de Segovia filling the office of magistrate, and [that] he knew about everything that the question states.

15.—[In reply] to the fifteenth question he said that he knew that the said Cristóbal de Segovia had returned to Popayán, where he had his Indians, and had heard it said that he had presented his certificate [showing him to be the holder] of a *repartimiento* to the representative [of the law] in order that he should hand over his Indians to him, and that he had not handed them over to him; and [that] he knew about all the rest of the matter mentioned in the question, because this witness [i.e. he] had likewise set out from Quito with Gonzalo de Pizarro to explore [the country for] cinnamon, whither the said Cristóbal de Segovia had gone.

16.—[In reply] to the sixteenth question he said that he knew about [the matter referred to in] it just as it is stated therein: asked how he knew about [the matter referred to in] it, he said that [it was] because this witness [i.e. he] was one of those who had taken part in everything that the question states.

17.—[In reply] to the seventeenth question he said that he knew about and had been a witness to what is related in this question, being as he was a man who had taken part in it all and had gone down it [i.e. the river]; and [he said] that [all] this that he had stated was what he knew and [was] the truth, and [was] common knowledge and well known [facts], under burden of the oath which he had taken; and he signed it with his name.—*Benito de Aguilar.*

Ginés Hernández, a witness brought in for this taking of testimony, having sworn in accordance with legal form and being questioned according to the contents of the said interrogatory, declared and testified as follows:

1.—[In reply] to the first question he said that he had known the said Cristóbal de Segovia for the past two and a half years, slightly more or less, by sight, [and] from dealings that he had had with him.

Being questioned by means of the general [questions], he said that he was twenty-two or twenty-three years old, slightly more or less, and that none of the general questions of the law affected him.

2.—[In reply] to the second question he said that he was not familiar with the matter set forth in this question, beyond having heard it recounted, with the exception that for the past two and a half years that he had known him he had seen him always active in military operations and doing what it was the duty of a loyal servant and vassal of His Majesty to do in the expeditions of discovery [in] which he had taken part.

3.—[In reply] to the third question he said that he did not know about this matter.

4.—[In reply] to the fourth question he said that he did not know about [the matter referred to in] it.

5.—[In reply] to the fifth question he said that he did not know about [the matter referred to in] it.

6.—[In reply] to the sixth question he said that he had heard recounted what is stated in this question.

7.—[In reply] to the seventh question he said that he had heard recounted what is stated in this question.

8.—[In reply] to the eighth question he said that he had heard recounted what is stated in this question.

9.—[In reply] to the ninth question he said that he was not familiar with [the matter referred to in] it.

10.—[In reply] to the tenth question he said that he was not familiar with [the matter referred to in] it because he had not been there.

11.—[In reply] to the eleventh question he said that he had heard the matter related.

12.—[In reply] to the twelfth question he said that he had heard many persons relate what is stated in this question.

14.*—[In reply] to the fourteenth question he said that he had heard many persons relate what is mentioned in this question and [that] it was common knowledge as such.

15.—[In reply] to the fifteenth question he said that he knew that the said Cristóbal de Segovia had gone out with the Governor Gonzalo Pizarro to explore [in search of] cinnamon, but that he did not know about the rest.

16.—[In reply] to the sixteenth question he said that he knew about [the matter mentioned in] this question just as it is stated therein: asked how he knew about [the matter mentioned in] it, he said that [it was] because he had been present at it all and [that] this witness [i.e. he] was one of those who had come on with the said Captain Francisco de Orellana.

17.—[In reply] to the seventeenth question he said that he was familiar with [the matter mentioned in] the question as it is stated therein because, as he had already stated, he had been present at it all; and [he said] that this was the truth and [was] what he knew under burden of the oath which he had taken; and he signed it.—*Gines Hernandez.*

The Comendador Cristóbal Enríquez, a witness brought in for this taking of testimony, having sworn in accordance with legal form and being questioned according to the contents of the said interrogatory, declared as follows:

1.—[In reply] to the first question he said that he had known Cristóbal de Segovia for the past three years, slightly more or less, by sight and [from] relations and dealings which he had had with him during the said time.

Being questioned by means of the general questions of the law, he said that he was twenty-seven or twenty-eight years old, slightly more or less, and that he was not a relative or an enemy of the said [Segovia].

2.—[In reply] to the second question he said that this witness [i.e. he] had heard it said many times that the said Cristóbal de Segovia had resided in the provinces mentioned in this question, and that he had been one of the conquistadors and colonizers of them as the said question states.

3.—[In reply] to the third question he said that in just this way he had heard the said Segovia relate the matter publicly.

4.—[In reply] to the fourth question he said that he was not familiar with [the matter mentioned in] it because this witness [i.e. he] had not yet crossed over to the Indies at the time that the events mentioned in the question took place.

5.—[In reply] to the fifth question he said that he had heard many persons relate the matter and that in just this way it was common knowledge that he [i.e. Segovia] had owned the said Indians in Nicaragua.

* [Ginés Hernández's answer to the thirteenth question is missing, at least as the document is published by Medina.—EDITOR.]

6.—[In reply] to the sixth question he said that what is stated in the question this witness [i.e. he] had not seen [take place, and that he knew nothing about this] other than that it was common knowledge and [a fact] well known among the conquistadors who had taken part in the conquest of Quito that the said Cristóbal de Segovia had been [one] of the first conquistadors of it [i.e. the country where Quito is], and that in the conquest he had always taken his part with his arms and [his] horse and [had] done what a good conquistador was bound to do, and [that] in view of his services they had granted him in *repartimiento* some Indians from among the best of the land; and [he said that] he had likewise heard it stated as common knowledge and [a fact] well known that the said Cristóbal de Segovia had left the said Indians behind in order to go on in company with the Governor Benalcázar and in the service of His Majesty, and [that] he knew that the Governor Francisco Pizarro had taken these said Indians away from him and had given them to some one else; and [he said that] this was what he knew regarding [the subject-matter of] this question.

7.—[In reply] to the seventh question he said that what he knew about [the matter referred to in] this question was that it was common knowledge and [a] well known [fact] that the said Cristóbal de Segovia had been one of the first conquistadors and colonizers of the provinces mentioned in this question, and [that] he knew that the said Governor Benalcázar, as [governors regularly do] for such a conquistador, had granted him a *repartimiento* of Indians in the city of Popayán, because this witness [i.e. he] had seen the certificates of the *repartimiento* which they had granted to him, and [that] he believed that these Indians of this *repartimiento* had been taken away from him, because he had been informed that they had come into the possession of another citizen, to whom Lieutenant Juan de Ampuya, so it appears, had given them; and that he had likewise heard it said that in the course of the said conquests they had killed the two horses of his mentioned in the said question, [horses] which were worth a great deal of money; and this [is what] he said concerning [the subject-matter of] this question.

8.—[In reply] to the eighth question he said that what was mentioned in this question he had heard related publicly by persons who had been associated with the said Cristóbal de Segovia and had had him as their leader in many expeditions into the interior which they had made.

9.—[In reply] to the ninth question he said that he did not know about [the matter referred to in] it, because it had not happened in the time of this witness [i.e. in his time].

10.—[In reply] to the tenth question he said that he did not know about [the matter referred to in] it, because it had not happened in his time; but [he said] that he believed that it had happened just as the question states, because of what he had heard said and [had] seen in connection with the said Cristóbal de Segovia.

11.—[In reply] to the eleventh question he said that he did not know about [the matter referred to in] it, because it had not happened in the time of this witness [i.e. in his time].

12.—[In reply] to the twelfth question he said that what is mentioned in the question he had not [actually] seen [take place], but that what is mentioned in the question was common knowledge and [a fact] well known among those who were familiar with the matter, and that he knew that as long as he had been acquainted with the said Cristóbal de Segovia he had seen him serve always well mounted and do what it was his duty to do [in a way becoming] to a loyal servant and vassal of His Majesty.

13.—[In reply] to the thirteenth question he said that he did not know about the matter mentioned in this question, but that he had heard it related publicly.

14.—[In reply] to the fourteenth question he said that he did not know about [the matter referred to in] it because it had not happened in the time of this witness [i.e. in his time].

15.—[In reply] to the fifteenth question he said that he had heard it said that the said Cristóbal de Segovia had petitioned the Lieutenant-General for certain Indians and [that] he knew that he had not given them to him; and [he said] that he [i.e. Segovia] did go out with the Governor Gonzalo Pizarro on an expedition of exploration [in search] of cinnamon, in whose party this witness [i.e. he] had [himself] gone along.

16.—[In reply] to the sixteenth question he said that he knew about the matter mentioned in this question, just as it is stated therein, as a man who had been present at it all and was one of those who had come on with Captain Francisco de Orellana.

17.—[In reply] to the seventeenth question he said that he likewise knew about what is mentioned in this question, being as he was a man who had taken part in it, and that when they had put into port on this island and on that of Cubagua they had been in great need of food and had endured much hunger and hardship; and [he said] that what he had stated was the truth and [was] what he knew and believed and had heard said, under burden of the oath which he had taken; and he signed it with his name.—*Cristobal Enriquez.*

The said Blas de Medina, a witness brought in for this taking of testimony, having sworn in accordance with legal form and being questioned according to the contents of the said interrogatory, made the following declaration:

1.—[In reply] to the first question he said that he had known the said Cristóbal de Segovia for the past six or seven years, rather more than less, by sight, from relations, and from dealings which he had had with him during the said time.

Questioned by means of the general [questions], he said that he was twenty-two years old, slightly more or less, and that none of the general questions affected him.

2.—[In reply] to the second question he said that all during the seven or eight [*sic*] years that he had known the said Cristóbal de Segovia he had known him in the provinces of Peru, where during the said time he had seen him serve His Majesty in exploring and colonizing new lands, and had seen him do what a good servant of His Majesty should do, and [had seen him] place himself in many critical situations and [positions involving] hardships and risks.

3.—[In reply] to the third question he said that what is mentioned in the question he had heard many persons relate.

4.—[In reply] to the fourth question he said that he had heard recounted what is mentioned in this question but did not [actually] know about it, because it had not happened in his time.

5.—[In reply] to the fifth question he said that what is mentioned in this question he had heard several residents of Nicaragua relate, wherefore this witness [i.e. he] believed what is mentioned in the question.

6.—[In reply] to the sixth question he said that he knew about [the matter referred to in] the question just as it is stated therein: asked how [he knew about it], he said that [it was] because this witness [i.e. he] had been in the province of Quito, where he had seen it [take place].

7.—[In reply] to the seventh question he said that he knew about [the matter referred to in] the question just as it is stated therein, except that he had not seen the two horses of his killed; but he had heard it related as [a thing] quite certain and had seen [the region] where they had killed them, and [that] the rest he knew because he had so witnessed it, and [he said that he believed that Segovia was telling the truth in the whole matter] because [he knew that] the said horses in those days were worth a great deal of money.

8.—[In reply] to the eighth question he said that he knew about [the matter referred to in] this question: asked how he knew about [the matter referred to in] it, he said that [it was] because he had taken part in it, and [that] several times this witness [i.e. he] had gone with the said Segovia to penetrate into the interior, [the latter] going, in fact, as the leader of some men, and [he said that] he had seen him bring many tribes around to terms of peace.

9.—[In reply] to the ninth question he said that he had not taken part [in the matter referred to], but that he had heard it related by many persons who had taken part in that which the question tells about.

10.—[In reply] to the tenth question he said that he had heard what is mentioned in the question related by many persons, wherefore this witness [i.e. he], so far as he was concerned, believed it, [that is] that it did happen as the question states.

11.—[In reply] to the eleventh question he said that he had heard what is mentioned in the question related by many soldiers who had been right there.

12.—[In reply] to the twelfth question he said that he knew that the said Cristóbal de Segovia had always served well mounted and had always been entirely obedient to the orders of his captains and very highly esteemed by them, and that he was a man [such] that they had always intrusted [to him] positions of command over men, and he had observed him doing what it was the duty of a good servant of His Majesty to do in the expeditions of conquest [during] which this witness [i.e. he] had been acquainted with him.

13.—[In reply] to the thirteenth question he said that he knew about [the matter referred to in] the question just as it is stated therein, because he had been right there, and [that] he knew that the said Cristóbal de Segovia was one of the first who had explored [that country] and founded the said town as a colony.

14.—[In reply] to the fourteenth question he said that he knew about the matter because he had heard it related by many soldiers who had been present at what is stated in this question.

15.—[In reply] to the fifteenth question he said that he knew about [the matter referred to in] it just as it is stated therein; asked how [he knew about it], he said that [it was] because he had seen the said Cristóbal de Segovia request the Lieutenant for certain Indians in Quito and [had observed that] he had not given them to him; and [he said that] he knew that from there he had set out with the Governor Gonzalo Pizarro on an expedition of exploration [in search] of cinnamon.

16.—[In reply] to the sixteenth question he said that he knew about [the matter referred to in] this question as it is stated therein, because he had taken part in it and was one of those who had come on down the river with Captain Orellana.

17.—[In reply] to the seventeenth question he said that he likewise knew about [the matter referred to in] this question because he was one of those who had come on down the said river and was now on this Island of Margarita, where they had put into port; and [he said] that [all] this that he had stated was what he knew, and believed, and had heard said, under burden of the oath which he had taken: and he signed it.—*Blas de Medina.*

And after the said declarations in the form of testimony had been obtained and received in the manner that has been stated, before the said justices of the peace, and in the presence of me, the said scrivener, there appeared the said Cristóbal de Segovia, and he requested that it be ordered that the said [complete] testimony be delivered to him in the commonly accepted form in order [that he might be able] to submit it to His Majesty, and wherever he might see that it best suited him [to do so], and that, in order that it might be valid and constitute true evidence, he [i.e. the regular justice of the peace] attach to it [the symbols, etc., of] his authority and his judicial sanction.

And later the said justices of the peace ordered me, the said scrivener, to draw off in the commonly accepted form one copy, or as many as the party might desire, of the said [complete] testimony, [saying] that they were ready to attach to them [the symbols, etc., of] their authority and judicial sanction in order that it [i.e. the testimony] might be valid and constitute true evidence in so far as there was legally any occasion for such.

And I, Rodrigo de Navarrete, scrivener of His Majesty and his notary public in his household and capital and in all his realms and dominions, by order of the said justices of the peace, and at the request of the said Cristóbal de Segovia, drew off this copy of the said [complete] testimony, just as it [i.e. the taking of testimony] took place before me: wherefore I made here this my mark to that effect.—In evidence of the truth.—*Francisco de Reyna.—Diego Xuarez.—Rodrigo de Navarrete*, scrivener of His Majesty.

# V

*Extracts from the judicial inquiry on the subject of the deserts and past services of Ginés Hernández, brother of Diego Hernández de Serpa, in connection with the exploration and colonization of the provinces of Loja and Piura, and afterwards in [the province of] Quito.\** Zamora de los Alcaides, February 14, 1564.

By means of the following questions shall be examined the witnesses who are or shall be brought in on behalf of Ginés Hernández, a citizen of the city of Zamora, in the taking of testimony *ad perpetuam rei memoriam* which he is having put through the court on the subject of what he has been doing in the service of His Majesty in these parts of the Indies for the past twenty-seven years.

1.—First, whether they know the said Ginés Hernández and Rodrigo de Ribadeneyra, District Attorney in the Royal [Court of] Justice in this city, and how long [they have known them]: let them tell what they know.

2.—*Item*, whether they know, believe, have observed, [or] have heard it said that the said Ginés Hernández has been in this realm of Peru a period of twenty-

---

* Archives of the Indies, "Patronato," case 1, shelf 5, bundle 23/7.

six years up to the present, slightly more or less, serving His Majesty in wars of conquest, exploring expeditions, and campaigns incidental to his service, and [in] important commissions and [on] other occasions which have arisen and [in connection with which] the responsibility has been placed upon him on behalf of His Majesty by his governors and captains: let them tell what they know [about this].

3.—*Item*, whether they know, etc., that approximately twenty-six years ago and [possibly] more the said Ginés Hernández went to the said city of San Miguel de Piura in this realm of Peru and took part in the conquest and pacification of Copiz and Cefrán and Goancabamba and part of the provinces of the Paltas, [all of which are] districts and [lands within a range of] jurisdiction now belonging to the city of Loja, which said city was founded at a period later than when the said Ginés Hernández had taken part in the said [war of] pacification: let them tell what they know [about this].

4.—*Item*, whether they know, etc., that the said Ginés Hernández, after playing a part in what is stated in the question preceding this one, left the said city of San Miguel to go, for the purpose of serving His Majesty, to the city of Quito, which is one hundred and twenty leagues away, where he arrived at a time when that [city] had not long been founded, and [when] many provinces [now] within its jurisdiction [were] in revolt, and many residents, and [read: "in fact"] nearly all of them, together with the natives, were very poor; and [that] that was at the time when Captain Lorenzo de Aldana went to the said city with a commission from the Marquis Don Francisco Pizarro, in which [city] he stopped and resided a long time, helping to keep it up and going off to the wars of conquest and pacification of the said provinces which had risen up and were in revolt, and [which] every day kept revolting; and [that] these said wars of pacification were instrumental in bringing it about that [even] in those days, thanks to them, the said city of Quito came to be one of the most important in these parts, and the natives of that province advanced and are [still] advancing along the lines of great material development, increase in numbers, and culture, and [that] among them there is being gathered a very great harvest in the field of evangelical teachings and things connected with our holy faith, and [that] they are wealthy in their possession of abundant lands and goods, and [that] consequently the citizens have become prosperous, as a result of which [condition] a great service [is being rendered] to God Our Lord and to His Majesty, and [that this is a great aid] to his [i.e. His Majesty's] levies of one-fifth [which] have been greatly increased: let them tell what they know [about this].

5.—For the fifth [question], [let them be asked] whether they know, etc., that the said Ginés Hernández left the said city of Quito to [go and] serve His Majesty under Captain Gonzalo Díaz de Pineda, who went off, with a commission from the Marquis Don Francisco Pizarro, on the expedition of exploration headed for Pelayo and Chalcoma, as a consequence of the numerous reports that were current regarding emeralds and [other forms of] riches [to be found there]; which said expedition of exploration [was a failure, for], after a great deal of time had been wasted on it and the men had become all worn out and reduced to a state of want, the said land was not found, owing to the fact that it [i.e. the country where this land was supposed to be] was really very rough, rugged and hilly; on which said expedition the said Ginés Hernández went at his own expense and on his own initiative and served as a loyal vassal of His Majesty: let them tell what they know [about this].

6.—*Item*, whether they know, etc., that, having come back from the said expedition of exploration explained in the question preceding this one, the said Ginés Hernández returned with the said Captain to the said city of Quito in order to go off to the exploration and conquest of the provinces of Quijos, Zumaco, and La Canela, to which provinces he went off with the said Captain on account of there being current many reports about them and on account of its being [considered to be] very important country: and [that] so he endured great hardships in it [i.e. in that country], until he finally came out in the border-land districts of Quito, and [that] from there they [i.e. Gonzalo Díaz de Pineda and Ginés Hernández] went and joined up with Captain Lorenzo de Aldana, who was coming with a force of men by way of [territory under] the jurisdiction of the governor of Popayán to found the city of Pasto; and [that] by the efforts of those men who, including myself, came with the said Captain of ours and of those whom the said Lorenzo de Aldana brought with him, there was founded the said city of Pasto, which is forty leagues away from Quito.

7.—*Item*, whether they know, etc., that the said Ginés Hernández, having gone through what is stated above, went forth to serve His Majesty under Captain Alonso Hernández in the conquest and pacification of the province of Yumbo, which at that time was in revolt, because, as everybody knew, there had been called together in council the chief of this province named Bitara and the chiefs of the provinces of Otavalo and Quito, and other chiefs and notables of those provinces in general had communicated with one another and agreed to revolt and to massacre the Spaniards, which [situation] was brought to a close and was calmed down and was smoothed out by the carrying out, in the way that it was carried out, of the said [war of] pacification and conquest, in consequence of which the whole country became settled down and quieted, and [that] this is the reason why there has never been any further general disturbance among the said natives: let them tell what they know [about this].

8.—*Item*, whether they know, etc., that the said Ginés Hernández, after serving in the affair mentioned in the question preceding this one, went forth from the city of Quito to serve His Majesty under Captain Lorenzo de Aldana, and went off to the province of Tomebamba to clear up the grievance of the natives in the matter of certain complaints which they were lodging against Captain Vergara and his followers, [this captain being the one] who had come in from the expedition of exploration of Los Bracamoros; and [that], when the said Lorenzo de Aldana went to the said province of Tomebamba to put a stop to these annoyances which the said Vergara was causing the natives in the said province of Tomebamba, which is fifty leagues away from Quito, and as soon as the said Vergara heard of his coming, the followers whom he [i.e. Vergara] had with him came away and he himself ceased causing the said annoyances, with the result that the natives obtained much profit and relief and were thereafter satisfied: let them tell what they know [about this].

9.—*Item*, whether they know, etc., that, after he had played his rôle in what is stated above, the said Ginés Hernández went off to serve His Majesty under Captain Rodrigo Núñez de Bonilla in the conquest and pacification of the provinces of Macas and Quisna and Tuna, and others which were within the same territorial limits, which were in revolt, [the natives] having killed certain Spaniards; which said provinces, along with the native inhabitants of them, were rightly chastised and were calmed down and pacified and came under the power of, and obedience to, His Majesty; let them tell what they know [about this].

10.—*Item*, whether they know, etc., that, at the termination of that [which is stated] in the question preceding this one, the said Ginés Hernández, having returned to the said city of Quito, left it to [go and] serve His Majesty with the Governor Gonzalo Pizarro, who in the name of His Majesty had been commissioned by the Marquis Don Francisco Pizarro, his brother [to head a new expedition], and [that] the said Ginés Hernández went with him a second time to the said provinces of La Canela and Zumaco and Quijos, in which provinces, after they had gone in there, much suffering was endured from want of supplies and there died from hunger the greater part of the men and they reached the point of being obliged to eat their horses; and [that] in spite of these hardships and of the fact that the country was hilly and rugged they kept on exploring the said provinces, from which said expedition of exploration there redounded a great service to [the glory of] God Our Lord and of His Majesty, on account of there having been founded in the said country four cities and [because] every day [this region] is being colonized farther and farther on: let them tell what they know [about this].

11.—*Item*, whether they know, etc., that, after he [i.e. Ginés Hernández] had endured the hardships mentioned in the question preceding this one and after the said provinces had been explored and [there had thus been encountered] many native inhabitants [in the regions] where at the present time the said cities are founded, the said Gonzalo Pizarro sent out Captain Francisco de Orellana, in prolongation of the said exploration, in a brigantine, and with him the said Ginés Hernández [and others], who, [starting out] with the said brigantine and some canoes down the river which they call the Marañón, [were to] explore the country and look for food; and [that] so they did go down the said river, which is one of the [most] remarkable things in the world, and came out in the Northern Sea, having covered more than one thousand five hundred leagues down the said river; along which they discovered great nations and settlements and countries of great riches and of abundant natural resources, [so vast] that they [i.e. the expeditioners], because of their being so few in number, could not conquer them: and [let the witnesses be asked] whether they know that there was built another brigantine as a means for them to escape from the great danger that they were constantly experiencing on account of the uninterrupted fighting that the natives forced upon them and as a means of protecting themselves against the fury of the river, which was so great that they could not turn back upstream, rather they continued on down the said river until they came out at the sea, and they proceeded along its shore for the four hundred leagues, approximately, which must make up the distance from the mouth of the said river to the islands of Cubagua and Margarita, where they arrived and found the city which the Spaniards have founded there: and [let the witnesses be asked] whether they know that the carrying out of this [voyage of] discovery was a very important accomplishment, because they [thus] discovered the greater part of the land that there is in Peru, and to His Majesty there was rendered a remarkable service: let them tell what they know [about this].

12.—*Item*, whether they know, etc., that, after the completion of the expedition of discovery [related] in the question preceding this one, the said Ginés Hernández returned to the Nombre de Dios coast and crossed over and took ship at [a port on] the Southern Sea, and proceeded to the Peruvian coast, and from there to the territory of Popayán and to that of Quito, whence he went forth to serve His Majesty under Captain Rodrigo de Ocampo in conquering and pacifying the provinces of Lita and Quilca, which had been in revolt for many days, and [that] this was at his own expense and on his own initiative: let them tell what they know [about this].

13.—*Item*, whether they know, etc., that the said Ginés Hernández, after his return to the said city, went forth from it to serve His Majesty with the revenue collector Pero Martín Montanero, who was starting out to pacify the province of Canaribamba, which is something like seventy leagues from Quito and was at that time [within] its jurisdiction, in which [province] the natives were in revolt, for at that time the Indians of the provinces of Chaparra and Viriayanca, who [at that time] were people dwelling in adjoining districts and now belong to the jurisdiction of the city of Loja, had massacred many Spanish traders and had robbed them of all that they were bringing from the coast of Túmbez to the city of Quito, [over the route] which was at that time the main highway; and [that], thanks to the fact that the said [expedition of] pacification was carried out, the roads became safe and they [i.e. the expeditioners] subdued the said natives, and [that], by means of this said [expedition of] pacification and [during] the time that was employed in it, there were explored in the said provinces of Canaribamba [and] Tomebamba, where there is now situated the city of Cuenca, the rich mines of the river which they call Santa Barbola, from which [mines] there has been extracted a great amount of gold, and to His Majesty there has been rendered a great service and his levies of one-fifth have been increased: let them tell what they know [about this].

14.—*Item*, whether they know, etc., that the said Ginés Hernández was in the said city of Quito at the time when Captain Rodrigo de Salazar hoisted his banner on the side of His Majesty and killed Captain Pedro de Puelles, who was in revolt there against the service of the King [and] who was a captain under Gonzalo Pizarro and was holding the said city; and [let the witnesses be asked] whether they know that the said Ginés Hernández went forth with the said Captain Salazar following the royal standard as far as the valley of Jauja, which is forty leagues from the city of Lima [and is the place] where the President Pedro de la Gasca was, and [that] he took his stand there under the royal standard, and went on following it [and] serving His Majesty as far as the valley of Xaquixaguana, where there was fought the battle in which the said Gonzalo Pizarro was routed and justice was wreaked on him and on his followers and [that] in all this he [i.e. Ginés Hernández] took part in the service of His Majesty: let them tell what they know [about this].

15.—*Item*, whether they know, etc., that, at the conclusion of the affair stated above, the said Ginés Hernández returned to the said city of Quito with the said Captain Rodrigo de Salazar, with the idea in mind of going off to establish some colonies in [places which had been seen during] the conquest and exploration of Quijos, Zumaco, and La Canela, [on] which [expedition] he had gone at an earlier date, and [that] because at that time the said [project of] colonization did not materialize, he set out from the said city on the expedition of exploration to Macas, where Captain Hernando de Benavente was [and] where now a new city has recently been founded, which said expedition of exploration he abandoned with the said captain on arriving in the province of Tomebamba, with the intention of going back to resume the exploration through some section where there would be a better approach for penetrating into the country: let them tell what they know [about this].

16.—*Item*, whether they know, etc., that the said Ginés Hernández proceeded with the said Captain Hernando de Benavente from the said province of Tomebamba to the city of Loja to join up with Captain Alonso de Mercadillo, with which men he went off to the conquest and exploration of [the region where] the said city of Zamora [has been founded], [as far as a place] where, just inside the border of the country, the said Captain Alonso de Mercadillo had a certain force of men: let them tell what they know [about this].

17.—*Item*, whether they know, etc., that the said Ginés Hernández took part in this said [expedition of] conquest and exploration with the said captains, Hernando de Benavente and Alonso de Mercadillo, now twelve years since, serving in the said conquest and in the [work of] pacification consequent upon it under the said captains and under the other captains and governors who have succeeded them, serving with his arms and [his] horses, performing and obediently executing what he was ordered to do by the said captains and judicial authorities, and [that all this] has been beneficial to the service of His Majesty and to the welfare and pacification of the country.

18.—*Item*, whether they know, etc., that, as a result of the said [expeditions of] conquest and pacification, the said city of Zamora was founded and has been kept going and is [still] being kept up, and the natives are coming into [possession of] a knowledge of our holy Catholic faith, and there has been suppressed among them the [custom of] eating human flesh, as [read: "for"] they were formerly accustomed to eating it and used to kill one another and eat one another and were constantly at war with one another; and [that] within the past six years, slightly more or less, there have been discovered, six leagues from the city and in other parts under its jurisdiction, very rich gold mines in rivers and on mountainsides, from which there have been extracted nuggets of one thousand five hundred pesos [in value], and of six hundred, and of five hundred, and of two hundred, slightly more or less: [in addition to which] a great quantity of finer gold has been extracted and there is [still] being extracted a great amount [of it]; from all of which [activity of his] there results [a great] service to His Majesty, as well as a great increase in his royal levies of one-fifth: let them tell what they know [about this].

19.—*Item*, whether they know, etc., that the said Ginés Hernández has been and [still] is a citizen of the said city of Zamora ever since it was founded and has kept up and is keeping up his household on a large scale and maintaining the rank of citizen with his arms and [his] horse, constantly supporting in his house honorable men who help to keep up the town, all at his own expense and on his own initiative: let them tell what they know [about this].

20.—*Item*, whether they know, etc., that, considering the rank and obligations of the said Ginés Hernández, and to enable him to support [properly] what he is supporting and be esteemed as a gentleman, the Indians that he has as a *repartimiento* are decidedly few; and that, not only for this reason but also in view of the fact that the city of Zamora is one of the most expensive in these parts [to live in], because provisions have to be brought in from outside, he is in need of being favored by His Majesty with another [and] greater kindness: let them tell what they know [about this].

21.—*Item*, whether they know, etc., that the said Ginés Hernández is a person of rank, [and] that as such he has always been esteemed and [has] developed his connections and personal relations with individuals of importance, and that [it is] as to a person of this sort [that] they have always intrusted and are [still] intrusting important positions to him in which he has served His Majesty, such as [those of] justice of the peace and magistrate many times and treasurer of His Majesty, and [that he is telling the truth when he claims] to have held other government offices which are customarily bestowed upon persons of importance, and that in them he has been considered to be a good and upright judge and has administered the said offices with great solicitude and [careful] directing, in such a way that he has shown himself to be very truly a servant of His Majesty and a protector of his dominions: let them tell what they know [about this].

22.—*Item*, whether they know, etc., that the said Ginés Hernández is a good Christian and a [good] Catholic fearful of God and obedient to His commands and to those of the Holy Mother Church and [a man] zealous in [looking after] the affairs related with the service of God and of His Majesty, and is a peace-loving person and is well liked and is solicitous for the preservation and protection of these natives, both on the occasions when he has been a detachment leader in the [expeditions of] pacification and conquest, and in [times of] peace and quiet, looking after the interests of the state: let them tell what they know [about this].

23.—*Item*, whether they know, etc., that as a partial reward for the said services which the said Ginés Hernández had rendered to His Majesty there were granted to him by proxy by Captain Alonso de Mercadillo five hundred Indians as an *encomienda* within the bounds of the territory belonging to the said city of Zamora, and [that this grant was] confirmed by the Viceroy Don Antonio de Mendoza, and [that] on top of this the Marqués de Cañete granted him as [an additional] *encomienda* two hundred more, and that [the said Ginés Hernández], having gone [out there] to inspect the country, found that he had suffered losses, because he found, and [now actually] possesses, only one hundred Indians, slightly more or less, with which, as has been stated, he can not support himself, not only because the Indians [i.e. the Indian men] are few in number but also because the people [who make up the families, etc.] of the said Indians are wretched and poor and live without clothing for their bodies and are a people who turn in no revenue whatsoever beyond that which by means of the laborious-ness and assistance of the said Ginés Hernández he [i.e. the latter] can obtain; and [let the witnesses be asked] whether they know that for this reason the said Ginés Hernández is very poor and plunged into debt and is in need of being aided by His Majesty in order to get himself out of debt: let them tell what they know [about this].

24.—*Item*, whether they know, etc., that all the services mentioned in the questions of this interrogatory the said Ginés Hernández has performed for His Majesty at his own expense and on his own initiative, and [that] in everything he has served him very loyally, without having done a single thing to His Majesty detrimental to his interests, either at any period or in any of the disturbances that there have been in this realm: let them tell what they know [about this].

25.—*Item*, whether they know, etc., that the said Ginés Hernández is a person of such qualifications that on him will be very fittingly conferred any favor that His Majesty may extend to him and that in direct proportion to his services and his rank he possesses a natural talent and merits for such a thing: let them tell what they know [about this].

26.—*Item*, whether they know, etc., that the said Ginés Hernández, on account of the great expenses which he has incurred in serving His Majesty in what is stated in the questions preceding this one, is poor and in such great need that he can not go or send [someone in his stead] to Ciudad de los Reyes to have this taking of evidence executed by the Royal Audiencia which has its seat there, in view of the fact that it is more than two hundred leagues away from this city and the roads are of [the sort which entails] many hardships, and in view of the fact that there is required a large sum of gold pesos for that purpose: let them tell what they know [about this].

Thus it was necessary to have the said taking of evidence executed in this city, because the said Ginés Hernández was unable to go to the said Royal Audiencia, and [if it had not been done here] he would have lost out in his just cause and would have failed to inform His Majesty of the services which he has rendered, for, as has been stated, he is very poor and needy, and his just cause would have come to naught.

27.—*Item*, whether they know that all that is stated above is common knowledge and known facts and public talk and [matters of] general report, and considered and esteemed and commonly reputed as such: let them tell what they know [about this].—*Gines Hernandez*.

Done in the city of Zamora de los Alcaides in the realms and provinces of Peru, on the fourteenth [day] of February, One Thousand Five Hundred and Sixty-four.

Diego Gómez.—[In reply] to the eleventh question he said that he knew about [the matter referred to in] it as it is stated therein: asked how [he knew about it], he said that [it was] because this witness [i.e. he] with his own hands had helped to build the brigantine on which the said Captain Francisco de Orellana and the said Ginés Hernández and fifty soldiers had embarked in order to go down the said Marañón River to look for food, as the said Gonzalo Pizarro had ordered them [or him, i.e. Orellana] to do; which said soldiers this witness [said that he] had seen hoist sail and start off down the said river and [that], when they had not had any news from them for more than a year, they had taken it for granted that they had died, for at a later period than when they had sent them off in search of food, because they were suffering great want, and [a want] so great that they had been eating the horses from hunger, after they had remained [there] awaiting the return of the said Captain with the said fifty soldiers for forty-odd days, they had been compelled to turn back to a land of peace and [go] in search of supplies; and [that] after many months, when there had come back to this realm of Peru a certain number out of several soldiers from among the above-mentioned, they had learned from them that the said Ginés Hernández and the rest who had gone with him had had to endure the hardships and dangers and periods of hunger which the question mentions, and [that it was] for this reason [that] he knew about the matter.

Álvaro de Sepúlveda.—[In reply] to the eleventh question he said that what he knew about [the matter referred to in] it was that he had seen how the said Gonzalo Pizarro had sent the Captain Francisco de Orellana that the question tells about, in the brigantine and canoes as it is explained therein, down the river which they call the Marañón in search of food, and that [he knew that in this way] he [i.e. Orellana] had explored some country; and [that] among the soldiers whom he [i.e. Orellana] had taken with him he had seen that one was the said

Ginés Hernández, for he had seen him get into the boat and go away with the rest, who all together went off in quest of what he has already stated, and [that] when they had not returned at the end of more than forty days, as he recalled it, the said Gonzalo Pizarro had gone on in pursuit of his journey, on which they had been delayed many days and had had to endure unbearable hardships which, on account of their being numerous and [full] of great perils [too horrible to tell about], he did not relate: and this [he said was what] he knew about [the matter mentioned in] this question.

Diego de Herrera.—[In reply] to the eleventh question he said that what he knew about [the matter referred to in] it was that at the time that the question states this witness [i.e. he] had seen how the said Governor Gonzalo Pizarro had sent Captain Francisco de Orellana with a brigantine and a certain number of canoes down the Marañón River in search of food and had given him for the purpose in hand forty or fifty soldiers, and among them the said Ginés Hernández, all of whom this witness [i.e. he] had seen get into their boats and start off down the said river, and [he said that] they had not come back again because, as it had been learned afterwards, they had gone on and come out at the Northern Sea; that, as for the distance they had traveled from the time that they had separated from the said Gonzalo Pizarro until they had reached the sea, [he understood that] they had covered more than one thousand five hundred leagues, during all of which enterprise, [so] this witness [i.e. he] had been told, by several of the soldiers who had gone with the said Captain Orellana, after they had come back to this realm, they had suffered great hardships and want and discovered many realms and [the abodes] of many natives and a great many other things in addition to what the question states, and [he told] of how the said Marañón River was one of the most stupendous things that there were in half a world, because they said that at the approach to the sea it was more than thirty leagues wide, and [that] farther up [it was] sixty, and that, [if he were asked to give his opinion about the importance] of their having discovered such vast territories, [he would say that] the service which the above-mentioned men had thereby rendered to His Majesty could not fail to be a signal one: and [he said] that this [was what] he knew about [the subject-matter of] this question.

Ruy Vázquez Parra.—[In reply] to the eleventh question he said that what is stated in the question the said Francisco de Isásaga and Pedro de Ibarra and Álvaro de Sepúlveda had related to this witness [i.e. to him] as quite true, and [that] since that time he had heard it said that two fine cities had been founded in the course of the said expedition, [and] that the one was named the city of Baeza and the other [the city] of Ávila: and [he said] that this [was what] he had to say [in reply] to this question.

Bernabé Fonseca.—[In reply] to the eleventh question he said that everything which the question states this witness [i.e. he] had heard related, as a very commonly reported and very well-known fact, by Francisco de Isásaga, who was one of those who had gone in company with the said Ginés Hernández in the said brigantine and canoes which the question mentions and explains about, along with other soldiers, down the said Marañón River, until they had come out at the Northern Sea; that, as they had estimated it, they may well have covered, in the [course of what is] said above, more than one thousand five hundred leagues, and that in going down the said river they had discovered all the land and peoples that the question mentions and had endured the hardships and the sufferings from want mentioned therein, until they had finally landed at Cubagua, and from there had returned to this realm: and [he said] that this [was what] he knew about [the subject-matter of] this question.

Pedro de Ibarra.—[In reply] to the eleventh question he said that all that the question states this witness [i.e. he] had heard related as common [knowledge] and very well-known [facts] by many soldiers who had gone in company with the said Ginés Hernández down the Marañón River at the time that the question says that this had taken place, just as, and in the form and manner that, it is explained therein.

Martín Sánchez.—[In reply] to the eleventh question he said that all that the question states this witness [i.e. he] had been informed of, [it being told to him] as [a] very commonly reported and very well-known [fact], by many soldiers of the said Gonzalo Pizarro at the time that they had come back from the said expedition, this witness [i.e. he] having sought to find out about the said Ginés Hernández and this Captain Francisco de Orellana whom the question mentions, because this witness [i.e. he] had [formerly] been a soldier in his company and had [now] become anxious to find out about him in order to go and serve under him, and [he told] how the said soldiers whom he had already mentioned had told him that that was not possible in view of the fact that he [i.e. Orellana] had gone off in a brigantine with fifty soldiers down the river in search of food and [with the end in view] of exploring some country, and [how the said soldiers had told him] that they did not think that he had gotten back so quickly, because he had decided in his own mind not to stop until [he reached] the Northern Sea, a proposal which in fact he did carry out, precisely in the manner and form that the question sets forth: asked how he knew about it [all], he said that [it was] due to the reasons which he had already stated and also because the said Ginés Hernández and other soldiers from among those whom the said Orellana had taken along with him had told it [all] to this witness [i.e. to him], just after they had returned to this realm of Peru, after they had gone over all the distance which the question states and endured the hardships and sufferings from want mentioned therein; and [he said that it was] for this reason [that] he knew about the matter as he had stated.

# VI

*Extracts from the judicial inquiry on the subject of the deserts and past services of Pedro Domínguez Miradero.\* Quito, September, 1564.*

In the city of San Francisco del Quito in these realms of Peru, on the twenty-sixth day of the month of September in the year One Thousand Five Hundred and Sixty-four, before the very illustrious licentiate Fernando de Santillán, former President of this Royal Audiencia, he being present in its royal court-rooms, there appeared Pedro Domínguez Miradero, and he delivered the petition and interrogatory whose contents are as follows:

Very powerful Sir: I, Pedro Domínguez Miradero, a citizen of this city of San Francisco del Quito, do come before Your Highness and do declare that:

* Archives of the Indies, case 1, shelf 5, bundle 35/19.

some thirty years ago I crossed over to these parts of the Indies with Don Pedro de Lugo, your [Highness'] Adelantado and Governor, and ever since that time down to the present have served Your Highness in these provinces, inasmuch as it was under your [Highness'] captain Luis Bernal and his lieutenant Juan Greciano [that I served] in exploring Guaca and Nore and Buritica and Caramanta, and the province of Ancerma, which I helped to settle and pacify and conquer, and from there I set out in company with them to pacify the city of Cali under Captain Miguel Muñoz, for the natives belonging to it were in revolt against your [Highness'] royal service; and when this matter had been attended to, in view of the report that I had received to the effect that the Indian natives belonging to this city of San Francisco del Quito were in revolt against your [Highness'] royal service, I came here in company with Captain Benavente, where we found Captain Rodrigo Martínez* de Bonilla, and with him and under your [Highness'] royal standard I took part in the expeditions of conquest and pacification in Macas and Quisna and Cuna and Cangai and other provinces [for the subduing] of the Indian natives, belonging to this city of San Francisco del Quito, that had been given to its citizens as *encomiendas;* and, when that which has just been stated had been attended to, I went forth from this city with Gonzalo Pizarro, who at that time was in your [Highness'] royal service, on the expedition of exploration to Zumaco and La Canela and El Dorado, and on the said expedition of exploration, on the way down the Marañón River, because the said captain of yours [read: "of Your Highness'"], Gonzalo Pizarro, had an [excellent] opinion of my personal qualities, he sent me in company with Captain Francisco de Orellana, along with fifty men, in a boat and twenty-two canoes, to explore the country down the river, and, we not being able to go back by the same river owing to the force of the currents and the [heavy] rains and the [bad] weather conditions and the skirmishes with the Indians, I traveled on for four [*sic*] months without stopping until I came out at the Northern Sea; suffering from terrific spells of hunger and from hardships and from [many] sorts of want, we finally came to port on the Island of Margarita, whence I departed in order to [go and] better serve Your Highness.  I came over to the Southern Sea, and, having heard that in Santiago de Guayaquil the natives of that province and of the island of Puná were in revolt against your royal [Highness'] service and that they had slain the bishop, Friar Vicente de Valverde, and the Christians who were with him there, I took part in the campaign for the pacification and conquest of the said province and island under orders of Captain Diego de Urbina and Gómez Destacio, his lieutenant, and I helped to settle it [i.e. all that general region], conquer it, reconstruct it, and reduce it [to obedience] to your [Highness'] royal service; and, when what has just been stated had been attended to, having heard that the Indians, belonging to the city of Quito, of the provinces of Quilcaylita and Caguasqui were in revolt against your [Highness'] royal service, I set out in company with your [Highness'] captain, Rodrigo de Campo, on the expedition of pacification of the said province; and, when what has just been stated had been attended to, in view of what I had heard about the mines of Santa Barbola River, I went to them, and through my thorough diligence and industriousness I was instrumental in bringing it about that many mines were discovered out of which your [Highness'] royal levies of one-fifth were increased, and from there I came on to

*[Read "Núñez," here and wherever the name occurs in the rest of the document.—Translator.]

this city of Quito, where, I being in it in [the interests of] your [Highness'] royal service, having received news that Gonzalo Pizarro had formed a conspiracy against your [Highness'] royal service, and Pedro de Puelles, Gonzalo Pizarro's captain, being in this city of Quito and holding it under tyrannical rule and under his control and command on behalf of the said Gonzalo Pizarro, a certain number of followers having been rounded up [to take a stand] against your [Highness'] royal service, and Captain Rodrigo de Salazar being at that time in this said city [and], having a [just] conception of me personally and of other servants of Your Highness, he hoisted his standard in defence of your [Highness'] royal service and, aided by your [Highness'] servants, he put to death the said Captain Pedro de Puelles, and in that affair I took part under your [Highness'] royal standard, and in consideration of the favorable opinion which he got of my personal qualities he made me a squadron-chief in charge of eighty arquebusiers; and, when this service had been rendered to Your Highness, the said Rodrigo de Salazar, having received news to the effect that Doctor La Gasca, your [Highness'] President, was coming up along the Southern Sea towards Lima [to launch an attack] against Gonzalo Pizarro, sallied forth from the city of Quito with three hundred men, and I [was] with him under your [Highness'] royal banner as squadron-chief in charge of the eighty arquebusiers, [and he proceeded] as far as the valley of Jauja, where he joined up with the said President La Gasca, and from there we marched all together as far as the valley of Xaquixaguana, where there was fought the battle against the tyrant Gonzalo Pizarro, and in it I took part under your [Highness'] royal banner with the said rank of squadron-chief until we defeated him and justice was wreaked on him and on his followers; and from there I set out, with the permission of Doctor La Gasca, for this province of Quito with the end in view of going to settle Quijos and La Canela along with Captain Rodrigo de Salazar, who had been duly commissioned for the said purpose by the said Doctor La Gasca; and, as a result of the fact that the said Captain Rodrigo de Salazar did not get the said expedition under way, I stayed in this city of Quito, to which there came at this time Antonio de Oznayo [i. e. Osnayo] as *corregidor*, and at this time there rose up in revolt the Indians of Lita and Quilca and Caguasqui and they killed the man to whom they as an *encomienda* belonged, along with some other Spaniards, and the said Antonio de Oznayo, the *corregidor*, set out to [undertake] the punishment and pacification of the said provinces with eighty men, and he took me along with him, in which campaign I took part [as a man enrolled] in your [Highness'] royal service; and, while the said *corregidor* of yours [read: "of Your Highness'"], Antonio de Oznayo, was engaged in the said expedition of pacification in the said provinces, he received notice from your [Highness'] President and the Judges of your [Highness'] Royal Audiencia in Lima to the effect that Francisco Hernández Girón had revolted against your [Highness'] royal service, his [i.e. Antonio de Osnayo's] orders being to observe great care and watchfulness in this city of Quito and in its territory; and when he received the said news he left the said provinces and came on to the town of Carangue which is in this said province of Quito, and there he pitched his camp, and being in his tent [at night] he sent for me at midnight by one of his pages and, having heard of the many and the loyal services which I had performed for Your Highness, having confidence in me, he informed me of what your [Highness'] President and Judges had written to him, and he placed his person and his equipage in my hands, and he charged me and requested me to pick out from his expeditionary force the soldiers who, in my opinion, were loyal servants of His Majesty to be his [i. e. Osnayo's] bodyguard, over which [as a body] and over whom [as individuals] he appointed me commander, and he intrusted to me the service of His Majesty and the guarding of his [i.e. his own] person; and I at once started to carry out what he had thus intrusted me with, and I picked out for him the number of soldiers that in my opinion was about right for such an enterprise, and, with me exercising the commission that he had given to me, [the whole affair] being secret, without there being imparted any information about it to any person whatsoever [i.e. to any other person in the place or in Quito], he got out of Carangue with the men that he had in his equipage, and I got him into the city of Quito, where, his person being [carefully] guarded in it [i.e. in the city], he called a meeting of the city council and announced to the city corporation, the court officials, and the municipal council board the news which he had received regarding the revolt of Francisco Hernández [Girón]; and constantly thereafter, until the news of the routing of the said Francisco Hernández Girón had been received, he kept me in this city of Quito in his entourage and in his house with the commission which he had given me, I serving Your Highness in all this affair as a good and loyal vassal; and, this affair being settled, there came to this city the Governor Gil Ramírez, who led an expedition from this city into Quijos and La Canela, and I went with him as commander for him and helped to conquer, pacify, and colonize [the district in which has been founded] the city of Baeza; and, the said service having been performed, I came back to this city of San Francisco del Quito with the said Governor Gil Ramírez to recruit men and assemble munitions; and, while I was in this city occupied with what has just been stated, Captain Rodrigo Martínez* de Bonilla was authorized to act in the capacity of governor in the said provinces of Quijos and La Canela, with whom I went into the said city of Baeza, and after this city had been established as a colony the Indian natives belonging to it rebelled, and I was appointed commander [of a force of men] by the said Captain Rodrigo Martínez de Bonilla, and [by way of] serving Your Highness I brought them around to terms of peace and reduced them [to obedience] to your [Highness'] service; and following the end and death of the said Rodrigo Martínez de Bonilla, your [Highness'] governor, there was appointed governor Melchor Vázquez de Ávila, who in your [Highness'] royal name and in his stead sent into the provinces of Zumaco and La Canela Captain Andrés Contero with one hundred and fifty men, and with him and under your [Highness'] royal standard I took part in the campaign at my own expense in order to serve Your Highness, serving as a commander in the said expedition; and with these said captains, and in the regions and places stated, I have steadfastly remained under your [Highness'] standard and in your [Highness'] royal service, serving with my person, [my] arms, and [my] horses, at my own expense and on my own initiative, and furnishing an inspiring example to other soldiers in your [Highness'] royal armies and to your [Highness'] captains in the matter of what ought to be done [on any given occasion], as a man who understood the matter; and, because for none of these services [have I been]† rewarded and [because] I wish that notice of them be brought to the attention of Your Highness, in order that as compensation for them Your Highness may grant me the favors which I deserve, I request and beseech Your Highness to order that the witnesses

* [See asterisk footnote, p. 292, *supra*.—TRANSLATOR.]
† [Added by Medina.—EDITOR.]

whom I shall bring forth be examined according to the contents of this my interrogatory, and to order that what they shall say and testify to be given to me all certified in commonly accepted form, in such a way that it may constitute true evidence, in order [that I may be able] to place it in Your [Highness'] royal hands, to the end that, when by Your Highness it shall have been considered [Your Highness], heeding his royal conscience, in consideration of the merits of my services, may grant me the favors to which in return for these [services] I aspire; and for this purpose I request that in conformity with your [Highness'] royal decree your [Highness'] attorney-general be notified [to take proper action], and in whatever may be required I implore your [Highness'] royal intervention.—
*Pedro Dominguez Miradero.*

.   .   .   .   .   .   .   .   .   .   .   .   .   .   .   .   .   .   .   .   .   .   .   .   .   .

Interrogatory.—By means of the following questions shall be examined such witnesses as have been summoned to appear on behalf of Pedro Domínguez Miradero in connection with [the judicial inquiry covering] the services which he has rendered to His Majesty in these parts of the Indies.

.   .   .   .   .   .   .   .   .   .   .   .   .   .   .   .   .   .   .   .   .   .   .   .   .   .

Question 6.—*Item*, whether they know that, when what has just been stated had been attended to, I left this city of San Francisco del Quito with Governor Gonzalo Pizarro, who at that time was in the service of His Majesty, on an expedition of exploration to Zumaco and La Canela and El Dorado, and [that] in the course of the said expedition, on the way down the Marañón River, the said Governor Gonzalo Pizarro, having an [excellent] opinion of my personal qualities, sent me in the service of His Majesty with Captain Francisco de Orellana, in a boat accompanied by twenty-two canoes and with fifty men [in them], to explore the country down the river, down which, not being able to go back upstream on account of the force of the currents and the heavy rains and the [bad] weather conditions and the skirmishes with the Indians, we traveled on for four [*sic*] months without stopping, enduring many hardships, spells of hunger, and sufferings from want, [the members of the expedition] eating, for lack of food supplies, their doublets and cow-hides and soles of shoes and boots and buskins and stirrup-straps and other nasty things which hunger and want forced upon them [for nourishment], in spite of all of which, thanks to the ingenuity which I, the said Pedro Domínguez Miradero, displayed not only in navigating the Marañón River but also [in steering our course] in the Northern Sea when we got out into it, cheering up the soldiers who went along in the same group with me, through the instrumentality of God and of another [i.e. a new] boat which he [i.e. Orellana] ordered to be built on [the shores of] the said Marañón River because of the need which we had of it as a means of safeguarding the lives of the men during the skirmishes with the natives, we escaped with our lives after much hardship and finally reached the end of our journey at Margarita, where we landed on the island of Cubagua (*sic*), more [nearly] dead than alive, and in such a state that the inhabitants of it were amazed to see us: let them tell what they know [about this].

.   .   .   .   .   .   .   .   .   .   .   .   .   .   .   .   .   .   .   .   .   .   .   .   .   .

Very powerful Sire: I, Pedro Domínguez Miradero, do declare: that in a petition which I submitted to Your Highness I did set forth the numerous and very loyal services which I have performed for Your Highness in these parts of the Indies during the past thirty years, for the purpose of having a taking of testimony [relative to these facts] executed for me, in order that Your Highness, being made cognizant of them, might grant me the favors which I deserve as compensation for them; and since they are numerous and [are] of the sort that I have shown them [to be] and [inasmuch as] I have spent a great many gold pesos in your [Highness'] royal service, I beg and beseech Your Highness to order that as compensation for them I be given an annual income of six thousand pesos in good [i.e. assayed (?)] gold in the form of revenue from some Indians who are good for it [i.e. that amount] and [that], until there shall be some [i.e. some Indians] free [for assignment as an *encomienda*], they [i.e. the six thousand pesos] be paid to me out of your [Highness'] royal chest; and, because as your [Highness'] loyal vassal and servant in the commissions which I have had [to carry out] by [orders of] your [Highness'] captains in the campaigns and battles in which I have taken part, I have performed some very remarkable feats, placing my life in jeopardy, such as was my climbing up into a very tall tree and [one] dangerous to climb up into and surrounded by enemies, from [the top of] which I discovered the land of Ancerma, and, [this land being thus] discovered, that was the occasion for capturing it and founding the city of Ancerma and other towns which were established in it [i.e. in that land] in your [Highness'] royal name; and [at one place] on the Marañón River I captured a fortress from a large number of Indian natives who had fortified themselves in it in order to kill us and block the narrows formed by the Marañón River and the bridge over it, which [fortress], together with the said bridge, I captured, and I passed through with the boats and [with] the men forming our party, thanks to which action we escaped with our lives; and in the campaign of Xaquixaguana, in the battle which was fought against Gonzalo Pizarro, I performed some notable services for Your Highness and [read: for example, when] I took away from one soldier whom I captured a helmet and a sword and a shield; and in return for the said services I beseech Your Highness, in addition to what is stated above, to do me the favor of [bestowing upon me] the title of regularly commissioned captain of Your Highness, with a vote in the council meetings of [all] the towns in which I may happen to be, because [I feel entitled to this privilege] as a man who understands the art of war [as it should be waged] in your [Highness'] royal service; and for the sake of being able to make a good personal appearance, and as a coat of arms, [I request the privilege of using] the tree and the fortress and the Marañón River and the bridge, the helmet and the shield and the sword which I captured, all in your [Highness'] royal service; and [I request] that I and my relatives and descendants may be able to have them and place them as a coat of arms on our houses, on our seals, and on our ornamental covers: in reference to all of which full evidence will be placed before Your Highness by means of the judicial inquiry which I am endeavoring to have put through, which for this purpose I do beg to have undertaken, and for this purpose, etc.—*Pedro Dominguez Miradero.*

. . . . . . . . . . . . . . . . . . . . . . .

Reply of the witness Juan Agraz to question 6:—[In reply] to the sixth question this witness said that he knew that the said Pedro Domínguez Miradero was one of the soldiers who had gone off in company with Gonzalo Pizarro to the provinces of Zumaco and La Canela and to the Marañón River, and [that] in it [i.e. on this expedition] he had served as a good soldier at his own expense, and [that] he knew that he was one of those who had gone down the Marañón River in company with Captain Orellana, because this witness [i.e. he] had [himself] gone with the said Gonzalo Pizarro and had seen the said Pedro Domínguez embark with the said Orellana to [go and] explore the said river, and that they could not have failed to have to endure many spells of hunger and [many] hardships, for the reason that they [i.e. these things] had been endured up to that point [i.e. until Orellana's departure from Gonzalo Pizarro's camp]: and this [was what] he knew [about this matter] and gave as his reply.

Reply of the witness Benito Barreda to the same question:—[In reply] to the sixth question this witness said that he knew and had [actually] seen that the said Pedro Domínguez had gone with the said Gonzalo Pizarro on the expedition of exploration and pacification among the Indians of Zumaco and La Canela and [along] the Marañón River, and [that] he had seen how the said Pedro Domínguez had gone with the said Orellana down the river to explore country, and that this witness [i.e. he] considered, so far as he was concerned, that owing to the fact that the currents were so strong they would not have been able to turn back upstream with the brigantine, and that in all this affair he had seen him serve in a very distinguished manner, on whatever occasion had presented itself, as a good soldier, and that they had endured many spells of hunger and sufferings from want, and that this witness [i.e. he] knew and had seen that they had eaten, in the course of the said expedition, driven to it by the great hunger, everything that is specifically mentioned in the question.

Reply of the witness Alonso de Cabrera to the same question:—[In reply] to the sixth question this witness said that he knew about [the matter referred to in] it as it is stated therein: asked how he knew about [the matter referred to in] it, he said that [it was] because this witness [i.e. he] was one of those who had gone on the said expedition with the said Gonzalo Pizarro and was also one of those who had gone down the said river with the said Captain Orellana, where he had been a witness to everything that the question mentions and had seen the said Pedro Domínguez serve and toil as a good soldier: and [he said that] this was what he knew [about the matter].

Reply of Captain Alonso de Bastidas:—[In reply] to the sixth question he said that what he knew about [the matter referred to in] the question was that at the time when the said Gonzalo Pizarro had been in this city on the point of starting out on the expedition of exploration which the question tells about he had seen the said Pedro Domínguez go off with the said Gonzalo Pizarro, and [that] a year and a half later, slightly more or less, this witness [i.e. he] had seen come back to this city the said Gonzalo Pizarro and many [other] Spaniards who had gone off with him, [now] quite worn out and broken down; and [that, having] asked about the men who were missing, he had been given to understand, and so it was [generally reported as] common [knowledge] and [a] well-known [fact], that Francisco de Orellana had gone on down the river and the said Pedro Domínguez with him, and that at the end of a fairly long time the said Pedro Domínguez had come back to this city; "from whom" [this witness went on to say], "as well as from a certain Alonso de Cabrera, and later on in Lima from Father Friar Gaspar de Caravajal [sic] and from other persons who had gone on down the river, I heard and came to understand that the said Pedro Domínguez had gone with them and that he had toiled very hard and had displayed great ingenuity in the building of a large boat which they [i.e. the expeditioners] had built, and [that] they had finally come to port and to the end of their journey on [the island of] Margarita"; and [that], after the said Pedro Domínguez had come to this city, this witness [i.e. he] had seen him very much handicapped, suffering from injuries to his hands, and [that] he [i.e. Pedro Domínguez] used to say that [it was] from the [hard] work that he had done in building the boats; and likewise [that he had understood] that they had had many skirmishes with the Indians in pirogues and canoes and had suffered excessive hardships: and this [is what] he gave as his reply to the question.

Reply of the witness Bonifaz de Herrera:—[In reply] to the sixth question he said that he knew, through having seen it [come about], that the said Pedro Domínguez had gone off with the Governor Gonzalo Pizarro, because this witness [i.e. he] had [himself] gone with him on the expedition which the question tells about, and had seen how the said Pedro Domínguez had gone off with Captain Orellana down the Marañón River, and [that] this witness [i.e. he] had remained behind with the said Gonzalo Pizarro; and [that] in this way he did not know [for a fact] what had happened after that.

# VII

*Extracts from the judicial inquiry on the subject of the merits and past services of Juan de Illanes.** Quito, September, 1568.

In the city of San Francisco del Quito, in the realms of Peru, on the sixteenth day of the month of September of the year One Thousand Five Hundred and Sixty-eight, before the President and Judges of the Audiencia and Royal Chancery of His Majesty situated in this city, to wit: Doctor Gabriel de Loarte, who as the senior judge presides in it, and the Licentiate García de Valverde and Doctor Pedro de Hinojosa, judges of the said Royal Audiencia, they being assembled for a public hearing, and in the presence of me, Gómez de Moscosso, clerk of the court in it, there appeared Juan de Illanes, a citizen of this city, and he presented a petition which reads in this manner:

Very powerful Sir: I, Juan de Illanes, a citizen of this city of Quito, do declare that: it was something like thirty-four years ago, slightly more or less, that I crossed over to these parts to serve Your Highness, and hence I have served Your Highness in the conquest and colonization of [the district which is now] the city of Santiago de Guayaquil and in the campaign in, and on the expedition of exploration to, La Canela under Gonzalo Pizarro, and I went down the river [with Gonzalo Pizarro as far as he went], and I served Your Highness in the discovery of the Marañón River under Captain Francisco de Orellana, finally coming out at Cubagua, and afterwards I served Your Highness among the followers of your [Highness'] viceroy Blasco Núñez Vela in Ciudad de los Reyes until they took him prisoner; and, in the days when this city was being tyrannized by Gonzalo Pizarro, I served Your Highness at the time that it was brought back [into obedience] to your [Highness'] royal service, and I served Your Highness in the following of President La Gasca in the battle which was fought against Gonzalo Pizarro, and afterwards I served Your Highness in the conquest and pacification of the settlements of Lita and Quilca and Caguaqui, which are within

* Archives of the Indies, 76-6-8.

the territorial limits of this city; and at the time when Francisco Hernández Girón rose up in revolt in this realm against your [Highness'] royal service, I remained in the village of Chimbo* belonging to this city under orders from its *corregidor*, guarding that pass with men whom I had received for that purpose; and I have served Your Highness in other affairs which have come up in connection with your [Highness'] royal service with my arms and [my] horses and [my] servants, all at my own expense and on my own initiative, to do which I have spent a huge sum of gold pesos without there having been paid to me anything whatsoever out of your [Highness'] royal exchequer and without my having done anything detrimental to the interests of Your Highness in any of the affairs that have taken place in this realm [directed] against your [Highness'] royal service; and up to the present I have not been rewarded or compensated for my services, and I am [now] poor and old, and have children, [and am] suffering from [lack of] means of support: and since I am taking the liberty of beseeching Your Royal Person to do me the favor of [bestowing upon me] an annual income of four thousand pesos, I beseech Your Highness, in accordance with what has been ordered through your [Highness'] royal decree, to order your [Highness'] President and Judges of this your [Highness'] Royal Audiencia to have it [i.e. the Audiencia] put through in due form the judicial inquiry on the subject of what is stated above and express its opinion in it [i.e. in the conclusions of the inquiry], and [I request] that they [then] send it [i.e. the whole document] to Your Royal Person in order that he may bestow [such] favors upon me [as he may see fit], and I beg for justice, and in whatever may be required, etc.—*Juan de Illanes*.

Witness.—In the city of San Francisco del Quito, on the twenty-fourth day of the month of September of the said year One Thousand Five Hundred and Sixty-eight, the said Doctor Pedro de Hinojosa, in connection with the judicial inquiry on the subject of the past services of Juan de Illanes, caused to appear before him Captain Álvaro de Paz, to whom he administered the oath, etc.

Being questioned whether this witness [i.e. he] knew, had seen, or [had] heard that the said Juan de Illanes had served His Majesty in these realms or in other parts in connection with the quarrels that had arisen in the Indies or in the expeditions of conquest and colonization, he said: that he knew that the said Juan de Illanes had been and [still] was a servant of His Majesty, because for the past thirty years that he had known him he had seen him serve His Majesty, in particular in the conquest and colonization of [the district which is now] the city of Santiago de Guayaquil, as a soldier of Francisco de Orellana, and [that] under the said captain he had gone off on the expedition of exploration to the province of Las Esmeraldas; and [that] during all this this witness [i.e. he himself] had been with the said Captain Orellana and had seen that the said Juan de Illanes had served in it [all] as a very good soldier, without any help or any expense money, but at his own expense and on his own initiative, because this witness [i.e. he] had had personal relations and intercourse during the said time with the said Juan de Illanes; and [that] later on, this witness [i.e. he] being in this city, he had seen that the said Juan de Illanes had gone off in company with Gonzalo Pizarro in the service of His Majesty on the expedition of exploration of La Canela and the Marañón River; and [that] a year and a half later, slightly more or less, this witness [i.e. he] had seen the said Gonzalo Pizarro come back from the said expedition with a part of the men that he had sent off [into that country], who were all worn out

---

* [See asterisk footnote, p. 119, *supra* —EDITOR.]

and shattered, and [that] this witness [i.e. he] had inquired about the said Juan de Illanes, inasmuch as he had not seen him come back, and [that] they had told this witness [i.e. him] that he [i.e. Juan de Illanes] had gone on down the Marañón River along with Captain Orellana, which [river] the said Gonzalo Pizarro had sent him to explore, and [that] afterwards he had seen him in this city; and [that] from him, as well as from Pedro Domínguez and from Alonso de Cabrera, this witness [i.e. he] had learned that the said Juan de Illanes had gone out through [the mouth of] the said Marañón River.

Witness.—And coming next after what is stated above, in the said city of Quito, on the twenty-fifth day of the said month of September of the said year One Thousand Five Hundred and Sixty-eight, the said Doctor Hinojosa, in connection with the said judicial inquiry, caused to appear before him Alonso de Cabrera, a citizen of the city of Cuenca, by whom was taken and [to whom] was administered the oath in legal form, and he did it very well and without omitting any detail, and the following questions were put to him:

Being asked how old this witness [i.e. he] was and how long a time he had now been in the Indies and whether he knew Juan de Illanes, a citizen of this city of Quito, and since when [he had known him], and where and in [just] what parts [of the Indies] he had made his acquaintance, and whether he was a relative or an enemy of his and [whether] he was affected by any of the general questions which were put to him, he said that this witness [i.e. he] was fifty years old, slightly more or less, and that he had been and [had] resided in the Indies for thirty years out of this total, and [that] this witness [i.e. he] had been residing in these realms of Peru and had known Juan de Illanes, a citizen of this city, for the past twenty-seven years, slightly more or less, and [that] he had always known him during all this time in these realms of Peru, and that he was not a relative or an enemy of his, and that he was not affected by any of the general questions.

Being asked whether this witness [i.e. he] knew, had seen, and [read: "or" (?)] [had] been given to understand that the said Juan de Illanes had served His Majesty on the occasion of the quarrels which had arisen in detriment to the royal service in these parts, and in expeditions of conquest and colonization and in other affairs, he said that he knew that the said Juan de Illanes was a servant of His Majesty, because this witness [i.e. he] had heard many persons say that the said Juan de Illanes had taken part in the founding of the city of Guayaquil and in the subduing of the natives; and that this witness [i.e. he] had seen that the said Juan de Illanes had gone off with Gonzalo Pizarro in the service of His Majesty on the expedition of exploration to La Canela and the Marañón River, because the said Gonzalo Pizarro had undertaken the said expedition in the name of His Majesty, and [that] the said Juan de Illanes had gone off [with it] as a soldier, where [i.e. in which said regions] he had remained away on the said expedition for two years, slightly more or less, and [that] there had been endured numerous and severe hardships, and [that] as a result of it [all] there had died many soldiers out of those whom the said Gonzalo Pizarro had taken along; and [that, while they had been] engaged in the said exploring and conquering, under orders of the said Gonzalo Pizarro, Captain Rodrigo (*sic*) de Orellana had gone in a brigantine down the Marañón River, with more than fifty soldiers, to explore the country farther inland, and [that] among these had been the said Juan de Illanes and this witness [i.e. he himself], because he had taken part in the said expedition [of Orellana's]; and [that] the said Rodrigo (*sic*) de Orellana, [after thus] going down the river, had not been able to go back up to where the said Gonzalo Pizarro was on account of the currents of the said river and [on account of] the freshets, and so they had gone on down the river, for a distance which, as this witness [i.e. he] thought, must have been more than a thousand leagues, until they had come out at the Northern Sea, and by following the coast had gone to Cubagua; and [that] along the said river there had been many hardships and dangers to put up with, owing not only to the water but also to the fighting Indians, with whom they had had many encounters, and [that] they were the first Spaniards who had navigated and explored the said river and had furnished some information about it; and [that], after they had come out in the Northern Sea, this witness [i.e. he] and the said Juan de Illanes had returned to these realms of Peru, etc.

Witness.—And next in order after what is stated above, in the said city of Quito, on the twenty-seventh day of the month of September of the said year, the said Doctor Hinojosa, a judge of His Majesty's, in connection with the said judicial inquiry, by lawful procedure caused to appear before him Pedro Domínguez Miradero, a citizen of this city of Quito, to whom he administered and [from whom] he received the oath in legal form, and he [i.e. Pedro Domínguez Miradero] did it well and without omitting any detail, and the following questions were put to him:

Being asked how old this witness [i.e. he] was and how long he had been residing in these realms of Peru, and whether he knew Juan de Illanes, a citizen of this city, and how long [he had known him], and where and in [just] what parts [of the Indies he had cultivated his acquaintance], and whether he was a relative or an enemy of his, or [whether] any of the general questions affected him, he said that this witness [i.e. he] was more than fifty years old, and that since the time when he had crossed over to these realms of Peru there might have elapsed twenty-eight years, and [that] he had known the said Juan de Illanes for the past twenty-seven years, slightly more or less, and [that] the acquaintanceship had been kept up in these realms of Peru and in expeditions of exploration and conquest carried on in the Indies, and that none of the general questions affected him.

Being asked whether this witness [i.e. he] knew, had heard, or [had] been given to understand that the said Juan de Illanes had ever served His Majesty in expeditions of conquest, [in] colonization enterprises, and in connection with the quarrels which had arisen in these parts, or in other affairs, he said: that this witness [i.e. he] knew that the said Juan de Illanes was a servant of His Majesty and had [long] been one, because this witness [i.e. he], during the past twenty-seven years that he had known him, had seen him serve His Majesty in many ways in the expedition to, and exploration of, La Canela and the Marañón River under Gonzalo Pizarro, who had gone off to explore the said provinces in the service of His Majesty, and [that] one [of the members of the expedition] had been the said Juan de Illanes, who had launched out down the river with Captain Orellana, [the latter having started out] under orders from the said Gonzalo Pizarro to explore [certain] regions, and that they [i.e. Orellana and his men] had not been able to turn back and had [therefore] gone on down the river exploring country, [for a distance] which was more than two thousand leagues, because this witness [i.e. he] had been in the service there with the said Gonzalo Pizarro and was one of those who had gone with the said Captain Orellana down the said river; and [that] in all this affair great hardships had been endured owing to fighting and to hunger spells, and [that] they were the first Spaniards who had explored the said country, and [that] in this way they had finished up in the Northern Sea at Cubagua and had then returned to these realms of Peru, without lingering on the way any longer than was necessary for making the journey; and [that] two years after that, slightly more or less, the said Gonzalo Pizarro had risen up and had rebelled against the service of His Majesty in these realms of Peru, and [that], there being in this city of Quito, on behalf of the said Gonzalo Pizarro, Pedro de Puelles, who in his name was holding it under tyrannical rule, a certain number of soldiers under Captain Rodrigo de Salazar had put him to death and had reduced the city [to obedience] to the service of His Majesty, and [that] when the cry "The King!" had been raised, the said Juan de Illanes had quickly come forward to serve on the occasion that had presented itself with his arms and [his] horses; and [that] at that time news had been received how the Licentiate La Gasca was coming in the name of His Majesty to reduce these realms [to obedience] to his royal service, and [that] the said Juan de Illanes had hastened to join the said President La Gasca, in company with the said Captain Rodrigo de Salazar, and had been in the service of His Majesty in company with the said President La Gasca as far as the valley of Xaquixaguana, where the battle had been fought against the said Gonzalo Pizarro by the said Licentiate La Gasca and his followers, [and] where the said Gonzalo Pizarro, along with his followers, had been killed and defeated, and [where] he [i.e. La Gasca] had wreaked justice upon them, and [that] in the said battle the said Juan de Illanes had taken part in the service of His Majesty and had served at his own expense and on his own initiative with his arms and [his] horse, as a good soldier, for this witness [i.e. he] had been at the said battle in the service of His Majesty and had taken part in it and had seen the thing come about and transpire as he had explained it [all]; and [that], when the punishing of the said Gonzalo Pizarro and of his associates and followers had been carried out, the said Juan de Illanes had come on to this city and from it had gone off with the *corregidor* Antonio de Oznayo on the expedition of conquest to Lita and Quilca and had gone and had taken along two soldiers with him at his own expense, in order that they might likewise serve in the affair stated above, and that the name of the one was Barragán, and of the other, Gutiérrez, and [that] he and the two soldiers had served His Majesty in the above-mentioned affair, because this witness [i.e. he] had been a member of the said expedition of conquest and had seen the thing come about and take place; and [that] this witness [i.e. he] had heard many persons, in particular Alonso Martín Namirado, say that the said Juan de Illanes had taken part in the conquest and colonizing of [the district where today stands] the city of Santiago de Guayaquil under Captain Orellana, and [that] just so it was [all] common [knowledge] and [a fact] well known to many people.

Being asked if this witness [i.e. he] knew, had heard, or [had] seen that the said Juan de Illanes had ever done anything detrimental to the interests of His Majesty in connection with the past quarrels or in other affairs, he said that he did not know nor had seen nor [had] heard that he had ever gone against the interests of His Majesty, because if he had ever gone against them this witness [i.e. he] was of the opinion that he would have learned about it, because of his being an old-timer in this country and having had personal dealings with the said Juan de Illanes [and because of] their having been associated in expeditions of conquest and exploration, as he had explained.

Being asked if he knew or had heard that to the said Juan de Illanes, as compensation for his services, they had [ever] granted any Indians as an *encomienda*, any expense money, any income from revenues temporarily not assigned, or [income accruing to him] in the royal household, or [whether he knew] by what trade he had supported himself, or from what [source of] gain he had drawn profit in this country, he said that the said Juan de Illanes had [always] served His Majesty as a soldier in this country, and had been a good one, and was not a man having a trade; [that he was a man] to whom this witness [i.e. he] was not aware of and had not heard that there had ever been granted in return for his services any Indians as an *encomienda*, or any income or any expense money, save that the said Juan de Illanes had married in this city a widow who through inheritance from her first husband possessed a *repartimiento* within the territorial limits of this city, [but that] this witness [i.e. he] did not know how much income it brought in, beyond the fact that he had heard that it was not much; and [he said that] through the said wife of his, after he had married, he had been living and was [still] living on the said *repartimiento;* and that the said Juan de Illanes was a man highly honored, and as such had been a regular justice of the peace in this city, and a magistrate, and [had] held offices of rank, because this witness [i.e. he] had seen it [all]; and [that], in return for his services [and] in consideration of his qualities as a man, this witness [i.e. he] was of the opinion that he [i.e. Juan de Illanes] was worthy [of the claim that he was making] that His Majesty, being [so well] served [by him], as compensation for his services grant him the favor of an income of six thousand pesos in this realm; and that this was what he knew and believed [about this matter], and was the truth, according to the oath which he had taken, under burden of which he stood by his statement and vouched for it, and he signed it with his name, and [so did] the said doctor who was present at the giving of testimony of this said person.—*Pedro Dominguez Miradero.—Doctor Pedro de Hinojosa.*—Before me, *Gomez de Moscoso.*

Witness.—In Quito, on the twenty-eighth [day] of the said month of September of the said year, the said judge, in connection with the said judicial inquiry, by lawful procedure caused to appear before him Pedro Quintero, a merchant, a citizen of this city, to whom he administered and [from whom] he received the oath in legal form, and he [i.e. Pedro Quintero] did it well and without omitting any detail; and, on being questioned on the matter which has been stated, he made the following statements: . . . he said that what he knew was that the said Juan de Illanes had taken part in the conquest and colonizing of [the district where today stands] the city of Santiago de Guayaquil, which is in these realms of Peru, as a soldier under Captain Orellana, because this witness [i.e. he himself] had gone at the time of the said conquest to the said city of Santiage de Guayaquil and had seen come about and take place what he had stated; and [that] this witness [i.e. he] had seen that Gonzalo Pizarro had gone off in the service of His Majesty on the expedition of exploration to La Canela and the Marañón River, [a territory] about which many reports had circulated, and [that] he had taken with him a large number of soldiers, and [that] among them had gone along the said Juan de Illanes in the service of His Majesty, etc.

Witness.—On the fifth of October of the said year there appeared Pedro Moreno Morillas, and, after taking the oath, etc., he made the following statements:

Being asked whether he knew and [read: "or" (?)] had seen or [had] heard that the said Juan de Illanes had served His Majesty, and in what affairs and [in what] connections, he said: that during the past thirty-one years during which he had been acquainted with him this witness [i.e. he] had seen him serving His Majesty on whatever occasion had presented itself, because this witness [i.e. he] had seen him serve in the conquest and colonizing of the province of Puerto Viejo under Captain Gonzalo Dolmos, and in the province of Guayaquil under Captain Francisco de Orellana, because this witness [i.e. he himself] had been a member of the said expedition of conquest and colonization and had seen that he [i.e. Juan de Illanes] had served in it as a good soldier; and [that] following the said conquest the said Juan de Illanes had come on to this city of Quito, from which it was common [knowledge] and [a] well known [fact] and a matter beyond doubt that the said Juan de Illanes had gone off in the service of His Majesty, along with Gonzalo Pizarro, on the expedition of exploration to La Canela and the Marañón River, and was one of those who had gone on out [the mouth of] the said river with Captain Orellana, etc.

Witness.—And next after what is stated above, on the sixth day of the said month of October of the said year, etc., there appeared Captain Francisco Dolmos, and after taking the oath, etc., he made the following statements:

Being asked whether this witness [i.e. he] knew and [read: "or" (?)] had heard that the said Juan de Illanes had served His Majesty in these realms of Peru and in other parts, and in what affairs and [in what] connections, and where, and in [just] what parts [of the country], he said that during the last thirty years, slightly more or less, during which he had been acquainted with the said Juan de Illanes in these realms of Peru he had seen him serve His Majesty in the conquest of the province of Guayaquil as a soldier under Captain Francisco de Orellana, because this witness [i.e. he] had [himself] seen it [all take place] in just this way; and [that] afterwards this witness [i.e. he] had learned from many persons that the said Juan de Illanes had gone on the expedition of exploration to La Canela and the Marañón River in the service of His Majesty, along with Gonzalo Pizarro, and [that] he was one of those who [in taking part] in the said expedition of exploration had gone out down the river with Captain Francisco de Orellana; and [that] afterwards he had seen him come back from the said expedition worn out and shattered, and [that] he [i.e. Juan de Illanes] had related to him the progress and outcome of it, etc.

# VIII

*Judicial inquiry\* on the subject of the deserts and past services of Alonso de Cabrera, a citizen of the city of Quito.† August, 1569.*

Very powerful Sire: I, Alonso de Cabrera, a citizen of this city of Quito, do hereby come before Your Highness and declare: that I have good cause, in conformity with my rights, to have put through the court a judicial inquiry in this your [Highness'] Royal Audiencia on the subject of what I have accomplished in serving Your Highness over a period of nearly thirty years just ending, in these

---

\* [Read: "*Extracts from the judicial inquiry,*" etc.—EDITOR.]

† Archives of the Indies, "Patronato," case 1, shelf 5, bundle 27/11, section 6.

realms of Peru, in order that, in consideration of the said services, Your Highness may command that there be granted to me whatever favor Your Highness may see fit [to grant me]; I beg and beseech Your Highness to order that there be received [the detailed statement of facts forming the basis of] the judicial inquiry which I shall furnish relating to the matter, your [Highness'] attorney-general being summoned [to take the proper action] for that purpose, and I beg Your Highness to order that the witnesses whom I shall bring in be examined by means of the following questions:

1.—First, whether they know the said Alonso de Cabrera and how long [they have known him]: let them make a statement [regarding this].

2.—*Item*, whether they know that the said Alonso de Cabrera first came to this city when it had only recently been established as a colony by Spaniards and [that] in the maintaining [of it] and in the pacifying [of the native inhabitants] of it he served His Majesty on every occasion that presented itself, and whether they know that within two or three years after that he went off with Gonzalo Pizarro as a member of the expedition and [party of] exploration to La Canela, where he endured many hardships and spells of hunger, on which said expedition the said Alonso de Cabrera went at his own expense and on his own initiative with his arms and [his] horse, and [that] continuing the said journey he went with Captain Francisco de Orellana down the Marañón, and [that] during the said expedition of discovery there were undergone great dangers and hardships owing to the fact that the country was [largely] uninhabited, out of which [country] they [eventually] made their way to port and ended up all worn out at Cubagua, a territory under a governor's jurisdiction distinct from [that of] these realms of Peru, in all of which [affair] he served His Majesty as a good and loyal vassal: let them make a statement [regarding this].

3.—*Item*, whether they know that after what is related in the questions preceding this one was over, the said Alonso de Cabrera came back to these realms of Peru by way of Panama, and [that] right after he had arrived in this city, within the next six days, there being [at that time] in it Pedro de Puelles, Gonzalo Pizarro's captain, in a certain raid that was carried out under the pretext that an attempt was going to be made to kill the said Pedro de Puelles,* [the organizers of this raid treating him, i.e. Alonso de Cabrera] as a man whom they looked upon as suspicious and [one] who had never been [associated] with them nor followed the cause of the said Gonzalo Pizarro, certain captains of the latter who happened to be in this said city took away from the said Alonso de Cabrera the horse which he possessed and [his] arms and arrested him and held him a prisoner under a guard of arquebusiers, and along with him many other soldiers, all on account of their being loyal men and servants of His Majesty, with the intention of executing them all, whereby the said Alonso de Cabrera and the others incurred great danger of losing their lives: let them make a statement [regarding this].

4.—*Item*, whether they know that, at the time when this city was being tyrannized by Gonzalo Pizarro and by his captain and lieutenant Pedro de Puelles, Captain Rodrigo de Salazar started a movement for bringing it back [into obedience] to the service of His Majesty and for putting the said Pedro de Puelles to death, and how he did so, and [how], for the reason that he considered the said Alonso de Cabrera to be a [loyal] servant of His Majesty, he acquainted him with

---

* [As it does not seem probable that Cabrera meant to say that it was Pedro de Puelles who was looked upon as a suspicious individual in this connection, it is assumed, for the purpose of the present translation, that a comma should have been inserted here in the original.—EDITOR.]

the scheme, and [also informed] other friends of his, with whom he had talked the matter over, and [how] in this way the said Alonso de Cabrera maintained secrecy in the matter which had been imparted to him by him [i.e. by Rodrigo de Salazar] until a banner was hoisted in the name of His Majesty; and [that] the said Alonso de Cabrera, right at the same time, sallied forth on the public square of this city among the first with his arms and [his] horse, [serving with the loyalists] until it [i.e. the city] was reduced [to obedience] to the service of His Majesty and they had wreaked justice on the said Pedro [de] Puelles: let them make a statement [regarding this].

5.—*Item*, whether they know that, after the said Pedro de Puelles, the said Gonzalo Pizarro's captain, had been put to death, the said Alonso de Cabrera left this city following in the tracks of President La Gasca and caught up with him at the Abancay bridge, from which point he went on in company with him, serving him on every occasion that presented itself in matters connected with warfare, as far as the valley of Xaquixaguana, where the battle was fought against the said Gonzalo Pizarro, and [that] the said Alonso de Cabrera was there in the service of His Majesty under his royal standard right up to the time when the said Gonzalo Pizarro was routed and justice was wreaked upon him and upon his followers: let them tell what they know [about this].

6.—*Item*, whether they know that, after the said punishment had been meted out to the said Gonzalo Pizarro and the others [who had been] his followers in Xaquixaguana, the said President La Gasca went off to the city of Cuzco and stayed there, engaged in punishing a large number of those who had taken part in the rebellion of the said Gonzalo Pizarro and in creating [order] and putting these realms in order so that they might be peaceful and [remain] in humble obedience to His Majesty, for a period of five months, slightly more or less, and [that] the said Alonso de Cabrera during all the said period of time remained in the said city of Cuzco in association with him; let them make a statement [regarding this].

7.—*Item*, whether they know that, following what is stated above and [following] the inflicting of defeat and the wreaking of justice upon the said Gonzalo Pizarro and his followers, the said Alonso de Cabrera again came back to this city of Quito, and [that] while he was staying in it he heard from the head justice of the peace about Francisco Hernández Jirón [i. e. Girón], and [that], as a consequence of the esteem in which the said Alonso de Cabrera was held, Antonio de Hoznayo [i. e. Osnayo], the *corregidor* in this said city at that time, commissioned him to [go and] stay in the pass of Tomebamba, [in the] province of Los Cañares, where nowadays the city of Quito* is founded, as guardian and commander of that pass, because of its being an important one, in order that he might form an idea as to what was to the best interests of the service of His Majesty [out there], in which said station he remained performing his duty with all diligence and care until news was received that the said Francisco Hernández [Girón] was defeated: let them make a statement [regarding this].

8.—*Item*, whether they know that, in view of the fact that Alonso de Cabrera was a person who has stood the test for truthfulness and nobility of character and trustworthiness, and [was] such a [loyal] servant of His Majesty, there have been bestowed upon him offices and positions of honor, such as [that of] revenue collector and [that of] inspector of the royal exchequer of His Majesty in this

* [Read "Cuenca."—TRANSLATOR.]

city of Quito, and in that of Cuenca [the office of] treasurer of the royal exchequer and [that of] lieutenant to the *corregidor* and [that of] regular justice of the peace, of which said offices he has given a very good account and reckoning [in accordance with his reputation] as a person of this sort: let them tell what they know [about this].

9.—*Item*, whether they know that the said Alonso de Cabrera in all that which is stated above has served His Majesty with all faithfulness and care, without doing anything detrimental to that service on any occasion at any time, [serving] at his own expense and on his own initiative, undergoing great hardships and sufferings from want and dangers, and [that] he has never been remunerated or compensated and has never been given anything out of the royal exchequer, and, on the other hand, [has never received] any mode of sustenance, or a *repartimiento* of Indians, [and]* [that] in consideration of the said services and of his [high] social rank he is worthy and deserving of any favor that His Majesty may see fit to grant him, and [that] as reward and compensation for the said services of his any favors that His Majesty may grant him will be fittingly given out [in being conferred] upon him: let them make a statement [regarding this].

10.—*Item*, whether they know that the said Alonso de Cabrera is an acknowledged hidalgo and is considered and looked upon as such and has a reputation to that effect among all the persons who have known him and do know him, and [that], as [is to be expected in the case of] such [a person], the governors and judges and the other [high] officials of the courts of these realms and provinces of Peru have had a high regard for him as a person of such a rank, and [that] in contrast with the said [high] social rank of his he is poor and does not possess wherewith to support himself: let them tell what they know [about this].

11.—*Item*, whether they know that all that which is stated above is common [knowledge] and [a] well known [fact] and [a matter of] every-day conversation and [general] report: let them tell what they know [about this].

And when the said taking of testimony shall have been completed, I beg and beseech Your Highness to order that the whole thing be given to me in commonly accepted form for the safeguarding of my rights, attaching to it [the symbols, etc., of] your authority and power of decree, on the strength of which I am appealing for justice, and to whatever extent it may be necessary I solicit your [Highness'] royal intervention.—*Alonso de Cabrera.*

On the twenty-seventh day of the month of August of the year One Thousand Five Hundred and Sixty-nine there appeared Pedro Domínguez Miradero, a citizen of San Francisco del Quito.—[In reply] to the second question he said that he knew about [the matter referred to in] it as it is stated therein, because this witness [i.e. he] had seen how the said Alonso de Cabrera had arrived at this city [when it had been only] recently founded by the Spaniards, and that he had aided in maintaining [it], and [that] in the pacification [of the native inhabitants] of it he had served His Majesty on every occasion that had presented itself, as a good and loyal vassal, and [that] within three years from that time, slightly more or less, he had seen how the said Alonso de Cabrera had gone with Gonzalo Pizarro as a member of the expedition and [party of] exploration to La Canela, where he had suffered, just as this witness [i.e. he himself] and all those who had gone with Gonzalo Pizarro on the said expedition had done, great hardships and hunger spells, on which said expedition the said Alonso de Cabrera

* [Added by Medina.—EDITOR.]

had gone at his own expense and on his own initiative with his arms and [his] horse; and [that] continuing on the said journey he [i.e. Alonso de Cabrera] had gone under Captain Francisco de Orellana down the Marañón River; and that during the said expedition of discovery there had been encountered great dangers and hardships from fighting and spells of hunger, owing to the fact that the country was [largely] uninhabited, out of which [country] they had made their way to port and had ended up all worn out, finally coming by way of the sea to Cubagua, a territory under a governor's jurisdiction of its own, because it was close to Santo Domingo: in all of which [enterprises] the said Alonso [de] Cabrera, as he had already stated, had served His Majesty as a good and loyal vassal; and this [was what] he said in reply to this question.

Captain Alonso de Bastidas, a citizen of the city of San Francisco del Quito.— [In reply] to the second question he said that what he knew and had seen [in regard to the subject-matter] of this question was that for the past twenty-eight years, possibly, slightly more or less, this witness [i.e. he] had known him [i.e. Alonso de Cabrera], [and that it was as long ago as that that] he had come to this said city, where he had found the said Alonso de Cabrera and had learned and had been given to understand that for a long time already he [i.e. the latter] had been in this city; and that, in view of the fact that this witness [i.e. he] had [always] looked upon him as being the honorable man that he, the said Alonso de Cabrera, was, and [as a loyal] servant of His Majesty, he felt convinced that on every occasion that had presented itself in connection with the service of His Majesty and the maintenance of this city he had certainly served him well and loyally; and that within a few days after this witness [i.e. he] had arrived in this city he had seen how Gonzalo Pizarro had come to it with a large force to set out [from there] to explore the provinces of Quijos, Zumaco, and La Canela, and "at the time when the said Gonzalo Pizarro left this city to go and explore the said provinces," [he went on to say,] "I saw how the said Alonso de Cabrera went forth from this city to go and serve His Majesty, along with the said Gonzalo Pizarro and the other men whom he [i.e. the latter] took along with him, well fitted out with his arms and [his] horse and well equipped with the other things [that were] needed, like any honorable person and [one] of distinction, [serving] at his own expense and on his own initiative," because this witness [i.e. he] had not heard or been given to understand that any aid or expense money had ever been paid to him; and that a year and a half after the said Gonzalo Pizarro had set out from this city, slightly more or less, the said Gonzalo Pizarro had returned to this said city with a part of the men who had gone off with him [now] quite worn out, and the said Alonso de Cabrera had not come back with him, and [that], when this witness [i.e. he] had inquired from many of those who had come with the said Gonzalo Pizarro about the said Alonso de Cabrera, they had told him how he had gone on down the Marañón River in a brigantine with Francisco de Orellana and with other persons; and [that] a certain period of time later there had come to this city the said Alonso de Cabrera by way of Panama, and [that] from him himself as well as from Juan de Illanes, a citizen of this city, as also from Pedro Domínguez Miradero, as likewise from Father Friar Gaspar, of the Order of Saint Dominic, who had all gone down the Marañón River, [he had obtained information, and] they had told this witness [i.e. him] (and he had heard and had been given to understand [the same thing] by them all) how they had gone on down the said Marañón River, and that they had finally come to port at Cubagua, and that during the said voyage down the said Marañón River they had endured numerous and excessive hardships due to hunger and to skirmishes which the natives had forced upon them; and [that] this witness [i.e. he] had seen the said Father Friar Gaspar de Caravajal [*sic*] with one eye knocked out, [adding] that people said that it was in the course of a skirmish that they [i.e. the Indians] had knocked it out with a blow with a stick which they had dealt him, wherefore this witness [i.e. he] gave credence to [what they stated regarding] the hardships and skirmishes that they had had: and this [was what] he gave as his reply [to this question].

Juan de Illanes, a citizen of said place of residence.—[In reply] to the second question he said that what he knew [in regard to the subject-matter] of this question was that this witness [i.e. he] had seen how within a short time after this city had been founded by Spaniards there had come to it the said Alonso de Cabrera, where on whatever occasion had presented itself he had served His Majesty; and that two or three years afterwards, slightly more or less, this witness [i.e. he] had seen how the said Alonso de Cabrera had gone with his arms and [his] horse, at his own expense and on his own initiative, with Gonzalo Pizarro on the expedition which he [i.e. the latter] led to La Canela, in the course of which there had been endured many hardships and hunger spells; and [that] later this witness [i.e. he] had seen how the said Alonso de Cabrera had been one of those who went with Captain Francisco de Orellana down the Marañón River, where he had likewise undergone great hardships and risks for his life, owing to the fact that the country was [largely] uninhabited, and [how] they had come to port and ended up quite worn out at Cubagua, a territory under a governor's jurisdiction distinct from [that of] these realms of Peru, throughout all of which the said Alonso de Cabrera had suffered many hardships and had served His Majesty as a good and loyal vassal of his: and this [was what] he said [in reply to this question].

Captain Rodrigo de Salazar.—[In reply] to the second question he said that this witness [i.e. he] remembered having heard that which this question states recounted by persons whose names he did not remember, and that in connection with this question he did not know anything else; and this [was what] he gave as his reply to it.

Bonifaz de Herrera, a citizen of the city of Quito, etc.—[In reply] to the second question this witness said that what he knew in regard to [the subject-matter of] this question was that this witness [i.e. he] knew and had seen that the said Alonso de Cabrera had come to the said city of Quito [many years back], the said city of Quito [having at that time been] only recently founded, because this witness [i.e. he] and the said Alonso de Cabrera had come [there] together; and that this witness [i.e. he] knew and had seen that the said Alonso de Cabrera had gone on the expedition to La Canela and the Marañón with Gonzalo Pizarro, who at that time was governor on the said expedition,[*] following which [departure] he had remained away on the said expedition for a period of two years, slightly more or less, [including the time spent] on this expedition and on the voyage of exploration, [in country] where there had been encountered vast unsettled regions and where there had been endured great hunger spells and hardships and losses and [where] there had died a considerable number of Spaniards who had gone off with

* [These last four words appear to be an unintentional repetition.—EDITOR.]

the said Gonzalo Pizarro, owing to the fact that the country was very rugged and uninhabitable to a very large extent; and [that] consequently those who had survived and had returned with the said Gonzalo Pizarro to the said city of Quito had come in naked and quite worn out and ill; and [that] the said Alonso de Cabrera had gone off in a brigantine with Captain Francisco de Orellana, who had set out with fifty men to look for food to succor the expeditionary force, following [the return of] which this witness [i.e. he] had in the course of time learned from the others who had gone with the said Captain Orellana that they had all been unable to come back with the said relief on account of the many uninhabited regions and the fighting Indians that they had come upon, and [that] this witness [i.e. he] had likewise learned from those who had gone with the said Alonso de Cabrera and with the said Captain Orellana that they had reached their destination quite worn out and naked and ill, whereby this witness [i.e. he] had been given to understand that they had endured great hardships, and [that] this witness [i.e. he] knew about it [all] because this witness [i.e. he] and the said Alonso de Cabrera had been billet companions on the said expedition up to the time when the said Alonso de Cabrera had departed with the said Captain Orellana, as he had already stated, in the said brigantine; and that this witness [i.e. he] had seen the said Alonso de Cabrera during the said expedition [serving] honorably with his arms and [his] horse, and that this witness [i.e. he] had never heard, nor had seen, nor had been given to understand that the said Governor or any other person had ever given him any aid or expense money for the said expedition, but that [on the contrary] the said Alonso de Cabrera, as an honorable person and a servant of His Majesty, had gone on the said expedition at his own expense and on his own initiative; and that this [was what] he knew and gave as his reply to this question.

Zebrián de Moreta, a citizen and a resident of the city of Quito.—[In reply] to the second question this witness said that what he knew [in regard to the subject-matter] of this question was that this witness [i.e. he] had seen that the said Alonso de Cabrera had gone on the expedition and voyage of exploration to La Canela and the Marañón River with Gonzalo Pizarro, and [that] he [himself] had been associated with him on the said expedition [i.e. until Orellana separated from Gonzalo Pizarro], in which [whole] affair he had served His Majesty with his arms and [his] horse, and [that he knew that] during the said [voyage of] exploration there had been endured great hardships; and [that] this witness [i.e. he] knew [all] this because this witness [i.e. he] was one of the soldiers who had taken part in the said expedition and had seen that it had taken place as he had stated; and [that] this was what he knew regarding [the subject-matter of] this question and gave as his reply to it.

# IX

*Expedition down the Marañón River and all that happened during it, together with other remarkable things deserving to be known which have come to pass in the Western Indies of Peru. Dedicated to the most blessed Prince, Don Philip III, our master.** [By Toribio de Ortiguera, probably 1581.]*

\* National Library of Madrid, Department of Manuscripts, J–143. The extracts here published are printed from a copy which has been very kindly placed at my disposal by my learned friend Don Marcos Jiménez de la Espada. [Medina has dealt with Ortiguera's history, of which he here

## [INTRODUCTION]

Enlightened and most happy Prince, our master and [our] refuge, strong wall and protection for our Catholic faith: A very righteous thing it is that Your Highness learn about and understand the affairs of his kingdom, and among them the things which happened on the expedition down the Marañón River, and others that have come to pass in the Western Indies [which are] subject to Your Highness, not only [in order that Your Highness may see what remains to be done] for the [complete] conquest and exploration of them, but also in order that such persons as may come to know about them [i.e. the things which have come to pass there] may be made to understand and see the punishment that was meted out to the guilty ones, and in order that those now living and those to come after them may learn a lesson inculcated at the cost of the lives of others, the good and loyal vassals bending their efforts towards taking courage for performing deeds worthy of note and [for] serving Your Highness with the loyalty and fidelity that are due to him, and those who are not such [being impressed in such a way that], if there come to them some evil thought, they will repress it, contemplating the end and final destination which Lope de Aguirre and his adherents came to, and [also] Francisco de Santisteban with the two Rodrigo Méndez's and their followers, along with the others with whom this history is to deal, for inasmuch as I was present in the city of Nombre de Dios in the realm of Tierra Firme [which is a part] of the Indies of the Western Seas in the service of the ever invincible King Don Philip, my master, and most beloved father of Your Highness, [engaged] in the guarding and keeping of that city and realm, [serving] to the best of my limited ability, [during] the year [of struggle] against the stubborn rebellion of Lope de Aguirre and his followers that it [i.e. the city] went through in 1561, and then in the following year in the city of Panama, belonging to the New Kingdom proper, against the rebellion of the two Rodrigo Méndez's and Francisco de Santisteban, until they were defeated and put to death in [furtherance of] his [i.e. Your Highness' father's] service, and their mad acts of insolence [were] paid for in punishment, and yet with no more rigor than their grave crimes deserved, I constantly sought for an opportunity to establish my residence in Peru, to which country I later did go with the same purpose [in mind, i.e. of serving the King] and [following up] the good beginning which I had made, coming forward promptly in full earnestness and with all my strength on all occasions which arose in connection with the service of His Majesty, with my arms and [my] horse, at my own expense, not only in the positions of state which I held, but also outside of them, without ever having perpetrated an act of disloyalty in anything during all the time that I was there, which was up to the end of the year eighty-five [1585], in the accomplishment of all of which I spent twenty-four years out of the period of fullest bloom and exuberance in my life; and it appearing to me to be a very righteous thing to take [upon myself]

quotes the introduction and Chapter 15 dealing with Orellana's expedition, in Chapter 3 of his Introduction, p. 29, *supra*. The entire account, as has been pointed out in the editorial addition to Medina's footnote 44 on p. 29, has been published, since Medina wrote his book, by M. Serrano y Sanz in his *Historiadores de Indias* (2 vols., Madrid, 1909: they form Vols. 13 and 15 of the *Nueva biblioteca de autores españoles*), Vol. 2, p. 305–422: see pp. 305–306 and 327–331. The passage dealing with Gonzalo Pizarro's expedition proper (beginning with "Gonzalo Pizarro, proceeding with his expedition . . ." *infra*, p. 314, and ending with ". . . in quarters with his expeditionary force," *infra*, p. 315) had been published by Jiménez de la Espada in *Ilustración Española y Americana* for August 22, 1894, p. 110.—EDITOR.]

a little more labor and set about serving Your Highness, I decided to record in writing some of the most noteworthy things that happened in my time in those lands, in order that Your Highness might know about them and be informed of the great amount and long stretch of land that he possesses today [already] conquered and colonized from the river La Hacha in Tierra Firme, down to the end of the rich and very warlike province of Chile, over an expanse of more than one thousand two hundred leagues lengthwise, [running from] north [to] south, wherein are included great multitudes of Indian natives of those [various] lands, within which [lands] there are many towns and cities founded by Spaniards, their conquerors and mighty tamers; and [I shall tell about] the incalculable riches in gold and silver and fine emerald mines, together with great fisheries supplying the finest pearls, evidence of which [riches] is furnished by the very large fleets which every year come in from this New World [laden] with them and with many other trade products which are raised over there; and likewise [I shall speak of] the great spread [of territory belonging to the natives but still to be explored] and great numbers of Indians that there are at the present time still to be conquered and subdued, together with a description of their land [so far as it has been explored] and what it has been possible to get at and find out in regard to it over an expanse of one thousand two hundred leagues measured lengthwise, on the banks of the great Marañón River, which arises in the province of Peru and finally empties into the Northern Sea in the region of the Island of Margarita, in which [great expanse of country], taken with the great width of this most powerful river from one bank to the other, there could be colonized a long and very wide realm having large gold and silver mines and many other sources of profit which time and opportunity will gradually reveal, in the opinion of all those who have observed the situation (and it would even be quite advisable that occupation be provided in this way for a great number of people that there are idle in Peru); I beseech Your Highness, with all the humility and respect that I can [muster], to receive this little gift that I am offering to him, which I am presenting with the sincerest expression of good will that is possible for me; and if I had anything else greater and of more value and more appreciable to give, I would do so with the same good will: may it please God Almighty [to grant] that Your Highness may see it [i.e. the said region of the Marañón River] peaceful and in mild subjection under [the laws which govern] his royal patrimony, along with the further addition [to it] of many other realms and dominions, in order that His holy name may be glorified with the conversion of all the souls that there are there on the way to perdition in the midst of their idolatries and vain sacrifices, for lack of some one to preach to them and teach them the things of our holy Catholic faith; for with [the thought of] this alone, and [that] of my having furnished Your Highness with information leading to its being done, I shall remain quite well repaid for my labors.   In Seville, [probably 1585].*—*Toribio de Ortiguera.*

.   .   .   .   .   .   .   .   .   .   .   .   .   .   .   .   .   .   .   .   .   .   .   .

## Chapter XV

How Gonzalo Pizarro set out from the city of Quito for the conquest of the provinces of Quijos, Zumaco, and La Canela, and what happened to him on this expedition, and how his captain, Francisco de Orellana, went with 54 companions down the Marañón River all the way to the Northern Sea, and what befell them on the journey.

* [See editorial addition to footnote 44 of the Introduction, p. 29, *supra.*—Editor.]

It was in the month of February of the year of the birth of Our Redeemer and Savior Jesus Christ 1540* that Gonzalo Pizarro set out from the city of San Francisco del Quito for the conquest and colonization of the provinces of Quijos, Zumaco, and La Canela; and as at that time he was so powerful and influential in Peru by dint of the fact that his brother was the Marquis Don Francisco Pizarro, colonizer and discoverer of this land, there followed him in that undertaking a large number of the noblest and most prominent people of the realm, up to a total of 280 men, [a figure worth noticing] for, when one considers the small number of Spanish persons that there were in the land then, it was a great achievement to have been able to get them together, and with them 260 horses, [and it must be borne in mind] that [the price of] the one which cost the least in those days exceeded 500 gold pesos of 22 and one half carats, and others double that much, because, as it was in the first period of the discovery of this realm, those which there were [in the country] were few. Along with [all] this he took a goodly number of arquebuses and crossbows with a large supply of munitions and implements of war, together with many slaves and Indians to perform their menial tasks, they all [thus forming] a very magnificant body of men and one well prepared for any adventure that might lie in their path. This territory is on the same general east and west line as Quito, toward the sunrise, across the great mountain range that follows on down from Santa Marta right at its start from the Northern Sea, as one comes from Spain to Tierra Firme; and it runs on as a continued prolongation from there down to the extreme end of Chile and to the Straits of Magellan over a distance of more than 1300 leagues [from] north [to] south. In this territory there have been founded up to the present† the cities of Baeza, Ávila, and Archidona within an area 30 leagues in circumference, which as places lying within a governor's jurisdiction belong to Melchor Vázquez de Ávila, [the latter two of] which [cities] were founded much later [than] Baeza, [for this last named had been founded] in the year 1558 by Governor Rodrigo Núñez de Bonilla, a former citizen of Quito, and after the latter's death, there had succeeded [in the office of governor] in it [i.e. Baeza] Melchor de [sic] Vázquez de Ávila, who, while he was governor of the province of Quito in the year 1592 (sic),‡ had sent out as his lieutenant and captain-general Andrés Contero, who went out to conquer and settle it [i.e. this section of the country] with 300 men well equipped at his own expense and on his own initiative, in which [enterprise] he spent more than 30 thousand pesos and founded the cities of Ávila and Archidona, which were given up as colonies at the end of 17 or 18 years after their founding as a result of the fact that the Indians subject to them had revolted and had massacred all the Spaniards [i.e. the Spanish men who had settled there] and [all] the women that there were in them without leaving a single person alive, except just one little girl about 6 years old, razing and burning the cities, as we shall learn, when the [proper] time and circumstance shall furnish us with a reason for bringing it in, from the history of their founding, of the revolt [which destroyed them], and of their re-building, together with [some account] of their re-builders and of the punishment which was inflicted upon the

* [This should read 1541. See the sequence of dates as developed in Medina's Introduction, Chapters 5 and 6, pp. 36–57 *supra*. On the date of Pizarro's departure from Quito, see pp. 46–47.—EDITOR.]

† [Medina, followed by Serrano y Sanz, has here inserted in the text a bracketed note to the effect that the time referred to here can not be earlier than the year 1585. See footnote 44, p. 29, *supra*, of the Introduction.—EDITOR.]

‡ [Read "1562."—TRANSLATOR.] [Serrano y Sanz prints "1562."—EDITOR.]

insurgents. Gonzalo Pizarro, proceeding with his expedition, after he had gone ahead for several days, came to the village of Zumaco, where there has since been founded in the service of His Majesty the city of Ávila. From this village he went on to the valley of the Coca, through which runs a beautiful and abundantly flowing river; determining to look for a place where he could cross it with the greatest amount of safety and least amount of damage to his expeditionary force, he followed the stream along its banks for three leagues, [to a place] where he found on his right a considerable stretch of narrows and a fall which the river forms between two cliffs [leaving a space between them] of thirteen feet in width, at which spot he ordered to be built a good wooden bridge over which he might take his expeditionary force and supply trains with entire safety; and when it had been crossed over, they continued on their journey downstream for a distance of some ten leagues. After them [i.e. the ten leagues] they came upon a fine savana, which is as much as [to say] a cleared stretch of fields, where there was a village called Guema, having few inhabitants and a certain supply of foodstuffs, thanks to which the army became refreshed, and this [savana] was something like three leagues long. At the lower end of this stretch of fields they came upon another savana, a smaller one, of upwards of a league and a half [in length], which was very fertile and abounded in different sorts of fruit and foodstuffs produced by the soil. Here the expeditionary force gave itself over to resting and to refreshing itself, and from there Gonzalo Pizarro sent Don Antonio de Ribera, his campmaster, with the number of men that the latter thought he needed, to explore the country along the banks of this river farther down; and he, having gone on something like 10 leagues, found right on its shores a fair-sized settlement, and, without getting into any encounter or trouble with the Indians inhabiting it, he went back and informed Gonzalo Pizarro of what the situation was, in consequence of which he [i.e. Gonzalo Pizarro] broke camp and left these savanas, heading for the new settlement, where they arrived without any damage to them or any incident that is worth relating. And when they had come to it they set about finding a method of approach to the Indians in such a way that they should not come to a break, and thanks to trinkets and to trade-offerings of salt, which among them is prized highly, and to iron axes and iron machetes, they [i.e. the Indians] began to bring them food in the form of many kinds of fish and maize and yucca [i.e. manioc] and sweet potatoes and other food products that were to be had in the land. After they had been staying there a few days, as the river was wide, gentle, and deep-flowing, [and one] up and down which the Indians navigated in canoes, Gonzalo Pizarro felt that it would be well to build a brigantine in order that there might better and more easily be explored the secrets of this river. The matter was made the subject of a discussion, and they all agreed that it was a sane and fitting idea. The task was started, the Indians helping to cut the timber and bring it in, together with the materials and [various odd] things needed for its construction; and thereby they aided our Spaniards in a friendly way, both in the work on the boat and in supplying them with foodstuffs in return for their trade-offerings: and the Spaniards being now assured of the kind friendly attitude which the Indians were manifesting toward them, they went out to fish in the river, where they caught a great deal of fish, because it [i.e. the river] was very well stocked with it, and they killed with their arquebuses many turkeys and ducks. With the one and the other [of these two forms of food] and with the maize and yucca they nourished themselves plentifully. With this excellent convenience in facilities [to help them], God saw fit to permit them to build a brigantine water-tight and strong, although not very large, and they launched it on the river in a short time. This village, to which they gave the name of *El Barco* [i. e. The Boat], is situated on the shores of this river, on the left, on a high bank, safe from the freshets that are usual with the winter rains, and is estimated to be about 70 leagues from the city of Quito, as far as which place [i.e. the village in question], and even farther up, the Indians were seen to navigate this river in canoes; and for this reason those who saw it maintain that one could sail all the way from Spain as far as this village and even farther, across the sea and up this river, were this country explored. With the construction of this boat completed, Gonzalo Pizarro decided that there should be placed in it and in some of the canoes as many as 25 Spaniards from among the sick soldiers that they had on their hands, as well as the impedimenta of the army, in order to lighten [the burden of] the men and the menials composing it [i.e. the expeditionary force], with an arrangement to the effect that the rest of it should follow on by land and [that] the boat should sail on down the river in company with the canoes that were going along with it, and [that] those on land and [those on the] river should always all go and spend the night together, avoiding letting the ones get drawn away and separated from the others, in order that from the brigantine the expeditionary force might supply itself with the things needed. This arrangement and this method were kept up for a distance of 50 leagues, in the course of which they found along the shores of it [i.e. of the river] several settlements from which they kept supplying themselves with the food that they needed, and when once these had been passed they came upon an uninhabited region, and when their supply of food again ran short [they recalled that], according to the account and information which they had been given, at a distance of four days journeying farther ahead there was a settlement where there was a plentiful supply of food, of which they were already in need; for which reason Gonzalo Pizarro ordered Francisco de Orellana, one of his captains, to pick out whatever number of men he thought would be right and to embark with them in the brigantine and in three of the canoes that they had, throwing out the clothing equipment and things belonging to the expeditionary force, in order that they might go more lightly laden, and [directed them] to go and look for this land and bring to him in all haste an account of what the situation was, together with the largest quantity of food that there was to be had. He [i.e. Orellana] at once selected 54 soldiers, and among them Father Carabajal [*sic*], of the Order of Saint Dominic, with which men he embarked [and started off] in pursuit of his errand. From there Gonzalo Pizarro turned back up the river to the nearest settlement that he had left behind him, [first] giving orders to Orellana to the effect that there he would find him in quarters with his expeditionary force. The people dwelling along this river have faces with very regular features and have good physiques, and are [well] dressed, wearing cloaks and tunics hand-painted in various designs and colors, and the women have clothes with the same painted designs. Among the men there were some who wore gold medal-like pieces on their breasts, and the women [wore] ear-hoops of the same [metal] hanging from their ears, and other pieces [of ornamentation] hanging from their noses and throats. The weapons which they have are "macanas," which are sticks cut from black palm-trees, long like broadswords, having both [sharpened] edges and a point, which [weapons] they handle prettily and nimbly, and [they also have] spears to be thrown. Let us leave Gonzalo Pizarro with his men in this camp, and let us go back to Francisco de Orellana, who was proceeding onward in his navigating with his [men], which party continued on for nine entire days without discovering any inhabited spot, at the end of which they came upon a village of as many as 200 inhabitants [belonging to the tribe] called the *Arimaraeses*, where they found a good supply of food in the form of maize, yucca, and sweet potatoes, and fish and many kinds of fruit. They leaped out on land, formed in good order for whatever eventuality might befall them, and without meeting with any check or obstacle whatsoever they were given a kind reception by the Indians, notwithstanding the fact that the two groups did feel distrustful of each other as [they naturally would] of strange people. In this village they stayed three months waiting for Gonzalo Pizarro, throughout which [time] the Indians extended kind treatment to them, giving them of the goods which they possessed. They [i.e. the Spaniards] were informed of the existence of other settlements not far away from this one, inland, [inhabited by people] with whom the inhabitants of this village carried on their trading enterprises and barterings. When the 3 months had gone by, and as Gonzalo Pizarro did not come, Captain Francisco de Orellana and his soldiers entered into consultation on the subject of whether it would be a good thing to go back to the expeditionary force where they had left Gonzalo Pizarro, or [on the contrary] continue on their journey until they should get to see the end of this river, and go out to sea. And as they talked the matter over, all or the greater part of them objected very strongly to [any suggestion of their] being able to go back up the river; others remarked that, considering the large number of persons who had remained behind with Gonzalo Pizarro and the small amount of food that they still had on hand, there could be no possibility of their [still] being where they had left them, because they could not find nourishment for themselves there, or [read: "and" (?)] they were probably all dead from lack of food supplies. But all [these remarks] were [merely] arguments which they were putting forth in [support of] their case, for they could with ease have gone back up the river with the brigantine, according to information which I obtained from some of those who took part in the affair, who were persons of reputation and good faith, such as were the Governor Andrés Contero, and Juan de Vargas, treasurer of the royal exchequer of Guayaquil, and Andrés Durán Bravo, head justice of the peace in this city, and Captain Juan de Llanes (Illanes), a citizen who holds an *encomienda* within the jurisdiction of the city of Quito, and Pero* Domínguez Miradero. And at the conclusion of all these agreements among themselves, they decided to go off down the river to look for the sea, for that was what best fitted in with the desires of the greater part of them. In accordance with this decision they left this village, and at the end of six days of navigation they came to a stop on the island of the *Cararies*, which is the one as far as which history has told us that García de Arce penetrated, and following after him the whole expedition of Governor Pedro de Orsúa, at which place the Indians came forth to meet them [i.e. Orellana and his men] with an offering of peace, in spite of their never having seen any Spaniards owing to the fact that Captain Francisco de Orellana and his men were the first from among all those who have gone down this river. Our Spaniards set about humoring and regaling these Indians as persons of whom they had need, and in view of the kind attitude of friendship and the facilities which they found among them, and [in view of the fact] that the river was very wide and the brigantine which they had with them [was] small, and [realizing] that they could not navigate with safety in the canoes, they decided to build another brigantine there, which

* ["Pero" is a familiar form of "Pedro," the given name of Domínguez Miradero used elsewhere in the Documents and in the Introduction.—EDITOR.]

idea they immediately started to carry out; and thanks to the fine [energy in the, gathering and preparation of materials with which the Indians favored them] within 50 days they had it ready, sails and all, and at the end of them [i.e. the 50 days] they left this province, and continuing on their voyage they came upon many Indian villages, both on the shores of the river and on the islands, for there are many [of these] in the middle of it; they likewise found many cultivated fields and fruit orchards, from which they kept getting the things that were needed by them for their voyage and [their experiment in] navigation, without ever daring to mingle with or get into a quarrel with the Indians, owing to the fact that the Spaniards who were there were few in comparison with the large number of Indians that there were.  Farther on down they came upon some villages [which had been] burned: the reason for this was that the Indians of this province were at war with the Indians of the province of Machifaro* (which lies farther on towards the sea), who [were the ones who] had burned and sacked them.  They found among [the articles of food used by] these Indians, along with other kinds of fruit, a sort of black and white grape (a very tasty thing), plenty of honey from bees, [and] many kinds of baked and dried fish, [and] all the Indians [were] greatly decked out, clad in cloaks and tunics hand-painted in various colors; there was found in their homes a [kind of] crockery which they employ, very thin and smooth, glazed and with colors shading off from one into another, in the style of that which is made in China.  It is a country producing much cotton, [this being the material] with which they caulked the brigantine; and in place of tar the Indians furnished them with a form of gum called "mene," which, mixed with fish grease, was sufficient [as a substitute to enable them to calk the brigantine in such a way] that it should be secure and water-tight.  There was a great abundance of maize, wild yucca, and sweet potatoes and yams, kidney-beans and peanuts; many peppers and gourds, and a great quantity of fruit, in [all of] which it [i.e. the country] is very rich; many turkeys and ducks and *pansies*,† which they ate and [which] they caught in great numbers.  The Indians of this province considered it to be something impossible for so small a number of Spaniards as formed the company of Francisco de Orellana to manage to hold out against the great number of natives belonging to Machifaro and against the other tribes inhabiting territories bordering on theirs.  At last, continuing on their journey, they came upon an uninhabited area, and at the end of seven days of navigating through it they came suddenly upon a very large and beautiful settlement—for in this way [i.e., using the term "beautiful"] they speak of it [when it is a village noteworthy] for its size—called Machifaro, from which a few Indians in canoes came out on the river to meet them, and they gave them to understand that their chief and overlord desired to see them and find out of what nationality they were and whither they were bound and what they were looking for; [and they indicated to them] that they should leap out on land. The Spaniards moved on in their brigantines in the direction of the shore, although with considerable caution, formed in good order, their arquebuses loaded, their matches lighted, their crossbows with cords drawn back and with their arrows in them.  At the time, then, that they pulled in there, as soon as they had gotten up to the village, as the chief saw them [to be] of different dress and aspect from all the other people that he had [ever] seen, and all bearded (for the Indians are

---

* [Carvajal (p. 190, *supra*), says "Machiparo."—EDITOR.]

† [This (if it is not the name of a fowl) is possibly the same word as *pangi*, which, according to the Index of the *Encyclopaedia Britannica* (14th ed.), is another name of the puma.—EDITOR.]

not), to a certain degree he revered them, and, [the Spaniards] employing courtesy with them, he ordered them [i.e. his subjects] to leave a section of the village free, with all the food that there was in it, which consisted of a large quantity of maize and yucca and fresh fish [prepared] for consumption by them and [in their] style, without any sort of salt, for they bake it and dry it over the fire in such a way that it can [nevertheless] be kept for many days; there were [also] a large number of pools filled with turtles, which the Indians kept fattened up for their eating and pleasure, fed on maize, and they were very fat, tasty, and good. When the Spaniards saw that they were in a country so plentiful and [well] stocked, they began to collect food with much greediness and disorderliness and to store it on board the brigantines. When the barbarous Indians perceived their greediness and lack of self-control they got into formation for a fight, and (all unexpectedly [to the Spaniards]) with one swoop there fell upon our Spaniards such a horde of Indians armed with "macanas" and lances and [protected by] shields made from the skins of crocodiles and manatees which covered them from head to feet, and so sudden and so unthought of was the [whole] business, that they [i.e. the Indians] found them [i.e. the Spaniards] away from their posts and separated from one another, busying themselves in their living quarters: in such a manner did they fall upon them that before they [i.e. the Spaniards] could get together they [i.e. the Indians] wounded several of them; but just as soon as they [i.e. the Spaniards] were united they rushed with great impetus upon the Indians, taking away from them their weapons and their shields, which [in turn] were a great protection to them [i.e. to the Spaniards] [as they manoeuvred] so that they [i.e. the Indians] might not kill them. In this fray they wounded and killed many Indians, and this became the excuse with which many more assembled for the purpose of avenging them; and, in view of the great mass of men that started to come on, it became imperative for the Spaniards to get into their boats in the best order that they could, without there being killed any one of them, although the greater part of them were wounded. As soon as they were in their boats, they [i.e. the Indians] came all around them on the river in more than four hundred canoes and pirogues, which kept delivering a fierce attack against them on one side and on the other, and when they [i.e. the Spaniards] saw themselves so hard pressed, they tied the two brigantines together in order that they [i.e. the Indians] might not be able to come in between them, and they distributed themselves along the sides of the boats in good order with their arquebuses and crossbows, with which they made some good shots, wounding and killing many of the enemy, whereby they instilled in them great fear as a means of forcing them not to come in close to them; and so great was the fright which they acquired from seeing [men] being wounded and killed [in conjunction] with the roar of the arquebuses, and [this] without knowing what it was nor seeing what was wounding them and killing them, that they took to dropping down on hearing the crack of the arquebuses; but no matter how quickly they did this, still there were killed [or]* wounded those whom the bullets or the small shot struck, owing to which cause they did not dare to come up close to them, for otherwise it would have been impossible for a single one of the Spaniards to prevent himself from being made a prisoner or from being killed, because there was for every one of them a hundred Indians, [so that their destruction would have been inevitable] had it not been that God in a miracle chose to watch over them. And in spite of all the damage that was being inflicted

---

* [Added in the text as printed by Medina.—EDITOR.]

upon them, they followed them down the river that afternoon [i.e. the afternoon of that day] when they [i.e. the Spaniards] had taken to their boats, and for two days more with their nights, during which they kept on navigating as hard as they could. During all this time the shores of the river [in this province] of Machifaro were [seen to be] inhabited, which fact could be observed by day owing to the brightness [of the sun] and by night owing to the many torches and illuminating fires which the Indians made on land [and] which produced a great deal of light. These people are naked, both men and women; their war implements are "macanas", arrows and lances, and shields made out of the skins of large crocodiles and of a certain kind of fishes called manatees, which are as large as calves and so tough that a dart shot from a crossbow can not pierce them; and they [i.e. these shields] were of great utility to the Spaniards, both for use against the inhabitants of this country and against those whom they came upon farther on. The country is partly sparse forest land and partly open savanas; there are in it the kinds of foodstuffs mentioned above, and nuts and large quantities of honey from bees, and wild pigs and tapirs. Prior to their reaching this province, as they were coming down through the uninhabited section which has been described, one of the soldiers being engaged in cleaning a nut belonging to a crossbow, it [i.e. the nut] fell from his hands into the river, and it came about that on the following day, they being engaged in fishing after having moved on for a good stretch, they caught a large fish, and on opening it up they found in its stomach the crossbow nut which had fallen into the river, so that it seems as if God through miracles, in such a predicament as this, was furnishing them with aid against their enemies. From this province Friar Diego (*sic*) de Carvajal, of the Order of Preachers, came out wounded in one eye, in consequence whereof he remained [thereafter] blinded in one eye. From here on down they came upon many more settlements, keeping always to the right, [through territory] where they did not dare to stop or investigate the secrets of the land, [or do anything] beyond merely seizing food in the most convenient spots according as they thought wise to do so, because they were few in numbers in comparison with the great horde of Indians that there were [there]. On the canoes and houses of some of these Indians they found painted some objects quite similar to [what one sees on] those [i.e. the houses] of the Incas of Cuzco and, on others, ewes and sheep [like those] of Peru; and, upon inquiring of them through the interpreters whom they were taking along what those paintings meant, they were told by them that off in the interior of the country there existed that sort of people and [those kinds of] animals, they [i.e. the interpreters] pointing to some lofty mountain ranges which are visible from the river. The few Spaniards who went along with Francisco de Orellana could not get to see anything else, nor reconnoiter it [i.e. the country] towards the interior, owing to the fear which the Indians of Machifaro had instilled in them; they merely saw many settlements along the river and its islands, which are in great numbers. They assert that the tide runs up the river for more than 100 leagues. Francisco de Orellana came out in the Northern Sea [and proceeded] to the Island of Margarita; and, liking the land [which he had passed through] and the peoples inhabiting it, he went off to Spain [and] begged His Majesty the Emperor Charles V, the King our master, for a commission to conquer it; he gave it to him along with the title of Adelantado, and, going over to undertake it [i.e. the conquest] with a large armed expedition, he [i.e. Orellana] went up the river past a great stretch of country [and] came upon a settlement which is on the right as one proceeds up the river, where he landed and [where] the Indians extended a kind welcome to him; he sent scouts into the interior of the country, and, the enterprise being at this stage of progress, as Francisco de Orellana was [now] an old man, there came over him an illness from which he died, whereupon [the expedition together with] the campaign [that had thus been launched] went to pieces. The Spaniards turned back down the river, and, although the persons who had gone off to reconnoiter the country brought back to them [i.e. the other members of the expedition] good accounts of it and of the numerous tribes and fine ones that there were there, they refused to establish colonies or do anything but turn back; and [this stand being] realized by a certain number of those who had gone inland to explore the country, they [i.e. these latter] refused to go with them, rather they remained in it, [a total of] 18 Spaniards, there being no indication that they have ever turned back up to the present, [the fact being that] on the contrary it has been reported that they were [seen] settled down off in the interior in that general region at the time that Lope de Aguirre went down through there in the year 71.* Let us return, now, to Gonzalo Pizarro and his men, who had remained behind waiting for the provisions which Captain Francisco de Orellana was to bring to them: as he did not come back with these, and [as] the hunger was so great, it became absolutely necessary for them to eat up their horses little by little, and eventually there were soldiers in such a condition that they gradually accepted the expedient of bleeding the horses once a week and cooking their blood with herbs in the morions which they wore, and of cooking it in this way along with the herbs and all; and this they did in order that their food supply might not give out so soon; in consequence of which situation it became absolutely necessary for Gonzalo Pizarro to go back to Quito, where he finally came out again at the end of two years, during which time he had been in very desperate straits, without having at that time come upon the country that he was looking for (and [I may add] without its having been found up to the present time), nor the rich mines which Huainacapac, to whom Peru was [once] subject, owned there, about which there are many reports in circulation and [which] would be easy to discover, if [only] there were some interest and industriousness [for undertaking it], according to what those who understand the matter have to say; but those who have means for being able to do it do not wish to put themselves to the trouble, and those who desire [to undertake] it do not possess what is needed for undertaking it; and on this account this enormous wealth lies hidden until God shall be pleased that it be discovered.

# X

*Transcript of a document on whose filing wrapper is written: "The petition which Orellana presented, together with the opinions of the Council."†—1543.*

## [ORELLANA'S PETITION]

S[acred] C[esarean] C[atholic] M[ajesty]:

I, Captain Francisco de Orellana, a native of the city of Trujillo, which is in these realms, do declare that: twenty-seven years ago, and [a little] more, I crossed over to the Indies, and I took part in the [expeditions of] exploration

* [Read "1561."—TRANSLATOR.]

† General Archives at Simancas, State Papers, bundle 61, fol. 19.

in the provinces of Peru, and there and in other parts of the Indies I have rendered many services to Your Majesty in many honorable commissions with which I was charged, both as captain and as governor's lieutenant, [and] of which I have given a good account, as may be seen from affidavits drawn up in the said regions and [so easily at hand] that, if it be necessary, I shall present them here; and in view of the fact that, in continued furtherance of the desire which I have always had of serving Your Majesty, I set out from the provinces of Quito with Gonzalo Pizarro on the [expedition of] exploration to the valley of La Canela, and for that purpose used up on horses and arms and ironware and also articles of barter more than forty thousand pesos, and went following after him until I caught up with him, and [because], while I was engaged in exploring with the said Gonzalo Pizarro and when I had gone with a certain number of companions down a river to look for food, it was God's will that with the current of the river we should be carried off down the said river for more than two hundred leagues, to a place whence we could not turn back, and as a consequence of this difficult situation, and because of the considerable amount of information which I had obtained regarding the great size and wealth of the country, and for the sake of serving God and Your Majesty and of exploring those vast provinces and bringing the peoples inhabiting them around to a knowledge of our holy Catholic faith, and of placing them under the rule of Your Majesty and of the Royal Crown of these realms of Castile, disregarding the danger to myself, and without [having in view] any personal gain whatsoever for myself, I launched forth on the adventure of trying to find out what there was in the said provinces, in the course of which enterprise there was discovered and there was performed [all] that which Your Majesty has become acquainted with through the account that I have laid before him covering it and [which] is also attested by several affidavits which I have with me; and considering the fact that the matter has been and [still] is as great [as], and [even] greater than, any matter ever [heard of] from the point of view of [extent of] population and [vastness of] country, and that the natives inhabiting it [i.e. this country] will [in this way] be able to come into [possession of] a knowledge of our holy Catholic faith, because the greater part of them are intelligent people, I beseech Your Majesty to see fit to give it to me as territory to be held by me as governor in order that I may explore it and colonize it on behalf of Your Majesty, and, in case Your Majesty grants me the favors which I shall state below, I offer myself for undertaking what follows, for the sake of serving God and Your Majesty:

In the first place, I shall take over, at my own expense, to the said land [forming a part] of these realms and of the Islands and Tierra Firme of the Indies five hundred men and two hundred horses and mares, and with these men I shall take along clerics and friars who have led good lives, those whom Your Highness shall be pleased [to select], in order that the land may be explored and colonized, and I shall distribute them in [such] regions and places as it shall be thought best [to select].

[I request] that for this purpose Your Majesty order that I be aided out of his royal exchequer in these realms to the amount that he may think best for the time being, which [amount] I shall bind myself to pay back within the limit of time that he may deem best.

*Item*, that Your Majesty grant me the distinction of the rank of perpetual governor, [this title to be reserved] for me and for an heir after my days, with jurisdiction over all that which I shall explore and colonize, with a salary of four thousand ducats per year.

*Item*, that of [the profit to be derived from] whatever [territory] I may so explore and colonize, out of the revenues and forms of income which Your Majesty shall acquire in the said land, he grant me the favor of [the right to withhold] one-tenth of the whole for all time for myself and for my heirs.

*Item*, that in the said lands which I shall so explore and colonize there be accorded [to me] the favor [of a grant, to hold good] for all time for me and for my heirs, of thirty leagues of land, with dominion and with civil and criminal jurisdiction [over it] and with [the use of] the revenues and sources of income which may come to exist in the said land, and that this be in the region which Your Highness shall deem most proper, [provided] that it be neither of the best nor of the poorest [land available], and [that this be] with the title that Your Majesty shall see fit [to grant], in conformity with my [high] social rank and [my long line of] descent and [my] past services.

*Item*, that he grant me the favor of the chief constableship of the said provinces for the duration of my life and of that of the said heir of mine.

*Item*, that he grant me the favor of the position of commander of four forts which are to be built in the said province in the region which I shall designate as the one which is suitable [for that purpose] from the point of view of the service of Your Majesty, [the said position of commander being reserved] for me and for my heirs, with a commander's salary of one thousand ducats per year.

*Item*, that there be granted to me the favor of membership in the Order of Santiago, inasmuch as in me there are found united the personal qualifications which are required, and that along with the said membership there be allotted, [from revenues] in the said provinces, whatever salary Your Highness may deem appropriate.

*Item*, that as a reward for what I and my companions accomplished serving Your Majesty in this [aforesaid] expedition, he have the kindness to grant that the positions to which appointments will have to be made for [service in] the said provinces be filled by appointments made from among those persons who are expert and competent for them.

*Item*, that in view of the fact that the countries [composing this vast territory] are numerous and belong to different tribes, and [that] they could not be explored and colonized or be brought around to a knowledge of our holy Catholic faith save through an intimate association with the Spaniards and with the friars and clerics, a free hand be allowed me in order that I may divide up into *repartimientos* such [land] as I shall in this way explore and colonize for assignment among those who are to go along with me, because in no other way will it be possible to work out at present what tributes they are to pay.

*Item*, that Your Majesty grant to the said lands and to those [persons] who go over to them the favor of [exemption from] all the duties [usually levied on goods taken] from here and into that country on everything that they shall take over to them [i.e. to those lands] for a period of twenty years.

*Item*, that the favor be done to me of the grant of permission to take over from these realms and from those of Portugal two hundred negroes exempt from all taxes, for neither now nor at any [later] time is it just that there be in the said land any [other] slaves of one form or another.

*Item*, I request Your Majesty to grant me all the other favors that are regularly granted to the other governors, in view of the importance of the undertaking and of the great size of the country; and [I can give assurance] that Your Majesty is destined to be very well served thereby and these realms greatly benefited.

## [OPINIONS OF THE COUNCIL OF THE INDIES]

After examination in Council [meeting] of this petition comprising [several] articles and of the account by the said Captain Orellana, the opinion has been arrived at that, according to the [said] account and [judged from] the location in which this river with the lands that he says he has discovered is, it might be a rich country and one by [the occupation of] which Your Majesty might be rendered a service and the Royal Crown of these realms be enhanced; and for this reason it is the opinion of the greater part of the Council that it is advantageous to the service of Your Majesty that the banks of this river be explored and settled and taken possession of by Your Majesty, and that this be done within the shortest time and with the greatest amount of diligence possible, because, in addition to the service which is rendered to God Our Lord by the bringing of the natives of that land to a knowledge of our holy Catholic faith and evangelical law, upon which until now they have been without any enlightenment whatsoever, it is desirable in this way as tending toward the enhancement of the Royal Crown; and in case this is not done with promptness there might result a considerable amount of difficulty, because, according to what this man says, he ended up by coming out by a large river which is in [that part of the Indies known as] the Brazil coast, which lies inside the line of demarcation [of territory] belonging to the most serene King of Portugal, although it is our conviction that he must have gone out by the Marañón River, whose mouth, according to the most recent mariners' charts, is inside the line of demarcation for Portugal, [the fact of the case being, however,] that up to now he [i.e. Orellana] has not finished explaining the matter; and as [it is no secret that] this man Orellana landed in Portugal, we know that the King held him there fifteen or twenty days, acquainting himself in very great detail with the facts in connection with this voyage of discovery and making advantageous offers to him in an effort to get him to stay there, it being his intention to make use of him in this matter; and now, according to a letter which the officials of the House of Trade in Seville have written to the Prince, it is said that news has been received to the effect that in Portugal a military expedition is being fitted out for the purpose of proceeding up this river; and it seems as if it must be true, because once before already, some three or four years ago, through the diligence of the treasurer Hernán Dálvarez he [i.e. Hernán Dálvarez] organized a certain military expedition for the purpose of going in there from [some place on] that coast, and it was lost; and it also seems quite likely to us that, so far as may be judged from the indications that have been given out on the part of the King of France of a desire to look into matters connected with the Indies, if this thing should come to his notice he might have covetous designs in connection with it; and, after consideration of the advantages and difficulties mentioned, as well as of others that are familiar to Your Majesty, and [in view of the fact] that so far as the kind treatment of the natives is concerned and so far as seeing to it that no injury be done to them Your Majesty has already looked after all that by means of his new laws and decrees, it is the opinion of the majority of us that this [expedition of] exploration and colonization be carried out, and that it be intrusted to this [man] Orellana on account of his having discovered it [i.e. this river] and on account of his being informed on the subject, and [that he go] under obligation to see to it that they [i.e. the persons joining the enterprise] observe the laws and decrees which Your Majesty has ordered to be set up, and moreover that he also be compelled to observe, in the same way as the said laws and decrees, the instructions which will be attached at the end of [the list of] the things which in our opinion ought to be granted to him; and that there be appointed a person of distinction, confidence, and solid conscientiousness to go along as inspector and enforcer of everything that the said governor is under obligation to live up to, in addition to the clerics who are to go along, to whom it [i.e. the same function] is also to be intrusted; and that, provided Your Majesty deem it wise that this be done, there be granted to him the following things:

That he be given the title and power of governor over whatever [territory] he shall explore on that one of the [two] banks of the river which he shall designate, with a salary of five thousand ducats per year [to be taken out] of what there may come to exist in the country [in the form of revenue], with such restrictions as the Council may think best.

The title of Adelantado for him and for his heir.

The command of two forts which he is to build, [this to hold good] for himself and for his heirs, with a salary of one hundred and fifty thousand maravedis for each one [of the two forts].

The chief constableship for him and for a son of his after his days.

A twelfth part of all the revenues and sources of income that Your Majesty is to acquire in that [expanse of territory] which he shall so explore, exclusive of costs, provided that it do not exceed one million maravedis per year, [this to hold good] for himself and for his heirs.

Exemption from duty charges on everything that he, together with the persons who are to go along with him and also those who are to go over later to settle, shall take along to that land, for a period of ten years.

Permission to take over eight negro slaves exempt from all taxes.

[All this] on condition that he observe the said new laws and decrees, and in addition [adhere to] the following instructions:

In the first place, that he take over from Castile three hundred men of Spanish nationality, approximately one hundred [of them] as cavalrymen, the rest as infantrymen, so that it may be a sufficiently large number and force to colonize as it advances and [still] defend itself.

*Item*, he must take along material for building the two boats which will be needed for transporting the horses and men down* the river.

*Item*, he shall not take along in the [said] boats any native Indians from the provinces of Peru, unless it be an occasional young boy whom the Spaniards who are in the party may have brought up, and [even] for this an authorization must be made out for the Viceroy of Peru in order that he [in turn] may so authorize it.

*Item*, he must take along as many as eight friars, who shall attend to the converting [of the natives] and to making reports to the said person whom Your

*[From this phrase and from some of the instructions which follow it will be seen that the members of the Council apparently got the impression that Orellana was to lead the new expedition down the river as he had done before, and not up it from its mouth. Medina does not comment upon this point.—EDITOR.]

Majesty will send [with him], to which person, as well as to the statements furnished by the friars, entire credence is to be given.

Likewise, he shall take along the [usual] officials of Your Majesty, [appointed with the understanding] that one is to be of higher rank and [deserving] of greater confidence [than the others], in order that he may be an inspector [to keep watch] over how the laws and decrees of Your Majesty, as well as what is contained in these detailed orders, are complied with and executed; to which officials Your Majesty will order salaries to be paid.

*Item*, he shall give his attention to founding, using the persons whom he is to take along with him, two towns, one at the approach to the inhabited country, on the upper part of the river, or wherever he shall think best, and another somewhere along the very last part and nearer to the mouth of the river, choosing for them the most healthful and the pleasantest sites, and these in provinces where there is abundance and in places where they can be supplied with provisions [by boats going] up the river.

*Item*, he shall take along tackle and rigging for fitting out two caravels, which he shall build after having begun to colonize, and he is to send them off the one in advance of the other, which caravels shall go out by the mouth of the river, having on board persons who shall be able to take soundings and take note of the bay formations at the mouth and along the whole river and of the landmarks in order that the entrance may be recognized [by others coming after them], and shall look into the matter of the routes and the course of navigation back to Castile, taking the latitudes, so that just as soon as the caravels shall have come back with an account of the country and of what has just been stated people may go [over there], and whatever colonies shall have been established may start trading, and colonizing posts may be established from the mouth of the said river on.

[The following is] what he must heed without fail:

That he see to it that he pick out the sites and sections of country for establishing the said settlements in places where there will be no infringement upon the rights and interests of the Indians; and, in case this can not be done, let them be chosen with the consent of the Indians or with such circumspection as the inspector and the clerics shall deem wise.

*Item*, that neither he nor those of his party shall take away from the Indians any married woman or child* or any other woman whatsoever, nor shall they take from them gold or silver or cotton or feathers or [precious] stones or any other article that they may possess, unless it be by bartering and upon the handing over of payment, and [even then only] after the establishing of the conditions of barter and amount of payment in accordance with what shall be the opinion of the said person and the clerics.

But we do give our consent [to the following, namely] that when the food which they are to take over from here shall have given out they shall be permitted to ask [the Indians] for some with offers of barter, giving them some article in exchange for these supplies; and in cases where this [method] may fail them, they may appeal to them for the said food with entreaties and kind words and means of persuasion, in such a way that they shall never go so far as to take it by force, except after all these means, as well as the others which the inspector

* [Masculine here, but feminine in the corresponding passage in the next document (p. 332, *infra*).—Editor.]

and the friars, together with the Captain, may advise, shall have been tried out; because when they are in extreme need, then they may without injustice seize it [i.e. any kind of foodstuffs] wherever they shall find it.

Likewise is he to understand that in no way whatsoever is war to be waged against the said Indians, nor is he to furnish any cause for such a thing, nor is there to be one [i.e. a war] unless it be [when there is need of their] defending themselves, [and even then] with that restraint which the situation requires; rather they are to be given to understand how Your Majesty is sending them [i.e. the expeditioners] solely to teach them and instruct them, and not to fight, but to impart to them a knowledge of God and of our holy Catholic faith and [to train them in] the obedience which they owe to Your Majesty.

*Item*, he is to observe the decrees and laws which are ordered promulgated on the subject of not making any Indian whatsoever a slave or a *naboría*,* but [he is] to regard them as free, just as Your Majesty commands [with respect to] this matter; which [decrees and laws] are to be attached here.

*Item*, he who shall kill or wound an Indian is to be punished in accordance with the laws of these realms, without there being taken into consideration the fact that the delinquent is a Spaniard and the slain or wounded person an Indian; for, as it has been stated, they are free men and vassals of Your Majesty.

*Item*, in proportion as he shall progress in pacifying the land he shall gradually reduce the amount of food and sustenance which each village must furnish, and those foodstuffs and commodities [which the Indians are to hand over] the said Governor shall divide up among the Spaniards who are to settle in the said land, distributing to them all such commodities in accordance with the laws and decrees which have been promulgated.

And inasmuch as it is the will of Your Majesty [as expressed] by these decrees that all the Indians come to be under his royal protection, in order that they may be spared and instructed in the faith, no occasion is to be allowed to arise serving as an excuse wherewith a Spaniard may hold Indians [in subjection], or maltreat them, or prevent their becoming Christians; nor is any object to be taken away from them, as has already been stated, except in accordance with the foregoing stipulations.

[On the other hand it shall be ordered] that, if by chance some overlord or notable person of those lands, having heard about the greatness of Your Majesty, whom they are to obey, should wish to offer some present to Your Majesty of his own free will, he [i.e. Orellana] receive it and [that] they [i.e. the proper persons] send it to Your Majesty.

Doctor Bernal is of the opinion that this colonizing of [the banks of] the river ought not to be intrusted to this Captain, because, he being a poor man, as they tell him that he is, and one trained in the kinds of warfare that have been practiced in the Indies, and taking along with him from them [i.e. from the Indies] men accustomed to that sort of thing, going on the expedition with arms and under pressure of want, he [i.e. Doctor Bernal] does not believe that he will live up to the serious instructions that will be given to him, and [that] the natives of the land will get stirred up, and will hate the Christian religion and the supreme rule of Your Majesty, and there will result the [same] outrages or a large part of them, as [have been perpetrated elsewhere] up to now; and that from his point of view it would be advisable to send first a peacefully inclined captain and [to

*[I.e. free servant.—TRANSLATOR.]

send him] without soldiers, and with clerics who would try out all the good and [most] feasible means for bringing the land around to the service of God and to obedience to Your Majesty, and [that], after these attempts had been made, he should bring back a more detailed account of the nature of the land and of the people, and [also] of what would have been accomplished with them [i.e. the people], and of what it would be advisable to undertake, in order that, after examination of all this, Your Majesty might give orders for taking action in the case with fuller information and knowledge at hand regarding the whole matter.

The Licentiate Gutierre Velázquez is of the opinion that the agreement which Captain Orellana is negotiating with Your Majesty be put through with all the conditions which are laid down in it, except on two points [on] which he is of the opposite opinion; and the one [recommendation of his] is that the said Captain Orellana do not take over more than one hundred and eighty men and [only] seventy of these as cavalrymen, and this on account of the great amount of damage which the soldiers, when they are numerous, do on these expeditions of exploration, especially when obliged, as they would be in this case, to cross over from Puerto Viejo to the headwaters of the river, [through country] which is already subdued and colonized and under the rule of Your Majesty; and the other [matter] is [this: he persists] in the opinion that they must not take the food away from the Indians by force there where they are to go to settle and explore, but by means of articles of barter until they shall be peacefully inclined; and [the procuring of food] being [a difficulty to be overcome] by the use of articles of barter, in order that it may be done at less cost there must not be so many soldiers [to feed]; and [with the latter] not wresting from them anything which is their property, or any food, but [rather] bartering with the Indians, and the friars, along with the interpreters whom they are to take with them, telling them and preaching into them about how they are coming to them to explain to them our holy Catholic faith and the dominion which Your Majesty holds over them and [making it clear to them] that they are not going to do them any harm whatsoever, he [i.e. Gutierre Velázquez] is convinced that they will be made to feel at ease and will receive them well and will become converted to our holy Catholic faith and [will be willing] to become subjects of Your Majesty, and little by little they [i.e. the expeditioners] can go on colonizing; and [read: "but"], if they [i.e. the expeditioners] begin by taking away from them by force their means of sustenance, they [i.e. the natives] will think that they are going to do them greater injuries, and they will flee, and there will ensue greater troubles, and it will not be within the power of the Captain or of the soldiers not to pursue them; and even this number of soldiers which he [i.e. Gutierre Velázquez] mentions he thinks will be difficult to hold back from making war on them and [from committing] extensive outrages, all the more [serious] if they are many more in number; and if this should come about, he is of the opinion that there would not be accomplished so well that which the service of God and of Your Majesty calls for, and [this he believes would be true] even though Your Majesty should do the Captain the favor of [crediting to his account an amount equivalent to] the greater part of what the objects of barter would cost, he himself advancing [the money for] them, and even though they [i.e. the sums spent by him on these objects of barter] were to be paid back to him later out of the taxes [levied], within the territory which is to be explored and colonized, on the villages which are to be set aside as sources of revenue payable directly to Your Majesty, in which he [i.e. Gutierre Velázquez] thinks* that there will be [enough] for all, both for the colonizers [in payment of] what they [i.e. the leaders of the enterprise] shall be under obligation to give them and for paying back whatever may be due to the Captain as reimbursement for [the cost of] the objects of barter, [and] that he will be paid back within a short time; and [he says] that he thinks it better [that the number of men be reduced] than that the soldiers should start right in at once by taking the food away from the Indians by force, whereby [i.e. by which plan of Gutierre Velázquez's] there will not result from their taking it by force the outrages already mentioned. (*Here follow five signature flourishes.*)

# XI

*Articles of agreement which were drawn up in favor of Francisco de Orellana fixing the conditions for the exploration and colonization of New Andalusia.*† Valladolid, February 13, 1544.

The Prince [orders]:—In view of the fact that you, Captain Francisco de Orellana, did report to me that you have served the Emperor and King my master in the conquest and pacification of the provinces of Peru and of other parts of the Indies and that, in further pursuance of the desire which you have always had of serving His Majesty, you went forth from the provinces of Quito with Gonzalo Pizarro on the expedition of exploration to the valley of La Canela, and that for that purpose you used up on horses and arms and ironware and also articles of barter more than forty thousand pesos and went following after him until you caught up with him, and that while you were engaged in exploring with the said Gonzalo Pizarro and when you had gone with a certain number of companions down a river to look for food, owing to the effect of the current you were all carried off down the said river for more than two hundred leagues, to a place whence you could not turn back, and that, as a consequence of this difficult situation and because of the extensive information which you had obtained regarding the great size and wealth of the country, disregarding the danger to yourself and without [having in view] any personal gain whatsoever for yourself, for the sake of serving His Majesty you launched forth on the adventure of trying to find out what there was in those provinces, and that in this way you visited and found large settlements, and you submitted to the Council of the Indies an account of the successive stages of this voyage, signed with your name; and [in view of the fact] that you, owing to the desire which you have [to continue to devote yourself] to the service of His Majesty and to [seeing to it] that the Royal Crown of these realms is enhanced and to [striving to bring it about] that the peoples that there are along the said river and in the lands come into [possession of] a knowledge of our holy Catholic faith, have requested to return to the said land to finish exploring it and to colonize it, and that [it is proposed that] for that purpose you shall take over from these realms three

---

*[The text as printed by Medina reads: "I think."—EDITOR.]

† Archives of the Indies, 139–1–1, book No. 1, folio 216v. [This document had previously been published in the *Colección de documentos inéditos relativos al descubrimiento . . . de América y Oceanía*, Vol. 23 (Madrid, 1875), pp. 98–110. The text of Medina's edition appears to be more accurate than this one. Muñoz's extract of the document had already been published in Vol. 7 (1867) of the same collection, pp. 552–555.—EDITOR.]

hundred men of Spanish nationality, one hundred as cavalrymen and the rest as infantrymen, and such material as will be necessary for building boats, and eight clerics to take charge of the education and conversion of the natives of the said land, all this at your own expense and on your own responsibility, without there being on the part of His Majesty or of the kings who shall come after him any obligation to pay you back or to settle for the expenses which you shall have incurred in it, beyond what is going to be credited to you by the terms of this agreement, and [whereas] you have begged me to do you the favor of [conferring upon you] the title and power of governor over whatever [territory] you may explore on one of the banks of the said river, whichever one you may designate, [I have looked into this matter,] covering which I have ordered to be drawn up in your favor the following contract and articles of agreement:

First, that you be bound and [that] you bind yourself to take over from these realms of Castile on the expedition of exploration and for the colonizing of the said land, which we have ordered to be called and named New Andalusia, three hundred men of Spanish nationality, one hundred [of them] as cavalrymen and two hundred as infantrymen, [a total] which seems to be a sufficiently large number and force for colonizing progressively and defending yourself and your men.

You likewise bind yourself to take over material for building the boats which will be needed for taking the horses and soldiers up* the river.

*Item*, [it is understood] that you shall not take along nor allow to be taken along in the boats any native Indians from any part of our Indies, Islands and Tierra Firme, unless it be an occasional one as interpreter and not for any other purpose whatsoever, under penalty of [a fine of] ten thousand gold pesos to be paid into our chamber and treasury.

Furthermore, that you be under obligation to take along and that you [actually] do take along as many as eight clerics, any that may be given to you and may be designated by those who are members of our Council of the Indies, in order that they may take charge of the education and conversion of the natives of the said land; which clerics you are to take over at your own expense, and [you are] to furnish them the necessary means of support.

*Item*, you are to give your attention to founding, using the persons whom you are to take along with you, two towns, one at the approach to the inhabited country inside the entrance to the river up which you are to lead your expedition, the nearest [possible] to the entrance, wherever it shall seem desirable to you and to the said clerics and to our officials of the said land, and another in the interior of the country, wherever it shall be most convenient and most appropriate, choosing for them the most healthful and the pleasantest sites that can be had and in provinces where there is abundance and in places where they can be supplied with provisions [by boats going] up the river.

You likewise bind yourself to go in, for the purpose of carrying out the said exploration and colonizing, through that mouth of the river through which you came out, and to take over from these realms two caravels or ships to go in through the mouth of the said river, which [two ships] you are to send up the river, the one in advance of the other, just as soon as you shall go in through the said mouth and shall anchor in order to repair your outfit, and on board these [two

* [As compared with the mistaken assumption underlying the recommendations of the Council of the Indies (see asterisk footnote, p. 324, *supra*), the present document correctly assumes that Orellana intended to enter the Amazon from its mouth.—Editor.]

ships there shall be] a few peacefully inclined persons and some clerics with the mission to take the necessary steps for persuading the natives that may be found to exist in the said land to adopt an attitude of peace, and [there shall be] also some expert persons who shall be able to take soundings and take note of the bay formations at the mouth and along the whole river and of the landmarks in order that the entrance may be recognized [by others coming after them], and [who] shall look into the matter of the routes and the course of navigation and shall take the latitudes, and [within a certain period of time] after one [ship] shall have gone off you shall send the other to do the same thing [with respect to the Indians etc., but] to go farther ahead, and the other one [i.e. the first one to start out] is to come back to make a report on what it shall have found, in such a way that by all means care is to be taken not to come to an open break with the Indians.

Likewise [it is to be understood] that if some governor or captain shall have explored or colonized some section in the said land and [along the said] river where you are to go, and shall be in it at the time that you shall arrive there, you shall not do anything in detriment to the interests of the one whom you may thus find in the said land, nor shall you make trouble by going into any portion of whatever [territory] he may have explored and colonized, even though you may find this to be inside the limits of your jurisdiction as governor, so that there may be avoided those disturbances which have hitherto arisen out of such situations, both in Peru and in other parts, and you shall advise us of what it may seem [proper to do], in order that you may be given orders in a case of this sort as to what you are to do.

Likewise you shall take care not to invade the islands which are in the said river with any soldiers, [and you shall have no authority to do anything with these islands] beyond being permitted to send clerics there to bring them [i.e. the inhabitants] by peaceful means around to obedience to us and to teach them matters connected with our holy Catholic faith, because these [islands] do not come within your jurisdiction as governor, and you are to trade with them [i.e. the inhabitants] exclusively by bartering.

And because between the Emperor-King my master and the most serene King of Portugal there exist certain treaties and agreements regarding the [line of] demarcation and the dividing up of the Indies, and also with regard to the Moluccas and the Spice Islands, I order you to observe them [i.e. these agreements] as worded in their texts and not to lay your hands on anything that belongs to the said most serene King.

On condition that you, the said Captain Francisco de Orellana, carry out and execute the things stated above, and each one of them, according as and in the manner that it [i.e. the matter] is stated in the articles [herein] included above, and that you observe the new laws and decrees issued by His Majesty and the other terms which shall be included [herein] below, we promise to do for you and grant to you the following favors:

In the first place, I give permission and power to you, the said Captain Francisco de Orellana, whereby on behalf of His Majesty and in the name of the Royal Crown of Castile and Leon you may explore and colonize the bank of the said river on the side which is at the left [as you go up] from the mouth of the river through which you are to go in there, which is in the direction of the River Plate, this being within the limits of the demarcation [of territory] belonging to His Majesty.

*Item*, in the belief that it is essential to [the proper functioning of] the service of God Our Lord, and by way of adding prestige to your person, we agree to give you the title of Governor and Captain-General with jurisdiction over whatever [territory] you may explore on the said bank to the left of the said river, with [its water front of] two hundred leagues of the shore of the said river as the crow flies, whatever ones [i.e. whatever two-hundred-league stretch] you may select within three years after you shall enter the country with your expedition, for all the [rest of] the days of your life, with a salary of five thousand ducats per year; which [sum] you are to [begin to] count as salary due to you from the day when you shall hoist sail in the port of Sanlúcar de Barrameda to proceed on your journey, and it is to be paid to you out of the revenues and sources of income belonging to His Majesty in the land and provinces which you shall thus explore and colonize; and, in case that in them [i.e. these provinces] there should not be any revenues or sources of income within the said period of time, His Majesty shall not be bound to order that you be paid anything toward it [i.e. salary due]: and the rest of the said bank that you may explore you shall hold under your jurisdiction as governor and [under your] judicial authority until the time when His Majesty shall order otherwise.

*Item*, he [i.e. His Majesty] does you the favor of [conferring upon you] the title of Adelantado of whatever [land] you may so explore on the said bank on which you are thus to be Governor, [the said favor to hold good] for you and for a successor of yours, such a one as you may designate.

Likewise we shall grant you the favor of [an appointment to] the office of Chief Constable in the said lands, [the said favor to hold good] for you and for a son of yours after your days, such a one as you may designate.

*Item*, we give you permission whereby, in conformity with the opinion and consent of the officials of His Majesty in the said land, you may build in it two stone forts in the regions and locations [in] which it will be most advantageous [to erect them], provided that it be the opinion of yourself and of the said officials of ours that they are necessary for the protection and pacifying of the said land; and we do you the favor of [placing in your hands] the command of them for all time, [this to be] for you and for your heirs and successors, with a salary of one hundred and fifty thousand maravedis per year for each one of the said forts; which said salary you are to be entitled to draw from the time that they shall both be built and finished and closed in [and shall be approved] after inspection by the said officials of ours, which [forts] you are to build at your own expense, without there being on the part of His Majesty or of the kings who shall come after him any obligation to pay back to you whatever you may spend on the said forts.

I furthermore do you the favor of [allowing you to withhold] one twelfth of all the revenues and earned profits which His Majesty is to collect each year in the lands and provinces which you shall so explore and colonize in accordance with [the terms of] this agreement, exclusive of costs, provided that these do not exceed one million maravedis per year; which said favor I grant to you [to hold good] for you and for your heirs for all time.

Likewise we shall give you permission and power whereby you may be allowed to take over, and [whereby] you do take over to the said land, you or whoever may have your authorization, from these our realms and dominions, or from the realm of Portugal and Cape Verde Islands or [from] Guinea, eight negro slaves exempt from all taxes.

*Item*, we exempt you and the persons who may go with you now over to the said land, and those who may go over later to settle in it, [on condition] that [this be] before the expiration of the time limit represented by the next ten years that shall elapse and shall be counted from the day corresponding to the date of these articles of agreement, from paying any duty charges on anything that they may take over for the furnishing and stocking up of their homes in the said lands.

And whereas the Emperor-King my master, having been informed of the need that there was for prescribing and putting in order a few things which were quite appropriate as being conducive to the good government of the Indies and to a kind treatment of the natives thereof and to an [equitable] administration of justice, has ordered certain laws and decrees to be promulgated, which we are ordering to be given to you in print, signed by Juan de Sámano, Secretary to His Majesty, you are to observe the said laws and decrees as a whole and in all details, according as and in the manner that the text reads in them and in each one of them, and in addition the other things which will be stated below, [these latter being instructions which you are to follow out] without fail and which are the following:

*Item*, you shall take care to select, for the purpose of establishing the settlements which you are to establish, sites and regions where there shall be no infringement upon the rights and desires of the Indians of the said land; and in case they can not be established [in this way], let it [i.e. the site for each settlement] be taken [possession of] with the consent of the said Indians, or with such circumspection as the inspector who is to go along with you to see how that which is stipulated in this agreement is carried out, as well as the said clerics, shall think advisable.

Likewise [you shall see to it] that neither you nor any individual from among those who are to go along with you take away from the Indians, nor that there be taken away [from them by any persons coming over after you], any married woman or daughter or any other woman at all, and that there be not taken away from them any gold or silver or cotton or feathers or [precious] stones or other article that the said Indians may possess, unless it be through bartering and upon the handing over to them of payment in the form of another article which is worth that [which is so obtained], and [also unless] the [trading with] barter goods and the payment [for articles purchased in this way] [are] being effected in accordance with what shall be the opinion of the said inspector and clerics [as to the conditions], under penalty of death and the loss of one's goods [as the punishment to which] he who does the contrary [may be liable]; but we do give our consent [to the following, namely] that when the food which you and the persons going with you are to take along shall be all used up, you be permitted to ask the said Indians for some with offers of barter, giving them some object in exchange for it [i.e. for whatever you are getting in this way]; and [that], whenever this [method] may fail you, by means of entreaties and kind words and acts of persuasion you beg them for the said food, in such a way that at no time shall recourse be had to [the practice of] taking [anything] away from them by force, unless it be after all the said means shall have been tried out, as well as such other ones as the said inspector and clerics and you may advise, for, in the event of your being in extreme need, the said food may be seized wherever it may be found.

*Item*, [you are to understand] that in no way or manner is war to be waged against the said Indians, nor is any cause for such to be furnished, nor shall there be allowed to exist any [war], unless it be in defending yourself [and your men, and even then] with that restraint which the situation requires; rather we order that they be given to understand how we are sending you solely to teach them and instruct them, and not to fight, but to impart to them a knowledge of God and of our holy Catholic faith and [to inform] them of the obedience which they owe to us: and if by chance the Indians should turn out to be so haughty that, not heeding the advances and peace exhortations with which you shall have approached them, they will still come at you and attack you in a warlike fashion, you having no other means of escaping and defending yourselves against them, save by breaking with them, [then] you shall follow this latter course with the greatest amount of restraint and moderation and with the least number of fatalities and injuries to them that is possible; and all the articles of wear and also objects of adornment that you may lay hands on, [and any other pieces] that are not arms of offense and defense, [things acquired in this way] both by you and by those who are to go along with you, you shall gather up, and you shall have them returned to the said Indians, telling them that you wish there had not been inflicted upon them the damage they shall have received, and that it was their fault for not having been willing to believe you, and that you are sending back to them those things which are theirs, because you have no inclination to kill them or maltreat them or take their belongings away from them, [and that you are seeking nothing] save a friendly understanding with them and redemption for them in the service of God and of His Majesty; because, if you do [all] this in this way, they will acquire great faith and confidence in what you shall have said and may say relative to this matter.

Likewise, [it is ordered] that any Spaniard whatsoever who may kill or wound any Indian shall be punished in conformity with the laws of these realms, without there being taken into consideration the fact that the delinquent is a Spaniard and the slain or wounded person an Indian.

*Item*, [it is ordered] that in proportion as you shall progress in pacifying the land you shall gradually reduce the amount of food and sustenance which each Indian village must furnish, and the foodstuffs and commodities which the said Indians are to hand over you shall divide up among the Spaniards who are to settle in the said land, distributing to them all such commodities in accordance with the said laws, and the most important district capitals you shall set aside [as sources of revenue exclusively] for the Royal Crown.

And for the reason that, as you shall see by the said laws, it is the will of His Majesty that all the Indians come to be under our protection, in order that they may be spared and be instructed in the things pertaining to our holy Catholic faith, you must not allow any occasion to arise serving as an excuse wherewith a Spaniard may hold Indians [in subjection], or maltreat them, or prevent their becoming Christians, or take any object away from them except by bartering and according as and in the manner that it is stipulated.

*Item*, [it is ordered] that if by chance some overlord or notable person of the said land, having heard about His Majesty, whom they are to obey, should wish to offer some present to His Majesty of his own free will, you be permitted to receive it, and [it is ordered that] you send it, taking every precaution and care, to His Majesty.

Therefore, by these presents, you, the said Captain Francisco de Orellana, carrying out that which is stated above, at your own expense and according as and in the manner that it is expressed above, and observing and complying with, and causing to be observed and complied with, what is embodied in the said new laws and decrees, as well as all the other instructions which we might order to be drawn up and followed with reference to the said land and with respect to the kind treatment and the conversion to our holy Catholic faith of the natives thereof, I do declare and promise that these articles of agreement and everything embodied in them will be lived up to in your favor, as a whole and in all details, in the form in which it is [all] stated above: and in the event of your not executing and fulfilling it [i.e. your part] in this way, His Majesty shall not be bound to live up to or fulfill in your favor that which is stated above, or any part of it; rather he will issue orders to punish you and to proceed against you as against a person who does not live up to and fulfill [what he has agreed to] and [who] transgresses the commands of his king and natural master. And as covering all this we order these presents to be delivered, signed by my hand and countersigned by Juan de Sámano, Secretary to His Majesty. Dated in the city of Valladolid the thirteenth day of the month of February of the year One Thousand Five Hundred and Forty-four.—*I the Prince.*—(*Countersigned by Sámano, and initialed by the Bishop of Cuenca and Gutierre Velázquez and Gregorio López y Salmerón.*)

# XII

*Declaration in writing by which Francisco de Orellana bound himself to live up to the articles of agreement drawn up in his favor and bearing upon the exploration and colonizing of New Andalusia.** Valladolid, February 18, 1544.

In the city of Valladolid, on the eighteenth day of the month of February of the year One Thousand Five Hundred and Forty-four, before me, Ochoa de Luyando, scrivener of Their Majesties, and before the witnesses whose names are written below, there appeared Francisco de Orellana, and he said: that whereas the Prince our master has ordered that there be drawn up in his favor a certain contract and [certain] articles of agreement, which are noted down above in this book, relative to the conquest and colonizing of certain lands and provinces which it has been ordered to call and name the province of New Andalusia, in the manner that it [i.e. this whole project] is stated at greater length in the said articles of agreement, to which he referred; therefore, [he declared] that he bound himself— and he did bind himself—to hold to, live up to, and carry out all that which by [the terms of] the said articles of agreement and contract he is under obligation to live up to and carry out, and [that he bound himself to observe] the new laws and decrees promulgated by His Majesty, which he acknowledged having received from the secretary Juan de Sámano, and [to comply with] all the instructions and special commissions from Their Majesties that may be issued to him, [he being otherwise] liable to the penalties specified in the said articles of agreement and new laws [and] instructions and special commissions: and by way of guaranteeing that he will so hold to, live up to, and carry out all this, he did pledge his person, and his household and landed belongings owned and to be owned, and he conceded full authority [over him] to all and any judges and judicial bodies of

*Archives of the Indies, 139-1-2, book No. 2, folio 10v.

Their Majesties, not only in these realms and dominions, but also in the Indies, [both the] Islands and Tierra Firme, in the Western Seas, under no matter whose jurisdiction they [i.e. the judges, etc.] may be, to which jurisdiction he did subject himself, in particular [did he subject himself] to that of the gentlemen composing the Council of the Indies and [to that] of the officials who have their headquarters in the city of Seville in the House of Trade for the Indies, he renouncing, as [in fact] he did renounce, his own [right of] jurisdiction and dominion and [his right to avail himself of] the law *Sic convenerit de jurisdictione*, in order that by the application of the full rigor of the law, which [in its working] shall be the quickest and most expeditious [possible], he may be forced to execute it [i.e. his part of the agreement], just as if by the final decision of a duly qualified judge he were sentenced to do so and [as if] the said decision were handed down in a case tried [in court] and allowed by him; in which connection he did renounce, [as being] in his favor and of aid to him, all and any laws, privileges, and rights that may be in his favor, including the law and right which says: "No general renunciation that a man may formulate with respect to the law shall be valid": in confirmation of [all of] which he did so give his consent before me the said scrivener and before the witnesses whose names are written below, on the said day [of] the said month and year, there being present as witnesses Martín de Ramoyn and Cristóbal Maldonado and Andrés Navarro. And by way of confirmation he signed it here with his name.—*Francisco Orellana.*

# XIII

*Five letters by Francisco de Orellana, belonging to the year 1544, dealing with the preparations for his expedition to the Amazon River and with the difficulties which beset him in his attempts to get under way.** Seville, May to November, 1544.

## [1]

S[acred] C[esarean] C[atholic] Majesty:—In another letter, I wrote to Your Majesty giving a full account of the state in which matters were in connection with my [proposed] expedition to New Andalusia, the pacification of which [land], [together with] the conversion and governing of its inhabitants, has been intrusted to me by Your Majesty, [and] begging Your Majesty to do me the favor of ordering that I be furnished with a sufficient number of guns to equip six or seven caravels, [to be taken] both from [the supply of] those that are in this city and [from those that are] in the neighboring districts; and in this same way I again beseech [Your Majesty] to order that this equipment be supplied, since it is a very important matter and one of such a nature that Your Majesty will be rendered a great service thereby; and, inasmuch as in the course of time, while negotiations are going on, people [always] discover something new, it has now come about that there are no sailors to be found who are willing to go on this expedition, and, although there are many of them about, they make excuses, from which [attitude] there results much harm to us because of the delay that they might cause us and because of other consequences; and inasmuch as this is an undertaking whereby God Our Lord and Your Majesty will be rendered a service, I beseech Your Majesty to order that the proper steps be taken whereby I, or whoever may have

*Archives of the Indies, 143-3-12.

my authorization, may be able to compel and force any sailors whatsoever that may be found here to go along with me on this expedition, paying them in return their just and due salary, and [to see to it that], if need be, the courts of justice favor me and assist me in this matter.

I likewise beg to inform Your Majesty that there is not to be found a single Castilian sailor who knows the coast [in the region] of the river for which my expedition is [being planned], [there being] only the Portuguese who possess a great familiarity with it as a consequence of the continuous navigating in which they are engaged in those parts; and so for this reason, as well as on account of the fact that they do their navigating in light and well fitted-out ships, it is advisable to take them along on this expedition; and because in this connection some obstruction might be placed in their way by the justices of the towns and by the sea guards, on account of their being foreigners, I beseech Your Majesty to be so kind as to order that the said Portuguese sailors with whom I shall have made a contract, without any hindrance or obstruction at all in the form of some prohibition which there may exist standing in the way of this, be allowed and permitted to take out and take along with them in any of Your Majesty's ships and caravels and brigantines the men, arms, and munitions, horses and other things needed on this expedition, and that on the way back from this enterprise they be permitted to load upon the said vessels all the Brazil-wood, sugar, and hides, as well as other merchandise, that they may wish to on the Island of Santo Domingo and in other parts, and that they enjoy for just this once all the privileges and liberties which the natives* enjoy and are in a position to enjoy, because, the matter being arranged in this way, a very great favor will be done to me and it will serve toward getting me started away from here around St. John's Day, God being willing, while otherwise it [i.e. my departure] will be delayed longer and the number of persons who are waiting around will dwindle considerably; and since this is a matter which is connected with the service of Your Majesty, and [since] so far as I myself am concerned all is being done that my strength is equal to, and even more [than that], Your Majesty ought to order that this be arranged within a short time, inasmuch as God has seen fit to grant me complete health, such as I have at present, which is for the purpose of being better able to serve Your Majesty, since my aim and my desire are none others. Seville, May 9, [in the] year One Thousand Five Hundred and Forty-four. Y[our] S[acred] C[esarean] C[atholic] Majesty's very faithful and humblest servant.—*Francisco Dorellana.*

[2]

[Sacred] C[esarean] C[atholic] Majesty:—In other letters I have besought Your Majesty to do me the favor of ordering that a few guns be supplied to me for equipping six or seven caravels, which I need for carrying out the expedition which Your Majesty saw fit to order me to undertake, having as its objective the conversion and pacification of New Andalusia, and in reply to this I was told that there was no source from which they could be supplied: I wish I were in a position such that I could serve Your Majesty in this expedition without causing any annoyance; but it is not possible to avoid causing this [annoyance], because the required guns I can not get if Your Majesty does not supply them: and so it is that I beseech Your Majesty to order that it [i.e. the supplying of guns] be attended to, since it is a matter which means so much for his service, and since

*[I.e. the Spaniards themselves.—TRANSLATOR.]

in the case of our not taking some along there may result for us considerable harm, and it will serve to furnish an excuse for my being held up here, and [will bring it about] that the men will dwindle away to such a degree that the expedition will not be able to be carried out.

I likewise begged Your Majesty to do me the favor of ordering that permission be given to any Portuguese pilots and sailors who might be familiar with the coast of Brazil to go on this expedition, because among the native [Spaniards] there is not to be found anyone who talks intelligently about it or [who] knows it; in reply to all of which I was told that the petition was denied, and word was sent in writing regarding this matter to Your Majesty's officials who have their headquarters in the House of Trade of this city to the effect that they should look for a pilot of the sort that there was need of, to go on this expedition; they did so, and they spoke to the one who was recommended to them from up there, and this man talks less intelligently about the coast than any other: and, while Your Majesty does order that no Portuguese shall go over on this expedition, may he at least see fit to grant permission to some Portuguese pilot who may be willing to go [and] upon whom is to be placed every bit of restriction that Your Majesty may see fit [to demand] in order that he may do nothing contrary to the service of Your Majesty, and in this matter there will be observed all the vigilance and care that there is occasion for; for Your Majesty may be sure that apart from the Portuguese pilots there is not a single one who knows about navigating over there, [or at least who knows about it] as well [as they do] through the uninterrupted experience which they have been having in those parts; and, since it means so much to us to take along a person who knows about this business, may Your Majesty see fit to order that it be arranged, or as he may think best.

I likewise beseech Your Majesty to be so kind as to order that I be granted the favor of one hundred slave licenses, [these slaves to be] exempt from all taxes, as an aid toward meeting a certain part of the many expenses which I am encountering in connection with this expedition and [which] I have already incurred, for I for my part am putting into it all my strength and ability, and I shall always do so in whatever has to do with the service of Your Majesty as a very faithful and true servant.

I likewise beg to inform Your Majesty that I am making all possible haste to get started away from here within a short time, and I have already put out into the river two ships and two caravels, and I am expecting every day another boat which I still lack, in addition to which no other is needed for the expedition, and there are likewise being built six brigantines for [use on] the river, the best fitted-out that it is possible to have: and this is what has been accomplished up to now in the service of Your Majesty, and as to what shall have been accomplished from now on, I shall send to Your Majesty an account covering it. Seville, the thirtieth of May, [in the] year One Thousand Five Hundred and Forty-four. Y[our] S[acred] C[esarean] C[atholic] Majesty's very faithful and humblest servant.—*Francisco Dorellana.*

[3]

S[acred] C[esarean] C[atholic] Majesty:—In other letters I have besought Your Majesty to be so kind as to order that I be allowed to have a Portuguese pilot for this expedition which I am undertaking at the command of Your Majesty with a view to the conversion and pacification of New Andalusia, the reason being that these people are expert in navigating along the coast of Brazil as a result of their having kept at it [i.e. navigating in those parts] without interruption; and, since this is not being allowed on account of the difficulties that might be created thereby for Your Majesty, I beg [Your Majesty] to be so kind as to order that the creditors of a certain Rentería and [of a certain] Francisco Sánchez, pilots, persons expert in navigating, about whom I have already informed Your Majesty in another letter, grant an extension of credit to them for the debts which they owe them, during the time, which will be short, that they shall be away on this expedition, for at the present time they have no means with which to pay, and what they owe is principally [in the form] of [premiums due on] bills of exchange, and interest; because, if this is not done, at the present time there can not be had, in their stead, any pilots at all who know anything [about the coast of Brazil], nor have your officials who have their headquarters in the House of Trade of this city supplied any, as they were ordered to do by Your Majesty, and it would be a great nuisance if my departure were put off for lack of a pilot. May Your Majesty order that it be arranged in this way, for the sake of the great service that can be rendered thereby to Your Majesty.

I likewise [beg to inform Your Majesty that I] have heard how certain persons have given out reports to the effect that I am treating very poorly the persons who are associated with me and [that] other things are being done which do not seem right, and [I wish to say that], if those who have written and publicly uttered all this were servants of Your Majesty to the same degree that I am, they would not do so; but I am quite confident that when, so far as my own responsibility is concerned, there shall have been completed [all] that which there may be any occasion for undertaking in the service of Your Majesty, there will be a feeling of gratitude toward me, and that no one will be able to create a situation whereby through [the spreading of] some false tale I shall be made to feel uneasy, since up to the present time I have sacrificed, and am ready to sacrifice [again], my person and my property through all the hardships that I have endured and expect still to endure in order better to serve Your Majesty; and if anything whatsoever in all that I have done and have reported on to Your Majesty shall be found to be detrimental [to his service], may Your Majesty order that I be punished for it, and may he order that the same be done to those who may venture to make such statements; because if anything more is desired in addition to what I have already stated, [let it be recalled that] I little needed to pledge my person to the extent of more than four thousand ducats, as up till now I have done, for the sake of putting in complete order the affairs of the expedition, as they are at the present time, which [expedition] will set out very shortly, and [all this] with little assistance from those who are going along on it, as has already been explained. Seville, the twenty-eighth of June, in [the year] One Thousand Five Hundred and Forty-four. Y[our] S[acred] C[esarean] C[atholic] Majesty's very humble and loyal vassal who kisses Your Majesty's feet and hands.—*Francisco Dorellana.*

[4]

S[acred] C[esarean] C[atholic] Majesty:—If there has been on my part a certain amount of negligence in the matter of submitting to Your Majesty an account of the progress of my affairs, this has been due to the fact that there has not been any up till now of the sort that I wish there were, and also to the worry and busy time that I have had in working for the saving and the quick expediting of [the affairs of] my expedition; and, after I had gone through many trials, God has seen fit to grant such a one [i.e. such a quick expediting, etc.] that there is [now] nothing whatsoever lacking out of what is needed for the expedition, because a cavalier [who is] a relative of mine, named Cosme de Chaves, a native of Trujillo, a servant of Your Majesty, has lent succor and aid to the amount of one thousand ducats; and, besides this, certain Genoese merchants, through the intercession and kind friendship and negotiating of Vicencio de Monte, Your Majesty's revenue collector, have likewise come to my aid with two thousand five hundred ducats toward the expediting of my affairs, which persons have offered a larger sum, in case it be needed; there are being applied all the diligence and solicitude that my strength is equal to in order that everything that is required as part of my equipment for my getting under way may be perfect and in sufficiently large quantities, so that I may be able better to serve Your Majesty, as I have always had (and [still] have) a full determination [to do], along with the desire not to make any mistakes in anything connected with what Your Majesty has ordered me to do; and for all my good progress I give thanks to Our Lord, for He has directed it as a thing which means so much to His service and to that of Your Majesty, without there being contributed toward it all any further assistance than what I am stating here. I am making all possible haste in order to get started away from here, and I shall do so in the shortest time that it can be done, and in due time, Our Lord being willing. Seville, the twenty-second of October, One Thousand Five Hundred and Forty-four. Y[our] S[acred] C[esarean] C[atholic] Majesty's very faithful and loyal vassal.—*Francisco Dorellana.*

[5]

S[acred] C[esarean] C[atholic] Majesty:—In the last letter which I wrote to Your Majesty I reported on the state in which preparations were for sending off the expedition which I am undertaking at the command of Your Majesty with a view to the conversion and pacification of the natives of the province of New Andalusia, and on how, with my attention fixed on this, so as better to perpetuate myself and be able to serve God Our Lord and Your Majesty in that land, I married; and since in other [letters] I have given a long account of how in my negotiations I have had powerful enemies, and [these] in various connections, bent on obstructing an enterprise such as this one is, which means so much to the service of God Our Lord and of Your Majesty, in this one I shall not go into details any more than to remark that those who have attempted to achieve this [i.e. the obstructing of the enterprise], now that they perceive the excellent progress that is being made in connection with whatever is needed, are at present pursuing very much more eagerly their evil purpose and intention, all to the detriment of the service of Your Majesty and to the demoralization of the men whom I am taking along; [in all of] which, because it is being done in such a concealed and tricky manner, there cannot be designated any particular person, [nor can one go] beyond speaking from conjectures and emphasizing the harm which their works are doing, because, if certain things have not been fully worked out in short order, it has been on account of this worm which has been in our midst; and because there is some possibility that the aforesaid individuals, pursuing their mean purpose and intention, have given out reports and will [continue to] give out reports, about certain things, which are more intended to serve their purpose of justifying their intentions than to contribute to the service of Your Majesty and to the quick expediting of this expedition, not only in the matter of the aid which the Genoese have proffered but also in other negotiations of a similar character, I beseech Your Majesty [to give orders to the effect] that, since at all times it has been and is my intention and determination to serve Your Majesty with every solicitude and with perfect fidelity, as I have been doing, confidence be had in me, [and that people be assured] that whatever may have been done and shall be done toward facilitating my getting under way will turn out to be a service to God Our Lord and to Your Majesty and a boon to the natives of that land and to those who are going to settle in it and pacify it, as [it will appear when] Your Majesty will be able to order the whole matter to be looked into and made known through the official communication and the person that I shall send [to him] just as soon as my departure is on the point of taking place, which will be within a short time [now] thanks to the aid of Our Lord, who I hope will grant in all respects the successful outcome which I desire for the sake of the service of Your Majesty. Seville, the twenty-first of November, One Thousand Five Hundred and Forty-four. Y[our] S[acred] C[esarean] C[atholic] Majesty's very loyal and very faithful vassal.—*Francisco Dorellana.*

# XIV

*Seven letters by Friar Pablo de Torres to the Emperor on the subject of the preparations for Orellana's expedition.** Seville, August to November, 1544.*

## [1]

Sacred, Cesarean, and Catholic Majesty:—On the twenty-seventh of August I received a letter from the most serene Prince my master dated the twenty-third of the same [month] in Valladolid, and I was astonished [to learn] that my letters addressed to Your Majesty, written on the eighth of August, had not reached their destination there, and I at once went to the House of Trade and talked with García de León, Your Majesty's scrivener in that House, to whom on the eighth of August I had handed over the bundle of letters of mine addressed to Your Majesty (and he had taken upon himself and had offered [to send it on] with the mail which was leaving that same day), and I found that neither with that mail nor with any other had he sent it on, I know not whether [it was] through forgetfulness, or for what reason [ it was], and I took it away with me; and this I am now again sending off with the present package,† which contains [accounts of] what had taken place down here up to that time, in order that Your Majesty may see that there has not been on my part either negligence or blame, but on the contrary a great deal of solicitude and labor; and to such an extent [is

*Archives of the Indies, case 143, shelf 3, bundle 12.

†[The choice of this last word has been dictated by the context. The original, as deciphered by Medina, is "later", which he prints with a (*sic*) to indicate, apparently, that he did not understand the word. Nor does the present editor understand it. It is hardly possible that "later" is a slip of the pen for "letra", for the latter word is feminine and Friar Torres had a masculine word in mind, as is shown by the form of the definite article preceding, and probably also by the relative pronoun which follows, although it is possible that the antecedent of this latter is the "bundle of letters" mentioned above. Perhaps, after all his precaution, Medina misread the word, which in the manuscript may be *lator*, i.e. "bearer" (cf. Italian *latore*, and note that according to the last paragraph of Medina's footnote 196 in the Introduction Friar Torres had served in Italy as a young man).—EDITOR.]

this true] that I am performing the duties not only of inspector but [also] of preacher and confessor, because when I arrived here I found the whole affair in a very upset and even desperate condition, and by the grace of God it has been well straightened out, although it makes me feel ashamed to have to say this, but I am compelled to say it by the blame which the Prince my master is putting upon me; and, God Our Lord interceding, Your Majesty may rest assured that, wherever I may be in the name of Your Majesty, there shall not be allowed any unjust, ugly, or careless doings, and worry may be set aside; and, in order that it may be seen that this is the case, let Your Majesty be informed that I arrived here on the third of August and on the eighth sent off the bundle of letters addressed to Your Majesty with the [list of] items which are mentioned therein, and since that time there has been added, over and above all that mentioned on the list and in the letter in the first bundle, sixty additional butts of wine, and fifty cows, which will be taken on board at the Island of Santiago. On the twenty-third was begun the loading of the hard-tack, and by the end of next week the galleon completely loaded will be sent to Sanlúcar, and at the rate of one per week, or at intervals of ten days, the remaining two ships and the caravel [will follow], in order that by the end of September, should it please God, everything may be expedited; and owing to the dissension and to the secret and sly factions that have come into existence here between Maldonado and those who accepted his views on the one hand, and the rest who were for the Adelantado and [the real interests of] the enterprise on the other, it was brought about that not only did certain ones, who were persons that had been helping a great deal toward the success of this enterprise, go off with the first fleet that departed for the Indies, but also many have become exasperated who are here in Seville [and] who had made up their minds to go, [and] who are [now] hesitating until they see whether the vessels are finally to be fitted out, and [this applies] even to many who both in Granada and in the rest of Andalusia were determined to go; and, to remedy this, captains have been dispatched to round up all those who are to go, very hurriedly, in order that, God aiding, [the preparations for departure of] the enterprise may be completed. I cannot yet console myself [when I think] that, after I had let pass the opportunity of sending my letters addressed to you through the intermediary of the Asistente, or in the Cardinal's bundle, or by some other reliable methods, and after I had handed them over for the sake of greater security to García de León, an official of the House of Trade, and had so specifically placed them in the hands of a person so sure, there should have been displayed so much carelessness that letters addressed to Your Majesty should not have been sent on with the care it behooves one to exercise in connection with the service of Your Majesty, [all] through the fault of the one who accepted them for the purpose of sending them up there.

I have tried to persuade the Adelantado that in no case, if that were possible, ought our expedition to touch at the Cape Verde Islands, for the reason that by means of favors, gifts, and entertainments men know how to undo whomever they will and get them [i.e. other persons] into difficulties: I say this because a certain very rich man of Portuguese nationality, who lives in Portugal, promised the Adelantado when he was there on his way through to Your Majesty's capital that he would give him 150 (I mean fifty) cows [when he should arrive] at the Island of Santiago, one of the Cape Verdes, and that that man's [i.e. his] son, who is here in Seville and is to go along with the Adelantado, would go and have them delivered in order to [be entitled to] go along on this enterprise: I should not like this to turn out to be a mere trick* for obstructing what is to be done. May Your Majesty give orders to the effect that neither shall this son of the other [i.e. the aforesaid] man go along on this expedition nor shall any beef or any other foodstuff be taken on at those islands, because this enterprise is looked upon with suspicion and hated in other parts [of the world]: [but] in this whole matter I yield to whatever Your Majesty shall order.

I made arrangements, after I wrote the other bundle of letters which was not forwarded, to have an announcement called out by the crier to the effect that those who had funds to hand over [as passage money] for the voyage should place them in a discount bank in order that they might not be spent except up to the amount that it was necessary to do so in connection with the expedition, and that has been done, as I gave notice that it would be done, and still with objections on the part of almost all of them.

Likewise, I took the necessary steps to have Cristóbal de Zaguirre,† who is furnishing the food supplies and the provisions for the expedition, sign an agreement to load them on board and have them [all] loaded on board by the 22nd of September, in order that the fleet might go on down to Sanlúcar, [and this I succeeded in doing] notwithstanding the fact that they [i.e. the organizers of the expedition] would not dare [to attempt] to make him sign [such] an agreement.

Likewise, I have figured out what is still lacking toward the rounding out of the [stipulated] amount of foodstuffs, in order to [be in a position to] make them round it out later and [in order to make them] search in the meantime for what is still lacking according to stipulations.

Likewise, I have arranged to have the captains go to Granada and throughout all Andalusia to bring in the men who have been prevailed upon to enroll for this enterprise and had become hesitant with regard to it.

Likewise, I have seen to it that the merchants, by means of contracts, help to hurry this expedition along toward its being sent on its way, and everything possible is being done, thanks to my pleading with them all.

And with regard to the orders of the Prince my master to the effect that no money shall be taken from those whom the Adelantado is to take along with him on this expedition, let Your Majesty be informed that on account of his poverty the aforesaid, having spent on expenses in connection with the expedition all that he has and [ever] did have in the form of funds in order to feed them and buy ships and not charter them, has been receiving money from those who were planning to go along, making arrangements with them some at the rate of ten ducats each, others fifteen ducats, others a larger or a smaller amount, as is customarily done in [the organizing of] other expeditions, and this [is] for ship-stores and transportation, and what he has been taking in from this source he has been turning to use in the interests of the expedition or as he has deemed best. If Your Majesty is of the opinion that this must not be done, the expedition will not be able to be carried out, for it is in this way that they are all carried out, even though the fitter-out may be rich; he wants the passengers to pay for only these two things, transportation and food, and this is the way that those who go to New Spain and to all the Indies pay. May Your Majesty decide on what orders

---

*[In Medina's text the word printed here is *mucípula*. Can this be a misprint for *manipula*, derived from *manipular*? In any case, the present translation of "a mere trick" is a conjecture based on the context.—EDITOR.]

†[Called "Aguirre" in a subsequent letter.—EDITOR.]

he gives with regard to this matter, for I, by way of regularizing the method and making it seem reasonable, in order that no acts of deceit might be perpetrated and on the other hand in order that the men might not back down, in the announcement which I caused to be called out by the crier in the name of the Adelantado inserted a clause to the effect that each one should provide himself with ship-stores and that for transportation he should go and make arrangements with the masters of the ships, in order that they [i.e. the ships] might be paid for out of that [source of funds], because they are not yet entirely paid for at the present time; and, inasmuch as this is an undertaking which the Adelantado is to carry out relying upon his own resourcefulness, I have not demanded of him a statement of what he has taken in up to now nor [of what he has] paid out, because I have no authority to do so, and [also] for the sake of not furnishing him any excuse for being suspicious of me [and imagining] that I have no confidence in what he is doing, or for saying that I am insulting him; but I watch and see what he is doing and I request him, politely, to tell me what he is doing and how much he is spending over and above what I see and learn about, and, what is more, in private conversation, whenever there is a good reason for that, I tell him what Your Majesty [himself] might tell him and even [what] the one receiving his confession [might tell him], and whenever it is necessary [I do this] before all; the truth is that he has not contradicted me in any matter which is for the good of the undertaking or in keeping with the service of Your Majesty up to now: we all of us who are down here do the things that it behooves us to do for the success of this undertaking, by the grace of Our Lord, by sheer strength of muscle, and the delay that was brought about in connection with this enterprise here in Seville, and the unusual weather conditions that prevailed up till May, and the fleet which departed for New Spain and the Indies—[all this] produced a great [deal of] hindrance to this [expedition] of ours, and with the manifestations of passion and the prattlings that have been rife among these men of ours it has not been possible to accomplish any more: there had been [actually] signed on for transportation up to now as many as one hundred men, and of those having considered going [there were] more than three hundred, but they are waiting until we load on the foodstuffs, and this is being done: of all that shall be done I shall notify Your Majesty in a letter to follow this one. Your Majesty's purser and Your Majesty's inspector, as they have been here a long time, are quite short of funds, and their case requires that Your Majesty think of them in their difficult situation. This is the state in which things are with regard to this expedition; I trust to God that the situation will get better day by day. As to my replying definitely whether there exists an absolute certainty that this voyage is to become a reality, I really don't know; but of the probability of it I am convinced, for there are the required ships for four hundred men with ample room, [there are] foodstuffs and provisions to the value of two thousand ducats and more, exactly as he [i.e. the Adelantado] is under contract [to provide], [and I may add] that in case of need he will provide more: we are expecting aid from some merchants, for an agreement upon that subject is being worked out; [we are expecting] persons to sign on for transportation totaling more than one hundred and fifty men; when there shall have been paid off the nine hundred and fifty ducats which are still due toward the full settlement of payment for the ships, there will remain nothing in the way: and, what is more, we are expecting the arrival of the Treasurer, who is to come with a group of thirty or forty men, who are bringing, so it is affirmed, material for them to fit out a caravel or a ship all by themselves: all this is [partly] in actual existence and [partly] within sight as things that may be counted upon: Our Lord aiding, we believe that our expedition will be [completely] organized by the end of September, because even the private food supplies will be plentiful, and, when the loading on board of everything is completed, a statement correct to a quarter of a hundred-weight of hard-tack will be submitted to Your Majesty. I have drawn up an estimate of what is needed for the voyage and of what we have on hand and of what is still lacking, and in this whole affair what ought to be done shall be done, exactly as if there were ten supervisors: right away this week I shall give my attention to the matter of constructing the brigantines which we are to take along all cut out and fitted and placed as ballast in the holds of the ships, together with their full sets of nails and their rigging, which they [i.e. the builders] are under contract to deliver to us at the rate of one finished [brigantine] every ten days.

No further activities [on my part] for the present will be devoted to any part of what is stated above until Your Majesty has seen by these letters what is being done down here, and may Our Lord grant to the entirely invincible person of Your Majesty every occasion to rejoice over the exaltation of the holy Catholic faith and the enhancement of the imperial greatness.—Seville, the twenty-seventh of August, [in the] year One Thousand Five Hundred and Forty-four.—The humblest of Your Majesty's chaplains, who kisses his sacred feet.—*Friar Pablo de Torres*, Ordinis Praedicatorum.—To the entirely invincible most happy Emperor our master.

[2]

Sacred, Cesarean, and Catholic Majesty:—On the eighth day of the present month I received a letter from the enlightened Prince our master, and [I beg to give assurance that] everything mentioned in it will be executed just as His Highness orders, although in truth nothing is being omitted in all that it is men's duty to do in the service of Your Majesty, because all of Your Majesty's officials are doing their duty and everything in their power toward the expediting of this enterprise, and their services are more extensive in scope than mine, and it is my wish that they meet with the success which it is hoped will be granted by Our Lord, whom I pray to guide this enterprise along lines in keeping with His service and with that of Your Sacred Majesty. The state in which [the progress toward launching] the expedition is now is this: within four days from now, and perhaps even sooner, we shall so expedite matters that the galleon will go off to Sanlúcar all ready to get under way, and then the caravel will be loaded, while the [large] ship can not be entirely loaded here, rather the loading will be begun here and will have to be finished outside, because its great size does not permit any other arrangement; and because the officials [of the House] of Trade asked me for a statement not only of what has been done [in this whole matter], but also of what it seems advisable to do, and of what is still lacking, with the intention of sending the whole thing to Your Majesty, I gave them the inventory and list of what Aguirre has promised to deliver and of what is needed and is still lacking toward the supplying of [all] that, and a list also of what would be needed for organizing any expedition composed of three hundred men, two hundred [of them] infantrymen and one hundred horse, for a duration of six months, on the basis of what the prices are now in Seville for the articles required, and even then [with these articles] kept down to reasonable quantities, and [on the basis of] guesswork [with regard to prices there] where what is not to be had here could be procured; and inasmuch as Your Majesty is going to see all that in the inventory which with my own hand I delivered to the officials of the House of Trade, signed with my name too, for them to send to Your Majesty, I shall accordingly not explain it here a second time: the truth is that, inasmuch as, subsequently to the other letters which I wrote to Your Majesty, it has come about that Cosme de Chaves, step-father of the Adelantado Orellana, is helping out the step-son to the amount of one thousand five hundred ducats towards [the expenses of] this enterprise, selling for that purpose thirty thousand maravedis worth of annuity or of quit-rent in order to raise that amount, and inasmuch as from the Almendralejo and Maestrazgo regions* there are coming in, including hidalgos and people of all sorts, as many as sixty men who have their minds already made up for [going on] this expedition, [and] who are so well-to-do that they even wanted to purchase a ship and foodstuffs for themselves, and [who finally], after hearing about our well-advanced preparations and excellent equipment, will come here, and [in view of the fact that I have been] informed that people are approaching the Adelantado here with marriage proposals, and also that in Seville and throughout all Andalusia there are many persons inclined to take part in this enterprise, though it [i.e. this inclination] is nothing more [for the present] than [a desire] to see if a beginning is being made toward getting under way and really preparing for the departure, and [persons] who do not dare show themselves in order not to be held back by friends, kinsmen, [and] immediate relatives, I am hopeful that the thing will materialize, which, if right from the start, as I have said, it had been steered clear of passions and worldly pastimes, which wreck the soul and destroy prestige, would certainly have attracted investments to an amount far in excess of the cost of fitting out the expedition: now we are keeping out of sight to the best of our ability, and I no longer allow myself any repose. May Our Lord bless the most just person of Your Majesty with universal dominion in keeping with His holy service, as we all desire.—Seville, the eleventh of September, in the year One Thousand Five Hundred and Forty-four.—The humblest of Your Sacred Majesty's chaplains, who kisses his sacred feet.—*Friar Pablo de Torres.*

[3]

Sacred Cesarean Catholic Majesty:—The loading of the galleon was completed on the seventeenth of September, and it is still waiting in the river, and the caravel is being loaded now, and [that is the best that can be expected considering that] there is so much dallying and delay in sending off this expedition, not through lack of solicitude and toilsome efforts that we are putting into it, but because it has not been possible to get hold of the funds to finish paying for either the caravel or the ship, and a large number of men are refraining from signing on for transportation because they do not see the ship and the caravel paid for in full and this [is how they feel] with their fear about paying in their money and [with their fear] lest afterward [if they do pay it in] the enterprise fail to materialize for the present: for the money to be raised on Cosme de Chaves' thirty thousand [maravedis worth] of annuity or quit-rent no funds were found in Seville, and [so] he went off to Trujillo to see if they could be had there: here the Genoese and other merchants proposed a contract designed to facilitate the raising of

---

*[On the Almendralejo and the Maestrazgo see the editorial footnotes respectively on pp. 134 and 120, *supra*, the latter under ''Ortiz (Alonso)''.—Editor.]

funds for getting the expedition started, and, what with article this and article that and conditions and reservations and clauses on advice of counsel to guarantee their security, they keep adding on, they never stop, although we beg them and urge them [to consider] what in all justice and conscience ought to and can be done; they are ready to sign the terms which they have fixed, although the Adelantado and our group will not sign without consulting the officials of the House of Trade: I am sure that, if the ships were already paid for, many persons would come who have here, [in the interests of such persons who may eventually come in] from several sections of the country, spies to watch what we are doing, as for example from the Maestrazgo, and from the Almendralejo, and from Malaga, and Granada, and Jerez, and the Condado:* there are persons going or desirous of going on this expedition whom it is not advisable to allow to go, because, in proportion as those who are to cross over there are better behaved and more virtuous, so much the better will there be accomplished that which appertains to the service of God and to the advancement of the interests of Your Sacred Majesty, whom I beseech to issue orders to the officials of the House of Trade to the effect that they shall not allow to cross over on this voyage such persons as may not be peacefully inclined and self-restrained as it is proper [that they should be], because on other occasions, no heed having been paid to a contingency of this sort, mutiny and revolt have broken out in some expeditions among those who had gone along on them, and there has not been derived from them the beneficial result which God and Your Majesty strive for: if the preparations were completed, the voyage would be begun at once, because there are now blowing levanters and gregales, which people here call "easters" and "east-nor' easters." I have been advised that the King of Portugal is fitting out an expedition for the Cape of St. Augustine,† an unusual thing, because there there is nothing worth fitting out an [armed] expedition for, because the French and anybody else go there to get Brazil wood without any interference at all, and that cape and that of St. Roque† are places where this expedition of ours is practically bound to head for, because, if it edges off to the right of this region, the current will hinder the progress of the fleet, and, if it gets off to the left, it will encounter west winds from land, [a circumstance] which will compel it to go out around the Cape of Good Hope; and, if there should be encountered any resistance in that region, it would be necessary [for our own men in turn] to put up a resistance: I can not understand for what purpose an [armed] expedition is being undertaken for that region: I shall write to Your Majesty stating whatever else may be found out relative to this matter. In regard to this expedition of ours, I am doing all that I can, without any sparing of fatigue and labor, as all those who are here on the lookout perceive, as if I were the fitter-out of the enterprise. In other letters I wrote to Your Majesty urging him to decide what was to be done in regard to a certain number of points; may Your Majesty give orders covering all this, and may Our Lord further exalt the very happy lot of Your Majesty by giving him universal dominion to the benefit of His holy service.—Seville, the twenty-eighth of September, in the year One Thousand Five Hundred and Forty-

*[By "the County" may be meant the County of Niebla, the territory of which, centering around the town of Niebla, lay between Seville and Palos in the basin of the Río Tinto.—EDITOR.]

†[Cape St. Augustine and Cape San Roque lie at the northeastern extremity of South America, the latter at the very corner of the continent and the former about 200 miles farther south along the south-trending coast. Cape St. Augustine is also mentioned in Juan da Sámano's letter to Francisco de los Cobos: see the Introduction, p. 25, *supra*.—EDITOR.]

four.—Your Sacred Majesty's humblest chaplain, who kisses his imperial feet, *Friar Pablo de Torres*, of the Order of Saint Dominic.

## [4]

Sacred Cesarean Catholic Majesty:—It must be more than two weeks ago that the galleon was loaded, and in order not to incur the double expense of [supporting] sailors here and in Sanlúcar we did not send it on down there, and it stayed here in the river, outside [the city] and farther downstream than all the other ships, all ready to start off, and in the meantime the caravel was dressed down and rigged and the loading of it was begun; and at the same time, in order to finish paying for the ship and [also in order to pay off] the remainder of what was still owed on this same caravel, and [in order to get money] for everything that was needed for the expediting of the enterprise, measures were being taken in every possible way, [our agents] seeking to procure funds by the giving of bills of exchange, or through loans, or by means of notes payable out of the profits of the enterprise, [attempting to negotiate] with native and foreign merchants, having merchandise delivered to them in such large quantities that from it, when sold at a price less [than cost], money could be raised, they offering as security Cosme de Chaves' quit-rents and annuities, not only the thirty thousand maravedis worth of these titles but also sum totals in quit-rents amounting in value to more than two thousand ducats, and [yet], neither through sales [of bills of exchange (?)], nor through the furnishing of security, nor through loans, nor through reduction sales, [with our agents] pleading with exchange brokers and "curb" brokers, nor by any other method has it been possible to get hold of even enough cash to finish paying for the vessels, wherefore many persons have declined to sign on for transportation, and even, in the case of those who were inclined and who we knew had made up their minds to go on this journey, to come here to Seville, on which account I wrote to Your Majesty that I could see very little likelihood that this expedition would materialize unless there should be forthcoming more aid than I can see; and reflecting and groping about in my mind [in an effort to determine] to what is to be attributed the fact that so much painstaking and labor and so good a beginning as had been made are not producing results, I find that there is no explanation other than that there must be, and I firmly suspect that there can not fail to be, a person or [several] persons who are working [to bring it about] that this enterprise be not carried out and are obstructing it with all their skill and with all their might, saying bad things about it and exaggerating the dangers and belittling either it or the persons who are going on it, because in the afternoon we will have some agreement all mapped out with some merchants, and by the next morning we find them with their minds changed. We find people willing to give trust [sufficiently to enable us] to get from them the things which we need, and shortly after we perceive that some one has caused us to lose our credit and they are not willing for anything in the world to aid us without being paid cash, or to wait even an hour, yet formerly they waited for days and were paid; we perceive that persons who were disposed to take part in this enterprise, as they publicly announced [that they would do] and [as] they were preparing [to do], without any cause whatsoever back down; we see that the treasurer who was to come here, and those persons who were to come with him from the Almendralejo and from the Maestrazgo in such large numbers that they wanted to purchase a ship and foodstuffs all by themselves, as it was learned here in Seville, and who sent word that they wanted to come, have given up coming, and people who had been signed on for this purpose in Jerez and in the Condado also are giving it up; I perceive that the Genoese merchants ([and be it noted] that they themselves came forward with an agreement relative to the supplying of funds for the undertaking without being asked, when they saw that we were so diligently hurrying along the loading and when it [i.e. this loading] became a known fact) have now withdrawn, and those who did not crawl out of doing what they had promised laid down such conditions afterwards that it is plainly to be seen that they are sorry [that they promised anything]: these and many other indications there are from which I can judge that what I am saying is the truth; and hence I believe that all this is traceable either to a [single] person or to [several] persons who are striving either to take charge of this enterprise themselves or to have friends of theirs take charge of it, or to some person to whom it is irksome that the Emperor our master be rendered this service and enjoy the profit that is expected to be forthcoming from this source and who finds no better expedient for the time being than to wreck this expedition from the start, or [it may be] that it is both of these considerations combined, and even though it were both of them [read: "even though these two considerations would suffice to explain everything" (?)] there might be others in addition to these: I leave that for Your Majesty to judge. In the meantime I am working away with the merchants and other persons to see if I can obtain something [in the way of funds] in order to make some progress with this enterprise; and because I wrote to Your Majesty the other day at greater length, I have nothing more to say now than to [add that I] pray that Our Lord will bless the entirely invincible person of Your Majesty with universal dominion to the benefit of His holy service.—Seville, the sixth of October, [in the] year One Thousand Five Hundred and Forty-four.—Your Sacred Majesty's humblest chaplain, who kisses his imperial feet, is [the writer].—*Friar Pablo de Torres*, Ordinis Praedicatorum.

[5]

Sacred Cesarean Catholic Majesty:—[Although it is some time] since I notified Your Majesty of how I had given to the officials of the House of Trade three inventories which they requested of me to send on to Your Majesty (and I gave them to them signed with my name), I have not had any letter [the contents of which were such] that I might learn from it how Your Majesty received them: one was [a statement] of the equipment and supplies which we had on hand for this enterprise, the second, of what was still lacking, the third [was an estimate of] what articles and supplies all told were needed for fitting out an expedition to be made up of two hundred infantrymen and one hundred light horse for a duration of six months; and I also wrote about where funds could be raised on behalf of the Adelantado for supplying what was still lacking, and I reported on the state [of preparation] which the expedition had reached and how for lack of funds nothing more was being done in connection with it; now Cosme de Chaves has come in with the amount of cash required in order that the ships may be paid for, and, when they are paid for, we shall begin to take in the men who have not yet dared to sign on for transportation and, moreover, whom we have not wanted to take in until the ships should become ours: every effort and every device are being tried out with the merchants and townspeople with a view to making the enterprise materialize: I beseech Your Majesty, since he is cooperating with his favor and prestige, and that is the main thing, to give orders to help out with anything at all toward pushing it along; and inasmuch as I have sent other despatches to Your Majesty, and in them [brought up] a certain number of matters which call for decision by Your Majesty, may he order that steps be taken [immediately] toward carrying out what he orders that there be done with regard to them.—May Our Lord prosper and preserve the Cesarean and Imperial person of Your Majesty in the exercise of universal dominion to the benefit of His holy service.—Seville, the ninth of October, in the year One Thousand Five Hundred and Forty-four.—Of Your Sacred Majesty's chaplains the humblest, who kisses his sacred feet.—*Friar Pablo de Torres*, of the Order of Saint Dominic.

[6]

Sacred Cesarean Catholic Majesty:—The necessity of hurrying on account of the closing of the mails does not leave me time enough to write as fully as I should like to, [or do] more [than state] that it must be a week ago that there arrived here a man from Portugal who said that he had seen an expedition being fitted out in Portugal for the Amazon, and he brought a letter for a certain Portuguese who is here, in which he was called back to go on it; and it is being organized in the name of a certain man of Castilian nationality who came over from the Indies on the invitation of the King; this matter, as a rumor or in the guise of confidential and secret information, was at once reported to the officials of the House of Trade: I beseech Your Majesty, since up to now this enterprise has been so completely deprived of recognition and so utterly ignored, to take a more personal interest in it from now on, and [I trust] that Your Majesty will bestow upon it some more special favor, for we see that very frequently what costs little is dear [in the long run]. The Genoese here sent around invitations to one another to get together for the purpose of helping out this expedition, and they requested as a method of dealing with them that Vicencio de Monte be sent to them in order that he might negotiate with them, and the Adelantado did send him to them, and he [i.e. Vicencio de Monte] closed [certain] agreements with them without my seeing them, and when I did get to see them they did not seem satisfactory to me, and I said nothing about it in order not to upset anything connected with the negotiation, having in mind to consult Your Majesty on the subject of this whole affair, and I obtained a copy of them, and since this has been in my hands they have made changes and modifications as they have seen fit and [have] inserted unreasonable clauses in them [i.e. in the agreements], and I reprimanded the revenue collector [i.e. Vicencio de Monte] for not having kept me posted on what was being done and for not having given me a copy of all the articles of agreement, and [I reprimanded] the Adelantado also to the end that all the articles of the said agreement might be examined in common among us and that we might negotiate with the Genoese and come to an understanding among ourselves with the consent of all parties, in order that on the one hand the laws and statutes of Your Majesty might not be violated and that they might be observed above everything else, and [in order that on the other hand] those sponsoring the enterprise might know what they were going to have to sign and agree to; and until now no statement about this has been given to anybody among those who are to take part in this enterprise: and in order to avoid giving rise to squabbles and slanderings I hold my tongue, and [also in order] not to frighten away the Genoese: just now an effort is being made to have drawn up the contract with the Genoese covering these articles which they have already signed, and I am not concerning myself with this matter because the terms which have been outlined do not seem to me to be just and because they are contrary to the laws and statutes of Your Majesty, [and I shall not do anything] until I know Your Majesty's orders. I enclose one of the copies in order that Your Majesty may decide what his orders are in the matter. In the three ship purchases which have been made here nothing has been right, and I have had nothing to do with them [i.e. these purchases] because at the time I was not here: now the large ship has been abandoned, because it was found to be unseaworthy, and at the time when there were funds available to finish paying for it I insisted on looking it over thoroughly and I found it to be damaged, and already certain other individuals knew about that and had not told me about it; but they were not among those who were to take part in the enterprise, and I reprimanded those who had purchased it [demonstrating to them] that they had not purchased one fulfilling the conditions stipulated, and [yet] when I came here they told me that it was sound and in good condition and that there was no defect in it; the purchase was made without plan, without order, absolutely blindly, and with little understanding: at present the Adelantado and those who sold it to him are litigating, and this is not as I should advise, because we are much to blame and there is not being done what needs to be done for the enterprise and we are wasting time on lawsuits: may God look after everything. There has been purchased another small ship, of one half the tonnage which the [large] ship [had], and I have just now sent the Inspector of the House of Trade to look it over, inasmuch as I had sat down to write this letter, because, although they did not inform me of the purchase, I want to have an idea what it is, and then, too, I am expecting an answer to the letters which I have written to Your Majesty, and I expect to write [then] at greater length. I say nothing more for the present beyond informing Your Majesty of how there has arrived here the Treasurer Francisco de Ulloa, [who has come here] because he was summoned, and [I shall merely add] that all are doing everything in their power in order that the enterprise may make headway. May Our Lord bless the imperial person of Your Majesty with universal dominion to the benefit of His holy service.—Seville, the twenty-third of October, in the year One Thousand Five Hundred and Forty-four.—Of Your Sacred Majesty's chaplains the humblest, who kisses his imperial feet and hands, is [the writer].— *Friar Pablo de Torres*, of the Order of Saint Dominic.

[7]

Sacred Cesarean Catholic Majesty:—After I had written my last despatch, there was brought to me a confirmation of what is going on in Portugal, [I mean the matter] about which I have already written to Your Majesty. The following are fitting out an expedition: Don Juan de Almeda, son of the Count of Brandes, and a certain Diego Núñez de Quesada, who brought over there from Peru a goodly supply of funds; and, because Don Juan de Almeda fell ill, in his place they put in Don Juan de Sandi, [and it is said] that they look upon him as very much of a swaggerer and [one] who takes around with him and receives in his house cutthroats and seditious individuals, and [that] such men as these he has selected to take part in this enterprise. The ships which they have fitted out are four in number: two of them are quite large, each one being of as many as two hundred tons, and the other two [are] smaller than they; they carry a great number of bronze guns, and munitions in such great plenty that they tell me that they have powder enough to be able to fight any large fleet; a large supply of foodstuffs; the weapons and munitions they say the King is furnishing, and the expenses [are being met by] the fitters-out, and it is possible that everything is being taken care of by the King; the report [that is allowed to circulate] regarding the expedition is [that it is] for Brazil, and the truth [of the matter is that it is] for [the same destination as] our own expedition, because in Lisbon they are searching about for persons who have been on the coast [over there], and they even talked with and urged to go along with them one of those who had gone down the river with the Adelantado Orellana, [a man] who went over there [i.e. to Lisbon] from here because he had been involved in the slaying of a man here in Seville, and had fled thither: they have warrants from the King for drafting men and requisitioning whatever they may need in all the localities which the King of Portugal possesses on that coast, and they are to build there some brigantines for going along the coast. They promise to divide up and distribute in shares the provinces that may be won there, in order to get people to flock to them [i.e. to the organizers of this expedition], keeping it secret that they are going to the river and publicly announcing [that they are going] to Brazil: I am told that in order to deceive the spies they are taking along barter goods in the name of the King. They say that the expedition is being organized very well and that it will start out this month and will stop at the Cape Verde Inlands in its course and there will stock up anew on salt beef. Your Majesty will find out about this more specifically from his ambassador who is at the court of Portugal, which [at the present time] is sojourning in the city of Evora, and it must be twenty-five days ago that Don Juan de Sandi went from Lisbon to Evora to have an interview with the King. Your Majesty will look into the matter and will send orders down here as to what the proper thing to do is.

As regards the affairs of our own expedition, may Your Majesty be informed that the Adelantado has married, despite my attempts to persuade him [not to], which were many and well founded, because they did not give him any dowry whatsoever, I mean not a single ducat, and he wants to take his wife along over there, and even one or two sisters-in-law [also]: he alleged as an argument on his side that he could not go off without a woman, and [that it was] in order to have a female consort [that] he wanted to marry; to all this I replied at considerable length in the manner that one was bound to reply as a Christian, and in a manner that harmonized with the interests of this enterprise, to the end that we might not burden the expedition with women and with expenses on their account. He has been considering appointing as his [lieutenant-]general and as his deputy one of the persons who arranged his marriage, not a suitable man for the office or even a suitable one to go along on the voyage, over which project of appointment there certainly would have been some hard feelings if it had not been forestalled. He fixed his choice for a campmaster upon a Genoese, in defiance of the laws and of the will of all, who are vexed at the setting of an Italian over these men; at first the plan as discussed was to have him go along [merely] as the representative of the Genoese to collect their shares [of the profits] which they are demanding, and for this purpose permission had to be asked of Your Majesty on account of his being a foreigner, and on top of this he [i.e. Orellana] made him campmaster, and they tell me that he handed some funds over to him; he said nothing to me about this. and I reprimanded him before all the officials for this and for other things. Of everything that needs to be done for this expedition and for the directing of it I shall notify Your Majesty just as soon as he shall give orders as to what is to be done with regard to the articles of agreement proposed by the Genoese.

The Adelantado is so kind-hearted that every time that a person tells him something he believes it and acts on it, and [he fails to see that] so much gentleness at times is of little profit to one. The ships which we possess have no guns mounted upon them; what [sort of ships] they are, I have already written to inform Your Majesty. The Adelantado shuns me as much as he can to avoid keeping me posted on what is being done, because I reprimand him for it, and with reference to what I think he is doing over and above what he has promised to do and signed an agreement to do, inasmuch as I do not know what orders Your Majesty is going to give relative to [his complying with] the agreement, I am undecided as to what I must do. There has arrived just now a ship belonging to the fleet coming back from the Indies, which people say got separated a few days ago from the convoy where the others were: may Our Lord bring it [i.e. the fleet] safely in and may He bless the imperial person of Your Sacred Majesty with universal dominion.—Seville, the twentieth of November, [in the] year One Thousand Five Hundred and Forty-four.—Of Your Sacred Majesty's chaplains the humblest, who kisses his imperial feet and hands.—*Friar Pablo de Torres*, of the Order of Saint Dominic.

Subsequently to the writing of this letter there arrived here in Seville Don Juan de Sandi, the captain of the expedition being organized in Portugal, and immediately, although [it was] night, I notified the officials of the House of Trade: this was on the twenty-first of the present [month]; I imagine that he has come here either to spy [on us] or to entice away from among ours a few men who, they imagine, possess some familiarity with the [Amazon] River.

# XV

*Passage from a letter written by the officials in Seville to the Prince on the subject of the preparations for Orellana's expedition.* April 4, 1545.

In regard to the orders which Your Highness gives to the effect that we all three go to Sanlúcar, taking along with us at the same time Friar Pablo de Torres, and [that] we inspect the expeditionary fleet of the Adelantado Orellana, and [that we find out] whether the articles of agreement have been complied with in the matter of what he is under obligation to comply with and [of what he is] to take along with him on it [i.e. on the expedition], [that] we get him under way and send him off, and [that], if not [i.e. if the articles of agreement have not been complied with], we notify Your Highness about whatever may be still lacking, and [that] in the meantime we hold up his departure until Your Highness shall transmit his orders as to what it is his pleasure that there be done in the matter, [we beg to report as follows]: At the time that we received Your Highness' letter Friar Pablo de Torres was not in Seville, for he had gone to Sanlúcar, and, be-

*Archives of the Indies, "Indiferente General," case 143, shelf 3, bundle 12.

cause people told us that they were expecting him every day and in order not to miss him on the way, we sent a messenger off to him with the request that he should let us know the situation in which the expeditionary fleet was, and whether he was to stay there: he came away just as soon as he had received our letter, and after his arrival in this city, and we three being about to depart for Sanlúcar, we together with Friar Pablo de Torres received a letter from Your Highness, dated the twentieth of the past [month], in which he [i.e. Your Highness] orders us, along with the Marquis of Cortes, Asistente in this city, to inquire about the possible total value of that which the English took off from the ship which came from the Indies [and] of which Francisco Gallego was the master, and how much the ship and merchandise were worth which they seized from the French inside the port of Sanlúcar, and to have an attachment put upon the property belonging to any English people that there were in this city and in the ports of this district up to the said total value, and one third more; and, in view of all this and of the order covering it which Your Highness directed to be sent to us, we went and had a talk with the Marquis of Cortes and we came to an agreement with him whereby one of us, namely Juan de Almansa, should remain behind to look after this matter; and the other two of us, namely the Treasurer and the Purser, with this arrangement agreed upon, went off to Sanlúcar, where, when we had arrived there, we inspected the vessels which the Adelantado Orellana has in that port, which are three in number, and we saw the supplies and the equipment and the guns which had been procured for them, and in Sanlúcar we found out about the men that he had and about another caravel which he has in the port of Santa María, which [caravel] one of us, namely the Purser, went and inspected, and because we concluded that the vessels lacked a certain amount of equipment and a certain number of guns, and likewise lacked supplies, we gave the Adelantado a statement of what we thought that he still lacked, in order that he might have the matter attended to, because without it [i.e. what they still lacked] the ships were not in condition to sail as they ought to; and we likewise saw the articles of agreement with him which Your Highness ordered to be drawn up, in order to see what under the terms of these he is under obligation to do, and it appears from them, just as we wrote to Your Highness in our last letter, that he is under obligation to take over three hundred men, and that one hundred of them are to be cavalrymen: in reply to [our inquiry about] this he said that he could not take along so many horses, nor [said he] could there be found room on board the ships for more than sixty horses at the most, and that the number of horses that he could take from here would be as many as twenty-four or twenty-five, and that he intended, [during his stop] in the Canary Islands and in the Cape Verde Islands, where he is to touch, to take on board there as many more horses as he would be able to take along; and that [as for] the total of three hundred men, he had that many there in Sanlúcar and in Seville and in the villages of the above-mentioned region; and that, as for the two boats the material for building which he is under obligation to take along, he was taking along everything in the way of nails and journeymen [in that line of work] that were needed, and that the lumber and rigging required for that purpose were to be had much more advantageously at the mouth of the [Amazon] River, where it was their [i.e. the expeditioners'] intention to build them, and that quite apart from all this he was taking along the lumber all cut out and the rigging for two brigantines.

In regard to the eight clergymen [he said] that he would take them along as he had contracted to do, and these are here in Seville waiting for the time when this expeditionary fleet shall be sent on its way.

And [he told us] that as for the caravels which he was to take along [to be used in going] up the river, all four ships which he was taking along were suited to that purpose.

And so far as the articles of agreement are concerned, it does not seem to us that by [virtue of] them he is under obligation to do anything else in Spain; and in view of what we have stated [above], both as regards his not complying with the terms of the agreement in the matter of the number of the horses and as regards his not having the ships thoroughly equipped, we served notice on him that, under penalty of a fine of ten thousand ducats and of the loss of the official positions and the favors which His Majesty has bestowed upon him, he was not to go off or leave that port until Your Highness should order that action be taken in the matter as Your Highness might think best, and just so he said that he would follow instructions, and notice of this order was served on him in the presence of Friar Pablo de Torres and of ourselves, in absolute secrecy, because if the men had learned that we were ordering him to be held back, they would have all left him and the expedition would have been ruined. What in our opinion is still needed for the hastening of this expedition in order to finish getting it started on its way and complete all the arrangements is something like one thousand ducats at the least; and this sum, according to what we have been told, we believe will be made up between those who have helped him out in the organization of this expedition and the passengers who are going along on it; but it will be necessary for Your Highness to give orders for the making up of the deficiency in the matter of horses; and also [Your Highness will probably have to make some special dispensations in Orellana's favor] because he is very seriously handicapped by a shortage of pilots and masters, for the reason that, since it [i.e. the expedition] is for an unfamiliar country, he can not find any competent pilots or masters, particularly any who are natives of these realms, and he has a Ragusan as master of the flagship, and with him a few more seamen from his country, and some Levantines, and the majority of the remainder of the seamen that he has are Flemings and Germans and [only] a few Spaniards; he did have a few Englishmen and Portuguese, whom we compelled him to discharge, and as for the Levantines and the Ragusans, although we told the Adelantado that he could not take them along and that we would not consent to their going along without permission from Your Highness, we did not try to have them put off from the ships, because, if he were to dismiss that Ragusan master, there would not be a single person left on the ships capable of looking after any one of them, and that would only be the cause of the ships' being wrecked [right there] in the port on account of their not having the full complement of men as required: in this whole matter may Your Highness order that action be taken along the lines that he may see fit to have the matter of the sending off of this expedition handled. Nothing else occurs [to us] on which it is our duty to report to Your Highness in this connection, save that it is our opinion that, if this expedition is not sent on its way within a short time, it will wear itself out of its own accord and will become disintegrated, because, since the men have been here for so long a time already, they are quite exhausted and broken down.

# XVI

*Four royal orders relating to various matters connected with Orellana's expedition.** From September, 1544, to April, 1545.

[1]

The Prince [says]:—Adelantado Don Francisco de Orellana, Governor and Captain-General of New Andalusia:—Through letters from Friar Pablo de Torres, general inspector for that [aforesaid] province, I have become posted on where you are at [in the progress which you are making] with your expedition and on the excellent prospects that there are for that undertaking, wherewith I have been well pleased, because I hold it to be certain that through your going over to that land Our Lord will be rendered a great service and the natives of it will be brought around to a knowledge of our holy Catholic faith; and, as you have already been given to understand, it is because the said Friar Pablo is the person that he is, and [a man] of so much experience and of such a righteous life and [one who serves as such a good] example, that His Majesty appointed him to the said position of general inspector; and there being combined in him, in the way that they are combined, so many good qualities, it is well that you always get advice from him on whatever you may have to undertake, because we hold it to be certain that he will advise you to do that which is right for the service of God and of His Majesty: and hence I charge you and order you to take counsel with the said Friar Pablo on whatever you may have to do connected with the work of launching this expedition and with the other matters which have been intrusted to you, and to accept his opinion, for thereby His Majesty will be rendered a service.

And because it might come about that a certain number of Portuguese might want to cross over with you to the said province of New Andalusia, and [because] it is believed that that would be a source of trouble, be warned [hereby] to avoid taking any of them along.—Valladolid, the fourth of September, in the year One Thousand Five Hundred and Forty-four.—*I the Prince.*—Countersigned by Pedro de los Cobos; initialed by Bernal and Velázquez and Gregorio López.

[2]

The Prince [says]:—Adelantado Don Francisco de Orellana, Governor of the Province of New Andalusia, and our officials appointed to positions there:—A story has come to me [the substance of] which is that people are saying that you are entering into a certain contract with a certain number of merchants covering certain aid which they are offering to furnish for [the purpose of making possible] the expedition which you, [speaking now to] the said Adelantado, are organizing for the exploration and colonizing of the said province, and that some of the articles of the said contract are in contradiction with the articles of agreement which the Emperor-King my master ordered to be drawn up in your favor authorizing the exploration of the said province, [this whole business, however, being something] which we do not consider to be true, because, after giving you such explicit orders relative to the observance and maintaining of what is set down in the said articles of agreement, we do not believe that you men will start anything new or make any contract whatsoever contrary to any aspect of it [i.e. the agreement]; and because, as you know, it is our will that the said articles of agree-

*Archives of the Indies, case 139, shelf 1, bundle 2.

ment be adhered to as a whole and in all details and that no action be taken or permitted contrary to them in any matter whatsoever, I order you to make no contract whatsoever with any merchant or other person contrary to the tenor and import of what is stated in the said articles of agreement and of the terms written into them; and if you should have occasion to make any contract, let it be [worked out in such a way that you will] not [be] going against what is stated in the said articles of agreement in any matter whatsoever: you shall first lay it before Friar Pablo de Torres, general inspector for the said province, to whom His Majesty has specifically assigned [the task of insisting upon] the observance of the said articles of agreement, along with other things appertaining to his service; for he, as a person of so much experience, will see what can be done about the matter and will say what he thinks about it, in order that nothing may be done in violation of the said articles of agreement; because no matter in what respect something might take place contrary to [what is stipulated in] them, His Majesty would be rendered a very bad service, and he would order steps to be taken in the matter as the case would require.—Valladolid, the fifth of November, in the year One Thousand Five Hundred and Forty-four.—*I the Prince.*—Countersigned by Pedro de los Cobos; initialed by Bernal and Gutierre Velázquez and Gregorio López.

[3]

The Prince [says]:—Devout Father Friar Pablo de Torres, chaplain to the Emperor-King, my master, and general inspector for the province of New Andalusia:—I have seen two letters, one [of which] is of the xxviiith of last month and [the other] of the ninth of the present month, together with the report which you sent relating to the doubts which existed in your mind, and I shall order that a reply to this matter be given to you in this letter.

2. The care which you are taking to notify me of the stage of preparation in which this expedition is [is something which] I am indebted to you for, and so I charge you to do this for the duration of time that you shall be in that city; and in regard to the aid which you ask me to order to be contributed in order that the undertaking may make some headway, at the present time there is no possibility of helping out with any money at all, because, as you have probably become well aware, the needs of His Majesty have been and are so great that they do not permit it.

3. As to what you say on the subject of its not being desirable that there go on this expedition turbulent individuals and persons who lead wicked lives, I am sending orders to the officials of His Majesty who have their headquarters in the House of Trade for the Indies not to allow to cross over with the said expedition such persons as you may deem best not to let cross over, as you will see by the order which accompanies this letter. You shall give notice of it [i.e. of the order].

4. Regarding the doubt which you say that you entertain as to whether there would not be some objection to permitting, for the present, that [both] stallions and mares be taken over together to that province of New Andalusia where you are going, here the opinion prevails that there is no such [objection] and that on the contrary it is well that they do be taken over [together], and hence there is no occasion for discussing this matter.

5. With regard to the other doubt which you say that you entertain in connection with the opinion which you hold to the effect that it would be well for the Spaniards, even though it were iron, steel [*sic*], or some other metals not known to the Indians yielded by the mines which they might find there, not to

exploit them [i.e. not to mine any metal] unless it be gold or silver, just now is not the time to talk about that: when you are over there you will be able to send word about the opinion that you may have as to what procedure it is advisable to follow; and [you shall] do the same in the matter of what you say relative to the idea that it is not advisable that arms of any sort be manufactured over there and that those that there could be any need for be taken over from here.

6.  As to the question about not giving arms to the Indians, and not selling them to them, and not trading them off with them in exchange for anything whatsoever, what you say has appeared to me to be right; and consequently I have ordered that a decree be issued covering this question, which [decree] I am ordering sent along with this letter: you shall take care to have this complied with.

7.  As regards what you say to the effect that it is not advisable that for the time being any Spaniard show or teach the Indians, [at least] for the next few years, any artisan's trade, [or how to do anything] except merely to serve God and obey His Majesty and till the soil, here the opinion is held that on the contrary there is an advantage in their giving their attention to artisan's trades, they having [fixed] hours and [a regular amount of] time for giving their attention to Christian teaching; and [you shall] arrange to have [this] done in this way.

8.  With regard to what you say relative to the opinion which you hold that it is desirable that no Spaniard over there be allowed for the present to possess or to order made any gold chain, or ring, or medal, or any object in gold, and [that] no silversmith or goldsmith over there be allowed to make objects out of gold for [wearing on] garments and use [as utensils], you and the Governor and His Majesty's officials shall talk over what is going to seem advisable to do in this matter, and whatever you may all think is right, that we order to be done.

9.  I have noted what you say relative to the question of whether the officials of His Majesty, who are the Treasurer, the Purser, [and] the Revenue Collector, are to pay the Adelantado Orellana for transportation, and [whether] any other official of His Majesty [is to do so], and how large a load [in personal effects] each one will be allowed to put on board in addition to food: along with this letter I am directing that there be sent an order to the effect that the officials of the House of Trade shall not permit that any innovation be introduced in this matter and that the thing be done just as it has been done in the case of other expeditionary fleets.

10.  With regard to what you say [to the effect that] it will be advisable that the Governor, before leaving these realms, present before the Council the persons whom he may be intending to appoint as his lieutenants, in order that they may be approved by it, you shall carefully see to it that the said Governor select for the said offices persons such as it shall be proper to appoint; and, in case he should not carry this out in this way, you shall advise me of it, in order that action may be taken as the case may require.

11.  And with regard to what you say in connection with the idea that it would be a good thing for Cosme de Chaves to go along on this expedition, because that would mean a particular protection and defense for the Indians, there is no occasion for taking any action in the matter here, because there where you in person are going, to whom His Majesty has already intrusted the protection and sheltering of the Indians, it is not necessary to intrust this matter to some other individual in particular: and consequently we beg you to exercise in this matter the care that we are confident that you will show.—Valladolid, the xviith day of

the month of October, in the year One Thousand Five Hundred and Forty-four.—
*I the Prince*.—Countersigned by Pedro de los Cobos; initialed by the Cardinal
of Seville and by Bernal, Velázquez, Gregorio López.

[4]

The Prince [says]:—Venerable and devout Father Friar Pablo de Torres, chaplain to the Emperor and King, my master, and his general inspector for the province of New Andalusia:—I have seen your letter of the eighth of the present month, in which you give me an account of how you went with the officials of the House of Trade to Sanlúcar to inspect the expeditionary fleet which the Adelantado Orellana has fitted out for the purpose of going to the said province of New Andalusia, and, in view of what you and the said officials have written to me regarding the matter, I have given orders to the said officials to the effect that, as soon as the said Adelantado should have complied with what they ordered him to comply with, they should let him go on his way, as you will hear from them. I charge you, in order that this may be put into execution, to do for your part whatever you may see to be proper; and, because for your journey you will find yourself in need of supplying yourself with a certain number of things, I am directing that an order be sent to you so that the officials of the House of Trade down there may pay you fifty ducats on account towards what you are to get from the position which you are going to occupy as general inspector.

In connection with what you say to the effect that the said Adelantado Orellana has made Vicencio de Monte, the revenue collector for the said province, his lieutenant-general and [that] to a brother of the said Monte he has given the office of chief constable, I am sending word to the said Adelantado ordering him not to give the said positions to the above-mentioned [individuals] or to any other foreigner whatsoever, [that is to say, to any persons] other than natives of these realms, as you will see by the order which accompanies this letter: you shall cause him to be duly notified of it [i.e. of the order], and you shall advise me with regard to the fulfilment of it.—Valladolid, the eighteenth day of the month of April, in the year One Thousand Five Hundred and Forty-five.

And because through your letters we have been made to understand that it is not advisable that a certain few persons go along on the expedition, we are sending orders to the officials to the effect that, [as regards] the persons whom you shall designate [as individuals] about whom you possess information [making it evident] that it is not desirable that they cross over, they [i.e. the authorities] shall not let these go or cross over with the expedition: you shall exercise the care that it is proper [that you exercise] in this matter, just as it is placed in your hands.—
*I the Prince*.—Countersigned by Sámano; initialed by the Cardinal, Bernal, Gutierre Velázquez, Gregorio López.

# XVII

*Record of the statement made by Francisco de Guzmán, who came in on the caravel named "Concepción" (the master of which is Pedro Sánchez, a citizen of Cadiz) and who is one of those who went away with the Adelantado Orellana.** No date.*

He says that: Orellana started out on the eleventh of May from Sanlúcar de Barrameda: he started out with four ships complete, on board which he carried

*Archives of the Indies, "Patronato," 2-5-1/14, No. 1, section 15.

away four hundred fighting men: he went and made port at Teneriffe, where he stayed three months: from there he went with the same fleet to Cape Verde [Islands], where he stayed two months, and as a consequence of the fact that the region was infected with disease, there died there ninety-eight persons from among those who had joined his expedition, and there must have stayed behind as many as fifty who were not in condition to continue on the journey: of the four ships which he had at the start it was necessary to dismantle one in order to fit out the others with hawsers and anchors, because in the above-mentioned port he had lost eleven anchors at the time that he had left there. He departed from the said port [i.e. from the Cape Verde Islands] with three ships, on board each of which he had from sixty-seven to one hundred persons, steering his course toward the coast of Brazil: the weather conditions were very unfavorable to him, and all on board would have perished if it had not been for a heavy downpour of rain, from which source they supplied themselves with a certain amount of water; and amidst this hardship and struggling one [ship] put in toward land, [the persons on board] saying that they had no water, which ship had on board seventy-seven persons, people in good health, and eleven horses, and one brigantine, regarding which said ship up to the present time nothing more has ever been heard: with our two ships which were left, thanks to a north wind, we again worked our way back up over the distance that we had edged off from our course on account of the adverse weather conditions. We went and reconnoitered the shoals of San Roque, and taking our bearings from the shore we went in close, on the lookout for the Marañón; and as far as a hundred leagues down the coast, [all] within half a degree [of latitude], twelve leagues out at sea we came upon fresh water, where Orellana said that in there was the river out through which he had passed. On the following day, the day of Saint Mary of the O, we went ashore inside [the mouth of] the river on two islands which we found there, inhabited, where there was given to us in exchange for our barter goods a full supply of food in the form of maize and cassava and fish and a variety of fruit produced in the land. There several persons from among us told the said Orellana, considering that the members of his party were quite worn out from the hardships which they had gone through, and likewise because eleven of his horses were quite run down on account of their having drunk only two *azumbres* [i.e. about a gallon] of water per day, and since that land was just the place to revive his men and his horses, and because it would be a good idea to have one of the brigantines which he had brought over there put together for the purpose of reconnoitering the principal branch up which they were to go with the vessels . . . *; and in reply to this he told us that he knew that the country was quite thickly settled and that there would be plenty of facilities for doing what is stated above: and so we went ahead with two vessels as much as a hundred leagues up the river, where we came upon four or five Indian cabins [and] where we stopped [in order to]† build a brigantine, and we struck a country [so poor] that there was little food to be had [in it], in consequence whereof there died on our hands there fifty-seven persons. We stayed there engaged in building the brigantine three months: we set out from there with the brigantine and one of the ships, for the other one had been broken up to supply the nails and the planking of the brigantine. The navigating which we did in this way was to the south, and in order to look for

*Something is wanting here in the original.
†[Inserted in the text as published by Medina.—Editor.]

the principal branch it was necessary to sail to the southeast, and when we had proceeded on for twenty leagues, at a time when we were anchored, the heavy current of the tide caused one of the hawsers that we had [out] to break, in consequence whereof we could not avail ourselves of the ship [any longer], except [to the extent of using] the nails for a [small] boat, whereupon we broke her up; and with this equipment we went off to a miserable Indian settlement, where out of boards from boxes we built a small boat in which to continue on our way: it took us two and a half months to build it, and at this place [where we started to build it] as many as thirty of us were left behind, and Orellana went away, saying that he was going to look for the principal branch of the river, and, at the end of twenty-seven days completely gone by, not finding it he came back to where we were, and, perceiving that short of thirty days from then we would not be able to launch the boat, he went off again saying that he was ill and would not be able to wait for us, and that, by way of saving time, inasmuch as he did not have men [enough] to be able to set up a colony, he wanted to go back again to look for the branch of the river and go up as far as the point of San Juan to barter for a certain amount of gold or silver to send to His Majesty, and that if we felt like following him after our boat should be built, we should find [him]* somewhere around there; and in this way we stayed behind building the boat and we applied ourselves so skilfully to establishing friendly relations with the chiefs of that country that they used to come and sell food to us by barter; and so it was that, at the time that we launched the boat, a certain chief went away with us in [one of a group of] six canoes, giving us in exchange for our barter goods all the food that we needed, and we giving them [i.e. this chief and his subjects] to understand that we were going to make war on those [i.e. the inhabitants] of Caripuna, because from statements of theirs we had come to realize that they were their enemies; and in this way they took us up the river for a distance of thirty-seven leagues as far as the islands of Marribuique and Caritán, and from there on [we no longer needed (?)] that chief, who supplied us with so much food that it became necessary for us to get away from there on account of there not being room for it all in the boat, because during the three days that we were there [i.e. on the journey thus far (?)] never did there cease to be alongside us anywhere from sixty to a hundred canoes; and there that chief stopped who had been going along with us, and [then] the chief of the [island of] Marribuique went along and showed us the way; and thus we resumed our voyage up the river for a distance of over thirty leagues at least, [to a place] where we found three important branches, and going on farther up we found all that great quantity of water to belong to one branch, which must be all of twelve leagues wide; and because the boat was letting in a lot of water and because we were short of oarsmen, on account of our being few in numbers, and also because we were running short of barter goods, perceiving that we could not render any service to His Majesty [by going on], and for the sake of safeguarding our persons, we agreed among ourselves to turn back; and so, steering our course down the river for a distance of forty leagues, we came upon a section of country which we took to be mainland, which [section of country] was composed of very large savanas and of land well taken up by sown fields producing foodstuffs [and] belonging to the same Indians: down through the middle of this country there runs an estuary which seemed to us to come from a highland, and by it the greater part of this country

*[Inserted in the text as published by Medina.—EDITOR.]

can be irrigated, [that is to say] by the estuary: this country the Indians call Comao, and they came forth to meet us in an attitude of peace and gave us in exchange for our barter goods cassava and maize in great plenty, sweet potatoes and yams, fish, ducks and hens and cocks of [the same breed as in] Spain: here there was found a turkey of [the same sort as is found in] Spain. In this country there were villages comprising sixty and seventy cabins: there penetrated ten or twelve men from among our number for a distance of four or six leagues into the interior of the country; they brought back in exchange for their barter goods fifty and a hundred Indians laden with food: at the time of our departure there remained behind from among our number six men, of their own free will and because they considered the country to be a good one; four leagues farther down the river a sailor turned back and left us, and three soldiers in the small boat which we had with us went back, [so] we became convinced, with the others; and so it was that we sailed on down the river [and out to sea] until we came to Margarita, where we found Orellana's wife, who told us that her husband had not succeeded in getting into the main branch which he was looking for, and [that] consequently, [and particularly] on account of his being ill, he had made up his mind to come to a land of Christians: and [that] during this time, when he was out looking for food for the journey, the Indians shot seventeen of his men with arrows. From grief over this and from his illness Orellana died somewhere up the river: this river [here] trends from north to south, the coast runs from east to west; the latitude having been taken there where we went in and there where we came out, it [i.e. the river] has a width of mouth of fifty-seven leagues: it must be borne in mind that this whole river is full of islands.

Orellana's wife went along with her husband on the whole trip up to the time when he died, and [then] she came on to the [island of] Margarita, where this passenger found her and [where] she told him [i.e. Francisco de Guzmán] what he states above.*

# XVIII

*Extracts from a judicial inquiry, put through the court in Lima in the month of December, 1558, on behalf of Diego Muñoz Ternero, covering services rendered in connection with the expedition of Francisco de Orellana to New Andalusia.†*

In the City of the Kings [i.e. Lima] in these realms and provinces of Peru, on the twentieth day of the month of December in the year One Thousand Five Hundred and Fifty-eight, before the president and judges of the Royal Audiencia and Chancery which in the name of His Majesty are established in this said city, and before me, Francisco de Caravajal, clerk of the court in the said Royal Audiencia, Diego Muñoz Ternero, a clerk of the court in it [i.e. in the same Royal

---

*It can be plainly seen that this last paragraph was added on to the document, in a handwriting of the time and, apparently, in the Council chamber.

†Archives of the Indies, "Patronato," 1-4-12/17, section 10. In spite of what I said on page 7 of the present volume, Don Pedro Torres Lanzas, First Assistant to the Keeper of Records in the Archives of the Indies, has recently had the kindness to call my attention to the existence of these files. I take advantage of this opportunity to acknowledge publicly in this place my gratitude towards Señor Torres Lanzas for his kindness on this occasion as well as on other occasions when he has favored me with his very valuable coöperation.

Audiencia], presented a petition and [a series of questions arranged as] articles, the wording of which is as follows:

Very powerful Sire:—I, Diego Muñoz Ternero, your [Highness'] scrivener and [clerk] of the court in this Royal Audiencia, do declare: that I have good reason for causing to be executed a taking of testimony relative to what I have accomplished in serving Your Highness ever since I crossed over to the Indies invested with the office of governor's scrivener in New Andalusia, the colonizing and conquest of which were intrusted to the Adelantado Don Francisco de Orellana, and afterwards in this realm. I beg Your Highness [to order] that it [i.e. the petition] be received, and that the witnesses be questioned by means of the following questions:

1.—Under the first question, whether they know the said Diego Muñoz Ternero.

2.—*Item*, whether they know that in the year forty-four [i.e. 1544] I was appointed by His Majesty chief scrivener to the governor in New Andalusia, the colonizing and conquest of which were intrusted to the Adelantado Orellana, [my appointment being] in recognition of my ability and breadth of knowledge.

3.—*Item*, whether they know that in the city of Seville, at the time when I was associated with the said Adelantado, he put forth a great effort in forming the fleet for the said expedition, buying ships and arms and munitions, and attending to other necessary matters, spending what [wealth] he possessed: and [that] in connection with that I had a great deal of work [to do] and expense [to bear] during the period of one year that the said Adelantado was there.

4.—*Item*, whether they know that I embarked on a ship belonging to the said fleet and came over on the said expedition, eventually reaching the great river Marañón; and [that] on the way, not only on the islands of Teneriffe and Cape Verde, but also in the course of the sailing [over the sea], we put up with many hardships and dangers and much suffering from the lack of food and other things, and [that] every day [we were] on the verge of perishing.

5.—*Item*, whether they know that after we had proceeded a considerable distance inside [the mouth of] the said river with two ships, the said Orellana had them broken up and [that] he fitted out one of the brigantines which he had brought over in lumber [all cut out], by means of which we went about exploring [to see] what there was up the said river.

6.—*Item*, whether they know that after we had located the shore of the said river, on account of its being lined with great shoals which extend far out into the water, at the entrance we were on the verge of being wrecked.

7.—*Item*, whether they know that after we had entered the river, having passed by the first [sections of country inhabited by] Indians, we came upon great swamp lands and wild forests and uninhabited regions, and went for many days without striking an inhabited district, and [that] when we did strike one, owing to the great shortage of food which we suffered from, there died a great number out of the said party, and others the Indians killed in the skirmishes which we had with them while searching for food.

8.—*Item*, whether they know that, after what is stated above was over, we being on peaceful terms with certain Indians, the said Orellana announced that he desired to go in the said brigantine and with a certain number of persons belonging to the said party to do some exploring farther up the river, and [gave orders to the effect] that we should remain behind on one of its islands, [saying] that he would come back promptly and would tell us what we were to do.

9.—*Item*, whether they know that, after the said Orellana had departed with a certain number of the said men, in view of the fact that he was staying away a long time and no news was being had of him, we built a boat at the cost of much [hard] work, in which we went a very long way up the said river in search of the said Orellana, getting as far as the province of Caripuna, and on account of our having obtained no news of him, and on account of there being actually not more than twenty-eight persons in our party all together, we agreed among ourselves to turn back down the river, and [that] both on our way up the river and on our way down it we experienced many close calls and dangers.

10.—*Item*, whether they know that for building the said boat we lacked many of the accessories needed, and [that] it was built at the cost of much [hard] work, and [that] it let in a great amount of water, so that it seemed as if it would be impossible to navigate in it.

11.—*Item*, whether they know that, being aware that if we made up our minds to stay somewhere along the course of the said river and not go out to sea [and on] to whatever place the current along the coast might carry us, we could not escape with our lives, because the Indians would massacre us, we agreed among ourselves to go out to sea in spite of the great risk.

12.—*Item*, whether they know that out of the small number of men composing our party who had remained behind there, eleven of them made up their minds to remain behind [and live] among the Indians and not go out to sea, because of their being convinced, as they were convinced, that we could not escape from there alive by any means, and [that] they ran away from us, and [that] in any attempt to look for them we should surely all have been lost, and [that] consequently we came away without them.

13.—*Item*, whether they know that after we had gotten out to sea the flood tides hurled us back again among the mangrove swamps, from which it was considered to be impossible to extricate one's self, according to the opinion held by Francisco López, from Cadiz, the pilot who took us into the said river.

14.—*Item*, whether they know that, sailing along the coast, owing to the fact that the boat was such a wretched one we were many times on the point of sinking, and [that] we underwent very great hardships, from which we had no respite by day or by night, emptying water out of it [i.e. out of the boat] with the pump and also with various sorts of vessels; and [that] we endured great hunger, and [that this was] due to the shortage which existed in [the supply of] food on account of there being no place from which to obtain some or find some.

15.—*Item*, whether they know that in spite of the said hardships we reached the Island of Margarita and there found the wife of the said Orellana and the persons who had gone off with him, and from them learned that, though he was supposed to go up the river, as he had told us, he had turned down the river headed for the said island, and on the way had died, [all of] which being sufficient cause for our becoming infallibly lost, without [the possibility of] there ever being heard any news about us, inasmuch as there was no salvation [for us] by going on overland, and [particularly in view of our] not knowing where we could come to a haven [of rescue], and [also for the reason] that to go down and out by the sea was an undertaking fraught with so much danger, as has been stated: and [that] hence those who had come on with him considered us as dead and lost, and [looked upon it] as something extremely difficult [to do] to be able to get out of there.

16.—*Item*, whether they know that as a result of the great hardships already related those of us who came on in the said boat remained [for some time] on the said Island of Margarita very ill and at the point of death.

. . . . . . . . . . . . . . . . . . . . . . . .

The first witness, Francisco Orellana.—The said Francisco de* Orellana, residing in this City of the Kings [i.e. Lima], a witness accepted in connection with the said judicial inquiry and taking of testimony, relative to [past] services, which are being put through the court by normal legal procedure at the request of the said Diego Muñoz Ternero, having taken the oath in due legal form and being questioned by means of the general questions of the law and by means of the [questions here designated as] articles for which he was admitted, made the following statements:

1.—Under the first article he said that he had known the said Diego Muñoz Ternero over a period of from fourteen to fifteen years down to the present, slightly more or less [as to the] time, not only in the realms of Spain but also in these of Peru and in other parts of the Indies, by sight and to speak to, by dealings, and by personal relations.

Questioned by means of the general questions of the law, he said that he was over fifty-five years of age, and that he was not a relative of the said Diego Muñoz Ternero, and [that] none of the remaining general questions of the law affected him personally or offended him.

2.—Under the second article he said that he knew that the said Diego Muñoz Ternero had been appointed chief scrivener to the governor in New Andalusia quite possibly as long ago as the article states, slightly more or less, and [that] he knew that the said governorship and colonizing and conquest had all been intrusted to the Adelantado Orellana; all of which this witness [i.e. he] knew because he had come over as a servant of the said Adelantado on the expedition which he had organized for the said conquest; and this [is what] he said in answering under this article.

3.—Under the third article he said that he knew and had seen that there had taken place that which is related in it, because, as he had already stated, this witness [i.e. he] had been a servant of the said Adelantado Orellana and had resided [while] in his service in the said city of Seville during the time that he [i.e. Orellana] had been in it, and had helped to accomplish that which the article tells about, and had seen how the said Diego Muñoz had been engaged in the affair stated above during the time mentioned in the said article, slightly more or less; and [he said that] he believed that he [i.e. Diego Muñoz] had spent on it a part of what [wealth] he possessed, for the reason that in this same way other soldiers had done so who had come over with the said Adelantado on the said expedition: and this [is what] he said in answering under this article.

4.—Under the fourth article he said that he knew about the matter referred to in the said article because he had been a witness to, and a sharer in, the hardships which had been put up with and endured on the said voyage; and [that] on [the ships of] the said expeditionary fleet he had seen the said Diego Muñoz Ternero, who had put up with them all [i.e. the hardships].

5.—Under the fifth article he said that he knew [that] what is recounted in the said article had come to pass and had taken place just as it is explained in it,

*[Thus in the text as printed by Medina, possibly as a result of a printer's error, if not of a purely mechanical error by Medina himself. This man must not be confused with the Adelantado.— EDITOR.]

because he had witnessed it with his own eyes and had taken part in it and had seen the said Diego Muñoz [taking part in it] as the article states.

6.—Under the sixth article he said that he knew about the matter as it is stated therein because [he remembered that] at the entrance to the said river they had lost the anchors of the ships in which the expeditionary force had crossed over and had been on the verge of being shipwrecked, and [that] because of the lack of anchors they had been in the habit of anchoring with guns, and [that] the greater part of these they had lost on the reefs and shoals that extend out into the water along the shore of the said river: and this he said in answering under this article, because he had been a witness to it.

7.—Under the seventh article he said that he knew and had [actually] seen that the said Adelantado Orellana, after he had gone into the said river, had sent a brigantine with a certain number of men to reconnoiter the [Indian] settlements that there were inside [the mouth of] the said river, and had seen how among those who had gone in the said brigantine one was the said Diego Muñoz Ternero; and [that] they had proceeded on for a great distance through uninhabited country and swamp lands, and in the way that the article states, and had endured terrific hunger and suffering owing to the great shortage of food which they had experienced; and [that] the situation had become so serious that several of those who had gone in the said brigantine had died from the hardships and hunger which they had endured: all of which this witness [said that he] knew because he had taken part in what the said article states, along with the rest who had been there.

8.—Under the eighth article he said that he knew about, and had been a witness to, that which the said article relates, because he had seen the said Adelantado go off and explore in a brigantine along with a certain number of soldiers up the said river, and [he said] that the rest had remained behind on an island, to which persons the said Adelantado had said what the article states, because this witness [i.e. he] had been present [there] and had remained behind on the said island, because he had been the man in charge of dealing out food to the soldiers out of that which they purchased by barter from the Indians of the land: and this [was what] he said in answering under this article.

9.—Under the ninth article he said that he knew [that] what is stated in the said article had come about and had taken place just as it is explained in it, because he was one of those who had built the said brigantine and gone up and back in it, and in it [had taken part] in that which is related in the said article, and had seen that there had been undergone considerable toil and suffering, and that in [all] this the said Diego Muñoz had been right there among the other soldiers who had taken part in it.

10.—Under the tenth article he said that he knew about the matter referred to in it and had been a witness to the fact that many times they had steered into estuaries of the said river for the purpose of repairing the said boat in which they had been proceeding, on account of the large amount of water that it had been letting in, for they had not been able to make it water-tight owing to their lack of [proper] materials and tools for building the said boat and brigantine; in which [brigantine], in spite of great hardships, they had reached the said Island of Margarita, which is a part of Cubagua.

11.—Under the eleventh article he said that he knew that for fear of that which the said article states they had made up their minds to quit the said island [in the Amazon where they were camped] in spite of the risk and the chance which he had already mentioned, [and had gone on] until they had reached the said Island of Margarita: and this [was what] he said in answering under this article.

12.—Under the twelfth article he said that he knew about the matter related in the said article because, when he had gone to look for food [as provisions] for proceeding out to sea and had penetrated into the interior on the mainland, he had seen [how] there had remained behind the soldiers of whom mention is made in the said question and articles; and [that] they had spoken to this witness [i.e. him] to get him to remain there with them, and [that] he had not been willing to, [that] on the contrary, on getting back to the boat, he had told his companions about the decision which the said soldiers had arrived at of remaining in that country, and [that] this witness [i.e. he] and the rest of the companions had gone back again to the land [i.e. the mainland] to look for them and had many times come upon the places round about where they had been in the habit of going and had never found them, and [that] on the other hand the said soldiers had not come in answer to the cries which they had called out to them, and so had stayed there, and [that] this witness [i.e. he] and the said Diego Muñoz and the rest of the companions had come away to the said boat in which they had been navigating.

13.—Under the thirteenth article he said that he knew that it [i.e. the matter referred to] had come about and had taken place exactly as the said article states, and [that] those who had been coming along that way had considered it as certain that they would not escape alive, and [that] this witness [i.e. he] and others, friends and companions of his, had gone around looking for something out of which to build rafts in order to be able to get away from there on a chance, because they had considered it as certain that the said boat was not going to be able to get out from among the said mangroves on account of the heavy swell and sea surf that there were in among them.

14.—Under the fourteenth article he said that he knew about the matter related in the said article because it had come about and had taken place exactly as it is explained therein; and this witness had already related this matter under the articles preceding this one, to which he referred back.

15.—Under the fifteenth article he said that he knew about the matter related in the said article because when this witness [i.e. he] and the said Diego Muñoz and the rest of the companions had arrived at Margarita, they had found on that island the wife of the said Adelantado and some other soldiers who had come with her, all of whom had been amazed to see them, because they had been considering them as lost and dead; and [he said that] the said soldiers who were on the said island had told them how the said Adelantado, finding himself to be a very sick man, [and the few men with him] had agreed among themselves to turn back down the river, as [indeed] he had turned back, and that before he had been able to get out to sea he had died.

16.—Under the sixteenth article he said that he had seen how out of the total number of soldiers who had come in the said boat to the said Island of Margarita the majority of them had fallen sick, and among them the said Diego Muñoz, and [how] he [i.e. Diego Muñoz] had been at the point of death, as the article states, as a result of the hardships, hunger spells, and sufferings which he had already stated [that] they had endured during the said journey . . .

. . . and [he said] that what he had stated was the truth, under burden of the oath which he had taken, and in [all] this matter he confirmed and vouched for his statements, his declaration being read to him, and he did not sign it because he said that he did not know how to write: he made this declaration before me, Francisco López, His Majesty's scrivener.

The second witness, Antonio Pérez de Vibero.—The said Antonio Pérez de Vibero, residing in this capital, a witness accepted in connection with the said judicial inquiry, having sworn in due legal form and being questioned by means of the general questions of the law and by means of the [questions here designated as] articles for which he was admitted, made the following statements:

1.—Under the first article he said that he had known the said Diego Muñoz Ternero since the year [One Thousand] Five Hundred and Forty-five right down to the present, which makes about thirteen years, [or] a slightly longer or shorter period of time.

Questioned by means of the general questions of the law, he said that he was forty years old, slightly more or less [in an exact reckoning of] time, and that he was not a relative of the said Diego Muñoz Ternero and [that] not any of the remaining general questions of the law had any direct effect upon this witness [i.e. upon him].

2.—Under the second article he said that what he knew about the matter referred to in the said article was that he had seen the said Diego Muñoz Ternero come over as secretary to the Adelantado Orellana and as chief scrivener to the governor in New Andalusia, because he had seen take place in his presence all the business transactions which the said Adelantado had handled from [the time when he was in] the port of Sanlúcar, where this witness [i.e. he] had made his acquaintance, to [the time of his arrival in] the Amazon River, the conquest of which said [region] this witness [i.e. he] knew [had been]* intrusted to the said Adelantado Orellana; and this witness [said that he] had gone with him on the said expedition into the interior and voyage of exploration: and this [was what] he said in answering under this article.

3.—Under the third article he said that he had heard the said Diego Muñoz Ternero recount what is stated in the said article.

4.—Under the fourth article he said that he knew about the matter referred to in the said article just as it is stated therein, because he had seen it [all] come about and take place just as it is explained therein, as a consequence of his having come over, as he had come over, on the said expedition; and [he said that] he had undergone the hardships which the article mentions, along with the said Diego Muñoz and the rest of the soldiers who had come over on the said expedition.

5.—Under the fifth article he said that what he knew about the matter related in the said article was that, when they had gone in, with two ships which were still left out of the four which had started out from Seville carrying the said expedition, [a certain distance] up the Marañón River and [read: "or" (?)] the Amazon, the said Adelantado [and his men], after they had moved on and [had] proceeded for a certain number of days with the said ships up the said river, had gone ashore in the neighborhood of some Indian cabins which they had come upon and had there built the brigantine; [and that] they had started out with it and with the other ship [i.e. that one out of the two which they had not sacrificed

*[Inserted in the text as printed by Medina.—EDITOR.]

for material needed to build the brigantine] to do some exploring up the river, and [that] within a few days after that the other ship [i.e. the one just mentioned] had been broken up, and out of its lumber a boat had been built: and this [was what] he said in answering under this article.

6.—Under the sixth article he said that he knew about the matter related in the said article because he had seen that it had [all] come about and had taken place just as it is explained therein.

7.—Under the seventh article he said that what he knew about that which is related in it was that in the course of the said exploring there had been found in the middle of the said river many swampy islands and a few covered with vast forest lands, in which there had died many of the said persons making up the expedition from ills and sicknesses which it had fallen to their lot to contract as a result of the hardships and hunger spells which they had undergone during the said expedition of exploration; all of which this witness [i.e. he] had seen with his own eyes, and [he said that] he had been ill as a result of enduring the said hardships and sufferings, in which the said Diego Muñoz Ternero had had a share like the rest of the soldiers.

8.—Under the eighth article he said that he knew about that which is mentioned in the said article because he had seen that it had come about and had taken place exactly as it is stated and explained therein; and this witness [said that he] was one of those who had remained behind on the island of which mention is made in this article, and [that] in the same way the said Diego Muñoz Ternero had remained behind on the said island.

9.—Under the ninth article he said that he knew about that which is related in the said article because he had taken part in it along with Diego Muñoz Ternero and the rest of the soldiers who had remained behind on the said island and [had helped] in the building of the said boat; in all of which [he said that] he had seen that numerous and very great and [even] excessive hardships and sufferings had been endured, because in order to build the said boat they had gone for nails and other needed materials to the ship which had been abandoned as a wreck a league or a league and a half away from there, and that they had kept going back and forth on errands of this sort many times, and [also] to the forest to cut lumber for the said task, and had been in the habit of carrying it on their backs: and [he said that] in the excursion upstream and back which they had made, following the said river in the said boat, they had encountered infinite hardships and enormous risks for their lives.

10.—Under the tenth article he said that with regard to what [is mentioned] in this question he would say what he had already said in connection with the question preceding this one, to which [statements] he referred back, and that he knew that there had been lacking many things needed for the task of building the said boat, in consequence whereof they had realized every day that they were in danger of losing their lives through lack of lashing ropes and through the excess of water which the said boat was letting in.

11.—Under the eleventh article he said that he knew that that which is related in the said article had come about and had taken place exactly as it is explained therein; and that, even if the Indians had not killed them, if they had remained on the said island they would have died off and [all] perished from hunger, because there was no food whatsoever to enable them to sustain themselves.

12.—Under the twelfth article he said that he knew about that which is related in the said article, just as it is explained therein, and that he had heard those who stayed there say that they were staying behind out of fear lest just as soon as [in any attempt to get away from where they were] they should start out [they would not be able to escape with their lives], and [that] the rest who had come on in the said boat had heard them say that they were staying behind out of fear lest just as soon as they should go out to sea they would not be able to escape with their lives: and this [was what] he said in answering under this article.*

13.—Under the thirteenth article he said that what he knew about that which is related in the said article was that one afternoon when they had gone out to sea in the said boat, almost at nightfall, they had found themselves high and dry owing to the fact that the tide had run out, and [that] afterwards, when the tide had come in, it had carried the said boat up into a swampy inlet, causing a great risk to them, and [that] there they had been held for two or three days enduring considerable suffering caused by mosquitoes.

14.—Under the fourteenth article he said that he knew that it [i.e. what is told in this article] had come about and had taken place exactly as it is explained therein, because this witness [i.e. he] had come on in the said boat, just as he had already stated under the articles preceding this one, to which he referred back.

15.—Under the fifteenth article he said that in the said boat, and amidst the hardships and dangers which he had already mentioned, they had reached the Island of Margarita, where they had found the wife of the Adelantado Orellana and a certain number of soldiers who had gone off with him in the brigantine, all of whom had been amazed when they had seen them [come in], because they had considered them as lost and dead; and [he said that] they had told this witness [i.e. him] and the others who had made the voyage in the said boat all the rest which the question tells about: and this [was what] he said in answering under this article.

16.—Under the sixteenth article he said that he knew, and had been a witness to, the fact that some of those who had come on in the said boat to the said island had become sick and had fallen ill upon arriving there, and [all] from the hardships and sufferings which they had endured on the said journey . . .

. . . and [he said that] everything which he had stated was the truth, under burden of the oath which he had taken; and [that] in everything that he had stated and declared he had seen [that] the said Diego Muñoz Ternero had taken part and had shared the said hardships, dangers, and sufferings and illnesses, like the rest who had been right there, and in [all] this matter he affirmed and vouched for [the truth of] his statements, [his declaration] being read to him, and he signed it with his name.—*Antonio Perez de Vibero.*—He made this declaration before me, *Francisco Lopez*, His Majesty's scrivener.

A witness, Juan Griego.—The said Juan Griego, a shipmaster and pilot, who said that he was a native of Greece, residing in this city, a witness brought in on behalf of the said Diego Muñoz, having sworn in due legal form and being questioned by means of the questions for which he had been brought in, made the following statements:

---

*[This rather involved paragraph is marked with a "(*sic*)" in the text as published by Medina. For the sake of the translation offered here, admittedly none too satisfying, it has been assumed that the verb form "sabían" which follows the first "de miedo desque" ("out of fear lest just as soon"), difficult to understand as "they knew" or "they should know," is an error for "salían."—EDITOR.]

1.—[In reply] to the first question he said that he had known the said Diego Muñoz for more than fourteen years, slightly more or less.

General [questions of the law].—Questioned by means of the general questions, he said that he was thirty-five years of age, slightly more or less, and that he was not a relative or an enemy [of the said Diego Muñoz], and that none of the general questions which had been put to him affected him personally.

2.—[In reply] to the second question he said that he knew about [the matter referred to in] the question just as it is stated therein: asked how he knew about [the matter referred to in] it, he said that [it was] because this witness [i.e. he] had [actually] seen that the Adelantado had been wont to call him the secretary and scrivener of the said province and its governor, and [that] in the same way all the rest of the persons who had come over on the said expedition [had been in the habit of speaking of him], and [that] as in the presence of the said scrivener this witness [i.e. he] had seen that all the business transactions had been handled and not in the presence of some other person [as witness], and [that] as such [a functionary] he had been looked upon and considered.

3.—[In reply] to the third question he said that he likewise knew about [the matter referred to in] it just as it is stated therein: asked how he knew about [the matter referred to in] it, he said that [it was] because this witness [i.e. he] had been a sailor on the flagship on board which the said Adelantado had sailed away on the said expedition, and [that] he had seen [all] this come about and take place just as the question states, and [that] for this reason he knew about it.

4.—Under article four he said that he knew about [the matter referred to in] the question just as it is stated therein because this witness [i.e. he] had taken passage and had come over on the said expedition with the said Adelantado and [with] Diego Muñoz on board a [certain] ship, and [that] he had been a witness to it [all] in the way that the article explains it.

5.—Under the fifth article he said that in the same way he knew about [the matter referred to in] the question just as it is stated therein: asked how he knew about [the matter referred to in] it, he said that [it was] because he had seen it [all] come about and take place just as it says in the question.

6.—Under the sixth article he said that he knew about [the matter referred to in] the question just as it is stated therein because this witness [i.e. he] had seen [that they had met with difficulties], after they had located the shore of the said river, on account of its being lined with great shoals which extend, for the most part, [far] out into the water, and [that] at the entrance they had all been on the verge of being wrecked.

7.—Under the seventh article he said that he knew about [the matter referred to in] the question just as it is stated therein: asked how he knew about [the matter referred to in] it, he said that [it was] because he had seen it [all] come about and take place just as it says in the question; and [that] he had taken part in all the rest of the skirmishes which had been fought.

8.—Under the eighth article he said that in the same way he knew about [the matter referred to in] the article just as it is stated therein because he had seen it [all] come about and take place just as the article states, and [that] this witness [i.e. he] had gone with the said Adelantado Orellana in the brigantine which the question mentions.

9.—Under article nine he said that what he knew about [the matter referred to in] it was that, as he had already stated, this witness [i.e. he] had gone with the said Governor as far as a hundred and fifty leagues on up, and [that] when they had come back they had not found the said Diego Muñoz nor the rest of the men where the said Adelantado had left them, "and we went about in search of them," and [that] afterwards the said Governor got out of [the valley of] the river and [that] they [i.e. Orellana's followers] came into port at Margarita; and [he added that] while he had been there this witness [i.e. he] had [actually] seen that the said Diego Muñoz, together with the rest of the party, had put into port on the said island, where he had seen them and [where] they had told him that they had endured what the article states.

10.—Under article ten he said that that which is stated in the article was the truth, because at the time that the said Governor had separated from them he had not left them anything in the way of facilities or materials for [building] the boat which the article mentions, and [that] for this reason he knew about the matter.

11.—[In reply] to question eleven he said that that which is related in the article was the truth and [that] he knew about it, because the said Governor and this witness [i.e. he] together had come out by the same way and had incurred much risk, and [that it was] for this reason [that] he knew about it.

12.—Under article twelve he said that that which is related in the article he had heard the said Diego Muñoz and others tell about at the time when they had all become re-united and had met one another on the said Island of Margarita, and that this [was what] he knew in connection with the question.

13.—Under article thirteen he said that he knew about the matter referred to in the article for the reason that the same thing had happened to this witness [i.e. to him] and to the rest of them at the time when they had come out of the said river.

14.—[In reply] to question fourteen he said that this witness [i.e. he] believed and considered as certain that they had endured the hardships which the article mentions, because the others had gone through the same thing; and [that] just in this way this witness [i.e. he] had heard it related by the said Diego Muñoz and by the pilot [of whom]* mention is made in the article preceding this one, [and who had stated] that what is recounted in this article had [really] taken place.

15.—Under article fifteen he said that he knew about [the matter referred to in] the question just as it is stated therein: asked how he knew about [the matter referred to in] it, he said that [it was] because this witness [i.e. he] was one of those who had gone with the said Governor and had come out [of that region], and [that] he [i.e. the said Governor] had died on the way, "and we came into port on the said Island of Margarita," just as the article states, and [that] he had seen [all this], and [that] it was for this reason that he knew about [the matter related in] it [i.e. the question].

16.—Under article sixteen he said that he knew about [the matter referred to in] the question just as it is stated therein: asked how he knew about [the matter referred to in] it, he said that [it was] because he had seen it [all] come about and take place just as the article says.

A witness, Francisco de Ulloa.—The said Captain Francisco de Ulloa, a citizen of the city of Concepción in [territory included in] the provinces of Chile, having sworn in due legal form and being questioned, in accordance with the contents of the questions for which he was admitted, made the following statements:

*[Inserted in the text as printed by Medina.—EDITOR.]

1.—[In reply] to the first question he said that he had known the said Diego Muñoz for the past fifteen years in these realms and in Spain and [as a man who had taken part] in Orellana's expedition.

General [questions of the law].—Questioned by means of the general questions, he said that he was fifty-five years of age, slightly more or less, and that none of the [general] questions affected him personally.

2.—[In reply] to the second question he said that he knew that the said Diego Muñoz Ternero had left the city of Seville in the year that the question says as chief scrivener for New Andalusia, the colonizing and conquest of which had been intrusted to the Adelantado Orellana, because this witness [i.e. he] had seen him perform the duties of the said position of chief scrivener in association with the said Adelantado.

3.—[In reply] to the third question he said that this witness [i.e. he] had seen the said Diego Muñoz for a certain length of time in the said city of Seville working at what the question says and aiding the said Adelantado; and that there [it was quite certain] that he [too] could not have failed to incur expenses, inasmuch as all those who were to come had incurred expenses, because they had waited around close on to a year before starting out from the said city of Seville.

4.—[In reply] to the fourth question he said that he knew about [the matter referred to in] the question just as it is stated therein because this witness [i.e. he] was one of those who had come over with the said expedition, and [that] there had been encountered many hardships and perils, and [that] they had been many times on the verge of perishing, particularly on one occasion, not to mention many others, which was when on board the ship [on] which the said Diego Muñoz and this witness [i.e. he himself] were sailing they had been for nine days stranded on a shoal, until they had gotten out of their perilous situation with the aid of a cockboat belonging to the said ship, in which they had gone off among some Indians, where they had built another [and] a larger one [i.e. a larger boat], in the course of the four or five months that they had stayed there.

5.—[In reply] to the fifth question he said that what he knew was that one of the ships, which was the one on board which the said Adelantado had come over, had been stranded on a beach, out of which [damaged ship] he had built a brigantine, in which he had gone about doing what the question states, and [that] the said Diego Muñoz [had gone] with him a large part of the time, and that with the other ship they had purposely run on a beach to wreck her because one of the hawsers which they had been using on her had broken and they had not been able to do anything else.

6.—[In reply] to the sixth question he said that he knew and had been a witness to the fact that after they had gone up into the said river, the first [sections of country inhabited by] Indians having been passed by, they had come upon great swamp lands and a few uninhabited districts and vast forest lands, and that, owing to lack of food and to illnesses which they had had to put up with, and being without remedies for all that, there had died a considerable number of persons, and [that their situation had been made all the more desperate] on account of a few whom the Indians had killed [when they had been out] looking for food.

8.*—[In reply] to the eighth question he said that he knew and had seen that,

*[There is irregularity in the numbering of Francisco de Ulloa's answers. The answer here numbered 5 contains Ulloa's replies to questions 5 and 6, while the answer numbered 6 corresponds to question 7, and there is no answer numbered 7 in the text as printed by Medina.—EDITOR.]

after what is stated above was over, they being practically on peaceful terms with certain Indians, the said Orellana had announced that he desired to go in the said brigantine and with a certain number of persons out of the said party to do some exploring farther up the river, and [had given orders to the effect] that the others should remain behind on one of its islands, [saying] that he would come back promptly and would tell them "what we were to do."

9.—[In reply] to the ninth question he said that, as he had already stated, after he [i.e. Orellana] had run the said ship on a beach to break it up, they had built the said boat in order to remedy their situation, "in which we went, after the departure of the said Orellana, in search of him up the said river with the men that the question mentions," and [that] they had moved about for a certain period of time, now in certain provinces, now in others, and [that] inasmuch as they had not found the said Orellana, and in view of the limited means which they had at their disposal for remedying their situation, they had decided among themselves to go back down the river, in which undertaking they had many times run a great risk of losing their lives: all of which this witness [said that he] knew because he had taken part in it all.

10.—[In reply] to question ten he said that everything stated in the question was the truth, because this witness [i.e. he himself] had taken part in it all.

11.—[In reply] to question eleven he said that likewise that which is related in the question was the truth, because, as he had already said, he had taken part in it and had been a witness to it; and that it seemed as if, in view of the small number of persons that there were in their group, the Indians could have killed them, and [that] they [i.e. the Spaniards] could not have prevented it owing to the small numbers that made up their group, if God in His mercy had not seen fit to protect them.

12.—[In reply] to question twelve he said that what he knew was that out of the said group of persons who had been in the said boat in which this witness [i.e. he] and the said Diego Muñoz had come away, there had remained behind ten or eleven Christians from among the said companions who had been going about among the Indians in the said boat, and [that] never had they been able to find them [again], although they had devised means and tried them out in an attempt to locate them; and [that] he did not know the reason why they had remained behind, [and that he had nothing further to add] beyond the fact that he thought that it was on account of the hardships and dangers which their imagination had pictured to them in regard to what was ahead of them.

13.—[In reply] to question thirteen he said that it was true that "after we had gone out to sea," the flood tides had hurled them back again among the said swamps covered with mangroves, from which they had gotten out, away from there, a few days afterwards at the cost of great toil and surrounded by danger.

14.—[In reply] to question fourteen he said that he knew, and that it was true, that while sailing along the said coast they had endured great hardships and [had met with] perils endangering their lives, not only as a result of the fact that the boat was a very wretched and a very small one, and one letting in much water, [so leaky, in fact,] that they had been constantly busy emptying it out with the pump and other utensils, but also on account of the hunger which they had endured.

15.—[In reply] to question fifteen he said that he knew about [the matter referred to in the] question because [it was a fact that] this witness [i.e. he] and the rest had put into port at Margarita, where they had found the wife of Orellana and had learned from her and from the others the rest of the matter stated in the question.

16.—[In reply] to question sixteen he said that it was true that after arriving at the said [island of] Margarita some had fallen ill, and [that] one [of these], not to mention others, was the said Diego Muñoz, who had been ill for a while.

# XIX

*Extracts from a judicial inquiry on the subject of services rendered by Juan de Peñalosa and bearing on Francisco de Orellana's expedition to New Andalusia, put through the court in the city of Panama on the 16th of February, 1572.*\*

1.—In the first place, whether they know the said purser Juan de Peñalosa, and how long since up to the present time.

2.—*Item*, whether they have ever heard about the expedition which, now twenty-five years [back], the Adelantado Orellana organized for the conquest and exploration of [territory along] the Marañón River, which, with its name changed, they now call the River of the Adelantado Orellana, and whether they know that it must be as long ago as the said twenty-five years, slightly more or less [by an exact reckoning of] time, that the said Adelantado Orellana started out from the realms of Spain to undertake the said conquest and exploration with four hundred and fifty men and four captains, and [that] one of them [i.e. of the latter] was the said Juan de Peñalosa, who at his own expense, taking along with him two servants of his, volunteered to go and did go, under orders of the said Adelantado, to serve His Majesty on the said expedition and came to the aid of the said Adelantado with a considerable amount of personal wealth towards getting the said expedition under way, and [that] in this form it is [all] common [knowledge] and [a] well known [fact].

3.—*Item*, whether they know that by the time the said Adelantado Orellana had arrived at the Cape Verde Islands there had become ill on the way a great many of his followers from among those whom he was taking along in his party for the purpose of the said conquest, in consequence whereof, [or rather] in consequence both of illnesses and of hardships which they had put up with on the way prior to reaching the said islands, a certain number of captains and men remained behind on them, as a consequence of the fact that they [i.e. the islands] were as thoroughly infected with disease as they [generally] are and as a result of there having fallen ill on their hands the great majority of the persons making up the expedition; and [whether they know that] the said Juan de Peñalosa, as a loyal vassal of His Majesty and one zealous [in furthering the interests] of his royal service, still continued to follow the said Adelantado Orellana right up to the final outcome of the said expedition, and [that] in this form it has [all] been and still is common [knowledge] and [a] well known [fact].

4.—Whether they know that, when they had reached the said Marañón River, the said Adelantado Orellana, and with him the said Captain Juan de Peñalosa, in the course of the said exploration and conquest endured great hardships from hunger spells and from illnesses, and that here they ate the horses which they.

\*Archives of the Indies, 1-6-2 /25.

had brought along as well as the dogs, within a period of eleven months while they were wandering about [like] lost [men] up and down the said river, during which time there died [at various places] along the said river the said Adelantado and the great majority of the persons who were taking part in the said [expedition of] conquest, [with the result] that there escaped alive only forty-four men, one of whom was the said Juan de Peñalosa; and [that] in this way those who were spared were left worn out and shattered after the said expedition and went off and came into port, all of them, on the Island of Margarita, together with Doña Ana de Ayala, the said Adelantado's wife.

A witness, Ana de Ayala, Orellana's widow.—In Panama, on the fifteenth day of the month of March in the year One Thousand Five Hundred and Seventy-two, the said purser Juan de Peñalosa brought in as a witness in connection with the said judicial inquiry Doña Ana de Ayala, a widow, the former wife of the Adelantado Orellana, staying in this city, who took the oath in due legal form, under burden of which she promised to tell the truth, and being questioned she made the following statements:

1.—[In reply] to the first question she said that she had known the said purser Juan de Peñalosa since a time twenty-five years back, which was when the above-mentioned had been appointed captain by the Adelantado Orellana, this witness's [i.e. her] former husband, at the time when the above-mentioned [i.e. Orellana] went off on the expedition into the interior up the Marañón River.

General [questions of the law].—Questioned by means of the general [questions] of the law she said that she was thirty-five years of age (*sic*), slightly more or less, and that the general [questions] did not affect her personally.

2.—[In reply] to the second question she said that she knew about [the matter referred to in] the question just as it is stated therein because this witness [i.e. she] knew, as the former wife of the Adelantado Orellana, that it must have been at a time as far back as the said twenty-five years which the question mentions that the said Adelantado Orellana had gone off under orders from His Majesty for the conquest and exploration of [the territory along] the Marañón River, which under a changed name is called the River of the Adelantado, with the [number of] followers mentioned in the question, together with the captains [mentioned], and [that] this witness [i.e. she] had seen how one of the four captains whom the said Adelantado, her husband, had appointed for the said expedition was one [who was none other than] the said Juan de Peñalosa; and that, inasmuch as His Majesty had not given the said Adelantado any aid or financial backing, the said Captain Peñalosa could not have failed to come to the aid of the said Adelantado, just as all the other captains and leading persons had been coming to his aid, and that this witness [i.e. she] had seen that the said Captain Peñalosa had been looked upon as, and taken along as, a man of great worth and skill and [had gone into the enterprise] with the servants that the question mentions.

3.—[In reply] to the third question she said that this witness [i.e. she] knew about [the matter related in] the question just as it is stated therein because it [really] had happened in the way that, and just as, the question states it; and [that] so it was that this witness [i.e. she] had seen how, owing to the fact that the captains and men had fallen ill, there had remained behind the greater part of them on the islands and in the regions which the question mentions, and [that] she knew [that] out of only four captains who had been accompanying the said expedition so far three had remained behind, and [also] the camp-master, one of which said captains was a first cousin of the said Captain Peñalosa; and [that], notwithstanding all this, this witness [i.e. she] knew that the above-mentioned had continued on his way with the said Adelantado her husband right up to the end which it [i.e. the expedition] came to, as a man of great courage and a servant of His Majesty and one zealous [in furthering the interests] of his royal service, enduring very great hardships caused by heavy rainfalls and hunger spells, [adding] that in that country there are a great many [heavy rainfalls]; and this [she said was what] she knew bearing upon the question.

4.—[In reply] to the fourth question she said that this witness [i.e. she] knew about [the matter referred to in] the question just as it is stated therein because [she recalled] that it had [all] come to pass in the way that, and just as, it [i.e. the question] states it; and [that] it was in this way that this witness [i.e. she] knew how in the course of the said exploring and [campaign of] conquest up and down the Marañón River the said Adelantado Orellana and the rest of the persons who were in his party, including the said Captain Peñalosa, had endured very great suffering from hunger and illnesses, because she knew that the said hunger had reached the point where they had eaten the horses which they had been taking along, as well as the dogs, within a period of eleven months while they had been wandering about [like] lost [men] in [the region of] the said river, during which time the greater part of the expeditioners had died, and among their number the said husband of hers; and this witness [i.e. she, said that she] knew that there had escaped alive only the said forty-four men, one of whom was the said Captain Juan de Peñalosa; and [she said that] in this way this witness [i.e. she] knew that in general they had all come out of it broken down, and in this way had all come into port, in company with this witness [i.e. her], on the Island of Margarita; and this [she said was what] she knew relative to the question, . . . and she signed it with her name.—*Ana de Ayala*.

A witness, Antonio Pérez de Vibero.—In the City of the Kings [i.e. Lima], on the twenty-seventh day of the month of June in the year One Thousand Five Hundred and Seventy-two, [there appeared in the courtroom] the said Antonio de Ávila, in the name of Juan de Peñalosa, his brother, and he presented before the illustrious Licentiate de Monzón, a judge of His Majesty's in the Royal Audiencia in this said city, who had been put in charge of the judicial inquiry covering the services which he [i.e. Juan de Peñalosa] claims to have performed for His Majesty in these realms, the witnesses of whom it was his intention to make use, for he was beseeching His Worship to call them into court in his official capacity and to question them in connection with the judicial inquiry introduced here in this case: and to the said end the said judge promptly caused to appear before him Antonio Pérez de Vibero, to whom the oath was administered and from whom it was received in legal form, over a representation of a cross, upon which he placed his right hand, [as a guarantee that] he would tell the truth with regard to whatever he might know and be asked about; and he said "Yes, I swear," and "Amen," and he promised to tell the truth; and being questioned in accordance with the contents of the interrogatory introduced in this case, he made the following statements:

1.—[In reply] to the first question he said that he had known the said purser Juan de Peñalosa for the past twenty-five years, slightly more or less, [as a man whom he had seen] holding the office of purser for His Majesty in Tierra Firme, in Nombre de Dios.

2.—[In reply] to the second question [he said] that this witness [i.e. he] knew and [that] it was true and [that] he had seen that, quite possibly twenty-five years back, slightly more or less, he [i.e. Juan de Peñalosa] had gone off to take part in the expedition to the Marañón [led] by the Adelantado Orellana, he [i.e. Juan de Peñalosa] being [at that time] in Spain, and [had had a share] in the conquest and exploring [of territory along the banks] of it [i.e. of the Marañón], because this witness [i.e. he] had [himself] come over on the said expedition to the said Marañón River; and [that] as far back, probably, as the said length of time the said Adelantado Orellana had set out on the said expedition with four hundred and fifty men, slightly more or slightly fewer, although this witness [i.e. he] had not counted them, and that he [i.e. Orellana] had taken along with him a certain number of captains, and that among these latter he had discerned the said Juan de Peñalosa, as he was called and as he was known in his relations with other persons, and [that] he [i.e. Peñalosa] had gone with the said Adelantado Orellana, he and all the rest [being men] who had [joined] at their own expense; and [that] it had been commonly reported that the captains and many of the soldiers were aiding the said Adelantado with money and goods towards the fitting out of the said expeditionary fleet, out of their own belongings, and that he thought that the said Juan de Peñalosa [had done] the same; and [that] inasmuch as the said expedition had afterwards gone all to pieces in consequence of the heavy mortality, [it had not worked out in such a way that] each man succeeded in getting back the amount of the account which had been opened in his name; and this [was what] he said in reply to the question.

3.—[In reply] to the third question he said that what is stated in it was true, just as it is explained therein, because this witness [i.e. he] had seen that just as soon as they had arrived at Cape Verde there had fallen ill on his hands a large number of persons out of those whom the said Adelantado was taking along with him on the said expedition, at which place there had died a large number of them and there had remained behind there [a certain number], not only soldiers but also [several] captains from among those whom he had taken along up to that point, and [that] the land was thoroughly infected with disease; and [that] the said Juan de Peñalosa, although he had witnessed all that which is told above, and [in spite of his] having to put up with hardships in the way that such servants of His Majesty [have to], had still continued on the said expedition with the said Adelantado, as a good soldier [and] servant of His Majesty, and had still continued to follow him through everything that had come up right to the end and outcome of the said expedition: and this [was what] he said in reply to the question as a person who had taken part in the whole affair and had seen that it had [all] happened just so.

4.—[In reply] to the fourth question he said that he knew about [the matter referred to in] the question in just the form in which it is stated therein, because this witness [i.e. he] had been right there during the whole affair; and that the said Juan de Peñalosa and the rest who were along had endured numerous and very severe hardships and hunger spells, and [that in this latter respect matters had gone] so far that they had eaten the dogs and the horses that had come that far, in the way that, and just as, the question states the matter and explains it; and [that] there, in the course of the said expedition, there had died almost all of those who had been taking part in the said expedition, including the Adelantado himself and many others, for very few were those who had escaped alive, who might have been as many as fifty persons in number, not many more, and [that] one of those who had escaped alive was the said Juan de Peñalosa; and [that] so it was that those who escaped alive had gotten out of the said expedition shattered and broken down, and had gone off and put into port, [practically] doomed [men], on the Island of Margarita, where there had [also] come into port the wife of the said Adelantado; and [he said that] he was very sure of that which is told above, in his capacity of a person who had taken part in it all and had seen that it had happened in this way.

A witness, P. Núñez Villavicencio.—And subsequently to what is related above, in the said City of the Kings [i.e. Lima], on the thirteenth day of the month of July in the year One Thousand Five Hundred and Seventy-two, the said judge, in connection with the said judicial inquiry covering the services which Juan de Peñalosa claims to have performed for His Majesty in these realms, caused to appear before him Pero Núñez Villavicencio, a resident of this City of the Kings, to whom the oath was administered and from whom it was received in legal form and over a representation of a cross, upon which he placed his right hand, under burden of which [oath] he said "Yes, I swear," and "Amen," and he promised to tell the truth; and being questioned in accordance with the contents of the interrogatory introduced in this case for his use, he spoke and testified as follows:

1.—[In reply] to the first question he said that he had been well acquainted with the said purser Juan de Peñalosa for the past twenty-seven years, slightly more or less.

2.—[In reply] to the second question he said that what he knew and [what] had happened was that in the year Forty-five [i.e. 1545], sometime during the month of May, the Adelantado Don Francisco de Orellana had started out from the bar of Sanlúcar to go in search of the Marañón River and the province of the Amazons with four ships, and [that there had been] on board them a goodly number of followers, and [that] he had taken along with him seven captains, among whom one, [as one] of their number, had been the said Juan de Peñalosa; and that he [i.e. the latter], for the said purpose and with the intention of serving His Majesty, had come on the said expedition at his own expense, and [that] he [i.e. the witness] considered it as certain that he [was the type of person who] would aid and [that] he [actually] had aided the said Adelantado with a part of his personal wealth, just as the rest of the captains had done who went out there; and this [was what] he said in reply to the question.

3.—[In reply] to the third question he said that he knew, and [that] it was true, and [that] this witness [i.e. he] had seen that, when [the members of]* the said expedition had arrived at the Island of Santiago in the Cape Verdes, there had fallen ill and died a large number of persons, and [that] several captains had stayed behind there ill and in a bad physical condition, and [that] this witness [i.e. he] was one of those who had ended up by being very sick and at the point of death; and [that] he had been a witness to the fact that the said Juan de Peñalosa had [there] embarked with the said Adelantado Don Francisco de Orellana and had gone off with him on the said expedition to follow out the plans for the said exploring, and that, this being now finished, a certain number of years later, this witness [i.e. he] being in the province of Tierra Firme and [in the town of]

*[Inserted in the text as printed by Medina, for the sake of the plural verb.—Editor.]

Nombre de Dios, there had arrived in it the wife of the said Adelantado Don Francisco de Orellana together with a certain number of men who had escaped alive after the said expedition, because all the ships had been wrecked somewhere up the said Marañón River and the Adelantado Don Francisco de Orellana [had] died, and [that] like doomed [men] these had come into port there at Nombre de Dios; and [that] from these he had heard how the said Peñalosa had taken part in the whole expedition and had served as a leading person in all [the events connected with] the said [expedition]; and that in exactly the same way he had heard the same thing about the chief pilot, whose name was Francisco López, who had come back to the world of civilization in this province of Peru; and this [he said was what] he knew relating to this question.

4.—[In reply] to the fourth question he said that he had heard many persons who had found their way out after this expedition say that everything which the question states had taken place, and in the way that, and just as, it is recounted and reads in it; and [that] this was common [knowledge] and [a] well known [fact] and [was] what he had to say in reply to the question.

# APPENDIX
# SELECTIONS FROM OVIEDO

# APPENDIX

SELECTIONS FROM OVIEDO'S "HISTORIA DE LAS INDIAS"
BEARING ON ORELLANA'S TWO EXPEDITIONS

## EDITOR'S FOREWORD

The reasons for which it has been thought advisable to add this Appendix to the present English version of Medina's book on the first voyage down the Amazon have been stated in the editor's additions to footnote 1, p. 8 above. There only remains to offer a few explanatory remarks about the selections from Oviedo's *Historia general y natural de las Indias*, etc., here presented for the first time, it is believed, in English translation, and to venture, on the basis of the scanty information that can be gathered from Medina's book and from Oviedo himself, an opinion regarding the relation between the version of Friar Carvajal's *Account* published by Medina and the one which Oviedo inserted in his history.

Gonzalo Fernández de Oviedo, as Medina points out (p. 28, *supra*), was the first of the historians or chroniclers of the Indies to write about Orellana's voyage down the Amazon, as well as, though very briefly, about that conquistador's later expedition to New Andalusia. The six chapters of varying lengths from Oviedo's own pen that contain the story of Orellana belong to the last section of his work. This deals with a single general topic, namely the history of New Castile (or Peru) from the organization of the expedition of discovery and conquest under Francisco Pizarro and Diego de Almagro down to and including the battle of Xaquixaguana (April 8, 1548) and constitutes Books XLVI–XLIX (or Part III, Books VIII–XI) of the work. Oviedo put the material of these four books together in final form during the latter part of a sojourn in Spain which extended from October, 1546, to the beginning of the year 1549, writing the next-to-the-last chapter (and perhaps others) in the month of December, 1548, in Seville, where he was waiting to take passage back to the New World. The frequency with which Oviedo uses the expression: "in this city of Santo Domingo," etc., or one very similar to it, is evidence that he had written the greater part of his account of these events back in that city, of whose fortress he was the governor, and that in incorporating it in his *Historia* he did practically no revising.

Thus, of the six chapters with which we are concerned here (Book XLIX, Chapters 1 to 6), the second was certainly written in Santo Domingo ("in this city of Santo Domingo," says Oviedo, p. 384, and again on p. 385). The third and fourth chapters, the subject-matter of which was drawn very largely from the same sources as the story briefly sketched in the second chapter, were probably written in the same place and at the same time. These sources are: (1) the oral account given to the author by Orellana himself during the latter's brief stop in Santo Domingo where he and a certain number of his companions had arrived in November or December, 1542, supplemented by what was told to Oviedo, probably on various occasions and perhaps, for the most part, only after Orellana had continued on his way to Spain, by several other members of the expedition, of whom there were "more than ten" in the city at the time that Oviedo was writing, since in the passage where he uses this figure (p. 383) he is undoubtedly referring to the specific individuals, "other hidalgos and commoners," of whom he speaks (p. 573) in the few remarks of his own which he adds after reproducing Friar Carvajal's account; (2) letters written in August, 1542, received in Santo Domingo from Popayán, giving the first news of the return to the region of Quito of the remnants of Gonzalo Pizarro's expedition to the Land of Cinnamon; (3) a copy of Carvajal's account, received by Oviedo on a date which is not known, but presumably prior to Oviedo's last interview, if not with Orellana himself, at least with some of the companions who lingered on in that city, for this seems to be what Oviedo means by the adverb "since" when he says (p. 384): " . . . in addition to that which . . . a devout friar of the Order of Saint Dominic wrote down, I have since learned . . . from Captain Francisco de Orellana and from other cavaliers and hidalgos. . . . " Oviedo must have noted down practically from dictation certain details which he must have obtained from these men, inasmuch as they are not to be found in Carvajal's account, such as the list of the names of the men composing Orellana's party, the list of (fantastic?) names of native rulers, vassals of the "Amazons," in Chapter 4, etc.; but, however recent, at the time that he was actually writing this all out, his latest interview with one or more of these men may have been, it seems as if a considerable period of time must have elapsed since the arrival of Orellana in Santo Domingo, because, if this had been a recent event, on the one hand Oviedo would most probably have said, in recording the date, merely "Monday" instead of "one Monday" (he says it this way twice, p. 384 and p. 573), and on the other hand he would not have been confused in regard to the month, saying, as he does, in one case that it was November and in the other that it was December, in each case giving a date (the 22nd and the 20th respectively) which did not fall on a Monday in that year.

It would seem, then, that 1543, and not the very beginning of that year either, is the earliest possible date at which Oviedo could have written these three chapters; and the *terminus ad quem* for their date of composition must be around the middle of the year 1546, shortly after which the author was absent from Santo Domingo, having sailed for Spain in August.

Inasmuch as the first news of the failure of Orellana's expedition to New Andalusia could not have reached a Spanish colony before November or December, 1546 (see Medina, p. 150f., *supra*), Oviedo must, of course, have written his short Chapter 5 dealing with this enterprise after his arrival in Spain. (This is why, in speaking of the coming of a few of the survivors to the land which was really his home, he no longer uses the phrase quoted above, but says merely: "on our island of Hispaniola.") His source of information for this chapter was possibly nothing more than the letter of the Licentiate Cerrato, dated Santo Domingo, January 25, 1547, of which Medina speaks in footnote 205 (p. 151, *supra*). Chapter 6 was likewise written in Spain (cf.: "in the province which, [located] in *this* Spain of ours," etc., p. 390), at a time when Oviedo had not yet heard that La Gasca had put an end to Gonzalo Pizarro's tyranny; that is, it must have been written, if not in 1547, then certainly in 1548, but at all events prior to December 8 of the latter year, when Oviedo first heard (see p. 455) of the battle of Xaquixaguana. As for Chapter 1, there seems to be no internal evidence by which one may determine either the place or the date of its composition; but as it is not much more than an introduction to the other five, it seems probable that Oviedo wrote it at the time that he was putting all of this material into final shape for publication.

Of these six chapters, the last, which is likewise the longest, has a very special interest: it is a sort of essay by itself, being Oviedo's attempt to present, without bias, a fairly complete but nevertheless succinct statement, written apparently with no documents before him except his own work, of all the circumstances leading up to and in part resulting from the separation of Orellana's party from the main body of the expeditionary force and the consequent "discovery" of the Amazon River; and it bears a certain resemblance to a brief summing up of events in Medina's Introduction in the present volume (specifically, pp. 90–96, *supra*), but with the important difference that, whereas Medina is preoccupied with refuting the charge of treason leveled against Orellana by the historians, Oviedo focuses his attention upon Gonzalo Pizarro, holding the latter largely responsible for the situation then existing in Peru, and only incidentally, and dispassionately, qualifying Orellana's act as that of "a man in revolt" (p. 393).

Upon obtaining a copy of Friar Carvajal's account of Orellana's voyage down the Amazon, Oviedo seems to have decided at once (see Chapter 2 of the translation below) that this was exactly the kind of story that could form a chapter of that section of his *General and Natural History of the Indies* which, though now designated as Book L (or Part III, Book XII), is really a sort of appendix under the title of "Misfortunes and Shipwrecks." In the first edition of Part I of Oviedo's work, the last pages of which left the press of the famous Seville printer Juan Cromberger on the last day of September, 1535, this part of the volume contains (if one may trust the reprint of Salamanca, 1547) eleven stories of shipwrecked men, the last one, or Chapter 10 of Book XII of Part III in the modern edition edited by José Amador de los Ríos, being a very long account of the wrecking, on the rocks of a barren island belonging to a group which Oviedo calls the Scorpion Islands, of the ship which was bearing the Licentiate Alonso Zuazo from Santiago de Cuba to Mexico on a mission to Hernando Cortés, the concluding paragraphs of the story dealing with a part of Zuazo's subsequent career. According to Medina (p. 12f., *supra*), Friar Carvajal arrived in Seville toward the end of that year, 1535, and he probably lived in that city most of the time during the following year, until he sailed for the Indies, as Medina shows good reason for believing, at the beginning of 1537. In view of these circumstances it would be difficult to believe that Friar Carvajal had not read, before coming to the New World, Part I of Oviedo's history, concluding with the story of Alonso Zuazo, which, with its many manifestations on the part of the author of a belief in divine intervention on several occasions in behalf of the shipwrecked men, could hardly have failed to leave a clear impression upon the mind of the Dominican friar. He must have known also that Oviedo had been appointed official chronicler of the Indies (since 1532: see Amador de los Ríos, Introduction in Vol. 1 of the modern edition of Oviedo, p. lviii) and that a royal decree had been issued requiring all governors and *adelantados* in the Indies to send to Oviedo all accounts of "new discoveries" (see Amador de los Ríos, *loc. cit.*, p. lxv). Thus it would seem as if Friar Carvajal must have been prepared in advance to make a contribution to the official chronicler's history in case he should find himself a member of a party engaged in a "discovery," particularly if the party had experiences somewhat similar to those of the shipwrecked Alonso Zuazo and his companions. The occasion did present itself, as we know, for within five years after he had left Seville he found himself a member of an expedition whose greatest sufferings, as in the case of Alonso Zuazo's party, were caused by the difficulty of obtaining food and whose escape from destruction on many occasions, to the mind of the devout priest, would not have been possible if God had not extended His protecting hand just as He had done for Alonso Zuazo and his small company. If it was with this story somewhat vaguely in mind that Friar Carvajal wrote his account of the trying experiences which Orellana and his men met with in their voyage down the Amazon, it is little to be wondered at that Oviedo found it ready to be inserted practically (perhaps absolutely) intact as a chapter in his "Misfortunes and Shipwrecks."

But at what moment did Friar Carvajal actually compose this account? Medina says (p. 10, *supra*) that the expeditioners realized the advisability of noting down day by day the incidents of the voyage, it being "precisely this task which Friar Carvajal took upon himself." Are we to understand from this that, according to Medina's interpretation of some statement of Carvajal's or of some source of information for which he furnishes no reference, that the Dominican friar wrote the greater part of the account as the expedition proceeded on its way? Or does Medina mean merely that Carvajal jotted down a few notes, not literally day by day, but from time to time, writing up the account later on the basis of these notes? The first of these alternatives is probably to be rejected at once because of the frequency, particularly in the version in Oviedo, with which Carvajal refers, as he writes, to subsequent events or incidents that happened on the voyage: as these references appear to be an integral part of the composition, and not interpolations, the account must have been written after the voyage was all over. As to whether Carvajal, when the time came for writing his account, was able to avail himself of notes taken during the journey, there does not seem to be any proof. Nor, in fact, is it necessary to assume that he needed any such notes. For it will be noticed that the chronology of the voyage is most accurately established when the time of occurrence of a given event or incident is an important religious feast-day, or a few days before or after one of these days, or a date readily calculable from such a feast-day not far removed; while after St. John the Baptist's day (June 24) until nearly the middle of August, during which period there are no great religious feast-days, the chronology becomes confused, as Medina himself observes (footnote 144, p. 103, *supra*). All this seems to indicate that Friar Carvajal, who throughout the entire voyage had been exceedingly zealous in the performance of his duties as a priest, relies, when it comes to fixing the date of an event or incident, upon his recollection of his activities in connection with an approaching or recent religious celebration of some sort; and he is very vague about dates when there is no religious feast-day closely following or preceding the event which he is recording. If he had any notes at all, they were perhaps nothing more than what could be scribbled in the margins of some sort of calendar, or of a missal or other small book of that sort. As for the many details which he frequently gives in connection with major events, these were not difficult to recall, so vivid were the impressions which had been made upon his mind both by the terrible hardships and dangers that had been undergone and by the many new and wonderful things that had been seen. But it is probable that he lost little time in consigning all this to writing as soon as he had come to a place where he had some facilities for doing so; that is, he probably composed his account not very long after he had arrived, in company with his weary companions, early in September, 1542, on the island of Cubagua, where Oviedo, in Santo Domingo, learned two or three months later from Orellana or some of his companions that Carvajal had stayed behind to rest for a while before returning to Lima. There is nothing in the statement by Oviedo (pp. 573-574) to indicate whether or not he had yet received the particular copy óf Carvajal's account which he was to transcribe for use in his *Historia*, but it seems probable that Carvajal must have written at least one of the various versions before he rested. In this latter connection, it is quite possible that rumors had already reached Cubagua to the effect that Gonzalo Pizarro, now back in Peru, was accusing Orellana of treason, in which case he would be quick to realize the advisability of sending to the official chronicler a truthful account of what had happened before Gonzalo Pizarro could send in one which would tell, to use a phrase by which Carvajal seems to be referring to just such an eventuality, "just the opposite of what we have experienced and seen" (p. 234 f., *supra*).

No autograph manuscript of Carvajal's account seems to have been preserved, for Medina is of the opinion (footnote 4, p. 9, *supra*) that the manuscript belonging to the Duke of T'Serclaes is not in the author's handwriting. It will therefore probably never be known how closely one or the other of the two existing versions of the account follows the original. It does not seem probable, however, that the original was any longer or more detailed than the extant versions, for the reason that Carvajal tells us, in a statement that has been preserved in the last paragraph of each of these, that he has only sketched the story. (The words "epitomized and shortening," in the version in Oviedo, can hardly mean that this version is an abridgment of the other version which has come down to us: the latter, if it were printed in the same format as the modern edition of Oviedo, would be only three or four pages longer than the former.) Medina (p. 8, *supra*) seems to have an opinion regarding the relation of the version in Oviedo, if not to Carvajal's original redaction, at least to the copy which he (Medina) is publishing for he says that the chronicler, in inserting Carvajal's account in his *Historia*, made "some changes." Unfortunately, Medina does not tell us on what authority he makes this statement: he may possibly have reached this conclusion merely on the basis of the fact that the differences between the texts of the two versions are striking and are to be explained on the theory that Oviedo in many cases substituted for what Carvajal had written some parts of the oral versions which he obtained from the "companions" with whom he talked in Santo Domingo. But before anything further can be said on this point, it will be necessary to look into these differences.

At the very beginning of the two versions of the account the text of the one is so entirely different from that of the other that one is forced to the conclusion that they cannot possibly be derived from a common original text. But after six pages of the version published by Medina, or nearly three pages of the version in Oviedo, in a passage which tells the story of the great disappointment felt by the expeditioners when, after certain among them thought that they had heard the sound of drums, it was found that this was all an illusion, one suddenly finds that the phraseology of the one version, when examined in detail, is almost identical with that of the other, so much so that for the corresponding passages in question there can be no doubt that there must have been a common source. This approximate identity of texts runs on for the equivalent of about one page of the *Account* printed by Medina, after which the texts again become entirely different in phraseology and partly in content, only to become nearly identical in another pair of corresponding passages a little farther on. This alternating of closely identical and entirely distinct texts for corresponding passages continues through the entire account, but with a great predominance, from the point of view of length, of corresponding passages showing the latter peculiarity. In addition to these textual differences between the two versions, there are also those resulting from the fuller treatment, in certain cases, of a given episode in the one version as compared with that in the other, and those which are due to the omission of a certain amount of matter from the one or the other of the two versions, and a few apparently intentional differences of style which will be briefly discussed in the paragraph below. As stated above, there is no essential difference in length between the two versions. There are but slight variations in the chronology of events in the two versions. The only logical explanation of this state of affairs, since there seems to be no reason for questioning the authorship in either case, is that Carvajal himself wrote his account twice, but with his first manuscript (or a copy of it) before him while he was writing the second version, copying the first with only slight changes in phraseology whenever he was satisfied with the text before him, but most often revising his own work completely, perhaps occasionally rectifying an error. If this hypothesis is correct, then there seems to be no reason for assuming, with Medina, that Oviedo tampered with the account when he adopted it as a chapter in his history, particularly in view of the manner in which, after transferring the account to his own work, he praises the Dominican friar both for his truthfulness and for his knowledge of "things of the Indies" (p. 574).

Certain additional considerations will warrant at least a conjecture as to which of the two versions was written first. In the version first published by Medina the approach to the subject in hand is direct and abrupt; the first encounters with the Indians, both peaceful and hostile, in which the qualities of Orellana as a leader are made to appear to advantage, are related in greater detail than in the other version; in the next-to-the-last paragraph Carvajal expresses the conviction that the river down which the expedition had come was the Marañón. It would seem as if this version were more in the nature of a report suitable for submission by Orellana to the Council of the Indies. If this is so, then it must have been written as quickly as possible and a copy of it made and handed over to Orellana, who, of course, may have had occasion to introduce a few changes in it in order to be able to present it as his own report or account. On the other hand, the other version shows signs of having been composed at a time when the author had a little more leisure for this kind of work. (One might be tempted to interpret an expression which occurs in the second paragraph, namely: "to these regions of the Antarctic or Southern Hemisphere," as meaning that Carvajal was now back in his home in Lima; but it is more probable that the demonstrative adjective in this expression, with the noun which it modifies, means "these regions that I am talking about," namely "New Castile, otherwise known as Peru," mentioned five or six lines above.) It opens with a certain display of learning and a search for rhetorical effect, these two characteristics reappearing several times throughout the account in the form of alleged quotations from the Scriptures and passages cited from Latin authors, of a speech by Orellana to his men (imitation of the style of Livy), etc.; it omits certain minor incidents (such as the first accident, namely when the boat struck a log in the river), little matters which perhaps seemed insignificant on second thought; a little more attention seems to be given to matters of natural history, geography, etc., and to the arts and crafts of the natives; toward the end of the account (p. 572) the author seems to leave to the judgment of a person better informed than himself the question of whether the river down which the expedition had made its way was the Huyapari (Orinoco) or the Marañón. In short, this version has every appearance of having been written for the specific purpose of being sent to the chronicler of the Indies for inclusion in his *Historia*. If this is the case, this is plainly the second or revised version, and it was probably sent, either by request (though Oviedo nowhere implies that) or on the author's own initiative, from the island of Cubagua before the Dominican friar left there to return to Lima, since it was in Oviedo's hands in time to enable him to supplement the information which it contained by the oral accounts of some ten of Orellana's companions before these had had time to scatter.

H. C. H.

OVIEDO'S DESCRIPTION OF GONZALO PIZARRO'S EXPEDITION TO THE LAND
OF CINNAMON, ORELLANA'S DESCENT OF THE AMAZON, AND
ORELLANA'S SUBSEQUENT EXPEDITION TO NEW ANDALUSIA

## BOOK XLIX [= PART III, BOOK XI]

### [381]* CHAPTER I

*In which is taken up the matter of how and by whom the city of San Francisco [Quito]
was founded; and how Captain Sebastián de Banalcázar, who was stationed
there by order of the Marquis Don Francisco Pizarro, without permission left
the country to go to Spain, where he was commissioned Governor of Popayán;
and how the Marquis sent Gonzalo Pizarro, his brother, to Quito, and how he
[i.e. Gonzalo Pizarro] went off in search of cinnamon and of the king or chief who
is called El Dorado. And how it was a matter of accident that the Marañón River
was discovered and [first] navigated from the inland part [of its course] down,
from its sources all the way to the Northern Sea, by Captain Francisco de Orellana,
accompanied by a certain number of companions, whose names will be told, along
with other details which are useful in connection with this history.*

Captain Diego de Ordaz† was put in charge of the undertaking whose aim was
the exploring and colonizing of [the region of] the Marañón River, and the ill
luck that attended it throughout was related in Book XXIV of these historical
accounts. But in order that the reader may be informed about what has since
been found out regarding this river and in what way [this knowledge has been
obtained], it is fitting [to record] and it is worthy of being pointed out that  .   .
.  .   .   .   .   .   .   .   .   .   .   .   .   .   .   .   .   .   .   .   .   .   .   .   .   .   .   .   .   .   ‡
.   .   .   And this man [Sebastián de Benalcázar] [382] founded the city of
San Francisco [Quito], which is the first town that came into existence having
Christians [as citizens] and the most important one that exists at the present
time in the said province of Quito: and this man Benalcázar right from that time
heard many reports about cinnamon, and, according to statements which he made
to me in this city of Santo Domingo, when he was on his way back from Spain
after being commissioned governor of Popayán, it was his opinion that off in the
direction of the Marañón River there was some to be found, and that that cinnamon ought to be taken over to Castile and to Europe by way of the said river,
for, according to indications which the Indians had given him regarding the
route, he felt that he could not make a mistake, unless the information given
to him was false; which [information] he considered to be sure and [reliable in

---

*[Boldface figures represent the page numbers in Vol. 4, Madrid, 1855, of Oviedo's *Historia
general y natural de las Indias*, etc., edited by José Amador de los Ríos and published by the Real
Academia de la Historia. Placed here where the corresponding pages in the *Historia* begin, these
numbers, as stated in the footnote on p. 8 above, are intended to facilitate locating the passages
cited in Part I of the present work.—EDITOR.]

†[On this expedition, undertaken in 1531, see Note 21 to Carvajal's *Account*, pp. 241–242, *supra*.
—EDITOR.]

‡[In the omitted passage Oviedo refers to the quarrel between Francisco Pizarro and Almagro
(see pp. 39–40, above) and to the events preceding the founding of Quito in 1534.—EDITOR.]

view of its having been obtained] from many Indians. When this captain departed from here, he had made up his mind to go look for it [i.e. cinnamon]; but, as Gonzalo Pizarro had already set out with a considerable head start (or during the time that Benalcázar was occupied here in these parts) in quest of cinnamon likewise, there resulted from the search for it the finding of it, as well as [the discovery] of the Marañón River from the inland end and of the sources of that great river, in the way in which it will be told in the following chapter.

## CHAPTER II

*Being a continuation of the matter which is spoken of and noted down in the heading of the preceding chapter, and of the reports which circulate regarding King El Dorado, and [of] how and in what unexpected way the Marañón River was discovered by Captain Francisco de Orellana, and [how] with fifty Spaniards he navigated it right down to the Northern Sea; and [of] how Gonzalo Pizarro got back to Quito after heavy losses, which included the greater part of the Christians whom he had taken along on the expedition in search of cinnamon; and at the same time there will be touched upon a few matters, in addition to what is [already] recounted, which are appropriate in connection with the development of this history.*

. . . . . . . . . . . . . . . . . . . *

[383] Now when the Marquis Don Francisco Pizarro learned that Benalcázar had left [the province of] Quito without his permission, he sent there Captain Gonzalo Pizarro, his brother, and he [i.e. the latter] took possession of that city of San Francisco [Quito] and of a part of that province, and from there he decided to go and search for cinnamon and for a great monarch who is called El Dorado (concerning whose wealth there are many rumors in these parts).

Upon being questioned by me as to the reason why they call that monarch Chief El Dorado or King El Dorado,† the Spaniards who have been in Quito and have come here to Santo Domingo (and at the present time there are more than ten of these men in this city) say that what has been gathered from the Indians is that that great lord or monarch constantly goes about covered with gold ground [into dust] and as fine as ground salt; for it is his opinion that to wear any other adornment is less beautifying, and that to put on pieces or a coat of arms hammered out of gold or stamped out or [fabricated] in any other way is [a sign of] vulgarity and a common thing, and that other rich lords and monarchs wear such things when it pleases them to do so; but to powder one's self with gold is an extraordinary thing [to do], unusual and new and more costly, inasmuch as what one puts on in the morning every day is removed and washed off in the evening and is cast away and thrown to waste on the ground; and this he does every day of his life. And it is a garment [of a sort] which, as he goes about clad and covered in this way, does not cause him any hindrance or bother, nor are the handsome proportions of his body and its natural form concealed or injured [thereby], [things] on which he prides himself greatly, thus not putting on any other clothing or any [form of] raiment. I would rather have the sweepings from

*[The omitted passage deals with the defection of Benalcázar from his superior, Francisco Pizarro.—EDITOR.]

†[I.e. the Gilded Chief or King.—EDITOR.]

the chamber of this monarch than that of the great melting establishments that have been set up for [the refining of] gold in Peru and [any other] that may exist in any part of the world. Thus it is that this chief or king is reported by the Indians to be an exceedingly wealthy and important overlord, and [it is further related that] with a certain resin or liquid which has a very fine odor he anoints himself every morning, and upon that ointment sets and sticks the gold ground [into dust] and as fine as is required for what has been stated, and his whole body is then left covered with gold from the soles of his feet to his head and as bright as a gold coin fashioned by the hand of a skilled artisan regularly comes out. And it is my belief that if that chief is accustomed to doing that, he must possess some very rich mines of that particular quality of gold, for in Tierra Firme I have seen considerable quantities of it, which we Spaniards call "flying," and [it is] so fine that what has been stated above could very easily be done [with it].

Gonzalo Pizarro believed that if he went off in that direction the outcome of his expedition was bound to be a successful and fruitful journey by water, to the very great advantage of the royal revenues and [looking toward] the aggrandizement of the state and of the patrimony of His Cesarean Majesty and his successors, and also a means whereby the Christians who were to see the enterprise through to the end might come to be very rich men. In order to accomplish this, with two hundred and thirty men on horse and on foot he went off to the headwaters of the Marañón River, and they found cinnamon trees; but it was in small quantities and on trees very far apart and in rugged and unsettled country, so that their enthusiasm with regard to this cinnamon was chilled, and they lost hope of finding it in abundance (at least for the time being). But although this is what some of those who took part in that affair thought, others from among the same individuals have told me personally that they do not believe that the cinnamon is in small quantities, inasmuch as it is shipped to many ports. And granted that the trees of this sort which they saw are wild and that nature makes them grow all by themselves, the Indians say that off in the interior people cultivate them and look after them, and [that] they are much better, and give a greater quantity and a far superior quality of the product.

They eventually found themselves faced with such a great shortage of supplies that hunger caused them to weaken in other matters requiring attention; and, in order to try to find food, Captain Gonzalo Pizarro sent off, in command of fifty men, Captain Francisco [384] de Orellana, and this man could not come back, because a certain river down which he had gone was so cold [sic]* that within two days they found themselves so far separated from Gonzalo Pizarro's army that it seemed best to this Captain and his companions to proceed onward with the current in order to go in search of the Northern Sea with the idea in mind of [at least] getting out of there with their lives. That is what he gave me to understand, but others say that he could have turned back, had he so wished, to where Gonzalo Pizarro had stopped, and this I believe, for reasons that will be set forth farther on. This group of men, which thus went off with Captain Francisco de Orellana, and he were the ones who discovered and [the ones who first] saw the course of this Marañón River, and they navigated down it a greater distance than any

---

*[This peculiar use of "cold" must have seemed odd to Medina, for he likewise put a "(sic)" after it in citing this passage in his Introduction (see *supra*, p. 83). If the Spanish word for "cold" is not due, in the present case, to an error in the printing of Oviedo's text, it may have connoted, when applied to a stream of water, the idea of swiftness resulting from the increase in the volume of the water produced by the rapid melting of snows.—EDITOR.]

other Christians who had ever traveled up and down it, as will be set forth in greater detail and at greater length in the last book of these historical accounts, [i.e.] in Chapter XXIV. This navigation and experience had been entered upon unintentionally and turned out to be so extraordinary that it is one of the greatest things that ever happened to men; and, because this voyage and discovery of the Marañón will be described *ad plenum* where I have said, I shall not stop here to discuss the matter, except for certain particulars which, in addition to that which as an eyewitness a devout friar of the Order of Saint Dominic wrote down, I have since learned in this city of Santo Domingo from Captain Francisco de Orellana himself and from other cavaliers and hidalgos who came in with him.* These particulars the said friar did not write down in his account because he did not remember to do so, or [because] it did not seem to him that he ought to concern himself with them; I shall tell it all as I heard it from this captain and his companions. And although the points brought up may not be presented [here] in as orderly a manner as they ought to be, they will be set down [as facts] just as true, and just as plainly [expressed], as they told them to me: some in response to my specific questioning, others as they themselves gradually recalled them.

And because it is not right that after a feat so remarkable, after such a long and dangerous voyage, the names of those who took part in it all should be forgotten and passed over in silence, I shall put them down here, for I saw a certain number of those men in this city of ours, where Captain Orellana and ten or twelve of them arrived one Monday, the twentieth of the month of December† in the year One Thousand Five Hundred and Forty-Two. But because, in addition to the fifty companions who separated from Gonzalo Pizarro's expeditionary corps under Captain Orellana, there were others who went aboard this same boat to go and wait for the rest of the army in a certain place where the said Captain Gonzalo Pizarro was to go shortly, I shall include in my account all those who took part in this [expedition of] navigation, and these were the following:

ENUMERATION OF THE MEN WHO WITH CAPTAIN FRANCISCO DE ORELLANA LEFT
GONZALO PIZARRO'S EXPEDITIONARY CORPS AND WENDED THEIR WAY DOWN
THE GREAT MARAÑÓN RIVER

In the first place,

1. Captain Francisco de Orellana, a native of the city of Trujillo, in Estremadura.

[Then,]

2. The Comendador Francisco Enríquez, a native of the city of Cáceres.

3. Cristóbal de Segovia, a native of Torrejón de Velasco.

4. Hernán Gutiérrez de Celis, a native of Celis, in the Montaña.

5. Alonso de Robles, a native of the town of Don Benito, which is a part of Medellín, [and] the lieutenant of this expedition.

---

*[It is possible that at least a part of these particulars, which would have been so useful in connection with the principal subject of investigation treated in the present volume, were not noted down by Oviedo after all: cf. the footnote, by Oviedo's editors, to the caption of Chapter III below.—EDITOR.]

†[On p. 573 Oviedo gives the date of Orellana's arrival in Santo Domingo as Monday, November 22. Medina (*supra*, p. 125) adopts this second date, apparently not having noticed the discrepancy between the two statements in Oviedo, or that each of these two dates fell on a Wednesday (on the correct correlation between week day and date in general, see editorial addition, pp. 58-59 above, to footnote 94).—EDITOR.]

6. Alonso Gutiérrez, from Badajoz.

7. Juan de Arnalte.

8. Juan de Alcántara.

9. Cristóbal de Aguilar, a half-breed, the son of the Licentiate Marcos de Aguilar and of an Indian woman, by whom he had him on this island of Hispaniola, and a young man handsome of person and an honest fellow.

10. Juan Carrillo.

11. Alonso García.

12. Juan Gutiérrez.

13. Alonso de Cabrera, a native of Cazalla.

[385]    14. Blas de Aguilar, an Asturian.

15. Juan de Empudia, a native of Empudia, who was killed by the Indians.

16. Antonio de Carranza, a citizen of Frías, who was likewise killed by the Indians.

17. García de Soria, a citizen of Soria, who was also killed by the Indians.

18. García de Aguilar, a native of Valladolid: he died during the voyage.

19. Another Juan de Alcántara, from the *maestrazgo** of Santiago: he also died during the voyage.

20. Juan Osorio, from the Maestrazgo*: he, too, died during the voyage.

21. Pedro Moreno, a native of Medellín: he also died of illness.

22. Juanes, a Biscayan, a native of Bilbao: he also died of illness.

23. Sebastián de Fuenterrabía: he died [after falling] ill during the voyage.

24. Juan de Rebolloso, a native of Valencia, the Cid's city: he died of illness.

25. Álvar González, an Asturian, from Oviedo: he died of illness.

26. Blas de Medina, a native of Medina del Campo.

27. Gómez Carrillo.

28. Hernán González, a Portuguese.

29. Antonio Hernández, a Portuguese.

30. Pero Domínguez, a native of Palos.

31. Antonio Muñoz, from Trujillo.

32. Juan de Illanes, a native of the town of Illanes in Asturias.

33. Perucho, a Biscayan from Pasages.

34. Francisco de Isásaga, a Biscayan, the scrivener of the expedition, a native of San Sebastián.

35. Andrés Martín, a native of Palos.

36. Juan de Palacios, a citizen of Ayamonte.

37. Matamoros, a citizen of Badajoz.

38. Juan de Arévalo, a citizen of Trujillo.

39. Juan de Elena.

40. Alonso Bermúdez, from Palos.

41. Juan Bueno, a native of Moguer.

42. Ginés Hernández, from Moguer.

43. Andrés Durán, from Moguer.

44. Juan Ortiz, from the Maestrazgo.

45. Mexía, a carpenter, a native of Seville.

46. Blas Contreras, from the Maestrazgo.

47. Juan de Vargas, from Estremadura.

48. Juan de Mangas, from the port of Santa María.†

*[See asterisk footnote, p. 120, *supra*.—EDITOR.]

†[See asterisk footnote, p. 139, *supra*.—EDITOR.]

49. Gonzalo Díaz.
50. Alexos González, a Galician.
51. Sebastián Rodríguez, a Galician.
52. Alonso Estéban, from Moguer.
53. Friar Gaspar de Carvajal, of the Order of Preaching Friars, a native of Trujillo.
54. Friar Gonzalo de Vera, of the Order of Mercy.

These are, all told, including Captain Francisco de Orellana, fifty-four persons, of whom fifty, as has been stated, set out with him to search for food and reconnoiter the country; and the friars and the rest* were being taken along in the same boat to wait for the army [at a location] where Captain Gonzalo Pizarro had ordered [them to wait] and [where] he himself was to go within a few days. And of the number that has been stated three were killed by the Indians and eight died natural deaths, so that the number of deceased men was eleven.

It is now known, through letters which came after this Captain Orellana had arrived in this city of Santo Domingo, written in the city of Popayán on the thirteenth of August in the year One Thousand Five Hundred and Forty-Two, that that Captain Gonzalo Pizarro sent this Captain Francisco de Orellana on ahead with the said fifty men to look for food for all of them, to a lake which [lies in a country that] is thoroughly settled, where it is said that there is very great wealth, in order that he might investigate the resources of the country, and that he ordered him to wait there; and that within a few days Gonzalo Pizarro himself, bringing the rest of his men, arrived there where he had ordered him to wait almost as soon [386] as Orellana had. And as he did not find him or the men, he came to the conclusion that the said Orellana and his companions, in a spirit of evil-mindedness, had gone off down a very mighty river in search of adventure in a boat or brigantine which they had with them (to look for [a way out to] the Northern Sea); and [hence it was apparent] that Gonzalo Pizarro had been tricked, because in the boat there had been taken along the powder and all the munitions which he had for his fighting forces, and it has even been stated in writing that the men in the boat also carried off a great wealth of gold and [precious] stones. Whether or not such was the case, as these letters say, will be found out as time goes on.

Here, this captain and his followers publicly stated that they had come here poor and that it had not been within their power to go back to the said Gonzalo Pizarro, even if they had tried to, on account of the swiftness [of the current] of the river and for the reasons which will be set forth at greater length in the friar's account. And so, no matter how all that came about, Pizarro was compelled, just as soon as he realized that he was in a desperate situation, to turn back towards Quito; and all along the way, until his arrival there, there were eaten more than a hundred horses and many dogs that they had taken along with them; and in this way he got back to the city of San Francisco [Quito]. And the letters further state that it was reported that Gonzalo Pizarro had founded a colony somewhere off there, and that he was making [out of this] a pretext for the need of gathering together more men and horses, and [read: but] that [in reality] his return to Quito had been for the purpose of finding out what condition

---

*[Subtracting, from the total of fifty-four, one for Orellana, fifty for his companions, and two for the priests, we find that the number of persons whom Oviedo here designates as "the rest" must have been one! Two paragraphs below, however, Oviedo, admits that there were others whose names could not be recalled.—EDITOR.]

the country was in and of informing himself about the affairs of President Vaca de Castro and Don Diego de Almagro;* but what was considered to be nearer to the truth was that this Captain Gonzalo Pizarro had come back a ruined man, because out of two hundred and thirty men that he had taken along there came back only one hundred, most of them broken down and ill; and these latter and those who escaped [with their lives by going] down the river with Francisco de Orellana are thought to be still alive, and the rest dead, these latter, if the truth be told, being more than eighty-seven in number; for into the boat with Orellana went more than these companions have stated, men whose names are not recalled.

In view of this misfortune which befell Gonzalo Pizarro, letters further state that Captain Sebastián de Benalcázar was making great haste to organize an expedition and obtain an authorization to go in search of El Dorado: what is to become of this, time will tell, and [this must wait now] in order that [material for] it may be gathered and written up where that administration of Benalcázar as governor is the special topic to be treated; and until then let the matter rest and let us go back to our story of Quito and to the account which this Captain Francisco de Orellana and his followers give [us] of these lands.

## CHAPTER III

*In which is presented an account of the nature of the land and the people of the province of Quito, and of what the cinnamon trees which Gonzalo Pizarro and the Spaniards saw are like, and of the great size of the Marañón River, and of the numerous islands that there are in it.†*

The land of Quito is fertile and quite generally inhabited, and the natives of that province and of its neighboring territories are warlike and of handsome figure, and the city of San Francisco [Quito], which is the principal town where there are Christians in that administrative territory, lies at a little less than four degrees the other side of the equinoctial line.‡

In their battles and campaigns the Indians are in the habit of carrying banners, and [of employing] well-trained squads, and [of using] trumpets and bagpipes (or [at least] certain musical instruments which sound [387] very much like bagpipes) and drums and rebecs; and [they adorn] their persons with beautiful plumes; they fight with sticks and "estoricas"§ and lances thirty palms long and with stones and slings.

---

*[I.e. Diego de Almagro the Lad (see footnote on p. 251, *supra*).—Editor.]

†At the end of this caption the original reading was as follows: "And of the idol-worship and rites and ceremonies which the Indians adhere to in some provinces; and additional particulars which Captain Francisco de Orellana and those who under his command separated themselves from Gonzalo Pizarro's expeditionary force testified to and [which] I heard from them *vivâ voce*." This has been crossed out, apparently by the hand of Oviedo. [With regard to this editorial comment by Amador de los Ríos it may be observed that Oviedo may have meant to cross out only the last few phrases of all this, it being his intention, perhaps, to note down the "additional particulars" elsewhere—an intention which he does not seem to have carried out.—Editor.]

‡[The true latitude of Quito is 13′ S., or about a quarter degree south of the equator.—Editor.]

§[In the version of Friar Carvajal's story copied by Oviedo, p. 555 (see p. 423 below), we find as a synonym for "estorica" the Spanish word "amiento," which means "strap" or "thong." The "estorica," therefore, seems to have been a leather strap tied to a stick that was hurled, being presumably attached to one end and serving either to guide the stick, like the feathers of an arrow, or, if it was a long strap, to enable the warrior to pull the stick back after the blow had been struck. The term seems to be used here, as well as in other passages in Carvajal's *Relación*, to designate the weapon itself.—Editor.]

I learned from this Captain Orellana and his companions that the country where the cinnamon trees grow is seventy leagues east of Quito; and fifty leagues, slightly more or less, west of Quito is the Southern Sea and the Island of Puná.* The leaves of these trees are a very fine spice, as well as the cup of the nut which it [i.e. this tree] bears as its fruit; but neither the nut nor the bark of the tree is as good a one [i.e. spice]. They are trees as tall as olive trees, and their leaves [are] like those of the laurel, [though] somewhat wider; the color of the leaves comes closer to being green than those of the olive tree and shades off towards a yellow color. The trees which the Spaniards saw on this expedition of Gonzalo Pizarro's were few in number and far apart the ones from the others, on mountain ranges and in barren and rugged country: with the spice derived therefrom they were quite pleased as regards its taste and good quality, [it being] very fine cinnamon, though differing as a product from that which has hitherto been commonly exported to Spain and Italy from the Levant and is used throughout the world. The shape of this [cinnamon], I mean of those cups of the fruit, which is the best part of it, is a subject which I have already treated in Book IX, Chapter XXXI, and I even drew a picture showing their shape.† But quite disappointed, in the end, were these soldiers over the small quantities which they found of this cinnamon, and from this fact it has come about that some have said that it is in exceedingly small quantities, while others say just the opposite in view of the fact that it is carried to many [distant] parts and [nearby] provinces; but [whether it is to be found there] in large quantities or in small quantities time will reveal, just as it has revealed [the facts in regard to] the gold on this our Island of Hispaniola, where there passed many years after the Spaniards had come here during which they found only a small quantity of gold, and afterwards there were discovered and there are now in existence many very rich mines and [these are located] in many parts of the island, and there have been taken out of them countless thousands of pesos worth of gold, or [sic] never will it be exhausted or run out until the end of the world; and this is what might also happen in [the matter of] the abundance of the supply of this cinnamon.

As to the great size of the Marañón River, I was assured by Captain Francisco de Orellana and his followers, who came here, that a thousand two hundred leagues before it reaches the sea its width at places is two and three leagues; and, as they came on down it, [they perceived that] it constantly broadens out and its volume becomes greater owing to the many other waters and rivers which pour into it from one and the other of its two banks; and that seven hundred leagues before emptying into the sea its width is ten leagues and more. And from here on its breadth increases more and more all the way down to the sea, where it goes out through many mouths, forming many islands, the number of which [mouths], as well as [that] of these islands, these discoverers never found out nor could at that time comprehend. But all maintain that, as numerous as those mouths are all the way to the main coast to the east and to the west, what falls in between

---

*[Reckoning the league as 3⅔ statute miles (see, above, p. 47, asterisk footnote) the stated distance from Quito to the Pacific is reasonably correct if measured along the main outlet route, i.e. southwestward to the Gulf of Guayaquil, at the head of which lies the Island of Puná. The cited distance from Quito to the cinnamon country is doubtless much exaggerated, probably owing to the tendency to overestimate distances on advancing through the trackless wilderness.—EDITOR.]

†[An editorial footnote here calls attention to the fact that this picture is Figure 1 on Plate 4 at the end of Volume 1 of this edition of Oviedo.—EDITOR.]

can [all] be said to be the river, and there are forty leagues or more of mouth and fresh water, and this [i.e. the fresh water] enters [into the sea] breaking up the salt [water]; and when one is another twenty-five leagues out from the shore there is drawn up fresh water out of that which pours out of the said river.

They came upon and saw countless islands inhabited and completely occupied by people using various sorts of weapons, and [on] some, [men] who fight with sticks and "estoricas" and "macanas," and on others, with bows and arrows; but the arrowmen have no [baneful] herb until [one gets down to] those who are two hundred leagues back from the sea, for from there down they shoot [arrows smeared] with it and employ it as a diabolical and most vicious poison.

All these people are idolaters, and they worship the sun and offer up to him doves and turtle-doves and *chicha*, which is the wine that they drink made out of maize and cassava, and other [388] beverages of theirs; and they place it [i.e. the offering] before their idols, which are a few statues and figures representing persons of great stature. They sacrifice, from among their enemies, a few of those whom they capture in war, in the following manner: they cut off the hands [of some] at the wrists and of others at the elbows, and in this condition they keep them until they die; and after they are dead they roast them on hurdles or grills and make powder out of them and throw it to the wind; and also out of their prisoners they keep a certain number in order to make use of them as slaves. They do not eat human flesh anywhere along the said river until [one gets down to] the arrowmen that use the [baneful] herb, who are Caribs and [who] eat it with great pleasure.

When the natives ([those who dwell] in the provinces higher up than the arrowmen [just mentioned]) die, they are wrapped in cotton blankets and buried in their own homes. They are a people of considerable foresight, and they keep provisions on hand until the time when they take in the next harvest, and they have others in store in lofts or on hurdles raised above the ground the height of a man and [read: or] as high as they see fit; and they keep there their maize and their biscuit (which [latter] they make out of maize and cassava mixed together or bound with a paste), and a great deal of roasted fish, and many manatees, and game meat.

In their houses they use ornaments, and they have very pretty mats made out of palmleaf, and earthenware in large quantities and of a very good quality. They sleep in hammocks; the houses are well swept and clean, and are built of wood and covered with straw. This [statement] about the houses holds true [for those] down on the coast or not far in from the sea; and in some places up the river they are built out of stone; the doors of the houses they [make it a point to] have facing in the direction where the sun rises, for some reason in connection with their ceremonies.

The land of Quito is fertile, supplying the food products already mentioned and likewise all the kinds of fruit which are known [to grow] in Tierra Firme; it is healthful and with good air and good water and a temperate [climate], and the Indians [are] of good physique and of a better color or less swarthy than those along the coast of the Northern Sea. There are many sorts and good qualities of herbaceous plants, and some like those in our Spain; and the ones which these Spaniards, the companions of Orellana, and he say that they have seen [down there] are nightshade, vervain, purslane, sweet basil, cress, sow thistles, edible thistles, penny-royal, and blackberry bushes; and many others it is believed [are there] which these are not familiar with and [it is probable] that time will bring them to our knowledge. Among the animals [which they saw] they say that there are many deer and does and cows [and] tapirs and ant-eating bears and rabbits and sloths and jaguars and pumas and all the others which are common in Tierra Firme, domestic and wild (not to mention those large Peruvian sheep and the other smaller ones), and armadillos and polecats of the species that emits an offensive smell, and opossums and the native dogs, which do not bark.

## CHAPTER IV

*In which is presented an account of the dominion of Queen Conorí and the Amazons, if Amazons they ought to be called, and of her government and great power and vast dominion, and of the overlords and monarchs who are subject to the said queen; and of the great monarch named Caripuna, within whose dominion they say that there is a great wealth of silver and other commodities, wherewith is concluded the account of the discoverers who journeyed by water down the Marañón River under Captain Francisco de Orellana.*

In that account which I have said Friar Gaspar de Carvajal wrote, [and] which is copied in Chapter XXIV of the last book of these histories of the Indies, among other noteworthy matters he says that there is a dominion belonging to women who live by themselves without males, and [that] they act as soldiers in [time of] war and are powerful and wealthy and own vast provinces. Already in several sections of this *General History of the Indies* mention has been made [**389**] of a number of regions where women are absolute rulers and hold sway over their [respective] nations and render justice in them and bear arms, whenever there is any occasion for doing so, an example being the case of that queen named Orocomay, as I related the matter and described it in Book XXIV, Chapter X. And similarly, in connection with [the creation of] the administrative territory of New Galicia and the conquest of the same, [a case of this sort of thing may be seen], as has been stated in Book XXXIV, Chapter VIII, dealing with the dominion of Ciguatán, and there they [i.e. the women] may well be called Amazons (if I have been told the truth); but they do not cut off their right breasts, as did those whom the ancients called Amazons, as it is claimed by Justin, who says that they used to burn off their right breasts in order that they might not hinder them in shooting with the bow. Both the one and the other matter touched upon in these historical accounts of mine relative to Orocomay and Ciguatán are unimportant in comparison with what these men who came down the Marañón River say is common gossip with respect to the women whom these men call Amazons. From an Indian whom this Captain Orellana took along with him ([and] who afterwards died on the Island of Cubagua) they learned that in the country where these women are ruling persons there are contained and included [stretches of territory having a total length of] more than three hundred leagues inhabited by women, these latter having no men among them, over all of which [territory] as queen and supreme ruling lady there is just one woman, whose name is Conorí [and] who is very [strictly] obeyed and respected and feared within her realms and outside of them, [that is to say,] in those which are contiguous to [the territory ruled over by] her; and she holds in subjection many provinces which obey her and consider her as their supreme ruler and render service to her, as her vassals and tributaries; these [contiguous realms] are [well] populated, as for example that region over which there rules a great overlord named Rapio. And [there is] another [region] which has another monarch, who goes by the name of Toronoy. And another province which has another overlord whom they call Yaguarayo. And another which has another who goes by the name of Topayo; and another which is ruled over by another male [ruler], Qüenyuco. And [there is] another province, one which, or one whose overlord, is called Chipayo; and another province which has another overlord who goes by the name of Yaguayo.

All these overlords or monarchs are great overlords and they rule over great stretches of country and are subject to the Amazons (if Amazons they ought to be called) and render service to them and to their queen Conorí. This commonwealth belonging to these women lies in Tierra Firme, between the Marañón River and the River Plate, the correct name of which is the Paranaguazu.

On the left as these Spaniards and their captain Francisco de Orellana came on down the Marañón River they say that there is a great overlord [ruling over a territory] facing the country of the Amazons, with the river in between: that monarch is named Caripuna and he holds in subjection and possesses a great expanse of country; and subject to him are many other overlords who obey him, and his country is very rich in silver. But inasmuch as clearness [in all this matter] and detailed information are not to be had in a more accurate form at the present time, I wanted to set down [just] this much here, not because it rounds out [the discussion of what was going on in] the administrative territory of Peru, but as a record in connection with what may happen later on and [what may] need to be told about, when these regions and territories shall have become better known and [shall have been better] explored, and because, as has been stated, it is thanks [only] to these Spanish hidalgos who set out from Quito that there has been made known and [there has been] discovered that which has been related [here]. And so, in order that he may better understand the matter, I would advise the reader, when in his reading he has reached this point, without going on any further to turn to Chapter XXIV of the last book of this *General History of the Indies*, in order that he may have the satisfaction of being better familiarized with the discovery of this Marañón River and with what was seen along its course by Captain Francisco de Orellana and by the men who in company with him were participants in a [feat of] navigation so great and so new [to human experience] and so dangerous. And as to whatever else may come to light in connection with this affair, let us give heed to what time shall reveal and shall advise us about in order that further additions may be made to the history of the Marañón, and also to that of [the province of] Quito, which is the special subject that is being treated here.

## [390] CHAPTER V

*In which are treated the unsuccessful operations and the death of Captain Francisco de Orellana, as well as of many others who, having placed their trust in his words, lost their lives [as a consequence thereof].*

This Captain Francisco de Orellana went off* with something over four hundred men and an excellent military organization and equipment, having been appointed

*[I.e. he started out from Spain on a new expedition to the Amazon, 1545–1546: see Chapter 10 of Medina's Introduction in the present volume.—EDITOR.]

adelantado and governor [of a stretch of territory along the course] of the Marañón River; and he touched at the Cape Verde Islands, where, partly as a result of sickness of various sorts, partly in consequence of his poor leadership, he lost a large part of the men that he was taking along. And as [best] he could, notwithstanding the hardships that befell him, he pushed on in search of those Amazons whom he had never seen and whom he had talked so much about throughout Spain, whereby he had deprived of their senses all those covetous individuals who followed him; and finally he reached one of the mouths through which the Marañón River empties into the sea. And there he died, as did the greater part of the company that he had brought with him; and those few who were left over, later, [though now] ruined men, reached a port of safety on our island of Hispaniola, as has been said above.* And because this captain accomplished nothing that is worthy of any praise in his favor or that deserves any thanks, let there suffice for you, reader, this brief account of the wretched fate which this cavalier met and [through] which his evil ideas came to nought, as might be expected from the brains which had set them in motion. And let us go on to other bloody and unsavory stories which time and the progress of this undertaking of mine bring to mind.

## CHAPTER VI

*In which is presented a summary treatment of the questions which arose leading to the wars that took place in the lands and [in general the region of] the southern seas improperly called Peru; which [conflict] has been a great obstacle to [the proper functioning of] the service of God and of His Cesarean [Majesty] and Their Catholic Majesties and [has worked] to the detriment of the crown and royal scepter of Castile, as well as of the Spaniards themselves and of the native Indians dwelling in those parts.*

. . . . . . . . . . . . . . . . . . . . . . . . .
. . . . . . . . . . . . . . . . . [392] . . . . .†

With these conditions [laid down], I say that the Licentiate Vaca de Castro, after he had crossed over tò Peru, was urged to proceed to the province of Quito; which territory, constituting the jurisdiction of a separate governor, Gonzalo Pizarro said that his brother the Marquis Don Francisco Pizarro, by virtue of power and authorization coming from Their Majesties, had handed over to him and renounced [into his hands], [this grant including] both the territorial division known as Quito, and what belongs to Pasto and La Culata, or the bay and port and island of Puná, along with several other settlements, and that he held all that

*[This reference has not been found. Is Oviedo here confusing these persons with the few men who, in company with Orellana, had proceeded to Santo Domingo at the conclusion of the first voyage down the Amazon?—EDITOR.]

†[The omitted passages, embracing a page and a half on pp. 390–392, deal mainly with the perversity and self-seeking of the Pizarros—Gonzalo, Hernando, and Francisco—characteristic of the "strifes and ill-spent efforts of the impassioned captains and soldiers who used up their lives in such squabbles." The account of these civil wars should be made brief, says Oviedo, for "it behooves him who writes about them to make it a point to express the truth using few words, he being actuated by thoroughly good intentions and free from the prejudices which might arise and throw themselves across his path to interfere with the very substance of the surest and most accurate intelligence, on which hinges the power and beauty of a history that shows no bias."—EDITOR.]

as belonging to him. And being now in Quito, he received reports about the valley where the cinnamon grows and about the lake [on whose shores was the home] of King or Chief El Dorado, and he decided to go and explore it [i.e. all this region], being informed (by Indians) that it was a place abounding in great wealth; he got under way at great expense to himself and after assembling more than two hundred men whom he took along with him for this purpose, partly on foot and partly on horseback, crossing over mountains very rugged and traversed by no roads, making some [i.e. roads] by hand with great difficulty and at the cost of excessive hardships, crossing numerous and large rivers and building bridges across them by dint of hitherto untried skill and at a remarkable risk, until they came out in a province that is called Zamaco, which is seventy leagues away from Quito, where on account of the fatigue and other failings they were compelled to halt in order to reorganize this army; and they found there a plentiful supply of food, although the country is a rugged one and one of great forest tracts and broken lands, and swamplands are not lacking among them. The natives are people who wear no clothes, and their houses [are] in the woods, far apart the ones from the others.

After they had rested and gathered together a certain amount of provisions, these Spaniards moved forward in the quest for cinnamon, taking along with them several interpreters who said that they would take them as far as there [i.e. where the cinnamon grew]; and in order that they might not all have to undergo hardships, Gonzalo Pizarro gave orders that there should go along with him (and those guides) as many as eighty companions, and that the rest should await his return. And in this way he advanced for sixty days on foot, [traveling this way] because the country was so rough that they could not take horses.

At the end of the said number of days the cinnamon trees were found: these are tall (and there are also short ones) and very far apart the ones from the others and [are] found in out-of-the-way places in rough forested country; their leaves, as well as a certain quantity of flower-buds which they have, have a cinnamon taste; neither the bark nor the rest has a pleasant taste, nor, [as a matter of fact], does it taste of anything but wood. And as the trees which they saw were few in number, they were not pleased with what they had found, being of the opinion that the profit to be derived from [the exploitation of] the cinnamon was slight in comparison with the great amount of hard labor [required] in going after it in a country so sparsely settled.

From there they moved on to another province which is called Capüa, and from there Gonzalo Pizarro sent for the men whom he had left behind; and he went on as far as another country which is called Güema, whence he crossed over to another province whose name is Oguama, the inhabitants of which dwell along the shore of a mighty river, and their houses are right down on the water's edge, although separated the ones from the others. The people of this tribe keep in contact with one another by going up and down along that shore in boats, and they wear cotton blouses; and the country off in the interior is very hard to travel about in, on account of the numerous marshes that there are in it.

There, Gonzalo Pizarro caused a brigantine to be built [393] for the purpose of crossing to the other side of that river and transporting the sick and the arquebuses and the crossbows and other weapons and munitions and other things required for his enterprise, [this brigantine to be so used] in conjunction with fifteen canoes which the Spaniards had captured there from the natives of the country.

And they proceeded onward with this fleet, although they did not fail to encounter a certain number of canoes that got in their way [to resist their advance]; but as soon as the Indians would see the brigantine and [hear] the detonation of the arquebuses, they would flee.

The greater part of the Christians were proceeding along on the banks of the river, [thus likewise] getting on in their journey; and one day Gonzalo Pizarro's lieutenant, Captain Francisco de Orellana, said to him that the guides were saying that down where they were heading for there was a great stretch of uninhabited country, and that it was not advisable to push on without first halting and procuring a supply of provisions for use in pushing on with their enterprise, and this was done. But the amount of provisions which they managed to get together was small. Thereupon Captain Orellana said to him that he, by way of rendering a service to Their Majesties and to the said Gonzalo Pizarro, would go down the river in the brigantine and canoes and with sixty men, as far as the junction of certain rivers where it was reported that food would be found, and would collect all that he possibly could and would come back to the main expeditionary force within ten or twelve days, and [that he was of the opinion] that Gonzalo Pizarro and [the rest of] the men should push on down the river, and that he, Orellana, would shortly return back up the river with the relief in the form of food supplies; and [he concluded by saying] that in this way the army would be kept alive and their [or his, i.e. Pizarro's] purpose could be carried out without [any inconvenience caused by] a lack of provisions.

It seemed to Gonzalo Pizarro that the proposal which Orellana was making was a good one, and he granted him permission and gave him the men and whatever else seemed proper and had been requested by him, and he gave orders to him to the effect that, at the expiration of the time which he had said, he should turn back, and that he should in no case go beyond the junction of the rivers where the guides said that they were sure to find food; and, because Gonzalo Pizarro had to cross over two great rivers, he told him to leave for him four or five canoes out of those which they were taking with them, so that those who were proceeding with him [i.e. Pizarro] might be able to cross over; and Orellana told him that he would do all that, and he departed. And instead of leaving the canoes [at that spot] and [instead of] coming back with the provisions, he went off down the river with the companions that Gonzalo Pizarro had given him, and he carried off the weapons and the iron implements and everything else; and, being now a man in revolt, he went off in search of [a way out] to the Northern Sea.

When Gonzalo Pizarro perceived that Orellana was overdue and was not coming back, and that he was without news of him beyond the fact that [he knew that] he [i.e. Orellana] had gone as far as the junction of the two rivers, where there were found huts and other signs showing that he had been there, he, Pizarro, found that he had been tricked; and he said that Francisco de Orellana had shown the greatest cruelty that any faithless man could indulge in, in abandoning Gonzalo Pizarro [i.e. him] and the others in those wildernesses among so many rivers and without food, for they had none other but some heads of "bihaos"* and a few palm kernels; and the shortage of food was so great that they were

---

*[In the glossary of "American terms used by Oviedo," compiled by the Academy of History's editor and inserted near the end of the volume from which the present extracts are taken, "bihao" is defined as "a certain plant whose leaves were used by Indians to cover their houses or huts." Furthermore, the word appears to be identical with "bijao," which is defined in modern dictionaries as "a musaceous plant," i.e. a plant belonging to the banana and plantain family.— EDITOR.]

obliged to eat a large number of dogs and more than a hundred horses and thousands of little beasts of the lizard family and poisonous victuals, in consequence
whereof a number of companions died and others came out of it weak and ill.

When Gonzalo Pizarro reached the junction [already referred to], he with the
men that he still had left [in good condition] got into five canoes which he had
captured, and taking a small number of companions he decided to go look for
food for himself and for them; and one day's journey from there, up the [other]
river from the junction, they found food, and with the news of this [prospective]
relief he went back to the expeditionary corps; but all of one accord told him
that they would die rather than go on any farther. Heeding this decision of
theirs, by means of those canoes he got the men across the great river* within
eight days with much toil and at a risk of no less proportions, and they found
maize and yucca there where the guides had said that food would be found. There
the force was reorganized and they rested several days, and having gone forward
[again] they passed through another large [394] area of uninhabited country,
harassed by a great shortage of provisions and [hence by] hunger, and such [was
this latter] that they finished eating the horses that they still had left, to the
number of more than eighty, and several [more] Spaniards died. Oh ye sinful
men, to what ends do your greedy aims and your vain desires bring you! And how
imprudently do you subject yourselves to such unbearable sufferings, and how well
do your guilty acts and your mad deeds deserve these!

On many days it fell to the lot of these Spaniards to have to cross over numerous
and large rivers and to build bridges and rafts for that purpose, and at times to
walk through the water up to their knees, up to their belts, and even higher. In
short, they had penetrated into the interior more than two hundred leagues, and
on the return journey the distance was much greater before they finally got back
to Quito; and by this time the Licentiate Vaca de Castro had passed that way,
and had caused himself to be accepted as the governor of Quito and of all the
rest [of the territory] that Gonzalo Pizarro had held as falling within his jurisdiction as governor; and there he [i.e. Gonzalo Pizarro] learned of the death of
the Marquis his brother, and he was told that Don Diego de Almagro the Lad
was refusing to obey the King's orders. Wherefore Gonzalo Pizarro thought
best to go look for President Vaca de Castro, taking with him as many as seventy
companions just as they had come back from the expedition which the [i.e. this]
history has [already] told about, and with the intention of obediently performing
whatever he might be ordered to do, according to what he himself wrote to his
friends in his letters; and I saw one of these dated at Tomebamba, in the land of
Quito, the third of September of the year One Thousand Five Hundred and
Forty-two.†

This, then, was the background for the flight and revolt of Captain Francisco de
Orellana and the cause of there having been seen, [for the first time by white men],
that Marañón River in the way that is told in the last book of these historical
accounts, which tells about shipwrecks, [namely,] Chapter XXIV.

*[Oviedo's editor prints: "the río Grande"—EDITOR.]
†[This is the letter which is published as Document I in this book, p. 245 ff. *supra.*—EDITOR.]

*[The subject of] which is something more than a shipwreck, because it deals with a miraculous event, in which [chapter] there is presented a specially composed account of the very remarkable and mighty river called the Marañón, down which Captain Francisco de Orellana and other hidalgos journeyed in boats, along the course of which river they spent eight months before finally coming to a land where there were Christians, [having traveled] more than two thousand leagues, and came to the Island of Pearls (otherwise known as Cubagua) which is in this general section of the seas; and from there the said Captain came on to this city of Santo Domingo on the Island of Hispaniola accompanied by a few soldiers belonging to his party, sharers in his hardships and witnesses of everything that will be set down here in the form in which it has been recorded in writing by a devout and reverend father of the Order of Preaching Friars, named Friar Gaspar de Carvajal, who was right there in person to take part in it all, [and] whose version or brief sketch [of it], reproduced here, runs as follows:*

Oblivion has deprived many men of compensation and payment for their services, and memory has heightened the worth of those who have obtained a reward for their works from monarchs, as the Holy Scriptures remind us in the case of David in the house and in the court of the ungrateful King Saul, and of Mordecai at the court and home of the resplendent King Ahasuerus; and in this connection I could cite other authorities and [other] authentic examples, which, [however], I am omitting for the sake of avoiding profuseness.

I shall merely state, or [rather] I insist on saying [at least this much], that we should not know a great deal now about the noteworthy deeds of the Romans if there had not been someone to write them down, as [did], for example, Titus Livius in his *Decades*, and [also] other authors; and, although these men knew how to do it better than I, still they had to be informed first by persons who, from having been eye-witnesses, could testify to [the truth of] what they [i.e. the writers] in choice words and a polished style gave to the public and handed down to everlasting memory for those to come after them, who [are] we who now read and [those who in the future] will read their treatises.  That is the way that I, having in mind nothing more than to communicate the truth to him who may wish to know about the matter and read my plain and simple account, without circumlocutions, with that straightforwardness with which the man of the church is duty bound to testify to what he has seen, and in the way in which that man [should do] to whom God saw fit to assign a part in this peregrination, shall relate a story just as it happened, in so far as I was in a position to follow it and in part

*[Part II of the present volume was already in page proof when this translation was undertaken. The reader will understand that, owing to this circumstance, it was not always possible, when this new opportunity led to a more satisfactory rendering, to change identical passages in the translation of the version of Carvajal's account published by Medina (Part II of the present volume) to conform strictly with the present translation of the version published by Oviedo. —Editor.]

grasp its significance; and furthermore [I wish to do this] because it seems to me that I should not be heeding the dictates of my conscience in failing to make this specially composed account accessible to whoever may wish to know the facts regarding the hardships which have been endured by Francisco de Orellana and fifty companions whom he led away from the expeditionary force of the governor of Quito, Gonzalo Pizarro, the brother of the Marquis Don Francisco Pizarro, governor of New Castile, otherwise known as Peru, on behalf of His Cesarean Majesty the Emperor-King, our master. This Captain Gonzalo Pizarro went off into the interior of the country having as his aim the conquest and exploration of the province of La Canela, because a certain quantity of cinnamon, through the agency of the Indians and after being passed on from one person to another, had come to Quito and to these regions of the Antarctic or Southern Hemisphere, where there were Spaniards scattered about and [where] they came to know about it; and it stirred up considerable interest, because it was thought that from the finding of trees and spices of this kind there was bound to result a great service to God through the conversion of the Indians who controlled the supply of it [i.e. the cinnamon], as well as a considerable benefit and [source of] increase [of revenue] for the Royal Exchequer, and many other advantages and unknown possibilities that were expected [to come ultimately out] of this new undertaking. And as this governor and his men were going down a certain river, he was informed that the country on ahead was uninhabited and lacking in provisions for the army which he was taking along with him; and because of the necessity of being prepared to cope with the situation in the event of a shortage of supplies such as indicated, it was agreed between Governor Gonzalo Pizarro and Captain Francisco de Orellana, and with [the approval of] other well-qualified members of that expeditionary force, that it was not an advisable thing to do to push on any farther until the physical nature of [the country along] the way should have been investigated, and, if that was possible, until [**542**] the army should have been provisioned with maize and all the supplies that could be found, because [already] there was a great shortage, nay, a considerable lack, of food.

With this end in view, the said Captain set out from the camp, taking with him the fifty men of whom mention was made above: he and his men suffered innumerable hardships and privations in the form of [protracted] hunger spells and periods of destitution, and in various places they had encounters with Indian warriors on the said river and off it, [people] of quite different tongues and belonging to [distinct] tribes, as we shall relate further on.

I shall not take upon myself to recount the risks and privations which this same Captain, prior to this moment, had incurred when he came, following in the tracks of the said Captain Gonzalo Pizarro and [trying] to find him, all the way from his home, [thus] abandoning his fixed residence and the life of ease which he had been keeping up with considerable honor and profit to himself, for he was the governor's lieutenant-general [residing] in Villa Nueva de Puerto Viejo and [performing the functions of governor] of the city of Santiago [i.e. Guayaquil], which he had founded and [whose site, with its surrounding territory, he had first] conquered at his own expense and on his own initiative, and which is in Peru, where he owned many Indians, and good ones, by right of grant, and other property and livestock and everything necessary for becoming a man of high rank and power if he had contented himself to remain at home accumulating wealth. But being a cavalier who desired to make better use of his time and his person and serve God and his King, or else because God had chosen him for an event and [a voyage of] discovery so noteworthy, he did not value his repose as highly as going to see [for himself] and have a share in, and ascertain for himself, the outcome of an undertaking as glorious as people said it was to find that cinnamon; and consequently he abandoned his place of residence and set out to overtake the said Gonzalo Pizarro's expeditionary force in the province of Moti,* and before arriving there he had to cross over lofty and rugged mountains where dwelt Carib or savage Indians, and over numerous and mighty rivers, and through the province of Zumaco which is inhabited by warlike Indians, taking with him only twenty companions, which men, as well as he himself, met with no end of immeasurable hardships, for he lost over forty thousand gold pesos in horses and munitions and fighting equipment, or in other words fourteen horses and all his clothing and bedding and everything [else] that he had started out with, so that all he had left in the end was three horses.

His companions lost the horses and the clothing and bedding which they had, nor did there fail to fall to his [i.e. Orellana's] lot and theirs many trying woes, consisting both of [long] spells of hunger and numerous encounters and real battles by which their advance was resisted along the way; and although it was from this Captain and his followers who had gone through it [all] that I heard about it and [consequently] consider it absolutely true, I do not care to go to the trouble of relating that which I neither witnessed nor had any share in to one single degree, while† in what follows from this point on I took part along with Captain Francisco de Orellana and his fifty companions [in the voyage] down the river, the reason for our separating from the expeditionary force being the one already stated, [namely that of] going off in search of inhabited country and of food, in a boat and several canoes, in which there were likewise taken along a few loads of clothing and bedding belonging to the expeditionary force, together with a few sick men, and it must be added that I was one of these [sick persons]; and as I was unable to travel either on foot or on horseback, I got into the boat [with the intention of staying with the party] until we should reach an inhabited section of country, believing that the expeditionary force and the entire army would be able to come on as far as there, and there likewise got into the boat another clergyman belonging to [the Order of] Our Lady of Mercy, whose name was Friar Gonzalo de Vera.

We set out from the camp on the second day of the Feast-tide of the Nativity of Our Redeemer Jesus Christ, Monday, the year and the day being the second of One Thousand Five Hundred and Forty and Two,‡ and proceeded down the river which rises in the province that is called Atunquijo, its source being thirty leagues from the Southern Sea, through which [province] we had already passed with the entire army of Governor Gonzalo Pizarro.

With this river other mighty rivers unite, such as the one they call the Cosanga (by which we also passed), as well as another which is called the Payamino, and the Canela; and, in spite of the fact that [the current of] the river down [543] which we were going was so swift in consequence of this [i.e. of the increase in the

*[The other version of Carvajal's account (p. 168, above) has Motín.—EDITOR.]

†[This is a somewhat forced translation of the "que" of the original, and is based in part on the assumption that a comma not in the original should be inserted after the preceding word.—EDITOR.]

‡[For Medina's conjecture regarding the last element of this figure and his interpretation of the entire expression used here to indicate the date of the start of Orellana's expedition proper, see Introduction, footnote 94, p. 58, *supra.*—EDITOR.]

volume of water resulting from the flowing in of the streams just mentioned], the seamen who happened to join our party, [these being included] in the figure fifty which has been mentioned, kept charting the river and taking notes, and they calculated our daily runs and affirmed that each day, rowing downstream, we navigated twenty-five leagues or more. In this way we moved on for three days without [coming upon] any inhabited section of country. O almighty God, how erring and foolish men are, and how far removed [they are] from comprehending or [even] divining the end to which their wanderings and calculations are going to come!

Seeing that we had set such a great distance between us and [the main body of] the expeditionary force and that there had now been used up our small supply of provisions which we had laid in, [a supply altogether too small] for a journey as uncertain [from the point of view of length] as the one that ours had turned itself into, so completely the reverse of what we thought at first, [we realized that it was not advisable to go on much farther]; and the Captain and the companions talked over the difficulty of turning back [from there], and [the question of] the lack of food, and [how], when we had left the [main] expeditionary force, we had thought that on the following day or on that [same day] we would find food and some sort of village; but, being confident that there could not fail to be some sort of settlement not far away, it was decided that we should go ahead. But neither on the next day nor on the following one was there found or did we see any trace or sign of a settlement, and in accordance with the view of all I said the Saint's mass, commending to God Our Lord our persons and our lives and beseeching His Divine Majesty, unworthy man though [I was], through that holy and most sacred mystery, that Our Redeemer might deliver us from such manifest hardship and [eventual] destruction as that was coming to look like now, and, although we did wish to go back upstream, it would have been impossible to do more than three leagues a day on account of the swiftness and the heavy current of the stream. To attempt to go by land was useless and out of the question; consequently, we were in great danger of death because of the excessive hunger that we were enduring; and so, after taking counsel and [weighing] opinions as to what should be done, talking over our affliction, a decision was arrived at and we chose of two evils the lesser, so it seemed to us, which was to go on downstream, rowing for all our strength was worth, trusting that Our Lord through His mercy would conserve it [i.e. our strength] until He should show us a way out, and that He would not permit our destruction.

In the meantime, lacking other victuals, we were eating leather from the seats and bows of saddles, and also the leather from game [on the outside] of the chests or hampers whose covering was made out of it, in which we were transporting the little clothing and bedding that we had, and a few tapir skins, not to mention the soles and [even whole] shoes that could be found among the members of the party; and, though there was no sauce other than hunger itself, this latter created in them [i.e. the men] a taste [for these things] and such an appetite [for them] that up to the point where we could stand it no longer these dishes of a sort so new were tolerated in order that this wretched flesh of ours might be sustained. A few companions ate herbs with which they were not familiar, and these were the worst off of all; and they reached the point where it was thought that they would not escape with their lives, and [yet] God saw fit to allow them [i.e. their lives] to be saved by means of a little oil that was found among certain medicines that happened to be on board, and which belonged to the surgeon of the expedition.

Because of this suffering which has been mentioned a certain number of the companions were quite disheartened, and the energies of these men the Captain, as he was a courageous cavalier, bolstered up to the best of his ability, inspiring hope in them by means of a countenance so pleasant and words so kind that it seemed as if God were favoring him with a special gift for cheering them up and helping them to put up with their suffering, and there is no doubt that he did a great deal of good in this way.

On New Year's Day it seemed to certain of the companions who were going along in one of the canoes belonging to our convoy and fleet that they heard drums, and this was announced among them all, and some said that it was true; others said that they could not hear it [i.e. the sound], but they became somewhat happier over this new ray of hope, and we pushed on with greater diligence than was customary with us, and, as [**544**] in truth neither on that day nor on the following one were any drums heard, they came to the conclusion that what had been said about their having heard drums was [the result of] imagination, and the outcome of it was that both those who were sick and the well became downhearted. And as God Our Lord is the father of mercy and of all consolation, who restores and helps him who calls on Him in the time of real need, it being Monday evening (this being the eighth day that we had been journeying on), while we were eating— inasmuch as we now had nothing else left to eat—a little wheat and flour which I had brought along for hosts, Indian drums were heard very plainly, and in our estimation they were some five or six leagues away from where we were, and after we had convinced ourselves [that it was true] by [appealing to] the ears of all, by which it [i.e. the sound] was being perceived more and more distinctly each hour, the Captain straightway ordered us to keep watch, and so it was that by quarters, as the custom is among well-trained men engaged in warfare, the watches were assigned with great care, a thing which had not been done before all down through the uninhabited section of country and along the journey which we had pursued so far.

The next day, in the morning, the Captain commanded that all be on the alert and arm themselves and have ready the three arquebuses and four or five cross- bows that there were among the companions; because, although in truth in the case of not one of the Spaniards was there [any tendency to manifest but] little worry as to what he had to do, the Captain had his own [worry] and that of all [the others], and consequently in every detail pertaining to his position [of com- mander] he performed very well the duty of an energetic and prudent man.

It turned out that on the next day, Tuesday, which made nine days from the time that we had left the expeditionary force, we arrived at a village situated in a country inhabited by Indians who are called Irimarais, in which country God willed that we should find a plentiful supply of maize and a certain amount of cured fish and large quantities of "aji";* and both during that day and on the following one the Captain had all the maize in the village collected with the idea in mind of going back to the expeditionary force, if that could be done, after load- ing that maize into the boat and the canoes; and for that purpose he ordered that there be unloaded the clothing and bedding which that boat was carrying and that they load it up, and the canoes, too, with maize; but although his intentions were good and [his aim was] to relieve Gonzalo Pizarro's army with provisions, there was no possibility of putting the plan into execution or of taking that supply of food up the river, and that is what the seamen in our party gave as their opinion,

*[I.e. red Indian dwarf pepper.—EDITOR.]

[saying that it could not be done] even if the boat and the canoes were to go not laden at all: notwithstanding which he [i.e. the Captain] decided that five or six men and a few tractable Indians and two negroes that there were there to help row should set out with that food relief and carry letters to Governor Gonzalo Pizarro informing him of what had been happening up to that moment. And in order that the Spaniards might be all the more willing to do that, he promised them one thousand castellanos; and [read: but] among all the men there were found only three who said that they would go, on condition that they were given three crossbowmen to go with them; men so inclined, [however], were not to be found, because they feared the death which was sure [to come] to them on account of the long time that it was bound to take them to get back to where they had left the camp or the expeditionary force, to go as far as which point was a feat which they could not perform in forty or fifty days, even though they met with no mishap, and [because they were convinced that], inasmuch as those forming the main army [back there] where Gonzalo Pizarro had halted had no food and no place from which to obtain any, he [i.e. Gonzalo Pizarro], on the other hand, of necessity must have turned back to look for inhabited country in order not to [let his whole expeditionary force] die of hunger; and [they maintained that] these men who were to go up the river with this message were bound not to escape perishing either, even though no Indians molested them, for there was this added consideration that there could not be had any [guarantee of] safety from the natives of the country and from [the dangers lurking on] the shores along which they were to work their way back.

In view of all these objectionable features [of the plan] and many others which are not mentioned here the trip was given up; and then there is the fact that all the companions petitioned the captain not to go back [**545**] up the river or send those men up, for the reason that they were now two hundred leagues from the expeditionary force; and, according to the opinion held [by these petitioners], in view of the shortage of provisions [causing the precarious situation] in which they had left the [main] army, there was reason to believe that it had probably turned back to search for food and that these men [about whom I have been speaking], even though they were to go [back up], would not find the camp and Christian folk anywhere along the whole river: and in view of all this they begged and urged Captain Francisco de Orellana to change his decision and follow another course and [stated] that they would all follow him as their Captain; and [they besought him] to bend his efforts, as a cavalier [and] in accordance with the obligation which was upon him, towards delivering them from the danger and manifest desperate situation in which he and all [the rest] found themselves, and to listen to advice, and to allow to be done that which would be most fitting as tending toward bringing about their salvation and the remedying [of the situation], putting upon him the responsibility for the lives of all by saying that he alone would be to blame if he attempted anything different.

The Captain, having heard the opinion of his men and recognizing that what they were saying to him was true, and [admitting] that they were right both as regards what has been stated and with respect to the dreadful [stretch of] uninhabited country through which we had passed, adhered as a prudent man to the views of the companions, and desisted from carrying out his own wish, which was to succor [the men back there in the precarious situation resulting from] the great shortage of provisions, in which Gonzalo Pizarro's army had been left; but, since that could not be done, he gave thanks to God for everything, who in His mercy permitted the Indians from the districts round about that stopping-place [of ours] to come [to us] in a peaceful mood, and just like friends some gave us fish in exchange for barter goods, others brought in birds and a certain quantity of "monkey-cat" meat; and in that village this worn-out company of ours got a [good] rest, not only those who were sick, but also the well.

In this village of Imara we stayed forty days, approximately, [waiting] to see if news could be had in some way or other from our men forming the [main] expeditionary force; and, as this was not possible and as it was not possible, either, for us to escape [from there] alive except by continuing on our way and in the direction of the Northern Sea, setting out to find it [by going] down the river, all the members of the party acquiesced in this decision, and [it was decided] that a brigantine should be built for this purpose large enough to carry thirty men, and that the remaining twenty should go in the boat [which we already had]; and, in order that no time might be wasted in idleness, [it was agreed] that nails should be made and that a certain number of men should go get timber for this piece of work; and in this way the task was begun.

During that period of time that they were there, each one creating strength out of weakness and taking necessity as his master, there being no craftsmen who were expert in this or that trade, some were engaged in making charcoal in spite of their not being charcoal burners, others in cutting and bringing in wood in spite of their not being woodcutters, others making nails in spite of their not being smiths, and others in working the bellows of the forge; and [with the aid of] God, being [as He is] the father and the ruler and the one who made up for the skill which the ones and the others lacked, within a few days two thousand nails of good quality were made out of the chains and horseshoes and [other] iron materials which were found scattered among the company.

A wonderful thing to behold was the [spirit of] brotherly affection and obedience and diligence with which we few men who were together there dealt with one another and aided one another with a [manifestation of] comradeship and love [both] heartfelt and bright; but [one should remember that], as the angel said to Esdras, "However much men may love their neighbors, God loveth them more." And in just this way did [the manifestations of] His mercy prove this to be true in our case in this journey [of ours], so long and so dangerous and one the like of which had never been heard of. [But] let us come back to [the story of] our journey.

I say[, then,] that we departed from this stopping-place, our task being completed, on the feast day of the Purification of Our Lady, which by another name they call Candlemas, on the first day of February of the year already stated, [i.e.] One Thousand Five Hundred and Forty-two. And [the reason why] we did not stay there longer [was] because the Indians had become rebellious, and for more than fifteen [546] days they had not been coming [to us] to barter goods, and [much] less had they been furnishing food, and the supply of maize which had been found in this village was diminishing. And, continuing on our journey, we went off to find a settlement called Aparia, which [name] is [likewise that of] a prominent overlord of that [settlement] and the province to which it belongs, and it [i.e. the province] is situated on both sides of the river; Captain Francisco de Orellana had entertained this man very nicely, and with the idea of bringing him around to [an attitude of] friendship toward the Christians had given him some "chaquira"* (for that is the name which is given to the strings of beads and [other] things which the Indian men and women wear around their necks as ornaments and [in lieu of] jewels), and in addition to all this he had also given them [i.e. to Aparia and his associates or subjects] other articles [consisting of pieces] of clothing, [back] in the stopping-place where the nails were made, because he had come to visit us there and on that occasion a certain amount of food had been brought by this captain†, whose home was on a river which unites with the one whose waters we navigated. And because of its [i.e. this other river's] strong current and [because] it emptied in with such a great onrush and force, ours [i.e. our force, our strength] was not sufficient for going up through it in the boat and the canoes‡ to take possession of the settlement, although we heard the drums and saw many Indians in canoes ready to defend the landing place; rather, we barely escaped drowning in getting past the junction of the rivers in [the midst of] a great jam of logs which the current had brought down. And so it was that against our wishes we passed on to go in quest of food supplies; and, although we did come upon a few small villages, they were without their inhabitants and the people [who had dwelt there were] up in arms [ready to fight us] and their houses [had been] burned down by order of the overlord who has been mentioned, in consequence whereof our privations and our hunger were becoming greater and greater and our strength and our energies were gradually weakening, because [what was really] inhabited country was for us uninhabited country and waste land, although there was still to be found a certain quantity of yucca and "aji" in the pools, for that is the term which they use there in speaking of the inclosures formed by means of [piled up] stones [and] belonging to the plots of cultivated land.

Under conditions of this sort we pushed on along the shores and through the country belonging to the settlements owned by this chief, and that was a long distance, owing to the fact that his is an extensive dominion; and, driven on by the fear that that small quantity of maize which we still had left was going to fail us soon, we moved on during the day as long as the sun and the daylight held out for us, all rowing as hard as our bodily weakness permitted, because, as we had no pilot, nor had any Christians ever made that journey, nor had there ever existed a navigator's chart with a description covering that part of the world, it was necessary to rest or at least not to push on during the night; inasmuch as [even] by day [the risk attending] the journey which we were making was concealed from us, by night we could have run into more dangers and it would have been a [show of] lack of prudence and a rash procedure to move on beyond where the [setting] sun had left us.

*[In the glossary of American words at the end of the volume from which the present translation is made "chaquira" is defined as follows: "a bracelet, a string of [pieces of] mother-of-pearl or of mother-of-pearl shells, [these being] ornamented with little plaques of gold." From a passage further on in Friar Carvajal's account (p. 564), where mention is made of a gourd which, after being filled with "diamonds and pearls, and jingle bells," was thrown into the water as a sop to some inhospitable Indians, it will be seen that the word has, at least for Carvajal, the general meaning of "trinkets." It is used with the feminine singular definite article in the passage just mentioned and appears to have a collective meaning in all passages in which it occurs in the present account.—EDITOR.]

†[It seems probable that in this passage "capitán" is a scribal (or printer's?) error for "señor," or possibly "cacique" as in the next paragraph.—EDITOR.]

‡[The text says: "with it" (and this pronoun can only mean the river) "through" (or "by") "the boats and canoes." The above translation is based on the assumption that the prepositions "with" and "through" have been interchanged.—EDITOR.]

A great misfortune and [one that brought about] no little vexation befell us, and [one which] caused [us] no little sadness, [one] in which we saw, for the time being, forebodings of our destruction [sooner or later] and [indications of] the improbability of our being able to save our corporeal lives: we are talking [here] about something which we know [for a fact] and we are testifying to the truth of something which we [actually] saw [take place]. One afternoon it came about that we bivouacked up a small inlet or brook which extended back from the shore of the main river whose course we were following in our journey, [whither we had gone] to catch a few small fish, and that two canoes of ours passed by and went ahead; in them were eleven Christians from our company, who, believing that the Captain and the rest of us Spaniards had gone on ahead, continued on their journey all that night and the next day and another [day], so that for two days and two nights they did not stop moving; and, as the river was very wide and kept splitting up into many arms (for at some places there emptied in a certain number of rivers while at others there flowed out others and they [i.e. these latter] kept breaking up [into separate courses]), the suspicion arose, and most of the men even claimed that it was something [absolutely] certain, that those companions must have gotten lost or have died at the hands of the Indians; and we without them were running a considerable risk, both because our company and our strength were [thus] being reduced and because among those men were persons quite essential [to us] and [several companions] well trained in matters pertaining to Indian warfare.

So great was the sadness on the part of us who were still left that I shall not be able [to find words with which] to emphasize the matter to an extent equal [547] to that to which we were affected by it; and [therefore I shall content myself with saying that] in consequence of this many made vows and promises of pilgrimages and of alms and of periods of prayer, and with great sincerity addressed petitions to God and to His glorious most Holy Mother, and [as a result of their] beseeching [Him] on behalf of those companions in order that they might not meet with destruction, Our Father of Mercy and Our Savior willed and saw fit that we should find them two days later, they having come to a stop on account of the Indians whom they had caught sight of in canoes on the river, and having become sure in their own minds that we had not gone on beyond that point; and [it was] out of fear of the Indians and due to their not daring to go into the settlements [that] they had come to a stop and an opportunity had been given to us to overtake them, [an event] which was no small piece of luck, rather [it was] a very great one and a good one for all of us, for just as soon as we saw them from a long way off (and things desired always have [this about them, that] the accomplishment [of the desire is] in doubt until they are [actually] obtained and that fear is set aside), some believed it was not they, others said it was, [these latter] trusting their sight. And when the truth was finally established, unbounded was the rejoicing on the part of all after we [i.e. the two groups] had succeeded in recognizing each other; and some for joy could not hold back their tears.

As soon as we had finished rejoicing for a short time over this renewal of life and this [occasion for mutual] consolation, the Captain, like a prudent man and one zealous in looking after the health of all, straightway gave orders to land in order to grant the men a respite from the fatigue and the hardships endured; and so we stopped early that day, and the following day also was used up in conversation and [in the putting and answering of] questions, as if it had been more than a year since we [two groups] had seen each other. There the Captain issued orders to all the companions who were traveling in canoes to the effect that, under heavy penalties, they should not draw away from the boat a space or distance of [more than] a crossbow shot, in order that there might not arise another mishap like the one which was now over.

On the following day we came upon a few Indian huts which had [once] been abandoned, not far from a large village, in which [latter] we slept that night; and it was one having more than sixty dwellings; and, so it appeared, a few days prior to this they [i.e. its inhabitants] had heard about our coming and out of fear had left the village to go [back] to those huts, to which the Captain ordered a few companions to go in the canoes in order to speak to the Indians and reassure them. And he took the proper measures to see to it that no Spaniard out of those whom he sent [on that mission] should get out on land or resort to any mistreatment of them, but that on the contrary in the kindest way that they could they should ask them for food and should hail them and encourage them to come in a peaceful mood and in all security to the Captain [i.e. to him]; and it pleased God that this should be so done in a peaceful manner. They brought back from there a few turtles of the very large variety, and that was something that could not fail to arouse curiosity, for we were [now] very far away from either the northern regions or the southern regions where such aquatic animals are usually found; and they also brought parrots, [all of] which [food] was sufficient to enable the companions to dine plentifully that night.

On the following day, just as soon as the sun was up, the Indians came in a peaceful frame of mind to talk to the Captain; and we learned from these persons that we were [now] in country belonging to Aparia the Great, and that from here on there were many settlements, and that the villages were not burned down as was the case with those which we had found thus far, a fact that explains why we had been having such a vast stretch of country without inhabitants to traverse during the nineteen days that we had been advancing since [leaving] the Irimais and Aparia the Lesser, during which time the companions had to a certain degree suffered from privations, which I am omitting from my story in order to avoid diffuseness.

On Saint Eulalia's day. there having already gone by eleven days of February since we had departed from the place where the nails were made, two rivers united with the river we were navigating, and they were wide, in particular the one which came in on the right side as we came downstream, which did away with and completely mastered the other river, and it seemed as if it swallowed it up within itself, because it came on with such fury and with so great an onrush that it was a thing of much awe and amazement to see [548] such a jam of trees and dead timber as it brought along with it, such that it was enough to fill one with the greatest fear [just] to look at it, let alone to go through it.

This junction of these three rivers was given the name of Saint Eulalia Confluence; many of those in this party of ours which was on its way down through there stated that they were convinced that it [i.e. the great stream just mentioned] was the river [which flowed down] from the Maca sierras; and it was so wide from bank to bank from here on that it seemed as though we were navigating launched out upon a vast sea.

From the moment when we had reached the settlements belonging to Aparia, [that is to say] after the nineteen days which we have already spoken of, we kept skirting along past some fair villages, in which we found maize and a certain quantity of fish, [and] especially turtles, and a few "guacamayos," which are parrots of the large sort [and] which the Indians are accustomed to having in their houses for the pleasure which they get out of them and [also] in order to pluck their feathers and put these to some use; and, as for us, we wanted them for the pot. These people were so far reduced from savagery that, although they hid their goods and their wives and their children outside of the villages, the men came to exchange articles for barter with us and brought us foodstuffs.

On Sunday, the twenty-sixth of February, [as we were] proceeding along on our journey down the river and [following] our usual course, there came out to meet us a certain number of Indians in two canoes, and they brought us ten or twelve very large turtles, [this being an instance] in which it seemed quite plain to us that God had sent out persons to be the means of the safeguarding of our lives, for after receiving the payment in the form of barter goods which the Captain ordered to be handed over to them in exchange for the turtles the Indians were quite happy, both in view of the good price that was given to them and because they perceived with what good will we treated them. And they rejoiced greatly to see that our Captain understood their tongue, for this was no small piece of good fortune [as one of the means] toward keeping us alive and toward bringing us out to a haven of clear understanding [regarding our situation] and [enabling us] to come [eventually] to a land of Christians; for, had he not understood it, neither would the Indians have come forward to meet us, nor should we have built, either, a brigantine such as we did build; but as God was pleased that such a great [venture into the] unknown should be carried to a conclusion and [the unknown] be made known, in order that to His Cesarean Majesty a report might be given covering what we saw and what was discovered, at the cost of so much hardship and in the manner here described, because by no other method or [use of] force or [expenditure of] human energy was it possible that it [i.e. what was found out by these adventurers] be made known, had not God put His hand to it [then] or whenever it might be His will [that this should be done], many centuries and years having elapsed [beforehand]; it was in this way that His divine providence willed and allowed that there should be given to us the Captain [who was] so fit and so expert, for in truth it seems as if God Our Lord had been keeping him in reserve for a purpose so great, because his skill and his good-naturedness and his diligence were to a large extent the means of our succeeding [so] well. [For the reader should know that] with great perseverance, after he came to these Indies, he always made it a point to get to understand the tongues of the natives and made his own elementary primers for his guidance; and God endowed him with such a good memory and excellent natural aptitude, and he was so expert in interpreting, that, notwithstanding the numerous and varying tongues that there are in those parts, although he did not understand all the Indians entirely and perfectly, as he wanted to, still, as a result of the perseverance which he applied to this matter, devoting himself to this practice, he was always understood in the end, and he himself understood quite accurately so far as the matter in hand concerned us.

I frankly recognize that I have taken in hand a matter which calls for more tranquillity of mind and [more] skill than there is in me for writing about these things in a manner so fitting and so careful from the point of view of style that to those of average understanding they will bring pleasure and [even] to [persons possessing] lofty judgments and to learned men will not be displeasing; but as

Tullius says: "[To write about] great things in elegant style is child's play; to explain them simply and clearly is the task of the wise man who understands." But as the Holy Scriptures say: "It is God alone who giveth a mouth and wisdom to men."[*]

[549] This Captain of ours, seeing that the river [now] divided into two arms, asked those Indians who had come in the [two] canoes [mentioned above] down which of the two arms we were to go, and they answered in their language and said: "Follow along where we shall go." And, as the Captain understood them, he ordered us to go the way the Indians were steering; and the result was that we went down that arm of the river from which we had considerably swerved, and if those guides had not come [to meet us] we should have gone down the main current of the river and should have passed on beyond the place of headquarters in which resided the chief and overlord of all that country, [a mistake] which could not have been unattended by a great risk of [our losing] our lives. As it was, we followed on after the Indians in their two canoes as stated until we came to the large settlement, where we found that overlord or monarch accompanied by many Indians; these latter, as soon as they perceived that we were headed for where they were, at once all got into their canoes and fell into position like men ready to fight; and Captain Francisco de Orellana in a like manner ordered the Christians to be on the alert with their weapons in their hands and with the crossbows and arquebuses all ready, in case matters should come to a break, inasmuch as the Indians showed signs of wanting to attack us. And thus in good order we reached the landing-place of the village, and the Captain and our men leaped out on land; and the Indians, seeing our boldness [and] filled with amazement, drew in closer, and the Captain spoke to them in their language and told them to leap out on land and have no fear at all, and they did so, showing by their countenances that they were pleased with our coming there. And at once they took out of their canoes a great quantity of foodstuffs, such as turtles, and in addition many kinds of fish, and a few roasted partridges and monkeys. These partridges are identically like those of our Spain, except that the former are so large that any one of them is larger than a pair of those in Castile, and the taste of them [is] no less delicate.

Captain Francisco de Orellana, perceiving the very polite manners of the Indians, addressed a few words to them, giving them to understand that we were Christians and worshipped and believed in a single and true God, who created the heavens and the earth, and [that] we were vassals of the Emperor of the Christians, the great King of Spain, called Don Carlos our master, to whom belonged the territory and dominion in which all the Indians dwell, as well as other dominions and kingdoms numerous and vast, and [that] it was by his command that we were engaged in reconnoitering that land in order to make a report to him on what we had seen in it. All this they seemed to listen to with keen attention and [great] enjoyment and to absorb in their minds up to the last detail, [manifesting interest] in everything that was being said to them, and after the captain had ceased speaking it seemed as if the listeners were content; and, they being [now] all silent, that monarch of theirs asked the Captain who we were, either showing [thereby] that he had not entirely understood what had been said to him or desiring to be better

---

[*][Carvajal may possibly have had in mind Proverbs, 2, 6: "For the Lord giveth wisdom; out of His mouth cometh knowledge and understanding."—The supposed quotation from Cicero has not been located.—EDITOR.]

informed about what was being told to him; and he asked to know where we were going, by way of seeing if the Captain showed any discrepancy in his words; the latter told him in reply the same things that he had already explained to him, and, in addition to [all] that, he told him that we were children of the Sun, and that we were going [to go on] down the river, for that was the course as planned.

This piece of news the Indians were much pleased to hear and they marveled greatly [at it], manifesting great joy, taking us to be saints or celestial beings, because all those peoples worship the Sun and hold him to be their god, whom they themselves call "Chise"; and, from that moment on, they did not refuse a single thing out of all those that the Captain asked them for.

With this much accomplished, he sent the Indians away, giving them many articles [taken from his supply] of barter goods, and they, greatly pleased, got into their canoes and with a very great deal of shouting pulled away and steered out into the open part of the river and left the whole village cleared [of its inhabitants], [550] in which place we found lodgings for ourselves. When the Captain had perceived the excellent conveniences and natural resources of the country and the favorable attitude which the Indians manifested toward us, he decided to build another brigantine, and the work was started at once, and there was found among us a woodworker who, although his trade was far from being ship-building, succeeded in directing and supervising the work in such a way as to get the brigantine built. And so the Captain took the necessary steps toward having apportioned out among [a part of] the companions, by groups, the frames and planks and timber pieces that were to be cut out and brought in, and others he ordered to make charcoal, and others to set up the forge which an ingenious companion made, for all that he was no blacksmith. But all that was accomplished with much difficulty, because among us there were no blacksmiths or trained artisans for the work that had to be done, nor were the companions accustomed to such lines of work as these; but, notwithstanding their inconveniences, Our Lord endowed all of them with skill for whatever was required, and they encouraged one another and worked with a great deal of willingness, perceiving that they were doing this in order [ultimately] to save the lives of all. And if we had gone on down from there using [only] the canoes, coming, as we afterwards did, upon warlike people, we could neither have defended ourselves nor gotten out of the river in safety; and thus it became quite evident that God enlightened [the mind of] the Captain so as to bring it about that the brigantine should be constructed in the village that has been mentioned, because farther on there were no conveniences or a [proper] place [for doing so], nor would there have been a [suitable] time for building it, when one considers the lack, not only of foodstuffs, but also of lumber and of a stopping-place as well fitted to our purpose as this one was; because [there] the Indians kept coming in every solitary day and bringing us things to eat, such as manatees and turtles, as well as other kinds of fish [properly speaking], in exchange for the barter goods which the Captain gave them. The result was that during all the time that we stopped there we did not fail to have provisions in plenty; and so the companions, thanks to this restorative nourishment, had strength to work at the task, both those who devoted themselves [to it] most assiduously and the rest of them, because the ones and the others longed to see the end of these hardships and get to a place where we might rest.

In addition to all our sufferings [already mentioned] there was another one, a very annoying one, which the natural conditions of the place that we were in caused us, and that was [one which necessitated the following arrangement, namely] that [there where], by hour shifts, any given man from among those who were engaged in the task [had to be], in order for him to be able to work at it [at all] it was necessary that another, and at times even two, should drive the mosquitoes away from him by means of a pair of fans made out of feathers which the Indians gave us; for they [i.e. the mosquitoes] were so numerous and so annoying and so mean that we were unable in any other way to aid [one another] or protect [ourselves] from such a plague except by having those "fly-shooers": a man could not even eat except when another one fanned the mosquitoes away from him, or, moreover, perform any task except under cover of the tent or awning which one had constructed for himself, out of the cotton blankets which we had, in order to be able to sleep. As numerous were the mosquitoes, large ones and small ones, both by day and by night, by which we were tormented, as it is written [that the insects] of the plagues of Egypt [were]. And [yet] God did not see fit to fail us, inasmuch as the craftsman and improvised task-master displayed such exceptional ability [in working things out] with those who helped him that a very good brigantine was built for going out to sea and for journeying by water down the river, a much better one than the boat which we had been using [and] which the same craftsman had built.

In this same stopping-place we spent the entire season of Lent, when all the companions confessed their sins to us two friars who were there; and I preached every Sunday and every feast day and Maundy Thursday and Good Friday and Easter, to the best that God Our Lord chose to grant me understanding. And relying upon His divine aid I endeavored, to the best of my ability, to comfort and encourage those brothers and companions, reminding them that they were Christians and Spaniards, and that they were rendering a great service to God and to the Emperor our master in carrying on the enterprise and in patiently bearing up under the [551] present hardships and under those to come, until they should complete this novel voyage of discovery, particularly in view of the fact that this was a matter upon which their reputations and their lives depended. And so it was that with this end in view I said what I thought best [to say] as fulfilling my mission and [the duties of one who wears the priestly] garb and also because my [own] life depended upon the successful outcome of our peregrination, as did that of those who were listening to me.

I also preached on Quasimodo Sunday and I can truthfully testify that not only the Captain but also the companions were possessed of so much loftiness of spirit and saintliness of devotion toward Jesus Christ Our Savior and His Holy Faith that it was plainly shown [to us] by Our Lord that it was His will to succor us. And the Captain, in fact, kept ordering me and requesting me to preach to them, and they all attended to their devotions with great fervor of faith, as persons who had great need of asking God for His mercy.

The time it took to build this brigantine and to repair the boat which we already had was forty-one working days, leaving out the Sundays and feast days and Maundy Thursday and Good Friday and Easter, when the companions did not work; among these latter there were many who had never in their lives taken an ax in hand to cut [something] with it, and [they therefore are all the more worthy of praise for the reason that] they displayed considerable ingenuity in [doing] everything that they were ordered [to do].

A wonderful thing to see was the willingness with which the Indians kept coming to bring us things to eat, as well as cotton and tar and resin with which to calk these vessels; and I consider it to be a remarkable thing that on Sundays and feast days and during Easter Week they brought in foodstuffs in greater abundance [than at other times], so that it seemed as if all their lives they had been servants to Christians.

As soon as the finishing touches had been given to the construction work on, and the fitting out of, these vessels, Captain Francisco de Orellana, having consulted those men whose opinions ought to be taken into consideration, decided that the time had come to continue on the journey; and he appointed to be his lieutenant a certain hidalgo, a competent man and one of much energy, named Alonso de Robles, who, when we later came to countries where the Indians were warlike, used to land with a few companions, every time that the Captain ordered him to do so, to go look for food for the whole party, and the Captain used to stay behind to guard the brigantines, which were our only real asset, next to God.

We departed from the stopping-place and the village of Aparia aboard the brigantines on the eve of the Evangelist Saint Mark's Day, the twenty-fourth of the month of April of the above-mentioned year One Thousand Five Hundred and Forty-two, and we came on down past the settlements belonging to that dominion of Aparia without encountering any warlike Indians; on the contrary, the chief himself came to talk to us and bring us food on Saint Mark's Day, which we celebrated in one of his villages. And the Captain extended very kind treatment to him and gave him some "chaquira," as well as to all the rest of the Indians who had come with him, because the purpose and desire of our Captain was to see to it, if that was possible, that there should [be caused to] remain among that barbaric people a friendly attitude [toward us] and [a sense of] pleasure as a consequence of their having come to know us, and no dissatisfaction at all, because thereby God and our King and master would be rendered a service, so that later on, when it should please His Cesarean Majesty [to take such steps], the land might with greater facility be made familiar with our Sacred Scriptures and [our] Holy Faith and the banner of Castile and be found more tamed for pacification and for being reduced to the [state of] obedience that would be in keeping with the requirements of his royal service, because at the same time that in this whole matter everything that had to be done was being done with tact and clearness [of foresight], what was equally necessary for the sake of our own preservation was the kind treatment to be dealt out to the Indians in order [for us] to be able to go forward, and it were not well that the expedient of arms should be resorted to save when [recourse to] self-defense could not be avoided. Because of this, although we found the villages abandoned, the Indians, seeing the kind treatment that was being extended to them, throughout [552] the whole province and territory of Aparia provided us with sustenance, [especially that form of] food consisting of manatees and fish, in exchange for our barter goods.

Within a few days the Indians ceased [coming] to barter [with us], and by this we recognized that we were [now] outside the dominion and tribal domains of Chief Aparia; and the Captain, fearing what could [at any moment] happen [to us now], ordered that the brigantines proceed with greater speed than they had been regularly doing hitherto. And one day, in the morning, when we had just departed from a small village, there sallied forth toward us, out in the middle of the river, a few Indians in a canoe, and they came close up to the brigantine where the

Captain was, and one of them came on board; and believing that he would [be just the man to] guide us to an inhabited country, the Captain ordered him to be taken along as a guide; and five days later, seeing that that Indian did not know the country and that [what looked like (?)] villages on the banks of the river were being missed by us, ordered him to be set free and given a canoe in which to return home.

From here on, we journeyed over a course attended by more hardships and past country more completely abandoned by its inhabitants than before, ([this latter circumstance being] due to the freshets), because the river led from one wooded section to another wooded section and only with difficulty could there be found [at times] a dry stopping-place for sleeping, because the river overflowed its course and inundated everything; and for this reason we were obliged to sleep on board the brigantines [which were] tied up to the trees along the shore; and we were also annoyed by the mosquitoes and by the lack of food, for the companions were not catching small fish to eat as they had been doing in the other uninhabited sections of country. And proceeding along under these conditions, one day at noon we came to an elevated spot which seemed to have been an inhabited place at one time, and the river [here] showed some indication of being a good place to catch fish; and we stopped there on the day of Saint John Ante-portam-latinam, which is the sixth of May.

There an incident occurred which I should not have dared to write down if it had not been observed by so many witnesses who were right there; and this was that a certain companion who has already been mentioned, named Mexía, shot with a crossbow at an iguana which was in a tree close to the river, and the nut sprang out of the stock of his crossbow and fell into the river, and a fish swallowed it; and that same afternoon, [the men] feeling that there was no chance of being able to get the nut back, and the whole company, indeed, being greatly grieved because one crossbow thus remained useless, a certain companion cast a hook out into the river and pulled up the very fish which had in its belly the very nut referred to. In that way the crossbow was repaired, for which there was great need later on, because next to God it was the crossbows that saved our lives.

When twelve days of the month of May of the year One Thousand Five Hundred and Forty-two had now gone by, we arrived at the settlements forming the province [under the rule] of Machiparo, concerning which [province] we had received reports as far back as [the village of] Aparia the Great; and we had also been informed of the existence of another dominion [the ruler of] which was called Omaga* [and] which borders upon the country belonging to this Machiparo.

Here there sallied forth to meet us many Indian warriors in their canoes [fully] manned and fitted out with shield protection. It was all so sudden that they caught us at a time when the arquebusiers happened to have their powder wet, and we could not call upon them then to defend us; but the crossbows made up for this deficiency in such a way that they compelled the Indians to retreat, and they [i.e. the Indians] gave us an opportunity to make port at the nearest village, although they first put up a resistance for a period of half an hour, both on water and on land, until there fell five or six Indians wounded by the arrows [of our crossbows]; and also of great assistance was an arquebuse which a certain Biscayan companion had in his possession.

---

*[The same form is used in the equivalent passage in Medina's version of Carvajal, p. 190 *supra*, Later in that version (pp. 200 and 202, *supra*), the more usual form Omagua is used.—EDITOR.]

The landing place having been captured, the Indians pulled out into the offing or open part of the river; and, as we had come to have a shortage of provisions for our nourishment, the Captain ordered the lieutenant to go with a certain number of companions and run through the village [to look for food]. This was done, and there were encountered a few Indians who put themselves on the defensive, [553] of whom the companions killed several and wounded many, and our men were victorious; and they brought back a large quantity of fish and a few turtles, and they told the Captain that the village was intact and that the Indians had not carried off their [supplies of] foodstuffs, and that there were more than a thousand turtles in inclosures and in wells filled with water. At once Captain Francisco de Orellana ordered a captain* to go with a certain number of companions and gather up the very largest quantity of foodstuffs that could be had, because he was planning to rest there five or six days in order to let the men recuperate after the hardships endured.

When these Spaniards got there they found that the Indians had taken up strong positions, and [with the idea of] protecting the food supplies they [i.e. the Indians] started a fight with our men, and these latter [grappled] with the attacking Indians and twice forced them to retreat; and, [with our men] observing that they were again reforming in spite of the fact that they [i.e. our men] had wounded or killed several of the Indians, they [i.e. the latter] paid no heed to this, but on the contrary displayed considerable courage; however, inasmuch as four or five of the companions were now wounded, and in particular one man (who died eight days after that), it became necessary for those Spaniards to draw back to where Captain Francisco de Orellana was, in another village, coming by way of a gully. At this time and at this conjuncture when the Indians fell upon the ten companions, from another part of the settlement they also fell upon the Captain and us who were with him, [we having become] careless in consequence of the fact that the said ten companions were out there somewhere, thinking [as we did] that our backs were protected and that the Indians would not attack us at two places [at the same time]: for this reason a few had disarmed themselves, and that is nothing to wonder at in view of the hardships and ceaseless toils that we had undergone in rowing, and practically fasting throughout the [period of] hunger [when we were] in the uninhabited country, and spending bad nights, and harassed by the mosquitoes. For these reasons, then, the Indians had an opportunity to come right in to where we, with the Captain, were in quarters, without being perceived and without encountering any resistance whatsoever. It [i.e. the approach of the Indians] was perceived by just one man, who gave the alarm and took a stand all alone against the whole body of Indians, holding them in check and receiving many blows with sticks which they hurled at him; and, protected by his shield and with his sword in his hand, he fought with a valiant spirit, and, as a result of his having no other arms, they wounded him by means of a blow with a stick, and, if he had not been promptly succored, they would have killed him; for the Indians were numerous and very well armed, and [besides] with arms of a strange sort and never before seen by Christians, because they [i.e. the Indians]

*[No mention is made elsewhere, in either of the two versions of Friar Carvajal's account, of another man in Orellana's party having the rank of captain. According to the other version (p. 193, *supra*) it was Cristóbal de Maldonado (i.e. de Segovia) who was ordered on this foraging foray. De Segovia doubtless was an officer of rank in the expedition, as indicated by his being the third in the list of members of the expedition in the present version (p. 393, *supra*) and by his career prior to the expedition (see pp. 121–122, *supra*).—EDITOR.]

were covered from head to feet with little shields made out of the skins of manatees, and these were such that a crossbow would not pierce them.

As soon as that Spaniard had been succored, our men attacked the enemy with so much intrepidity that they killed and wounded many of them, and they made the rest retreat in their canoes, and they [i.e. the Indians] pulled away and put out into the open part of the river at a loss to themselves, although all that was not accomplished without [the shedding of] blood of the Spaniards, because six companions came out of it badly wounded, some with their arms and others with their legs pierced, in addition to other slight and less dangerous wounds which they received in this fight. God saw fit to have mercy on us [in so far as it was through His intervention] that those Indians did not have any poisonous herb [with which to poison their arrows]; for, if they had had that, they would have inflicted so much damage upon us that we should have been left reduced in numbers by fully one tenth, and even by one fifth, after this first perilous clash of arms which we had with these people [and] which it was thought God had willed that we should meet with in order to arouse us [from our carelessness], for which [kindness of His] we must give Him infinite thanks.

On that same day the Captain sent an officer in command of a certain number of companions to seize a pass in a gully in a wooded section, occupied by the Indians, from which point they were doing most of their shouting, quite close to where we were quartered; and our Spaniards met with resistance, and, indeed, a Biscayan [**554**] arquebusier was wounded, [who was] a good soldier; and for this reason the officer sent back to ask for more men, because the Indians were numerous and occupied strong positions. But, as the Captain was a prudent man, he sent orders to the officer to retreat, because this was no time for them to endanger the life of a single Spaniard, nor was there any call for doing so; nor, [as he said], were either he or [the rest of] these Christians going [on this journey] to conquer the country, nor was his intention, now that God had brought him down this river, other than to discover those provinces so completely unknown to the Christians, in order that at the proper time, whenever the divine will should so decree, the Emperor our master might send out whomever it pleased [him] to conquer and subdue those barbaric peoples. And so on that [same] day, after our men had been called back, the captain made a brief harangue to them all, as follows:

"Gentlemen, brothers, friends, and companions of mine: Great confidence have I in God and in His Glorious Mother, and you too will do well to have such, that thanks to the good luck [that regularly attends enterprises carried out in the name] of the Emperor-King our master, our voyage is destined to terminate in a delivrance from destruction; and, in order that this may come true, we must not allow any delays or linger [on the way] but on the contrary pursue our course diligently, since our efforts are directed towards serving our monarch, now that we plainly see that [it was] in [keeping with] his good fortune (though not [through any order issued by him directing us] to come to reconnoiter or explore these hitherto unknown lands, or [to undergo] the hardships past or present or still to be looked forward to) [that] God was keeping you and me in reserve for this trial of our persons, inasmuch as we left Captain Gonzalo Pizarro's expeditionary force with an entirely different intention, and [that was] to return to him promptly. So it is that God is manifestly showing us that it is His will that we carry out this enterprise of exploration and that we keep on in this voyage upon which we are [launched]; and for the sake of the successful outcome of all this it is necessary that we value highly the life of every Spaniard in our company. That is the reason why I have called the men back; and I for my part tell you that I do not value my own safety as highly as I do that of the least among you who are here present with me; and so it behooves each one of you, in good harmony and in [brotherly] love, to feel that the life of one is that of all, and [that] that of all [is] that of any given individual; and [I warn you] that, so far as it shall be within our power to continue to advance on our way out and not have any fighting or recourse to arms, that must be done; and [that], whenever necessity shall demand something different and there shall be no possibility of avoiding warfare, each one must do what it is his duty to do, as I believe and [even] know for a certainty that you are going to do and are obliged [to do], in order that God, on seeing our good endeavor, may grant that through His grace we may succeed, [thereby] rendering a service unto Him, in serving the Emperor our master and in conferring honor upon the father-land and upon our persons through this memorable [voyage of] discovery which we are making, and [that] we may be able to deliver an account of what we have [already] seen and of what there still remains for us [to see] from here on until through the action of divine pity we shall come safely to a land where there are Christians, and [that] we may be able to impart the news of a voyage [of a kind] so unheard of [until now], so new [in human experience], so great and so worthy of being remembered by the men of these times and of the times to come, and [one] which has prospects of being so exceedingly useful to the royal crown of Castile, in order that our King may bestow favors upon us and [that] at the proper time the reward for our sufferings may be forthcoming, and in order that for all time the matter may remain written down in the memory of those who live today and of those who shall be born, a sure title to honor, an imperishable monument to you and to us. Get ready, gentlemen, because my decision is to leave this place, and let each one load what food he has into the boats, for we have as intercessors for us the Mother of Jesus Christ Our Savior and the glorious Saint James, patron and protector of Spain and the Spaniards."

As soon as Captain Francisco de Orellana had finished his warning and talk on the subject of peace, spoken or delivered by him better than [555] written down here, the companions all together, with much willingness and in good spirits and with contentedness, set about getting started again on our journey, [bent on] continuing on down that enormously great river, God alone being the pilot. And [it was] at the time when the sun was going down [that] we departed from that stopping-place; and scarcely had we pulled away from the shore and proceeded out into the open part of the river, when the Indians came toward us with great shouts and cries and with many trumpets and drums, and with banners unfolded, and hurling many sticks with "estoricas" or leather straps against the brigantines [and] at us, so that it was necessary for our Spaniards to defend themselves; and with the arquebuses and crossbows they made the Indians humble that barbaric and impetuous fury which they were displaying, [these weapons] causing [con-siderable] damage among them. And it [i.e. the return fire from our side] was such that they fared poorly in their boldness without learning any lesson therefrom, because in spite of that they did not cease following us [for a long time] from there on, although somewhat humbled by fear of the arquebuses and crossbows.

Here it was plainly shown to be [by an act of] divine providence that there had been found the nut of the crossbow in the belly of the fish, as was stated above, in order that by means of it [i.e. the crossbow] and of the others [in our possession] our deficiency [in the matter of weapons] might be made up for and those [occasions on] which we had [need] of the crossbows during this journey [might be faced without danger]; because, if we had not had them for use in defending ourselves, the Indians were quite sufficient in numbers, on the water and on land, to kill us all many times over, even if we had been more numerous. In this way these Machiparo Indians kept following us for two days and two nights, chasing us to the accompaniment of many shouts and haranguings and with a fleet or armed squadron of more than a hundred canoes, and they did not cease following us until they drove us beyond their settlements, which in our estimation extended over a stretch of more than sixty leagues; and in the villages, on land, there appeared to be a great mass of people.

The women of these Machiparo people used to throw earth and dust into the air, in a manner [such] that we imagined this to be a form of sorcery.

It was impossible to count all the villages of this province of Machiparo, because those which we passed by in the night could not all be seen, and [also] because, as a matter of fact, we were fleeing; but it was all high land, an upland characterized by a rich vegetation down along the shore. Off in the interior of the country it was not possible to see what there was. From this point on we always found the country hostile. I do not recount here the special feats performed by several of the companions, of whose personalities prior to this not much notice had been taken; and [read: but] ever since then, they have been looked upon as brave men, because, inasmuch as it was nothing less than life [itself] that was at stake for them, each one strove to distinguish himself and [yet] let necessity restrain his courage, [they thus] doing all that [any] honorable men and veterans and chosen soldiers could do.

After these Machiparo people had ceased pursuing us, we moved on nine or ten leagues as far as a village which was situated upon an elevated spot [and] which we thought was the frontier [town] of the settlements and dominion ruled over by Omagua. There the Indians made a stand on the bank of the river, armed with sticks and "estoricas," and some of them had wooden shields; and Captain Francisco de Orellana ordered that that [river] port be captured, because there was [now] a shortage of provisions [that was beginning to have its effect on us], for they [i.e. those which we had laid in] had now become practically exhausted. And in order that they [i.e. the Indians] might [be compelled to] leave the landing-place clear for us, there were fired at them a few arquebuse and crossbow shots from the brigantines, and they [i.e. our men] wounded several of the Indians, and [the wounding of] these men thus gave us our opportunity by enabling the lieutenant to leap out on land and go in pursuit of the Indians until they should drive them out of the dwelling quarters. And in this village we slept two nights because we had to make up ship-stores consisting of biscuits and roast a few turtles which we had been carrying along with us from the time that we had left [the country of] Machiparo, for the Captain said that we should have to move on with all the haste that it was possible [to make].

Now that I have just had an occasion to speak of biscuit, and [in view of the fact that our having] this [556] biscuit will seem odd to those who do not know about it or have never seen what it is, not being made of wheat flour, it must be pointed out that there the Indians had great quantities of large cakes made out of cassava baked hard like biscuit, and also some made out of a mixture of maize and yucca, which makes a good [kind of] bread.

To return to the story, I [next] state that on Sunday after the Ascension of Our Redeemer Jesus Christ, many of the men being occupied, as has been stated, in making up their ship-stores, the Indians came in canoes to attack our brigantines, which were in the harbor, and hurled many sticks into them and placed in a very difficult situation a few companions who happened just then to be on board. But the crossbowmen immediately hurried to the rescue and killed several Indians, and they kept shooting arrows at them so fast that they [i.e. the Indians] decided to take to flight and let us make up our ship-stores. We stayed there three days.

On Tuesday, the sixteenth of March* of the year already stated, we departed from this village, and we went on, constantly passing in sight of inhabited country on one side and on the other of the river. Whenever the Captain saw that we were short of provisions, he would have some one go ashore in some small village where less resistance would be met with to seize some foodstuffs. It was God's pleasure that notwithstanding our worries and unlucky experiences and lack of restorative nourishment all our wounded should get well, and out of all those who had been wounded in [the land of] Machiparo none died except a certain companion named Pedro de Empudia, [and in this case it was] on account of the unreasonableness and disorderly behavior which he himself indulged in.

In one village, which was situated on an elevated spot, where we decided to seize some food for our use during the holiday season of Whitsuntide, we found a great deal of porcelain, very well manufactured, with various kinds of painting on them, and glazed, jars as well as many other [kinds of] vessels. This village came to be called by us Loza†, because in truth there was a great deal of it there and [it was] of a very beautiful sort. There were also seen indications that there were gold and silver in the country, because on a few projectile weapons or "estoricas" we saw some inlaid and [found some of these] ornamented with some. A copper hatchet was found there, like those which the Indians in Peru use.

There were found in a "galpón"‡ or [entrance to a] large mansion two tall idols, having the stature of giants, woven out of palm leaves, and they had big ears like the Incas of Cuzco. We did not dare to sleep there, because there were many highways, and very wide ones, which led into the interior of the country, [and] which indicated that that village was one to which many people came and that there were in its outskirts, or [perhaps] quite close by, many settlements and numerous inhabitants. Consequently we went off to the hillside and woods to sleep, leaving a proper guard on board the boats and anchoring [these latter] at some distance from shore. In this port food enough was seized to last to the next one, where the Captain gave the command to go ashore [again].

At this place the inhabitants of the country waited [for us to come up to them], including both the women and the children, for they neither took to flight nor

*[Medina (infra, p. 102: cf. footnote 142) has called attention to the fact that "March" must be an error for "May." Furthermore, "sixteenth" appears to be an error for "twenty-third," since the incident mentioned in the preceding paragraph occurred on the Sunday after Ascension, i.e. on May 21, in a village where, says Carvajal, Orellana spent three days, these being, apparently, Sunday the 21st, Monday the 22nd, and Tuesday the 23rd, on the last of which dates the expedition again got under way.—EDITOR.]

†[I.e. Porcelainville.—EDITOR.]

‡[Defined, in the glossary provided by Oviedo's editors, as a "portico."—EDITOR.]

defended the landing-place, as those of the village of Loza had done; in this stopping-place a few Indian women were seized to make bread for the companions, and a few boys [were taken] to serve as interpreters; and because the inhabitants of this village were so docile, it came to be called Bobos Village.*

We left there and [from now on] kept passing by much better looking settlements [than heretofore], and we passed by [the mouth of] a river that emptied into the one which we were navigating, on the right as we came down, [the land bordering upon] which [tributary], down around the mouth, was thickly covered with villages of a very pretty aspect and cool [in the midst of groves] of [common] fruit trees as well as of guava trees and custard-apple trees and [plants bearing] large beans and other sorts [of trees, etc.] And the Captain decided that we should not stop there, on account of the large number of Indian inhabitants that could be seen [going about on land].

From that place there came out many canoes which, keeping at a certain distance away from us, followed us down the river, [their occupants] shouting at us in a way which seemed to indicate that they were convinced that we were persons who did not dare to let them catch up with us.

On the Monday after Whitsunday [557] we passed in sight of a village which had many landing-places and many a grove of fruit trees and more than five hundred houses, and there were seen to be many inhabitants along the landing-places ready to defend the harbor and the village, and the name given [by us] to the latter was Pueblo Vicioso;† and the Captain would not let us stop there, because that could not have been done without considerable danger of [the shedding of] blood.

On that day, the twenty-ninth of May, the Captain had the men make port in a small village, there being no resistance whatsoever [here] on the part of the Indians, and from there on we saw indications of the existence of savanas, for the huts were roofed over with straw of [the kind that grows in] savanas. And it was believed that they must bring it [there] from the inland country, toward which went out many roads which undoubtedly led to the other villages situated away from the river in the interior of the country; and our Captain did not decide to send anyone to explore the country off in the interior, because of the [small number of] men that he had there, for there were not even as many as fifty companions, because in truth the Spaniards who were there could not cope with the Indians in that kind of undertaking, and, if our men had become divided, we should have been completely annihilated.

Every day we could see, so far as we were able to observe [in the course of our forays], an increase in the natural wealth of the land from the time when we had arrived at [the settlements belonging to] Machiparo, and never again did we come upon uninhabited country: on the contrary, we found a certain amount of salt and duck meat and parrot meat belonging to the Indians.

On Saturday, the eve of Holy Trinity, the Captain gave orders to make port in another village for the purpose of obtaining foodstuffs, and although the Indians put themselves on the defensive, in spite [of that], and at some loss to them, it was captured. There there were found a few fowl of the sort known in Castile, whereby it became evident that Christians had come to this river, although we did not know what river it was.

*[I.e. Stupidville.—EDITOR.]
†[I.e. Viciousville.—EDITOR.]

This same day, having now left this place and pursuing our journey, we saw [that] inside the mouth of another large river on the left, which emptied into the one down which we were going, the water [was] black or very turbid, as if coming from swamps or a lake, and for this reason we named it Río Negro; which [river] flowed so abundantly and with such swiftness that for a distance of more than ten leagues the one water was distinguishable from the other, because that down through which we were coming was reddish as a result of the many freshets [which had stirred it up]. On this day we saw other villages not very large.

The following day, which was Trinity, the Captain and all [the rest] celebrated the holiday in some fisherman's quarters in a village that was on a hillside. We found much fish [there], a thing which was a help and a great relief for the Spaniards, because [many] days had passed since we had hit upon such lodgings. This village was situated on a high spot back from the river as if on the frontier facing other tribes who made war upon them, because it was strongly fortified and surrounded by a palisade of heavy timbers; and just as this village was [about to be] captured [by us], the Indians decided to defend it and took up a strong position inside that inclosure and started to fight, and as the necessity that existed [for us] of seizing some food supplies was [very] great, the Spaniards got their weapons ready and attacked like intrepid lions, set on finding some food and capturing the inclosure, and the village was taken, and they [i.e. the Spaniards] laid in a stock of foodstuffs to make up for the shortage from which they had been suffering.

On Monday, the fifth day of June, we left the village which has just been mentioned, all the time passing by very large settlements and provinces and procuring food as best could be done whenever we lacked it. And on this day we made port in a village in which there was found, on a public square, in a place of worship dedicated to the Sun, a large hewn tree trunk ten feet around, carved in relief, and all of one piece, whence the reader will be able to imagine how large a tree that must have been out of which such a piece was cut. That design which was [to be seen] on that hewn tree trunk was, as has been stated, carved out in relief, and represented a round wall tower with two doors, and at each door were two columns, and on [**558**] the sides of the tower were two lions with ferocious looks, which turned their glances backwards as though suspicious of each other. These held between their forepaws and claws the entire structure which was carved there in half relief, in the middle of which there was a circular space with a hole [in the middle], through which, as an offering to the Sun, they poured *chicha*, which is the wine which those people drink, and the Sun is the one whom they worship as their god; this *chicha* worked its way down to the bottom of that block of wood and ran out on the ground. In short, the structure was a thing well worth seeing and [furnished] evidence as to [the existence of] the large cities that there are off in the interior of the country: that is what all the Indians gave [us] to understand. On this same public square stood a building isolated [from all others] and large, [for use in connection with the worship] of the Sun, where the Indians perform their ceremonies and rites. In it there were found many robes made out of feathers of divers colors, [these feathers being] fastened into, and woven together upon, cotton [cloth], and [they were] very attractive [robes], which the Indians put on to celebrate their festive occasions and to dance, whenever they came together there for some holiday affair or rejoicing, in front of their idols. All around the hewn tree trunk that has been mentioned the Indians offered up their sacrifices in their unholy ritual.

In another village, a very large one, a league long, composed of an unbroken row of dwellings and [other] buildings, the Indians very boldly defended the harbor against our attack and took a stand there like brave men; and the fight lasted nearly half of the time of one watch* before our Spaniards could leap out on land, and undoubtedly they [i.e. the Indians] would have inflicted considerable damage upon us, if it had not been for the crossbows and arquebuses, for these made them fall back so that the Christians might get out of the water. There were found there a large quantity of maize and a few fowl.

Having departed from this large settlement, we passed by other large villages where the Indians stood waiting in battle array, like a warlike people, with their weapons and their shields in hand, crying out to us; and from out beyond [their reach] our arquebusiers and crossbowmen were able to fell many Indians, because there was a great multitude of them and they formed a huge wall and they [i.e. our men] shot at them as [if they were shooting] at a target. And as they [i.e. the Indians] were not accustomed to the odor or the effect or the sound of arquebuses or crossbows, they [did not make any effort to get under cover, but] waited longer than they should have done in the manner that has been stated; nevertheless, in view of [the size of] the countless horde of people that we could see, we passed by well out from shore, leaving them the information about us which has been mentioned [i.e. showing them what we could do to them], although the fact of the matter is that we had no occasion for stopping there. And for this [same] reason, continuing on down our river, we passed by other villages having such powerful defenses that we did not dare [to try] to stop in them: these are on the left side of the river as we came down it, upon a rather high hillside, from which they cried out to us and challenged us.

On Wednesday, the day before Corpus Christi, which by count was the seventh day of the month of June, the Captain gave orders to make port at a small settlement which was on the same hillside up from the banks of the river, and this was done without any resistance whatsoever [on the part of the natives]; and there was found there fish in very large quantities, [which was being] roasted on barbecues or gridirons, [there being] such a great supply of this that the brigantines could have been loaded up with fish. And as the village was small, seeing that its inhabitants were not about to molest us or engage us in battle, all the companions begged Captain Francisco de Orellana, as a favor, to celebrate in that village the festival of Corpus Christi; and, although against his will (for all that he wanted to do was to go on into the wilderness and woods to sleep, for the sake of our safety), he was obliged to yield in the matter in order to please us who were requesting this of him, and he chose sleeping quarters for that night in the village. And just as the sun was going down, the Indians came to attack us, the Captain and the companions being then engaged in having supper; but, just as soon as the enemy were detected, four Spaniards took up positions to defend us and fell upon the Indians, and they did this with such a display of valor that the Indians took to flight, and some of them threw themselves [559] into the water, because they [i.e. our men] did not allow them an opportunity to get into their canoes; and in view of this latter circumstance it was believed that, since the Indians were few in

---

*[Literally translated, the original has: "nearly half of the time of a quarter of hour." The translation adopted above, based in part on the assumption that the last four words may possibly mean: "a quarter by (ship's) time," i.e. one of the four periods into which daylight time was divided (on board ship), corresponds roughly to the statement in the other version of Carvajal's account (*supra*, p. 206) that the fight lasted "more than an hour."—EDITOR.]

number, they dared not come back at us. When this was over, our men lay down to sleep, but not without first posting sentinels, as is regularly done at such times; and shortly after midnight, during the watch belonging to the first guard, many Indians fell upon us from two directions and hurled many sticks upon our awnings and tents, and they wounded two Spaniards.

These Indians were men from other villages in the neighborhood of, and quite close to, the one in which we were [in quarters]; and, when the sentinels had given the alarm, the companions went forth to meet the Indians and fell upon them with great vigor and put them to flight; and, as they were more familiar with the country than the Spaniards [were], they got away safely. The result was that, although the object of the attack was accomplished, there was caught only one Indian, whom a companion had wounded with [all] that fury [that the circumstances called for, namely] in such a way that one knife blow alone was all that was necessary; and so they let him go back to the Indians, in order to inspire more fear in them, because he went off with his back all opened up. That night the Captain ordered a certain number of Christians to lay an ambuscade by going off into the woods and [hiding] close to the road by which those Indians had come [before], he believing that they would return with a much larger number of men; and the greater part of the companions did not go to sleep during the whole night, nor did the Captain, in order to be prepared and ready for whatever might happen. Thus it was that our desire to rest there was turned into [something which was just] the reverse of that for us, and the rest which we had expected to find or take in those quarters was converted into fearful watching; for the whole country is very thickly populated, and there was reason to suspect that the Indians, realizing that it was only a small number of Christians [that they had to contend with], inasmuch as they had had the courage to fight when few in numbers, [would imagine that] when assembled in large numbers they could attack us more successfully.

With the arrival of morning, which we had been waiting for with considerable longing, the Captain caused a few Indians who had been captured in that village to be punished by hanging, because it was considered certain that [it was] through notice given by them and through their spying [that] the others had come, who had expected to kill us [as we were] sleeping; and he caused to be burned all the houses of that village, to which, at the moment that we had arrived there, we had very joyfully given the name of Corpus Christi Village.

As soon as the next day following this skirmish or night battle had dawned, the Captain with [all the men on board] the brigantines started out; and at midday we went ashore in the bramble growth or [sort of] woods [which was] not far from our boats, in order that the men might rest. And from there on, the Captain never permitted us to sleep in an inhabited place, but [commanded] that forays into the dwelling districts should be made and food seized during the day, and that at night we should go off to bivouac in the woodlands in order to eat what had been won, having first established a good watch; and, if any other method of procedure had been followed, it would not have been possible to get away or move forward, among so many thousands of barbaric people and such warlike ones, in the way that such a small company as we were did move forward on a journey so long and so toilsome. And if the Captain had not been so careful and so diligent and [had not been a man] of so much experience, considering the way in which the Indians constantly strove to bring about our death, undoubtedly they would have put an end to us; but he made it his aim to have peace and to make barter exchanges with the natives along the shores wherever that was [thought to be] the best thing to do, and to seize foodstuffs wherever the conditions were such that [the use of] fine skill on his part would mean success. But [it is true] also [that] in other places they [i.e. the natives] would not listen to him or hear us, but [remained firm in their desire to] resort to the use of arms to injure us, and even most frequently they were in the habit of attacking us without our having given them any cause for it, and by force compelled the Christians to fight and all contribute their share toward the cost and [thus] purchase the food at a high price. I am telling the truth when I say that there were among us a few so weary of this kind of life and of the long journey that, if their consciences had not kept them from so doing, they would not have failed to remain behind among the Indians, and [read: but] those in whom this weakness and small-mindedness could be suspected were men of little account; but, although in [the cases of] **[560]** such as these a certain amount of baseness [of character] was feared, there were others so full of manhood that they did not let them fall into such an error, [men] from whose [air of] confidence and [display of] vigor they took courage, and they put up with more than they could have endured if there had not been some men of real worth there among us.

All this is nothing to be amazed at, considering the vast expanse of country that we had gone over in our journey down along the shores and [in and out among] the bends of this river, which, according to a true calculation, we had already navigated for a distance of over a thousand leagues before arriving at Corpus Christi Village, and as yet it was not known how much we still had to go before we should reach the salt water and the sea [that extends along the full length] of the coast which this continent has up toward the north, whither we were going in search of it [i.e. of the sea]. In this way, navigating as heretofore and passing by some very large settlements which we could see on either shore of the river, at times our advance through the country was effected fairly easily, because [in the forays through] the villages which we were in the habit of seizing in order to look for food supplies, although our soldiers would find them poorly provisioned* on account of their being small ones, [still] there would be found in them a great deal of maize and a certain quantity of fish and some tame parrots.

On Tuesday, the thirteenth day of June of the above-mentioned year One Thousand Five Hundred and Forty-two, we passed by a village [which was quite] large and [was] situated on high land, a very strong one, which showed by its style that it was the frontier of other provinces, because the houses were different from those that we had seen in the other villages which we had left behind us.

This settlement was a large one and [was probably even] much larger than [could be determined from] what we could see of it from the river, and because of certain shoals and marshes and places where grass grew which we encountered in our way we were unable to make port [there]; but the next day, Wednesday, we reached another village where the men stood waiting and [where] the women [stayed] inside their huts. But for all this there was no lack of men to defend the landing-place against our attack with their bows and arrows, and [read: but] they lacked steadfastness in the resistance which they attempted for a moment to put up in the face of our attack; because just as soon as a certain number of

---

*[Such, at least, appears to be the meaning of "huérfanos," the literal translation of which is "orphans."—Editor.]

companions leaped out on land the Indians fled, [not without] having wounded a Spaniard from among our number; but he did not incur any danger, because there was no poison [in use] among those who fought with [bows and] arrows. And, thanks to the skill of an arquebusier and following the orders of the Captain, a large hut was set on fire, in order that the Indians might take fright and in order that with reduced risk for the Christians a certain quantity of provisions might be seized to enable us to continue on our journey. And after a few Indians had fortified themselves inside that house, they made up their minds not to come out, but to put up a defense by shooting many arrows from there, and as a result of their stubbornness they were all burned inside, with a few women and children, not being willing to surrender or get away from that danger; and for that reason this settlement came to be called [by us] Quemados* Village. There were found there some ducks, chickens, parrots, and a small quantity of fish.

From here on a certain suspicion was felt among us that there was poison [in use] among the Indians of that country, because many arrows and sticks were found to be smeared with a certain kind of sticky substance; and the Captain ordered that an experiment be made, wherein, although it seemed like a sort of act of cruelty to perform the experiment upon a person who was not to blame in the matter, his intention was none other than to find out the truth and take away from the Christians their fear of the poison. And with this end in view, they injected into the arms of an Indian woman who was on board [one of] the brigantines [some of] that [substance] which was supposed to be poison of the death-dealing sort which the Indians employ in many parts of the continent; and, as she did not die [from the effects of it], those who had been frightened were freed of the uncertainty, and all received much pleasure from such a good piece of news.

On the Friday following, a certain number of villages were caught sight of on the left bank of the river as we were proceeding, which were situated rather high up on an upland; and farther back in the country at a distance of something like half a league could be seen a large village on a slope of a hill, and it was supposed that farther back in the interior of the district [561] which included those settlements there must be many others. And from this village which has just been mentioned the Indians came forth in a canoe to look us over and scrutinize us, and they came alongside the brigantine on board which the captain was, pointing off towards the villages of the province, and we did not succeed in understanding them; but, according to what we were finally able to make out from the signs [which they were making], in that neighborhood and to the left as we came on down were the Christians who got lost from Captain Diego de Ordaz's expeditionary fleet† in the course of the enterprise which he had undertaken to found colonies on the Marañón River; and the Indians said, or [at least] gave the impression, that there were many more Christians [there] than the number included in our party, and also [that they were] white men and wore beards. And that was the truth, for from the caravels which Diego de Ordaz had sent on ahead more than three hundred men became lost; and it is believed that they are the ones that these Indians were trying to inform us about, and that they must be lost [there], [living as] settlers and under the rule of some important overlord.

*[This word means "burned people."—Editor.]

†[On this expedition, undertaken in 1531, see note 21 to Carvajal's *Account*, pp. 241–242, *supra*.—Editor.]

The Captain offered some "chaquira" and a certain quantity of cloth [in the form] of cotton blankets to these Indians in the canoe with whom the conversation had been held, and they refused to accept it;* and so they went back to where they had come from.

The next day in the morning, [and] right away early in the morning [too], there came out towards us many Indians in canoes and in battle formation, with the intention of driving us away from their villages, shouting at us and threatening us with their bows and arrows. In those villages they have (and we saw [them]) many poles and large sticks of timber stuck up in the ground, and on top of them [were] placed heads of Indians, fastened [there] as trophies or as tokens [meaning] that that tribe must be respected, or as a souvenir of their victories or as war reminders.

On the Saturday following, we made port in a village in which there was found a considerable stock of foodstuffs; and it [i.e. the village] was captured without any resistance [on the part of the enemy], because the Indians had not taken a stand. From this village there went out many roads into the interior of the country, and there were discovered there arrows of the kind that go whistling through the air when they [i.e. the Indians] shoot them; and from this village on we saw abundant signs of savanas and of land not overgrown with trees, for on the banks of the river there were plants and herbs [of the sorts] that regularly grow in fields and savanas.

On Monday, farther on down, we made port in a village in which we found a great quantity of maize in hampers [and] buried in ashes in order that it might keep and be protected from weevils. There was likewise found [there] a large quantity (and a good quality) of oats, out of which the Indians make bread and very good *chicha*, resembling beer; and [this was in addition to] a great abundance of provisions of other sorts that was found there. There was a very large storage and dispensing establishment that the Indians had in this place, [this being] for some purpose which we did not succeed in understanding about, or [perhaps it was] for the purpose of supplying from there, as from a custom-house, other parts [of the country], because there were likewise many cotton hammocks [there];† and, although few people could be seen about, those whom we did see were clad in cotton. There was found there a temple or a building quite different from all the others, because there were inside it many military adorn-ments in the form of cuirasses and other pieces for all parts of the body; and [hanging] above all these were two mitres, very well made and with [only] natural skill, and [yet] in such a way as to be quite like those which bishops and prelates have as a part of their pontifical robes; they were made out of woven cotton and [were] of [various] colors.

We moved on from this village and went off to a section of country on the other side of the river in order to sleep in the woods or bushy places, as it was our custom to do. And there came there many Indians in canoes, shouting at us, but several of them were wounded by our arquebusiers; and, as they did not like the detona-tions, nor the odor of the smoke either, they left us alone and went away.

*[Interpreted literally, this singular pronoun means that the Indians refused only the cloth, but it is probable that by a sort of looseness of construction this pronoun is meant to include the *chaquira* also.—EDITOR.]

†[Possibly we are to understand that these hammocks were for the use of men who, coming from a long distance to get provisions, would be obliged to spend the night there before returning to their own villages.—EDITOR.]

On the following Tuesday, the twenty-second day of the month of June, we saw a great deal of inhabited country off in the direction (or on the bank of the river) to the left as we were coming downstream; but [562] during that whole day there was no possibility of going over to follow the other shore on account of the excessive choppiness of the rough waves, and [these were] as broken and as restless as [any that] could be seen at sea.

On Wednesday, the twenty-third of the month, we captured a village which was situated up an inlet, where a savana or plain more than two leagues long as measured along the river bank came to an end: it [i.e. the village] had a ground plan laid out in such a way that it was all one street, and the houses on the one side and on the other [were] placed in a very orderly fashion. In that place there was a great deal of maize and a certain quantity of cassava bread made out of a mixture of maize and yucca. There were [also] found a few ducks and parrots. To this settlement our Spaniards gave the name of Escondido* Village, [i.e. the village hidden] on the inlet where the savana was, because it was not visible [from the river].

On the Thursday following we made port in a small village which was at the beginning [i.e. at the far end (?)] of the savana, which [village] appeared to be [temporary (?)] quarters and cottages belonging to the [the inhabitants of] other villages; we found there a great deal of salt and maize, and [read: but] no other food supplies, because the Indians had carried them all away. On this same day the men on board the small brigantine landed at a medium-sized village, where there was a great deal of maize, and [read: but] no other kind of food whatsoever. This village was also situated on a savana and had some [of the conveniences of a good] stopping-place; but the Captain immediately ordered the men to get into the boat, and we moved on to look for some village that would be likely to be a good place for us to obtain a supply of some sort of meat and fish for the celebration and gladdening of that day [of] so special [a nature], which was [that] of the glorious herald of Jesus Christ, John the Baptist. And God willed that on rounding a bend which the river made we should see on the shore ahead several large villages, from which a certain number of Indians came forth in canoes toward us; and, when they were near, within a crossbow shot from the brigantines, the Captain began to call to them, using peace signals, to which they, whether they understood them or not, did not reply; on the contrary, they began to shout, and they showed signs [of what their attitude was] by threatening us with their bows and arrows. And, perceiving their arrogance, the Captain ordered that they [i.e. our men] shoot at them with the crossbows and arquebuses, and in consequence of this they [i.e. the Indians] fled toward their villages. At the same moment there came out many armed with [bows and] arrows from among the trees along the shore of the river, talking very loud and as if vexed, going through all sorts of contortions with their bodies, indicating thereby that they looked upon us with scorn; and we thought that they must be drunk, because these tribes of people very frequently indulge [heavily] in wine and [other] beverages which they are accustomed to [drinking], and they consider this a smart thing to do; and in this way, like inflamed intoxicated men, they waited stationed at intervals along the bank of the river, transformed, as it were, into lions, having no fear of the arquebuses and crossbows. And as fast as the brigantines advanced toward

*[This word means "hidden." In Medina's version (p. 212, above) the hamlet is called the Village of the Street.—EDITOR.]

the villages, [just] so fast did they move up toward the other fighting armed force which stood ready to defend the landing place; but, as our need of [replenishing our] supplies was spurring us on, the Captain ordered that the landing-place be captured, and consequently the Spaniards turned the prows towards where the main body of the horde of foes stood, urging the squad armed with arquebuses to work with all the speed that was possible, and the crossbowmen did the same; and that was carried out in a manner [so effective] that the enemy allowed a certain number of the Spanish companions to leap out on land. In this place were seen Indian women with bows and arrows who did as much fighting as the Indian men, or [even] more, and they led on and incited the Indian men to fight; and, when *they* wanted [to have the fight go on], they, using the bows and arrows as sticks, would even drub those who started to flee, and they served as captains, commanding those warriors to fight, and placed themselves in the front ranks and held others [of the fighting men] in position so that they would stand firm in the battle, which was entered into very resolutely. And because this practice is as foreign to women as [the very nature of] the female sex requires [that it should be] and may appear to be something very unusual to the reader who may happen to see [i.e. read] this account of mine, I [wish to] state, by way of clearing myself [of any charge of untruthfulness], that I am talking about something which I [actually] saw; and [from] what we succeeded in finding out and [from what] was [**563**] considered to be the truth, it is [evident] that these women who fought there like Amazons are those about whom, in numerous and diverse accounts, for a long time already there has been circulating a widespread report in these Indies or in these parts, [a report] circulated in many different forms, regarding these warlike women. These have sovereignty, and jurisdiction over life and property, and absolute power of their own in this province, and [the seat of their rule is] not far from there [where we were, and there they lead a life] away from, and independent of and without association with, male beings; and those whom we saw were a few administrators and inspectors of their government, who had come there to keep watch on the shore. They are tall and of a robust build, and [go about] naked, [except for their] having a small clout which they wear in front of their more privy parts; but in time of peace they go about clad in robes and woven goods made out of cotton, thin and very graceful.

In this way, to return to [the story of] the fight, the Spaniards fell upon the Indians, wounding and killing many of them, until they drove them out of the village; and the arquebusiers and crossbowmen killed many, and no less damage did the companions who were on land inflict [upon them], because the Indians met their attack with great courage, and so determined [were they] in the resistance which they put up that it was a marvelous thing [to behold]. There an Indian was captured who told about many things and special matters with reference to the country off in the interior, as will be stated at the proper time: which Indian the Captain took aboard his brigantine, because he [i.e. the Indian] was a man of good understanding, and every day [thereafter] he related wonderful things. Several companions came out of this battle or fight wounded, for they [i.e. the Indians] managed to hit them aboard the brigantines at the time when the landing-place was captured, and me too they hit in the side with an arrow, which went in as far as the hollow part, and had it not been for the folds in my clothes, through which the arrow first passed, they would have killed me. But as there was no poison [on the arrows] in that province, no one died [from his wounds].

The fighting being now over and the Indians having fled, the Captain ordered the men to get into the boats, and we resumed our customary navigating down the familiar river, and we passed by a village only a short distance from the one which has just been spoken of; and, as we had not found anything in the first one but maize, for of this we regularly found an abundance in all the villages, the companions requested the Captain to do them the favor of letting us [read: them] make port there, in this second harbor, to look for some food [i. e. meat or fish]; and the Captain did not want to do it, but I, at the same time as the companions, requested him to do it as a favor, because no inhabitants were in sight and it might be that some sort of fish or meat would be found there. And, although we had now gone on ahead for quite some distance past the village, the Captain ordered the brigantines to turn back toward the harbor; and, inasmuch as we were now going skirting along upstream close in toward the shore and the Indians were [hidden] in ambuscades in the grass and the tree-covered areas, divided up into squadrons and [assigned in these formations to different] posts, they found it easy to shoot at the brigantines in a way that made it seem like a shower of arrows; but, as the Spaniards had been prepared [for this sort of thing] ever since [they had left the province of] Machiparo [and] had with them some good shields of the sort which the Indians use [back] in that province, made out of manatee skins, and very large and strong, as has been stated above, they hit no one but me, for Our Lord permitted them, because of my faults, to plant an arrow shot over one of my eyes, the arrow passing through my head and sticking out two fingers' length on the other side behind my ear and slightly above it; from which wound, besides losing the eye, I have endured much suffering and worry, and even now I am not free from pain, although Our Lord, without my deserving it, has been kind enough to grant me life so that I may mend my ways and serve Him better than I had served Him hitherto. At that point the men in the smaller boat leaped out on land; and the Indians were so numerous that they now had them surrounded, and, if the Captain had not come to their aid with the large brigantine, they [**564**] would have been done for and the Indians would have carried them off, in spite of the fact that the Christians were using their hands to good advantage, for they were fighting like lions. So it was that the Captain called them back; and when he saw me wounded, he gave orders for the brigantines to pull out, and he abandoned [the attempt to capture] the village, because there were many fighting men [there] and thoroughly stubborn ones, in order that they might not kill some of his companions, for he well understood the necessity of not daring to face the aid [which was bound to come to the Indians] in view of the fact that the country is densely inhabited (and [furthermore] there was the obligation of saving the lives [of the companions]), for one village was not [more than] half a league distant from another, and [in the case of] many of them [there was] even less space [between] than I am stating. All along that side of the river, on the right as we were navigating downstream, back in the land there were villages, and the physical nature of the country was seen to be excellent, in that there were not only savanas, but also uplands and slopes and hills cleared of trees. So it was that, when this affair was over, the Captain gave orders to cross over to the other side of the river with the brigantines in order to get away from the inhabited country, and for this reason many settlements were not caught sight of at all, numbering more than those that we did see. The name of Punta de San Juan*

*[I.e. Dawn of Saint John's Day.—EDITOR.]

was given to that province [by us], because it was on his [i.e. Saint John's] day that we arrived there, on which day, in the morning, I had preached in praise of such a glorious and most holy herald of Christ; and I hold it to be certain that it was through his intercession that God granted me life.

As we pulled out into the open part of the river, the Indians from those villages kept following us; but they did not dare to come very close up to the brigantines for fear of the arquebuses and crossbows. And that night we went over to the other shore of the river to sleep, and [yet] the Captain did not allow anyone to go on land, because it [i.e. the land] was not [known to be] safe; and the Indians of Punta de San Juan did not come to attack us that night, and we passed it in that way and slept with the brigantines moored to the trees, without getting out on land. In this same way we moved on after that always on our guard until we got out of this province, which is more than one hundred and fifty leagues long [as measured] along the shore [of the river].

On the following day, the twenty-fifth of June, we passed within sight of a certain number of large villages belonging to the same province, from which [villages] there came out many Indians, in canoes numbering more than two hundred, very large ones equal in size to pirogues; and these villages were situated on some very beautiful and very cool islands having high land and savanas, among which islands there are some with a shore [length] of fifty leagues and more, and [these are] very densely populated. And these large canoes kept coming nearer and nearer every hour, until they had the brigantines surrounded on all sides, so that, in order that our men might not let themselves be killed with impunity, it was necessary to bring the powder and the crossbows into play; and, when the Indians had begun to get a taste of the fruit of the arquebuses, they drew away and from a long distance off continued to follow us all that day, until they had driven us out of the inhabited country.

In the afternoon, on the same day, the Captain, desiring peace with those Indians in order to see if we could take a rest in some wooded section of country, decided to offer them a certain quantity of *chaquira* as barter goods or as a sign of a friendly attitude [on our part], and with this end in view he ordered to be thrown out in a gourd a certain number of diamonds and pearls, and jingle bells, and other articles of that sort and [things] which among us are not esteemed very highly and [yet are such] that in other parts of these Indies the Indians value them and look upon them as being of considerable worth; and, when the gourd had been thrown into the water in the direction of where the Indians were in order that they might see it, while we were holding off at a short distance a canoe came up to the gourd containing the *chaquira*, and they [i.e. the Indians in this canoe] picked it up and showed it to the other Indians, and they valued it so little that it became evident to us that they were making fun of it. And for this reason they did not stop following us until, as has been stated, we had gone on beyond their villages, which, as a matter of fact, on account of their being [so] numerous could not be counted, and furthermore no attempt was made to do this [counting] because they did not leave us alone long enough for us to do so.

That night we went off to get our sleep in an [565] oak grove which was situated in a savana, where we were not without fearful apprehensions, because [on the one hand] they [i.e. some Indians] came by water in two canoes to observe us and [on the other hand] on land there were many roads. At this place the Captain questioned the Indian who has been mentioned about the natural conditions and [general] character of the country, and he said that back in the interior there were many tribes of people and great overlords and [large] provinces, among which [latter] he said that there was one very large province inhabited by women, [and] that there were no males [living] with these; and [he said] that [the inhabitants of] all those lands do homage to them [i.e. these women] and [their chiefs] are tributaries to them, and that he himself had gone there many times to do homage; and that they have houses built of stone, and that on the inside of the houses, as far down as half a man's height [from the ground up], the walls all around are covered with silver plaques; and [that] the roads by which those who engage in business there come in [are] closed off on the one side and on the other with high walls and at given distances apart have archways, and they [i.e. those who go there to trade] have duties to pay to the guards who are stationed at these places for that purpose. And this Indian said that there were great quantities of sheep [there] of the same large variety as in Peru, and a very great wealth of gold, because all those women who were ruling mistresses had eating services made out of this (while the other women belonging to the plebeian class occupying a lower station used for their eating service vessels made of wood), and they all wore clothes made out of very fine wool. This Indian stated furthermore that from a country far away [from their own], from provinces where these women carried on war, by the use of force they brought the Indian men to their own country, particularly those belonging to a great overlord who was called the White King, for the purpose of taking pleasure with them in [the satisfying of] their carnal desires in the multiplying of their race, and kept them with them for some time until they had become pregnant and [then], after they had become aware that they had conceived, sent them back to their country; and, if they later gave birth to male children, they either killed them or sent them to their fathers, while if it was a daughter that they [read: any given one of them] gave birth to, they [read: she] raised her by giving suck to her and instructed her in the arts of war.

Concerning these women we had always heard a very great number of reports all along the course of this journey, and [even] before we had left Gonzalo Pizarro's expeditionary force it had been looked upon as a certainty that this dominion in the hands of women of this sort did exist. And among ourselves we gave them the name of Amazons, [though] improperly: for "Amazon" in the Greek language means: "having no breasts," in order that they might have nothing to hinder' them in shooting with the bow, according to what Justin writes at greater length about this matter.* But these women that we are dealing with here, although they do use the bow, do not cut off their breasts nor do they burn them off, albeit in other matters, such as in taking men unto themselves for a certain period of time for the propagation of their kind and in other respects, it does seem as if they imitate those whom the ancients called Amazons.

This Indian, in the account that he gave of those women, said nothing that disagreed with what other Indians had been telling [us] in [the country where we were still members of] Gonzalo Pizarro's expeditionary force [proper], and [even] before that, in Quito and in Peru: rather, here they [i.e. the Indians] told much more [than was needed to convince us]; for ever since [we had left] the chief of Coca, [a territory] which is within fifty leagues of Quito [and] which is situated at the headwaters of the river, one thousand five hundred leagues, slightly more or less, from these other villages about which this Indian was talking, we had been accept-

*[See Justinus (the abbreviator of Trogus Pompeius), Book II, Ch. 4.—EDITOR.]

ing this story as an absolutely true and proven one, because the majority of the Indians who were captured all said the same thing, and some without being questioned about it. This Indian said that [the place where] we had left these women behind us [was] in a very thickly settled [country along a] river which emptied into this one that we were navigating, on the right as we came on down.

Proceeding on our customary journey, eager to arrive at a country where there were Christians in order to be able to rest from our past, present, and forthcoming hardships, we encountered people more and more warlike every day and [people] who extended worse receptions to us, among which peoples [there was] one tribe [which] came out to attack us in a large number of canoes, [the occupants of which were] stained black by an artificial process consisting of the use of ink; and for this reason our Spaniards gave them the name of black or sooty tribe. These men came out from several very large provinces on the [**566**] left side of the river down which we were proceeding; which people are located in the midst of very fine natural surroundings in the form of a country composed of uplands and savanas, and they are persons of very large physical proportions, like Germans or [even] larger [types]. We did not make port in any village belonging to those people, because the Captain did not permit it, in spite of the fact that for several days we had been eating nothing but bread, for fear lest they might kill one or more of his Christians, as well as on account of the fact that the villages were very large ones and because it was his desire to get those few men that he had with him out of there in safety.

A few days later we arrived off a certain small village, where the Captain gave orders to make for land in order to look for foodstuffs, and the landing-place was easily taken possession of, in spite of the fact that the Indians resisted the attack; but after a few moments they fled to another village which was situated farther down, where we likewise made port. And neither in the one nor in the other was there found any maize or meat or fish. In this second village the Indians offered resistance in a very courageous manner, like men who sought to protect their homes, for, although the landing place was captured from them, that was not accomplished without loss to us; and before the Spaniards had leaped out on land, they [i.e. the Indians] had wounded a Christian on board [one of] the brigantines with an arrow; and at the moment that it struck him he felt great pain, and it was immediately evident that he was mortally wounded, and he confessed his sins and set his soul aright. It was a thing that inspired great pity [in us] to see him; for the foot in which he had been wounded turned very black, and the poison gradually made its way up through the leg, like a living thing, without its being possible to head it off, although they applied many cauteries to it with fire, wherefrom it was plainly evident that the arrow had been dipped in a most noxious poison; and when it [i.e. the poison] had mounted to his heart, he died, being in great pain until the third day, when he gave up his soul to God who had created it. The name of this companion was Antonio de Carranza. The Indians of these villages were engaged in a war with those [adjoining them] up the river, and they were in the habit of defending their country against the others by means of this poison, which their adversaries did not have; and for this reason they [i.e the latter] were unable to destroy them, in spite of the fact that they were a much larger tribe than these others.

From here on, we were in much greater terror than before, on account of our fear of the poison; and we went to get our sleep in a savana where there were a few oak trees; and there the captain had some railings, like a rim, built on the brigantines, as high as up to a man's chest, and covered with the cotton and woolen blankets which we had brought along, in order to protect us from the arrows which the Indians were now shooting at the brigantines. From this spot could be seen, three leagues inland from the river, on the sloping skirt of a wooded mountain range, some large settlements which shone white, and the country had the appearance of being a very good one.

We stayed at this stopping-place a day and a half; and at the end of this period of time there was heard a bird which had alighted on the top of an oak tree, close to where we were; which [bird], in a manner indicating very great urgency, seemed to us to be saying clearly and distinctly in its cry: "huír, huír, huír."* And this little bird said this many times, for all during this journey we used to hear it, whenever we were near an inhabited spot; and it used to say as plainly as a man could say: "buhío, buhío, buhío," which means "hut, hut, hut." And it was a marvelous thing [to see] how the companions rejoiced when they would hear it, particularly if we were then experiencing a shortage of provisions.

In [the offing of] this stopping-place there appeared in canoes some Indians who had come down out of an arm of the river visible to us and [approached] with a great deal of shouting and [in] an attitude indicating that it was their determination to find out what our Spaniards were equal to; but, upon [our] shooting at them with the arquebuses and crossbows, they turned about [and proceeded] to go back into the same arm of the river, and the Captain and all [the rest] of us suspected, inasmuch as those men were few in number, that they had come to observe us and form an estimate of us, like spies, and indeed that is what they were, as it afterwards became evident. And [**567**] consequently the Captain ordered the brigantines to depart at once, and we went that night, to get our sleep, over to the other shore of the river, where we slept [with] the boats moored to the trees; and that was undoubtedly [decided upon by us with] the [special] permission of God, who did not grant that we should find a dry spot [anywhere] on land in order to get out on it, for if we had slept [only after pulling up] out of the water that night, the Indians would have attacked us. And it was clearly perceived that that was what they had decided to do, as it was afterwards seen; and [read: for] that very night our watches actually heard the Indians talking on land, for they were going about [there] looking for us; and it must be believed that without fail, if they had found us on land and [read: or] even [where we were, i.e.] on board the brigantines they would have placed us in [a position where we should have undergone] the last [stage of our] suffering and [there can be no doubt] that there would not have remained from among our number anyone who could have given [to the outside world] the news of what had been happening to us, in view of the death-dealing poison which the Indians possess from that point all the rest of the way down to the sea, which may be a distance of two hundred and fifty leagues; all the way up which [distance] the flowing or rise of the tide extends. The total count of leagues that there are from Corpus Christi Village to this province where the poison was used, according to the calculations of those who kept charting the shores and [the course of] our journey, may be three hundred leagues, not much more or less.

Then, as soon as it was day, the Captain commanded that the brigantines pull out from among the trees where they were moored; and we had not moved on

*[Or "huí, huí, huí" according to Medina's version of Carvajal's Account: see *supra*, p. 225.— EDITOR.]

even as far as a crossbow shot when, just as we put in our appearance at the entrance to an arm of the river, we saw coming out a fleet composed of a great number of canoes, and very large ones [they were], as large as pirogues, which had been waiting for us there with the intention of forcing a battle upon us; and, if they had found us sooner, the damage done to us would have been greater, since we were unable to get away from there or make our escape as unscathed as we should have wished, because they surrounded our brigantines on all sides and shot many arrows into them; and if it had not been for the arquebusiers and crossbowmen, who compelled them to draw away, we should have suffered great loss.

On this occasion there were fired with the arquebuses two remarkable shots which saved our lives and had the effect of inducing the enemy to retreat into the distance. One shot was such that it hit a number of Indians, and they became excited to such a degree that the canoe capsized and sank, and they, [a group of] fully twelve or thirteen Indians who were [thus] obliged to abandon it, went swimming about in the water, and their friends in the other canoes were not able to come to their rescue, for they were now fleeing on account of the havoc which the arquebuses were producing among them, in spite of the fact that they were some distance away. The other shot a Biscayan companion fired, by means of which he felled two other Indians.

This battle was a very remarkable thing to watch, because the brigantines followed up the Indians who swam off, and they [i.e. the Spaniards] shot [at some of them] with the crossbows, and others they hit with lances, with the result that not one of those men escaped from being killed at the hands of the Spaniards, or [from being] drowned, [I mean] of those who fell out of the canoe which capsized. And in this way the victory was won, although on this trying occasion one Spaniard was mortally wounded by an arrow shot which they planted in one of his thighs; and it all happened in the following way, [namely] that, as the arrow had been shot from afar off, the arrow point penetrated such a short distance into his thigh that it dropped off by itself after it had struck him; but the poison which it had on it was so vicious that twenty-four hours later he was dead. This companion's name was García de Soria.

We came on down the river from where it has just been said, skirting along the shore on the right side as we followed our course, and [with] the Indians in their canoes still in pursuit of us, [though] holding off at a good distance, until they saw us out of [the country which includes] their settlements: these we caught sight of, on that day, on the same side of the river back inland, where there could be distinguished some very large villages and high land and [land] of a very fine appearance, from which [villages] there came forth many warriors and women and children to see us, as something which was new to them. And the Indian men [568] kept uttering cries, and the women and children kept beating the air with pairs of fans resembling fly-shooers, and kept jumping and dancing, executing many gestures and contortions of their bodies, manifesting great delight and joy, like people who had come out victorious in that they had driven us out of their country. Upon the high bank of the river there stood more than five thousand warriors belonging to that most barbaric host, and more rather than fewer, scattered along at intervals by squadrons.

That day and the following one we continued to move on in sight of some very fine country [made up] of hills without trees, and there could be seen a few stretches of land having bright red soil and [some] savanas quite thickly covered with dwellings on the left side of the river as we proceeded on our journey. And the Indian who had given information about the Amazons said that in this country which we could see there was a very great overlord who held these provinces and [these] lands in subjection, and that there was a very great quantity of silver there, and that all [the inhabitants] have utensils made out of it in their houses; and indeed it did seem as if in the country [that I am talking about] there must be all that which the interpreter said, judged from what we ourselves saw.

A few days later we captured a village on that same left side of the river, and [there we found that] the Indians had carried away their foodstuffs, because they had been notified about us.

From this place we went off to get our sleep upon a high bank of the river, [on the edge of a stretch] of land having no trees, like savanas, [and it was] broken country; and the woods or, more properly speaking, the groves in this country, are growths of cork oaks and evergreen oaks and white oaks, and these three kinds of trees [are] like, and [in fact] just the same as, those of our Spain.

From this place the Captain, perceiving the beautiful richness of vegetation of the country, sent a certain number of companions out to inspect it, and he ordered them not to get more than a league away and to bring him a report on what they saw. And so they went; and, having come back, they said that the country got better and better toward the interior, and that they had [nevertheless] not dared to go farther away from the shore on account of the many [beaten] tracks that they had found made by Indians, who must have come along there [sometime] to hunt or fish, [though perhaps not recently] because the tracks were not freshly made ones; but they showed signs of being [regularly] traveled over, and it might be that they had [just] been altered by the effect of some [heavy fall of] dew or a shower that had made them look as if they had [last] been followed many days back in spite of their [really] having been freshly trodden. There was found there a burned-down village, and the Indian interpreter said that the Indians from the interior of the country had done it [i.e. burned the village].

At this stopping-place we stayed two days, because it looked like a country that would cheer one up, and [also because of our desire] to renew our courage and to rest before continuing on our journey; and then, right after we started off, we struck out among islands that are really a part of the river's course, which are too numerous to count and in some cases very large, navigating among which calls for highly skilled mariners or pilots able to decide where to go in and where to come out, because they [i.e. the islands] make [the river divide up into] many arms; and for this reason we did not manage or find out how to reach the mainland [again] all the way down to the sea.

We were continually finding on these islands villages in large numbers, and many more we missed seeing on account of our being unable to skirt along the mainland, for we neither caught sight of it nor succeeded in reaching it over the distance of more than one hundred and fifty leagues that we navigated in among the islands.

The Indians dwelling in these villages are Caribs and they eat human flesh, for there was found in them [i.e. in the villages] flesh roasted on barbecues or gridirons, as they kept it on hand [ready] to eat, and it was readily recognized as the flesh of a human being, because there were among other pieces of it a few feet and hands that had belonged to a human being. And in one village there was found a shoemaker's awl, with the thread and brass sheath that go with it, whence it was understood that the Indians of that country knew of the existence of Christians.

In another settlement there were found two crudely fashioned imitation brigantines, hung up, which the Indians had put together to look like copies, these having the proportions and shape which [569] a real brigantine ought to have, [objects] which in my opinion must have been made [and placed there] in remembrance of some victory or for some other purpose connected with something they wished to remember, and [it was evident] that the Indians had seen brigantines, since they had learned how to shape and imitate them so well and so nearly like [real ones].

A thing well worth seeing are the pictures which all the Indians along this river put on the vessels which they use for their [household] service, both clay and wooden ones, and on the gourds out of which they drink, both [because] of the exquisite and beautiful leaves and the carefully drawn figures, and in [view of] the excellent skill and [thorough] organization [of labor] that is required in [making] them; and they apply colors to them and make them stay on very well, and these [colors] are very good and very fine, each one being of a special kind and [different in] shade. They manufacture and fashion large pieces out of clay, with relief designs, [in the style] of Roman workmanship; and so it was that we saw many vessels, such as bowls and cups and other containers for drinking, and jars as tall as a man, which can hold thirty and forty and [even] fifty arrobas,* very beautiful and made out of a very fine quality of clay.

In short, all their hand-made products show that they are a people very keen and of excellent mental faculties, and the objects which they manufacture would make a very good showing in the eyes of the highly accomplished artisans in that profession in Europe, and wherever they [i.e. people] might get to see them [i.e. these objects].

We eventually had to make port in a certain village where we were caught in a very difficult situation, [accompanied by] hazard and danger, because, at the entrance to the harbor, as a result of the rising of the tide we failed to see a large number of tree trunks which were below [the surface of] the water [and] of which the small brigantine ran afoul, and as a consequence of that crash one of its planks was stove in and it [i.e. the brigantine] began to go to the bottom, [sinking] until there remained only four finger widths of [the top of] the gunwales uncovered. Hence we were having [ill] luck by water and by land, and the Indians kept turning back upon our companions who had gone into the village and forced them to retreat in the direction of the brigantines; and it became necessary for the Captain to order that the Spaniards be divided [into squads], for we were in a position where a great deal of caution was required. And this is what was done: one half of the companions were occupied with fighting with the Indians, and others with floating the [small] brigantine, and others with guarding the large brigantine, guarding [against an attack from] the river, in order that by water the Indians might not inflict any damage upon us. It pleased Jesus Christ to help us and favor us, as He always did on this voyage which we like lost men had undertaken to carry out, without knowing where we were or whither we were going or what was to become of us. So it was that in a very special and complete manner it was made clear that God made use of His pity in our behalf; for without its being understood by anyone [among us] how it was done, the Divine Majesty, through

*[Of about four gallons each.—EDITOR.]

the working of His unbounded clemency and providence, showed us the way out of the difficulty and aided us by having it come about that the brigantine should be held aloft by a [submerged] tree trunk until it was possible to find out where the water was coming in and [until] it [i.e. the water] could be held back, by means of [pieces of] clothing and bedding materials, long enough [for them to be able] to master it and pump it all out; and at one and the same moment the brigantine was salvaged and the warriors took to flight, and there was an opportunity to haul the brigantine up on shore in order to mend the broken plank; and, during all the time that this was being done, the rest of the Spaniards were on guard and on the alert. O infinite and sovereign God, how many times did we find ourselves in trying situations and in moments of agony so close to death that, had it not been for Thy mercy and absolute power [to protect us], it would have been impossible [for us] to muster sufficient strength or [avail ourselves sufficiently of] the counsels of men in order to escape with our lives!

From this village that I was speaking about there was obtained a great deal of maize, as well as a large quantity of other foodstuffs and salt; and we went off to get our sleep that night farther on down our course, [having continued on] until we stopped [at a spot] where it seemed to us that we were going to be safe, the boats being tied or moored to some trees; indeed, we did not pull up to a landing-place until the following day, when we found one beyond the inhabited section of country, or, more properly speaking, [until we found] a patch of woods on the shore of the river, where the small brigantine was practically rebuilt. At that task we were occupied for eighteen days, undergoing [570] many hardships on account of the small quantity of provisions that there was on hand, although it was with considerable moderation and with rationing that we ate that which we had.

Once again, Our Lord here manifested the special care which He was exercising over us sinners, and He saw fit to provide for us in our [time of] shortage of food as in [the time of] all the others that I have told about. And that is how it was that, [the companions] being harassed by hunger and the strength of the Spaniards being diminished, it happened by the will of God that one day, toward evening, down the river, on the same side and close to the section of shore where the brigantine was being repaired, there came [floating] along the top of the water a very large tapir cow; and Captain Francisco de Orellana ordered a certain number of companions to go out into the river and bring in that cow. And that was done; and it was divided up among all, with the result that a goodly portion fell to the lot of each, whereby the sick received succor and the rest sustenance. There in that little camp nails were made for use in repairing both brigantines and in putting decks and upperworks upon them, for they had none, with the idea of getting them ready and [converting them into vessels] of such a sort that they might be fit to go to sea. This we went off to do on a beach, [arriving there] not many days after we had departed from this stopping-place; and, during the time that we were coming on down looking for the said beach and a spot having facilities and conveniences for repairing the brigantines, we made port in several villages where a certain quantity of fish was found but no maize; because the Indians value it [i.e. maize] highly along these shores, down near the sea, and whatever amount they had they had carried away [somewhere].

On Holy Savior's Day, which is the Transfiguration of Jesus Christ Our Redeemer, we found the said beach that we were looking for, where the brigantines were repaired quite satisfactorily, and with no little rejoicing on the part of our companions and [our] Captain; and all toiled as at a task which was as important to them as their very lives. This work on, and repairing of, the brigantines took up fourteen days [and these were days] of regular and continuous penance due to the great hunger [that we were enduring] and to the small amount of foodstuffs [on hand], because there was but a very small quantity of maize and there was a shortage of all the other victuals: the result being that our privation reached the point where we were eating by the ounce and [as when one is on a] diet, fearing [to have nothing left for] sailing on the sea; and each one was keeping a little roasted maize to take along, and ate [only] the tidewater food that he found after the tide had gone out, which consisted of a few snails, and very small ones [at that], and a few tiny crabs; and it [i.e. this kind of food] would have been no small [cause for] contentment, if of these things they had found all that they could have stuffed themselves with.

When the work on the brigantines was completed, we departed from this stopping-place, on the eighth day of the month of August, hungry, and fitted out none too well [but] in proportion to the conditions resulting from the limited means at our disposal; for there can be no doubt that many were the things that we lacked, both as regards sails for the brigantines, and rigging and everything else needed for navigating. And in order to make up, to a certain degree, for these deficiencies, we made the sails out of the Peruvian blankets that we had with us, which each one had been in the habit of pilfering from those Indians of his who had been with us; and in this way we proceeded under sail down the river with much toil and with a contrary wind, tacking and waiting for the tides in order to make better progress, and we constantly passed through [moments of] shuddering and fear on account of the many shoals that were encountered in the river. And what grieved us most was having no anchors for either one of the brigantines in order to [be able to] lie at anchor, waiting, as it was necessary to wait, for the tides [i.e. for the time] when the water should fall; and, as we anchored to buckets made of stone and of sticks,* it happened many times that the brigantines would drag [these crude anchors] along the bottom, with the risk of being smashed to pieces.

God in His clemency, not looking upon our sins, saw fit to bring us out of these dangers and to do us so many favors that [571] He did not permit us to die of hunger or suffer shipwreck, which we were very close to many times, finding ourselves aground or stranded in three palms of water; the result being that it was frequently necessary for all the companions to jump into the water in order to lift the brigantines out and push them off bottom to get them to float. And when one considers the [number of] times that they struck bottom, and the blows which they received from the sea amidships, it may surely be believed that God with His absolute power chose to save us, so that we might mend our ways or for some other mysterious purpose which His Divine Majesty kept to Himself, [and] which we mortals did not grasp.

On down the river we continually found villages with Indians, where we secured a certain amount of food, although only a small amount, because the Indians kept it hidden away; and, if we had not found it, at least [that which consisted]

---

*[These seven words are a literal translation of the original. Perhaps the meaning is: "buckets made of twigs, each with a [heavy] stone in it." Medina says [p. 105, *supra*]: "they tied the boats to stones . . ."—EDITOR.]

of maize in limited quantities and roots [i.e. tubers], we should all have perished from hunger. And thus it was that we came away very weak and very short of supplies from that stopping-place where the last part of the work of repairing the brigantines was done.

In the villages just mentioned the Indian men, being as they were a more docile people than those farther up, let us come to them, [being] without bows or arrows or any other kinds of weapons; and it seemed, from the signs and gestures which they made, pointing at the beards and features and clothes of the Christians, as if they were giving us to understand that not far away from there there were some lost or colonizing Spaniards. And this rumor, together with the signs [to that effect], persisted among the Indians of most of the villages which we came upon [from this time on] until we got away from the river, particularly at the mouth through which we came out of it, where we found a certain number of docile Indians living in a few villages which are right at the mouth: these came to the brigantines to exchange with us for our barter goods a small quantity of fish, like people who had done that on other occasions. These same Indians informed us in clearer terms that from that point there were three days of sailing along the coast to the place where those Christians were.

Before going out to sea we stopped at this mouth of the river one day and one night, where there were made a good hawser and a certain number of ropes for the riggings of the brigantines; and, as they had been made out of piecings, there was always some piecing to be done on them; and, if in one place we would succeed in securing certain things, in other places we would not find any. And, as the rest of the things with which we fitted ourselves out were imitations and made by the hands of men without experience and unaccustomed to such a profession, they lasted a very short time; and, as they were not to be found everywhere, it was necessary to keep on toiling and fitting [ourselves] out at random. In this manner, in one place the sail was made, in another the rudder, in another the pump, and in another the rigging, and in the case of each one of these things, as long as we did not have it, it meant being in great danger.

I am leaving out many other things we lacked, such as pilots and sailors and a compass, which are necessary things, for without any one of them there is no man, however devoid of common sense he may be, that would dare to go to sea, except ourselves, to whom this rambling voyage came by accident and not by our will.

It took us twenty-four days to get down to this mouth of the river, and during all of them it never rained where we were, nor did we encounter a heavy shower, and that was a special favor from God.

This mouth of the river, from cape to cape, is four leagues wide, and we saw other wider mouths than the one through which we went out to sea; and to the minds of experienced men, and in view of the pattern of the many islands and gulfs and bays which the river formed fifty leagues back before we got out of it, it was quite evident that there remained other mouths to the right as we came down, on which side we encountered a heavier and a rougher sea, although it was fresh water [there], than over the whole distance that we later traversed in salt water. And our one desire was to bend our efforts and find out how to reach the [real] country and main shore [572] on the left as we came down, in order to go out to sea by that route, because we believed that in this way we should come sooner upon the abodes of Christians, inasmuch as we were to proceed along the seacoast

on the left as we were coming down, until we should arrive at the Island of Cubagua or at some other settlement where there were Christians; and notwithstanding
all the diligence that was applied to searching for the mainland bordering upon
the river, never could it be reached: so that we were forced to go out between
islands on the one side and the other through the aforesaid mouth.

[As to] this exceedingly large river, with all my attempting with much eagerness
to get some information [regarding it] from men who have traveled about on this
coast of Tierra Firme and have gone up some of its rivers, I have not been able to
convince myself definitely which of two rivers it is, because some say that it is
the Huyapari* and others the Marañón; for there is a distance of four hundred
leagues to this Island of Cubagua from where we went out to sea; and, as we have
already seen, the whole river taken together, there where we entered it [i.e. the
sea], has a width of more than forty leagues, and there is a rise and fall [of the
tide] at the mouth of more than five fathoms. The total number of leagues that
there are from Corpus Christi Village to the place of the [first discovery by us of
the use of] poison must be three hundred leagues, a few more or less, and the total
count for our voyage, from where we started out as lost men down to where we
came upon the sea, is one thousand five hundred and fifty leagues. This [is]
without [counting] those [leagues] we had covered [at the time] when we decided
to go in search of the sea, because of our inability to go back to Gonzalo Pizarro's
camp, which makes an additional hundred and fifty leagues, so that the total
distance down to the sea is one thousand seven hundred leagues. So it is that,
[calculated in conjunction] with four hundred more [for those] which there are
[from the mouth of the river] to Cubagua, two thousand one hundred leagues is
the total length of this rambling journey of ours, which, as has been stated, was
undertaken unintentionally.

We passed out of the aforesaid river to begin our sea journey on Saturday, in
the morning before dawn, the twenty-sixth day of the month of August, and it
turned out to be such good weather for us that not once did it rain or did a squall
molest us. We proceeded onward by sea, the two brigantines [keeping] together
in convoy, for four days, and on the day of the Beheading† of Saint John the
Baptist, during the night, one brigantine got separated from the other in such a
way that we did not succeed in sighting each other until [we reached] Cubagua
(which under another name is known as the Island of Pearls), where the small
brigantine [i.e. the one which became separated from us], called the *San Pedro*,
arrived on Saturday the ninth day of the month of September, and [where] we, on
board the larger brigantine, called the *Victoria*, arrived the following Monday,
which brought us to the eleventh day of the same month, namely September.
And so it was that ([and] they no less than we, those in one brigantine and those
in the other), inasmuch as we had no pilots or [magnetic] needles or navigator's
charts, we became all confused in our navigating, and much more [seriously]

*[The Orinoco, as Oviedo explains in Book XXIV, Chapter 3, of his *Historia . . . de las
Indias* (Madrid, 1851–55 edition, Vol. 2, p. 216).—EDITOR.]

†[The Spanish word used here in the text from which the present translation is made is "cola-
ción," for which there is no definition, in the dictionaries at hand, that is acceptable from the
point of view of the context here. For this reason, the word which is found in the corresponding
passage in Friar Carvajal's *Account* as published by Medina (cf. p. 233, *supra*), namely "Degolla-
ción" (i.e. "Beheading"), is substituted for the purposes of the present translation. The civil date
of the religious feast day in question is August 29, and consequently, inasmuch as Friar Carvajal's
reckoning of "four days" includes the 26th, the correlation is correct.—EDITOR.]

those of us who were traveling in the larger brigantine; because those in the smaller brigantine lost four days of navigating, while we in the brigantine *Victoria* [lost] seven.

Those in the small brigantine were delayed on account of having tried to go into the Mouths of the Dragon, thinking that that was their route; and, if they had gone in, they would have found themselves caught in a gulf whence they would have been able to escape [only] with difficulty, as it happened to us, who, because of our sins, went in where they had not been able to enter, this [mistake of ours] being permitted by God who had chosen to save them from the peril in which we found ourselves, caught as in a gulf in a hellish corner for seven consecutive days and nights, the companions toiling away at the oars in the effort to get out of where we had gone in. And the wind was so [constantly] against us and so strong that it would make us lose in one hour what we had won in a whole day [of toiling]. There our food had become exhausted, and we saw ourselves caught by so great a shortage of supplies that he who managed to have ten grains of roasted maize considered that he was having a good meal for that day.

It was Our Lord's pleasure to bring us out of that prison which I have spoken of, and although, on getting out [of there], we had to put up with a calm for [573] a period of two days, we were happy, giving thanks to God, trusting in His mercy [and confident] that He would soon take us to where we should find people of our own race. And just as during our journey, long drawn out as it was, it was the Holy Spirit that always guided us, though our works did not deserve that, so now in a singular fashion, God Himself being our guide and our way, He led us, after the calms had left us, in two days straight to the city of Nueva Cádiz in Cubagua, where, as has already been stated, we found the companions who had come in on board the brigantine *San Pedro*; and it was no little [source of] joy for Captain Francisco de Orellana and the rest, for we did not know about them and we had come on [filled] with the fear that they had been caught in a gulf, just as we had done.

Of one thing I am persuaded and quite assured: that both to them and to us God granted great favors, and very special ones, in keeping us in safety all the way to that island, because we had been navigating along the most dangerous and the roughest coast that there is around this whole vast ocean. And had we gone out, on the contrary, in winter time, [escape from shipwreck after] our going out would have been looked upon as a miracle, [especially] if we had arrived [at a port as far away as] where we now are, [namely] in this city and [on this] island already mentioned, where we have furthermore been received by the few citizens that there are at present in it, as good parents are in the habit of receiving their children; and thereby they plainly show that they are men who have gone through similar hardships.

I, Brother Gaspar de Carvajal, the least of the friars of the sacred Order of our brother and friar, Father Saint Dominic, have chosen to take upon myself this little task of writing an account of the progress and outcome of our journey and navigation, not only in order to tell about it and make known the truth in the whole matter, but also in order to remove the temptation from many persons who perchance will feel inclined to relate or describe this peregrination of ours in a different way, or [even go so far as to publish] just the opposite of what we have experienced and seen. And it is true that in what I have written here I have done a considerable amount of epitomizing and shortening, because profuseness engenders distaste, and distaste gives rise to scorn and offsets the prestige and trust-worthiness which authentic accounts ought to reflect; but in this way I have sketchily and summarily related the truth in connection with everything that I saw and that happened to Captain Francisco de Orellana and to the hidalgos and commoners, or the fifty companions who separated from the expeditionary corps of Gonzalo Pizarro, Governor of Peru, otherwise known as New Castile. God be praised.

The historian and compiler* of these new data says:

I talked, in this city of Santo Domingo, with Captain Francisco de Orellana; and he arrived here one Monday, the twenty-second day of the month of November of the year One Thousand Five Hundred and Forty-two, and with him the Comendador Cristóbal Manrique, a native of the city of Cáceres, and Cristóbal de Cáceres, a native of the town of Torrejón de Velasco, and Alonso Gutiérrez, from Badajoz, and Hernán Gutiérrez de Celis, a native of the Montaña and, in fact, of the village called Celis. And I talked with other hidalgos and commoners who took part in that [voyage of] discovery under the said Captain Francisco de Orellana, a native of the city of Trujillo; and from him and from a few of the men I learned that amidst their perils and hardships, besides their own special devotions they always called on and remembered Our Lady of Guadalupe, and they even vowed and promised to go on a pilgrimage to her shrine when it should please the Mother of God to give them an opportunity to do so.

I have added this written record here because I am partial to the idea of furnishing evidence in connection with what I write; and I have longed to see that brother in religion, Friar Gaspar de Carvajal, of the Order of Preaching Friars, who wrote this account; and these cavaliers of hidalgo rank told me [574] that he had stayed behind to rest on the Island of Margarita. And I say that I should have been happy to see him and know him well; for to me it seems that such a one as he is worthy to write of things of the Indies, and that he should be believed by virtue of those two arrow shots, one of which tore out or destroyed one of his eyes; and with that single one [which he still has left], not to mention his personal prestige and qualities, which are very fine according to the affirmations of those who have had dealings with him, I would believe [him] more than [I would] those who, with two eyes and without knowing what they are talking about or understanding what the Indies are and without having visited them, staying at home in Europe, are continually babbling and have written down many tales, to which, in truth, I find nothing more fittingly comparable than the words of parrots, which, though they do speak, do not understand a single word of that which they themselves are saying.

*[This is Oviedo, introducing himself in the third person, as he frequently does throughout his history.—EDITOR.]

# INDEX

449

A CATALOG OF SELECTED
# DOVER BOOKS
IN ALL FIELDS OF INTEREST

# A CATALOG OF SELECTED DOVER
# BOOKS IN ALL FIELDS OF INTEREST

CONCERNING THE SPIRITUAL IN ART, Wassily Kandinsky. Pioneering work by father of abstract art. Thoughts on color theory, nature of art. Analysis of earlier masters. 12 illustrations. 80pp. of text. 5⅜ × 8½. 23411-8 Pa. $2.95

LEONARDO ON THE HUMAN BODY, Leonardo da Vinci. More than 1200 of Leonardo's anatomical drawings on 215 plates. Leonardo's text, which accompanies the drawings, has been translated into English. 506pp. 8⅜ × 11¼.
24483-0 Pa. $11.95

GOBLIN MARKET, Christina Rossetti. Best-known work by poet comparable to Emily Dickinson, Alfred Tennyson. With 46 delightfully grotesque illustrations by Laurence Housman. 64pp. 4 × 6¾. 24516-0 Pa. $2.50

THE HEART OF THOREAU'S JOURNALS, edited by Odell Shepard. Selections from *Journal*, ranging over full gamut of interests. 228pp. 5⅜ × 8½.
20741-2 Pa. $4.50

MR. LINCOLN'S CAMERA MAN: MATHEW B. BRADY, Roy Meredith. Over 300 Brady photos reproduced directly from original negatives, photos. Lively commentary. 368pp. 8⅜ × 11¼. 23021-X Pa. $14.95

PHOTOGRAPHIC VIEWS OF SHERMAN'S CAMPAIGN, George N. Barnard. Reprint of landmark 1866 volume with 61 plates: battlefield of New Hope Church, the Etawah Bridge, the capture of Atlanta, etc. 80pp. 9 × 12. 23445-2 Pa. $6.00

A SHORT HISTORY OF ANATOMY AND PHYSIOLOGY FROM THE GREEKS TO HARVEY, Dr. Charles Singer. Thoroughly engrossing nontechnical survey. 270 illustrations. 211pp. 5⅜ × 8½. 20389-1 Pa. $4.95

REDOUTE ROSES IRON-ON TRANSFER PATTERNS, Barbara Christopher. Redouté was botanical painter to the Empress Josephine; transfer his famous roses onto fabric with these 24 transfer patterns. 80pp. 8¼ × 10⅞. 24292-7 Pa. $3.50

THE FIVE BOOKS OF ARCHITECTURE, Sebastiano Serlio. Architectural milestone, first (1611) English translation of Renaissance classic. Unabridged reproduction of original edition includes over 300 woodcut illustrations. 416pp. 9⅜ × 12¼. 24349-4 Pa. $14.95

CARLSON'S GUIDE TO LANDSCAPE PAINTING, John F. Carlson. Authoritative, comprehensive guide covers, every aspect of landscape painting. 34 reproductions of paintings by author; 58 explanatory diagrams. 144pp. 8⅜ × 11.
22927-0 Pa. $5.95

101 PUZZLES IN THOUGHT AND LOGIC, C.R. Wylie, Jr. Solve murders, robberies, see which fishermen are liars—purely by reasoning! 107pp. 5⅜ × 8½.
20367-0 Pa. $2.00

TEST YOUR LOGIC, George J. Summers. 50 more truly new puzzles with new turns of thought, new subtleties of inference. 100pp. 5⅜ × 8½. 22877-0 Pa. $2.50

THE MURDER BOOK OF J.G. REEDER, Edgar Wallace. Eight suspenseful stories by bestselling mystery writer of 20s and 30s. Features the donnish Mr. J.G. Reeder of Public Prosecutor's Office. 128pp. 5⅜ × 8½.

24374-5 Pa. $3.95

ANNE ORR'S CHARTED DESIGNS, Anne Orr. Best designs by premier needlework designer, all on charts: flowers, borders, birds, children, alphabets, etc. Over 100 charts, 10 in color. Total of 40pp. 8¼ × 11.

23704-4 Pa. $2.50

BASIC CONSTRUCTION TECHNIQUES FOR HOUSES AND SMALL BUILDINGS SIMPLY EXPLAINED, U.S. Bureau of Naval Personnel. Grading, masonry, woodworking, floor and wall framing, roof framing, plastering, tile setting, much more. Over 675 illustrations. 568pp. 6½ × 9¼.

20242-9 Pa. $9.95

MATISSE LINE DRAWINGS AND PRINTS, Henri Matisse. Representative collection of female nudes, faces, still lifes, experimental works, etc., from 1898 to 1948. 50 illustrations. 48pp. 8⅜ × 11¼.

23877-6 Pa. $3.50

HOW TO PLAY THE CHESS OPENINGS, Eugene Znosko-Borovsky. Clear, profound examinations of just what each opening is intended to do and how opponent can counter. Many sample games. 147pp. 5⅜ × 8½.

22795-2 Pa. $3.50

DUPLICATE BRIDGE, Alfred Sheinwold. Clear, thorough, easily followed account: rules, etiquette, scoring, strategy, bidding; Goren's point-count system, Blackwood and Gerber conventions, etc. 158pp. 5⅜ × 8½.

22741-3 Pa. $3.50

SARGENT PORTRAIT DRAWINGS, J.S. Sargent. Collection of 42 portraits reveals technical skill and intuitive eye of noted American portrait painter, John Singer Sargent. 48pp. 8¼ × 11⅛.

24524-1 Pa. $3.50

ENTERTAINING SCIENCE EXPERIMENTS WITH EVERYDAY OBJECTS, Martin Gardner. Over 100 experiments for youngsters. Will amuse, astonish, teach, and entertain. Over 100 illustrations. 127pp. 5⅜ × 8½.

24201-3 Pa. $2.50

TEDDY BEAR PAPER DOLLS IN FULL COLOR: A Family of Four Bears and Their Costumes, Crystal Collins. A family of four Teddy Bear paper dolls and nearly 60 cut-out costumes. Full color, printed one side only. 32pp. 9¼ × 12¼.

24550-0 Pa. $3.50

NEW CALLIGRAPHIC ORNAMENTS AND FLOURISHES, Arthur Baker. Unusual, multi-useable material: arrows, pointing hands, brackets and frames, ovals, swirls, birds, etc. Nearly 700 illustrations. 80pp. 8⅜ × 11¼.

24095-9 Pa. $3.75

DINOSAUR DIORAMAS TO CUT & ASSEMBLE, M. Kalmenoff. Two complete three-dimensional scenes in full color, with 31 cut-out animals and plants. Excellent educational toy for youngsters. Instructions; 2 assembly diagrams. 32pp. 9¼ × 12¼.

24541-1 Pa. $4.50

SILHOUETTES: A PICTORIAL ARCHIVE OF VARIED ILLUSTRATIONS, edited by Carol Belanger Grafton. Over 600 silhouettes from the 18th to 20th centuries. Profiles and full figures of men, women, children, birds, animals, groups and scenes, nature, ships, an alphabet. 144pp. 8⅜ × 11¼.

23781-8 Pa. $5.95

25 KITES THAT FLY, Leslie Hunt. Full, easy-to-follow instructions for kites made from inexpensive materials. Many novelties. 70 illustrations. 110pp. 5⅜ × 8½.
22550-X Pa. $2.50

PIANO TUNING, J. Cree Fischer. Clearest, best book for beginner, amateur. Simple repairs, raising dropped notes, tuning by easy method of flattened fifths. No previous skills needed. 4 illustrations. 201pp. 5⅜ × 8½.
23267-0 Pa. $3.50

EARLY AMERICAN IRON-ON TRANSFER PATTERNS, edited by Rita Weiss. 75 designs, borders, alphabets, from traditional American sources. 48pp. 8¼ × 11.
23162-3 Pa. $1.95

CROCHETING EDGINGS, edited by Rita Weiss. Over 100 of the best designs for these lovely trims for a host of household items. Complete instructions, illustrations. 48pp. 8¼ × 11.
24031-2 Pa. $2.95

FINGER PLAYS FOR NURSERY AND KINDERGARTEN, Emilie Poulsson. 18 finger plays with music (voice and piano); entertaining, instructive. Counting, nature lore, etc. Victorian classic. 53 illustrations. 80pp. 6½ × 9¼. 22588-7 Pa. $2.25

BOSTON THEN AND NOW, Peter Vanderwarker. Here in 59 side-by-side views are photographic documentations of the city's past and present. 119 photographs. Full captions. 122pp. 8¼ × 11.
24312-5 Pa. $7.95

CROCHETING BEDSPREADS, edited by Rita Weiss. 22 patterns, originally published in three instruction books 1939-41. 39 photos, 8 charts. Instructions. 48pp. 8¼ × 11.
23610-2 Pa. $2.00

HAWTHORNE ON PAINTING, Charles W. Hawthorne. Collected from notes taken by students at famous Cape Cod School; hundreds of direct, personal *apercus*, ideas, suggestions. 91pp. 5⅜ × 8½.
20653-X Pa. $2.95

THERMODYNAMICS, Enrico Fermi. A classic of modern science. Clear, organized treatment of systems, first and second laws, entropy, thermodynamic potentials, etc. Calculus required. 160pp. 5⅜ × 8½.
60361-X Pa. $4.50

TEN BOOKS ON ARCHITECTURE, Vitruvius. The most important book ever written on architecture. Early Roman aesthetics, technology, classical orders, site selection, all other aspects. Morgan translation. 331pp. 5⅜ × 8½. 20645-9 Pa. $6.95

THE CORNELL BREAD BOOK, Clive M. McCay and Jeanette B. McCay. Famed high-protein recipe incorporated into breads, rolls, buns, coffee cakes, pizza, pie crusts, more. Nearly 50 illustrations. 48pp. 8¼ × 11.
23995-0 Pa. $2.00

THE CRAFTSMAN'S HANDBOOK, Cennino Cennini. 15th-century handbook, school of Giotto, explains applying gold, silver leaf; gesso; fresco painting, grinding pigments, etc. 142pp. 6⅛ × 9¼.
20054-X Pa. $3.95

FRANK LLOYD WRIGHT'S FALLINGWATER, Donald Hoffmann. Full story of Wright's masterwork at Bear Run, Pa. 100 photographs of site, construction, and details of completed structure. 112pp. 9¼ × 10.
23671-4 Pa. $7.95

OVAL STAINED GLASS PATTERN BOOK, C. Eaton. 60 new designs framed in shape of an oval. Greater complexity, challenge with sinuous cats, birds, mandalas framed in antique shape. 64pp. 8¼ × 11.
24519-5 Pa. $3.95

THE BOOK OF WOOD CARVING, Charles Marshall Sayers. Still finest book for beginning student. Fundamentals, technique; gives 34 designs, over 34 projects for panels, bookends, mirrors, etc. 33 photos. 118pp. 7¾ × 10⅝. 23654-4 Pa. $3.95

CARVING COUNTRY CHARACTERS, Bill Higginbotham. Expert advice for beginning, advanced carvers on materials, techniques for creating 18 projects—mirthful panorama of American characters. 105 illustrations. 80pp. 8⅜ × 11. 24135-1 Pa. $2.95

300 ART NOUVEAU DESIGNS AND MOTIFS IN FULL COLOR, C.B. Grafton. 44 full-page plates display swirling lines and muted colors typical of Art Nouveau. Borders, frames, panels, cartouches, dingbats, etc. 48pp. 9⅜ × 12¼. 24354-0 Pa. $6.95

SELF-WORKING CARD TRICKS, Karl Fulves. Editor of *Pallbearer* offers 72 tricks that work automatically through nature of card deck. No sleight of hand needed. Often spectacular. 42 illustrations. 113pp. 5⅜ × 8½. 23334-0 Pa. $3.50

CUT AND ASSEMBLE A WESTERN FRONTIER TOWN, Edmund V. Gillon, Jr. Ten authentic full-color buildings on heavy cardboard stock in H-O scale. Sheriff's Office and Jail, Saloon, Wells Fargo, Opera House, others. 48pp. 9¼ × 12¼. 23736-2 Pa. $4.95

CUT AND ASSEMBLE AN EARLY NEW ENGLAND VILLAGE, Edmund V. Gillon, Jr. Printed in full color on heavy cardboard stock. 12 authentic buildings in H-O scale: Adams home in Quincy, Mass., Oliver Wight house in Sturbridge, smithy, store, church, others. 48pp. 9¼ × 12¼. 23536-X Pa. $4.95

THE TALE OF TWO BAD MICE, Beatrix Potter. Tom Thumb and Hunca Munca squeeze out of their hole and go exploring. 27 full-color Potter illustrations. 59pp. 4¼ × 5½. (Available in U.S. only) 23065-1 Pa. $1.75

CARVING FIGURE CARICATURES IN THE OZARK STYLE, Harold L. Enlow. Instructions and illustrations for ten delightful projects, plus general carving instructions. 22 drawings and 47 photographs altogether. 39pp. 8⅜ × 11. 23151-8 Pa. $2.95

A TREASURY OF FLOWER DESIGNS FOR ARTISTS, EMBROIDERERS AND CRAFTSMEN, Susan Gaber. 100 garden favorites lushly rendered by artist for artists, craftsmen, needleworkers. Many form frames, borders. 80pp. 8¼ × 11. 24096-7 Pa. $3.95

CUT & ASSEMBLE A TOY THEATER/THE NUTCRACKER BALLET, Tom Tierney. Model of a complete, full-color production of Tchaikovsky's classic. 6 backdrops, dozens of characters, familiar dance sequences. 32pp. 9⅜ × 12¼. 24194-7 Pa. $4.50

ANIMALS: 1,419 COPYRIGHT-FREE ILLUSTRATIONS OF MAMMALS, BIRDS, FISH, INSECTS, ETC., edited by Jim Harter. Clear wood engravings present, in extremely lifelike poses, over 1,000 species of animals. 284pp. 9 × 12. 23766-4 Pa. $9.95

MORE HAND SHADOWS, Henry Bursill. For those at their 'finger ends,'' 16 more effects—Shakespeare, a hare, a squirrel, Mr. Punch, and twelve more—each explained by a full-page illustration. Considerable period charm. 30pp. 6½ × 9¼. 21384-6 Pa. $1.95

SURREAL STICKERS AND UNREAL STAMPS, William Rowe. 224 haunting, hilarious stamps on gummed, perforated stock, with images of elephants, geisha girls, George Washington, etc. 16pp. one side. 8¼ × 11. 24371-0 Pa. $3.50

GOURMET KITCHEN LABELS, Ed Sibbett, Jr. 112 full-color labels (4 copies each of 28 designs). Fruit, bread, other culinary motifs. Gummed and perforated. 16pp. 8¼ × 11. 24087-8 Pa. $2.95

PATTERNS AND INSTRUCTIONS FOR CARVING AUTHENTIC BIRDS, H.D. Green. Detailed instructions, 27 diagrams, 85 photographs for carving 15 species of birds so life-like, they'll seem ready to fly! 8¼ × 11. 24222-6 Pa. $3.00

FLATLAND, E.A. Abbott. Science-fiction classic explores life of 2-D being in 3-D world. 16 illustrations. 103pp. 5⅜ × 8. 20001-9 Pa. $2.00

DRIED FLOWERS, Sarah Whitlock and Martha Rankin. Concise, clear, practical guide to dehydration, glycerinizing, pressing plant material, and more. Covers use of silica gel. 12 drawings. 32pp. 5⅜ × 8½. 21802-3 Pa. $1.00

EASY-TO-MAKE CANDLES, Gary V. Guy. Learn how easy it is to make all kinds of decorative candles. Step-by-step instructions. 82 illustrations. 48pp. 8¼ × 11.
23881-4 Pa. $2.95

SUPER STICKERS FOR KIDS, Carolyn Bracken. 128 gummed and perforated full-color stickers: GIRL WANTED, KEEP OUT, BORED OF EDUCATION, X-RATED, COMBAT ZONE, many others. 16pp. 8¼ × 11. 24092-4 Pa. $3.50

CUT AND COLOR PAPER MASKS, Michael Grater. Clowns, animals, funny faces...simply color them in, cut them out, and put them together, and you have 9 paper masks to play with and enjoy. 32pp. 8¼ × 11. 23171-2 Pa. $2.95

A CHRISTMAS CAROL: THE ORIGINAL MANUSCRIPT, Charles Dickens. Clear facsimile of Dickens manuscript, on facing pages with final printed text. 8 illustrations by John Leech, 4 in color on covers. 144pp. 8⅜ × 11¼.
20980-6 Pa. $5.95

CARVING SHOREBIRDS, Harry V. Shourds & Anthony Hillman. 16 full-size patterns (all double-page spreads) for 19 North American shorebirds with step-by-step instructions. 72pp. 9¼ × 12¼. 24287-0 Pa. $5.95

THE GENTLE ART OF MATHEMATICS, Dan Pedoe. Mathematical games, probability, the question of infinity, topology, how the laws of algebra work, problems of irrational numbers, and more. 42 figures. 143pp. 5⅜ × 8½.
22949-1 Pa. $3.50

READY-TO-USE DOLLHOUSE WALLPAPER, Katzenbach & Warren, Inc. Stripe, 2 floral stripes, 2 allover florals, polka dot; all in full color. 4 sheets (350 sq. in.) of each, enough for average room. 48pp. 8¼ × 11. 23495-9 Pa. $2.95

MINIATURE IRON-ON TRANSFER PATTERNS FOR DOLLHOUSES, DOLLS, AND SMALL PROJECTS, Rita Weiss and Frank Fontana. Over 100 miniature patterns: rugs, bedspreads, quilts, chair seats, etc. In standard dollhouse size. 48pp. 8¼ × 11. 23741-9 Pa. $1.95

THE DINOSAUR COLORING BOOK, Anthony Rao. 45 renderings of dinosaurs, fossil birds, turtles, other creatures of Mesozoic Era. Scientifically accurate. Captions. 48pp. 8¼ × 11. 24022-3 Pa. $2.50

JAPANESE DESIGN MOTIFS, Matsuya Co. Mon, or heraldic designs. Over 4000 typical, beautiful designs: birds, animals, flowers, swords, fans, geometrics; all beautifully stylized. 213pp. 11⅜ × 8¼. 22874-6 Pa. $7.95

THE TALE OF BENJAMIN BUNNY, Beatrix Potter. Peter Rabbit's cousin coaxes him back into Mr. McGregor's garden for a whole new set of adventures. All 27 full-color illustrations. 59pp. 4¼ × 5½. (Available in U.S. only) 21102-9 Pa. $1.75

THE TALE OF PETER RABBIT AND OTHER FAVORITE STORIES BOXED SET, Beatrix Potter. Seven of Beatrix Potter's best-loved tales including Peter Rabbit in a specially designed, durable boxed set. 4¼ × 5½. Total of 447pp. 158 color illustrations. (Available in U.S. only) 23903-9 Pa. $12.25

PRACTICAL MENTAL MAGIC, Theodore Annemann. Nearly 200 astonishing feats of mental magic revealed in step-by-step detail. Complete advice on staging, patter, etc. Illustrated. 320pp. 5⅜ × 8½. 24426-1 Pa. $5.95

CELEBRATED CASES OF JUDGE DEE (DEE GOONG AN), translated by Robert Van Gulik. Authentic 18th-century Chinese detective novel; Dee and associates solve three interlocked cases. Led to van Gulik's own stories with same characters. Extensive introduction. 9 illustrations. 237pp. 5⅜ × 8½. 23337-5 Pa. $4.95

CUT & FOLD EXTRATERRESTRIAL INVADERS THAT FLY, M. Grater. Stage your own lilliputian space battles. By following the step-by-step instructions and explanatory diagrams you can launch 22 full-color fliers into space. 36pp. 8¼ × 11. 24478-4 Pa. $2.95

CUT & ASSEMBLE VICTORIAN HOUSES, Edmund V. Gillon, Jr. Printed in full color on heavy cardboard stock, 4 authentic Victorian houses in H-O scale: Italian-style Villa, Octagon, Second Empire, Stick Style. 48pp. 9¼ × 12¼. 23849-0 Pa. $4.95

BEST SCIENCE FICTION STORIES OF H.G. WELLS, H.G. Wells. Full novel *The Invisible Man,* plus 17 short stories: "The Crystal Egg," "Aepyornis Island," "The Strange Orchid," etc. 303pp. 5⅜ × 8½. (Available in U.S. only) 21531-8 Pa. $4.95

TRADEMARK DESIGNS OF THE WORLD, Yusaku Kamekura. A lavish collection of nearly 700 trademarks, the work of Wright, Loewy, Klee, Binder, hundreds of others. 160pp. 8¾ × 8. (EJ) 24191-2 Pa. $5.95

THE ARTIST'S AND CRAFTSMAN'S GUIDE TO REDUCING, ENLARGING AND TRANSFERRING DESIGNS, Rita Weiss. Discover, reduce, enlarge, transfer designs from any objects to any craft project. 12pp. plus 16 sheets special graph paper. 8¼ × 11. 24142-4 Pa. $3.95

TREASURY OF JAPANESE DESIGNS AND MOTIFS FOR ARTISTS AND CRAFTSMEN, edited by Carol Belanger Grafton. Indispensable collection of 360 traditional Japanese designs and motifs redrawn in clean, crisp black-and-white, copyright-free illustrations. 96pp. 8¼ × 11. 24435-0 Pa. $4.50

CHANCERY CURSIVE STROKE BY STROKE, Arthur Baker. Instructions and illustrations for each stroke of each letter (upper and lower case) and numerals. 54 full-page plates. 64pp. 8¼ × 11.                                    24278-1 Pa. $2.50

THE ENJOYMENT AND USE OF COLOR, Walter Sargent. Color relationships, values, intensities; complementary colors, illumination, similar topics. Color in nature and art. 7 color plates, 29 illustrations. 274pp. 5⅜ × 8½.    20944-X Pa. $4.95

SCULPTURE PRINCIPLES AND PRACTICE, Louis Slobodkin. Step-by-step approach to clay, plaster, metals, stone; classical and modern. 253 drawings, photos. 255pp. 8⅛ × 11.                                    22960-2 Pa. $7.50

VICTORIAN FASHION PAPER DOLLS FROM HARPER'S BAZAR, 1867-1898, Theodore Menten. Four female dolls with 28 elegant high fashion costumes, printed in full color. 32pp. 9¼ × 12¼.                        23453-3 Pa. $3.95

FLOPSY, MOPSY AND COTTONTAIL: A Little Book of Paper Dolls in Full Color, Susan LaBelle. Three dolls and 21 costumes (7 for each doll) show Peter Rabbit's siblings dressed for holidays, gardening, hiking, etc. Charming borders, captions. 48pp. 4¼ × 5½. (USCO)                                24376-1 Pa. $2.50

NATIONAL LEAGUE BASEBALL CARD CLASSICS, Bert Randolph Sugar. 83 big-leaguers from 1909-69 on facsimile cards. Hubbell, Dean, Spahn, Brock plus advertising, info, no duplications. Perforated, detachable. 16pp. 8¼ × 11.
                                                                24308-7 Pa. $3.50

THE LOGICAL APPROACH TO CHESS, Dr. Max Euwe, et al. First-rate text of comprehensive strategy, tactics, theory for the amateur. No gambits to memorize, just a clear, logical approach. 224pp. 5⅜ × 8½.            24353-2 Pa. $4.50

MAGICK IN THEORY AND PRACTICE, Aleister Crowley. The summation of the thought and practice of the century's most famous necromancer, long hard to find. Crowley's best book. 436pp. 5⅜ × 8½. (Available in U.S. only)
                                                                23295-6 Pa. $6.95

THE HAUNTED HOTEL, Wilkie Collins. Collins' last great tale; doom and destiny in a Venetian palace. Praised by T.S. Eliot. 127pp. 5⅜ × 8½.
                                                                24333-8 Pa. $3.00

ART DECO DISPLAY ALPHABETS, Dan X. Solo. Wide variety of bold yet elegant lettering in handsome Art Deco styles. 100 complete fonts, with numerals, punctuation, more. 104pp. 8⅛ × 11.                            24372-9 Pa. $4.50

CALLIGRAPHIC ALPHABETS, Arthur Baker. Nearly 150 complete alphabets by outstanding contemporary. Stimulating ideas; useful source for unique effects. 154 plates. 157pp. 8⅜ × 11¼.                                21045-6 Pa. $5.95

ARTHUR BAKER'S HISTORIC CALLIGRAPHIC ALPHABETS, Arthur Baker. From monumental capitals of first-century Rome to humanistic cursive of 16th century, 33 alphabets in fresh interpretations. 88 plates. 96pp. 9 × 12.
                                                                24054-1 Pa. $4.50

LETTIE LANE PAPER DOLLS, Sheila Young. Genteel turn-of-the-century family very popular then and now. 24 paper dolls. 16 plates in full color. 32pp. 9¼ × 12¼.                                                24089-4 Pa. $3.95

KEYBOARD WORKS FOR SOLO INSTRUMENTS, G.F. Handel. 35 neglected works from Handel's vast oeuvre, originally jotted down as improvisations. Includes Eight Great Suites, others. New sequence. 174pp. 9⅜ × 12¼.
24338-9 Pa. $7.50

AMERICAN LEAGUE BASEBALL CARD CLASSICS, Bert Randolph Sugar. 82 stars from 1900s to 60s on facsimile cards. Ruth, Cobb, Mantle, Williams, plus advertising, info, no duplications. Perforated, detachable. 16pp. 8¼ × 11.
24286-2 Pa. $3.50

A TREASURY OF CHARTED DESIGNS FOR NEEDLEWORKERS, Georgia Gorham and Jeanne Warth. 141 charted designs: owl, cat with yarn, tulips, piano, spinning wheel, covered bridge, Victorian house and many others. 48pp. 8¼ × 11.
23558-0 Pa. $1.95

DANISH FLORAL CHARTED DESIGNS, Gerda Bengtsson. Exquisite collection of over 40 different florals: anemone, Iceland poppy, wild fruit, pansies, many others. 45 illustrations. 48pp. 8¼ × 11.
23957-8 Pa. $2.50

OLD PHILADELPHIA IN EARLY PHOTOGRAPHS 1839-1914, Robert F. Looney. 215 photographs: panoramas, street scenes, landmarks, President-elect Lincoln's visit, 1876 Centennial Exposition, much more. 230pp. 8⅜ × 11¾.
23345-6 Pa. $9.95

PRELUDE TO MATHEMATICS, W.W. Sawyer. Noted mathematician's lively, stimulating account of non-Euclidean geometry, matrices, determinants, group theory, other topics. Emphasis on novel, striking aspects. 224pp. 5⅜ × 8½.
24401-6 Pa. $4.50

ADVENTURES WITH A MICROSCOPE, Richard Headstrom. 59 adventures with clothing fibers, protozoa, ferns and lichens, roots and leaves, much more. 142 illustrations. 232pp. 5⅜ × 8½.
23471-1 Pa. $3.95

IDENTIFYING ANIMAL TRACKS: MAMMALS, BIRDS, AND OTHER ANIMALS OF THE EASTERN UNITED STATES, Richard Headstrom. For hunters, naturalists, scouts, nature-lovers. Diagrams of tracks, tips on identification. 128pp. 5⅜ × 8.
24442-3 Pa. $3.50

VICTORIAN FASHIONS AND COSTUMES FROM HARPER'S BAZAR, 1867-1898, edited by Stella Blum. Day costumes, evening wear, sports clothes, shoes, hats, other accessories in over 1,000 detailed engravings. 320pp. 9⅜ × 12¼.
22990-4 Pa. $10.95

EVERYDAY FASHIONS OF THE TWENTIES AS PICTURED IN SEARS AND OTHER CATALOGS, edited by Stella Blum. Actual dress of the Roaring Twenties, with text by Stella Blum. Over 750 illustrations, captions. 156pp. 9 × 12.
24134-3 Pa. $8.95

HALL OF FAME BASEBALL CARDS, edited by Bert Randolph Sugar. Cy Young, Ted Williams, Lou Gehrig, and many other Hall of Fame greats on 92 full-color, detachable reprints of early baseball cards. No duplication of cards with *Classic Baseball Cards.* 16pp. 8¼ × 11.
23624-2 Pa. $3.50

THE ART OF HAND LETTERING, Helm Wotzkow. Course in hand lettering, Roman, Gothic, Italic, Block, Script. Tools, proportions, optical aspects, individual variation. Very quality conscious. Hundreds of specimens. 320pp. 5⅜ × 8½.
21797-3 Pa. $5.95

HOW THE OTHER HALF LIVES, Jacob A. Riis. Journalistic record of filth, degradation, upward drive in New York immigrant slums, shops, around 1900. New edition includes 100 original Riis photos, monuments of early photography. 233pp. 10 × 7⅞. 22012-5 Pa. $9.95

CHINA AND ITS PEOPLE IN EARLY PHOTOGRAPHS, John Thomson. In 200 black-and-white photographs of exceptional quality photographic pioneer Thomson captures the mountains, dwellings, monuments and people of 19th-century China. 272pp. 9⅜ × 12¼. 24393-1 Pa. $13.95

GODEY COSTUME PLATES IN COLOR FOR DECOUPAGE AND FRAMING, edited by Eleanor Hasbrouk Rawlings. 24 full-color engravings depicting 19th-century Parisian haute couture. Printed on one side only. 56pp. 8¼ × 11. 23879-2 Pa. $3.95

ART NOUVEAU STAINED GLASS PATTERN BOOK, Ed Sibbett, Jr. 104 projects using well-known themes of Art Nouveau: swirling forms, florals, peacocks, and sensuous women. 60pp. 8¼ × 11. 23577-7 Pa. $3.95

QUICK AND EASY PATCHWORK ON THE SEWING MACHINE: Susan Aylsworth Murwin and Suzzy Payne. Instructions, diagrams show exactly how to machine sew 12 quilts. 48pp. of templates. 50 figures. 80pp. 8¼ × 11. 23770-2 Pa. $3.95

THE STANDARD BOOK OF QUILT MAKING AND COLLECTING, Marguerite Ickis. Full information, full-sized patterns for making 46 traditional quilts, also 150 other patterns. 483 illustrations. 273pp. 6⅞ × 9⅝. 20582-7 Pa. $5.95

LETTERING AND ALPHABETS, J. Albert Cavanagh. 85 complete alphabets lettered in various styles; instructions for spacing, roughs, brushwork. 121pp. 8¾ × 8. 20053-1 Pa. $3.95

LETTER FORMS: 110 COMPLETE ALPHABETS, Frederick Lambert. 110 sets of capital letters; 16 lower case alphabets; 70 sets of numbers and other symbols. 110pp. 8⅛ × 11. 22872-X Pa. $4.50

ORCHIDS AS HOUSE PLANTS, Rebecca Tyson Northen. Grow cattleyas and many other kinds of orchids—in a window, in a case, or under artificial light. 63 illustrations. 148pp. 5⅜ × 8½. 23261-1 Pa. $2.95

THE MUSHROOM HANDBOOK, Louis C.C. Krieger. Still the best popular handbook. Full descriptions of 259 species, extremely thorough text, poisons, folklore, etc. 32 color plates; 126 other illustrations. 560pp. 5⅜ × 8½. 21861-9 Pa. $8.50

THE DORÉ BIBLE ILLUSTRATIONS, Gustave Doré. All wonderful, detailed plates: Adam and Eve, Flood, Babylon, life of Jesus, etc. Brief King James text with each plate. 241 plates. 241pp. 9 × 12. 23004-X Pa. $8.95

THE BOOK OF KELLS: Selected Plates in Full Color, edited by Blanche Cirker. 32 full-page plates from greatest manuscript-icon of early Middle Ages. Fantastic, mysterious. Publisher's Note. Captions. 32pp. 9¾ × 12¼. 24345-1 Pa. $4.50

THE PERFECT WAGNERITE, George Bernard Shaw. Brilliant criticism of the Ring Cycle, with provocative interpretation of politics, economic theories behind the Ring. 136pp. 5⅜ × 8½. (EUK) 21707-8 Pa. $3.95

THE RIME OF THE ANCIENT MARINER, Gustave Doré, S.T. Coleridge. Doré's finest work, 34 plates capture moods, subtleties of poem. Full text. 77pp. 9¼ × 12.  22305-1 Pa. $4.95

SONGS OF INNOCENCE, William Blake. The first and most popular of Blake's famous "Illuminated Books," in a facsimile edition reproducing all 31 brightly colored plates. Additional printed text of each poem. 64pp. 5¼ × 7.  22764-2 Pa. $3.50

AN INTRODUCTION TO INFORMATION THEORY, J.R. Pierce. Second (1980) edition of most impressive non-technical account available. Encoding, entropy, noisy channel, related areas, etc. 320pp. 5⅜ × 8½.  24061-4 Pa. $5.95

THE DIVINE PROPORTION: A STUDY IN MATHEMATICAL BEAUTY, H.E. Huntley. "Divine proportion" or "golden ratio" in poetry, Pascal's triangle, philosophy, psychology, music, mathematical figures, etc. Excellent bridge between science and art. 58 figures. 185pp. 5⅜ × 8½.  22254-3 Pa. $4.50

THE DOVER NEW YORK WALKING GUIDE: From the Battery to Wall Street, Mary J. Shapiro. Superb inexpensive guide to historic buildings and locales in lower Manhattan: Trinity Church, Bowling Green, more. Complete Text; maps. 36 illustrations. 48pp. 3⅞ × 9¼.  24225-0 Pa. $2.50

NEW YORK THEN AND NOW, Edward B. Watson, Edmund V. Gillon, Jr. 83 important Manhattan sites: on facing pages early photographs (1875-1925) and 1976 photos by Gillon. 172 illustrations. 171pp. 9¼ × 10.  23361-8 Pa. $9.95

HISTORIC COSTUME IN PICTURES, Braun & Schneider. Over 1450 costumed figures from dawn of civilization to end of 19th century. English captions. 125 plates. 256pp. 8⅜ × 11¼.  23150-X Pa. $7.95

VICTORIAN AND EDWARDIAN FASHION: A Photographic Survey, Alison Gernsheim. First fashion history completely illustrated by contemporary photographs. Full text plus 235 photos, 1840-1914, in which many celebrities appear. 240pp. 6½ × 9¼.  24205-6 Pa. $6.00

CHARTED CHRISTMAS DESIGNS FOR COUNTED CROSS-STITCH AND OTHER NEEDLECRAFTS, Lindberg Press. Charted designs for 45 beautiful needlecraft projects with many yuletide and wintertime motifs. 48pp. 8¼ × 11. (EDNS)  24356-7 Pa. $2.50

101 FOLK DESIGNS FOR COUNTED CROSS-STITCH AND OTHER NEEDLE-CRAFTS, Carter Houck. 101 authentic charted folk designs in a wide array of lovely representations with many suggestions for effective use. 48pp. 8¼ × 11.  24369-9 Pa. $2.25

FIVE ACRES AND INDEPENDENCE, Maurice G. Kains. Great back-to-the-land classic explains basics of self-sufficient farming. The one book to get. 95 illustrations. 397pp. 5⅜ × 8½.  20974-1 Pa. $6.50

A MODERN HERBAL, Margaret Grieve. Much the fullest, most exact, most useful compilation of herbal material. Gigantic alphabetical encyclopedia, from aconite to zedoary, gives botanical information, medical properties, folklore, economic uses, and much else. Indispensable to serious reader. 161 illustrations. 888pp. 6½ × 9¼. (Available in U.S. only)  22798-7, 22799-5 Pa., Two-vol. set $17.00

DECORATIVE NAPKIN FOLDING FOR BEGINNERS, Lillian Oppenheimer and Natalie Epstein. 22 different napkin folds in the shape of a heart, clown's hat, love knot, etc. 63 drawings. 48pp. 8¼ × 11. 23797-4 Pa. $2.25

DECORATIVE LABELS FOR HOME CANNING, PRESERVING, AND OTHER HOUSEHOLD AND GIFT USES, Theodore Menten. 128 gummed, perforated labels, beautifully printed in 2 colors. 12 versions. Adhere to metal, glass, wood, ceramics. 24pp. 8¼ × 11. 23219-0 Pa. $3.50

EARLY AMERICAN STENCILS ON WALLS AND FURNITURE, Janet Waring. Thorough coverage of 19th-century folk art: techniques, artifacts, surviving specimens. 166 illustrations, 7 in color. 147pp. of text. 7⅞ × 10¾. 21906-2 Pa. $9.95

AMERICAN ANTIQUE WEATHERVANES, A.B. & W.T. Westervelt. Extensively illustrated 1883 catalog exhibiting over 550 copper weathervanes and finials. Excellent primary source by one of the principal manufacturers. 104pp. 6⅛ × 9¼. 24396-6 Pa. $3.95

ART STUDENTS' ANATOMY, Edmond J. Farris. Long favorite in art schools. Basic elements, common positions, actions. Full text, 158 illustrations. 159pp. 5⅜ × 8½. 20744-7 Pa. $3.95

BRIDGMAN'S LIFE DRAWING, George B. Bridgman. More than 500 drawings and text teach you to abstract the body into its major masses. Also specific areas of anatomy. 192pp. 6½ × 9¼. 22710-3 Pa. $4.50

COMPLETE PRELUDES AND ETUDES FOR SOLO PIANO, Frederic Chopin. All 26 Preludes, all 27 Etudes by greatest composer of piano music. Authoritative Paderewski edition. 224pp. 9 × 12. (Available in U.S. only) 24052-5 Pa. $7.50

PIANO MUSIC 1888-1905, Claude Debussy. Deux Arabesques, Suite Bergamesque, Masques, 1st series of Images, etc. 9 others, in corrected editions. 175pp. 9⅜ × 12¼. 22771-5 Pa. $6.95

TEDDY BEAR IRON-ON TRANSFER PATTERNS, Ted Menten. 80 iron-on transfer patterns of male and female Teddys in a wide variety of activities, poses, sizes. 48pp. 8¼ × 11. 24596-9 Pa. $2.25

A PICTURE HISTORY OF THE BROOKLYN BRIDGE, M.J. Shapiro. Profusely illustrated account of greatest engineering achievement of 19th century. 167 rare photos & engravings recall construction, human drama. Extensive, detailed text. 122pp. 8¼ × 11. 24403-2 Pa. $7.95

NEW YORK IN THE THIRTIES, Berenice Abbott. Noted photographer's fascinating study shows new buildings that have become famous and old sights that have disappeared forever. 97 photographs. 97pp. 11⅜ × 10. 22967-X Pa. $7.50

MATHEMATICAL TABLES AND FORMULAS, Robert D. Carmichael and Edwin R. Smith. Logarithms, sines, tangents, trig functions, powers, roots, reciprocals, exponential and hyperbolic functions, formulas and theorems. 269pp. 5⅜ × 8½. 60111-0 Pa. $4.95

HANDBOOK OF MATHEMATICAL FUNCTIONS WITH FORMULAS, GRAPHS, AND MATHEMATICAL TABLES, edited by Milton Abramowitz and Irene A. Stegun. Vast compendium: 29 sets of tables, some to as high as 20 places. 1,046pp. 8 × 10½. 61272-4 Pa. $21.95

REASON IN ART, George Santayana. Renowned philosopher's provocative, seminal treatment of basis of art in instinct and experience. Volume Four of *The Life of Reason.* 230pp. 5⅜ × 8. 24358-3 Pa. $4.50

LANGUAGE, TRUTH AND LOGIC, Alfred J. Ayer. Famous, clear introduction to Vienna, Cambridge schools of Logical Positivism. Role of philosophy, elimination of metaphysics, nature of analysis, etc. 160pp. 5⅜ × 8½. (USCO) 20010-8 Pa. $2.95

BASIC ELECTRONICS, U.S. Bureau of Naval Personnel. Electron tubes, circuits, antennas, AM, FM, and CW transmission and receiving, etc. 560 illustrations. 567pp. 6½ × 9¼. 21076-6 Pa. $9.95

THE ART DECO STYLE, edited by Theodore Menten. Furniture, jewelry, metalwork, ceramics, fabrics, lighting fixtures, interior decors, exteriors, graphics from pure French sources. Over 400 photographs. 183pp. 8⅜ × 11¼. 22824-X Pa. $7.95

THE FOUR BOOKS OF ARCHITECTURE, Andrea Palladio. 16th-century classic covers classical architectural remains, Renaissance revivals, classical orders, etc. 1738 Ware English edition. 216 plates. 110pp. of text. 9½ × 12¾. 21308-0 Pa. $11.95

THE WIT AND HUMOR OF OSCAR WILDE, edited by Alvin Redman. More than 1000 ripostes, paradoxes, wisecracks: Work is the curse of the drinking classes, I can resist everything except temptations, etc. 258pp. 5⅜ × 8½. 20602-5 Pa. $4.50

THE DEVIL'S DICTIONARY, Ambrose Bierce. Barbed, bitter, brilliant witticisms in the form of a dictionary. Best, most ferocious satire America has produced. 145pp. 5⅜ × 8½. 20487-1 Pa. $2.95

ERTÉ'S FASHION DESIGNS, Erté. 210 black-and-white inventions from *Harper's Bazar,* 1918-32, plus 8pp. full-color covers. Captions. 88pp. 9 × 12. 24203-X Pa. $7.95

ERTÉ GRAPHICS, Erté. Collection of striking color graphics: *Seasons, Alphabet, Numerals, Aces* and *Precious Stones.* 50 plates, including 4 on covers. 48pp. 9⅜ × 12¼. 23580-7 Pa. $6.95

PAPER FOLDING FOR BEGINNERS, William D. Murray and Francis J. Rigney. Clearest book for making origami sail boats, roosters, frogs that move legs, etc. 40 projects. More than 275 illustrations. 94pp. 5⅜ × 8½. 20713-7 Pa. $2.50

ORIGAMI FOR THE ENTHUSIAST, John Montroll. Fish, ostrich, peacock, squirrel, rhinoceros, Pegasus, 19 other intricate subjects. Instructions. Diagrams. 128pp. 9 × 12. 23799-0 Pa. $5.95

CROCHETING NOVELTY POT HOLDERS, edited by Linda Macho. 64 useful, whimsical pot holders feature kitchen themes, animals, flowers, other novelties. Surprisingly easy to crochet. Complete instructions. 48pp. 8¼ × 11. 24296-X Pa. $1.95

CROCHETING DOILIES, edited by Rita Weiss. Irish Crochet, Jewel, Star Wheel, Vanity Fair and more. Also luncheon and console sets, runners and centerpieces. 51 illustrations. 48pp. 8¼ × 11. 23424-X Pa. $2.75

YUCATAN BEFORE AND AFTER THE CONQUEST, Diego de Landa. Only significant account of Yucatan written in the early post-Conquest era. Translated by William Gates. Over 120 illustrations. 162pp. 5⅜ × 8½. 23622-6 Pa. $3.95

ORNATE PICTORIAL CALLIGRAPHY, E.A. Lupfer. Complete instructions, over 150 examples help you create magnificent "flourishes" from which beautiful animals and objects gracefully emerge. 8⅛ × 11. 21957-7 Pa. $3.50

DOLLY DINGLE PAPER DOLLS, Grace Drayton. Cute chubby children by same artist who did Campbell Kids. Rare plates from 1910s. 30 paper dolls and over 100 outfits reproduced in full color. 32pp. 9¼ × 12¼. 23711-7 Pa. $3.50

CURIOUS GEORGE PAPER DOLLS IN FULL COLOR, H. A. Rey, Kathy Allert. Naughty little monkey-hero of children's books in two doll figures, plus 48 full-color costumes: pirate, Indian chief, fireman, more. 32pp. 9¼ × 12¼. 24386-9 Pa. $3.50

GERMAN: HOW TO SPEAK AND WRITE IT, Joseph Rosenberg. Like *French, How to Speak and Write It.* Very rich modern course, with a wealth of pictorial material. 330 illustrations. 384pp. 5⅜ × 8½. 20271-2 Pa. $4.95

CATS AND KITTENS: 24 Ready-to-Mail Color Photo Postcards, D. Holby. Handsome collection; feline in a variety of adorable poses. Identifications. 12pp. on postcard stock. 8¼ × 11. 24469-5 Pa. $2.95

MARILYN MONROE PAPER DOLLS, Tom Tierney. 31 full-color designs on heavy stock, from *The Asphalt Jungle, Gentlemen Prefer Blondes,* 22 others. 1 doll. 16 plates. 32pp. 9⅜ × 12¼. 23769-9 Pa. $3.95

FUNDAMENTALS OF LAYOUT, F.H. Wills. All phases of layout design discussed and illustrated in 121 illustrations. Indispensable as student's text or handbook for professional. 124pp. 8⅛ × 11. 21279-3 Pa. $4.50

FANTASTIC SUPER STICKERS, Ed Sibbett, Jr. 75 colorful pressure-sensitive stickers. Peel off and place for a touch of pizzazz: clowns, penguins, teddy bears, etc. Full color. 16pp. 8¼ × 11. 24471-7 Pa. $3.50

LABELS FOR ALL OCCASIONS, Ed Sibbett, Jr. 6 labels each of 16 different designs—baroque, art nouveau, art deco, Pennsylvania Dutch, etc.—in full color. 24pp. 8¼ × 11. 23688-9 Pa. $3.95

HOW TO CALCULATE QUICKLY: RAPID METHODS IN BASIC MATHEMATICS, Henry Sticker. Addition, subtraction, multiplication, division, checks, etc. More than 8000 problems, solutions. 185pp. 5 × 7¼. 20295-X Pa. $2.95

THE CAT COLORING BOOK, Karen Baldauski. Handsome, realistic renderings of 40 splendid felines, from American shorthair to exotic types. 44 plates. Captions. 48pp. 8¼ × 11. 24011-8 Pa. $2.50

THE TALE OF PETER RABBIT, Beatrix Potter. The inimitable Peter's terrifying adventure in Mr. McGregor's garden, with all 27 wonderful, full-color Potter illustrations. 55pp. 4¼ × 5½. (Available in U.S. only) 22827-4 Pa. $1.75

BASIC ELECTRICITY, U.S. Bureau of Naval Personnel. Batteries, circuits, conductors, AC and DC, inductance and capacitance, generators, motors, transformers, amplifiers, etc. 349 illustrations. 448pp. 6½ × 9¼. 20973-3 Pa. $7.95

SOURCE BOOK OF MEDICAL HISTORY, edited by Logan Clendening, M.D. Original accounts ranging from Ancient Egypt and Greece to discovery of X-rays: Galen, Pasteur, Lavoisier, Harvey, Parkinson, others. 685pp. 5⅜ × 8½.
20621-1 Pa. $11.95

THE ROSE AND THE KEY, J.S. Lefanu. Superb mystery novel from Irish master. Dark doings among an ancient and aristocratic English family. Well-drawn characters; capital suspense. Introduction by N. Donaldson. 448pp. 5⅜ × 8½.
24377-X Pa. $6.95

SOUTH WIND, Norman Douglas. Witty, elegant novel of ideas set on languorous Meditterranean island of Nepenthe. Elegant prose, glittering epigrams, mordant satire. 1917 masterpiece. 416pp. 5⅜ × 8½. (Available in U.S. only)
24361-3 Pa. $5.95

RUSSELL'S CIVIL WAR PHOTOGRAPHS, Capt. A.J. Russell. 116 rare Civil War Photos: Bull Run, Virginia campaigns, bridges, railroads, Richmond, Lincoln's funeral car. Many never seen before. Captions. 128pp. 9⅜ × 12¼.
24283-8 Pa. $7.95

PHOTOGRAPHS BY MAN RAY: 105 Works, 1920-1934. Nudes, still lifes, landscapes, women's faces, celebrity portraits (Dali, Matisse, Picasso, others), rayographs. Reprinted from rare gravure edition. 128pp. 9⅜ × 12¼.
23842-3 Pa. $8.95

STAR NAMES: THEIR LORE AND MEANING, Richard H. Allen. Star names, the zodiac, constellations: folklore and literature associated with heavens. The basic book of its field, fascinating reading. 563pp. 5⅜ × 8½. 21079-0 Pa. $7.95

BURNHAM'S CELESTIAL HANDBOOK, Robert Burnham, Jr. Thorough guide to the stars beyond our solar system. Exhaustive treatment. Alphabetical by constellation: Andromeda to Cetus in Vol. 1; Chamaeleon to Orion in Vol. 2; and Pavo to Vulpecula in Vol. 3. Hundreds of illustrations. Index in Vol. 3. 2000pp. 6⅛ × 9¼. 23567-X, 23568-8, 23673-0 Pa. Three-vol. set $37.85

THE ART NOUVEAU STYLE BOOK OF ALPHONSE MUCHA, Alphonse Mucha. All 72 plates from *Documents Decoratifs* in original color. Stunning, essential work of Art Nouveau. 80pp. 9⅜ × 12¼. 24044-4 Pa. $8.95

DESIGNS BY ERTE; FASHION DRAWINGS AND ILLUSTRATIONS FROM "HARPER'S BAZAR," Erte. 310 fabulous line drawings and 14 *Harper's Bazar* covers, 8 in full color. Erte's exotic temptresses with tassels, fur muffs, long trains, coifs, more. 129pp. 9⅜ × 12¼. 23397-9 Pa. $8.95

HISTORY OF STRENGTH OF MATERIALS, Stephen P. Timoshenko. Excellent historical survey of the strength of materials with many references to the theories of elasticity and structure. 245 figures. 452pp. 5⅜ × 8½. 61187-6 Pa. $9.95

*Prices subject to change without notice.*

Available at your book dealer or write for free catalog to Dept. GI, Dover Publications, Inc., 31 East 2nd St. Mineola, N.Y. 11501. Dover publishes more than 175 books each year on science, elementary and advanced mathematics, biology, music, art, literary history, social sciences and other areas.

71
L.H